LESLIE H. FISHEL, JR.
Heidelberg College

BENJAMIN QUARLES
Morgan State College

The Black American

A Documentary History

Third Edition

SCOTT, FORESMAN AND COMPANY Glenview, Illinois
Dallas, Tex. Oakland, N.J. Palo Alto, Cal. Tucker, Ga. Brighton, England

Dedication

To my wife. — B.Q.
To Butch, the real and only "without whom." — L.H.F., Jr.

Grateful acknowledgment is given here for the illustrative material appearing in the book.

Courtesy of Bob Adelman, distributed by Magnum: 490; Courtesy of the Trustees of the British Museum: 8; Brown Brothers: 274, 356; Courtesy of The Chicago Historical Society: 1, 230, 249; Courtesy of The Chicago Public Library: 80, 82, 83, 201 (margin), 210, 259, 268, 269, 283, 287; Colonial Williamsburg: 38; Culver Pictures: 348, 354; Ellis Herwig from Stock Boston: 563; Chester Higgins from Rapho/Photo Researchers: 542, 585; *Frank Leslie's Illustrated,* June 27, 1863: 234; *Ladies Home Journal,* November 1896: 197; Library of Congress: 48, 207, 214, 216, 243, 246, 257, 446, 471; The Metropolitan Museum of Art, Rogers Fund, 1942: 143; Nacio Jan Brown/B.B.M.: 592; National Archives, U.S. War Department General Staff: 400; National Association for the Advancement of Colored People: 385; Reproduced with permission of The National Urban League, Inc.: 386; Courtesy of The Newberry Library, Chicago: 2, 15, 47, 109, 118, 127, 169, 201 (left); Courtesy of The New York Historical Society, New York City: 100, 200; The New York Public Library, The Berg Collection: 167, and The Schomburg Collection: 72, 136; Courtesy of The New York State Historical Association, Cooperstown, New York: 126; Nicholas Sapieha from Stock Boston: 573; United Press International: 402, 403, 434, 456, 463, 484, 524, 525, 534; Valentine Museum, The Cook Collection: 306, 307, 344; *Views of Slavery,* an American Anti-Slavery Society publication, courtesy of Dwight L. Dumond: 184; *The Western Citizen,* July 13, 1844: 132; Wide World Photos: 508, 517, 540.

Cover mural: Charles White

Library of Congress Cataloging in Publication Data

Fishel, Leslie H.
The Black American: A Documentary History

Published in 1967 and 1968 under title: The Negro American
Includes bibliography and index.
1. Negroes — History — Sources. I. Quarles, Benjamin, joint author. II. Title.
E184.6.F57 1976 973'.04'96073 75-20420
ISBN: 0-673-07970-8

Printed in the United States of America.

1 2 3 4 5 6 7 8 9 10 – NAP – 85 84 83 82 81 80 79 78 77 76 75

THE HAMPTON INSTITUTE MURAL

"The Black American's Contribution to Democracy" was painted by Charles W. White, a Chicago muralist. Formally presented to Hampton Institute on June 25, 1943, the mural depicts those black Americans who have fought against anti-democratic forces, symbolized by the figure in the center background clutching in a stranglehold laborers and machinery, the means of production, and by the colonial Tory in the lower left-hand corner, who destroys a bill by which the Continental Congress in 1775 sought to outlaw the sale or importation of slaves in America.

Crispus Attucks is shown falling before the guns of the redcoats in the Boston Massacre. Behind the British soldiers is Peter Salem, who killed Major Pitcairn of the British army at the Battle of Bunker Hill. Nat Turner (with flaming torch) and Denmark Vesey (on horseback) led armed revolts against slavery before Emancipation. They were inspired by a religious mysticism, represented by the angel with the sword.

Bearded Frederick Douglass is shown with the black soldiers he persuaded Abraham Lincoln to use in the Civil War. On the right, Sojourner Truth beckons freedom-loving slaves through the arch symbolizing the Underground Railway. Beyond her are Harriet Tubman, another underground worker, and Peter Still, who waves his declaration: "I will die before I submit to the yoke."

In the right foreground Booker T. Washington, George Washington Carver, Marian Anderson, Ferdinand Smith, Paul Robeson, and Leadbelly are easily recognizable. The group in the center foreground represents the contemporary black American family. The young man is holding a blueprint suggesting a society free of social wrongs, for which black Americans fight today.

Preface

In the twentieth century only the most recent events are remembered, yet these are rooted in the rich loam of the past. The sweeping changes that face us today can be seen in numerous prophetic signs, once hazy but now pointed. Realizing this, the careful reader will be able to place today's headlines in proper perspective. He will note, for example, that the civil rights confrontations of our times take on fresh meaning when viewed in relation to the Harlem Renaissance of the 1920's, to cries for Negro organization in Booker T. Washington's day, to the Negro convention movement and slave escapes before the Civil War.

An integral part of the American experience from the beginning, the Negro has left his stamp on his country's institutions. Since the founding of Virginia, he has been a factor in many of the major issues in American history. Far more than is generally realized, his role in American history was a positive one, as he spoke and acted of his own volition. But whether passive or active, this role of our most numerous ethnic minority has been deeply and variously expressed in American life and culture.

Few can deny that the past acts upon living individuals in myriad ways. The impress of family, community, and nation (and race, too) develops historically, yet it is no easy matter to make our contemporaries aware of these pervasive historical influences. Documents from the past can help to create this understanding and it is our hope that this volume will be an impetus to the never-ending dialogue between the reader and his past. While no one can relive the past, contemporary documents in the idiom of the time described dramatize the "humanness" of history and recreate the vitality and vigor which give old issues their rightful relevance to today's crises.

It is in this context that we offer this selection of documents. We believe that they demonstrate that the Negro has played a significant role in America's history. Sometimes this role was constricted to that of an issue, but even in these instances, the Negro, individually and collectively, was as active in his own behalf as circumstances permitted. Toward the middle and late nineteenth century, the Negro began more and more to take a hand in shaping his own destiny, and thereby the destiny of his region and his country. This story is only now becoming known.

We have selected documents from several points of view, realizing that no selection is an adequate substitute for a comprehensive review. We have chosen those documents which relate directly or indirectly to the two major themes of the book—the primary role of the Negro in American history and the importance of the Negro's own history. We have tried to include documents which are both informative and readable and which are not readily available elsewhere. While Mr. Quarles is primarily responsible for the first six chapters and Mr. Fishel for the final six chapters, this book is truly a joint product, representing as well as any joint work can the meeting of two independent minds.

The authors are deeply indebted to Robert L. Anderson, of Scott, Foresman and Company—a more knowledgeable, perspicacious and hard-working editor would be hard to find. Not the least of his burdens was the bloodletting task of reducing by nearly 50 percent the bulk of the original manuscript.

Mr. Fishel wants to acknowledge his great debt to Dr. David Thelen, now assistant professor of history, University of Missouri, for his assistance in screening documents, editing headnotes and offering perceptive counsel. He acknowledges also with thanks the time granted to him by the Board of Curators of the State Historical Society of Wisconsin to work on this book, the assistance of staffs of the Archives-Manuscripts Division and General Library of the Society, and especially the help of his administrative assistant, Mrs. Carl Wilhelm.

Mr. Quarles wants to acknowledge his indebtedness to the Morgan College Library personnel for the use of its facilities, including the xeroxing service, and to express thanks to his wife, Ruth Brett Quarles, for valued assistance.

PREFACE TO THE SECOND EDITION

In history books that cover the recent past it is standard practice to add portions to bring the work more nearly up to date. Such a step is particularly necessary if the additional years to be covered are marked by dramatic and significant change. Certainly in a general history dealing with the Negro American no justification would seem necessary for adding a chapter that covers the years since 1964. For in this span, brief as it was in the total range of this country's past, the black and white populations reacted and interacted on a scale unprecedented in our national experience.

If this most recent leg of the black pilgrimage could be characterized by a single word, that word would be "crisis." These years of the immediate past have embraced a series of crises—a ghetto crisis, a rural crisis, and, in its totality, a race-oriented national crisis. Among Negroes there has been an identity crisis, as illustrated, in its most constructive phases, by a deepening sense of pride in themselves. And over all these developments there has hung the cry of "black power," which to some young militants signified a farewell to nonviolence and a cultural and political autonomy tantamount to separation.

To cover a cross section of some of these developments is the purpose of the new chapter. Admittedly, selection is not easy when there is so much to choose from. There also are the hazards of attaining a proper perspective of events still so close upon us.

We have recast the title, replacing "Negro" with "black." This substitution is meant as an indication of our awareness of the expanded uses of the latter, not as any criticism of the validity of the former.

To this edition an index is added, a step that will add to the usefulness of the book in academic circles. In expanding this book, we hope that we have done more to meet the needs of all those who believe that Negro history and black studies are a growing and vital segment of the examination of the American experience.

L.H.F., Jr.
B.Q.

PREFACE TO THE THIRD EDITION

This Third Edition of *The Black American* extends our coverage to include the significant years of the early and mid-1970's. "We are on the threshold of a new dawn," wrote Martin Luther King, Jr., in the 1960's. But to blacks of the post-King era, the hopes of the slain leader seemed far from realization, since the overall rate of black progress remained stubbornly slow in such key areas as housing and employment. Black expectations became more tempered, as the ebullient mood of the sixties gave way to an attitude of "Wait and see." Not to be ignored was a smaller, less hopeful group of blacks who held to the viewpoint "It will never happen." But whether sanguine or pessimistic, black Americans of the seventies believed that their future would, in increasing measure, be what they themselves made of it.

Acting on this belief, black Americans began, as never before, to come together and pool their resources. Although still highly individualistic, they showed a greater spirit of intragroup cooperation. They looked to collective leadership, rather than to a single person or persons, to achieve their goals. Their outlook became broader, embracing local and national concerns not confined to their own racial group. Their range of interests extended to the international scene, although marked by a continuing and deepening interest in Africa. The clenched-fist gesture might be less in evidence, but the spirit of racial pride and assertion which it reflected still infused black leadership and life.

This Third Edition of *The Black American* differs from its immediate predecessor in several ways. The period from 1954 to 1968 is covered in one chapter, rather than two. Hence almost all of Chapter 13, covering the early and mid-1970's, is new. This edition also includes a bibliography, "Suggestions for Further Reading," which lists and briefly describes forty books. Arranged by chronological periods, this annotated bibliography should add to the overall usefulness of the book. Finally, the Third Edition carries some new photographs.

We have profited from the cogent comments and suggestions made by many teachers who have used this book in their classes, and we extend our sincere thanks to them.

L. H. F., Jr.
B. Q.

Contents

CHAPTER ONE

Seed from West Africa

CHAPTER TWO

The Revolutionary War Period

CHAPTER THREE

Slavery's Lengthening Shadow

CHAPTER SEVEN

The Burdens of Reconstruction

CHAPTER ELEVEN

The Negro in a Time of Democratic Crisis

CHAPTER TWELVE

New Peaks of Confrontation

CHAPTER THIRTEEN

Waves at Ebb Tide

CHAPTER ONE

Seed From West Africa

urtesy of Chicago Historical Society

INTRODUCTION

Seed from West Africa

The characterization of the United States as a "nation of nations" is timeworn, but the truth of the cliché is undeniable. Except for the native Indians, the inhabitants of this country have immigrated from virtually every region of the earth. Among the earliest immigrants were Negroes from the West Coast of Africa, twenty of whom landed at Jamestown in 1619, a year before the *Mayflower* reached Plymouth. These Negroes can in truth be numbered among the "Old Americans," those who first reached the English colonies.

Dark-skinned newcomers were destined to become an integral part of American history. Their numbers increased steadily, until at the end of the colonial period in 1775, Negroes comprised one sixth of the population of the British mainland settlements. The presence of the Negro markedly shaped the economic life and history of the thirteen English colonies, indelibly stamped their social attitudes, and importantly affected a host of related spheres from religion to military defense. "Negroes provided as much of the heritage of the American continent as any other group," writes anthropologist Paul Bohannan.

The territory from which the vast majority of Negroes came to the New World stretched for more than 3000 miles from the Senegal

River in the bulge of Africa to the southern tip of the present Portuguese Angola. Within the different physical environments of this expanse were found distinct variation in the physical structure of the inhabitants, a multiplicity of tongues, and diverse cultures.

Today a great body of historical information is becoming available for a revitalized study of Africa's rich precolonial past. Viewing tribal Africa as it was at the beginning of the modern period in 1500, the contemporary observer sees ever more clearly that it was not a scene of social chaos and stagnation, nor were its peoples little more than retarded children. Many myths about Africa are destined to disappear, among them the centuries-old belief that the inhabitants of the West Coast lived in barbarism and savagery before the coming of the Europeans.

West African political units ranged from individual village kinship groups to extensive empire-states like Songhay. The more complex of these had legal codes, armies, and courts. No matter what degree of sophistication the unit had attained, however, there was one universal political entity throughout the entire region—the family. Not an individual household unit, this kinship group comprised the hundreds of descendants of a common ancestor.

Though most Africans were not literate, they possessed a body of historical and even scientific knowledge, which they learned both from listening to the trained narrators who related their history and traditions and from observing keenly the world about them. A French trader, M. Adanson, was "amazed" by the knowledge that West Coast tribes had of the heavenly bodies. "The Negroes likewise pointed to me a considerable number of stars, that form the chief constellations," he wrote, "wherewith they are well acquainted."

In religion the Africans exhibited both diversity and unity. On the one hand, religion tended to be a tribal affair, with a special and unique intimacy between the group and its exclusive deities. But among Africans there was also a monotheistic inclination, a belief that there existed a single High God who had set the world in motion and whose power and dominion enriched all mankind. In the African religion art played an important role. Statuettes and masks of bronze, wood, or ivory were produced in profusion as adjuncts to the performances of religious and magical ceremonies, ritual being paramount in tribal Africa.

Art of every form and medium was primarily functional. More than an exercise in esthetics, art permeated West Coast culture and related to daily activity. The countless tribal dances illustrate this wedding of art and experience. Each served its own specific purpose, whether it was to observe a death or to petition for a good crop.

Regional variations were reflected in the occupation of the Africans. The river-dwelling tribes were fishermen or boatmakers, while the inhabitants of the grasslands were shepherds, tending sheep, goats, and cattle. Each village, wherever located, generally had its corps of skilled blacksmiths, potters, weavers, and shoemakers, who worked with the wood, ivory, iron, or leather. The natives carried on a lively trade, not only through barter, but through a monetary system based on cowrie shells. Almost everywhere the basic economy was agricultural. "The general Trade from which none but the Kings and principall persons are exempted, is Husbandry," wrote Englishman Richard Dobson of the Gambia Coast early in the 1600's.

One might well ask what became of these communities and civilizations that flourished in West Africa before European exploration, what forces plunged them into an eclipse that is only now lifting? While the Moroccan invasions of the sixteenth century unquestionably contributed to the cultural decline, the most important factor by far in this deterioration was the institution of New World slavery.

The modern traffic in African slaves began with the Portuguese, who inaugurated a systematic exploration of the African coastline shortly after 1400, under the farseeing and energetic Prince Henry the Navigator. The chief aim of these explorers was the expansion of trade. In 1441 Antam Goncalvez and his crew of twenty sailed down the coast of Africa in quest of a cargo of skins and oils. To prove to his sovereign that he had reached the lands beyond Muslim Africa, the young mariner decided to take some of the natives back to Portugal. Hence, when Goncalvez returned to Lisbon from Cape Bojador, he brought with him a new commodity—ten Negroes from the West Coast.

Within a decade Lisbon had become the center of a thriving trade in African slaves. A new era had begun not only for Portugal but for the entire western world. Although the rediscovery of Africa would result in a profitable trade in gold, pepper, and ivory, the chief prize was destined to be a fresh labor supply for the newly settled lands across the Atlantic.

Finding Africa to be a treasure house, the Portuguese tried to confine trade with that continent to themselves. For nearly a century they were successful, but beginning in the late 1500's the Portuguese monopoly began to crumble. The following century witnessed a massive intrusion by Swedes, Danes, French, Brandenburg Germans, Dutch, and English. During the mid-1600's the Dutch were the leaders in the slave-carrying trade, a position they gradually yielded to England.

England had shown an interest in the slave trade even before the discovery of the New World. In 1481 King Edward IV had petitioned the Pope to permit English merchants to journey to the West Coast. The alarmed Portuguese ruler managed to gain Edward's consent to dissuade the merchants from making the trip. But Edward's acquiescence was not copied by Elizabeth I and her successors, who shared the common European belief that African slavery was the cornerstone of overseas expansion, since it gained for the homeland not only the enormous profits of the slave trade itself, but the profits that the colonial possessions could yield through the use of slave labor.

Although the trading companies that secured slaves for the New World varied in nationality, their slave-trading operations were much the same. The first step was to obtain a grant of charter from one's sovereign. The company would then stock its ships with goods—textiles, metalware, and rum—and send them to previously acquired forts and stations in West Africa. The company's traders at these stations would arrange to do business with the native chief, their principal source for the supply of slaves.

The African potentates who were engaged in the slave trade were not fully aware of the long-range consequences of their acts. They had long been familiar with slavery, for the practice had existed among them from time immemorial. But this indigenous slavery had been on a relatively small scale. Moreover, in pre-European Africa, slavery carried no stigma of innate inferiority, a slave often rising to a position of trust and honor. But with the coming of the European traders, African slavery reached massive proportions, decimating whole tribes. In the span of three centuries and a half, West Coast Africa would lose from 18,000,000 to 24,000,000 of its best physical specimens, the only kind the slave traders wanted. Also, the Europeans were quick to formulate racial theories to justify the traffic, classifying Africans as "natural" slaves, foredoomed to such a lowly estate by their inborn backwardness.

But this train of events could hardly have been foreseen by the early native chiefs as they bargained with the traders. In this buying and selling, the chiefs and their agents generally showed great shrewdness. Even before negotiations began, they insisted on being showered with gifts. After the preliminaries, the exchange could proceed, the average healthy male bringing sixty dollars in merchandise.

When a shipload of slaves had been gathered up at the trading post, they were driven aboard, their destination the West Indies. The forty-day voyage across the Atlantic, the "Middle Passage," called for great endurance by crew and human cargo. Disease, particularly smallpox, took a high toll; the supply of food and water often ran out. The crew had to be alert for a slave mutiny, an occurrence that happened often enough to compel the trading companies to take out "revolt insurance" policies. Although the experienced trader, James Barbot, took precautions against a slave uprising, his Jamaica-bound ship, *Albion,* was the scene of a mutiny that cost the lives of nearly thirty slaves, many of whom, wrote Barbot, "leaped overboard, and drowned themselves in the ocean with much resolution, showing no manner of concern for life."

The West Indies, to which the great majority of slave ships were bound, were only a temporary home for many of the slaves, who would later be taken to the English mainland colonies. To these uprooted Africans the West Indies served as a "seasoning" post, where they were conditioned for the routines of slavery. West Indian slavery required as much stamina as the ocean voyage that had preceded it. The work in the sugar fields was hard, the food was poor and insufficient, and the slave codes were severe. "Like Israel in Egypt, all their service was with rigour," wrote the clergyman-historian W. J. Gardner in his study of Jamaica. But if the slave were lucky enough to survive a three-year seasoning period, he might be sold to the British colonies along the Atlantic seaboard.

By 1700 these mainland colonies furnished a ready market for slaves. White indentured servants—persons who had entered into a contract of servitude in order to reach America—were being displaced by Negroes. In the southern colonies black laborers were needed to produce the staples—first tobacco, then sugar cane, rice, and indigo. The provincial South also had its corps of slave artisans and craftsmen, Negroes having a virtual monopoly on the mechanic arts. "It is certain," writes Marcus Jernegan, "that the negro slave artisan was an important agency in the commercial development of the southern colonies."

No southern colony was prepared to survive without slaves. The founders of Georgia had hoped to keep slavery out of the province, but their arguments against slavery did not convince the settlers. Eventually the Georgia Trustees were compelled to grant the request that slavery be permitted. North Carolina did not lend itself readily to the production of the great agricultural staples, but it, too, wanted black laborers. "Great is the loss this Country has sustained in not being supply'd by vessells from Guinea with Negroes," wrote Captain George Burrington, on January 1, 1733, to the Lords of Trade and Plantations. "It is hoped some Merchants in England will speedily furnish this Colony with Negroes, to increase the Produce and its Trade to England."

The North, too, found use for Negroes. In the northern colonies the slave pursued the variety of vocations characteristic of a highly diversified economy. Negroes, slave and free, were employed as printers, rope makers, goldsmiths, silversmiths, and cabinet makers. To New England, however, the chief importance of the Negro was not as an employee, but as merchandise in the slave trade. Out of this trade grew a wealthy class of shippers and merchants. This trade spawned the great distilleries in Rhode Island and Massachusetts, rum being one of the indispensable commodities in the business. Moreover, the slave trade offered employment to innumerable seamen, thus strengthening the colonial merchant marine.

In colonial America the Negro played a role beyond that of a plantation worker and laborer-artisan. He was called upon to bear arms in times of crisis. The practice of arming Negroes was, as a rule, contrary to the laws debarring them from the militia. Slaves were excluded from military service because of their obligations to their masters and because of the fear of a servile insurrection.

To arm the Negro was indeed hazardous. But it was a necessary risk, even in a colony like South Carolina, where the black population was dangerously numerous, or in a colony like Georgia, which was exposed to enemies whom the Negroes might join. A slave enlistment law was passed in South Carolina in 1719, and in Georgia in 1772. The threat from outside—from the Indians, the French, or the Spanish—made it necessary either to ignore the laws against putting a gun in the hands of a Negro or to pass laws authorizing such a step.

In the English colonies the presence of the Negro led to fixed ideas concerning him as a type (if not a stereotype). He was regarded as a pariah, a man with natural shortcomings, and hence one who must be kept at arm's length. Holding such disdainful attitudes, the colonists passed laws against racial intermarriage. Maryland passed the first such law in 1664. By 1725 her example had been followed by six other colonies, including Massachusetts and Pennsylvania.

To some extent these laws, and the derogatory attitude that engendered them, stemmed from the fact that most Negroes were slaves. But the Negroes' lowly status does not wholly account for the prejudicial attitude toward them. For it is to be noted that this attitude was prevalent before slavery had taken firm root, and it existed in sections where Negroes were few. Moreover, in Latin America, where the Negro was also a slave, the concept of the black man as a permanent inferior never became part of the mores, as Frank Tannenbaum explains in his *Slave and Citizen.* In fine, although racial attitudes in British America grew largely from economic considerations, this was not the whole story.

For the concept of Negro inferiority so dominant in the English settlements had its psychopathological aspects. Whites found it comforting to view themselves as a superior breed. The need for a foil, an "out-group," was well served by the Negro. His land of origin, his cultural background, his skin color and other outward physical traits tended to set him apart, and hence to make him an object of prejudice. To have a class of permanent underlings was satisfying to the ego. And this superiority complex, with its expressions in law and in everyday life, went unchecked by Crown or church.

If the theory of the racial inferiority of the Negro was deeply rooted, this is not to say that he was without friends. Some whites, particularly those of Quaker persuasion, condemned slavery. Much of their opposition was based on its deleterious effect on the bondman himself. Other whites, Puritans and Anglicans, while not generally denouncing slavery, showed a deep concern for the spiritual welfare of slaves. Bent on insuring the slave a better life in the hereafter, they gave him religious instruction and, where the law permitted, provided schools for teaching him to read the Bible.

The total impact of this religious concern upon the Negro himself is difficult to assess. But it is not without significance that the first two articulate Negroes in America, poets Jupiter Hammon and Phillis Wheatley, were deeply religious. As Hammon wrote in a dedicatory poem to his fellow slave, "An Address to Miss Phillis Wheatley":

God's tender mercy brought thee here;
    Tost o'er the raging main;
In Christian faith thou hast a share,
    Worth all the gold of Spain.

1

THE GENUINE AFRICAN

The first Europeans to reach the West Coast of Africa were officials and traders, interested more in profit and loss than in native cultures. Moreover, they observed Africa's indigenous peoples with a Western eye, one that regarded a difference *in culture as an* inferiority *in culture. Nevertheless, an increasing body of material is becoming available for a study of Africa before the Portuguese, and today's historian is able to present a more balanced view of pre-colonial Africa than were his predecessors.*

Fifty years ago it was difficult to find a European who did not view African cultures with the "Western eye." A rare exception was Leo Frobenius, an ethnologist who brought to the study of Africa no preconceived notions of the inferiority of native cultures. A member of the German Inner African Exploration Expedition from 1910 to 1912, Frobenius capped his long career as an Africanist with the publication of a two-volume work, The Voice of Africa. *Frobenius began his study of West Coast cultures in 1891 after reading in a Berlin paper a purportedly learned article which stated that pre-colonial Africa had been a hopelessly backward region. In the passage below, written in 1899, Frobenius disputes this point of view.*

16th Century Ivory Mask of the King of Benin, Nigeria.

. . . We are ignorant of hoary Africa. Somewhat of its present, perhaps, we know, but of its past little.

We ethnologists have fared particularly ill. Far from bringing us answers to our questions, the travelers have increased our enigmas by many an addition so peculiar that astonishment has scarcely yet made room for investigation. For the pictures of the inhabitants and the specimens of their civilization are indeed questions. Open an illustrated geography and compare the "Type of the African Negro," the bluish-black fellow of the protuberant lips, the flattened nose, the stupid expression, and the short curly hair, with the tall bronze figures from Dark Africa, with which we have of late become familiar, their almost fine-cut features, slightly arched nose, long hair, etc., and you have an example of the problems pressing for solution. In other respects, too, the genuine African of the interior bears no resemblance to the accepted negro type as it figures on drug and cigar store signs, wearing a shabby stovepipe hat, plaid trousers, and a varicolored coat. A stroll through the corridors of the Berlin Museum of Ethnology teaches that the real African need by no means resort to the rags and tatters of bygone European splendor. He has precious ornaments of his own, of ivory and plumes, fine plaited willow ware, weapons of superior workmanship. Nothing more beautiful, for instance, can be imagined than an iron club carefully wound round with strips of metal, the handle covered with snake skin.*

---

*Leo Frobenius, "The Origin of African Civilizations," *Annual Report of the Board of Regents of the Smithsonian Institution . . . for the Year Ending June 30, 1898* (Washington, 1899), 637-638.

2

AFRICA IN THE SIXTEENTH CENTURY

Among the many travelers attracted to West Africa in the late Middle Ages was a Moor who had been born in Spain in 1494, had moved with his family to North Africa shortly thereafter, and had entered the Moroccan diplomatic service while still in his teens. In 1518 he was captured by Christian pirates, who were so impressed by his great learning and wide travel that they took him to Rome as a present for the Pope. The young Moor quickly won the favor of Leo X, who freed him, gave him a handsome pension, and conferred upon him his own name. When he was captured, this Leo Africanus, to use the name by which he is known to history, had with him a rough draft of the work to which he owes his fame, The History and Description of Africa and the Notable Things Therein Contained. *In 1526 Africanus completed this work, having rewritten it in Italian. John Pory, a scholarly friend of the eminent geographer, Richard Hakluyt, translated the volume into English in 1600. Leo's work gave to his contemporaries and to the world the first detailed account of the wide regions that he had traversed.*

This pathbreaking historical travelogue was based on a long caravan journey from 1513 to 1515 led by Leo's uncle, a diplomat-merchant like Leo himself. On this expedition Africanus gained a first-hand aquaintance of fifteen Negro kingdoms representing the flowering of the medieval Muslim civilizations in the Western Sudan. These kingdoms, with their imperial organization, their trade networks, their arts, their "great store of temples, priests, and professours," reveal an order of civilization comparing favorably with their contemporaneous European counterparts. The note of wonder that creeps into Leo's writings may have stemmed in part from astonishment, since he had shared the patronizing attitude of the Muslim toward the Negro. But he was a careful and trustworthy observer. "He is one of the few geographical writers of his age who can still be read, not merely for the purposes of the historian, or for entertainment—and he is good for both—but for actual information regarding the condition of the countries and the habits of the people described by him," writes Robert Brown, editor of the Pory-translated history by Africanus. In the passages that follow, the renowned traveler gives descriptions of Djenne (Ghinea), Melle, and Tombuto (Timbuktu).

A DESCRIPTION OF THE KINGDOME OF GHINEA

This kingdome called by the merchants of our nation Gheneoa, by the natural inhabitants thereof Genni, and by the Portugals and other people of Europe Ghinea, standeth in the midst betweene Gualata on the north, Tombuto on the east, and the kingdome of Melli on the south. In length it containeth almost five hundred miles, and extendeth two hundred and fiftie miles along the river of Niger, and bordereth upon the Ocean sea in the same place, where Niger falleth into the saide sea. This place exceedingly aboundeth with barlie, rice, cattell, fishes, and cotton: and their cotton they sell unto the merchants of Barbarie, for cloth of Europe, for brazen vessels, for armour, and other such commodities. Their coine is of gold without any stampe or inscription at all: they have certaine iron-money also, which they use about matters of small value, some peeces whereof weigh a pound, some halfe a pound, and some one quarter of a pound. In all this kingdome there is no fruite to be found but onely dates, which are brought hither either out of Gualata or

Numidia. Heere is neither towne nor castle, but a certaine great village onely, wherein the prince of Ghinea, together with his priestes, doctors, merchants, and all the principall men of the region inhabite. The walles of their houses are built of chalke, and the roofes are covered with strawe: the inhabitants are clad in blacke or blew cotton, wherewith they cover their heads also: but the priests and doctors of their law go apparelled in white cotton. This region during the three moneths of Iulie, August, and September, is yeerely environed with the overflowings of Niger in manner of an Island; all which time the merchants of Tombuto conveigh their merchandize hither in certaine Canoas or narrow boats made of one tree, which they rowe all the day long, but at night they binde them to the shore, and lodge themselves upon the lande.

Of the kingdome of Melli

This region extending it selfe almost three hundred miles along the side of a river which falleth into Niger, bordereth northward upon the region last described, southward upon certaine deserts and drie mountaines, westward upon huge woods and forrests stretching to the Ocean sea shore, and eastward upon the territorie of Gago. In this kingdome there is a large and ample village containing to the number of sixe thousand or mo families, and called Melli, whereof the whole kingdome is so named. And here the king hath his place of residence. The region it selfe yeeldeth great abundance of corne, flesh, and cotton. Heere are many artificers and merchants in all places: and yet the king honourably entertaineth all strangers. The inhabitants are rich, and have plentie of wares. Heere are great store of temples, priests, and professours, which professours read their lectures onely in the temples, bicause they have no colleges at all. The people of this region excell all other Negros in witte, civilitie, and industry; and were the first that embraced the law of Mahumet.

Of the kingdome of Tombuto

This name was in our times (as some thinke) imposed upon this kingdome from the name of a certain towne so called, which (they say) king *Mense Suleiman* founded in the yeere of the Hegeira 610, and it is situate within twelve miles of a certaine branch of Niger, all the houses whereof are now changed into cottages built of chalke, and covered with thatch. Howbeit there is a most stately temple to be seene, the wals whereof are made of stone and lime; and a princely palace also built by a most excellent workeman of Granada. Here are many shops of artificers, and merchants, and especially of such as weave linnen and cotton cloth. And hither do the Barbarie-merchants bring cloth of Europe. All the women of this region except maid-servants go with their faces covered, and sell all necessarie victuals. The inhabitants, & especially strangers there residing, are exceeding rich, insomuch, that the king that now is [1526], married both his daughters unto two rich merchants. Here are many wels, containing most sweete water; and so often as the river Niger overfloweth, they conveigh the water thereof by certaine sluces into the towne. Corne, cattle, milke, and butter this region yeeldeth in great abundance: but salt is verie scarce heere; for it is brought hither by land from Tegaza, which is five hundred miles distant. When I my selfe was here, I saw one camels loade of salt sold for 80. ducates. The rich king of Tombuto hath many plates and scepters of gold, some whereof weigh 1300. poundes: and he keepes a magnificent and well furnished court. When he travelleth any whither he rideth upon a camell, which is lead by some of his noblemen; and so he doth likewise when hee goeth to warfar, and all his souldiers ride upon horses.*

3

TRIBAL CLASS SOCIETY

Each African tribe, however classless it may have appeared to an outsider, had its own social ranks. At the head was the king, often considered sacred, to whom a portion of one's goods must be given. The number and the nature of the classes below the king varied, with slaves at the bottom of the social pyramid. Along the Ivory and Gold Coasts three dominant classes existed. These were described by William Bosman, a resident slave trader for the Dutch, writing in 1701 from the station at Elmina Castle to a friend in London. In the interests of his company, Bosman took trips up and down the coast and thus came to know the customs of the natives. These peoples had borrowed little from Islamic influences, having developed their own well-ordered political and social systems.

I have observed five degrees of men amongst the Negroes; the first of which are their kings or captains, for the word is here synonymous.

The second, their Caboceros, or chief men; which reducing to our manner of expression, we should be apt to call them Civil fathers, whose province is only to take care of the welfare of the city or village, and to appease any tumult.

The third sort are those who have acquired a great reputation by their riches, either devolved on them by inheritance or gotten by trade. And these are the persons which some authors have represented as noblemen; but whether they are in the right or not, shall hereafter plainly appear.

The fourth are the common people employed in the tillage of wines, agriculture and fishing.

The fifth and last are the slaves, either sold by their relations, taken in war, or come so by poverty.

These five being the only degrees which are to be found amongst the Negroes; let us enquire by what means they arrive at any of the three first.

First, the dignity of king or captain in most of these countries, descends hereditarily from father to son, and in defect of issue to the next male-heir; though sometimes so much regard is had to his

*Robert Brown, editor, Leo Africanus, *The History and Description of Africa,* trans. John Pory (New York, Burt Franklin, Publisher, no date), III, 822-824.

riches in slaves and money, that he who is plentifully stored with these, is often preferred to the right heir.

The inauguration of a king is not clogged with many pompous ceremonies; for coronations and coronation-oaths being here equally unknown, the new king is shewn to the people, and sometimes carried through his territories; and the whole affair terminates in one merry day: but in case of competitorship, when two pretend to that dignity at the same time; for confirmation of the loyalty of their followers, each pretender obliges his respective party to an oath of allegiance; without this happens all things run very smoothly, some offerings only made, as usual here on all solemn occasions. The principal men or Caboceros are commonly limited to a set number; but some of them dying, and the vacancies not filling, when upon assembling together they find their number too small, they chose out of the commonalty persons well advanced in years to compleat their number (for young men are seldom admitted into this honourable assembly), who are obliged to express their gratitude to their electing brethren by a present of a cow and some drink; after which they are lawfully admitted and confirmed. The custom of Axim obliges the candidate for this dignity to be a native of that country living at Axim, at least keeping a house there, inhabited by one of his wives, or some of his family, and sometimes residing there himself; which is somewhat like our being obliged to keep fire and light to preserve our right of citizens in Holland. If there be one alone, or several, he or they are all brought to our fort and presented to our factor, with a request that they may be admitted into their society; who, if he hath nothing to object against him, administers an oath to him on the Bible, obliging him to be and remain true to the Netherlanders, and to aid and assist them to the utmost of his power against all their enemy's whatsoever, whether Europeans or Negroes, and deport himself on all occasions as a loyal subject: after which he takes an oath, not unlike the former, respecting his own nation; both which oaths are confirmed by an imprecation, "That God would strike him dead if he swore contrary to his intentions, or doth not keep his oath"; in farther confirmation of which the Bible is held to his breast and laid on his head, which are the ceremonies used to render the oath obligatory: this done, the factor having registered his name, acknowledges him a member of their assembly, and admits him to all the rights, privileges, and advantages appendant thereto; and having made the due presents to his brethren, he is a Caboceer during his life. In other places on the coast the election of a Caboceer is somewhat different; but it being so well regulated at Axim, I shall content myself with describing that only.

The third sort of Negroes are those enriched either by inheritance or trade; who, to acquire a reputation and great name amongst their fellow-citizens, buy about seven small elephants' teeth, which they make into blowing-horns; upon which they cause their family to be taught all sort of tunes usual, according to the extravagant course of the country: which, when they have learned, they inform all their relations and acquaintance that they intend to shew their blowing-horns publicly, that they may come and make merry with them for several days together; whilst they, their wives, and slaves appear with as much pomp and splendour as is possible, borrowing gold and coral of their friends to make the greater show, and distributing presents amongst them: so that this extravagant ceremony becomes very expensive. This initiatory festival being over they are free to blow upon their horns at pleasure, which none are permitted who have not thus aggrandized themselves; but if they are inclined to divert themselves are obliged to borrow them. How contradictory is the course of things in this world! in some places men are obliged to beg hard and make interest for horns, whilst they come home to the houses of others as unexpected as undesired.

A Negro thus far advanced in honour, usually makes himself master of first one and then another shield: of which he makes a shew as public and pompous as that of the horns; and is obliged to lie the first night with all his family in battle array in the open air, intimating that he will not be afraid of any danger or hardship in defence of his people. After which he passes the next and the remaining days of the feast, which are generally about eight, in shooting and martial exercises, as well as dancing and all sorts of mirth; himself, his wives, and family being as richly drest as they possibly can; and all that he hath in the world exposed to public view, and removed from place to place. But this festival is not so expensive as the former; for instead of making presents, as usual in that, he here on the contrary receives very valuable presents; and when he designs to divert himself, or go to the war, he is permitted to carry two shields: a favour not allowed to any who hath not thus qualified himself.

These are the nobility which authors boast of on this coast; but that in reality they are not so is plain, because no person can ennoble himself, but must be so by birth, or by creation of another: in which they are both deficient; for by birth they are only slaves, and consequently widely distant from nobles, and they owe their advance only to themselves and their money; their port of honour here being always open to him who is rich enough to bear the expence. Besides, in other places nobility engages those honoured with it firmly in the public service of their King or country; which these are not the least concerned for, applying themselves to nothing but trade: but if any are fond of having them gentlemen and noblemen, I shall let them remain so. And it will not a little redound to my honour, that I have for several years successively been waited on by one of these noblemen in the capacity of a footman, without having the least respect to his nobility.

The fourth and fifth sort need no other account to be given of them, than that they are common people and slaves.*

---

*William Bosman, *A New and Accurate Description of the Coast of Guinea*, London, 1705, in John Pinkerton, ed., *A Collection of the . . . Voyages and Travels in All Parts of the World* (London, 1814), XVI, 392-394.

4

NATIVE INDUSTRY AND TRADE

Among the general descriptions of particular regions is one left by John Barbot, an agent-general of a French organization, the Royal Company of Africa and the Islands of America. In the 1680's Barbot spent many months, off and on, in the region between the Senegal and the Gambia Rivers, where the French had driven out the Portuguese. Barbot left a general description of the culture of the peoples along the Gambia Coast, who boasted well-fortified towns, corps of craftsmen in many fields, and a flourishing husbandry. Reading Barbot, one gets the impression of a stable, orderly pattern of life, not of a savage region occupied by still more savage people, nor of a land of eternal warfare between petty and backward tribal tyrants.

OF THE NATIVES IN GENERAL

The *Blacks* of *Gamboa* were formerly very savage, cruel and treacherous; but through long commerce with the *Europeans* they are now become pretty tractable; especially those about the sea-coasts, who are most civiliz'd, many of them understanding or speaking *Portuguese, English, French,* or *Dutch,* indifferently well.

Many of them take to some profession, and their wealth consists in slaves and gold, especially about Jagre.

The blacksmiths make all sorts of tools and instruments for tillage, *etc.* as also weapons and armour, being indifferent skilful at hardning of iron, and whetting it on common stones. Their bellows are made of two large reeds join'd together, in each of which is a stick, cover'd all over with small feathers, tied fast to it, so that drawing out and thrusting in the sticks with both hands, they blow and light the fire.

The weavers make great quantities of narrow cotton-cloth, which from the *Portuguese* name, they call *Panho,* of the same as has been mention'd at *Cabo Verde.* The best sort they call *Panhos Sakes,* being eight narrow slips stich'd together, generally white, clouded with flames. The second sort is of six narrow slips put together, called *Bontans,* about two yards long, and a yard and a half broad, curiously striped. The third sort is call'd *Barfoel,* of the same size, but coarser.

These cloths they sell to the *English* and *Portugeses;* one of the first sort for a bar of iron; three of the second for two bars; and two of the third for one bar: with which those *Europeans* trade at *Sierra Leona, Sherbro,* and on the south coast of *Guinea,* and purchase for them elephants teeth.

The husbandmen till the ground with a sort of tool, much like a small axe, but sharp. At certain times of the year every one of the *Blacks* is oblig'd to till the land, excepting only the king, the chief officers, the decrepit, and small children.

THEIR CLOATHING

Both men and women generally wear a sort of coat, or vest, made after the manner of a shirt, reaching down to the knees, with long wide open sleeves; and under it the men have drawers, after the *Turkish* fashion.

Maids and young women make several figures all over their faces, arms, breasts, and fingers, with hot burning irons, or needles, which at a distance look like a mezzo-relievo on the flesh; and this they reckon a mighty ornament.

THEIR HOUSES

Or huts, are much after the same form, and of the same materials as those describ'd at *Senega,* but neat and convenient, commonly made of a red binding clay, or earth, which soon hardens in the sun; and so well thatch'd or cover'd with rushes, or palm-tree leaves, ingeniously wove together, that neither the sun, nor rain can offend those within. At the village of *Bar,* the huts are generally smaller than at other places.

THEIR FOOD

Commonly consists of millet, fish, milk, rice, poultry and fruit. The *Portuguese Mulattoes* boil fowl and rice together. The way the *Blacks* use to dress their meat, is much the same as at *Senega;* and their drink is palm-wine, especially about the coast, near cape *Roxo;* but, for the most part, they are not very cleanly, either in their meat or drink.

THEIR TRADE

This is the employment of very many of the *Blacks,* either among others of their own complexion, or with the *Europeans,* making good advantage of it. The *English* and *French* deal with those that are about their settlements; and the *Portugueses* with those farther up the country, along the rivers, from *Cachau* to *Gamboa,* in the nature of interlopers.

Below, the African city of Loango as seen by Thomas Astley, on his travels in the eighteenth century. A major trading center, Loango had a palace, civic gardens, and even a royal wine house.

The *Blacks* do not only trade along the river *Gamboa,* in their canoos, but along the coast too, constantly attending the times of fairs and markets.

The fair at *Mansagar* is held under a hill, near the town, where some *Portuguese Mulattoes* have their dwelling; and thither is brought to the market abundance of salt, wax, elephants teeth, mats, cotton, golddust, of this the least, all sorts of cattle, goats, poultry, horses; and every *Monday* throughout the year there is a small market for provisions. Mats are properly the coin of the country, all other things being rated by the mats, for they know nothing of plate or money.

The fair kept twice a year at *Great Cassan* is both times very considerable, an almost incredible number of people resorting thither from all parts of the country, and vast quantities of all sorts of commodities being brought to it. The *Portugueses* resort to it very much to buy dry hides, elephants teeth, *etc.* for bugles and iron bars. They set out from *Cachau,* and other places on the south-side of *Gamboa,* at the beginning of the rainy season, and return not home till all is over.*

5

THE IMPORTANCE OF THE SLAVE TRADE TO ENGLAND

Within two decades after Goncalvez had brought the first Negroes to Lisbon, the slave trade had become an important component of European commerce. And with the discovery of America toward the close of the century, the African slave trade became a truly major enterprise. Now the Europeans had a vast new continent in which this fresh supply of black labor could be gainfully employed. The New World, with its great natural resources waiting to be tapped, was a boon to slavery, and the fostering mother of the slave trade.

The importance of the slave trade was persuasively set forth in a pamphlet published in England in 1745; its probable author was Malachy Postlethwayt, a staunch supporter of the traffic. Postlethwayt correctly appraises the great influence of the slave trade in quickening the tempo of England's economy. The West Indian slave trade was the source of much of the wealth that enabled England to become the mother of the Industrial Revolution. Postlethwayt does not mention, of course, the effect of the slave trade on African tribal life—that was something else again.

But is it not notorious to the whole World, that the Business of *Planting* in our *British Colonies,* as well as in the *French,* is carried on by the Labour of *Negroes,* imported thither from *Africa?* Are we not indebted to that valuable People, the *Africans,* for our *Sugars, Tobaccoes, Rice, Rum,* and all other *Plantation Produce?* And the greater the Number of *Negroes* imported into our *Colonies,* from *Africa,* will not the Exportation of *British* Manufactures among the *Africans* be in Proportion; they being paid for in such Commodities only? The more likewise our Plantations abound in *Negroes,* will not more

---

*John Barbot, *A Description of the Coasts of Nigritia, vulgarly called North-Guinea,* in A. and J. Churchill, eds., *A Collection of Voyages and Travels* (London, 1746), V, 77-78.

Land become cultivated, and both *better* and greater *Variety* of *Plantation Commodities* be produced? As those Trades are subservient to the Well Being and Prosperity of each other; so the more either flourishes or declines, the other must be necessarily affected; and the general Trade and Navigation of their *Mother Country* will be proportionately benefited or injured. May we not therefore say, with equal Truth, as the *French* do . . . that the general NAVIGATION of *Great Britain* owes all its *Encrease* and *Splendor* to the Commerce of its *American* and *African Colonies;* and that it cannot be maintained and enlarged otherwise than from the constant Prosperity of both those Branches, *whose Interests are mutual and inseparable?*

Whatever *other* Causes may have conspired to enable the *French* to beat us out of all the Markets in Europe in the *Sugar* and *Indigo Trades,* etc. the great and extraordinary Care they have taken to cherish and encourage their *African Company,* to the End that their *Plantations* might be cheaply and plentifully stocked with Negroe Husbandmen, is amply sufficient of itself to account for the Effect; for this Policy, they wisely judged, would enable them to produce those Commodities cheaper than we, who have suffered the *British* Interest to decline in *Africa,* as that of the *French* has advanced; and when they could produce the Commodities cheaper, is it at all to be admired that they have undersold us at all the foreign Markets in *Europe,* and hereby got that most beneficial Part of our Trade into their own Hands?

As their great Care and our great Neglect of the *African Trade,* has for many Years past given *France* the Advantage over us in *Planting;* so while the same *Cause* continues, Is it not impossible, in the Nature of Things that the *Effect* should cease, and our Trade return to its former flourishing State? All other Measures as they hitherto have, so always will prove only *temporary Expedients,* not *effectual Restoratives:* They have none of them struck at the Root of the Evil; nor is it possible to work a thorough Cure any other way, but by enabling the *African Company* effectually to maintain and support *British* Rights and Privileges on the Coast of *Africa* against the Encroachments of the *French,* and all other Rivals; and in Consequence thereof, by stocking our own Plantations with greater Plenty of *Negroes,* and at *cheaper Rates* than our Rivals would, in such Case, be able to do. . . .

As *Negroe Labour* hitherto has, so that only can support our *British* Colonies, as it has done those of other Nations. It is *that* also will keep them in due Subserviency to the Interest of their *Mother Country;* for while our Plantations depend only on Planting by *Negroes,* and that of such Produce as interferes only with the Interests of our Rivals not of their *Mother-Country,* our Colonies can never prove injurious to *British* Manufactures, never become independent of these Kingdoms, but remain a perpetual Support to our *European* Interest, by preserving to us a Superiority of Trade and Naval Power.*

---

*From *English Historical Documents,* Vol. X, 1714–1783, edited by David C. Douglas. Reprinted by permission of Eyre & Spottiswodde (Publishers) Ltd.

6

THE IMPERSONAL NATURE OF THE SLAVE TRADE

In rare instances a slave ship crossed the Atlantic without such mishaps as the loss of a single slave or crew member. More typical, however, was the voyage of the Dutch vessel St. Jan. *When she sailed from the island of Annobon, loaded with slaves, on August 17, 1659, the* St. Jan *had already lost her one cooper and one of her surgeons, and the cargo of slaves was suffering from malnutrition and dysentery. Both slaves and crew were put on short rations during the voyage as the result of leaky water casks that had gone dry, and 110 dead slaves had to be thrown overboard. When the ship foundered on a reef in the West Indies on September 24, 1659, the captain and crew abandoned her, leaving aboard the rest of the slaves, who were subsequently seized by a British privateer.*

From Curaçao, the skipper of the St. Jan, *Adriaen Blaes, filed a lengthy deposition to the Amsterdam Directors of the Dutch West India Company. The opening passage of this deposition, reproduced below, is significant not so much for the grim events that it relates as for the manner in which it demonstrates the completely impersonal nature of the slave trade, a business that tended to bring out the worst in those who engaged in it.*

DEPOSITION OF ADRIAEN BLAES
1659

Appeared Adriaen Blaes van der Veer, and says, that he was commanded by Johan Valckenburch, general of El Mina and the Gold Coast, on the 4th of March last to sail as skipper of the ship *St. Jan* from the roadstead of the Castle del Mina aforesaid, with commissary Johan Froon and the accompanying crew or sailors, in the company's service, to the Calabari or Rio Real, there to trade for slaves and to proceed with them, by order of the aforesaid general, to this place. In obedience to these orders, two hundred and nineteen slaves, big and little, were actually traded and purchased, wherewith we sailed in order to prosecute our voyage and carry out our instructions. Not obtaining at the Calabari such sufficiency of provisions as this voyage demanded, for the sustenance of the aforesaid slaves, we resolved to go to the highland of Ambosius where we were unable to procure any provisions, as was our desire. We therefore went to the River Camerones, where we obtained a few articles, but not as much as we wanted. Nevertheless, we pursued our voyage towards Capo de Lopo Gonsalves, at which place we took in wood and water, and thence stood across although experiencing great misery and want of food, to Anabo, where we got some provisions and went on our voyage and made land in the month of October last at the island of Tobago, the greater portion of the slaves having

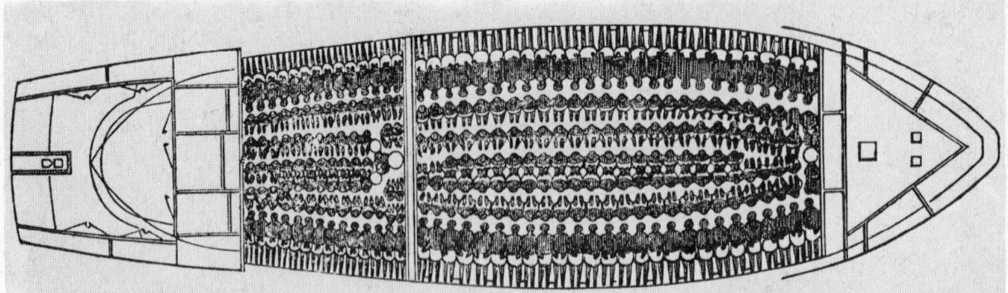

Crammed hull of a slave ship—as seen from above.

died from want and sickness, in consequence of such a very long voyage, so that we saved only ninety slaves, out of the whole cargo. Having taken in water and a few refreshments from the surrounding islands, we set sail from there, passing around the islands, and after we fixed our course on the first instant, west by south, we ran ashore, two hours before day, on one of the reefs of Rocus, on the north east side of the island. At day break, perceiving our danger, we saved ourselves with all the crew in the boat, leaving the negroes in the ship, taking our course to this place [Curacao], in order to inform the Hon'ble Director M. Beck of our misfortune.*

The Status of Negroes in Colonial America

7

THE SENTENCE OF JOHN PUNCH

Negroes had accompanied the early explorers of the New World in the 16th century, and it was only twelve years after the founding of Jamestown that black men made their appearance in the new colony of Virginia. The coming of the Negro in 1619 was quiet enough. Indeed, the time and place of his entry might have remained unknown, had not John Rolfe, tobacco planter and husband of Pocahantas, jotted down this single sentence in his record of events in early Jamestown: "About the last of August came in a dutch man of warre that sold us twenty Negars."

These first Negroes were indentured servants, not slaves. But within two decades the status of the colored inhabitants of the colonies was changing, with black servitude evolving into black slavery. The case of John Punch, which follows, was significant because of the disparity between the sentences of the two white men and that of Punch, who was sentenced to lifetime service, in effect slavery. This case takes on added significance from the fact that Virginia's experiences with her black population would furnish a guideline for the other colonies.

Re Negro John Punch, July 1640. "Whereas Hugh Gwyn hath . . Brought back from Maryland three servants formerly run away . . the court doth therefore order that the said three servants shall receive the punishment of whipping and to have thirty stripes apiece one called Victor, a dutchman, the other a Scotchman called James Gregory, shall first serve out their times with their master according to their Indentures, and one whole year apiece after the time of their service is Expired . . and after that service . . to serve the colony for three whole years apiece, and that the third being a negro named John Punch shall serve his said master or his assigns for the time of his natural Life here or elsewhere."†

---

*New York Colonial Manuscripts, State Archives, Albany, in Elizabeth Donnan, ed., *Documents Illustrative of the Slave Trade* (Washington, Carnegie Institution of Washington, 1930-1935), I, 145.

†Helen T. Catterall, ed., *Judicial Cases Concerning American Slavery and the Negro* (5 vols., Washington, Carnegie Institution of Washington, 1926-1936), I, 77.

8

LIFE SERVITUDE

Negro slavery had fully evolved in Virginia by 1661. A law of that year referred to Negroes as persons "incapable of making satisfaction by addition of time." This meant that there were Negroes who could not be punished by adding to their period of servitude, since they were already committed to service for the remainder of their lives. The provision is quoted below.

ENGLISH RUNNING AWAY WITH NEGROES.

Bee itt enacted That in case any English servant shall run away in company with any negroes who are incapable of makeing satisfaction by addition of time, *Bee itt enacted* that the English so running away in company with them shall serve for the time of the said negroes absence as they are to do for their owne by a former act.*

9

SLAVERY AND PREJUDICE

In early Virginia the Negro's deteriorating status extended to social relationships. He was not, it was commonly agreed, to be treated as a social equal. In 1664 Maryland passed a law stipulating that a white woman who married a slave would have to serve said slave's master as long as her husband lived. This law, which follows, set the pattern for other colonies, and for the antebellum South, in striking at Negro-white marriages.

AN ACT CONCERNING NEGROES & OTHER SLAVES

Bee itt Enacted by the Right Hon[ble]. the Lord Proprietary by the advice and Consent of the upper and lower house of this present Generall Assembly That all Negroes or other slaves already within the Province And all Negroes and other slaves to bee hereafter imported into the Province shall serve Durante Vita And all Children born of any Negro or other slave shall be Slaves as their fathers were for the terme of their lives And forasmuch as divers freeborne English women forgettfull of their free Condicōn and to the disgrace of our Nation doe intermarry with Negro Slaves by which alsoe divers suites may arise touching the Issue of such woemen and a great damage doth befall the Masters of such Negros for prevention whereof for deterring such freeborne women from such shamefull Matches Bee itt further Enacted by the Authority advice and Consent aforesaid That whatsoever free borne woman shall inter marry with any slave from and after the Last day of this present Assembly shall Serve the master of such slave dureing the life of her husband And that all the Issue of such freeborne woemen soe marryed shall be Slaves as their fathers were And Bee itt further Enacted that all the

---

*William H. Hening, ed., *The Statutes at Large: Being a Collection of All the Laws of Virginia, 1619-1792* (13 vols., Richmond, published by the State of Virginia, 1809-1823), II, 26.

Issues of English or other freeborne woemen that have already marryed Negroes shall serve the Masters of their Parents till they be Thirty yeares of age and noe longer.*

10

SLAVE CODES

Colonial America had a role for the Negro. But the presence of a servile population, presumably of inferior stock, made it necessary to adopt measures of control. As might be expected, the southern colonies had the most highly developed codes governing Negroes. In 1712 South Carolina passed "An Act for the better ordering and governing of Negroes and Slaves." This comprehensive measure served as a model for slave codes in the South during the colonial and national periods. The first twelve of its thirty-five sections are reproduced below.

AN ACT FOR THE BETTER ORDERING AND GOVERNING OF NEGROES AND SLAVES.

WHEREAS, the plantations and estates of this Province cannot be well and sufficiently managed and brought into use, without the labor and service of negroes and other slaves; and forasmuch as the said negroes and other slaves brought unto the people of this Province for that purpose, are of barbarous, wild, savage natures, and such as renders them wholly unqualified to be governed by the laws, customs, and practices of this Province; but that it is absolutely necessary, that such other constitutions, laws and orders, should in this Province be made and enacted, for the good regulating and ordering of them, as may restrain the disorders, rapines and inhumanity, to which they are naturally prone and inclined, and may also tend to the safety and security of the people of this Province and their estates; to which purpose,

I. *Be it therefore enacted,* by his Excellency, William, Lord Craven, Palatine, and the rest of the true and absolute Lords and Proprietors of this Province, by and with the advice and consent of the rest of the members of the General Assembly, now met at Charlestown, for the South-west part of this Province, and by the authority of the same, That all negroes, mulatoes, mustizoes or Indians, which at any time heretofore have been sold, or now are held or taken to be, or hereafter shall be bought and sold for slaves, are hereby declared slaves; and they, and their children, are hereby made and declared slaves, to all intents and purposes; excepting all such negroes, mulatoes, mustizoes or Indians, which heretofore have been, or hereafter shall be, for some particular merit, made and declared free, either by the Governor and council of this Province, pursuant to any Act or law of this Province, or by their respective owners or masters; and also, excepting all such negroes, mulatoes, mustizoes or Indians, as can prove they ought not to be sold for slaves. And in case any negro, mulatoe, mustizoe or Indian, doth lay claim to his or her

*William H. Browne, et al., ed., *Archives of Maryland* (65 vols., Baltimore, Maryland Historical Society, 1883-1952), I, 533-534.

freedom, upon all or any of the said accounts, the same shall be finally heard and determined by the Governor and council of this Province.

II. And for the better ordering and governing of negroes and all other slaves in this Province, *Be it enacted* by the authority aforesaid, That no master, mistress, overseer, or other person whatsoever, that hath the care and charge of any negro or slave, shall give their negroes and other slaves leave, on Sundays, hollidays, or any other time, to go out of their plantations, except such negro or other slave as usually wait upon them at home or abroad, or wearing a livery; and every other negro or slave that shall be taken hereafter out of his master's plantation, without a ticket, or leave in writing, from his master or mistress, or some other person by his or her appointment, or some white person in the company of such slave, to give an account of his business, shall be whipped; and every person who shall not (when in his power,) apprehend every negro or other slave which he shall see out of his master's plantation, without leave as aforesaid, and after apprehended, shall neglect to punish him by moderate whipping, shall forfeit twenty shillings, the one half to the poor, to be paid to the church wardens of the Parish where such forfeiture shall become due, and the other half to him that will inform for the same, within one week after such neglect; and that no slave may make further or other use of any one ticket than was intended by him that granted the same, every ticket shall particularly mention the name of every slave employed in the particular business, and to what place they are sent, and what time they return; and if any person shall presume to give any negro or slave a ticket in the name of his master or mistress, without his or her consent, such person so doing shall forfeit the sum of twenty shillings; one half to the poor, to be disposed of as aforesaid, the other half to the person injured, that will complain against the person offending, within one week after the offence committed. And for the better security of all such persons that shall endeavor to take any runaway, or shall examine any slave for his ticket, passing to and from his master's plantation, it is hereby declared lawful for any white person to beat, maim or assult, and if such negro or slave cannot otherwise be taken, to kill him, who shall refuse to shew his ticket, or, by running away or resistance, shall endeavor to avoid being apprehended or taken.

III. *And be it further enacted* by the authority aforesaid, That every master, mistress or overseer of a family in this Province, shall cause all his negro houses to be searched diligently and effectually once every fourteen days, for fugitive and runaway slaves, guns, swords, clubs, and any other mischievous weapons, and finding any, to take them away, and cause them to be secured; as also, for clothes, goods, and any other things and commodities that are not given them by their master, mistress, commander or overseer, and honestly come by; and in whose custody they find any thing of that kind, and suspect or know to be stolen goods, the same they shall seize and take into their custody, and a full and ample description of the particulars thereof, in writing, within ten days after the discovery thereof, either to the provost marshall, or to the clerk of the parish for the time being, who is hereby required to receive the same, and to enter upon it the day of its receipt, and the particulars to file and keep to himself; and the clerk shall set upon the posts of the church door, and the provost marshall upon the usual public places, or places of notice, a short brief, that such lost goods are found; whereby, any person that hath lost his goods may the better come to the knowledge where they are; and the owner going to the marshall or clerk, and proving, by marks or otherwise, that the goods lost belong to him, and paying twelve pence for the entry and declaration of the same, if the marshall or clerk be convinced that any part of the goods certified by him to be found, appertains to the party inquiring, he is to direct the said party inquiring to the place and party where the goods be, who is hereby required to make restitution of what is in being to the true owner; and every master, mistress or overseer, as also the provost marshall or clerk, neglecting his duty in any the particulars aforesaid, for every neglect shall forfeit twenty shillings.

IV. And for the more effectual detecting and punishing such persons that trade with any slave for stolen goods, *Be it further enacted* by the authority aforesaid, That where any person shall be suspected to trade as aforesaid, any justice of the peace shall have power to take from him suspected, sufficient recognizance, not to trade with any slave contrary to the laws of this Province; and if it shall afterwards appear to any of the justices of the peace, that such person hath, or hath had, or shipped off, any goods, suspected to be unlawfully come by, it shall be lawful for such justice of the peace to oblige the person to appear at the next general sessions, who shall there be obliged to make reasonable proof, of whom he bought, or how he came by, the said goods, and unless he do it, his recognizance shall be forfeited.

V. *And be it further enacted* by the authority aforesaid, That no negro or slave shall carry out of the limits of his master's plantation any sort of gun or fire arms, without his master, or some other white person by his order, is present with him, or without a certificate from his master, mistress or overseer, for the same; and if any negro or slave shall be so apprehended or taken, without the limits aforesaid, with any gun or fire arms as aforesaid, such arms shall be forfeited to him or them that shall apprehend or take the same; unless the person who is the owner of the arms so taken, shall in three months time redeem the arms so taken, by paying to the person that took the same, the sum of twenty shillings.

VI. *And be it further enacted* by the authority aforesaid, That every master or head of any family, shall keep all his guns and other arms, when out of use, in the most private and least frequented room in the house, upon the penalty of being convicted of neglect therein, to forfeit three pounds.

VII. And *whereas*, great numbers of slaves which do not dwell in Charlestown, on Sundays and holidays resort thither, to drink, quarrel, fight, curse and swear, and profane the Sabbath, and using and carrying of clubs and other mischievous weapons, resorting in great companies together, which may give them an opportunity of executing any wicked designs and purposes, to the damage and prejudice of the inhabitants of this Province; for the prevention whereof, *Be it enacted* by the authority aforesaid, That all and every the constables of Charlestown, separately on every Sunday, and the holidays at Christmas, Easter and Whitsonside, together with so many men as each constable shall think necessary to accompany him, which he is hereby empowered for that end to press, under the penalty of twenty shillings to the person that shall disobey him, shall, together with such persons, go through all or any the streets, and also, round about Charlestown, and as much further on the neck as they shall be informed or have reason to suspect any meeting or concourse of any such negroes or slaves to be at that time, and to enter into any house, at Charlestown, or elsewhere, to search for such slaves, and as many of them as they can apprehend, shall cause to be publicly whipped in Charlestown, and then to be delivered to the marshall, who for every slave so whipped and delivered to him by the constable, shall pay the constable five shillings, which five shillings shall be repaid the said marshall by the owner or head of that family to which the said negro or slave doth belong, together with such other charges as shall become due to him for keeping runaway slaves; and the marshall shall in all respects keep and dispose of such slave as if the same was delivered to him as a runaway, under the same penalties and forfeiture as hereafter in that case is provided; and every constable of Charlestown which shall neglect or refuse to make search as aforesaid, for every such neglect shall forefit the sum of twenty shillings.

VIII. *And be it further enacted* by the authority aforesaid, That no owner or head of any family shall give a ticket to any slave to go to Charlestown, or from plantation to plantation, on Sunday, excepting it be for and about such particular business as cannot reasonably be delayed to another time, under the forfeiture of ten shillings; and in every ticket in that case given, shall be mentioned the particular business that slave is sent about, or that slave shall be dealt with as if he had no ticket.

IX. *And be it further enacted* by the authority aforesaid, That upon complaint made to any justice of the peace, of any heinous or grievous crime, committed by any slave or slaves, as murder, burglary, robbery, burning of houses, or any lesser crimes, as killing or stealing any meat or other cattle, maiming one the other, stealing of fowls, provisions, or such like trespasses or injuries, the said justice shall issue out his warrant for apprehending the offender or offenders, and for all persons to come before him that can give evidence; and if upon examination, it probably appeareth, that the apprehended person is guilty, he shall commit him or them to prison, or immediately proceed to tryal of the said slave or slaves, according to the form hereafter specified, or take security for his or their forthcoming, as the case shall require, and also to certify to the justice next to him, the said cause, and to require him, by virtue of this Act, to associate himself to him, which said justice is hereby required to do, and they so associated, are to issue their summons to three sufficient freeholders, acquainting them with the matter, and appointing them a day, hour and place, when and where the same shall be heard and determined, at which day, hour and place, the said justices and freeholders shall cause the offenders and evidences to come before them, and if they, on hearing the matter, the said freeholders being by the said justices first sworn to judge uprightly and according to evidence, and diligently weighing and examining all evidences, proofs and testimonies, (and in case of murder only, if on violent presumption and circumstances) they shall find such negro or other slave or slaves guilty thereof, they shall give sentence of death, if the crime by law deserve the same, and forthwith by their warrant cause immediate execution to be done, by the common or any other executioner, in such manner as they shall think fit, the kind of death to be inflicted to be left to their judgment and discretion; and if the crime committed shall not deserve death, they shall then condemn and adjudge the criminal or criminals to any other punishment, but not extending to limb or disabling him, without a particular law directing such punishment, and shall forthwith order execution to be done accordingly.

X. And in regard great mischiefs daily happen by petty larcenies committed by negroes and slaves of this Province, *Be it further enacted* by the authority aforesaid, That if any negro or other slave shall hereafter steal or destroy any goods, chattels, or provisions whatsoever, of any other person than his master or mistress, being under the value of twelve pence, every negro or other slave so offending, and being brought before some justice of the peace of this Province, upon complaint of the party injured, and shall be adjudged guilty by confession, proof, or probable circumstances, such negro or slave so offending, excepting children, whose punishment is left wholly to the discretion of the said justice, shall be adjudged by such justice to be publicly and severely whipped, not exceeding forty lashes; and if such negro or other slave punished as aforesaid, be afterwards, by two justices of the peace, found guilty of the like crimes, he or they, for such his or their second offence, shall either have one of his ears cut off, or be branded in the forehead with a hot iron, that the mark thereof may remain; and if after such punishment, such negro or slave for his third offence, shall have his nose slit; and if such negro or other slave, after the third time as aforesaid, be accused of petty larceny, or of any of the offences before mentioned, such negro or other slave shall be tried in such manner as those accused of murder, burglary, *etc.* are before by this Act provided for to be tried, and in case they shall be found guilty a fourth time, of any the offences before mentioned, then such negro or other slave shall be adjudged to suffer death, or other punishment, as the said justices shall think fitting; and any judgment given for the first offence, shall be a sufficient conviction for the first offence; and any after judgment after the first judgment, shall be a sufficient conviction to bring the offender within the penalty of the second offence, and so for inflicting the rest of the punishments; and in case the said justices and freeholders, and any or either of them, shall neglect or refuse to perform the duties by this Act required of them, they shall severally, for such their defaults, forfeit the sum of twenty-five pounds.

XI. *And be it further enacted* by the authority aforesaid, That if any person shall send his negro out of this Province, that hath killed another negro or slave, such person shall pay unto the master or owner of such negro, the full value of such negro so killed as aforesaid; and in case any person shall send, or cause to be sent, his negro out of this Province, that hath killed any white person, knowing the negro to be guilty of such crime, he shall forfeit the sum of five hundred pounds, to the executors of the person killed; to be recovered by action of debt in the court of common pleas in this Province, the action to be brought at any time within one year after the fact committed.

XII. *And it is further enacted* by the authority aforesaid, That if any negroes or other slaves shall make mutiny or insurrection, or rise in rebellion against the authority and government of this Province, or shall make preparation of arms, powder, bullets or offensive weapons, in order to carry on such mutiny or insurrection, or shall hold any counsel or conspiracy for raising such mutiny, insurrection or rebellion, the offenders shall be tried by two justices of the peace and three freeholders, associated together as before expressed in case of murder, burglary, *etc.*, who are hereby empowered and required to try the said slaves so offending, and inflict death, or any other punishment, upon the offenders, and forthwith by their warrant cause execution to be done, by the common or any other executioner, in such manner as they shall think fitting; and if any person shall make away or conceal any negro or negroes, or other slave or slaves, suspected to be guilty of the beforementioned crimes, and not upon demand bring forth the suspected offender or offenders, such person shall forfeit for every negro or slave so concealed or made away, the sum of fifty pounds; *Provided, nevertheless,* that when and as often as any of the beforementioned crimes shall be committed by more than one negro, that shall deserve death, that then and in all such cases, if the Governor and council of this Province shall think fitting, and accordingly shall order, that only one or more of the said criminals should suffer death as exemplary, and the rest to be returned to the owners, that then, the owners of the negroes so offending, shall bear proportionably the loss of the said negro or negroes so put to death, as shall be allotted them by the said justices and freeholders; and if any person shall refuse his part so allotted him, that then, and in all such cases, the said justices and freeholders are hereby required to issue out their warrant of distress upon the goods and chattels of the person so refusing, and shall cause the same to be sold by public outcry, to satisfy the said money so allotted him to pay, and to return the overplus, if any be, to the owner; *Provided, nevertheless,* that the part allotted for any person to pay for his part or proportion of the negro or negroes so put to death, shall not exceed one sixth part of his negro or negroes so excused and pardoned; and in case that shall not be sufficient to satisfy for the negro or negroes that shall be put to death, that the remaining sum shall be paid out of the public treasury of this Province.*

*Thomas Cooper and David J. McCord, eds., *Statutes at Large of South Carolina* (10 vols., Columbia, 1836-1841), VII, 352-357.

11

THE FEAR OF INSURRECTION

New York City, located in the colony with the largest slave population north of the Potomac, was the scene of the major servile plot in colonial America. The unusually severe winter of 1740-1741 had brought acute suffering to the poor whites and to the slaves. England was fighting Spain in the "War of Jenkins's Ear," and New Yorkers feared an attack in which the slaves might assist the enemy. Thus, when a series of fires broke out on the night of February 28, 1741, the citizens quickly concluded that a gigantic slave plot had reached its denouement. Fear and panic took over; before the city had recovered from its hysteria, more than 150 persons, including 25 whites, had been arrested.

Of the 134 Negroes brought to trial, 13 were burned alive, 18 were hanged, 70 were transported to the West Indies, and 33 were discharged. Below is part of the list of these defendants and their sentences, which was compiled by the court recorder, Daniel Horsmanden. It may be added that this scare did not lead to a pattern of repressive measures against slaves, since the growing number of white laborers in the middle colonies reduced the need for Negroes and, as a consequence, the fear of them.

A PARTIAL LIST OF NEGROES COMMITTED ON ACCOUNT OF THE CONSPIRACY*

NEGROES†	COMMITTED	ARRAIGNED	CONVICTED	CONFESSED	BURNT	HANGED	TRANSPORTED TO	DISCHARGED
Antonio (Spaniards)	6 April	13 June	17 June				Spanish W. Indies	
Augustine (Spaniards)	1 April	13 June	17 June					
Antonio (Spaniards)	1 April	13 June	17 June				Madeira	
Albany	12 May	8 June	10 June		12 June			
Abraham, a free Negro	1 June							
Adam	26 June			27 June			Madeira	
Brash	9 May	25 June		25 June			Madeira	
Bastian, alias Tom Peal	12 May	8 June	10 June	11 June			Hispaniola	
Ben	9 June	12 June	13 June		16 June			
Bill, alias Will	12 June	3 July						
Bridgewater	22 June	3 July		30 June			Madeira	
Billy	25 June	1 July		27 June			Hispaniola	
Braveboy	27 June	10 July		30 June			Madeira	
Burlington	3 July							15 July
Caesar	1 March	24 April	1 May††			11 May		
Cuffee	5 April	28 May	29 May		30 May			
Cuba, a Wench	4 April							5 July
Curacoa Dick	9 May	8 June	10 June		12 June			
Cato	9 May	15 July		22 June				
Caesar	9 May	3 July		22 June			Madeira	
Cuffee	24 May	6 June	8 June		9 June			
Caesar	25 May	6 June	8 June		9 June			
Cato	25 May	12 June	13 June			16 June		
Cook	26 May	6 June	8 June		9 June			
Cambridge	30 May	10 July		30 June			Cape François	
Caesar	30 May	26 June		27 June			St. Thomas, return'd	
Cato	9 June	16 June	19 June	27 June		3 July		
Caesar	9 June	3 July		2 July			Hispaniola	
Cato, or Toby	9 June	12 June	13 June			16 June		
Cuffee	22 June	15 July		2 July				

†The names of the masters or owners of the slaves have been omitted.
††Convicted of a robbery, but appears to have been a principal negro conspirator.

*Daniel Horsmanden, *A Journal of the Proceedings in the Detection of the Conspiracy . . . for the Burning of the City of New York in America, and Murdering the Inhabitants* (New York, 1744), 11-15.

12

THE GERMANTOWN PROTEST

The belief that slavery was justifiable and right was widely held in colonial America. But there were voices, however poorly heeded, crying out against the practice. As a rule these critics were of a deeply religious bent, persons who had not been able to reconcile slavery with their interpretation of Christian doctrine. In point of priority and sustained effort, the Quakers were leaders in opposing slavery. In February 1688, a Quaker group at Germantown, Pennsylvania, meeting at the home of a member, drew up a protest against slavery, the first of its kind in English-speaking America. This document, the historic Germantown Protest, advanced five reasons against human bondage.

This is to the monthly meeting held at Richard Worrell's:

These are the reasons why we are against the traffic of mensbody, as follows: Is there any that would be done or handled at this manner? viz., to be sold or made a slave for all the time of his life? How fearful and faint-hearted are many on sea, when they see a strange vessel, being afraid it should be a Turk and they should be taken and sold for slaves in Turkey. Now what is *this* better done than Turks do? Yea, rather it is worse for them which say they are Christians; for we hear that the most part of such Negroes are brought hither against their will and consent, and that many of them are stolen. Now, though they are black, we cannot conceive there is more liberty to have them slaves as it is to have other white ones. There is a saying that we shall do to all men like as we will be done ourselves; making no difference of what generation, descent or colour they are. And those who steal or rob men, and those who buy or purchase them, are they not all alike? Here is liberty of conscience, which is right and reasonable; here ought to be likewise liberty of the body, except of evil-doers, which is another case. But to bring men hither, or to rob and sell them against their will, we stand against. In Europe there are many oppressed for conscience sake; and here there are those oppressed which are of a black colour. And we who know that men must not commit adultery—some do commit adultery *in* others, separating wives from their husbands, and giving them to others: and some sell the children of those poor creatures to other men. Oh! do consider well this thing, you who do it, if you would be done at this manner—and if it is done according to Christianity! You surpass Holland and Germany in this thing. This makes an ill report in all those countries of Europe, where they hear of [it], that the Quakers do here handle men like they handle there the cattle. And for that reason some have no mind or inclination to come hither. And who shall maintain this your cause, or plead for it? Truly, we cannot do so except you shall inform us better hereof, viz.: that Christians have liberty to practise these things. Pray, what thing in the world can be done worse towards us than if men should rob or steal us away and sell us for slaves to strange countries; separating husbands from their wives and children. Being now this is not done in the manner we will be done at; therefore, we contradict, and are against this traffic of men-body. And we who profess that it is not lawful to steal, must, likewise, avoid to purchase such things as are stolen, but rather help to stop this robbing and stealing, if possible. And such men ought to be delivered out of the hands of the robbers and set free as well as in Europe. Then is Pennsylvania to have a good report; instead, it has now a bad one for this sake in other countries; especially whereas the Europeans are desirous to know in what manner *the Quakers* do rule in *their* province; and most of them do look upon us with an envious eye. But if this is done well, what shall we say is done evil?

If once these slaves (which they say are so wicked and stubborn men), should join themselves—fight for their freedom and handle their masters and mistresses as they did handle them before; will these masters and mistresses take the sword at hand and war against these poor slaves, like we are able to believe, some will not refuse to do? Or, have these Negroes not as much right to fight for their freedom as you have to keep them slaves?

Now, consider well this thing, if it is good or bad. And in case you find it to be good to handle these blacks in that manner, we desire and require you hereby lovingly, that you may inform us herein, which at this time never was done, viz., that Christians have liberty to do so. To the end we shall be satisfied on this point, and satisfy likewise our good friends and acquaintances in our native country, to whom it is a terror or fearful thing, that men should be handled so in Pennsylvania.

This is from our meeting at Germantown, held the 18 of the 2 month, 1688, to be delivered to the monthly meeting at Richard Worrell's.

Gerret Hendericks — Francis Daniel Pastorius
Derick op de Graeff — Abraham op de Graeff*

13

THE QUAKER CONSCIENCE

After the Germantown Protest, the Quaker conscience could never be wholly at ease with slavery. John Woolman of New Jersey was the greatest of the Quaker reformers who tried to persuade his coreligionists to give up their slaves. A clerk and conveyancer in a store at Mount Holly, Woolman had become a reformer when his employer had asked him one day to draw up a bill of sale for a slave. With the buyer waiting in the shop, young Woolman wrote the bill of sale. But the whole transaction set him to thinking, inevitably leading him to become a spokesman for the slave.

In 1754 Woolman put his views into print, issuing a pamphlet entitled Some Considerations on the Keeping of Negroes: Recommended to the Professors

---

*From *American Colonial Documents To 1776*, Vol. IX, edited by Merrill Jensen. Reprinted by permission of Eyre & Spottiswodde (Publishers) Ltd.

of Christianity of every Denomination. *The Philadelphia Quakers distributed this tract widely in the colonies and abroad. "No other antislavery document had hitherto received such extensive circulation in any language anywhere," writes a present-day authority, Thomas E. Drake. "It opened the way and set the pattern for pamphlets by Anthony Benezet on Africa and the slave trade, for later pamphleteering by John Wesley, Granville Sharpe, and Thomas Clarkson in England, and for the antislavery pronouncements by the Philadelphia Yearly Meeting itself." The excerpts below are from both the 1754 and the 1762 editions of* Some Considerations. *In theory all Quakers believed that "there was a little bit of God in everyone," including slaves. Woolman took it as his task to make his fellow-religionists bring their practices to conform to their beliefs.*

Some Considerations On the Keeping of Negroes.

Forasmuch as ye did it to the least of these my Brethren, ye did it unto me. Matt. xxv. 40.

As Many Times there are different Motives to the same Actions; and one does that from a generous Heart, which another does for selfish Ends:——The like may be said in this Case.

There are various Circumstances amongst them that keep *Negroes,* and different Ways by which they fall under their Care; and, I doubt not, there are many well disposed Persons amongst them who desire rather to manage wisely and justly in this difficult Matter, than to make Gain of it.

But the general Disadvantage which these poor *Africans* lie under in an enlight'ned Christian Country, having often fill'd me with real Sadness, and been like undigested Matter on my Mind, I now think it my Duty, through Divine Aid, to offer some Thoughts thereon to the Consideration of others.

When we remember that all Nations are of one Blood, *Gen.* iii. 20. that in this World we are but Sojourners, that we are subject to the like Afflictions and Infirmities of Body, the like Disorders and Frailties in Mind, the like Temptations, the same Death, and the same Judgment, and, that the Alwise Being is Judge and Lord over us all, it seems to raise an Idea of a general Brotherhood, and a Disposition easy to be touched with a Feeling of each others Afflictions: But when we forget those Things, and look chiefly at our outward Circumstances, in this and some Ages past, constantly retaining in our Minds the Distinction betwixt us and them, with respect to our Knowledge and Improvement in Things divine, natural and artificial, our Breasts being apt to be filled with fond Notions of Superiority, there is Danger of erring in our Conduct toward them.

We allow them to be of the same Species with ourselves, the Odds is, we are in a higher Station, and enjoy greater Favours than they: And when it is thus, that our heavenly Father endoweth some of his Children with distinguished Gifts, they are intended for good Ends; but if those thus gifted are thereby lifted up above their Brethren, not considering themselves as Debtors to the Weak, nor behaving themselves as faithful Stewards, none who judge impartially can suppose them free from Ingratitude.

* * *

To consider Mankind otherwise than Brethren, to think Favours are peculiar to one Nation, and exclude others, plainly supposes a

Darkness in the Understanding: For as God's Love is universal, so where the Mind is sufficiently influenced by it, it begets a Likeness of itself, and the Heart is enlarged towards all Men. Again, to conclude a People froward, perverse, and worse by Nature than others (who ungratefully receive Favours, and apply them to bad Ends) this will excite a Behaviour toward them unbecoming the Excellence of true Religion.

To prevent such Error, let us calmly consider their Circumstance; and, the better to do it, make their Case ours. Suppose, then, that our Ancestors and we had been exposed to constant Servitude in the more servile and inferior Employments of Life; that we had been destitute of the Help of Reading and good Company; that amongst ourselves we had had few wise and pious Instructors; that the Religious amongst our Superiors seldom took Notice of us; that while others, in Ease, have plentifully heap'd up the Fruit of our Labour, we had receiv'd barely enough to relieve Nature, and being wholly at the Command of others, had generally been treated as a contemptible, ignorant Part of Mankind: Should we, in that Case, be less abject than they now are? Again, If Oppression be so hard to bear, that a wise Man is made mad by it, *Eccl.* vii. 7. then a Series of those Things altering the Behaviour and Manners of a People, is what may reasonably be expected.

WHEN our property is taken contrary to our Mind, by Means appearing to us unjust, it is only through divine Influence, and the Enlargement of Heart from thence proceeding, that we can love our reputed Oppressors: If the *Negroes* fall short in this, an uneasy, if not a disconsolate Disposition, will be awak'ned, and remain like Seeds in their Minds, producing Sloth and many other Habits appearing odious to us, with which being free Men, they, perhaps, had not been chargeable. (1754)

SINCE Mankind spread upon the Earth, many have been the Revolutions attending the several Families, and their Customs and Ways of Life different from each other. This Diversity of Manners, though some are preferable to others, operates not in Favour of any, so far as to justify them to do Violence to innocent Men; to bring them from their own to another Way of Life. The Mind, when moved by a Principle of true Love, may feel a Warmth of Gratitude to the universal Father, and a lively Sympathy with those Nations, where Divine Light has been less manifest.

THIS Desire for their real Good may beget a Willingness to undergo Hardships for their Sakes, that the true Knowledge of GOD may be spread amongst them: But to take them from their own Land, with Views of Profit to ourselves, by Means inconsistent with pure Justice, is foreign to that Principle which seeks the Happiness of the whole Creation. Forced Subjection, on innocent Persons of full Age, is inconsistent with right Reason; on one Side, the human Mind is not naturally fortified with that Firmness in Wisdom and Goodness, necessary to an independent Ruler; on the other Side, to be subject to the uncontroulable Will of a Man, liable to err, is most painful and afflicting to a conscientious Creature.

It is our Happiness faithfully to serve the Divine Being, who made us: His Perfection makes our Service reasonable; but so long as Men are biassed by narrow Self-love, so long an absolute Power over other Men is unfit for them.

Men, taking on them the Government of others, may intend to govern reasonably, and make their Subjects more happy than they would be otherwise; but, as absolute Command belongs only to him who is perfect, where frail Men, in their own Wills, assume such Command, it hath a direct Tendency to vitiate their Minds, and make them more unfit for Government.

Placing on Men the ignominious Title SLAVE, dressing them in uncomely Garments, keeping them to servile Labour, in which they are often dirty, tends gradually to fix a Notion in the Mind, that they are a Sort of People below us in Nature, and leads us to consider them as such in all our Conclusions about them. And, moreover, a Person, which in our Esteem is mean and contemptible, if their Language or Behaviour toward us is unseemly or disrespectful, it excites Wrath more powerfully than the like Conduct in one we accounted our Equal or Superior; and where this happens to be the Case, it disqualifies for candid Judgment; for it is unfit for a Person to sit as Judge in a Case where his own Personal Resentments are stirred up; and, as Members of Society in a well framed Government, we are mutually dependant. Present Interest incites to Duty, and makes each Man attentive to the Convenience of others; but he whose Will is a Law to Others, and can enforce Obedience by Punishment; he whose Wants are supplied without feeling any Obligation to make equal Returns to his Benefactor, his irregular Appetites find an open Field for Motion, and he is in Danger of growing hard, and inattentive to their Convenience who labour for his Support; and so loses that Disposition, in which alone Men are fit to govern.

The *English* Government hath been commended by candid Foreigners for the Disuse of Racks and Tortures, so much practised in some States; but this multiplying Slaves now leads to it; for where People exact hard Labour of others, without a suitable Reward, and are resolved to continue in that Way, Severity to such who oppose them becomes the Consequence; and several *Negroe* Criminals, among the *English* in *America,* have been executed in a lingering, painful Way, very terrifying to others.

It is a happy Case to set out right, and persevere in the same Way: A wrong Beginning leads into many Difficulties; for to support one Evil, another becomes customary; two produces more; and the further Men proceed in this Way, the greater their Dangers, their Doubts and Fears; and the more painful and perplexing are their Circumstances; so that such who are true Friends to the real and lasting Interest of our Country, and candidly consider the Tendency of Things, cannot but feel some Concern on this Account.* (1762)

---

*John Woolman, *Some Considerations on the Keeping of Negroes* (Philadelphia, 1754), 1-3, 6-7; *Some Considerations on Keeping Negroes* (Philadelphia, 1762), 22-25.

14

THE NEW ENGLAND CALVINIST

In Calvinistic New England the first public plea against slavery was Samuel Sewall's three-page tract, "The Selling of Joseph," published in 1700. A merchant, churchman, magistrate, and judge, Sewall stood high in the social and business circles of Boston. Alarmed by the realization that slavery had taken root in New England and that the number of Negro slaves was increasing, Sewall was moved to write his pamphlet. A man of strong religious spirit, Sewall drew his title from the Biblical story of Joseph.

"The Selling of Joseph" follows the pattern of a Puritan sermon, with a statement of the text, followed by an elaboration sprinkled with Latin and Biblical quotations. There follows a list of objections with a rebuttal of each one. The pamphlet drew much criticism, since most Puritans believed that Negroes bore the curse of Cain, a sin for which their slavery was a way of atonement. But Sewall stood his ground despite criticism. In the excerpt that follows, the Latin passages have been omitted.

THE SELLING OF JOSEPH: A MEMORIAL.
BY THE HON'BLE JUDGE SEWALL IN NEW ENGLAND.

FORASMUCH *as* LIBERTY *is in real value next unto Life; None ought to part with it themselves, or deprive others of it, but upon most mature consideration.*

The Numerousness of Slaves at this Day in the Province, and the Uneasiness of them under their Slavery, hath put many upon thinking whether the Foundation of it be firmly and well laid; so as to sustain the Vast Weight that is built upon it. It is most certain that all Men, as they are the Sons of *Adam,* are Co-heirs, and have equal Right unto Liberty, and all other outward Comforts of Life. GOD *hath given the Earth (with all its commodities) unto the Sons of Adam, Psal.,* 115, 16. *And hath made of one Blood all Nations of Men, for to dwell on all the face of the Earth, and hath determined the Times before appointed, and the bounds of their Habitation: That they should seek the Lord. Forasmuch then as we are the Offspring of* GOD, *etc. Acts* 17. 26, 27, 29. Now, although the Title given by the last ADAM doth infinitely better Men's Estates, respecting GOD and themselves; and grants them a most beneficial and inviolable Lease under the Broad Seal of Heaven, who were before only Tenants at Will; yet through the Indulgence of GOD to our First Parents after the Fall, the outward Estate of all and every of their Children, remains the same as to one another. So that Originally, and Naturally, there is no such thing as Slavery. *Joseph* was rightfully no more a Slave to his Brethren, than they were to him; and they had no more Authority to *Sell* him, than they had to *Slay* him. And if *they* had nothing to do to sell him; the *Ishmaelites* bargaining with them, and paying down Twenty pieces of Silver, could not make a Title. Neither could *Potiphar* have any better Interest in him than the *Ishmaelites* had. *Gen.* 37, 20, 27, 28. For he that shall in this case plead *Alteration of Property,* seems to have forfeited a great part of his own claim to Humanity. There is no proportion between Twenty Pieces of Silver and LIBERTY. The Commodity itself is the Claimer. If *Arabian* Gold be imported in any quantities, most are afraid to meddle with it, though they might have it at easy rates; lest it should have been wrongfully taken from the Owners, it should kindle a fire to the Consumption of their whole Estate. 'Tis pity there should be more Caution used in buying a Horse, or a little lifeless dust, than there is in purchasing Men and Women: Whereas they are the Offspring of God.

Caveat Emptor!

And all things considered, it would conduce more to the Welfare of the Province, to have White Servants for a Term of Years, than to have Slaves for Life. Few can endure to hear of a Negro's being made free; and indeed they can seldom use their Freedom well; yet their continual aspiring after their forbidden Liberty, renders them Unwilling Servants. And there is such a disparity in their Conditions, Colour, and Hair, that they can never embody with us, & grow up in orderly Families, to the Peopling of the Land; but still remain in our Body Politick as a kind of extravasat Blood. As many Negro Men as there are among us, so many empty Places are there in our Train Bands, and the places taken up of Men that might make Husbands for our Daughters. And the Sons and Daughters of *New England* would become more like *Jacob* and *Rachel,* if this Slavery were thrust quite out of Doors. Moreover it is too well known what Temptations Masters are under, to connive at the Fornication of their Slaves; lest they should be obliged to find them Wives, or pay their Fines. It seems to be practically pleaded that they might be lawless; 'tis thought much of, that the Law should have satisfaction for their Thefts, and other Immoralities; by which means, *Holiness to the Lord* is more rarely engraven upon this sort of Servitude. It is likewise most lamentable to think, how in taking Negroes out of *Africa,* and selling of them here, That which God has joined together, Men do boldly rend asunder; Men from their Country, Husbands from their Wives, Parents from their Children. How horrible is the Uncleanness, Mortality, if not Murder, that the Ships are guilty of that bring great Crouds of these Miserable Men and Women. Methinks when we are bemoaning the barbarous Usage of our Friends and Kinsfolk in *Africa,* it might not be unreasonable to enquire whether we are not culpable in forcing the *Africans* to become Slaves amongst ourselves. And it may be a question whether all the Benefit received by *Negro* Slaves will balance the Accompt of Cash laid out upon them; and for the Redemption of our own enslaved Friends out of *Africa.* Besides all the Persons and Estates that have perished there.

Obj. 1. *These Blackamores are of the Posterity of Cham, and therefore are under the Curse of Slavery.* Gen. 9, 25, 26, 27.

Ans. Of all Offices, one would not beg this; viz. Uncall'd for, to be an Executioner of the Vindictive Wrath of God; the extent and duration of which is to us uncertain. If this ever was a Commission; How do we know but that it is long since out of Date? Many have found it to their Cost, that a Prophetical Denunciation of Judgment against a Person or People, would not warrant them to inflict that evil.

Obj. 2. *The* Nigers *are brought out of a Pagan Country, into places where the Gospel is preached.*

Ans. Evil must not be done, that good may come of it. The extraordinary and comprehensive Benefit accruing to the Church of GOD, and to *Joseph* personally, did not rectify his Brethren's Sale of him.

Obj. 3. *The Africans have Wars one with another: Our Ships bring lawful Captives taken in those wars.*

Ans. For aught is known, their Wars are much such as were between *Jacob's* Sons and their Brother *Joseph.* If they be between Town and Town; Provincial or National: Every War is upon one side Unjust. An Unlawful War can't make lawful Captives. And by receiving, we are in danger to promote, and partake in their Barbarous Cruelties. I am sure, if some Gentlemen should go down to the *Brewsters* to take the Air, and Fish: And a stronger Party from *Hull* should surprise them, and sell them for Slaves to a Ship outward bound; they would think themselves unjustly dealt with; both by Sellers and Buyers. And yet 'tis to be feared, we have no other Kind of Title to our *Nigers. Therefore all things whatsoever ye would that men should do to you, do you even so to them: for this is the Law and the Prophets.* Matt. 7, 12.

Obj. 4. Abraham *had Servants bought with his Money and born in his House.*

Ans. Until the Circumstances of *Abraham's* purchase be recorded, no Argument can be drawn from it. In the mean time, Charity obliges us to conclude, that He knew it was lawful and good.

It is Observable that the *Israelites* were strictly forbidden the buying or selling one another for Slaves. *Levit.* 25. 39. 46. *Jer.* 34. 8-22. And GOD gaged His Blessing in lieu of any loss they might conceit they suffered thereby, *Deut.* 15. 18. And since the partition Wall is broken down, inordinate Self-love should likewise be demolished. GOD expects that Christians should be of a more Ingenuous and benign frame of Spirit. Christians should carry it to all the World, as the *Israelites* were to carry it one towards another. And for Men obstinately to persist in holding their Neighbours and Brethren under the Rigor of perpetual Bondage, seems to be no proper way of gaining Assurance that GOD has given them Spiritual Freedom. Our Blessed Saviour has altered the Measures of the ancient Love Song, and set it to a most Excellent New Tune, which all ought to be ambitious of Learning. *Matt.* 5. 43. 44. *John* 13. 34. These *Ethiopians,* as black as they are, seeing they are the Sons and Daughters of the First *Adam,* the Brethren and Sisters of the Last ADAM, and the Offspring of GOD; They ought to be treated with a Respect agreeable.*

---

*George H. Moore, *Notes on the History of Slavery in Massachusetts* (Boston, 1866), 83-87.

15

RELIGIOUS INSTRUCTION FOR THE NEGRO

In New England, as elsewhere, the conversion of Negroes did not go unopposed. The argument was familiar: making a Christian of a slave might give him notions of social equality, or might even effect his loss as a servant. But the religious impulse was strong in New England, and the belief that the Negro had a soul to be saved would not be suppressed. In 1674 John Eliot, a friend to the Indian, turned his attention to Negroes, inviting their masters to send them to him once a week for religious instruction. In colonial New England clergyman-scholar Cotton Mather of Boston was the best known of the early advocates of religious instruction for slaves, opening a charity school for Indians and Negroes in 1717. After Mather's day it became increasingly common for a slave to be baptized and accepted into the church of his master. Ezra Stiles, the scholarly pastor of the Second Congregational Church in Newport (and later president of Yale), gave special instructions to his Negro communicants, as these entries from his diary of 1772 indicate.

[Feb.] 24. Compiling History. In the Evening a very full and serious Meeting of Negroes at my House, perhaps 80 or 90: I discoursed to them on Luke xiv, 16, 17, 18. "A certain man made — — Excuse." They sang well. They appeared attentive and much affected; and after I had done, many of them came up to me and thanked me, as they said, for taking so much Care of their souls, and hoped they should remember my Counsels. There are six or seven Negroe Communicants in the Baptist Churches in Town, 4 or 5 in the Church of England, seven in my Church and six or seven in Mr. Hopkins' Church: perhaps 26, and not above 30 professors out of Twelve hundred Negroes in Town.

[July] 10. Reading Origen contra Celsum. I have Eighty Communicants in my Church, of which seven are Negroes. I directed the Negroes to come to me this Evening; when three Negro Brethren and three Negro Sisters met in my Study. I discoursed with them on the great Things of the divine Life and eternal Salvation—counselling and encouraging and earnestly pressing upon them to make their Calling and Election sure, and to walk worthy of their holy profession, and especially to maintain a daily Intercourse with heaven in holy duties and divine Contemplation on the Love of Christ. Then we all fell upon our Knees together, and I poured out fervent Supplications at the Throne of Grace imploring the divine Blessing upon us, and commending ourselves to the holy Keeping of the Most High. We seemed to have the delightful presence of Jesus.*

---

*Frank B. Dexter, ed., *The Literary Diary of Ezra Stiles* (2 vols., New York, 1901), I, 213-214, 247-248.

16

PHILLIS WHEATLEY

It is not surprising that in Puritan New England the only Negro who attracted wide attention was the deeply religious Phillis Wheatley. Born in Africa, Phillis had been brought as a young girl to Boston, where she was purchased by John Wheatley and quickly won the affection of his family. Phillis learned easily how to read and write, and showed marked aptitude for study and reflection. She capped her early promise by publishing a volume of poetry in 1773, when barely twenty years old. This work, the second book of verse published by a woman in colonial America, bore the revealing title, Poems on Various Subjects, Religious and Moral. *The poem below strikes a characteristically devout note.*

ON BEING BROUGHT FROM AFRICA TO AMERICA

'Twas mercy brought me from my Pagan land,
Taught my benighted soul to understand
That there's a God, and there's a Saviour too:
Once I redemption neither sought nor knew.
Some view our sable race with scornful eye,
"Their colour is a diabolic die."
Remember, Christians, Negroes, black as Cain,
May be refin'd, and join th' angelic train.*

17

THE LOVE OF FREEDOM

Although a slave, Phillis Wheatley had never known want or hardship. She had never lacked affection, having been treated by the Wheatleys as one of the family. But despite the great kindness of her master and mistress, Phillis did not care to remain a slave. In a poem dedicated to the Earl of Dartmouth, whom she had met in London, Phillis accounted for her love of freedom. In this, as in her quest for self-improvement, Phillis Wheatley was a typical American of the period that ushered in the Revolutionary War.

TO THE RIGHT HONORABLE WILLIAM, EARL OF DARTMOUTH,
HIS MAJESTY'S SECRETARY OF STATE FOR NORTH AMERICA, ETC.

Should you, my lord, while you peruse my song,
Wonder from whence my love of Freedom sprung,
Whence flow these wishes for the common good,
By feeling hearts alone best understood,
I, young in life, by seeming cruel fate
Was snatch'd from Afric's fancy'd happy seat:
What pangs excruciating must molest,
What sorrows labour in my parent's breast?
Steel'd was the soul and by no misery mov'd
That from a father seiz'd his babe belov'd:
Such, such my case. And can I then but pray
Others my never feel tyrannic sway?*

---

*Phillis Wheatley, *Poems on Various Subjects, Religious and Moral,* 18, 74.

CHAPTER TWO

The Revolutionary War Period

General Washington leans against a cannon and his trusted Negro servant Billy Lee holds his horse behind him. General of the army and servant-slave, both men represent forces of the Revolution. It will be only a few years and the colonies will be free. But for the slave-servants, the beginning is over a hundred years away.

INTRODUCTION

The Revolutionary War Period

Basically the roots of the American Revolution may be traced to a series of Parliamentary measures whereby England attempted to regulate the economic activities of her thirteen colonies and to exercise the controlling political authority over them. The British victory in the French and Indian War in 1763 sharpened the conflict between the mother country and the colonies. The British ministers felt that the colonists should bear a larger portion of the tax burden caused by the war and should help to support the large garrison force that the British military authorities were bent on keeping in America. The colonists, on the other hand, argued that a Parliament in which they were not directly represented hadn't the right to tax them, and they believed that they no longer needed the protection of His Majesty's armed forces.

In the widening rift between mother country and colonies during the decade of discontent (1765-1775) the leaders of thought in provincial America sought to justify their stand by stressing the doctrines of liberty and freedom. If these theories were derived from such philosophers of the eighteenth-century Enlightenment as John Locke, they assumed a freshness and urgency in the hands of men like James Otis and Patrick Henry. These revolutionary ideas received their most significant expression in the Declaration of Independence, primarily the work of thirty-three-year-old Thomas Jefferson. "All men are created equal," ran the stirring words, and are endowed with rights that cannot be taken away.

The slogans of liberty so widespread in America on the eve of the break with England had their effect on slavery, for the memorable phrases of the Declaration of Independence advocated a principle irreconcilable with the concept that regarded men as property. These slogans had a more immediate effect on the slaves themselves, particularly in New England. Here a slave might bring a "suit of service," asking the courts for his freedom and for compensation for past labors. The best known of these cases related to Jenny Slew of Ipswitch, Massachusetts, who in 1765 was awarded her freedom and the sum of four pounds by the highest court in the colony. In addition to filing freedom suits, New England Negroes sent petitions to the legislative assemblies, urging them to proclaim liberty throughout the commonwealth. Such group requests were invariably tabled inasmuch as they required the freeing of slaves *en masse* rather than individually, as in a suit of service.

Fortunately for the slave a more direct route to freedom emerged with the coming of the war between the mother country and the colonies. To become a soldier was a way to gain one's freedom, as it had been in colonial times. And in the opening weeks of the war, it seemed that there would be a role for Negro arms-bearers. In the first military engagement of the Revolution, the Battle of Lexington and Concord on April 19, 1775, a number of Negroes saw action. At nearby Boston two months later, Negroes took part in the Battle of Bunker Hill, among them Salem Poor, who was commended for his bravery, and Peter Salem, a veteran of Lexington and Concord, whose master had freed him to join the militia. "In the regiments at Roxbury," wrote General John Thomas to John Adams, "we have some

Negroes; . . . many of them have proved themselves brave." In Virginia, at the Battle of Great Bridge in December 1775, Negro William Flora was the last militiaman to leave his post, withdrawing amidst a volley of musket balls.

This early use of Negro soldiers proved to be short-lived; indeed, by the time of Flora's exploit, a pattern of exclusion had set in. The most forceful advocate of the no-Negroes policy was the newly formed Continental army, which did not want its ranks to become peopled with runaway slaves. Meeting at Cambridge, Massachusetts, on October 8, 1775, the high command agreed on a policy of exclusion for both slaves and free Negroes. The individual states took their cues. By mid-1776 every New England state had officially closed the door to Negro enlistments, while south of the Potomac the new recruiting laws were carbon copies of colonial statutes confining military service to whites.

The policy of excluding Negroes from the armies was based on the mistaken supposition that the war would be short. By the close of 1776 grim necessity forced the states and the central government to recast their thinking. The states took the lead, especially when Congress in 1777 began to fix quotas for each of them. As it became increasingly difficult to raise volunteer forces, local and state recruiting officers were inclined to meet their quotas by sending Negroes to Washington's army. Quietly reversing its policy, the Continental command accepted all Negroes sent by the states. The recruiting of Negroes was further stimulated by the system of substitution, through which a draftee could avoid service by producing someone to take his place. A black soldier was a common sight north of the Potomac after 1777. "The Negro can take the field in his master's place; hence you never see a regiment in which there are not a lot of Negroes, and there are well-built, strong, husky fellows among them," wrote a Hessian officer stationed at Cambridge in mid-December 1777.

The southward shift in the theatre of war in 1778 led Virginia and Maryland to reverse their Negro-exclusion policies. Unlike their sisters to the north, however, South Carolina and Georgia steadfastly refused to legalize Negro enlistments, even after the fall of Savannah late in 1778 and a congressional recommendation on March 29, 1779, that the two beleaguered states take immediate steps to raise 3000 able-bodied blacks.

A total of 5000 Negroes bore arms for America. Except in two instances they served in integrated units, fighting side by side with whites. These Negroes "made first-class soldiers," wrote historian Henry Belcher. "They distinguished themselves as good patriots again and again." Few families could equal the record of the Nickens's of Northern Neck, Virginia, nine of whom bore arms during the war. Few units were as striking in appearance or dress as that of the 545 Negroes from San Domingo who served with the French at Savannah. In Rhode Island it was voted that any able-bodied Negro, mulatto, or Indian slave, enlisting for service in the Continental army, should be "valued" and a certificate issued to his master, which, at the end of the war, would be turned over to the treasurer of the state of Rhode Island. The treasurer would compute the value of the certificate (the slave) at six per cent, which would be paid to the owner of the slave. This certificate was viewed as a promissory note. The slaves "enlisted" by their masters would serve in whatever capacity their new masters (the officers in the army) thought best. While many, as stated above, fought in integrated units, most worked as laborers.

Whatever the American reluctance to arm Negroes, there was no hesitancy in putting into their hands the tools of labor—shovel, spade, pickaxe, or hoe. As military laborers, Negroes constructed batteries, threw up entrenchments, and repaired roads. Military commanders sought or assumed authority to impress slaves. Negroes served as cooks and orderlies; some were employed as spies and guides. In the South, slaves were used as enlistment bounty, a reward for those who joined the army.

Service at sea attracted nearly 2000 Negroes, naval authorities being much more receptive to Negroes than were their military counterparts. In the competition for black recruits between the state and the Continental navies, the latter generally came out second. The Massachusetts legislature ordered that captured slaves be made to serve on state vessels. In the Chesapeake waters of Virginia and Maryland the use of Negro pilots (often impressed slaves) was not uncommon. Negroes swelled the ranks of the more than 20,000 seamen who manned the privateers.

Thousands of Negroes gained their liberty by running away to join His Majesty's forces. The British naturally tried to induce their enemy's slaves to seek freedom. The difficulty of recruiting English soldiers made the British doubly receptive to the coming of the blacks. The policy of inviting slaves to repair to the Crown forces was initiated in November 1775 by Lord Dunmore, last of the royal governors of Virginia. Within a few months Dunmore had been driven from Old Dominion waters, but the number of slaves who had tried to reach his lines was not lost on the British command. Henceforth the solicitation of Negroes became standard policy.

Americans countered by exercising increased vigilance over their slaves, threatening them with dire punishment for fleeing to the British, and removing able-bodied slaves from places near the theaters of war. Such precautions proved far less effective than their sponsors had hoped. By land and by sea the slaves made their way to His Majesty's forces.

These runaway slaves were not employed as soldiers by the British, except in isolated instances. On a few occasions, notably in the South, Negroes were used as shock troops. When slaves worked on entrenchments exposed to enemy fire, it was sometimes considered expedient to arm them for their own defense. Early in the war some British officers had toyed with the idea of masses of black troops, but such a policy was never adopted. The reason was simple: the available supply of able-bodied Negroes was too badly needed in noncombatant capacities.

Although some Negroes served as spies and guides, it was as military laborers that they found their widest use. The striking power of the British was markedly increased by the thousands of Negro carpenters, hostlers, miners, blacksmiths, and armorers. Lacking enough slaves, many commanders employed free Negroes, paying them two or three shillings a day. At sea as on land the British found use for Negroes, who swelled the ranks of ordinary seamen and took part in marauding expeditions. Most valuable of the seagoing Negroes were the pilots, with their intimate knowledge of the coastal waters.

At the war's end most of the Negroes who had served with the British sailed away with them—4000 from Savannah, 6000 from Charleston, and 4000 from New York. Major destinations were the West Indies and Nova Scotia. As their former slaves were being evacuated, the Americans bitterly accused the British of violating article seven of the treaty regulations, which stipulated that they withdraw without "carrying away any negroes or other property." For a quarter of a century Anglo-American relations would be poisoned by the controversy over these evacuated Negroes.

To the Negro in America, war's end brought some gains. To the slave soldier it brought freedom, often accompanied by a land bounty. Moreover, since the war had been waged in the name of liberty, many Americans were led to reflect seriously upon the impropriety of slavery. During the war anti-slavery sentiment became a moving force, highlighted by the law of March 1780 gradually abolishing slavery in Pennsylvania.

A war often brings unforeseen internal changes, in effect a social revolution. The Negro benefited from the impetus that the Revolutionary War gave to humanitarian movements. Organized religion experienced fresh impulses, which resulted in a sharp attack on established churches, an increase in religious freedom, and a deepened concern about the welfare of the Negro. The Quakers continued to show evidence of their interest in Negroes, and now they were joined by other denominations. Baptists began to welcome Negroes into their congregations and to license Negro preachers. One such was Jesse Peter, who in 1783 assumed the pastorate of the church at Silver Bluff, South Carolina, the first Negro Baptist church in the United States. Another licensee, the mulatto Joseph Willis, delivered the first Protestant sermon heard west of the Mississippi and later became the moderator of the Louisiana Association, the first statewide organization west of the Mississippi. In Methodist circles, founder John Wesley led the way by castigating human bondage in his *Thoughts on Slavery*, published in 1774. A feature of the early Methodist churches, as of the Baptist churches, was their racially mixed congregations; at the 1789 Methodist conference, 36 of the 51 churches reported colored members.

Another manifestation of interest in the Negro was the emergence of abolitionist societies. A primary goal of the pioneer Pennsylvania Society, reactivated in 1784, was to thwart evasions of the state law gradually abolishing slavery. In 1785 New York organized a similar society, with John Jay as president and Alexander Hamilton as secretary. By 1790 five additional statewide organizations had been formed, plus a number on the local level. In the main these societies worked for the abrogation of the slave trade, the gradual abolition of slavery, and the welfare of the free Negro.

Abolitionist and religious groups had some influence at state capitals. In 1784 Connecticut and Rhode Island passed gradual emancipation laws. Four years later New York permitted masters to free their slaves without becoming liable for them. In the South, too, opposition to slavery received vigorous support in the postwar years. Virginia in 1782 empowered a master to free his slave without first obtaining legislative permission. The Maryland assembly voted in 1785 to continue slavery, but the measure received 22 nays opposed to the 32 ayes.

But in the South as a whole, abolition, even in small doses, was foredoomed, since the economic interest in slavery and the slave trade outweighed all other sentiments. Leading clergymen like Francis Asbury and Thomas Coke might be antislavery to the core, but they could not carry their fellow religionists with them. To their dismay they found that the Church was forced to compromise with the world, and largely on the latter's terms.

During and immediately following the war, the central government lent no assistance to curbing slavery. The weakness of the Continental Congress and of the Confederation Congress that succeeded it led their members to avoid the explosive slavery issue. In 1784, however, the acquisition of a public domain beyond the Alleghenies compelled Congress to formulate an overall policy for the new lands. Passed on July 13, 1787, the Northwest Ordinance, in the last of its six articles, prohibited slavery in the territory north of the Ohio River. The first national enactment curbing slavery, this measure was to some extent a reflection of humanitarian sentiment, although it must be added that Southerners permitted the bill to pass because they did not believe that the territory in question had a climate suitable for the cultivation of tobacco and indigo.

The conservative outlook on slavery which generally characterized federal bodies was again evident at the Constitutional Convention of 1787. The men who met at Philadelphia were adept at the strategy of compromise. The southern delegates, willing participants in the game of *quid pro quo,* were ready to make concessions to achieve their ends: an extension of time for the foreign slave trade, the return of fugitives, and the counting of the slave population in determining the apportionment of seats in the House of Representatives. This last-named measure, the "three-fifths compromise," would loom large in the decades to come. But this the men in Philadelphia had no way of knowing.

The Revolutionary Philosophy of Freedom

18

THE SUPREMACY OF NATURAL LAW

In breaking with England, the colonists evoked a philosophy of freedom, a philosophy incompatible with slavery and other forms of discrimination. Many Americans sensed that they could not in good conscience condemn England for curtailing their liberties if they were themselves guilty of oppressing others. One of the first Americans to grasp the full import of the revolutionary philosophy was James Otis of Massachusetts. In 1761, as attorney for a group of Boston merchants who objected to the issuance of general search warrants ("writs of assistance") by British officials, Otis argued that a law was void if it ran counter to man's natural rights. Two years later he reaffirmed the supremacy of natural law in The Rights of the British Colonies Asserted and Proved. *In this treatise he discussed Negro slavery, warning against the danger of denying liberty to anyone.*

The Colonists are by the law of nature free born, as indeed all men are, white or black. No better reasons can be given, for enslaving those of any colour, than such as baron Montesquieu has humourously given, as the foundation of that cruel slavery exercised over the poor Ethiopians; which threatens one day to reduce both Europe and America to the ignorance and barbarity of the darkest ages. Does it follow that it is right to enslave a man because he is black? Will short curled hair, like wool, instead of Christian hair, as it is called by those whose hearts are as hard as the nether millstone, help the argument? Can any logical inference in favour of slavery, be drawn from a flat nose, a long or a short face? Nothing better can be said in favour of a trade, that is the most shocking violation of the law of nature, has a direct tendency to diminish the idea of the inestimable value of liberty, and makes every dealer in it a tyrant, from the director of an African company to the petty chapman in needles and pins on the unhappy coast. It is a clear truth, that those who every day barter away other mens liberty, will soon care little for their own.*

19

PETITIONS FOR FREEDOM

Negroes were quick to link the revolutionary slogans of the patriots to their own condition. They began to draft petitions like the one that follows. Neither the legislature of Massachusetts nor the governor was disposed to grant this request. The slaves sent a delegation to the latter to enlist his support, but Governor Thomas Hutchinson, a slave-holder himself, could hardly have been sympathetic. During the colonial period many Negroes had petitioned individually for their freedom. The petition below, however, is one of the very first issued in the name of many. It is to be noted that, despite its apologetic and deferential tone, the petition conveys unmistakably the yearning for freedom.

---

*James Otis, *The Rights of the British Colonies Asserted and Proved* (London, 1766), 43-44.

Boston, April 20th, 1773

Sir, The efforts made by the legislative of this province in their last sessions to free themselves from slavery, gave us, who are in that deplorable state, a high degree of satisfaction. We expect great things from men who have made such a noble stand against the designs of their *fellow-men* to enslave them. We cannot but wish and hope Sir, that you will have the same grand object, we mean civil and religious liberty, in view in your next session. The divine spirit of *freedom,* seems to fire every humane breast on this continent, except such as are bribed to assist in executing the execrable plan.

We are very sensible that it would be highly detrimental to our present masters, if we were allowed to demand all that of *right* belongs to us for past services; this we disclaim. Even the *Spaniards,* who have not those sublime ideas of freedom that English men have, are conscious that they have no right to all the services of their fellow-men, we mean the *Africans,* whom they have purchased with their money; therefore they allow them one day in a week to work for themselves, to enable them to earn money to purchase the residue of their time, which they have a right to demand in such portions as they are able to pay for (a due appraizement of their services being first made, which always stands at the purchase money.) We do not pretend to dictate to you Sir, or to the Honorable Assembly, of which you are a member. We acknowledge our obligations to you for what you have already done, but as the people of this province seem to be actuated by the principles of equity and justice, we cannot but expect your house will again take our deplorable case into serious consideration, and give us that ample relief which, *as men,* we have a natural right to.

But since the wise and righteous governor of the universe, has permitted our fellow men to make us slaves, we bow in submission to him, and determine to behave in such a manner as that we may have reason to expect the divine approbation of, and assistance in, our peaceable and lawful attempts to gain our freedom.

We are willing to submit to such regulations and laws, as may be made relative to us, until we leave the province, which we determine to do as soon as we can, from our joynt labours procure money to transport ourselves to some part of the Coast of *Africa,* where we propose a settlement. We are very desirous that you should have instructions relative to us, from your town, therefore we pray you to communicate this letter to them, and ask this favor for us.

In behalf of our fellow slaves in this province, and by order of their Committee.

Peter Bestes,
Sambo Freeman,
Felix Holbrook,
Chester Joie.

For the Representative of the town of Thompson.*

---

*From *A Documentary History of the Negro People in the United States,* Vol. I, by Herbert Aptheker. Copyright 1951 by Herbert Aptheker. Reprinted by permission of Citadel Press, Inc.

20

UNALIENABLE RIGHTS

The doctrine of natural law—that there is a sphere of human rights untouchable by government—was cogently expressed in the document by which the Americans justified their separation from Great Britain. The Declaration of Independence was not without flaw. Scholars of later generations would question the soundness of its theory. Moreover, there were contemporary critics who pointed out that the Declaration omitted any direct condemnation of slavery. In the original draft formulated by Jefferson, slavery had been listed in the catalogue of crimes charged to George III, but this passage was deleted by Congress. Despite any omissions, evasions, or weakness in theory, however, the Declaration of Independence was of major importance. It furnished a rallying cry to the Revolutionary generation. To the dispossessed of its day, and thereafter, it was simultaneously a beacon light, a fortress, and an armory. Below is a significant excerpt.

IN CONGRESS, JULY 4, 1776

THE UNANIMOUS DECLARATION OF THE THIRTEEN UNITED STATES OF AMERICA,

* * *

We hold these truths to be self-evident, that all men are created equal, that they are endowed by their Creator with certain unalienable Rights, that among these are Life, Liberty and the pursuit of Happiness. —That to secure these rights, Governments are instituted among Men, deriving their just powers from the consent of the governed, —That whenever any Form of Government becomes destructive of these ends, it is the Right of the People to alter or to abolish it, and to institute new Government, laying its foundation on such principles and organizing its powers in such form, as to them shall seem most likely to effect their Safety and Happiness.*

* * *

Uncertain Trumpet

21

CRISPUS ATTUCKS AND THE BOSTON MASSACRE

With the rift widening between England and her mainland colonies, it was not surprising that a resort to arms should result. The war did not come without casting its shadow before it. Of the prewar incidents, the Boston Massacre (March 5, 1770) was one of the most dramatic, and hence was of great propaganda value to the American patriots. Two of His Majesty's regiments were stationed in Boston, sent there to protect the unpopular customs officials. Goaded by taunts and jeers, the British soldiers, in a moment of panic, fired into the crowd. Eleven persons were hit, five of whom were to die, including Crispus Attucks, a Negro. Determined to make full use of the incident, the Boston patriots arranged a public funeral on March 8. The solemn parade to the Granary Burial Ground was witnessed by more persons than any other event in colonial America. A local newspaper, the Boston Gazette and Country Journal, *reported the affair.*

**The Declaration of Independence.*

Crispus Attucks owes his prominence in history to the attention which Attorney Adams devoted to him at the trial proceedings, and to the general belief that he was the one who struck British soldier Hugh Montgomery, thus touching off the firing by the troops. Andrew, slave of a Boston selectman, Oliver Wendell, was one of the witnesses who testified that Attucks was the assailant. The soldiers would be acquitted, but the Fifth of March would be celebrated as the chief American holiday until superseded by the Fourth of July. It may be added that a Crispus Attucks monument was erected on Boston Common in 1889, a step that the city took in response to petitions by Negroes. Included is the testimony of slave Andrew concerning Attucks

The Funeral

Last Thursday, agreeable to a general request of the inhabitants and by the consent of parents and friends, were carried to their grave in succession the bodies of Samuel Gray, Samuel Maverick, James Caldwell, and Crispus Attucks, the unhappy victims who fell in the bloody massacre of the Monday evening preceding!

On this occasion most of the shops in town were shut, all the bells were ordered to toll a solemn peal, as were also those in the neighbouring towns of Charlestown, Roxbury, etc. The procession began to move between the hours of four and five in the afternoon, two of the unfortunate sufferers, viz. Messrs. James Caldwell and Crispus Attucks who were strangers, borne from Faneuil Hall attended by a numerous train of persons of all ranks; and the other two, viz. Mr. Samuel Gray, from the house of Mr. Benjamin Gray (his brother) on the north side of the Exchange, and Mr. Maverick, from the house of his distressed mother, Mrs. Mary Maverick, in Union Street, each followed by their respective relations and friends, the several hearses forming a junction in King Street, the theatre of the inhuman tragedy, proceeded from thence through the Main Street, lengthened by an immense concourse of people so numerous as to be obliged to follow in ranks of six, and brought up by a long train of carriages belonging to the principal gentry of the town. The bodies were deposited in one vault in the middle burying ground. The aggravated circumstances of their death, the distress and sorrow visible in every countenance, together with the peculiar solemnity with which the whole funeral was conducted, surpass description.*

An account of the burial of the victims of the Boston Massacre—the coffin at far right is that of Crispus Attucks.

The Testimony of Slave Andrew

The people seemed to be leaving the soldiers, and to turn from them, when there came down a number from Jackson's corner, huzzaing and crying, damn them, they dare not fire, we are not afraid of them. One of these people, a stout man with a long cord wood stick, threw himself in, and made a blow at the officer; I saw the officer try to ward off the stroke; whether he struck him or not I do not know; the stout man then turned round, and struck the grenadier's gun at the captain's right hand, and immediately fell in with his club, and knocked his gun away, and struck him over the head; the blow came either on the soldier's cheek or hat. This stout man

*Merrill Jensen, op. cit., 749-750.

held the bayonet with his left hand, and twitched it and cried, kill the dogs, knock them over. This was the general cry; the people then crowded in, and upon that the grenadier gave a twitch back and relieved his gun, and he up with it and began to pay away on the people. I was then betwixt the officer and this grenadier; I turned to go off, when I heard the word fire; at the word fire, I thought I heard the report of a gun, and upon my hearing the report, I saw the same grenadier swing his gun, and immediately he discharged it. Do you know who this stout man was, that fell in and struck the grenadier? I thought, and still think, it was the mulatto who was shot.*

22

SALEM POOR, PATRIOT SOLDIER

One of the first engagements of the war was the Battle of Bunker Hill on June 17, 1775, an attempt by the British to occupy the heights of Boston. In the bloody day-long encounter, the British finally prevailed, but they suffered heavy casualties, losing more than one third of their men. One of the patriot soldiers in the battle, Salem Poor, was praised by fourteen officers, who sent a petition to the legislature on his behalf. Poor later served at Valley Forge and at White Plains.

The Subscribers begg leave to Report to your Hon[ble] House (which we do in justice to the Caracter of so Brave a Man) that under Our Own observation, We declare that a Negro Man Called Salem Poor of Col. Frye's Regiment, Cap[t] Ames Company—in the late Battle at Charlestown, behaved like an Experienced officer, as well as an Excellent Soldier, to set forth Particulars of his Conduct would be Tedious, We would only begg leave to Say in the Person of this Negro Centers a Brave and gallant Soldier. The Reward due to so great and Distinguished a Caracter, We Submit to the Congress— Cambridge, Dec. 5th 1775

Jon[a.] Brewer, Col.
[signed by 13 other officers]

To the Honorable General Court
of the Massachusetts Bay†

23

EXCLUSION OF BLACK SOLDIERS

During the early weeks of the war, Negroes were used as soldiers, but the practice was soon abandoned. Exclusion of slaves, and later of free Negroes, became the official policy of state governments, of the Continental army, and of the Congress. The first state to act was Massachusetts. The executive branch of that state, the Committee of Safety, passed the resolution below on May 20, 1775.

---

*Frederic Kidder, *History of the Boston Massacre* (Boston, 1870), 205.

†Original manuscript, Revolutionary Rolls, Collection, *Massachusetts Archives* (State House, Boston), CLXXX, 241.

When the Continental command (which included General Washington, Major Generals Ward, Lee, and Putnam, and Brigadier Generals Thomas, Spencer, Heath, Sullivan, Green, and Gates) held a council of war on October 8, 1775, one of the questions they considered was whether or not to enlist Negroes. They agreed not to accept either free or slave Negroes.

It did not take the military men long to win Congress over to their viewpoint on the issue of Negro soldiers. On October 23, 1775, General Washington met with three official representatives from Congress—Thomas Lynch, Jr., of South Carolina, Benjamin Harrison of Virginia, and Benjamin Franklin of Pennsylvania. At this meeting, attended also by civilian authorites from Massachusetts, Rhode Island, and Connecticut, the Negro was again rejected.

MASSACHUSETTS

Resolved, That it is the opinion of this committee, as that contest now between Great Britain and the colonies respects the liberties and privileges of the latter, which the colonies are determined to maintain, that the admission of any persons, as soldiers, into the army now raising, but only such as are freemen, will be inconsistent with the procedures that are to be supported, and reflect dishonor on this colony, and that no Slaves shall be admitted into this army upon any consideration whatever.*

THE CONTINENTAL ARMY

Whether it would be advisable to enlist any negroes in the new Army? or whether there should be a distinction between such as are slaves and those who are free?

Agreed, unanimously, to reject all slaves, and, by a great majority, to reject negroes altogether.†

THE CONTINENTAL CONGRESS

Ought not Negroes be excluded from the new enlistment, especially such as are slaves? all were thought improper by the Council of Officers.

Agreed, That they be rejected altogether.‡

Arms-Bearers for America

24

SLAVE ENLISTMENT IN RHODE ISLAND

By the summer of 1777, towns in New England, in order to fill their Continental quotas, began to enlist Negroes. If these recruits were free, they were given a cash bounty; if they were slaves, they were given their freedom. Noting the success of these practices, the state governments began to turn to black recruits. In May 1777, Connecticut permitted a drafted man to furnish a Negro substitute.

**The Journals of Each Provincial Congress of Massachusetts in 1774 and 1775, and of the Committee of Safety* (Boston, 1838), 553.

†*American Archives* (Washington, U.S. Superintendent of Documents, 1837-1853), ser. 4, III, 1040.

‡*Ibid.*, 1161.

The most forthright step was taken by Rhode Island, which, in February 1778, passed a slave enlistment bill. Such a proposal had been initiated by state officers serving in the Continental army. Through General Washington and Governor Nicholas Cook, their recommendation reached the General Assembly, which spoke as follows:

State of Rhode Island and Providence Plantations
February 14, 1778.

Whereas, for the preservation of the rights and liberties of the United States, it is necessary that the whole powers of government should be exerted in recruiting the Continental battalions; and whereas, His Excellency Gen. Washington hath enclosed to this state a proposal made to him by Brigadier General Varnum, to enlist into the two battalions, raising by this state, such slaves as should be willing to enter into the service; and whereas, history affords us frequent precedents of the wisest, the freest, and bravest nations having liberated their slaves, and enlisted them as soldiers to fight in defence of their country; and also whereas, the enemy, with a great force, have taken possession of the capital, and of a greater part of this state; and this state is obliged to raise a very considerable number of troops for its own immediate defence, whereby it is in a manner rendered impossible for this state to furnish recruits for the said two battalions, without adopting the said measure so recommended.

It is voted and resolved, that every able-bodied negro, mulatto, or Indian man slave, in this state, may enlist into either of the said two battalions, to serve during the continuance of the present war with Great Britain.

That every slave, so enlisting, shall be entitled to, and receive, all the bounties, wages, and encouragements, allowed by the Continental Congress, to any soldier enlisting into their service.

It is further voted and resolved, that every slave, so enlisting, shall, upon his passing muster before Col. Christopher Greene, be immediately discharged from the service of his master or mistress, and be absolutely FREE, as though he had never been encumbered with any kind of servitude or slavery.

And in case such slave shall, by sickness or otherwise, be rendered unable to maintain himself, he shall not be chargeable to his master or mistress; but shall be supported at the expense of the state.

And whereas, slaves have been, by the laws, deemed the property of their owners, and therefore compensation ought to be made to the owners for the loss of their service,—

It is further voted and resolved, that there be allowed, and paid by this state, to the owner, for every such slave so enlisting, a sum according to his worth; at a price not exceeding £120 for the most valuable slave; and in proportion for a slave of less value.*

---

*John Russell Bartlett, *Records of the State of Rhode Island and Providence Plantations in New England* (10 vols., Providence, published by the State of Rhode Island, 1856-1865), III, 358-360.

25

NEGROES IN THE CONTINENTAL ARMY

By the summer of 1778 the Continental army, like those of most of the states, was accepting Negroes. Indeed, a Negro was far more likely to serve in the Continental line than in the state forces. Service in the former was less preferable, since the period of enlistment was longer and the soldier had to be prepared to go to any theater of war, rather than remain within the borders of his own state. Since the Negro volunteer was not, as a rule, in a position to choose between the state and federal armies, he generally found himself in the latter. The official return below, signed by Adjutant General Alexander Scammell on August 24, 1778, gives the numbers as of that date.

RETURN OF THE NEGROES IN THE ARMY, 24TH AUGT. 1778

BRIGADES	PRESENT	SICK ABSENT	ON COMMAND	TOTAL
N. Carolina	42	10	6	58
Woodford	36	3	1	40
Muhlenburg	64	26	8	98
Scott	20	3	1	24
Smalwood	43	15	2	60
2: Maryland	33	1	1	35
Wayne	2			2
2: Pennsylvania				
Clinton	33	2	4	39
Parsons	117	12	19	148
Huntington	56	2	4	62
Nixon	26		1	27
Patterson	64	13	12	89
Late Learned	34	4	8	46
Poor	16	7	4	27
TOTAL	586	98	71	755

(*signed*) Alex Scammell, *adj. Gen.**

26

A DRAFT SUBSTITUTE

The Rhode Island slave enlistment bill led to the formation of a predominantly colored unit (except for its officers) for the Rhode Island First Regiment. Other states, including some south of the Mason-Dixon Line, had second thoughts about excluding Negroes from arms-bearing. Maryland's need for manpower led her to include the free Negro in the lists of draft eligibles and to authorize slave enlistments with the consent of their masters. Virginia, though not permitting slaves to bear arms, lifted the ban on free Negro soldiers. In Georgia there were instances, even if not numerous, of a slave serving as a draft substitute for his master. Austin Dabney of Burke County was an example. Freed to enlist to replace his master, Dabney served in Colonel Elijah Clark's artillery corps. In the Battle of Kettle Creek in 1779, Dabney's thigh was broken. Forty years later the Georgia legislature voted him 112 acres of land as a reward for his "bravery and fortitude . . . in several engagements and actions" against the British. Below is an attestation of Dabney's service.

*George Washington Papers (Library of Congress), LXXXII—volume entitled, "1778, Aug. 17-30."

State of Georgia

These are to certify, That Austin Dabney was an Inhabitant of this State prior to the Reduction thereof by the British Arms, and was a Refugee from the same, during which Time he cheerfully did his Duty as a Soldier and Friend to this and the United States.

Given under my Hand, this Second Day of Febr^{y} 1784,

Elijah Clark, Col.

By his Order W. Freeman*

27

THE RECOMMENDATION OF ALEXANDER HAMILTON

The Continental army became even more receptive to the use of Negro soldiers after the fall of Savannah and the British threat to subjugate the entire South. Army commanders and the Congress agreed that a request should be made to Georgia and South Carolina to enlist their slaves as soldiers. The proposal to make the southern Negro an arms-bearer had been vigorously advocated by two young officers on Washington's staff who had become friends, John Laurens of South Carolina and Alexander Hamilton. Writing from army headquarters on March 14, 1779, the latter directed a carefully reasoned letter to the President of the Continental Congress.

A LETTER TO JOHN JAY

Middlebrook, New Jersey
March 14, 1779

Dear Sir,

Col Laurens, who will have the honor of delivering you this letter, is on his way to South Carolina, on a project, which I think, in the present situation of affairs there, is a very good one and deserves every kind of support and encouragement. This is to raise two three or four batalions of negroes; with the assistance of the government of that state, by contributions from the owners in proportion to the number they possess. If you should think proper to enter upon the subject with him, he will give you a detail of his plan. He wishes to have it recommended by Congress to the state; and, as an inducement, that they would engage to take those batalions into Continental pay.

It appears to me, that an expedient of this kind, in the present state of Southern affairs, is the most rational, that can be adopted, and promises very important advantages. Indeed, I hardly see how a sufficient force can be collected in that quarter without it; and the enemy's operations there are growing infinitely serious and formidable. I have not the least doubt, that the negroes will make very excellent soldiers, with proper management; and I will venture to pronounce, that they cannot be put in better hands than those of Mr. Laurens. He has all the zeal, intelligence, enterprise, and every other qualification requisite to succeed in such an undertaking. It is

*Original manuscript, Georgia Department of Archives and History (Atlanta).

a maxim with some great military judges, that with sensible officers soldiers can hardly be too stupid; and on this principle it is thought that the Russians would make the best troops in the world, if they were under other officers than their own. The King of Prussia is among the number who maintain this doctrine and has a very emphatical saying on the occasion, which I do not exactly recollect. I mention this, because I frequently hear it objected to the scheme of embodying negroes that they are too stupid to make soldiers. This is so far from appearing to me a valid objection that I think their want of cultivation (for their natural faculties are probably as good as ours) joined to that habit of subordination which they acquire from a life of servitude, will make them sooner became soldiers than our White inhabitants. Let officers be men of sense and sentiment, and the nearer the soldiers approach to machines perhaps the better.

I foresee that this project will have to combat much opposition from prejudice and self-interest. The contempt we have been taught to entertain for the blacks, makes us fancy many things that are founded neither in reason nor experience; and an unwillingness to part with property of so valuable a kind will furnish a thousand arguments to show the impracticability or pernicious tendency of a scheme which requires such a sacrifice. But it should be considered, that if we do not make use of them in this way, the enemy probably will; and that the best way to counteract the temptations they will hold out will be to offer them ourselves. An essential part of the plan is to give them their freedom with their muskets. This will secure their fidelity, animate their courage, and I believe will have a good influence upon those who remain, by opening a door to their emancipation. This circumstance, I confess, has no small weight in inducing me to wish the success of the project; for the dictates of humanity and true policy equally interest me in favour of this unfortunate class of men. . . .

With the truest respect & esteem I am Sir Your Most Obed Servant

Alex Hamilton*

28

A SLAVE PILOT IN THE VIRGINIA NAVY

As was the case in the army, manpower shortages made the use of Negroes in the Continental and state navies inevitable. Naval commanders, who often had to put to sea dangerously undermanned, were not given to picking and choosing their crews. The Virginia navy, largest of the state navies in the South, outstripped all others in the use of Negro pilots. Negroes were "accustomed to the navigation of the River," as one official put it. Outstanding among these black pilots was Caesar, the slave of Carter Tarrant of Hampton. On one occasion Caesar was at the wheel of the schooner Patriot *when she captured a British brig,* Fanny, *carrying stores and supplies. In 1789 the legislature purchased his freedom.*

*From *The Papers of Alexander Hamilton*, Vol. 9, edited by Harold C. Syrett and Jacob E. Cooke, pp. 17, 18, 19. Reprinted by permission of Columbia University Press.

AN ACT FOR THE PURCHASE AND MANUMITTING NEGRO CAESAR.
(PASSED THE 14TH OF NOVEMBER, 1789.)

WHEREAS it is represented to this Assembly, that Mary Tarrant of the county of Elizabeth City, hath her life in a negro named Caesar, who entered very early into the service of his country, and continued to pilot the armed vessels of this state during the late war; in consideration of which meritorious services it is judged expedient to purchase the freedom of the said Caesar; *Be it therefore enacted by the General Assembly,* that the executive shall appoint a proper person to contract with the said Mary Tarrant for the purchase of the said Caesar, and if they should agree, the person so appointed by the executive shall deliver to the said Mary Tarrant a certificate expressing such purchase and the sum, and upon producing such certificate to the auditor of the accounts, he shall issue a warrant for the same to the treasurer, to be by him paid out of the lighthouse fund. *And be it further enacted,* that from and after the execution of a certificate aforesaid, the said Caesar shall be manumitted and set free to all intents and purposes.*

29

LAFAYETTE'S SPY

The American forces found use for a few Negro spies. Of these the best known was James, a slave of William Armistead of New Kent County, Virginia. With his master's permission, James took service with Lafayette when that young commander came to Williamsburg in March 1781. James made a number of trips to Portsmouth, hovering around the British camps and delivering letters to other spies. Lafayette was highly pleased and later drew up a written statement of commendation. The Virginia legislature voted in 1786 to purchase James' freedom. Forty years later, when Lafayette came to Richmond (October 1824), one of his welcomers was James, who long since had borrowed his hero's surname, styling himself "James Lafayette." The statement of commendation by General Lafayette read as follows:

This is to certify that the bearer by the name of James has done essential service to me while I had the honour to command in this State. His intelligences from the enemy's camp were industriously collected and more faithfully delivered. He properly acquitted himself with some important communications I gave him and appears to be entitled to every reward his situation can admit of. Done under my hand, Richmond, November 21st, 1784.

Lafayette†

---

*Hening, *op. cit.*, XIII, 102.

†Luther P. Jackson, *Virginia Negro Soldiers and Seamen in the Revolutionary War* (Norfolk, privately printed, 1944), 9.

30

SLAVE BOUNTY

Slaves were used as enlistment bounties, also. Indeed, a slave bounty was preferred to a bounty in paper money, which was always depreciating. A slave bounty compared favorably also with a land bounty, which might turn out to be a barren spot many miles away from its owner's domicile. In November 1780 the Virginia legislature debated a bill whereby each army recruit would be given a slave not less than ten nor more than forty years old. The measure was defeated, primarily because of the almost solid opposition of the planter aristocracy, from whom the slaves were to be purchased at unspecified prices. In South Carolina, however, a slave enlistment bill was passed early in 1782. The slaveowners did not object, since the slaves were to be obtained not from them, but from the confiscated estates of British sympathizers. The following is a passage from the South Carolina statute. The irony of rewarding one man for defending rights and liberties by giving him an individual stripped of rights and liberties was not apparent, it seems, to the legislators.

AN ACT TO PROCURE RECRUITS AND PREVENT DESERTION.

* * *

II. And as an encouragement to those who are willing to serve their country in the defence of her rights and liberties, *Be it further enacted,* by the authority aforesaid, That every ablebodied recruit between the age of sixteen and forty-five years, who shall enlist to serve for the term aforesaid, and shall be passed by one of the officers who shall be appointed by order of the continental General of this State to inspect recruits, shall be entitled to, and shall receive, for each and every year's service, the bounty of one sound negro between the age of ten years and forty, to be delivered to such recruit in the manner following, viz. one at the time of his being passed as aforesaid, another at the commencement of the second year's service, and the third at the expiration of the third's year's service; and if any such recruit shall die, be killed, or maimed, after the commencement of the third year, he or his heirs shall nevertheless by entitled to receive the same bounty as if he had served out the said third year. Provided nevertheless, that if the said recruit shall desert, he shall forfeit to the use of this State the bounty which he is entitled to by virtue of this Act.*

In His Majesty's Service

31

AN INVITATION TO SLAVES

Faced by a manpower shortage even greater than that of their American foes, the British were most receptive to the idea of using Negroes. The ones they had in mind were the able-bodied slaves of the American rebels. Possession of the slaves of the enemy was particularly satisfying, since it strengthened one's own striking

**The Statutes at Large of South Carolina, 1752-1786* (Columbia, 1838), 513-514.

power while simultaneously weakening his. From the first threat of trouble the British had contemplated the use of black auxiliaries; General Thomas Gage had raised the question as early as June 1775. It was Lord Dunmore, six months later, who took the formal step of inviting slaves to join the royal standard. Crown governor of Virginia during the critical months when the crisis between the colonists and England was coming to a head, Dunmore quit Williamstown in June 1775, taking refuge with the British fleet. In November of the same year, when it had become evident that reconciliation was unlikely, Dunmore issued the proclamation below.

A PROCLAMATION.

As I have ever entertained hopes that an accommodation might have taken place between *Great Britain* and this Colony, without being compelled by my duty to this most disagreeable, but now absolutely necessary step, rendered so by a body of armed men, unlawfully assembled, firing on His Majesty's Tenders; and the formation of an Army, and that Army now on their march to attack His Majesty's Troops, and destroy the well-disposed subjects of this Colony: To defeat such treasonable purposes, and that all such traitors and their abettors may be brought to justice, and that the peace and good order of this Colony may be again restored, which the ordinary course of the civil law is unable to effect, I have thought fit to issue this my Proclamation, hereby declaring, that until the aforesaid good purposes can be obtained, I do, in virtue of the power and authority to me given by His Majesty, determine to execute martial law, and cause the same to be executed throughout this Colony. And to the end that peace and good order may the sooner be restored, I do require every person capable of bearing arms to resort to His Majesty's standard, or be looked upon as traitors to His Majesty's crown and Government, and thereby become liable to the penalty the law inflicts upon such offences—such as forfeiture of life, confiscation of lands, &c., &c.; and I do hereby further declare all indented servants, Negroes, or others, (appertaining to Rebels,) free, that are able and willing to bear arms, they joining His Majesty's Troops, as soon as may be, for the more speedily reducing this Colony to a proper sense of their duty to His Majesty's crown and dignity. I do further order and require all His Majesty's liege subjects to retain their quit-rents, or any other taxes due, or that may become due, in their own custody, will such time as peace may be again restored to this, at present, most unhappy Country, or demanded of them for their former salutary purposes, by officers properly authorized to receive the same.

Given under my hand, on board the Ship *William,* off *Norfolk,* the 7th day of *November,* in the sixteenth year of His Majesty's reign.

DUNMORE.

GOD *Save the King.**

---

*Peter Force, ed., *American Archives . . . A Documentary History of . . . the American Colonies* (4th ser., 6 vols.; 5th ser., 3 vols.; Washington, 1837-1853), ser. 4, III, 1385.

32

GENERAL CLINTON'S PROCLAMATION

Dunmore was soon driven from his insecure and floating headquarters in Virginia waters, but not before many slaves had attempted to reach him. Their efforts, and the alarm that the proclamation raised among Americans, was not lost on the British commanders. Henceforth they welcomed able-bodied slaves; Dunmore's proclamation had initiated policy. Later this policy was more authoritatively stated, the most important instance being General Clinton's proclamation of 1779. This document was widely printed and reprinted in the loyalist press, particularly in Rivington's Royal Gazette. *Clinton's proclamation took on added significance as the theatre of war shifted to the South with its large slave population.*

PROCLAMATION.

WHEREAS, The Enemy have adopted a practice of enrolling NEGROES among their troops: I do hereby give Notice, that all NEGROES taken in Arms, or upon any military Duty, shall be purchased for a stated price; the Money to be paid to the Captors.

But I do most strictly forbid any Person to sell or claim Right over any NEGROE, the Property of a Rebel, who may take refuge with any part of this Army: And I do promise to every NEGROE who shall desert the Rebel Standard full Security to follow within these Lines any occupation which he shall think proper.

Given under my Hand, at Head-Quarters,
Philipsburgh, the 30th day of June
1779.
H. CLINTON.

By his Excellency's Command,
JOHN SMITH, Secretary*

33

THE LURE OF FREEDOM

The American authorities, civilian and military, took a number of steps to prevent slaves from going over to the British. Some states, like Virginia, established a detail of galleys which removed small craft from the waters. North Carolina tightened its system of slave patrols, exempting the patrollers from military duty. Many masters took the precaution of removing their slaves whenever the British came too close. Such measures met with only a limited success. The typical slave desired his freedom; to attain it he was ready to take a reasonable risk. Hence, thousands of slaves, lured by the fulsome promises of the British, made their way to His Majesty's lines. Richard Barnes of Leonard Town, Maryland, in a letter to Governor Lee on March 25, 1781, described the behavior of the Negroes when the British drew near.

---

*Royal Gazette (Rivington's, New York, July 3, 1779).

RICH[d] BARNES, LEO[d] TOWN HIS EXCELLENCY THO[s] SIM LEE ESQ[r]

* * *

I shuld be glad of your opinion whether it would not be advisable, whilst the Enemy are in the Bay to keep about sixty more men constantly patroling from one part of the Co[ty] to the other in order to prevent disatisfaction and the negroes going to the Enemy as from the late conduct of the Negroes when those Ships were in S[t] Marys I am well satisfied the greatest part of them that are in the Co[ty] would join them, as I am well informed upwards of twenty five offered themselves to those Ships the night they were in St. Marys. Your answer to the above will oblige Your Most ob[t] ser[t]*

34

LABORERS IN THE BRITISH ARMY

The Negro's greatest service to the British was as a laborer. All departments of the army used Negroes, frequently competing with one another in attempts to obtain them. In order to establish some uniformity in employment practices among the departments, the army command in South Carolina in 1781 issued a set of rules.

INSTRUCTIONS FOR THE OFFICE ESTABLISHED TO RECEIVE THE PAY OF NEGROES EMPLOYED IN THE DIFFERENT DEPARTMENTS, VIZ.

I. RETURNS to be given in to the Pay-Masters by the Heads of Departments, of the Negroes employed in the different Departments, by Families, specifying the Numbers, their Owners Names, and if in Arms against Government or if Loyalists.

II. Their Wages as fixed by a former Order, viz. Eight Pence per Day for common Labourers, and Eighteen Pence per Day for Artificers; two Women to be considered and paid equal to one labouring Man; to be lodged in the Hands of the Pay-Masters, Quarterly, by the Heads of Departments, in Order to pay the Loyalists for the Use of their Slaves, to Cloath them all and to establish a Fund for future Services.

III. The Receipts of the Heads of Departments to be Vouchers to the Pay-Masters for Cloathing supplied the Negroes.

IV. All the Negroes to have their Cloathing made up in Uniform; and all Negroes to be taken up who have not the proper Tickets from the Pay-Masters.

V. A certain fixed Allowance of Money to be paid Quarterly, upon a Certificate of their deserving it being given by the Foreman or Overseer, under which they have worked, countersigned by the Head of the Department, viz. To every common Labourer and to every two Women One Dollar per Month, to every Artificer, &c. &c. &c. Two Dollars per Month; which allowance is to be ascertained by the Tickets granted from the Pay-Office, specifying if an Artificer or common Labourer.

---

*William H. Browne, *op. cit.*, XLVII, 148.

VI. The Pay-Masters to Muster all the Negroes, once a Month, and when a Negro absents himself from any Department the Pay-Masters are to be reported to in writing, by the Head of the Department, which Report is to be produced to the Auditor of Accounts Quarterly, and a Copy of these Accounts to be delivered to all the Heads of Departments, who are also to be supplied with new Tickets, Quarterly.*

35

IMPRESSMENT OF NEGROES

The authorities sometimes had to resort to impressment to obtain slave labor. In Tory Georgia in 1780 Governor Wright had the legislature pass a measure authorizing the impressment of Negroes as laborers and, if the need arose, as soldiers. Wright described his activities in a letter to his superior in London.

GOV. SIR JAS. WRIGHT TO SEC. LORD G. GERMAIN.

1st Dec. 1780.
SAVANAH IN GEORGIA

MY LORD,

Inclos'd Your Lordship has the Triplicate of my Letter No. 32 & in consequence of the power vested in me, by the Bill which I assented to on the 30th of October last, I order'd out upwards of 400 Negroes, who have been at work fortifying the Town of Savanah ever since that Day.

We are making five Redoubts & Batterys & there is to be a Parapet made of Fascines & Earth from the River at Each End & on the Back of the Town. This Parapet is 10 foot wide & 7 foot high with a Ditch on the Outside 15 foot wide at Top 10 foot Deep & sloping to the Bottom 3 foot. I think the Redoubts will be finished & Each Parapet about half done, or say the whole 4 foot high by Christmas & I expect the works will be entirely finish'd in all January. This my Lord is a most inconvenient thing & a heavy Tax on the People, being one fourth part of all their Male Slaves for near or quite 3 Months, & when the work is complete I shall send Y[r] Lordship a Plan of the whole.

The present state of our strength will appear to Y[r] Lordship from my former Letters & from the Inclosed Address of the Members of His Majesty's Council.

The late Law also enables me to call out & arm Negroes in defence of the Province & to exercise further power over the Militia, but this only in time of *Alarms actually fired &* there are several things provided for which we thought necessary in these yet very perilous times.

---

*Original manuscript, Sir Henry Clinton Papers, Clements Library, University of Michigan.

I have the honor to be with Perfect Esteem

My Lord, Your Lordships
most obliged & obed[t] Serv[t]
JA. WRIGHT.

The R[t] Ho[ble] Lord Geo. Germain
His Majesty's Principal Secretary of State &c. &c. &c.
[Indorsed] R 17th February 1781.*

36

THE RESENTMENT OF SLAVEHOLDERS

To the British the most prized Negroes were the pilots. Seafaring Negroes of lesser skills were often used in the numerous forays into Chesapeake waters to seize enemy goods. The resentment of slaveholders toward their former slaves who warred against them can be imagined. A Negro who was captured while taking part in a marauding expedition was likely to be given the maximum sentence, as one of them found out.

[May 8th Prince Wm. Co.]

Indictment and trial of Mulatto Slave, called "Bill" alias "Will"; alias "William", of the Parish of Dettingen in Prince Wm. County, and the property of John Tayloe, Esq. late of Richmond County, for "Treason," in aiding and abetting, and felloniously and traiterously waging & levying war against the Commonwealth, in conjunction with divers enemies of the same, in an armed vessell &c—Upon trial by the Court of Oyer & Terminu, the following being present—

Henry Lee	William Carr	
Foushee Tebbs	Richd: Graham	Gents: Justices.
William Tebbs	William Brent	

the said Slave was found guilty and condemned to be hanged by the neck upon the public gallows, until dead—

Signed by
CUTHBERT BUELETT, Attoy: for
the Commonwealth, and
ROBT. GRAHAM, Clk. Court—†

37

THE PEACE TREATY AND HIS MAJESTY'S NEGROES

After Yorktown, as the war drew to a close and the British prepared to evacuate, their ranks were swollen by the Negroes who had been in their employ, and who were, almost to a man, bent on leaving with them. The Americans held that their

---

*_Collections of the Georgia Historical Society_ (8 vols., Savannah, Georgia State Historical Society, 1840-1916), III, 322-323. Reprinted by permission.

†W. P. Palmer, *et al.*, ed., *Calendar of Virginia State Papers* (11 vols., Richmond, published by the State of Virginia, 1875-1893), II, 90.

slaves should be restored to them. But the British commander, Sir Guy Carleton, was equally insistent that his government could not in good faith abandon the Negroes who had come into the British lines under the proclamations of freedom issued by His Majesty's officers. On April 15, 1783, Congress instructed General Washington to make arrangements to obtain American property, including slaves then in the hands of the British. Washington wrote to Carleton, suggesting a meeting, a request to which the latter agreed without enthusiasm. This important conference took place at Orange Town, New York, on May 6. The results were bitterly disappointing to Washington, who left convinced that the American slaves would never be returned, a conviction later affirmed. The opposing viewpoints on the return of slaves were clearly brought out in the official report of the meeting between the two high-ranking commanders.

SUBSTANCE OF A CONFERENCE BETWEEN GENERAL WASHINGTON AND SIR GUY CARLETON

Orange Town, May 6, 1783

. . . Sir Guy Carleton then observed . . . that in this Embarkation a Number of Negroes were comprised. General Washington thereupon expressed his Surprize that after what appeared to him an express Stipulation to the Contrary in the Treaty Negroes the Property of the Inhabitants of these States should be sent off; to which Sir Guy Carleton replied . . . He principally insisted that he conceived it could not have been the intention of the British Government by the Treaty of Peace to reduce themselves to the necessity of violating their Faith to the Negroes who came into the British Lines under the Proclamation of his Predecessors in Command, that he forbore to express his Sentiments on the Propriety of these Proclamations but that delivering up the Negroes to their former Masters would be delivering them up some possibly to Execution and others to severe Punishment which in his Opinion would be a dishonorable Violation of the public Faith pledged to the Negroes in the Proclamations that if the sending off the Negroes should hereafter be declared an Infraction of the Treaty, Compensation must be made by the Crown of Great Britain to the Owners, that he had taken Measures to provide for this by directing a Register to be kept of all the Negroes who were sent off specifying the Name Age and Occupation of the Slave and the Name and Place of Residence of his former Master.

General Washington again observed that he conceived this Conduct on the part of Sir Guy Carleton a Departure both from the Letter and Spirit of the Articles of Peace and particularly mentioned a Difficulty that would arise in compensating the Proprietors of Negroes admitting this infraction of the Treaty could be satisfied by such compensation as Sir Guy Carleton had alluded to, as it was impossible to ascertain the Value of the Slaves from any Fact or Circumstance which may appear in the Register, the value of a Slave consisting chiefly in his Industry and Sobriety and General Washington further mentioned a Difficulty which would attend identifying the Slave supposing him to have changed his own Name or to have given in a wrong Name of his former Master. In answer to which Sir Guy Carleton said that as the Negro was free and secured against his Master he could have no Inducement to conceal either his own true Name or that of his Master. Sir Guy Carleton then observed that he was not by the Treaty held to deliver up any Property but was only restricted from carrying it away and therefore admitting the Interpretation of the Treaty as given by Genl. Washington to be just he was notwithstanding pursuing a Measure which would operate most for the Security of Proprietors for if the Negroes were left to themselves without Care or Control from him Numbers of them would very probably go off and not return to the parts of the Country they came from, or clandestinely get on board the Transports in Manner which it would not be in his Power to prevent in either of which Cases and inevitable Loss would ensue to the Proprietors but as the Business was now conducted they had at least a Chance for Compensation; and concluded the Conversation on this Subject by saying that he imagined that the Mode of compensating as well as the Accounts and other Points with respect to which there was no express Provision made by the Treaty must be adjudged by Commissioners to be hereafter appointed by the two Nations.*

Postwar Federal Action

38

THE NORTHWEST ORDINANCE

Before the end of the war the northern states had taken action against slavery and the slave trade. The federal government moved more slowly, but in 1787 it passed the Northwest Ordinance, which, in Article Six, prohibited slavery north of the Ohio River. This was the first time that the national government had placed a check on slavery. Moreover, the opening clause of Article Six was destined to be repeated word for word in the subsequent organic laws of territories and states. And, as a fitting climax, these words would find further expression in the Thirteenth Amendment in 1865. Hence the brevity of Article Six of the Northwest Ordinance is no measure of its importance.

THE NORTHWEST ORDINANCE
JULY 13, 1787

Art. 6. There shall be neither slavery nor involuntary servitude in the said territory, otherwise than in the punishment of crimes whereof the party shall have been duly convicted: *Provided, always,* that any person escaping into the same, from whom labor or service is lawfully claimed in any one of the original States, such fugitive may be lawfully reclaimed and conveyed to the person claiming his or her labor or service as aforesaid.†

---

*John C. Fitzpatrick, ed., *Writings of George Washington* (39 vols., Washington, Government Printing Office, 1931-1944), XXVI, 402-405.

†F. N. Thorpe, ed., *Federal and State Constitutions* (Washington, Government Printing Office, 1909), II, 960.

39

THE CONSTITUTION AND THE SLAVE TRADE

The men who met at Philadelphia in the summer of 1787 to draw up a constitution for the new nation could not ignore slavery, although they managed to avoid the use of the word. Theoretically these men believed in freedom for everyone, but actually they found it hard to conceive of a society in which Negroes were of equal status to whites. Moreover, they regarded slaves as chattels, and they had no relish for any experiments impinging upon private property, which they held in reverence.

The convention found it necessary to consider questions concerning the foreign slave trade, the return of fugitives, and the apportionment of representation. Opponents of the foreign slave trade appealed in the debates to the principles of the American Revolution. But such sentiments were lost on the delegates from Georgia and South Carolina, states that had sustained heavy losses during the war and wanted to replenish their supply. The delegates reached a compromise which protected the foreign slave trade for twenty years. In 1807 Congress would pass an act prohibiting such trade, but this measure would be very poorly enforced. The compromise made by the convention appears in Article II, Section 9.

The Migration or Importation of such Persons as any of the States now existing shall think proper to admit, shall not be prohibited by the Congress prior to the Year one thousand eight hundred and eight, but a Tax or duty may be imposed on such Importation, not exceeding ten dollars for each Person.*

40

THE CONSTITUTION AND FUGITIVE SLAVES

The delegates to the Constitutional Convention were in general agreement that fugitives should be returned to their masters, a stipulation that had appeared even in the antislavery Northwest Ordinance. The provision is found in Article IV, Section 2, of the Constitution.

No Person held to Service or Labour in one State, under the Laws thereof, escaping into another, shall, in Consequence of any Law or Regulation therein, be discharged from such Service or Labour, but shall be delivered up on Claim of the Party to whom such Service or Labour may be due.†

**The Constitution of the United States of America,* Senate Doc. no. 170, 82nd Cong., 2nd sess. (Washington, 1953), 25.

†*Ibid.*, 31.

41

THE "THREE-FIFTHS COMPROMISE"

One of the major debates in the Constitutional Convention hinged on the use of slaves in computing taxes and fixing representation. Southern delegates held that slaves should be computed in determining representation in the House, but that they should not be counted in determining a state's share of the direct tax burden. The northern delegates' point of view was exactly the opposite. A compromise was reached whereby three fifths of the slaves were to be counted in apportionment of representation and in direct taxes among the states. Thus the South was victorious in obtaining representation for her slaves, even though delegate Luther Martin might rail that the Constitution was an insult to the Deity "who views with equal eye the poor African slave and his American master." The "three-fifths compromise" appears in Article I, Section 2.

Representatives and direct Taxes shall be apportioned among the several States which may be included within this Union, according to their respective Numbers, which shall be determined by adding to the whole Number of free Persons, including those bound to Service for a Term of Years, and excluding Indians not taxed, three fifths of all other Persons.*

42

THE FEDERALIST

The "three-fifths compromise" was based on the assumption that a slave had the dual quality of being both a chattel and a person. This paradox of man viewed as a person for some purposes and as property for other purposes was carefully analyzed in one issue of The Federalist, *a series of eighty-five political essays written in 1787 and 1788 by Alexander Hamilton, James Madison, and John Jay in order to win support in the state conventions called to vote upon the Constitution. The excerpt below is taken from essay number 54, generally credited to James Madison.*

February 12, 1788

To the People of the State of New York.

The next view which I shall take of the House of Representatives, relates to the apportionment of its members to the several States, which is to be determined by the same rule with that of direct taxes.

* * *

We subscribe to the doctrine, might one of our southern brethren observe, that representation relates more immediately to persons, and taxation more immediately to property, and we join in the application of this distinction to the case of our slaves. But we must deny the fact that slaves are considered merely as property, and in no respect whatever as persons. The true state of the case is, that they partake of both these qualities; being considered by our laws, in

---

Ibid., 19.

some respects, as persons, and in other respects, as property. In being compelled to labor not for himself, but for a master; in being vendible by one master to another master; and in being subject at all times to be restrained in his liberty, and chastised in his body, by the capricious will of another, the slave may appear to be degraded from the human rank, and classed with those irrational animals, which fall under the legal denomination of property. In being protected on the other hand in his life & in his limbs, against the violence of all others, even the master of his labor and his liberty; and in being punishable himself for all violence committed against others; the slave is no less evidently regarded by the law as a member of the society; not as a part of the irrational creation; as a moral person, not as a mere article of property. The Fœderal Constitution therefore, decides with great propriety on the case of our slaves, when it views them in the mixt character of persons and of property. This is in fact their true character. It is the character bestowed on them by the laws under which they live; and it will not be denied that these are the proper criterion; because it is only under the pretext that the laws have transformed the negroes into subjects of property, that a place is disputed them in the computation of numbers; and it is admitted that if the laws were to restore the rights which have been taken away, the negroes could no longer be refused an equal share of representation with the other inhabitants.*

The Early Abolitionist Impulse

43

THE HARMFUL EFFECTS OF SLAVERY

The Constitution of the United States is a notable piece of work, an achievement hard to overpraise. But it was drawn up by men of property and standing whose main concern was order and stability. These men did not speak in revolutionary accents, as had Patrick Henry and Thomas Jefferson, both of whom were conspicuously absent from the Constitutional Convention. Hence, for all their insight, the men at Philadelphia did not sense the theoretical dangers inherent in slavery, as Jefferson had sensed them. In the closing year of the war, Jefferson, in his Notes on Virginia, *had devoted some attention to slavery's harmful effects and had sounded a note of warning.*

It is difficult to determine on the standard by which the manners of a nation may be tried, whether *catholic* or *particular.* It is more difficult for a native to bring to that standard the manners of his own nation, familiarized to him by habit. There must doubtless be an unhappy influence on the manners of our people produced by the existence of slavery among us. The whole commerce between master and slave is a perpetual exercise of the most boisterous passions, the

*Jacob E. Cooke, ed., *The Federalist* (Middleton, Conn., Wesleyan University Press, 1961), 366-369.

most unremitting despotism on the one part, and degrading submissions on the other. Our children see this, and learn to imitate it; for man is an imitative animal. This quality is the germ of all education in him. From his cradle to his grave he is learning to do what he sees others do. If a parent could find no motive either in his philanthropy or his self-love, for restraining the intemperance of passion towards his slave, it should always be a sufficient one that his child is present. But generally it is not sufficient. The parent storms, the child looks on, catches the lineaments of wrath, puts on the same airs in the circle of smaller slaves, gives a loose to the worst of passions, and thus nursed, educated, and daily exercised in tyranny, cannot but be stamped by it with odious peculiarities. The man must be a prodigy who can retain his manners and morals undepraved by such circumstances. And with what execrations should the statesman be loaded, who permitting one half the citizens thus to trample on the rights of the other, transforms those into despots, and these into enemies, destroys the morals of the one part, and the amor patriae of the other. For if a slave can have a country in this world, it must be any other in preference to that in which he is born to live and labour for another: in which he must lock up the faculties of his nature, contribute as far as depends on his individual endeavours to the evanishment of the human race, or entail his own miserable condition on the endless generations proceeding from him. With the morals of the people, their industry also is destroyed. For in a warm climate, no man will labour for himself who can make another labour for him. This is so true, that of the proprietors of slaves a very small proportion indeed are ever seen to labour. And can the liberties of a nation be thought secure when we have removed their only firm basis, a conviction in the minds of the people that these liberties are of the gift of God? That they are not to be violated but with his wrath? Indeed I tremble for my country when I reflect that God is just: that his justice cannot sleep forever: that considering numbers, nature and natural means only, a revolution of the wheel of fortune, an exchange of situation, is among possible events: that it may become probable by supernatural interference! The Almighty has no attribute which can take side with us in such a contest.—But it is impossible to be temperate and to pursue this subject through the various considerations of policy, of morals, of history natural and civil. We must be contented to hope they will force their way into every one's mind. I think a change already perceptible, since the origin of the present revolution. The spirit of the master is abating, that of the slave rising from the dust, his condition mollifying, the way I hope preparing, under the auspices of heaven, for a total emancipation, and that this is disposed, in the order of events, to be with the consent of the masters, rather than by their extirpation.*

---

*Paul Leicester Ford, *The Writings of Thomas Jefferson* (10 vols., New York, G. P. Putnam, 1892-1899), III, 266-268.

44

THE PENNSYLVANIA SOCIETY

The spirit of humanitarianism engendered by the Revolution found expression in the formation of societies to abolish slavery. Experiencing a rapid growth in the decades after the war, these societies with their basically conciliatory approach attracted many men prominent in public life. The best known of these groups was the Pennsylvania Society, which, writes Dwight L. Dumond, "encouraged the organization of other societies; sent memorials (later called petitions) to Congress; publicized state laws relative to slavery and free Negroes; printed and distributed antislavery literature, both foreign and domestic; corresponded with prominent antislavery leaders in England and France; and initiated a policy of assistance to free Negroes and to those illegally held in bondage." The constitution of the Pennsylvania Society, setting forth its philosophy and its modus operandi, *became a model for others. Below is the preamble to the constitution.*

The Constitution of the Pennsylvania Society, for the promoting of the Abolition of Slavery, and the Relief of Free Negroes, Unlawfully Held in Bondage;

Enlarged at Philadelphia, April 23d, 1787.

It having pleased the Creator of the world, to make of one flesh all the children of men—it becomes them to consult and promote each other's happiness, as members of the same family, however diversified they may be, by colour, situation, religion, or different states of society. It is more especially the duty of those persons, who profess to maintain for themselves the rights of human nature, and who acknowledge the obligations of Christianity, to use such means as are in their power, to extend the blessings of freedom to every part of the human race; and in a more particular manner, to such of their fellow-creatures, as are entitled to freedom by the laws and constitutions of any of the United States, and who, notwithstanding, are detained in bondage, by fraud or violence.—From a full conviction of the truth and obligation of these principles—from a desire to diffuse them, wherever the miseries and vices of slavery exist, and in humble confidence of the favor and support of the Father of Mankind, the subscribers have associated themselves, under the title of the "Pennsylvania Society for promoting the Abolition of Slavery, and the Relief of free Negroes unlawfully held in Bondage."

* * *

The Present OFFICERS *of the* SOCIETY.

PRESIDENT,

BENJAMIN FRANKLIN.

VICE-PRESIDENTS,

JAMES PEMBERTON, JONATHAN PENROSE.

SECRETARIES,

BENJAMIN RUSH, TENCH COXE.

TREASURER,

JAMES STARR.*

**The Constitution of the Pennsylvania Society for Promoting the Abolition of Slavery, and the Relief of Free Negroes unlawfully held in Bondage* (Philadelphia, 1888), 3-7.

45

PETITIONS TO CONGRESS

In 1791, six of the state societies sent petitions to Congress. Two of these societies were located in states in which slavery was deeply rooted, Maryland and Virginia. Nevertheless, the petition of the latter was as forthright as any other.

To the Honorable the Congress of the UNITED STATES OF AMERICA—*The* MEMORIAL *of the* VIRGINIA SOCIETY, *for promoting the Abolition of Slavery, and the Relief of free Negroes, and others, unlawfully held in bondage, and for other humane purposes:* RESPECTFULLY SHEWETH,

THAT your memorialists, fully believing that "righteousness exalteth a nation," and that slavery is not only an odious degradation, but an outrageous violation of one of the most essential rights of human nature, and utterly repugnant to the precepts of the gospel, which breathes "peace on earth, goodwill to men;" they lament that a practice, so inconsistent with true policy and the unalienable rights of men, should subsist in so enlightened an age, and among a people professing, that all mankind are, by nature, equally entitled to freedom. But, more especially, that a trade to Africa, for the express purpose of enslaving and transporting that much-injured and oppressed people from their native country and connections, should be continued, or suffered, by any of the United States of America.

Your memorialists do, therefore, request, and earnestly intreat Congress to take the premises into consideration, and exert the powers they are possessed of, in passing such laws as may put a stop to, or discourage, so unrigheous a traffic; and alleviate, as much as possible, the horrors and cruelties generally practised in the prosecution of the trade, so contrary to every sentiment of humanity and justice, and destructive of the lives and temporal happiness of that unfortunate race of mankind. They conceive that an act so laudable, would well become the Representatives of a free people, and be pleasing in the sight of the merciful Father of all the families of the earth.

Signed, by appointment, and on behalf of the said Society, at their half-yearly meeting, held in the town of Manchester the 5th day of the 4th month, called April, 1791.

ROBERT PLEASANTS,
President.

Attest.
JAMES SMITH, *Secretary.**

**Memorials Presented to the Congress of the United States by the Different Societies Instituted for Promoting the Abolition of Slavery in the States of Rhode-Island, Connecticut, New York, Pennsylvania, Maryland and Virginia* (Philadelphia, 1792), 29-31.

46

PROPAGANDA FOR ABOLITION

The Pennsylvania Society publicized the accomplishments of outstanding Negroes, hoping thereby to refute the charge of innate racial inferiority. To this end, Benjamin Rush wrote a short piece about James Derham. One of the Pennsylvania Society's original founders, and a signer of the Declaration of Independence, Rush was a physician who somehow found time for a notable public career.

Philadelphia, Jan. 5, 1789

At a meeting of the Pennsylvania Society for promoting the abolition of slavery, and the relief of free negroes, unlawfully held in bondage—ordered, that the following certificates, communicated by dr. Rush, be published.

There is now in this city, a black man, of the name of James Derham, a practitioner of physic, belonging to the Spanish settlement of New Orleans, on the Mississippi. This man was born in a family in this city, in which he was taught to read and write, and instructed in the principles of christianity. When a boy, he was transferred by his master to the late dr. John Kearsly, jun. of this city, who employed him occasionally to compound medicines, and to perform some of the more humble acts of attention to his patients.

Upon the death of dr. Kearsly, he became (after passing through several hands) the property of dr. George West, surgeon to the sixteenth British regiment, under whom, during the late war in America, he performed many of the menial duties of our profession. At the close of the war, he was sold by dr. West to dr. Robert Dove, of New Orleans, who employed him as an assistant in his business: in which capacity he gained so much of his confidence and friendship, that he consented to liberate him, after two or three years, upon easy terms. From dr. Derham's numerous opportunities of improving in medicine, he became so well acquainted with the healing art, as to commence practitioner at New Orleans, under the patronage of his last master. He is now about twenty-six years of age, has a wife, but no children, and does business to the amount of three thousand dollars a year.

I have conversed with him upon most of the acute and epidemic diseases of the country where he lives, and was pleased to find him perfectly acquainted with the modern simple mode of practice in those diseases. I expected to have suggested some new medicines to him; but he suggested many more to me. He is very modest and engaging in his manners. He speaks French fluently, and has some knowledge of the Spanish language. But by some accident, although born in a religious family, belonging to the church of England, he was not baptised in his infancy; in consequence of which he applied, a few days ago, to bishop White, to be received by that ordinance into the episcopal church. The bishop found him qualified, both by knowledge and moral conduct, to be admitted to baptism, and this day performed the ceremony, in one of the churches in this city.

Philadelphia, November 14, 1788.*

47

LEMUEL HAYNES

Any account of the Negro during the Revolution and the first years of independence must recognize the emergence of a gallery of prominent personages. During the colonial period a few individual Negroes might become known locally, but their fame ended at the boundaries of their own communities, Phillis Wheatley excepted. The Revolutionary period, however, created a climate in which it became possible for an able Negro to escape obscurity. For among the new impulses strengthened by the Revolution was a new freedom of choice, a greater opportunity for the individual man or woman to be heard and respected. With all the emphasis on independence and independent effort, it is not surprising that at least a handful of Negroes should step out of the shadows, among them Lemuel Haynes, Benjamin Banneker, Paul Cuffe, and Prince Hall.

Of these early notables, Lemuel Haynes gained distinction as the first Negro to serve regularly as pastor to white congregations. A soldier in the Revolutionary War, Haynes left the army to study theology under private tutors. Licensed to preach in 1780, Haynes held Congregational pastorates in all-white churches in Connecticut, Vermont, and New York. His writings brought him fame; leading divines and college presidents were among his acquaintances. In the summer of 1785, while on the threshold of his career, he kept a diary that reveals something of his theological bent. Preceding these diary entries is a story, related by Haynes' biographer, of a parishioner whose prejudice changed to warm admiration.

Respecting his ministry here there is a striking fact, which I will relate in the language of a correspondent. "There is a man of my acquaintance who feels that he owes much, under God, to the preaching of Mr. Haynes while at Torrington. He was disaffected that the church should employ him, and neglected meeting for a time. At length curiosity conquered prejudice so far that he went to the house of God. He took his seat in the crowded assembly, and, from designed disrespect, sat *with his hat on*. Mr. Haynes gave out his text, and began with his usual impassioned earnestness, as if unconscious of anything amiss in the congregation. 'The preacher had not proceeded far in his sermon,' said the man, 'before I thought him the *whitest* man I ever saw. My hat was instantly taken off and thrown under the seat, and I found myself listening with the most profound attention.' That day was a memorable era in the life of this scorner, and the sermon was memorable for its piercing effects upon his conscience. Through the influences of the spirit of God, he was roused from his stupidity—convinced of his guilt and ruin—and led

**The American Museum* (Philadelphia, 1789), V, 61-62.

to look to Christ Jesus for salvation. He became a man of prayer and unexceptionable piety; and is now, if living, an elder in the church at the west."

Brief sketch of a Tour into the State of Vermont.

Torrington, July 26, 1785. Set out on my journey to the State of Vermont, accompanied by Mr. L. Loomis. May we be prospered, and have the Divine presence! Visited Mr. S. Banning, of Hartland, a young man of twenty-one, who appeared to be upon the borders of the eternal world. — Could not talk with him much about dying, his reason being gone. — Commended him to the Throne of Grace in prayer. — Heard, at the same time, of the sudden death of Mr. Wilder, an old acquaintance. — Went to visit the distressed family. — Discoursed with them on the importance of being prepared to meet sudden death. — Lodged at Granville.

July 28. Set out for Williamstown.—Dined with the Reverend Mr. Collins, Lanesborough.—Heard him discourse very sensibly on divinity.

July 29. Kept Sabbath with the Rev. Seth Swift, Williamstown, an exceedingly agreeable gentleman and faithful minister. — Am grieved for the unhappy divisions among his people, chiefly on account of public affairs. — Preached from Numb. xxi., 9; "And Moses made a serpent of brass, and put it upon a pole; and it came to pass, that if a serpent had bitten any man, when he beheld the serpent of brass he lived." And Tit. ii., 13; "Looking for that blessed hope and the glorious appearing of the great God, and our Saviour Jesus Christ." — The people were very attentive.

July 30. Called on the Rev. Job Swift, of Bennington.—Had an agreeable interview.

July 31. Lodged at Esquire Smith's, in Clarendon.

Aug. 1. Came to Rutland.

Aug. 2. Preached at Deacon Roberts's, from Matt. xiii., 44; "Again, the kingdom of heaven is like unto treasure hid in a field, the which, when a man hath found, he hideth, and for joy thereof goeth and selleth all that he hath and buyeth that field."

Aug. 3. Preached at Mr. Cornish's, from Tit. ii., 13. — Saw something of the power of God among the people.

Aug. 4. Visited a sick man — attempted to pray with him.

Aug. 5. Sabbath. Preached at Rutland, from 2 Pet. i., 10; "Wherefore the rather, brethren, give diligence to make your calling and election sure; for if ye do these things ye shall never fall." Numb. xxiii., 10. "Who can count the dust of Jacob, and count the fourth part of Israel? Let me die the death of the righteous, and let my last end be like his!" — The people gave remarkable attention.

Aug. 6. Went to Pawlet. — Preached for Rev. Mr. B——, from Zech. xii., 10; "And I will pour upon the house of David, and upon the inhabitants of Jerusalem," &c. — Met with Rev. Mr. Graves, of Rupert, and Messrs. Thomson and Tolman, candidates. — Had much conversation with them. — All seem to be zealous in the cause of the Redeemer. — Heard Mr. Tolman preach from 1 Cor. vii., 29; "The time is short."

Aug. 7. Heard Mr. Thomson preach to a sick woman, from Psal. 1v., 5, 6; "Fearfulness and trembling are come upon me, and horror hath overwhelmed me. And I said, Oh that I had the wings of a dove! for then would I fly away and be at rest." — Rode to Granville after sermon, in company with Mr. Thomson. — Visited a sick woman — prayed and conversed with her.

Aug. 8. Preached at Granville for Rev. Mr. Hitchcox. — Rode to Poultney. — Preached from Phil. iii., 13; "Brethren, I count not myself to have apprehended: but this one thing I do, forgetting those things which are behind, and reaching forth to those things which are before."

Aug. 9. Rode to Tinmouth, — preached, at 4 o'clock, from Col. iii., 4; "When Christ who is our life shall appear, then shall ye also appear with him in glory." — Visited the Rev. Mr. Osborne, who, on account of division, had stopped preaching. — Lodged with Judge Mattocks of that place. — Had a most agreeable opportunity with him.*

48

BENJAMIN BANNEKER

Benjamin Bannaker's
PENNSYLVANIA, DELAWARE, MARY-LAND, AND VIRGINIA
ALMANAC,
FOR THE
YEAR of our LORD 1795;
Being the Third after Leap-Year.
BANNAKER.
PHILADELPHIA:
Printed for WILLIAM GIBBONS, Cherry Street

Benjamin Banneker, mathematician and astronomer, began in 1791 the publication of a series of almanacs which would be widely read in the middle states during the 1790's. A household staple in early America, along with the Bible, almanacs were informative and entertaining, their content ranging from weather predictions to witty sayings. As described by a contemporary, Banneker was "a large man of noble appearance, with venerable hair, wearing a coat of superfine drab broad cloth, and a broad rimmed hat," and resembling Benjamin Franklin, another maker of almanacs. Banneker sent a pre-publication copy of his first almanac to Thomas Jefferson, then Secretary of State, who graciously acknowledged the gift, adding that "nobody wishes more than I do to see such proofs as you exhibit that nature has given to our black brethren talents equal to those of the other colors of men." A year later, President Washington, at the request of Jefferson, appointed Banneker to serve on a commission to lay out the projected national capital. Banneker's initial almanac was headed by a letter to the printers from James McHenry, a prominent Marylander who would later serve as Secretary of War in Washington's cabinet.

The Editors of the Pennsylvania, Delaware, Maryland, *and* Virginia Almanack, *feel themselves gratified in the Opportunity of presenting to the Public, through the Medium of* their *Press, what must be considered an extraordinary Effort of Genius*—a COMPLETE and ACCURATE EPHEMERIS for the Year 1792, *calculated by a sable Descendant of* Africa, *who, by this Specimen of Ingenuity, evinces, to Demonstration, that mental Powers and Endowments are not the exclusive Excellence of* white People, *but that the Rays of Science may alike illumine the Minds of Men of every* Clime, *(however they may*

---

*Timothy M. Cooley, *Sketches of the Life and Character of Lemuel Haynes, A. M.* (New York, 1837), 73-75.

differ in the Colour *of* their Skin) *particularly those whom Tyrant-Custom hath too long taught us to depreciate as a Race inferior in intellectual Capacity.—They flatter themselves that a philanthropic Public, in this enlightened Era, will be induced to give their Patronage and Support to this* Work, *not only on Account of its intrinsic Merit, (it having met the Approbation of several of the most distinguished Astronomers in America, particularly the celebrated Mr.* Rittenhouse) *but from similar Motives to those which induced the Editors to give this Calculation the Preference, the ardent Desire of drawing modest Merit from Obscurity, and controverting the long-established illiberal Prejudice against the* Blacks.

Though it becomes the Editors to speak with less Confidence of the miscellaneous Part of this Work, they yet flatter themselves, from their Attention to the variegated Selections in Prose and Verse, that their Readers will find it both USEFUL *and* ENTERTAINING, *and not undeserving of that Approbation which they have had the Happiness of experiencing for a Series of Years—an Approbation they are most ambitious of meriting, and which, they hope, will crown their present Wishes and Labours with Success.*

The Editors have taken the Liberty to annex a Letter from Mr. McHENRY, *containing Particulars respecting* Benjamin, *which, it is presumed, will prove more acceptable to the Reader, than anything further in the prefatory Way.*

"Baltimore, August 20, 1791.

"Messrs. CODDARD and ANGELL,

"BENJAMIN BANNEKER, a free Negro, has calculated an ALMANACK, for the ensuing year, 1792, which being desirous to dispose of, to the best advantage, he has requested me to aid his application to you for that purpose. Having fully satisfied myself, with respect to his title to this kind of authorship, if you can agree with him for the price of his work, I may venture to assure you it will do you credit, as Editors, while it will afford you the opportunity to encourage talents that have thus far surmounted the most discouraging circumstances and prejudices.

"This Man is about fifty-nine years of age; he was born in *Baltimore County;* his father was an *African,* and his mother the offspring of *African* parents.—His father and mother having obtained their freedom, were enabled to send him to an obscure school, where he learned, when a boy, reading, writing, and arithmetic as far as double position; and to leave him, at their deaths, a few acres of land, upon which he has supported himself ever since by means of economy and constant labour, and preserved a fair reputation. To struggle incessantly against want is no ways favourable to improvement: What he had learned, however, he did not forget; for as some hours of leisure will occur in the most toilsome life, he availed himself of these, not to read and acquire knowledge from writings of genius and discovery, for of such he had none, but to digest and apply, as occasions presented, the few principles of the few rules of arithmetic he had been taught at school. This kind of mental exercise formed his chief amusement, and soon gave him a facility in calculation that was often serviceable to his neighbours, and at length attracted the attention of the Messrs. *Ellicotts,* a family remarkable for their ingenuity and turn to the useful mechanics. It is about three years since Mr. *George Ellicott* lent him *Mayer's* Tables, *Fergusen's* Astronomy, *Leadbeater's* Lunar Tables, and some astronomic instruments, but without accompanying them with either hint or instruction, that might further his studies, or lead him to apply them to any useful result. These books and instruments, the first of the kind he had ever seen, opened a new world to *Benjamin,* and from thenceforward he employed his leisure in astronomical researches. He now took up the idea of the calculations for an ALMANACK, and actually completed an entire set for the last year, upon his original stock of arithmetic. Encouraged by this first attempt, he entered upon his calculation for 1792, which, as well as the former, he began and finished without the least information, or assistance, from any person, or other books than those I have mentioned; so that, whatever merit is attached to his present performance, is exclusively and peculiarly his own.

"I have been the more careful to investigate those particulars, and to ascertain their reality, as they form an interesting fact in the History of Man; and as you may want them to gratify curiosity, I have no objection to your selecting them for your account of *Benjamin.*

"I consider this Negro as a fresh proof that the powers of the mind are disconnected with the colour of the skin, or, in other words, a striking contradiction to Mr. *Hume's* doctrine, that "the Negroes are naturally inferior to the whites, and unsusceptible of attainments in arts and sciences." In every civilized country we shall find thousands of whites, liberally educated, and who have enjoyed greater opportunities of instruction than this Negro, his inferiors in those intellectual acquirements and capacities that form the most characteristic feature in the human race. But the system that would assign to these degraded blacks an origin different from the whites, if it is not ready to be deserted by the philosophers, must be relinquished as similar instances multiply; and that such must frequently happen cannot well be doubted, should no check impede the progress of humanity, which, meliorating the condition of slavery, necessarily leads to its final extinction.—Let, however, the issue be what it will, I cannot but wish, on this occasion, to see the Public patronage keep pace with my black friend's merit.

"I am, Gentlemen, your most obedient servant,

JAMES M'HENRY."*

**Benjamin Banneker's Pennsylvania, Delaware, Maryland, and Virginia Almanack and Ephemeris, For the Year of Our Lord, 1792* (Baltimore, 1791), 2-4.

49

PAUL CUFFE

Paul Cuffe was a shipbuilder, merchant, and sea captain. In 1780 he and his brother John led the fight of the Negroes of Dartmouth, Massachusetts, to obtain the right to vote. A Quaker, he financed a school building for the children of the community. His name can be linked to two continents, inasmuch as he was an exponent of colonization, transporting 38 Negroes to Sierra Leone, West Africa, in 1815, almost wholly at his own expense. His trip antedated the formation of the American Colonization Society and the founding of Liberia. Among the rare first-hand accounts of Cuffe is a eulogy, "A Discourse Delivered on the Death of Captain Paul Cuffe," by Peter Williams, a New York Negro who was then studying for the Episcopal priesthood. The address was given at the New York African Institution on October 21, 1817, six weeks after Cuffe's death.

In his person, Capt. Cuffe was large and well proportioned. His countenance was serious but mild. His speech and habit, plain and unostentatious. His deportment, dignified and prepossessing; blending gravity with modesty and sweetness, and firmness with gentleness and humility. His whole exterior indicated a man of respectability and piety. Such would a stranger have supposed him to be at the first glance.

To convey a further idea of him, it is necessary to recur to his history. He was born in the year 1759, on one of the Elizabeth Islands, near New Bedford. His parents had ten children—four sons and six daughters. He was the youngest of the sons. His father died when he was about 14 years of age, at which time he had learnt but little more than his alphabet; and having from thence, with his brothers, the care of his mother and sisters devolving upon him, he had but little opportunity for the acquisitions of literature. Indeed, he never had any schooling, but obtained what learning he had by his own indefatigable exertions, and the scanty aids which he occasionally received from persons who were friendly towards him. By these means, however, he advanced to a considerable proficiency in arithmetic, and skill in navigation. Of his talent for receiving learning, we may form an estimate from the fact, that he acquired such a knowledge of navigation in two weeks as enabled him to command his vessel in the voyages which he made to Russia, to England, to Africa, to the West India Islands, as well as to a number of different ports in the southern section of the United States. His mind, it appears, was early inclined to the pursuits of commerce. Before he was grown to manhood, he made several voyages to the West Indies, and along the American coast. At the age of 20, he commenced business for himself, in a small open boat. With this, he set out trading to the neighboring towns and settlements; and, though Providence seemed rather unpropitious to him at first, by perseverance, prudence and industry, his resources were so blessed with an increase, that, after a while, he was enabled to obtain a good sized schooner. In this vessel he enlarged the sphere of his action; trading to more distant places, and in articles requiring a larger capital; and thus, in the process of time, he became owner of one brig, afterwards of 2, then he added a ship, and so on until 1806, at which time he was possessed of one ship, two brigs, and several smaller vessels, besides considerable property in houses and lands.

* * *

In the year 1780, Capt. C. being just then of age, was with his brother John, called on by the collector to pay his personal tax. At that time the coloured people of Massachusetts were not considered as entitled to the right of suffrage, or to any of the privileges peculiar to citizens. A question immediately arose with them, whether it was constitutional for them to pay taxes, while they were deprived of the rights enjoyed by others who paid them? They concluded, it was not; and, though the sum was small, yet considering it as an imposition affecting the interests of the people of colour throughout the state, they refused to pay it. The consequence was, a law-suit, attended with so much trouble and vexatious delay, that they finally gave it up, by complying with the requisitions of the collector. They did not, however, abandon the pursuit of their rights; but at the next session of the Legislature, presented a petition, praying that they might have the rights, since they had to bear the burden of citizenship; and though there was much reason to doubt of its success, yet it was granted, and all the free coloured people of the state, on paying their taxes, were considered, from thenceforth, as entitled to all the privileges of citizens. For this triumph of justice and humanity over prejudice and oppression, not only the coloured people of Massachusetts, but every advocate of correct principle, owes a tribute of respect and gratitude to John and Paul Cuffe.

In 1797, Capt. Cuffe, lamenting that the place in which he lived was destitute of a school for the instruction of youth; and anxious that his children should have a more favorable opportunity of obtaining education than he had had, proposed to his neighbors to unite with him in erecting a school-house. This, though the utility of the object was undeniable, was made the cause of so much contention, (probably on account of his colour) that he resolved at length to build a school-house on his own land, and at his own expense. He did so, and when finished, gave them the use of it gratis, satisfying himself with seeing it occupied for the purposes contemplated.

* * *

But it was in his active commiseration in behalf of his African brethren, that he shone forth most conspicuously as a man of worth. Long had his bowels yearned over their degraded, destitute, miserable condition. He saw, it is true, many benevolent men engaging in releasing them from bondage, and pouring into their minds the light of literature and religion, but he saw also the force of prejudice operating so powerfully against them, as to give but little encouragement to hope that they could ever rise to respectability and usefulness, unless it were in a state of society where they would have greater incentives to improvement, and more favorable opportunities than would probably be ever afforded them where the bulk of the population are whites.

Under this impression, he turned his thoughts to the British settlement at Sierra Leona; and in 1811, finding his property sufficient to warrant the undertaking, and believing it to be his duty to appropriate part of what God had given him to the benefit of his and our unhappy race, he embarked on board of his own brig, manned entirely by persons of colour, and sailed to the land of his forefathers, in the hope of benefitting its natives and descendants.

Arrived at the colony, he made himself acquainted with its condition, and held a number of conversations with the governor and principal inhabitants; in which he suggested a number of important improvements. Among other things, he recommended the formation of a society for the purposes of promoting the interests of its members and of the colonists in general; which measure was immediately adopted, and the society named "The Friendly Society of Sierra Leona." From thence he sailed to England, where, meeting with every mark of attention and respect, he was favored with an opportunity of opening his views to the board of managers of the African Institution, who cordially acquiescing in all his plans, gave him authority to carry over from the U. States a few coloured persons of good character, to instruct the colonists in agriculture and the mechanical arts. After this he returned to Sierra Leona, carrying with him some goods as a consignment to the Friendly Society, to encourage them in the way of trade; which having safely delivered, and given them some salutary instructions, he set sail and returned again to his native land.

* * *

Scarcely had the first transports of rejoicing, at his return, time to subside, before he commenced his preparations for a second voyage; not discouraged by the labours and dangers he had past, and unmindful of the ease which the decline of life requires, and to which his long continued and earnest exertions gave him a peculiar claim. In the hope of finding persons of the description given by the African Institution, he visited most of the large cities in the union, held frequent conferences with the most reputable men of colour, and also with those among the whites who had distinguished themselves as the friends of the Africans; and recommended to the coloured people to form associations for the furtherance of the benevolent work in which he was engaged. The results were, the formation of two societies, one in Philadelphia, and the other in New York, and the discovery of a number of proper persons, who were willing to go with him and settle in Africa. But unfortunately, before he found himself in readiness for the voyage, the war commenced between this country and Great Britain. This put a bar in the way of his operations, which he was so anxious to remove, that he travelled from his home at Westport, to the city of Washington, to solicit the government to favor his views, and to let him depart and carry with him those persons and their effects whom he had engaged to go and settle in Sierra Leona. He was, however, unsuccessful in the attempt. His general plan was highly and universally approbated, but the policy of the government would not admit of such an intercourse with an enemy's colony.

He had now no alternative but to stay at home and wait the event of the war. But the delay, thus occasioned, instead of being suffered to damp his ardor, was improved by him to the maturing of his plans, and extending his correspondence, which already embraced some of the first characters in Great Britain and America. After the termination of the war, he with all convenient speed prepared for his departure, and in Dec. 1815, he took on board his brig 38 persons of the dispersed race of Africa; and after a voyage of 55 days, landed them safely on the soil of their progenitors.

It is proper here to remark that Capt. C. in his zeal for the welfare of his brethren, had exceeded the instructions of the institution at London. They had advised him not to carry over, in the first instance, more than 6 or 8 persons; consequently, he had no claim on them for the passage and other expenses attending the removal of any over that number. But this he had previously considered, and generously resolved to bear the burden of the expense himself, rather than any of those whom he had engaged should be deprived of an opportunity of going where they might be so usefully employed. He moreover foresaw, that when these persons were landed at Sierra Leona, it would be necessary to make such provision for the destitute as would support them until they were enabled to provide for themselves.

For this also he had to apply to his own resources, so that in this voyage he expended out of his own private funds, between three and four thousand dollars, for the benefit of the colony.*

50

PRINCE HALL

Prince Hall was born in Barbados and made his way in 1765 to Boston, where he served in the local militias and took part in the Battle of Bunker Hill. He became a Methodist minister in Cambridge and a spokesman for Negroes throughout Massachusetts. Hall was initiated into the Masonic order early in 1775 by a British military lodge then stationed in Boston. At the end of the war Hall and his followers, after a series of rebuffs, received a charter from the Grand Lodge of England, and Hall became master of the new branch. Even though the leader of one particular fraternal group, Hall's interests and his outlook were broad. Indeed, it was characteristic of all Negro spokesmen that their very position as leaders of a minority group tended to sensitize them to man's common humanity and to his indissoluble destiny. In a Masonic sermon in June 1797, Hall identified the Negroes with the larger community, revealing his belief that all men were one in God, and in the desire for freedom.

EXTRACT FROM A CHARGE DELIVERED TO THE AFRICAN LODGE, JUNE 24TH, 1797, AT MENOTOMY, (NOW WEST CAMBRIDGE,) MASS., BY THE RIGHT WORSHIPFUL PRINCE HALL.

Beloved Brethren of the African Lodge:

It is now five years since I delivered a charge to you on some parts and points of masonry. As one branch or superstructure of the foundation, I endeavored to show you the duty of a mason to a

*Benjamin Brawley, *Early American Negro Writers* (Chapel Hill, University of North Carolina Press, 1935), 103-108.

mason, and of charity and love to all mankind, as the work and image of the great God and the Father of the human race. I shall now attempt to show you that it is our duty to sympathise with our fellow-men under their troubles, and with the families of our brethren who are gone, we hope, to the Grand Lodge above.

We are to have sympathy, but this, after all, is not to be confined to parties or colors, nor to towns or states, nor to a kingdom, but to the kingdoms of the whole earth, over whom Christ the King is head and grand master for all in distress.

Among these numerous sons and daughters of distress, let us see our friends and brethren; and first let us see *them* dragged from their native country, by the iron hand of tyranny and oppression, from their dear friends and connections, with weeping eyes and aching hearts, to a strange land, and among a strange people, whose tender mercies are cruel,—and there to bear the iron yoke of slavery and cruelty, till death, as a friend, shall relieve them. And must not the unhappy condition of these, our fellow-men, draw forth our hearty prayers and wishes for their deliverance from those merchants and traders, whose characters you have described in Revelations xviii. 11-13? And who knows but these same sort of traders may, in a short time, in like manner bewail the loss of the African traffic, to their shame and confusion? The day dawns now in some of the West India Islands. God can and will change their condition and their hearts, too, and let Boston and the world know that He hath no respect of persons, and that that bulwark of envy, pride, scorn and contempt, which is so visible in some, shall fall.

* * *

Now, my brethren, nothing is stable; all things are changeable. Let us seek those things which are sure and steadfast, and let us pray God that, while we remain here, he would give us the grace of patience, and strength to bear up under all our troubles, which, at this day, God knows, we have our share of. Patience, I say; for were we not possessed of a great measure of it, we could not bear up under the daily insults we meet with in the streets of Boston, much more on public days of recreation. How, at such times, are we shamefully abused, and that to such a degree, that we may truly be said to carry our lives in our hands, and the arrows of death are flying about our heads.

* * *

My brethren, let us not be cast down under these and many other abuses we at present are laboring under,—for the darkest hour is just before the break of day. My brethren, let us remember what a dark day it was with our African brethren, six years ago, in the French West Indies. Nothing but the snap of the whip was heard, from morning to evening. Hanging, breaking on the wheel, burning, and all manner of tortures, were inflicted on those unhappy people. But, blessed be God, the scene is changed. They now confess that God hath no respect of persons, and, therefore, receive them as their friends, and treat them as brothers. Thus doth Ethiopia stretch forth her hand from slavery, to freedom and equality.*

---

*William C. Nell, *The Colored Patriots of the American Revolution* (Boston, 1855), 61-64.

CHAPTER THREE

Slavery's Lengthening Shadow

The slave auction was a common sight through the South before the Civil War. This sketch, which appeared in The Illustrated London News, *on November 29, 1856, depicts a slave sale in Charleston, South Carolina. The artist, Eyre Crowe, has created a cross section of society in the Slave South. The men being sold are on a platform, with the auctioneer working up a sale. Around the platform prospective buyers are examining the Negroes. One is tapping a black man's chest, another is commenting to his friend, two seem to be bidding, perhaps for the mother and child. In the crowd itself you can see the many forms of slave-servitude. An affluent white in the background seems to be speaking to his black man-servant. Sitting on the ground, one of the slaves—still wearing his striped hat—looks downcast while his new master bids for another.*

INTRODUCTION

Slavery's Lengthening Shadow

In the decades between the Revolutionary War and the Civil War an important change took place in the life of the South, a change based on the large-scale production of a new agricultural staple and on the necessity for a labor supply to cultivate it. The effect of this change on the relationship between the South and the North led eventually to an armed sectional clash.

The possibility of a war brought on by cotton and by slavery may have appeared remote during the decade immediately following the Revolutionary War. Many people at the time believed that slavery would decline. The South had suffered a great destruction of landed property during the final years of the war and had lost many of its slaves to the British, either by confiscation or by flight. The view that slavery was dying before the invention of the cotton gin, however, has been vigorously challenged. Recent scholarship has shown that postwar southern agriculture was not listless, but rather was experiencing a marked recovery. Rice and indigo production were on the increase, tobacco exports were higher than ever before, and the volume of shipping that cleared southern ports was nearly doubling.

Undeniably, however, both agriculture and slavery received great impetus from the introduction of cotton. The revolution of the textile industry by new weaving and spinning machines created an insatiable demand for cotton by factory owners at home and abroad. In 1793 the invention of the cotton gin, which removed the seeds from the closely adhering fiber, had an immediate and profound effect on the future of slavery. Cotton provided year-round employment for slaves; it was well-fitted for the slave-gang system of close supervision by white overseers; and it could be tended by laborers of all sorts and conditions, the old as well as the young, the strong as well as the infirm.

By 1860 cotton had made a deep impression on American life. In dollars and cents, it comprised 57 per cent of the nation's exports. The South's greatest commercial crop, it accounted for three quarters of all the Negro agricultural workers. Other staples also had a slave-labor base—tobacco, sugar, rice, and hemp. But it was cotton, more than all of these combined, that gave the slave his economic importance, as it had been cotton that had extended the domain of slavery.

For its expansion cotton required such virgin lands as were to be found in the lower South, the region that became the center of cotton cultivation. The labor supply came from the Atlantic slave states, mostly from Virginia, which exported an average of 10,000 slaves a year from 1830 to 1860. By 1820 the domestic slave trade had become a flourishing business. Slaves purchased in the upper South were either sent overland to the Mississippi or shipped by boat from the Chesapeake ports of Baltimore, Washington, and Norfolk. By either route, their destination was a slave market in New Orleans or another of the coastal ports on the Gulf of Mexico.

In supplying black laborers when and where they were needed, the domestic slave trade was supplemented by the practice of hiring. Averaging more than 50,000 a year, the hiring of slaves was a thriving business controlled by professional brokers, although on occasion a

trustworthy slave might be permitted to let his own time. Slave hiring was a boon to those employers who needed labor for a special task only, or for a limited period—day, week, month, or year. While some slaves were hired for cotton and sugar production, most of them performed nonagricultural tasks as domestics, stevedores, or factory workers. A slave who was trusted, skilled, and lucky might be permitted to "hire his own time," paying his master a fixed sum from his earnings.

As slavery took deep root in the South, the institution had to be justified. The result was the development of an elaborate proslavery argument, denying that slavery was an evil. Southern Congressmen, editors, and college professors entered the lists. Slavery, they contended, was based upon the biological inferiority of the Negro, his inability to handle the responsibilities of a free man. Because he had a master and a mistress to care for him, the slave, according to the spokesmen for the South, was contented with his lot; indeed, in most instances he was happy. Such arguments became a necessity to white Southerners who harbored lingering feelings of guilt.

Undoubtedly some of its proponents recognized that slavery had its drawbacks, its built-in evils. But if such sentiments might be confided privately, they could not be expressed publicly. Most of the defenders of the South's "peculiar institution," however, were convinced that slavery was, in John C. Calhoun's words, "a positive good."

Not only Southerners believed that slavery was a benevolent institution. Observers from the North and from across the Atlantic, focusing upon the bright side of the picture, expressed surprise upon witnessing the affectionate ties between some slaves and their masters. To these visitors the slave population appeared to be adequately housed, clothed, and fed, and wholly without complaint against their fate.

Other observers from the outside were more critical. Successful in penetrating the mask habitually worn by slaves in the presence of whites, such visitors professed to sense the deep, if unvoiced, desire for freedom. Other visitors disputed the familiar southern assertion that its bondmen were as well off as most of the working population elsewhere, a point of view that overlooked the particularly blighting effect of slavery upon the human spirit.

The actual lot of the slaves is not easy to assess, since their circumstances varied so greatly. Those who lived in the cities counted themselves fortunate, for they led a freer life than their plantation brothers. The master-slave relationship was weakest in the cities, where it was impossible to exercise the same machinery of control as in rural areas. "Slavery dislikes a dense population," wrote Frederick Douglass, and indeed the number of urban slaves tended to decline from decade to decade during the half century before the Civil War. The town slave had distinctive recreational outlets. Whether in Richmond or in Montgomery, he might have a taste of "high life." Richmond slaves had "champagne suppers," and Montgomery's more fashionable slaves received cards of invitation to free Negro balls to which no one was admitted except in full dress.

On the plantations not all slaves fared alike. The elite group comprised the domestics—mammy, housemaid, laundress, cook, butler, and coachman. This group had personal contact with the master and mistress, wore better clothes, and ate better food than the field hands. In speech, manner, taste, and habits the house slave was set apart, forming the plantation's "black aristocracy."

The lot of the field slave bore some relationship to the staple in which he worked. Generally a slave would rather work in tobacco or hemp than in cotton, and in cotton rather than in rice or sugar. A slave dreaded being sold down the Mississippi River, fearing that he might wind up on a Louisiana sugar plantation, where daily routine ran to sixteen hours of heavy labor, some of it in swampy terrain.

The attitude of his master, whether kind, indifferent, or hostile to his bondman, was also reflected in the lot of a slave. To some masters the welfare of their slaves was a matter of concern; a planter like Howell Cobb, of Houston County, Georgia, would enjoin his heirs to treat the Cobb Negroes with "all the justice and indulgence that is consistent with a state of slavery." But there were masters of a sadistic bent, given to tyrannizing their slaves.

The slave's outlook was shaped in part by the controls upon him—religious, legal, and psychological. Catechisms were provided for slaves, teaching them that the masters ruled from God. Although the religious instruction of slaves was indeed a form of indoctrination, some clergymen were genuinely concerned about their spiritual welfare. Among these was William Capers, who, as president of the South Carolina Missionary Society, directed slave missions in South Carolina and Georgia. This movement to bring the gospel to the plantation workers faced strong opposition from many masters, who feared that the circuit riders would somehow undermine slavery.

Some masters permitted the slaves to conduct their own religious services. A white person would be present, as the law required, to keep an eye on things. Out of the all-slave church came the Negro spirituals. In these religious songs the slave found a way of saying things he could not express otherwise; the words of many spirituals had a meaning unsuspected by one not in the know. Negro music was "a sort of secret password" into the lives of the slaves.

A more direct method of control than religious indoctrination was the exercise of the law. Each state had its own black codes. As a rule a slave could not testify against whites, and his acts or attempted acts against them were severely punished. Although a slave was a person, he was also a piece of property. Hence, in a court case involving a conflict between the slave's rights as a person and his status as a chattel, the magistrates invariably gave priority to the latter.

Because a slave was property first and foremost, legal marriage did not exist for him. A slave wedding was either a perfunctory service with a clergyman going through the motions, or it was a simple "jump de broomstick" in slave quarters. A few men were permitted to take mates on other plantations ("abroad wives"), but planters opposed this because of the time lost in travel. Obviously the institution of slavery did not encourage domestic ties. The instability of family life in slavery—its lack of legal sanction and its tolerance of promiscuity—would leave its mark after slavery itself had disappeared.

Some masters believed that the slaves might be better kept in line if recreation were provided occasionally. Slaves were permitted to hold dances, and they were generally given the Fourth of July as a holiday. Especially did they look forward to the Christmas season. Then they had a respite from their labors, a vacation ranging from three to seven days, depending on the master's generosity. Into these days the slave tried to crowd as many carefree hours as possible. "In visiting, riding, renewing old friendships, or perchance, reviving some old attachment, or pursuing whatever pleasure may suggest itself the time is occupied. Such is 'southern life as it is,' *three days in the year*, as I found it," wrote runaway slave Solomon Northup.

To control the slave the master employed blunt psychological tools. It was drilled into the slave that he was inferior to any and all whites, whom he was to hold in respect amounting to awe. The slave was taught that his peace rested in the master's will, and, hence, that unconditional submission was his rightful obligation, as it was his only permitted response. "The natural tendency of slavery," wrote Josiah Henson, who spoke from firsthand experience, "is to convert the master into a tyrant, and the slave into the cringing, treacherous, false, and thieving victim of tyranny."

The slave was expected to play a role, and he played it. But in behaving in a docile, childlike, loyal, dependent manner, did the slave actually become the thing he had to pretend to be? Had the mask become the man? Had the slave been so effectively brainwashed that he became in his own thinking the "Sambo" his master required? It is certainly not unlikely that the slave's lot made for some degree of infantilism on his part.

The more than 100,000 former slaves who bore arms in the Civil War, however, did not prove to have been shorn of their manhood; they did not behave like persons cowed in body or emasculated in spirit. Moreover, there is abundant evidence that the slave showed marked resentment at his fate, a resentment that in some instances took the form of outright resistance. The most common of his techniques of protest was his everyday resistance, his being as inefficient as he could without bringing the lash upon his back. Slaves were "a troublesome property," writes Kenneth Stampp in *The Peculiar Institution*. They worked in slow motion, which became even less animated when the overseer was at the other end of the field. They feigned illness or disability, some slave women seeming always to be plagued by "female complaints." More than one master suspected a poorly performing slave of "rascality," but the charge was not easy to prove. Common, too, among slaves was the undercover destruction of property, from the breaking of farm implements to the burning of barns.

The more adventurous slaves expressed their protest by flight. Runaways were, as a rule, under thirty, with males more numerous than females. Slave escapes were everyday occurrences, as readers of southern newspapers well knew. The demand by slaveholders for fugitive slave laws with teeth is proof of this tendency of the slave to take to his heels. Sometimes in making his escape the slave was assisted by the organized movement known as the Underground Railroad. But slaves in the deep South, where the tentacles of the Railroad did not reach, made their way as best they could without assistance. A large per cent of runaways were caught, but many reached their destinations in the North, in Canada, or in Mexico.

The most daring of the refractory slaves were the plotters of armed revolt. From colonial times to emancipation, there were some 250 slave revolts and conspiracies. The greatest of the uprisings took place in Southampton County, Virginia, and was led by Nat Turner. Nearly sixty whites were put to death before Turner and his seventy followers were captured.

The Southampton revolt shocked the South. From then on there were periodic insurrection panics. Undoubtedly, some of these scares were invented by whites bent on instituting greater control over Negroes. But there was no mistaking the deep-seated and lasting apprehension caused by Nat Turner, whose name was to be well remembered in the antebellum South for three decades.

The Internal Slave Trade

51

ADVERTISEMENT OF A SLAVE SALE

The buyers and the sellers of slaves made extensive use of newspaper advertisements—the former to make known their needs, the latter to publicize their merchandise. Charleston, South Carolina, one of the ports of call for steamers bound for the slave markets of New Orleans, was a leading slave trade center along the Atlantic seaboard. The City Gazette *of Charleston, under the date of March 10, 1796, carried the following notice:*

FIFTY PRIME NEGROES FOR SALE. To be Sold, on Tuesday the 15th March instant, by the Subscribers, before their office near the Exchange.

About fifty prime orderly Negroes; consisting of Fellows, Wenches, Boys and Girls. This gang taken together, is perhaps as prime, complete and valuable for the number as were ever offered for sale; they are generally country born, young & able very likely; two of them capable of acting as drivers, and one of them a good jobbing carpenter. The wenches are young and improving; the boys, girls and children are remarkably smart, active and sensible: several of the wenches are fitted either for the house or plantation work; the boys and girls for trades or waiting servants. The age, descriptions and qualifications of these negroes, may be seen at the office of the Subscribers, and of Brian Cape and Son, or of Treasdale or Kiddell, merchants, in Queen-street, who can give directions to those who desire it where the negroes may be seen.

These negroes are sold free from all incumbrances, with warranted titles, and are sold on account of their present Owner's declining the Planting Business, and not for any other reason; they are not Negroes selected out of a larger gang for the purpose of a sale, but are prime, their present Owner, with great trouble and expence, selected them out of many for several years past. They were purchased for stock and breeding Negroes, and to any Planter who particularly wanted them for that purpose, they are a very choice and desirable gang. Any Person desirous of purchasing the whole gang by private contract, may apply to Brian Cape and Son; the Terms if sold together will be made convenient to the Purchasers, and the Conditions of public sale (if not contracted for in the mean time, of which due notice will be given) will be very easy and accommodating, and which will be declared on the Day of Sale.

COLCOCK & PATERSON*.

52

THE AGONIES OF FAMILY SEPARATION

Among the inhumanities of the traffic in slaves was the separation of families. What it meant to him to stand on an auction block in Montgomery County, Maryland, was described by Josiah Henson, whose life served as an inspiration for Harriet Beecher Stowe's Uncle Tom's Cabin. *An unusual slave, Henson had doubled as superintendent of his master's farm and salesman of its produce in the markets of nearby Washington and Georgetown. In February 1825 Henson's master had placed him in charge of a convoy of seventeen slaves to be taken to Davis County, Kentucky. Learning later that his master considered selling him in the New Orleans slave markets, Henson made up his mind to flee to Canada, a step he took in September 1830. The experience related below took place many years earlier, when Henson was a small child.*

Common as are slave-auctions in the southern states, and naturally as a slave may look forward to the time when he will be put up on the block, still the full misery of the event—of the scenes which precede and succeed it—is never understood till the actual experience comes. The first sad announcement that the sale is to be; the knowledge that all ties of the past are to be sundered; the frantic terror at the idea of being sent "down south"; the almost certainty that one member of a family will be torn from another; the anxious scanning of purchasers' faces; the agony at parting, often forever, with husband, wife, child—these must be seen and felt to be fully understood. Young as I was then, the iron entered into my soul. The remembrance of the breaking up of McPherson's estate is photographed in its minutest features in my mind. The crowd collected round the stand, the huddling group of negroes, the examination of muscle, teeth, the exhibition of agility, the look of the auctioneer, the agony of my mother—I can shut my eyes and see them all.

---

*U. B. Phillips, ed., *Plantation and Frontier Documents* (2 vols., Cleveland, 1909), II, 57-58.

My brothers and sisters were bid off first, and one by one, while my mother, paralyzed by grief, held me by the hand. Her turn came, and she was bought by Isaac Riley of Montgomery county. Then I was offered to the assembled purchasers. My mother, half distracted with the thought of parting forever from all her children, pushed through the crowd, while the bidding for me was going on, to the spot where Riley was standing. She fell at his feet, and clung to his knees, entreating him in tones that a mother only could command, to buy her *baby* as well as herself, and spare to her one, at least, of her little ones. Will it, can it be believed that this man, thus appealed to, was capable not merely of turning a deaf ear to her supplication, but of disengaging himself from her with such violent blows and kicks, as to reduce her to the necessity of creeping out of his reach, and mingling the groan of bodily suffering with the sob of a breaking heart? As she crawled away from the brutal man I heard her sob out, "Oh, Lord Jesus, how long, how long shall I suffer this way!" I must have been then between five and six years old. I seem to see and hear my poor weeping mother now. This was one of my earliest observations of men; an experience which I only shared with thousands of my race, the bitterness of which to any individual who suffers it cannot be diminished by the frequency of its recurrence, while it is dark enough to overshadow the whole after-life with something blacker than a funeral pall.*

53

THE STATUS OF THE SLAVE TRADER

Not only were the newspapers used to advertise the sale of slaves, but newspaper offices themselves also served as meeting places between buyers and sellers, especially since many slave traders, whose business held a low place in public esteem, sought to attract as little attention as possible. A few traders belonged to old-line, respected families, but traders as a class were held in contempt by the southern gentry. The British traveler James Stirling, who toured the South in the spring of 1857, felt that, because the owners of slaves bore some of the responsibility for the traffic, they were trying to project their guilt upon someone else. In the following passage Stirling offers one explanation for the unpopularity of the "Trader."

The slave trade, though not universal in its application, is another hideous evil; and though many escape its grievous calamities, there are few who do not suffer from the dread of its application to themselves or those whom they love. So long as the slave trade continues there can be no sense of security for the slave, and without security it is a mockery to talk of happiness. This trade is a sore subject with the defenders of slavery. It is difficult to weave it handsomely in among the amenities of the patriarchal institution. They fain would make a scape-goat of the 'Trader,' and

*Walter Fisher, ed., *Father Henson's Story of His Own Life* (New York, Corinth Books, Inc., 1962), 11-13.

load all the iniquities of the system on his unlucky back. Men who own hundreds of slaves would scorn to meet on equal terms with a slave-trader. Now there seems little justice here. If slavery and the slave trade which it necessitates be in themselves right and proper, it is a wrong to visit with ignominy the instruments of the system. But conscience will not be put down; our intuitions are stronger than our logic, and the slave-owner has the 'noble inconsistency' to condemn his institution in the person of the agent who is essential to its existence.

The shame felt at the slave trade prompts the South to cry exaggeration. But the extent to which it is carried is conclusively proved by the statistics of the slave population, from which it appears that, during the last thirty years, the number of slaves has rapidly increased in the Southern or slave-buying States, while in the Northern or slave-breeding States, the slave population has been almost stationary. The following is the exact statement:—

Increase of Slave-Population, 1820-1850.

Average increase per cent. per annum.

Northern or slave-breeding States	.93
Southern or slave-buying State	5.93

Now it will hardly be asserted that the amenities of negro life on cotton, rice, and sugar plantations are so overwhelming as to account for a natural yearly increase of 5.93 per cent., while their brethren in the frontier States show only an increase of .93 per cent. The increased proportion, therefore, in the Southern Slave States, must be due to the importations of the 'Trader.'*

54

SLAVE HIRING

Slave hiring was an important appendage to the traffic in human merchandise. Common throughout the South, slave hiring was practiced in a variety of occupations. The selections that follow illustrate the use of hired slaves as ferry-boat hands on Chesapeake Bay and as lumbermen in Virginia. As the first excerpt indicates, some slaves were permitted to "hire their own time," while others were not. The excerpt concerning the lumbermen furnishes an example of slaves working with little supervision when an incentive existed.

TALK WITH A SLAVE.

In coming from Washington, on the ferry-boat, I had a talk with one of the slaves. I asked him how much he was hired for.

"I get $120—it's far too little. The other fellows here get $30 a month—so they has $21, and they only pays $10 for me."

"Why do you work for so little, then?" I asked, supposing, from what he said, that he was a freeman.

*James Stirling, *Letters from the Slave States* (London, 1857), 292-294.

"I's a slave," he said.

"Are the others free?"

"No, sir, but they hires their own time. Their mass'r takes $120 a year for them, and they hires out for $30 a month, and pays $9 for board—so they has $6 a month to themsel'es. I works as hard as them and I does n't get nothin'. It's too hard."

"Why do n't you hire out your time?" I asked him.

"Kase my missus won't let me. I wish she would. I could make heaps of money for myself, if she did."

"Why won't she let you hire your time?"

"Oh, kase she's a queer ole missus."

"What do your companions do with their money when they save it?"

"Oh, guess they *sprees.*"

"Would you if you had money?"

"No, sir."

"Do any of your friends save their money to buy their freedom?"

"Some on them as has a good chance has done it."

"What do you call a good chance?"

"When our owner lets us hire our time reasonable, and 'lows us to buy oursel'es low."

"What is the usual pay for laborers?"

"$120 or so—we as follows the water gets more. I won't foller it another year, 'kase it's too confinin'; but I'd allers foller it if my missus 'lowed me to hire my own time."*

SLAVE-LUMBERMEN.

The labor in the swamp is almost entirely done by slaves; and the way in which they are managed is interesting and instructive. They are mostly hired by their employers at a rent, perhaps of one hundred dollars a year for each, paid to their owners. They spend one or two months of the winter—when it is too wet to work in the swamp—at the residence of their master. At this period little or no work is required of them; their time is their own, and if they can get any employment, they will generally keep for themselves what they are paid for it. When it is sufficiently dry—usually early in February—they go into the swamp in gangs, each gang under a white overseer. Before leaving, they are all examined and registered at the Court-house, and "passes," good for a year, are given them, in which their features and the marks upon their persons are minutely described. Each man is furnished with a quantity of provisions and clothing, of which, as well as of all that he afterwards draws from the stock in the hands of the overseer, an exact account is kept.*

LIFE IN THE SWAMP—SLAVES QUASI FREEMEN.

Arrived at their destination, a rude camp is made, huts of logs, poles, shingles, and boughs being built, usually upon some place

---

*James Redpath, *The Roving Editor, or Talks with Slaves in the Southern States* (New York, 1859), 211-212.

where shingles have been worked before, and in which the shavings have accumulated in small hillocks upon the soft surface of the ground.

The slave lumberman then lives measurably as a free man; hunts, fishes, eats, drinks, smokes and sleeps, plays and works, each when and as much as he pleases. It is only required of him that he shall have made, after half a year has passed, such a quantity of shingles as shall be worth to his master so much money as is paid to his owner for his services, and shall refund the value of the clothing and provisions he has required.

No "driving" at his work is attempted or needed. No force is used to overcome the indolence peculiar to the negro. The overseer merely takes a daily account of the number of shingles each man adds to the general stock, and employs another set of hands, with mules, to draw them to a point from which they can be shipped, and where they are, from time to time, called for by a schooner.

At the end of five months the gang returns to dry-land, and a statement of account from the overseer's book is drawn up, something like the following:

Sam Bo to John Doe, Dr.

Feb. 1. To clothing (outfit) $5 00
Mar.10. To clothing, as per overseer's account 2 25
Feb. 1. To bacon and meal (outfit) 19 00
July 1. To stores drawn in swamp, as per
overseer's account 4 75
July 1. To half-yearly hire, paid his owner . . .50 00
$81 00

Per Contra, Cr.

July 1. By 10,000 shingles, as per overseer's
account, 10c. 100 00
Balance due Sambo. $19 00

which is immediately paid him, and which, together with the proceeds of sale of peltry which he has got while in the swamp, he is always allowed to make use of as his own. No liquor is sold or served to the negroes in the swamp, and, as their first want when they come out of it is an excitement, most of their money goes to the grog-shops.

After a short vacation, the whole gang is taken in the schooner to spend another five months in the swamp as before. If they are good hands and work steadily, they will commonly be hired again, and so continuing, will spend most of their lives at it. They almost invariably have excellent health, as do also the white men engaged in the business. They all consider the water of "the Dismals" to have a medicinal virtue, and quite probably it is a mild tonic. It is greenish in color, and I thought I detected a slightly resinous taste upon first drinking it. Upon entering the swamp also, an agreeable resinous odor, resembling that of a hemlock forest, was perceptible.*

The Proslavery Argument

55

THE UNIVERSAL LAW OF SLAVERY

*As a flourishing institution, slavery attracted a host of able defenders. Ranking high among them was the Virginia lawyer, George Fitzhugh, who wrote two books—*Sociology for the South; or the Failure of Free Society *(1854) and* Cannibals All! or, Slaves without Masters *(1857)—and several articles in justification of the South's way of life. If Fitzhugh had had his way, no critic of slavery would have been employed as a teacher in the South, and no book critical of slavery would have been permitted in the schools. Fitzhugh propounded a so-called universal law of slavery, a viewpoint stemming from his belief in the natural inequality of man. Fitzhugh's many-faceted argument included discourses on the characteristics of the Negro, his happiness in slavery, and the industrious habits of the master class.*

He the Negro is but a grown up child, and must be governed as a child, not as a lunatic or criminal. The master occupies toward him the place of parent or guardian. We shall not dwell on this view, for no one will differ with us who thinks as we do of the negro's capacity, and we might argue till dooms-day in vain, with those who have a high opinion of the negro's moral and intellectual capacity.

Secondly. The negro is improvident; will not lay up in summer for the wants of winter; will not accumulate in youth for the exigencies of age. He would become an insufferable burden to society. Society has the right to prevent this, and can only do so by subjecting him to domestic slavery. In the last place, the negro race is inferior to the white race, and living in their midst, they would be far outstripped or outwitted in the chaos of free competition. Gradual but certain extermination would be their fate. We presume the maddest abolitionist does not think the negro's providence of habits and money-making capacity at all to compare to those of the whites. This defect of character would alone justify enslaving him, if he is to remain here. In Africa or the West Indies, he would become idolatrous, savage and cannibal, or be devoured by savages and cannibals. At the North he would freeze or starve.

We would remind those who deprecate and sympathize with negro slavery, that his slavery here relieves him from a far more cruel slavery in Africa, or from idolatry and cannibalism, and every brutal vice and crime that can disgrace humanity; and that it christianizes, protects, supports and civilizes him; that it governs him far

*Frederick Law Olmsted, *A Journey in the Seaboard Slave States* (New York, 1856), 153-55.

better than free laborers at the North are governed. There, wife-murder has become a mere holiday pastime; and where so many wives are murdered, almost all must be brutally treated. Nay, more; men who kill their wives or treat them brutally, must be ready for all kinds of crime, and the calendar of crime at the North proves the inference to be correct. Negroes never kill their wives. If it be objected that legally they have no wives, then we reply, that in an experience of more than forty years, we never yet heard of a negro man killing a negro woman. Our negroes are not only better off as to physical comfort than free laborers, but their moral condition is better.

* * *

The negro slaves of the South are the happiest, and, in some sense, the freest people in the world. The children and the aged and infirm work not at all, and yet have all the comforts and necessaries of life provided for them. They enjoy liberty, because they are oppressed neither by care nor labor. The women do little hard work, and are protected from the despotism of their husbands by their masters. The negro men and stout boys work, on the average, in good weather, not more than nine hours a day. The balance of their time is spent in perfect abandon. Besides, they have their Sabbaths and holidays. White men, with so much of license and liberty, would die of ennui; but negroes luxuriate in corporeal and mental repose. With their faces upturned to the sun, they can sleep at any hour; and quiet sleep is the greatest of human enjoyments. "Blessed be the man who invented sleep." 'Tis happiness in itself—and results from contentment with the present, and confident assurance of the future.

* * *

A common charge preferred against slavery is, that it induces idleness with the masters. The trouble, care and labor, of providing for wife, children and slaves, and of properly governing and administering the whole affairs of the farm, is usually borne on small estates by the master. On larger ones, he is aided by an overseer or manager. If they do their duty, their time is fully occupied. If they do not, the estate goes to ruin. The mistress, on Southern farms, is usually more busily, usefully and benevolently occupied than any one on the farm. She unites in her person, the offices of wife, mother, mistress, housekeeper, and sister of charity. And she fulfills all these offices admirably well. The rich men, in free society, may, if they please, lounge about town, visit clubs, attend the theatre, and have no other trouble than that of collecting rents, interest and dividends of stock. In a well constituted slave society, there should be no idlers. But we cannot divine how the capitalists in free society are to put to work. The master labors for the slave, they exchange industrial value. But the capitalist, living on his income, gives nothing to his subjects. He lives by mere exploitations.*

---

*Harvey Wish, ed., *Ante-Bellum: The Writings of George Fitzhugh and Hinton Rowan Helper on Slavery* (New York, G. P. Putnam's Sons, 1960), 89, 113–114, 123–124.

56

THE HUMANIZING EFFECT OF SLAVERY

To the charge that slaves were treated cruelly, William Harper offered a rebuttal. Holder of high elective and appointive offices in South Carolina—Speaker of the House, supreme court judge, and chancellor—Harper had gained fame as a champion of states' rights. With the publication of his Memoir on Slavery *in 1837, he became even better known as a persuasive defender of another cherished institution in the South.*

But short of life and limb, various cruelties may be practised as the passions of the master may dictate. To this the same reply has been often given—that they are secured by the master's interest. If the state of Slavery is to exist at all, the master must have and ought to have, such power of punishment as will compel them to perform the duties of their station. And is not this for their advantage as well as his? No human being can be contented, who does not perform the duties of his station. Has the master any temptation to go beyond this? If he inflicts on him such punishment as will permanently impair his strength, he inflicts a loss on himself, and so if he requires of him excessive labor. Compare the labor required of the Slave, with those of the free agricultural, or manufacturing laborer in Europe, or even in the more thickly peopled portions of the non-Slave-Holding States of our Confederacy—though these last are no fair subjects of comparison—they enjoying, as I have said, in a great degree, the advantages of Slavery along with those of an early and simple state of society. Read the English Parliamentary reports, on the condition of the manufacturing operatives, and the children employed in factories. And such is the impotence of man to remedy the evils which the condition of his existence has imposed on him, that it is much to be doubted whether the attempts by legislation to improve their situation, will not aggravate its evils. They resort to this excessive labor as a choice of evils. If so, the amount of their compensation will be lessened also with the diminished labor; for this is a matter which legislation cannot regulate. Is it the part of benevolence then to cut them off even from this miserable liberty of choice? Yet would these evils exist in the same degree, if the laborers were the *property* of the master—having a direct interest in preserving their lives, their health and strength? Who but a drivelling fanatic, has thought of the necessity of protecting domestic animals from the cruelty of their owners? And yet are not great and wanton cruelties practised on these animals? Compare the whole of the cruelties inflicted on Slaves throughout our Southern country, with those elsewhere, inflicted by ignorant and depraved portions of the community, on those whom the relations of society put into their power—of brutal husbands on their wives; of brutal parents—subdued against the strongest instincts of nature to that brutality by the extremity of their misery—on their children; of brutal masters on apprentices. And if it should be asked, are not similar cruelties inflicted, and miseries endured in your society? I answer in no comparable degree.

The class in question are placed under the control of others, who are interested to restrain their excesses of cruelty or rage.

* * *

Is it not natural that a man should be attached to that which is *his own,* and which has contributed to his convenience, his enjoyment, or his vanity? This is felt even towards animals, and inanimate objects. How much more towards a being of superior intelligence and usefulness, who can appreciate our feelings towards him, and return them? Is it not natural that we should be interested in that which is dependant on us for protection and support? Do not men every where contract kind feelings towards their dependants? Is it not natural that men should be more attached to those whom they have long known—whom, perhaps, they have reared or been associated with from infancy—than to one with whom their connexion has been casual and temporary? What is there in our atmosphere or institutions, to produce a perversion of the general feelings of nature? To be sure, in this as in all other relations, there is frequent cause of offence or excitement—on one side, for some omission of duty, on the other, on account of reproof or punishment inflicted. But this is common to the relation of parent and child; and I will venture to say that if punishment be justly inflicted—and there is no temptation to inflict it unjustly—it is as little likely to occasion permanent estrangement or resentment as in that case. Slaves are perpetual children. It is not the common nature of man, unless it be depraved by his own misery, to delight in witnessing pain. It is more grateful to behold contented and cheerful beings, than sullen and wretched ones. That men are sometimes wayward, depraved and brutal, we know. That atrocious and brutal cruelties have been perpetrated on Slaves, and on those who were not Slaves, by such wretches, we also know. But that the institution of Slavery has a natural tendency to form such a character, that such crimes are more common, or more aggravated than in other states of society, or produce among us less surprise and horror, we utterly deny, and challenge the comparison. Indeed I have little hesitation in saying, that if full evidence could be obtained, the comparison would result in our favor, and that the tendency of Slavery is rather to humanize than to brutalize.

The accounts of travellers in oriental countries, give a very favorable representation of the kindly relations which exist between the Master and Slave; the latter being often the friend, and sometimes the heir of the former. Generally, however, especially if they be English travellers—if they say any thing which may seem to give a favorable complexion to Slavery, they think it necessary to enter their protest, that they shall not be taken to give any sanction to Slavery as it exists in America. Yet human nature is the same in all countries. There are very obvious reasons why in those countries there should be a nearer approach to equality in their manners. The master and Slave are often of cognate races, and therefore tend more to assimilate. There is in fact less inequality in mind and character, where the master is but imperfectly civilized. Less labor is exacted, because the master has fewer motives to accumulate. But is it an injury to a human being, that regular, if not excessive labor should be required of him? The primeval curse, with the usual benignity of providential contrivance, has been turned into the solace of an existence that would be much more intolerable without it. If they labor less, they are much more subject to the outrages of capricious passion. If it were put to the choice of any human being, would he prefer to be the Slave of a civilized man, or of a barbarian or semi-barbarian? But if the general tendency of the institution in these countries is to create kindly relations, can it be imagined why it should operate differently in this? It is true, as suggested by President Dew—with the exception of the ties of close consanguinity, it forms one of the most intimate relations of society. And it will be more and more so, the longer it continues to exist. The harshest features of Slavery were created by those who were strangers to Slavery—who supposed that it consisted in keeping savages in subjection by violence and terror. The severest laws to be found on our statute book, were enacted by such, and such are still found to be the severest masters. As society becomes settled, and the wandering habits of our countrymen altered, there will be a larger and larger proportion of those who were reared by the owner, or derived to him from his ancestors, and who therefore will be more and mored intimately regarded, as forming a portion of his family.

It is true that the Slave is driven to labor by stripes; and if the object of punishment be to produce obedience or reformation, with the least permanent injury, it is the best method of punishment. But is it not intolerable, that a being formed in the image of his Maker, should be degraded by *blows*? This is one of the perversions of mind and feeling, to which I shall have occasion again to refer. Such punishment would be degrading to a freeman, who had the thoughts and aspirations of a freeman. In general it is not degrading to a Slave, nor is it felt to be so. The evil is the bodily pain. Is it degrading to a child? Or if in any particular instance it would be so felt, it is sure not to be inflicted—unless in those rare cases which constitute the startling and eccentric evils, from which no society is exempt, and against which no institutions of society can provide.*

57

THE "MUDSILL" THEORY

James Henry Hammond, a wealthy plantation owner from South Carolina, in a Senate speech on March 4, 1858, set forth the "mudsill" theory—that a viable society is divided into two groups, one exercising superior functions, and the other exercising inferior ones. If the "mudsill" theory was not new in the South, it had never been more cogently expressed than by Hammond. No proslavery argument ever uttered in Congress received more attention, particularly from

*William Harper, *Memoir on Slavery Read Before the Society for the Advancement of Learning of South Carolina, at Its Annual Meeting at Columbia, 1837* (Charleston, 1838), 20-22.

Northern critics, who pointed out that Hammond's theory seemed to include some whites along with all Negroes.

In all social systems there must be a class to do the menial duties, to perform the drudgery of life. That is, a class requiring but a low order of intellect and but little skill. Its requisites are vigor, docility, fidelity. Such a class you must have, or you would not have that other class which leads progress, civilization, and refinement. It constitutes the very mud-sill of society and of political government; and you might as well attempt to build a house in the air, as to build either the one or the other, except on this mud-sill. Fortunately for the South, she found a race adapted to that purpose to her hand. A race inferior to her own, but eminently qualified in temper, in vigor, in docility, in capacity to stand the climate, to answer all her purposes. We use them for our purpose, and call them slaves. We found them slaves by the common "consent of mankind," which, according to Cicero, "*lex naturae est.*" The highest proof of what is Nature's law. We are old-fashioned at the South yet; slave is a word discarded now by "ears polite;" I will not characterize that class at the North by that term; but you have it; it is there; it is everywhere; it is eternal.

The Senator from New York said yesterday that the whole world had abolished slavery. Aye, the *name*, but not the *thing;* all the powers of the earth cannot abolish that. God only can do it when he repeals the *fiat*, "the poor ye always have with you;" for the man who lives by daily labor, and scarcely lives at that, and who has to put out his labor in the market, and take the best he can get for it; in short, your whole hireling class of manual laborers and "operatives," as you call them, are essentially slaves. The difference between us is, that our slaves are hired for life and well compensated; there is no starvation, no begging, no want of employment among our people, and not too much employment either. Yours are hired by the day, not cared for, and scantily compensated, which may be proved in the most painful manner, at any hour in any street in any of your large towns. Why, you meet more beggars in one day, in any single street of the city of New York, than you would meet in a lifetime in the whole South. We do not think that whites should be slaves either by law or necessity. Our slaves are black, of another and inferior race. The *status* in which we have placed them is an elevation. They are elevated from the condition in which God first created them, by being made our slaves. None of that race on the whole face of the globe can be compared with the slaves of the South. They are happy, content, unaspiring, and utterly incapable, from intellectual weakness, ever to give us any trouble by their aspirations. Yours are white, or your own race; you are brothers of one blood. They are your equals in natural endowment of intellect, and they feel galled by their degradation. Our slaves do not vote. We give them no political power. Yours do vote, and, being the majority, they are the depositaries of all your political power. If they knew the tremendous secret, that the ballot-box is stronger than "an army with banners," and could combine, where would you be? Your society would be reconstructed, your government overthrown, your property divided, not as they have mistakenly attempted to initiate such proceedings by meeting in parks, with arms in their hands, but by the quiet process of the ballot-box. You have been making war upon us to our very hearthstones. How would you like for us to send lecturers and agitators North, to teach these people this, to aid in combining, and to lead them?*

58

THE "PLURALITY" THEORY

Proslavery advocate John H. Van Evrie, a reputable physician of Washington, D.C., viewed the Negro as belonging to a lower order of man. Van Evrie's belief that the Negroes constituted a different species from the whites led him to support the "plurality" theory of the origin of mankind, which asserted that early man did not originate in a single center of creation.

The Negro is a man, but a different and inferior *species* of man, who could no more originate from the same source as ourselves, than the owl could from the eagle, or the shad from the salmon, or the cat from the tiger; and who can no more be forced by *human power* to manifest the faculties, or perform the purposes assigned by the Almighty Creator to the Caucasian man, than can either of these forms of life be made to manifest faculties other than those inherent, *specific,* and eternally impressed upon their organization.

We are no defender of "materialism," and utterly reject the impious doctrine, that the human soul is the *result* of organization, and therefore, perishes with it; but the identity of organism and functions, of structure and faculties, of form and capabilities, in short of *specific* organization and a *specific* nature, is a *fact* universal, invariable and indestructible.

The Caucasian brain measures 92 cubic inches—with the cerebrum, the centre of the intellectual functions, relatively predominating over the cerebellum, the centre of the animal instincts; thus, it is capable of indefinite progression, and transmits the knowledge or experience acquired by one generation to subsequent generations—the record of which is history.

The Negro brain measures from 65 to 70 cubic inches—with the cerebellum, the centre of the animal instincts relatively predominating over the cerebrum, the centre of the intellectual powers; thus, its acquisition of knowledge is limited to a single generation, and incapable of transmitting this to subsequent generations, *it can have no history*. A single glance at eternal and immutable *facts,* which perpetually separate these forms of human existence will be sufficient to cover the whole ground—thus, could the deluded people who propose to improve on the works of the Creator, and *elevate* the Negro to the standard of the white, actually perform an act of

**Congressional Globe,* 35th Cong., 1st sess., 962.

omnipotence, and, add 25 or 30 per cent. to the totality of the Negro brain, they would still be at as great a distance as ever from their final object, while the relations of the anterior and posterior portions of the brain remained as at present.

And were they capable of performing a second act of creative power, to diminish the posterior portion, and add to the anterior portion of the Negro brain, to make it in form, as well as size, correspond to that of the Caucasian man, they would even then, after all this effort, and all this display of omnipotent force, come back again to the starting point, for such a brain could no more be born of a negress, than can an elephant pass through the eye of a needle. Historical fact is in perfect accordance with these physiological facts, thus, while there are portions, nationalities or branches of the Caucasian race that have relapsed, become effete, decayed, lost—the *race* has steadily progressed, and from the banks of the Nile, to those of the Mississippi, civilization, progress, intellectual development, the *specific* characteristics of the Caucasian have alone changed locations. The Negro on the contrary is at this moment just where the race was four thousand years ago, when sculptured on Egyptian monuments. Portions of it in contact with the superior race have been temporarily advanced, but invariably, without exception, they have returned to the African standard as soon as this contact has ceased, or as soon as the results of amalgamation between them have disappeared.

The Abyssinians originally pure Caucasian, the Lybians, the Numidians of Roman history, and Ethiopeans, the two latter, and possibly the Lybians also of mixed Caucasian blood are often confounded with the Negro or the typical woolly haired, and thus it has been claimed that the latter were capable of progress; but it is a historical truth beyond contradiction or doubt even that the typical African, *the race now in our midst,* has never of its own volition passed beyond the hunter condition, that condition which it now occupies in Africa, when isolated from all other races.

The Creator has beneficently as wisely permitted amalgamation to a certain extent between the extremes of "humanity," the Caucasian and Negro—otherwise there would be slavery, oppression, brutality, death, but this is limited within fixed boundaries; thus, the Mulatto or Hybrid of the fourth generation, is as sterile as the mule or most *animal* hybrids are in the first generation.*

59

BENIGN SLAVERY ON A GEORGIA PLANTATION

Charles Lyell, the noted English geologist, was favorably impressed by the benign type of slavery that he witnessed at a Georgia plantation on one of his four visits to the United States. In his analysis of slave contentment, Lyell's insight

---

*J. H. Van Evrie, *Negroes and Negro Slavery: the First, an Inferior Race—the Latter, Its Normal Condition* (Baltimore, 1853), 28-29.

into human behavior may have fallen short of his insight into the world of nature. It may be noted, however, that Lyell's sympathies were with the North, rather than with the South, during the Civil War.

There are 500 negroes on the Hopeton estate, a great many of whom are children, and some old and superannuated. The latter class, who would be supported in a poor-house in England, enjoy here, to the end of their days, the society of their neighbors and kinsfolk, and live at large in separate houses assigned to them. The children have no regular work to do till they are ten or twelve years old. We see that some of them, at this season, are set to pick up dead leaves from the paths, others to attend the babies. When the mothers are at work, the young children are looked after by an old negress, called Mom Diana. Although very ugly as babies, they have such bright, happy faces when three or four years old, and from that age to ten or twelve have such frank and confiding manners, as to be very engaging. Whenever we met them, they held out their hands to us to shake, and when my wife caressed them, she was often asked by some of the ladies, whether she would not like to bring up one of the girls to love her, and wait upon her. The parents indulge their own fancies in naming their children, and display a singular taste; for one is called January, another April, a third Monday, and a fourth Hard Times. The fisherman on the estate rejoices in the appellation of "Old Bacchus." Quash is the name of the favorite preacher, and Bulally the African name of another negro.

The out-door laborers have separate houses provided for them; even the domestic servants, except a few who are nurses to the white children, live apart from the great house—an arrangement not always convenient for the masters, as there is no one to answer a bell after a certain hour. But if we place ourselves in the condition of the majority of the population, that of servants, we see at once how many advantages we should enjoy over the white race in the same rank of life in Europe. In the first place, all can marry; and if a mistress should lay on any young woman here the injunction so common in English newspaper advertisements for a maid of all work, "no followers allowed," it would be considered an extraordinary act of tyranny. The laborers begin work at six o'clock in the morning, have an hour's rest at nine for breakfast, and many have finished their assigned task by two o'clock, all of them by three o'clock. In summer they divide their work differently, going to bed in the middle of the day, then rising to finish their task, and afterward spending a great part of the night in chatting, merry-making, preaching, and psalm-singing. At Christmas they claim a week's holidays, when they hold a kind of Saturnalia, and the owners can get no work done. Although there is scarcely any drinking, the master rejoices when this season is well over without mischief. The negro houses are as neat as the greater part of the cottages in Scotland (no flattering compliment it must be confessed), are provided always with a back door, and a hall, as they call it, in which is a chest, a table, two or three chairs, and a few shelves for crockery.

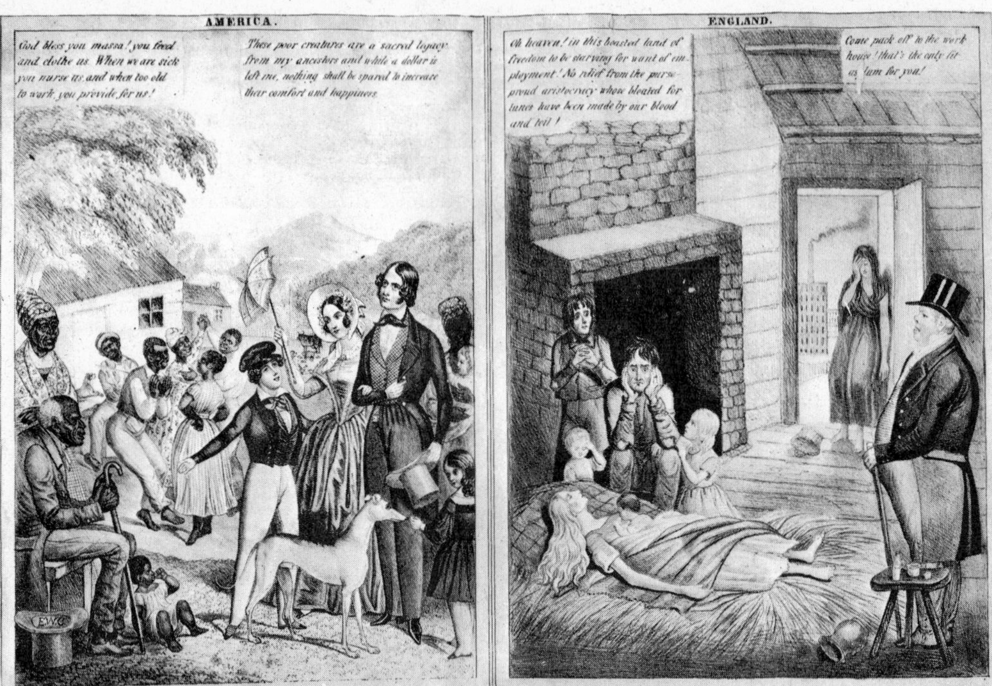

Such a cartoon today would be dismissed as calculated hypocricy. While such may have been true at this time, many people in both the North and the South believed in the "white man's burden."

On the door of the sleeping apartment they keep a large wooden padlock, to guard their valuables from their neighbors when they are at work in the field, for there is much pilfering among them. A little yard is often attached, in which are seen their chickens, and usually a yelping cur, kept for their amusement.

The winter, when the whites enjoy the best health, is the trying season for the negroes, who are rarely ill in the rice-grounds in summer, which are so fatal to the whites, that when the planters who have retreated to the sea-islands revisit their estates once a fortnight, they dare not sleep at home. Such is the indifference of the negroes to heat, that they are often found sleeping with their faces upward in a broiling sun, instead of lying under the shade of a tree hard by. We visited the hospital at Hopeton, which consists of three separate wards, all perfectly clean and well-ventilated. One is for men, another for women, and a third for lying-in women. The latter are always allowed a month's rest after their confinement, an advantage rarely enjoyed by hard-working English peasants. Although they are better looked after and kept more quiet, on these occasions, in the hospital, the planters are usually baffled; for the women prefer their own houses, where they can gossip with their friends without restraint, and they usually contrive to be taken by surprise at home.*

---

*Charles Lyell, *A Second Visit to the United States of North America* (2 vols., London, 1850), I, 353-356.

60

FREDERICK LAW OLMSTED

Lyell's rose-colored point of view was not shared by all travelers. Frederick Law Olmsted challenged the contention that the slaves in the South were better off than the laboring classes in other places. Although cool toward slavery, agriculturist Olmsted was a trained observer, who strove to describe things just as he saw them.

What advantage have the slaves, under this most enlightened and humane management, over the occupants of our poor-houses? In all the items of food, oversight, clothing, bedding, furniture, religious instruction, medical attendance, defense from quarreling—in everything except the amount of labor, and the provision of partners, our poor-houses provide (so far as I know, and I have visited not a few), at least equally well. But our laboring people are not generally anxious to be admitted to the poor-house. Far from it. They universally consider it a deplorable misfortune which obliges them to go to it. Our poor-houses are seldom crowded. They seldom, in the rural districts, contain any but a few imbeciles and cripples.

Louisiana is the only State in which meat is required, by law, to be furnished the slaves. I believe it is four pounds a week, with a barrel of corn (flour barrel of ears of maize) per month, and salt. In North Carolina the prescribed allowance is "a quart of corn per day." In no other States does the law define the quantity, but it is required, in general terms, to be sufficient for the health of the slave; and I have no doubt that suffering from want of food is exceedingly rare. The food is everywhere, however, coarse, crude, and wanting in variety; much more so than that of our prison convicts. In fact, under favorable circumstances, on the large plantations the slave's allowance does not equal either in quantity or quality that which we furnish the rogues in our penitentiaries. In the New Hampshire, Vermont, Massachusetts, Connecticut, and Pennsylvania state-prisons, the weekly allowance of meat (which is in variety—nor merely bacon) is always from one to three pounds more than that recommended by Mr. Collins, and which his slaves received with "much satisfaction," after "a stinted policy" had been given up, and three to five pounds more than that provided by Mr. Phillips. A greater variety of vegetables and condiments is also provided; and in New Hampshire, Vermont, and Pennsylvania, the quantity of potatoes or porridge furnished is officially reported to be "unlimited." Our laborers certainly do not generally look with envying eyes upon the comforts of a prison.

Does argument, that the condition of free-laborers is, on the whole, better than that of slaves, or that simply they are generally better fed, and more comfortably provided, seem to any one to be unnecessary? Many of our newspapers, of the largest circulation, and certainly of great influence among people—probably not very reflective, but certainly not fools—take the contrary for granted, whenever it suits their purpose. The Southern newspapers, so far as I know, do so, without exception. And very few Southern writers, on any subject whatever, can get through a book, or even a business or friendly letter, to be sent North, without, in some form or other, asserting that Northern laborers might well envy the condition of the slaves. A great many Southern gentlemen—gentlemen whom I respect much for their moral character, if not for their faculties of observation—have asserted it so strongly and confidently, as to shut my mouth, and by assuring me that they had personally observed the condition of Northern laborers themselves, and really knew that I was wrong, have for a time half convinced me against my own long experience. (And perhaps I should say that my experience has been gained, not only as an employer, in different parts of the North, but as a laborer; for I have been a farm laborer, associating and faring equally with the generality of Northern laborers, myself.) I have, since my return, received letters to the same effect: I have heard the assertion repeated by several travelers, and even by Northerners, who had resided long in the South: I have heard it publicly repeated in Tammany Hall, and elsewhere, by Northern Democrats: I have seen it in European books and journals: I have, in times past, taken its truth for granted, and repeated it myself. Such is the effect of the continued iteration of falsehood.

Since my return I have made it a subject of careful and extended inquiry. I have received reliable and unprejudiced information in the matter, or have examined personally the food, the wages, and the habits of the laborers in more than one hundred different farmers' families, in every free State (except California), and in Canada. I have made personal observations and inquiries of the same sort in Great Britain, Germany, France, and Belgium. In Europe, where there are large landed estates, which are rented by lordly proprietors to the peasant farmers, or where land is divided into such small portions that its owners are unable to make use of the best modern labor-saving implements, the condition of the laborer, as respects food, often is as bad as that of the slave often is—never worse than that sometimes is. But, in general, even in France, I do not believe it is generally or frequently worse; I believe it is, in the large majority of cases, much better than that of the majority of slaves. And as respects higher things than the necessities of life—in their intellectual, moral and social condition, with some exceptions on large farms and large estates in England, bad as is that of the mass of European laborers, the man is a brute or a devil who, with my information, would prefer that of the American slave. As to our own laborers, in the Free States, I have already said enough for my present purpose.*

---

*Frederick Law Olmsted, *op. cit.*, 699-702.

61

HARRIET MARTINEAU

In her Retrospect of Western Travel, *Harriet Martineau devoted one chapter to "Restless Slaves," challenging the notion that all was bliss among the bondmen. Miss Martineau had won fame in her native England for her social tracts in fictional garb. She had a keenly observant eye, although it should be mentioned that when she arrived in America in 1834, she brought with her a pronounced distaste for slavery.*

The traveller in America hears on every hand of the fondness of slaves for slavery. If he points to the little picture of a runaway prefixed to advertisements of fugitives, and repeated down whole columns of the first newspaper that comes to hand, he is met with anecdotes of slaves who have been offered their freedom, and prefer remaining in bondage. Both aspects of the question are true, and yet more may be said on both sides. The traveller finds, as he proceeds, that suicides are very frequent among slaves; and that there is a race of Africans who will not endure bondage at all, and who, when smuggled from Africa into Louisiana, are avoided in the market by purchasers, though they have great bodily strength and comeliness. When one of this race is accidentally purchased and taken home, he is generally missed before twenty-four hours are over, and found hanging behind a door or drowned in the nearest pond. The Cuba slaveholders have volumes of stories to tell of this race, proving their incapacity for slavery. On the other hand, the traveller may meet with a few negroes who have returned into slaveland from a state of freedom, and besought their masters to take them back.

These seeming contradictions admit of an easy explanation. Slaves are more or less degraded by slavery in proportion to their original strength of character or educational discipline of mind. The most degraded are satisfied, the least degraded are dissatisfied with slavery. The lowest order prefer release from duties and cares to the enjoyment of rights and the possession of themselves; and the highest order have a directly opposite taste. The mistake lies in not perceiving that slavery is emphatically condemned by the conduct of both.

The stories on the one side of the question are all alike. The master offers freedom—of course, to the worst of his slaves—to those who are more plague than profit. Perhaps he sends the fellow he wants to get rid of on some errand into a free state, hoping that he will not return. The man comes back; and, if questioned as to why he did not stay where he might have been free, he replies that he knows better than to work hard for a precarious living when he can be fed by his master without anxiety of his own as long as he lives. As for those who return after having been free, they are usually the weak-minded, who have been persuaded into remaining in a free state, where they have been carried in attendance on their masters' families, and who want courage to sustain their unprotected freedom. I do not remember ever hearing of the return of a slave who, having long nourished the idea and purpose of liberty, had absconded with danger and difficulty. The prosecution of such a purpose argues a strength of mind worthy of freedom.

The stories on this side of the question are as various as the characters and fortunes of the heroes of them. Many facts of this nature became known to me during my travels, most of which cannot be published, for fear of involving in difficulty either the escaped heroes or those who assisted them in regaining their liberty. But a few may be safely related, which will show, as well as any greater number, the kind of restlessness which is the torment of the lives of "persons held to labour," the constitutional description of the slave-class of the constituents of government.

Slavery is nowhere more hopeless and helpless than in Alabama. The richness of the soil and the paucity of inhabitants make the labourer a most valuable possession; while his distance from any free state—the extent of country overspread with enemies which the fugitive has to traverse—makes the attempt to escape desperate. All coloured persons travelling in the slave states without a pass—a certificate of freedom or of leave—are liable to be arrested and advertised, and, if unclaimed at the end of a certain time, sold in the market. Yet slaves do continue to escape from the farthest corners of Alabama or Mississippi. Two slaves in Alabama, who had from their early manhood cherished the idea of freedom, planned their escape in concert, and laboured for many years at their scheme. They were allowed the profits of their labour at over-hours; and, by strenuous toil and self-denial, saved and hid a large sum of money. Last year they found they had enough, and that the time was come for the execution of their purpose. They engaged the services of "a mean white"; one of the extremely degraded class who are driven by loss of character to labour in the slave states, where, labour by whites being disgraceful, they are looked down upon by the slaves no less than the slaves are by the superior whites. These two slaves hired a "mean white man" to personate a gentleman; bought him a suit of good clothes, a portmanteau, a carriage and horses, and proper costume for themselves. One night the three set off in style, as master, coachman, and footman, and travelled rapidly through the whole country, without the slightest hinderance, to Buffalo. There the slaves sold their carriage, horses, and finery, paid off their white man, and escaped into Canada, where they now are in safety.

They found in Canada a society of their own colour prepared to welcome and aid them. In Upper Canada there are upward of ten thousand people of colour, chiefly fugitive slaves, who prosper in the country which they have chosen for a refuge. Scarcely an instance is known of any of them having received alms, and they are as respectable for their intelligence as for their morals. One peculiarity in them is the extravagance of their loyalty. They exert themselves vehemently in defence of all the acts of the executive, whatever they may be. The reason for this is obvious: they exceedingly dread the barest mention of the annexation or Canada to the United States.

It is astonishing that, in the face of facts of daily occurrences like that of the escape of these men, it can be pleaded in behalf of slavery that negroes cannot take care of themselves, and that they prefer being held as property.*

62

ALEXIS DE TOCQUEVILLE

Alexis de Tocqueville, the French political writer, saw a deep and peculiar danger in modern slavery, a danger stemming from the difference in origin and in race between the master and the slave. Believing that slaves did not fully sense their plight, Tocqueville had no deep compassion for them as human beings. His numerous observations on the free Negro and the slave, therefore, while important as theoretical discussions concerning social injustice, the nature of democracy, and the tyranny of public opinion, never quite captured the human equation —the personal tragedies of the slave and of his master, the one unspoken and the other unsensed.

The Indians will perish in the same isolated condition in which they have lived; but the destiny of the Negroes is in some measure interwoven with that of the Europeans. These two races are attached to each other without intermingling; and they are alike unable entirely to separate or to combine. The most formidable of all the ills which threaten the future existence of the Union, arises from the presence of a black population upon its territory; and in contemplating the cause of the present embarrassments or of the future dangers of the United States, the observer is invariably led to consider this as a primary fact.

* * *

It is important to make an accurate distinction between slavery itself, and its consequences. The immediate evils which are produced by slavery were very nearly the same in antiquity as they are amongst the moderns; but the consequences of these evils were different. The slave, amongst the ancients, belonged to the same race as his master, and he was often the superior of the two in education† and instruction. Freedom was the only distinction between them; and when freedom was conferred, they were easily confounded together. The ancients, then, had a very simple means of avoiding slavery and its evil consequences, which was that of affranchisement; and they succeeded as soon as they adopted this measure generally. Not but, in ancient States, the vestiges of servitude subsisted, for some time after servitude itself was abolished. There is a natural prejudice which prompts men to despise whomsoever has been their inferior long after he is become their equal; and the real inequality which is

---

*Harriet Martineau, *Retrospect of Western Travel* (2 vols., London, 1838), I, 242-244.

†It is well known that several of the most distinguished authors of antiquity, and amongst them Aesop and Terence, were, or had been slaves. Slaves were not always taken from barbarous nations, and the chances of war reduced highly civilized men to servitude.

produced by fortune or by law, is always succeeded by an imaginary inequality which is implanted in the manners of the people. Nevertheless, this secondary consequence of slavery was limited to a certain term amongst the ancients; for the freedman bore so entire a resemblance to those born free, that it soon became impossible to distinguish him from amongst them.

The greatest difficulty in antiquity was that of altering the law; amongst the moderns it is that of altering the manners; and, as far as we are concerned, the real obstacles begin where those of the ancients left off. This arises from the circumstance that, amongst the moderns, the abstract and transient fact of slavery is fatally united to the physical and permanent fact of colour. The tradition of slavery dishonors the race, and the peculiarity of the race perpetuates the tradition of slavery. No African has ever voluntarily emigrated to the shores of the New World; whence it must be inferred, that all the blacks who are now to be found in that hemisphere are either slaves or freedmen. Thus the negro transmits the eternal mark of his ignominy to all his descendants; and although the law may abolish slavery, God alone can obliterate the traces of its existence.

The modern slave differs from his master not only in his condition, but in his origin. You may set the negro free, but you cannot make him otherwise than an alien to the European. Nor is this all: we scarcely acknowledge the common features of mankind in this child of debasement whom slavery has brought amongst us. His physiognomy is to our eyes hideous, his understanding weak, his tastes low; and we are almost inclined to look upon him as a being intermediate between man and the brutes* The moderns, then, after they have abolished slavery, have three prejudices to contend against, which are less easy to attack, and far less easy to conquer, than the mere fact of servitude; the prejudice of the master, the prejudice of the race, and the prejudice of colour.

It is difficult for us, who have had the good fortune to be born amongst men like ourselves by nature, and equal to ourselves by law, to conceive the irreconcileable differences which separate the negro from the European in America. But we may derive some faint notion of them from analogy. France was formerly a country in which numerous distinctions of rank existed, that had been created by the legislation. Nothing can be more fictitious than a purely legal inferiority; nothing more contrary to the instinct of mankind than these permanent divisions which had been established between beings evidently similar. Nevertheless these divisions subsisted for ages; they still subsist in many places; and on all sides they have left imaginary vestiges, which time alone can efface. If it be so difficult to root out an inequality which solely originates in the law, how are those distinctions to be destroyed which seem to be based upon the immutable laws of Nature herself? When I remember the extreme difficulty with which aristocratic bodies, of whatever nature they may be, are commingled with the mass of the people; and the exceeding care which they take to preserve the ideal boundaries of their caste inviolate, I despair of seeing an aristocracy disappear which is founded upon visible and indelible signs. Those who hope that the Europeans will ever mix with the negroes, appear to me to delude themselves; and I am not led to any such conclusion by my own reason, or by the evidence of facts.†

Variations in the Pattern

63

THE HOUSE SLAVE AND THE FIELD SLAVE

All slaves did not share the same lot; some were better off than others. City slaves might mix with free Negroes in church and at social affairs and might share in the excitements of urban life, thus leading a freer and more interesting life than slaves in a rural setting. And on the plantations not all bondmen were alike; a domestic living in the "big house" would have been most unwilling to change places with a field hand living along slave row. The English traveler James Stirling took note of the contrast between these two groups.

In judging of the welfare of the slaves, it is necessary to distinguish the different conditions of slavery. The most important distinction, both as regards numbers and its influence on the well-being of the slave, is that between house-servants and farm or field-hands. The house-servant is comparatively well off. He is frequently born and bred in the family he belongs to; and even when this is not the case, the constant association of the slave and his master, and master's family, naturally leads to such an attachment as ensures good treatment. There are not wanting instances of devoted attachment on both sides in such cases. There is even a danger that the affection on the part of the owner may degenerate into over-indulgence. It is no uncommon thing to make pets of slaves, as we do of other inferior animals; and when this is the case, the real welfare of the slave is sacrificed to an indiscriminating attachment. I was struck with the appearance of the slaves in the streets of Charleston on a Sunday afternoon. A large proportion of them were well dressed, and of decent bearing, and had all the appearance of enjoying a holiday. I was informed they were principally house-servants belonging to the town; and there could be no doubt the control of public opinion, natural to a large city, had exercised a favourable influence on the condition of these poor people.

The position of the field-hands is very different; of those, especially, who labour on large plantations. Here there are none of those humanizing influences at work which temper the rigour of the system, nor is there the same check of public opinion to control abuse. The 'force' is worked *en masse,* as a great human

---

*To induce the whites to abandon the opinion they have conceived of the moral and intellectual inferiority of their former slaves, the negroes must change; but as long as this opinion subsists, to change is impossible.

†Henry Reeves, trans., Alexis de Tocqueville, *Democracy in America* (2 vols., London, 1838), II, 214-217.

mechanism; or, if you will, as a drove of human cattle. The proprietor is seldom present to direct and control. Even if he were, on large estates the numbers are too great for his personal attention to details of treatment. On all large plantations the comfort of the slave is practically at the disposal of the white overseer, and his subordinate, the negro-driver. There are many estates which the proprietor does not visit at all, or visits perhaps once a year; and where, during his absence, the slaves are left to the uncontrolled caprice of the overseer and his assistants, not another white man, perhaps, being within miles of the plantation. Who can say what passes in those voiceless solitudes? Happen what may, there is none to tell. Whatever the slave may suffer there is none to bear witness to his wrong. It needs a large amount of charity to believe that power so despotic, so utterly uncontrolled even by opinion, will never degenerate into violence. It could only be so if overseers were saints, and drivers angels.

It is often said that the interest of the slave-owner is sufficient guarantee for the good treatment of the slave; that no man will voluntarily injure the value of his property. This reasoning assumes, first, that slave-owners will take an intelligent view of their own interests; and, secondly, that they will be guided by the passion of gain rather than by other passions. But we find the Cuba slave-owner working his slaves to death, at the rate of 3 per cent. per annum. And again, slavery is a system which evokes passions more powerful even than the love of gain. Against the action of these angry passions, the distant calculation of mere profit can avail but little with men of violent dispositions.

But even if we grant the restraint placed on the passions of the master by considerations of pecuniary interest, we cannot allow the same effect to be produced on the overseer. On the contrary, the interest of the overseer is to exhibit a large production as the result of his exertions; and the more remote consideration of being a prudent husbandman of his forces will only affect a superior mind. On this point I prefer giving the opinions of slave-owners themselves. In an articie in *De Bow's Review,* on the management of slaves, I find some interesting remarks on this subject, in a report to a committee of slaveholders. After pointing out the interest of the owners in the good treatment of their slaves, it continues:—'There is one class of our community to whom all the motives referred to, to induce us to kindness to our slaves, do not apply. Your committee refer to our overseers. As they have no property in our slaves, of course they lack the check of self-interest. As their only aim, in general, is to get the largest possible crop for the year, we can readily conceive the strong inducement they have to overwork our slaves, and masters are often much to blame for inadvertently encouraging this feeling in their overseers.'

It appears, then, that nothing but high principle on the part of the overseer could ensure the good treatment of the slave on large plantations. But all testimony concurs in representing the overseers as a very inferior class in point of character. A Virginian slave-owner used this language to Olmsted:—'They (the overseers) are the curse of this country, sir; the worst men in the community.' Yet these are the men on whom devolves, practically, the management of the great bulk of the agricultural slave population, in the cotton, rice, and sugar districts.*

64

THE ROLE OF THE DRIVER

The field hands, unlike the domestics, had few contacts with the master and the mistress. Authority over the field slaves and supervision of their work were responsibilities exercised by the overseer and the driver. Law or custom required that the overseer be white. His right-hand man was the driver, or foreman. A slave was carefully screened before he was made a driver. A component of the "power structure," the driver inevitably was heartily disliked by his fellow slaves. His role has been described by Olmsted.

It is the driver's duty to make the tasked hands do their work well. If, in their haste to finish it, they neglect to do it properly, he "sets them back," so that carelessness will hinder more than it will hasten the completion of their tasks.

In the selection of drivers, regard seems to be had to size and strength—at least, nearly all the drivers I have seen are tall and strong men—but a great deal of judgment, requiring greater capacity of mind than the ordinary slave is often supposed to be possessed of, is certainly needed in them. A good driver is very valuable and usually holds office for life. His authority is not limited to the direction of labor in the field, but extends to the general deportment of the negroes. He is made to do the duties of policeman, and even of police magistrate.

Where the drivers are discreet, experienced and trusty, the overseer is frequently employed merely as a matter of form, to comply with the laws requiring the superintendence or presence of a white man among every body of slaves; and his duty is rather to inspect and report, than to govern. Mr. X. considers his overseer an uncommonly efficient and faithful one, but he would not employ him, even during the summer, when he is absent for several months, if the law did not require it. He has sometimes left his plantation in care of one of the drivers for a considerable length of time, after having dis-

*James Stirling, *op. cit.*, 287-291.

charged an overseer; and he thinks it has then been quite as well conducted as ever. His overseer consults the drivers on all important points, and is governed by their advice.*

65

THE TASK SYSTEM

The overseer, assisted by the driver, determined the working capacity of each field hand. Some slaves, particularly the skilled, worked under the task system. Under this system, a slave was allotted a fixed amount of daily work (a "standardized task"), the completion of which permitted him to quit for the day. Again our guide is Olmsted's observant eye.

The field-hands are all divided into four classes, according to their physical capacities. The children beginning as "quarter-hands," advancing to "half-hands," and then to "three-quarter hands;" and, finally, when mature, and able-bodied, healthy, and strong, to "full hands." As they decline in strength, from age, sickness, or other cause, they retrograde in the scale, and proportionately less labor is required of them. Many, of naturally weak frame, never are put among the full hands. Finally, the aged are left out at the annual classification, and no more regular field-work is required of them, although they are generally provided with some light, sedentary occupation.

* * *

The field hands, are nearly always worked in gangs, the strength of a gang varying according to the work that engages it; usually it numbers twenty or more, and is directed by a driver. As on most large plantations, whether of rice or cotton, in Eastern Georgia and South Carolina, nearly all ordinary and regular work is performed *by tasks:* that is to say, each hand has his labor for the day marked out before him, and can take his own time to do it in. For instance, in making drains in light, clean meadow land, each man or woman of the full hands is required to dig one thousand cubic feet; in swamp-land that is being prepared for rice culture, where there are not many stumps, the task for a ditcher is five hundred feet; while in a very strong cypress swamp, only two hundred feet is required; in hoeing rice, a certain number of rows, equal to one-half or two-thirds of an acre, according to the condition of the land; in sowing rice (strewing in drills), two acres; in reaping rice (if it stands well), three-quarters of an acre; or, sometimes a gang will be required to reap, tie in sheaves, and carry to the stack-yard the produce of a certain area, commonly equal to one fourth the number of acres that there are hands working together. Hoeing cotton, corn, or potatoes; one half to one acre. Threshing; five to six hundred sheaves. In plowing rice-land (light, clean, mellow soil) with a yoke of oxen, one acre a day, including the ground lost in and near the drains—the oxen being

*Frederick Law Olmsted, *op. cit.*, 437-438

changed at noon. A cooper, also, for instance, is required to make barrels at the rate of eighteen a week. Drawing staves; 500 a day. Hoop poles; 120. Squaring timber; 100 ft. Laying worm-fence; 50 panels per hand. Post and rail do., posts set 2½ to 3 ft. deep, 9 ft. apart, nine or ten panels per hand. In getting fuel from the woods, (pine, to be cut and split,) one cord is the task for a day. In "mauling rails," the taskman selecting the trees (pine) that he judges will split easiest, one hundred a day, ends not sharpened.

These are the tasks for first class able-bodied men, they are lessened by one quarter for three quarter hands, and proportionately for the lighter classes. In allotting the tasks, the drivers are expected to put the weaker hands, where (if there is any choice in the appearance of the ground, as where certain rows in hoeing corn would be less weedy than others,) they will be favored.

These tasks certainly would not be considered excessively hard, by a Northern laborer; and, in point of fact, the more industrious and active hands finish them often by two o'clock. I saw one or two leaving the field soon after one o'clock, several about two; and between three and four, I met a dozen women and several men coming home to their cabins, having finished their day's work.

Under this "Organization of Labor," most of the slaves work rapidly and well. In nearly all ordinary work, custom has settled the extent of the task, and it is difficult to increase it. The driver who marks it out, has to remain on the ground until it is finished, and has no interest in over-measuring it; and if it should be systematically increased very much, there is danger of a general stampede to the "swamp"—a danger the slave can always hold before his master's cupidity. In fact, it is looked upon in this region as a proscriptive right of the negroes to have this incitement to diligence offered them; and the man who denied it, or who attempted to lessen it, would, it is said, suffer in his reputation, as well as experience much annoyance from the obstinate "rascality" of his negroes. Notwithstanding this, I have heard a man assert, boastingly, that he made his negroes habitually perform double the customary tasks, thus we get a glimpse again of the black side. If he is allowed the power to do this, what may not a man do?*

66

THE GANG SYSTEM

In most instances, however, the plantation slaves worked under the "gang" system, rather than by task. An example of the gang system, by which a slave might work from "can see 'til can't," was described by the much-traveled Englishman, James Silk Buckingham.

We visited one of the rice plantations in the neighbourhood of Savannah, and saw the conditions of the slaves on it with our own eyes. The estate was considered to be a valuable one, and under a

**Ibid.*, 433-436.

fair condition of management, not among the best nor among the worst, but just such an average plantation as we wished to examine. The dwellings for the negroes were built of wood, ranged in rows of great uniformity, raised a little above the ground, each building containing two or more rooms, with a fire-place for two. We saw also the nursery for the children, and the sick-room or hospital for those who were hurt or diseased, and we had communication with the overseer, and several of the people, from both of whom we learnt the following facts, as to their routine of labour, food, and treatment.

The slaves are all up by daylight; and every one who is able to work, from eight or nine years old and upwards, repair to their several departments of field-labour. They do not return to their houses either to breakfast or dinner; but have their food cooked for them in the field, by negroes appointed to that duty. They continue thus at work till dark, and then return to their dwellings. There is no holiday on Saturday afternoon, or any other time throughout the year, except a day or two at Christmas; but from daylight to dark, every day except Sunday, they are at their labour. Their allowance of food consists of a peck, or two gallons, of Indian corn per week, half that quantity for working boys and girls, and a quarter for little children. This corn they are obliged to grind themselves, after their hours of labour are over; and it is then boiled in water, and made into hominy, but without anything to eat with it, neither bread, rice, fish, meat, potatoes, or butter; boiled corn and water only, and barely a sufficient quantity of this for subsistence.

Of clothes, the men and boys had a coarse woollen jacket and trousers once a year, without shirt or any other garment. This was their winter dress; their summer apparel consists of a similar suit of jacket and trousers of the coarsest cotton cloth. Absence from work, or neglect of duty, was punished with stinted allowance, imprisonment, and flogging. A medical man visited the plantation occasionally, and medicines were administered by a negro woman called the sick-nurse. No instruction was allowed to be given in reading or writing, no games or recreations were provided, nor was there indeed any time to enjoy them if they were. Their lot was one of continued toil, from morning to night, uncheered even by the *hope* of any change, or prospect of improvement in condition.*

67

SIMON GRAY, FLATBOAT CAPTAIN

Some slaves exercised an unusal degree of responsibility, rivermen in particular. From 1845 to 1862 Simon Gray was a flatboat captain in command of crews of from ten to twenty men, who were engaged in transporting lumber between Natchez and New Orleans. An expert in both the art of flatboating and the

*James Silk Buckingham, *The Slave States of America* (2 vols., London, 1842), I, 132-133.

marketing of cypress lumber, slave Gray traveled about freely, carried fire-arms, and was paid a regular wage. It was his practice to submit written reports of his trips; the following, addressed to Andrew Dott on June 21, 1850, is typical.

I now write you these few lines to let you know that I am a little better than I was when I left. I have got along quite well with the boat so far and have delivered *Mr. Moss* bill [of lumber] according to order and taken a draft for the same. I stoped the boat from leaking in the evening [afternoon] of the 19th of this month. The bill [order] of Mr Allens, it is to come with H. K. Moss next bill. I have not made any collections as yet but have the promis of some this morning This letter that I send in your care I want to send to my wife, if you please.

Nothing more at preasant. I remain your umble servent &c.*

68

A SLAVE DENIED CONSENT TO MARRY

It should be noted that one of the partners in the firm that employed Simon Gray did not approve of bestowing so much responsibility upon a slave. The fact remains that however widely the slaves varied in the tasks they performed and in the responsibilities they carried, they all held one thing in common—the constant awareness that their destiny was in the hands of others. Such a condition of dependence might bring heartbreak, as Milo Thompson of Harrodsburg, Kentucky, found out. Unable to gain his master's consent to marry a slave of James G. Birney, Sr., the disappointed Milo wrote to the other party in waiting, expressing a hope that was not fated to be realized.

MILO THOMPSON (SLAVE) TO LOUISA BETHLEY

Oct. 15th 1834

Miss Louisa Bethley

I have got greatly disappointed in my expectations on next Saturday. I will be compelled to disappoint you at that time but I regret it very much. Master says I must put it off a little longer, until he can see farther into the matter. he says probably Mr. Birney may break up house keeping or something of the kind and he dont know what may become of you, for that reason we must defer it a little longer. I will come up and see you shortly and then we will make some arrangements about it. it is with great reluctance that I put it off any longer, but I am compelled to do it owing to the circumstances I have related. I shall remain your affectionate lover until death.

Milo Thompson†

*John Hebron Moore, "Simon Gray, Riverman: A Slave Who Was Almost Free," *The Mississippi Valley Historical Review,* Vol. 49 (Dec. 1962), 476.

†Dwight L. Dumond, ed., *Letters of James Gillespie Birney, 1831-1857* (2 vols., New York, D. Appleton-Century, 1938), I, 144. Reprinted by permission of the American Historical Association, Washington, D.C.

69

A SLAVE CATECHISM

Control of the slave was exercised through religion, whether encouraged as a type of escape from the trouble of the world or used as a form of indoctrination. The all-slave church gave birth to the spirituals with their apparent emphasis on a promised land in the hereafter. The spirituals, however, may not have been so "otherworldly" as, at first blush, they sounded. They were susceptible of double meanings, and undoubtedly many slaves interpreted the language of the spirituals in a manner unsuspected by white listeners. In slave-attended churches with white pastors, a special catechism, of which the following is an example, was prepared for the darker brother.

Q. Who keeps the snakes and all bad things from hurting you?
A. God does.
Q. Who gave you a master and a mistress?
A. God gave them to me.
Q. Who says that you must obey them?
A. God says that I must.
Q. What book tells you these things?
A. The Bible.
Q. How does God do all his work?
A. He always does it right.
Q. Does God love to work?
A. Yes, God is always at work.
Q. Do the angels work?
A. Yes, they do what God tells them.
Q. Do they love to work?
A. Yes, they love to please God.
Q. What does God say about your work?
A. He that will not work shall not eat.
Q. Did Adam and Eve have to work?
A. Yes, they had to keep the garden.
Q. Was it hard to keep that garden?
A. No, it was very easy.
Q. What makes the crops so hard to grow now?
A. Sin makes it.
Q. What makes you lazy?
A. My wicked heart.
Q. How do you know your heart is wicked?
A. I feel it every day.
Q. Who teaches you so many wicked things?
A. The Devil.
Q. Must you let the Devil teach you?
A. No, I must not.*

**Frederick Douglass' Paper*, June 2, 1854, from the *Southern Episcopalian*, Charleston, S.C., April 1854.

70

AN ACT PROHIBITING THE TEACHING OF SLAVES TO READ

To keep the slaves in hand it was deemed necessary to keep them innocent of the printed page. Otherwise they might read abolitionist newspapers that were smuggled in, become dissatisfied, forge passes, or simply know too much. Hence most states passed laws prohibiting anyone from teaching slaves to read or write. The North Carolina statute was typical.

AN ACT TO PREVENT ALL PERSONS FROM TEACHING SLAVES TO READ OR WRITE, THE USE OF FIGURES EXCEPTED.

Whereas the teaching of slaves to read and write, has a tendency to excite dissatisfaction in their minds, and to produce insurrection and rebellion, to the manifest injury of the citizens of this State: Therefore,

Be it enacted by the General Assembly of the State of North Carolina, and it is hereby enacted by the authority of the same, That any free person, who shall hereafter teach, or attempt to teach, any slave within the State to read or write, the use of figures excepted, or shall give or sell to such slave or slaves any books or pamphlets, shall be liable to indictment in any court of record in this State having jurisdiction thereof, and upon conviction, shall, at the discretion of the court, if a white man or woman, be fined not less than one hundred dollars, nor more than two hundred dollars, or imprisoned; and if a free person of color, shall be fined, imprisoned, or whipped, at the discretion of the court, not exceeding thirty nine lashes, nor less than twenty lashes.

II. *Be it further enacted,* That if any slave shall hereafter teach, or attempt to teach, any other slave to read or write, the use of figures excepted, he or she may be carried before any justice of the peace, and on conviction thereof, shall be sentenced to receive thirty nine lashes on his or her bare back

III. *Be it further enacted,* That the judges of the Superior Courts and the justices of the County Courts shall give this act in charge to the grand juries of their respective counties.*

Slave Attitudes

71

THE UNHAPPINESS OF SINGING SLAVES

Although some slaves appeared to have found their lot tolerable, Frederick Douglass, born in bondage on the Eastern Shore of Maryland, insisted that slaves as a class were unhappy, outward appearances to the contrary. Douglass offered as one example the behavior of the slaves from the Lloyd plantation who were sent to get the food rations for the month.

**Acts Passed by the General Assembly of the State of North Carolina at the Session of 1830-1831* (Raleigh, 1831), 11.

The slaves selected to go to the Great House Farm, for the monthly allowance for themselves and their fellow-slaves, were peculiarly enthusiastic. While on their way, they would make the dense old woods, for miles around, reverberate with their wild songs, revealing at once the highest joy and the deepest sadness. They would compose and sing as they went along, consulting neither time nor tune. The thought that came up, came out—if not in the word, in the sound;—and as frequently in the one as in the other. They would sometimes sing the most pathetic sentiment in the most rapturous tone, and the most rapturous sentiment in the most pathetic tone. Into all of their songs they would manage to weave something of the Great House Farm. Especially would they do this, when leaving home. They would then sing most exultingly the following words:—

"I am going away to the Great House Farm!
O, yea! O, yea! O!"

This they would sing, as a chorus, to words which to many would seem unmeaning jargon, but which, nevertheless, were full of meaning to themselves. I have sometimes thought that the mere hearing of those songs would do more to impress some minds with the horrible character of slavery, than the reading of whole volumes of philosophy on the subject could do.

I did not, when a slave, understand the deep meaning of those rude and apparently incoherent songs. I was myself within the circle; so that I neither saw nor heard as those without might see and hear. They told a tale of woe which was then altogether beyond my feeble comprehension; they were tones loud, long, and deep; they breathed the prayer and complaint of souls boiling over with the bitterest anguish. Every tone was a testimony against slavery, and a prayer to God for deliverance from chains. The hearing of those wild notes always depressed my spirit, and filled me with ineffable sadness. I have frequently found myself in tears while hearing them. The mere recurrence to those songs, even now, afflicts me; and while I am writing these lines, an expression of feeling has already found its way down my cheek. To those songs I trace my first glimmering conception of the dehumanizing character of slavery. I can never get rid of that conception. Those songs still follow me, to deepen my hatred of slavery, and quicken my sympathies for my brethren in bonds. If any one wishes to be impressed with the soul-killing effects of slavery, let him go to Colonel Lloyd's plantation, and, on allowance-day, place himself in the deep pine woods, and there let him, in silence, analyze the sounds that shall pass through the chambers of his soul,—and if he is not thus impressed, it will only be because "there is no flesh in his obdurate heart."

I have often been utterly astonished, since I came to the north, to find persons who could speak of the singing, among slaves, as evidence of their contentment and happiness. It is impossible to conceive of a greater mistake. Slaves sing most when they are most unhappy. The songs of the slave represent the sorrows of his heart; and he is relieved by them, only as an aching heart is relieved by its tears. At least, such is my experience. I have often sung to drown my sorrow, but seldom to express my happiness. Crying for joy, and singing for joy, were alike uncommon to me while in the jaws of slavery. The singing of a man cast away upon a desolate island might be as appropriately considered as evidence of contentment and happiness, as the singing of a slave; the songs of the one and of the other are prompted by the same emotion.*

72

THE SLAVES CONCEAL THEIR FEELINGS

Though it is not likely that the majority of slaves were as dissatisfied as the brooding, militant Douglass, it is difficult to determine what the average slave felt or thought. In part this was a consequence of his efforts to mask his true feelings. This trait of dissembling was detected by a Northerner, Mrs. A. M. French. Mother of seven, school teacher, and former editor of a religious publication, Mrs. French was a dedicated humanitarian, if somewhat eccentric in her manners. Her observations were based on the behavior of the Negroes at Port Royal in South Carolina, whence she had come with her husband in March 1862.

The slave, too, conceals. He is never off his guard. He is perfectly skilled in hiding all emotions. The downcast eye, dull when he wills it, conceals his opinions, the hearty laugh his grief. His Master knows him not, except, possibly, as to what brute force will best subdue him. Nothing is more apparent now that the mask is thrown off, than that owners never understood their slaves. They were accomplished tragedians, the dullest of them, as will in many cases appear, in this work. But lest some think we err, and that Masters and visitors did understand them, we give from SOUTHERN WORKS, extracts from the OFFICIAL REPORT of the rebellion under Denmark Vesey, of Charleston. It says:

"He was for twenty years a most faithful slave. He maintained such an irreproachable character, and enjoyed so much the confidence of the whites, that when he was accused of leading the rebellion, not only was the charge discredited, but he was not even arrested for several days after, and not till the proofs of his guilt had become too strong to be doubted. Not a symptom of the volcano raging within him had ever appeared, and on close investigation of his whole life, nothing could be adduced by witnesses but that once he had said, respecting his children, 'he wished he could see them free.' Yet for more than four years, the enterprise for the independence of the blacks had occupied his whole mind."

That the Colored men cannot be understood when they will it otherwise, is further proven from the same Report. It goes on to say:

"It is a remarkable fact, that the general good character of the leaders, except Gullah Jack, was such as rendered them OBJECTS

---

*Benjamin Quarles, ed., *Narrative of the Life of Frederick Douglass* (Cambridge, Mass., The Belknap Press of Harvard University Press, 1960), 36-38. Reprinted by permission.

LEAST LIABLE TO SUSPICION. Their conduct had secured them not only the unlimited confidence of their owners, but they had been indulged."

"But," continues the Report, "not only were the leaders of good character, and very much indulged by their owners, but this was VERY GENERALLY THE CASE, WITH ALL who were convicted, MANY OF THEM POSSESSING the highest confidence of their owners, and not one reputed of bad character."

We merely quote this from Southern records, as being more convincing to critics—not as more striking, than many instances we have found. Of course, no sensible slave would be so out of love with life, as to say to his Master, "I desire freedom." And the more he was plotting for it, the more loving and contented would he appear. So, in everything, long habit has inured them to deception. Often, they act the opposite of what they feel, as it seems almost involuntarily.

Their accuracy in reading character from the countenance and appearance is amazing. This has been their life-long study. The deep thought it engenders is taken for dullness. Then, many of them are hated, abused, sold for resembling their Master, with all the spirit of his family swelling and boiling within them.

How, then, could visitors comprehend them, especially when on good terms with their Masters?

There is no work extant respecting the Negro, but misrepresents him. Not one! Not even the works of those warmly enlisted in his favor, do him justice, or speak truly respecting him, at least, as he is, in America. Not one. The reason is obvious. The only light in which he could be seen, was that cast by slavery, for no other power had access, real access, to them. Many travellers, and others, may have imagined, they had access, saw things, as they were, but it will yet be universally acknowledged that THIS WAS NOT SO, and that, however candid, and open appearances were, they saw in these dark places, merely, but just what the Masters chose, they should see,

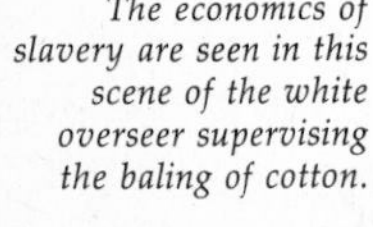

The economics of slavery are seen in this scene of the white overseer supervising the baling of cotton.

and nothing more. They heard just what tales the poor Colored, knew it was for their whole skin, and length of days, that they should tell, whatever appearances were. The "greenness" of the traveller, or transient resident, who imagines that a Negro would dare be sulky, or sad, in appearance, or otherwise than jovial, wants a name, or, that the Negro, would dare act himself, in any one way, freely.*

73

THE FLIGHT OF WILLIAM AND ELLEN CRAFT

A technique of protest common to the more adventurous spirits was flight, whether to Mexico, to Canada, to the northern states, or to the urban centers of the South. Most of the slaves who made the dash for freedom were assisted by the organized movement known as the Underground Railroad. This was a loosely knit network of stations, located at points a day's journey apart, to which fugitives would be brought by "conductors." Some slaves, particularly those in regions not served by the Railroad, struck out unassisted. Notable among these were William and Ellen Craft, whose dramatic escape became part of the folklore of the abolitionist crusade. Their story is told by William Wells Brown, himself a runaway, in this letter to William Lloyd Garrison.

One of the most interesting cases of the escape of fugitives from American slavery that have ever come before the American people, has just occurred, under the following circumstances:—William and Ellen Craft, man and wife, lived with different masters in the State of Georgia. Ellen is so near white, that she can pass without suspicion for a white woman. Her husband is much darker. He is a mechanic, and by working nights and Sundays, he laid up money enough to bring himself and his wife out of slavery. Their plan was without precedent; and though novel, was the means of getting them their freedom. Ellen dressed in man's clothing, and passed as the *master*, while her husband passed as the *servant*. In this way they travelled from Georgia to Philadelphia. They are now out of the reach of the blood-hounds of the South. On their journey, they put up at the best hotels where they stopped. Neither of them can read or write. And Ellen, knowing that she would be called upon to write her name at the hotels, &c, tied her right hand up as though it was lame, which proved of some service to her, as she was called upon several times at hotels to "register" her name. In Charleston, S.C., they put up at the hotel which Gov. M'Duffie and John C. Calhoun generally make their home, yet these distinguished advocates of the "peculiar institution" say that the slaves cannot take care of themselves. They arrived in Philadelphia, in four days from the time they started. Their history, especially that of their escape, is replete with interest. They will be at the meeting of the Massachusetts Anti-Slavery Society, in Boston, in the latter part of this month, where I

*A. M. French, *Slavery in South Carolina and the Ex-Slaves* (New York, 1862), 61-62, 159

know the history of their escape will be listened to with great interest. They are very intelligent. They are young, Ellen 22, and William 24 years of age. Ellen is truly a heroine.

Yours truly,
William W. Brown

P. S. They are now hid away within 25 miles of Philadelphia, where they will remain until the 6th, when they will leave with me for New England. Will you please say in the *Liberator* that I will lecture, in connexion with them, as follows:—

At Norwich, Conn., Thursday evening, January 18
At Worcester, Mass., Friday evening, January 19
At Pawtucket, Mass., Saturday evening, January 20
At New Bedford, Mass., Sunday afternoon and evening, January 28.*

74

NAT TURNER'S REBELLION

Armed revolt was the most spectacular, as it was the most desperate, of the slave's ways of striking back at his master. Slave uprisings had scant prospects of success, but hope never deserts the true revolutionary. Such a man was the slave preacher, Nat Turner, of Southampton County, Virginia. A man of intense religious fervor, and something of a mystic, Turner had led a puritanical personal life. To a New Testament dedication to love he added an Old Testament instinct for massive warfare against the hosts of evil. Permitted to move about and preach, Turner became known as the Prophet to his listeners, who believed that he had been chosen to lead them to a Promised Land.

In the summer of 1831, after receiving what he accepted as a sign from on High, Turner headed a revolt unparalleled in the United States. Turner was captured, but not until he and his followers had put to death some sixty whites. In an interview given while awaiting sentence, Turner spoke freely of himself and his plans. To Turner's remarks the reporter, Thomas R. Gray, appended a few observations of his own on the verdict of the court. The antebellum South never forgot Nat Turner. To outward appearances he had seemed docile and contented. The fear lingered that some other apparently satisfied slave would prove to be another Turner.

CONFESSION.

Agreeable to his own appointment, on the evening he was committed to prison, with permission of the jailer, I visited NAT on Tuesday the 1st November, when, without being questioned at all, he commenced his narrative in the following words:—

Sir,—You have asked me to give a history of the motives which induced me to undertake the late insurrection, as you call it—To do so I must go back to the days of my infancy, and even before I was born. I was thirty-one years of age the 2d of October last, and born the property of Benj. Turner, of this county. In my childhood a circumstance occurred which made an indelible impression on my mind, and laid the ground work of that enthusiasm which has terminated so fatally to many, both white and black, and for which I am about to

**The Liberator* (Boston), January 12, 1849.

atone at the gallows. It is here necessary to relate this circumstance—trifling as it may seem, it was the commencement of that belief which has grown with time, and even now, sir, in this dungeon, helpless and forsaken as I am, I cannot divest myself of. Being at play with other children, when three or four years old, I was telling them something, which my mother overhearing, said it had happened before I was born—I stuck to my story, however, and related somethings which went, in her opinion, to confirm it—others being called on were greatly astonished, knowing that these had happened, and caused them to say in my hearing, I surely would be a prophet, as the Lord had shewn me things that had happened before my birth.

* * *

And about this time I had a vision—and I saw white spirits and black spirits engaged in battle, and the sun was darkened—the thunder rolled in the Heavens, and blood flowed in streams—and I heard a voice saying, "Such is your luck, such you are called to see, and let it come rough or smooth, you must surely bare it." I now withdrew myself as much as my situation would permit, from the intercourse of my fellow servants, for the avowed purpose of serving the Spirit more fully—and it appeared to me, and reminded me of the things it had already shown me, and that it would then reveal to me the knowledge of the elements, the revolution of the planets, the operation of tides, and changes of the seasons. After this revelation in the year 1825, and the knowledge of the elements being made known to me, I sought more than ever to obtain true holiness before the great day of judgment should appear, and then I began to receive the true knowledge of faith. And from the first steps of righteousness until the last, was I made perfect; and the Holy Ghost was with me, and said, "Behold me as I stand in the Heavens"—and I looked and saw the forms of men in different attitudes—and there were lights in the sky to which the children of darkness gave other names than what they really were—for they were the lights of the Saviour's hands, stretched forth from east to west, even as they were extended on the cross on Calvary for the redemption of sinners. And I wondered greatly at these miracles, and prayed to be informed of a certainty of the meaning thereof—and shortly afterwards, while laboring in the field, I discovered drops of blood on the corn as though it were dew from heaven—and I communicated it to many, both white and black, in the neighborhood—and I then found on the leaves in the woods hieroglyphic characters, and numbers, with the forms of men in different attitudes, portrayed in blood, and representing the figures I had seen before in the heavens. And now the Holy Ghost had revealed itself to me, and made plain the miracles it had shown me—For as the blood of Christ had been shed on this earth, and had ascended to heaven for the salvation of sinners, and was now returning to earth again in the form of dew—and as the leaves on the trees bore the impression of the figures I had seen in the heavens, it was plain to me that the Saviour was about to lay down the yoke he had borne for the sins of men, and the great day of judgment was at hand.

* * *

Since the commencement of 1830, I had been living with Mr. Joseph Travis, who was to me a kind master, and placed the greatest confidence in me; in fact, I had no cause to complain of his treatment of me. On Saturday evening, the 20th of August, it was agreed between Henry, Hark and myself, to prepare a dinner the next day for the men we expected, and then to concert a plan, as we had not yet determined on any. Hark, on the following morning, brought a pig, and Henry brandy, and being joined by Sam, Nelson, Will and Jack, they prepared in the woods a dinner, where, about three o'clock, I joined them.

Q. Why were you so backward in joining them.

A. The same reason that had caused me not to mix with them for years before.

I saluted them on coming up, and asked Will how came he there, he answered, his life was worth no more than others, and his liberty as dear to him. I asked him if he thought to obtain it? He said he would, or lose his life. This was enough to put him in full confidence. Jack, I knew, was only a tool in the hands of Hark. It was quickly agreed we should commence at home (Mr. J. Travis') on that night, and until we had armed and equipped ourselves, and gathered sufficient force, neither age nor sex was to be spared, (which was invariably adhered to.) We remained at the feast, until about two hours in the night, when we went to the house and found Austin; they all went to the cider press and drank, except myself. On returning to the house, Hank went to the door with an axe, for the purpose of breaking it open, as we knew we were strong enough to murder the family, if they were awaked by the noise; but reflecting that it might create an alarm in the neighborhood, we determined to enter the house secretly, and murder them whilst sleeping. Hark got a ladder and set it against the chimney, on which I ascended, and hoisting a window, entered and came down stairs, unbarred the door, and removed the guns from their places. It was then observed that I must spill the first blood. On which, armed with a hatchet, and accompanied by Will, I entered my master's chamber, it being dark, I could not give a death blow, the hatchet glanced from his head, he sprang from the bed, and called his wife, it was his last word, Will laid him dead, with a blow of his axe, and Mrs. Travis shared the same fate, as she lay in bed. The murder of this family, five in number, was the work of a moment, not one of them awoke; there was a little infant sleeping in a cradle, that was forgotten, until we had left the house and gone some distance, when Henry and Will returned and killed it; we got here, four guns that would shoot, and several old muskets, with a pound or two of powder. We remained some time at the barn, where we paraded; I formed them in a line as soldiers, and after carrying them off to Mr. Salathur Francis', about six hundred yards distant, Sam and Will went to the door and knocked. Mr. Francis asked who was there, Sam replied it was him, and he had a letter for him, on which he got up and came to the door; they immediately seized him, and dragging him out a little from the door, he was dispatched by repeated blows on the head; there was no other white person in the family. We started from there for

Mrs. Reese's, maintaining the most perfect silence on our march, where finding the door unlocked, we entered, and murdered Mrs. Reese in her bed, while sleeping; her son awoke, but it was only to sleep the sleep of death; he had only time to say who is that, and he was no more. From Mrs. Reese's we went to Mrs. Turner's, a mile distant, which we reached about sunrise, on Monday morning. Henry, Austin, and Sam, went to the still, where, finding Mr. Peebles, Austin shot him, and the rest of us went to the house; as we approached, the family discovered us, and shut the door. Vain hope! Will, with one stroke of his axe, opened it, and we entered and found Mrs. Turner and Mrs. Newsome in the middle of a room, almost frightened to death. Will immediately killed Mrs. Turner, with one blow of his axe. I took Mrs. Newsome by the hand, and with the sword I had when I was apprehended, I struck her several blows over the head, but not being able to kill her, as the sword was dull. Will turning around and discovering it, despatched her also. A general destruction of property and search for money and ammunition, always succeeded the murders. By this time my company amounted to fifteen, and nine men mounted, who started for Mrs. Whitehead's, (the other six were to go through a by way to Mr. Bryant's, and rejoin us at Mrs. Whitehead's,) as we approached the house we discovered Mr. Richard Whitehead standing in the cotton patch, near the lane fence; we called him over into the land, and Will, the executioner, was near at hand, with his fatal axe, to send him to an untimely grave.

* * * .

I here proceeded to make some inquiries of him, after assuring him of the certain death that awaited him, and that concealment would only bring destruction on the innocent as well as guilty, of his own color, if he knew of any extensive or concerted plan. His answer was, I do not. When I questioned him as to the insurrection in North Carolina happening about the same time, he denied any knowledge of it; and when I looked him in the face as though I would search his inmost thoughts, he replied, "I see sir, you doubt my word; but can you not think the same ideas, and strange appearances about this time in the heaven's might prompt others, as well as myself, to this undertaking." I now had much conversation with and asked him many questions, having forborne to do so previously, except in the cases noted in parenthesis; but during his statement, I had, unnoticed by him, taken notes as to some particular circumstances, and having the advantage of his statement before me in writing, on the evening of the third day that I had been with him, I began a cross examination, and found his statement corroborated by every circumstance coming within my own knowledge or the confessions of others whom had been either killed or executed, and whom he had not seen nor had any knowledge since 22d of August last, he expressed himself fully satisfied as to the impracticability of his attempt. It has been said he was ignorant and cowardly, and that his object was to murder and rob for the purpose of obtaining money to make his escape. It is notorious, that he was never known to have a dollar in his life; to swear an oath, or drink a drop of spirits.

As to his ignorance, he certainly never had the advantages of education, but he can read and write, (it was taught him by his parents,) and for natural intelligence and quickness of apprehension, is surpassed by few men I have ever seen. As to his being a coward, his reason as given for not resisting Mr. Phipps, shews the decision of his character. When he saw Mr. Phipps present his gun, he said he knew it was impossible for him to escape as the woods were full of men; he therefore thought it was better to surrender, and trust to fortune for his escape. He is a complete fanatic, or plays his part most admirably. On other subjects he possesses an uncommon share of intelligence, with a mind capable of attaining any thing; but warped and perverted by the influence of early impressions. He is below the ordinary in stature, though strong and active, having the true negro face, every feature of which is strongly marked. I shall not attempt to describe the effect of his narrative, as told and commented on by himself, in the condemned hole of the prison. The calm, deliberate composure with which he spoke of his late deeds and intentions, the expression of his fiend-like face when excited by enthusiasm, still bearing the stains of the blood of helpless innocence about him; clothed with rags and covered with chains; yet daring to raise his manacled hands to heaven, with a spirit soaring above the attributes of man; I looked on him and my blood curdled in my veins.

* * *

The Commonwealth, *vs.* *Nat Turner.*	Charged with making insurrection, and plotting to take away the lives of divers free white persons, &c. on the 22d of August, 1831.

The court composed of ———, having met for the trial of Nat Turner, the prisoner was brought in and arraigned, and upon his arraignment pleaded *Not guilty;* saying to his counsel, that he did not feel so.

On the part of the Commonwealth, Levi Waller was introduced, who being sworn, deposed as follows: (*agreeably to Nat's own Confession.)* Col. Trezvant [the committing Magistrate] was then introduced, who being sworn, narrated Nat's Confession to him, as follows: *(his Confession as given to Mr. Gray.)* The prisoner introduced no evidence, and the case was submitted without argument to the court, who having found him guilty, Jeremiah Cobb, Esq. Chairman, pronounced the sentence of the court, in the following words: "Nat Turner! Stand up. Have you anything to say why sentence of death should not be pronounced against you?"

Ans. I have not. I have made a full confession to Mr. Gray, and I have nothing more to say.

Attend then to the sentence of the Court. You have been arraigned and tried before this court, and convicted of one of the highest crimes in our criminal code. You have been convicted of plotting in cold blood, the indiscriminate destruction of men, of helpless women, and of infant children. The evidence before us leaves not a shadow of doubt, but that your hands were often imbrued in the blood of the innocent; and your own confession tells us that they were stained with the blood of a master; in your own language, "too indulgent." Could I stop here, your crime would be sufficiently aggravated. But the original contriver of a plan, deep and deadly, one that never can be effected, you managed so far to put it into execution, as to deprive us of many of our most valuable citizens; and this was done when they were asleep, and defenceless; under circumstances shocking to humanity. And while upon this part of the subject, I cannot but call your attention to the poor misguided wretches who have gone before you. They are not few in number—they were your bosom associates; and the blood of all cries aloud, and calls upon you, as the author of their misfortune. Yes! You forced them unprepared, from Time to Eternity. Borne down by this load of guilt, your only justification is, that you were led away by fanaticism. If this be true, from my soul I pity you; and while you have my sympathies, I am, nevertheless called upon to pass the sentence of the court. The time between this and your execution, will necessarily be very short; and your only hope must be in another world. The judgment of the court is, that you be taken hence to the jail from whence you came, thence to the place of execution, and on Friday next, between the hours of 10 A.M. and 2 P.M. be hung by the neck until you are dead! dead! dead[!] and may the Lord have mercy upon your soul.*

**The Confessions of Nat Turner . . . As Fully and Voluntarily Made to Thomas R. Gray* (Baltimore, 1831), 7, 11-13, 18-19, 20-21.

CHAPTER FOUR

Negroes Without Masters

New York State Historical Association, Cooperstown, N.Y.

William Whipper, one of thousands of educated Negroes of the nineteenth century, was the son of a Negro servant girl and her white master. He grew up with his white half brother, helping in his father's lumber business in Pennsylvania. Eventually, Whipper inherited the business. A Negro without a master in the days when so many Negroes were slaves, Whipper was active in the abolitionist movement, helping to found an organization that was eventually to become The Americal Moral Reform Society. In 1837, twelve years before Thoreau's essay on Civil Disobedience, Whipper wrote an article for The Colored American, *entitled "An Address on Non Resistance to Offensive Aggression."*

INTRODUCTION

Negroes Without Masters

In pre-Civil War America practically all slaves were Negroes. But not all Negroes were slaves. These colored people without masters numbered 59,557 in 1790 and jumped to 488,070 in 1860. Of this nearly half a million nonslave Negroes, 250,787 were to be found in the South on the eve of the Civil War. Here they were known as "free Negroes" (a term which, strictly speaking, did not apply to the North after 1800, since virtually all of the Negroes in that section had been freed by then). Wherever he was to be found the free Negro exerted an influence, often negatively in the discriminations employed against him, but sometimes positively, as his own attitudes and actions affected the larger society.

Though the free Negro faced the high wall of color in Boston as well as in Charleston, the etiquette of race relations varied in its particulars from state to state, if not from community to community. As was to be expected, there were broad sectional patterns. In general, while the free Negro in the South found better job opportunities, he encountered more social and personal restrictions than the Negro in the North. A more accurate focus might be obtained, therefore, by viewing the free Negro in one sectional setting and then in another.

In the South the free Negro was unwanted, branded both a nuisance and a menace. He was regarded as a congenital delinquent, given to petty crime rather than honest labor, and hence likely to become a public charge. He was viewed as a threat to the institution of slavery, not only by arousing the slaves' dissatisfaction by his very presence, but by actively encouraging them to steal, to escape, and to plot against their masters.

All whites agreed that the free Negro must be kept in check. First and foremost of the controls required that he carry a certificate of freedom, stating his name, stature, complexion, and the manner in which his freedom had been obtained. A Negro without "free papers" was treated, as a rule, as a runaway slave. Even with his paper credentials in order, a free Negro risked servitude if he fell behind in his taxes, incurred debts, or was arrested as a vagabond.

Slave states formulated comprehensive codes of law concerning free Negroes. Invariably one section of these codes restricted the free Negro from moving from place to place. The Delaware code of 1852 stipulated that no free Negro not then located in Delaware could gain legal residence, and that those free Negroes who were residents could not return if they left the state for sixty days. Holding public office or voting was forbidden; in Delaware a free Negro who was merely present at any political gathering was guilty of a misdemeanor and fined $20.

Before the law the free Negro did not stand as an equal. In court, he could not testify against a white. In two states—Georgia and Florida—the law required the free Negro to have a white guardian to whom he had to report periodically. In seeking to assemble, even for religious purposes, the free Negroes faced a problem. In New Orleans the law-abiding, well-behaved First African Baptist Church had to constantly defend against the efforts of the civil and police authorities to issue ordinances of dissolution.

At nightfall the free Negro, like the slave, had to observe curfew. To use firearms, or any "warlike instrument," he had to obtain a special license; without one, he and the person who sold him the weapon would be fined. As might be expected, free Negroes were jim-crowed in public places and while traveling in public conveyances, even those as circumspect and well-to-do as William Johnson, a barbershop owner, landlord, and moneylender of Natchez, Mississippi.

Some free Negroes believed that they might find a better life by moving to the West. In 1816 a Richmond Negro, Christopher McPherson, wrote to Secretary of State James Monroe asking for a land grant from the federal government, to be paid for on easy terms. McPherson said that he spoke for "very many" free Negroes in Virginia and North Carolina. For a small number of free Negroes, the hardships they bore led them to prefer the lot of a slave as the lesser of two evils. Such was the case of William Bass of Marlborough, South Carolina, who in December 1859 petitioned the general assembly to permit him to take a master.

Despite legal and social proscriptions, the free Negro in the South was not without fair prospects of making a living. The perennial shortage of labor spelled opportunity for Negro workers in the mechanical trades. Some Negroes became well-to-do, such as Thomy Lafon, who amassed $500,000 in real estate. A fellow Louisianian, Cyprien Ricaud, owned ninety-one slaves on an Iberville Parish plantation, itself valued at a quarter of a million.

Masters like Ricaud and Martin Donatto of Plaquemine Brulé, Louisiana, owner of 75 slaves, were typical planters, viewing their bondmen as capital investments. But most Negro masters were small holders, and owned slaves who were relatives or close friends who, by law, would have had to leave the state if freed. The practice of caring for one another, particularly in sickness and death, was characteristic of the free Negro in the South. Benevolent societies were common, Baltimore having thirty-five in 1835. Free Negroes operated schools in cities like Charleston where the authorities winked at the law.

Leading in education, as in many other areas, were the Negroes in New Orleans, some of whom had gone to Paris for their schooling. New Orleans had two colored regiments—a militia which antedated the acquisition of Louisiana by the United States. A product of New Orleans, Norbert Rillieux, invented a vacuum-cup in 1846 which revolutionized sugar-refining methods. A year earlier a group of seventeen New Orleans Negroes published a 215-page anthology, *Les Cenelles,* 82 verses of which were written in French.

Although the Negro in the North may have been impressed by the achievements of southern Negroes, he would not have changed locales. He counted himself fortunate to be outside the cotton kingdom. But in one vital area he was at a comparative disadvantage with the southern Negro—in the world of work. In the North, the colored job-seeker faced bitter competition from whites, particularly the successive waves of immigrants. As a rule the Negro was restricted to the fields of domestic service and common labor. There were few Negroes holding skilled jobs inasmuch as white craftsmen would not take on a colored boy as apprentice. Even white businessmen, like Arthur Tappan of New York, who were sympathetic to Negroes, offered them only menial jobs. Trade unions barred Negro membership.

The Negro in the North faced legal disabilities. In five states he could not testify against whites; except in Massachusetts he was ineligible for jury service. Many states would not permit him to vote; New York would do so only if he owned real estate worth $250 or more. Even in communities which did not expressly forbid it by law, voting by Negroes was infrequent, public sentiment being a sufficiently strong deterrent. A few states prohibited his entry unless he could furnish bond as a guarantee of good conduct.

Throughout the free states the Negro faced discrimination in public places and on public carriers. Customarily only whites were admitted to theatres and concert halls, even when the performing artist might be Elizabeth Taylor Greenfield, the "Black Swan." In education the Negro faced more than ordinary difficulties. Negro students who visited white colleges seeking admission were invariably told, according to Theodore Wright, a Negro clergyman, "There is no rule to exclude you, but we think you had better not apply."

In private organizations the color line was even more sharply drawn. Church groups followed the general pattern of Negro exclusion. Even the Quakers, with their long record of anti-slavery activity, had Negro benches in their meeting halls. Sarah Douglass of Philadelphia, principal of the preparatory department of the Institute for Colored Youth, wrote in 1837 that she had not attended the Arch Street meeting for four years, although her mother went once a week and "frequently she has a *whole long bench* to herself."

But if the doctrine of white supremacy was held almost as tenaciously above the Mason-Dixon Line as below it, the Negro in the North fared better in the exercise of personal freedom and in the much greater opportunities for self expression. To begin with, since slavery had passed away in the North, a Negro without a master posed no threat to an established, flourishing institution.

This, combined with the sparseness of the colored population in the North, made for a degree of indifference, if not tolerance, not possible in the slave states.

Thus freed from constant surveillance, the Negro in the North founded organizations of his own. He had his mutual aid societies, like the Free African Society, established in Philadelphia in 1787, and the Sons of the African Society, established eleven years later in Boston. The most influential of the mutual aid groups were the secret fraternal orders like the Masons (founded in 1787) and the Odd Fellows (founded in 1843). Other organizations striving for racial betterment included the Negro literary societies, which numbered at least forty-five during the antebellum period. Negro improvement organizations stressed self-reliance; they exhorted their members to grasp those opportunities which did exist, and they pleaded with the improvident not to waste their earnings.

The most influential of the Negro organizations was the church. Unwilling to attend white churches because of their "Negro pews," worshippers formed congregations of their own. In 1816 Negro Methodists severed their organizational ties with whites. Among the Baptists there was a similar movement toward independence. The Negro church was a multi-purpose agency, serving not only as a temple of worship, but as a social center, a meeting place for reformist groups, a sanctuary for escaped slaves, and a schoolhouse.

Churchmen like Richard Allen were key figures in the colored convention movement, a movement designed to enlist concerted action of Negro leaders. Beginning in 1830 at Bethel church in Philadelphia, these conventions were held annually, with delegates from most of the free states. They addressed themselves to public issues affecting Negroes. National conventions were supplemented by those on the state and local levels. A California convention, for example, might address itself to such grievances as the state's refusal to let Negroes testify against whites, and to acquire unclouded title to landed property. Invariably, the conventions, whether national or local, discussed the colonization question. As a rule the delegates voted overwhelmingly against proposals for sending the colored people out of the country. But in the fifties, as the lot of the Negroes seemed to worsen, the colonization advocates among them appeared to expand their slim ranks.

To combat discrimination some Negroes formed separate, independent communities. Scattered throughout the northern states and Canada, such organized settlements sought to develop among their membership a sense of civic responsibility and a spirit of "do-it-yourself." Invariably they established schools, later adding manual labor instruction to curriculums. These all-Negro communities stressed moral uplift, exhorting the settlers to observe the Sabbath Day and to abstain from strong drink. Such groups were generally short-lived, due to faulty organization, inept leadership, or the hostility of the surrounding communities. But in truth most of them were conceived of as temporary projects designed to prove that the Negro was worthy of full membership in the larger society.

Just as some sympathetic whites had contributed funds to the all-Negro settlements, so others assisted Negroes in their local communities. In 1832 a group of whites in Hartford, Connecticut, founded a Benevolent Society for Colored Children designed to "take under care" orphans and youngsters whose parents were unable or unwilling to do so. In 1845 an Asylum for the Poor Colored Orphans of Ohio was chartered at Cincinnati, a local newspaper urging that whites support it because "our beautiful republican laws do not extend the same blessing to *colored* children that they do to *white*." In New York a group of whites founded a Negro home in 1840, supporting it by subscriptions, donations, and legacies. For the year 1851 the receipts totaled $15,875.

Despite his own problems the Negro in the North was not unmindful of the plight of the slave. "The free people of Color, with few exceptions, are true to their brethren in bond, and determined to remain by them whatever the cost," wrote John Scoble in 1853 in a letter from New York to his fellow members of the British and Foreign Anti-Slavery Society.

To strike at human bondage some northern Negroes adopted the pocketbook approach, pledging themselves to buy nothing grown or manufactured by slave labor. This free produce movement, although continuously and strongly advocated in reformist circles, was never effective. Generally it was too difficult to obtain a substitute for slave-labor products—cotton goods, sugar, and rice—except at a prohibitive cost. But even though the results were meager it was emotionally satisfying, no doubt, to be a member of the "Colored Free Produce Society of Pennsylvania," pledged to lessen the value of slave labor and to "destroy the gains of the hardened oppressor."

Many Negroes in the North assisted slaves in raising money to buy off their masters. These liberty-seeking efforts were noted by Theodore Weld in a letter, March 18, 1834, to Lewis Tappan, a fellow reformer: "Of the almost 3000 blacks in Cincinnati more than three fourths of the adults are emancipated slaves, who worked out their own freedom. Besides these, multitudes are toiling to purchase their friends, who are now in slavery."

Northern Negroes worked in the Underground Railroad—the organized movement designed to assist runaways. Levi Coffin, best known and most active of the white Underground Railroad organizers, employed Negroes in his operations, particularly after he moved to Cincinnati in 1847. "We have several trusty colored men—who owned no property and who could lose nothing in a prosecution—who understood Underground Railroad matters," wrote Coffin, "and we generally got them to act as drivers." The Underground Railroad was exciting with its stealthy night-rides, and dangerous with its prowling kidnapers. But once a slave reached safety he was made to feel that the risk had been well worth running. In some cases he would be showered with gifts and money (thus inducing some unscrupulous free Negroes to pose as runaways). In many cases he would be taken under the wing of a vigilance committee, whose purpose was to help him begin life as a free man.

LIBERTY LINE.
NEW ARRANGEMENT---NIGHT AND DAY.
The improved and splendid Locomotives, Clarkson and Lundy, with their trains fitted up in the best style of accommodation for passengers, will run their regular trips during the present season, between the borders of the Patriarchal Dominion and Libertyville, Upper Canada. Gentlemen and Ladies, who may wish to improve their health or circumstances, by a northern tour, are respectfully invited to give us their patronage.
SEATS FREE, *irrespective of color.*
Necessary Clothing furnished gratuitously to such as have "*fallen among thieves.*"
"Hide the outcasts—let the oppressed go free."—*Bible.*
☞For seats apply at any of the trap doors, or to the conductor of the train.
J. CROSS, *Proprietor.*
N. B. For the special benefit of Pro-Slavery Police Officers, an extra heavy wagon for Texas, will be furnished, whenever it may be necessary, in which they will be forwarded as dead freight, to the "Valley of Rascals," always at the risk of the owners.
☞Extra Overcoats provided for such of them as are afflicted with protracted *chilly-phobia.*

Primarily Negro-founded and Negro-run, vigilance committees sought to find a home and a job for the fugitive, and to protect him from seizure.

The northern Negro also actively participated in the abolitionist crusade, the organized effort to efface slavery from the American scene. His role in this significant movement will be noted in the chapter which follows.

The Free Negro in the South

75

SELLING NEGROES BACK INTO SLAVERY

Because he was an unwanted element, the free Negro in the South faced grave dangers and hardships. The most serious of these by far was the ever-present jeopardy to his freedom. In Maryland in 1816 a committee of Quakers journeyed to Annapolis with a petition to outlaw the practice of selling free Negroes back into slavery. Despite button-holing the members of the assembly and exhorting them individually, the Quakers' bill was rejected on the grounds that it endangered property in slaves. The Quakers took heart, however, by the closeness of the vote. Their petition follows.

TO THE GENERAL ASSEMBLY OF MARYLAND [1816]

The memorial of the representatives of the yearly meeting of Friends held at Baltimore, Respectfully Sheweth That your memorialists have views with much sympathy and commiserations, the sufferings to which certain descriptions of the affrican race continue to be subjected: the particular circumstances to which your memorialists are engaged to request the attention of the Legislature, is the mournful condition to which free persons of colour and such as are entitled to be free at a future time in this State continue to be exposed from persons who are engaged in the trade of supplying the Southern States with Slaves, being still in the practice under various circumstances of fraud evidence of carrying such out of the jurisdiction of the laws of this State.

Your memorialists are not insensible that this subject has from time to time received the attention of the legislature and that several laws have already been papered for the protection of these people and for the punishment of such persons as are detected in attempting to carry them off for the purpose of enslaving them; whilst your memorialists view with much satisfaction this evidence of the influence of justice and humanity they feel themselves bound to represent to the legislature that those laws are upon experience found to be insufficient to secure the objects proposed, and that some further and more effectual restraints are become necessary. Your memorialists, therefore earnestly solicit the further attention of the Legislature to the subject and that such further security may be extended to these suffering people as in its wisdom may be deemed expedient and proper.

Signed on behalf of the representatives aforesaid.

Evan Thomas, Gerald Brooke, Emnion Williams,
David Preston, Roger Brooke, Izak Procter,
Gerald T. Hopkins, John Janney, Edward Stabler,
Jonathan Ellicote, Philip E. Thomas, Elijha Tyson, George Ellicott.*

76

REMOVAL OF FREEDMEN

Every slave state made a strong effort to restrict the number of free Negroes. Hence these states, as a rule, required the removal of a slave who became free. Indeed, some Negroes held their wives or children as nominal slaves inasmuch as it would have been necessary to send them out of the state if they were emancipated. In Halifax, North Carolina, the plight of a family which included newly freed slaves was the subject of a letter to Senator Willie P. Magnum from Thomas Burges, a local attorney and former member of the state legislature. Dated March 26, 1832, the letter reveals the personal equation in the formal law, the flesh-and-blood consequences implicit in the detached language and sonorous tones of the statutes.

May I further trespass on your kindness by asking an additional favor—There resides in this village a Free man of color, of exemplary conduct & irreproachable character, who is a good Barber & musician, & has a Wife & five small children,—all of whom, by his industry, & economy, he has purchased from their former master—as he cannot liberate them by the laws of this State, he is very desirous to remove with his family, to some Town in the North Western States, where he can set his Wife & children free, raise & support

---

*Original manuscript from the Bliss Forbush Collection relating to the Quakers and Slavery, Morgan State College, Baltimore, Md.

them by his calling, & be exempt from the oppression & restraint necessarily incident to a slave holding State.—He has asked my advice as to the place of his removal, & being ignorant of the local laws of the Free States in relation to colored people, & not knowing where would be the most eligible spot to locate himself & pursue with most advantage his occupations, I have, of course, declined advising him on the subject.—But feeling considerable interest in his Welfare, I have taken the liberty to request of you to procure the necessary information from your acquaintances in congress, & write me the result—I propose myself taking an excursion, the ensuing summer, thro' some of the Western States, & if your report be favorable, this free fellow will accompany me—

* * *

Accept assurances of my esteem & respect—

T Burges*

77

PETITION FOR LUCY ANN

Lucy Ann, manumitted by will in King William County, Virginia, was ordered to leave the state upon pain of being returned to slavery. The case came to the attention of the legislature when her husband, a skillful pilot of the Chesapeake waters, sought relief in a petition dated December 19, 1825. It may be noted that although he was a Pamunky Indian and that his wife was of mixed parentage, these factors bore no legal weight.

Your petitioner, John Dungee, and Lucy Ann, his wife, who are free persons of colour residing in King William County ask permission most respectfully to represent to the legislature of Virginia. That your petitioner John Dungee (who is descended from the aborigines of this dominion) was born free and 'tis his birth-right to reside therein. That having many relations and connections in this section of the county in which he was raised, all his feelings and attachments have bound him to Virginia and he has never for a moment entertained the idea of leaving the land of his forbears. . . . . Your petitioner Lucy Ann is the illigitimate daughter of the late Edmund Littlepage Esq., a highly respected and wealthy citizen, who by his last will and testament and as an act of justice and atonement for an error of an unguarded moment bequeathed to his innocent offspring the boon of freedom and a pecuniary legacy of $1,000.00. . . . . During the last year your petitioners urged by the strongest and purest attachment to each other were lawfully united to each other in matrimony and fondly flattered themselves that they had the prospect of passing through life with a portion of happiness that is decreed to but few. Only a few months had passed away, however, before your petitioners were aroused from their halcyon state by being informed that by the laws of the land it

*Henry T. Shanks, ed., *The Papers of William Person Mangum* (5 vols., Raleigh, State Department of Archives and History, North Carolina, 1950-1956), I, 518.

was necessary that your petitioner Lucy Ann should remove from the Commonwealth or be sold into slavery. The intellegent and humane can at once imagine how appalling the information was to your petitioners, how frightful the consequence of a rigid and unbending enforcement of the law, how totally destructive of the right, the interest, and happiness, of your petitioners. An enumeration of the disasterious effects of the enforcement of the law in this case is almost unnecessary to your enlightened body, but they will briefly state, that if they are compelled to leave this land your petitioner John in a moment loses the labor of his life in acquiring an accurate knowledge of the Chesapeake Bay and of the rivers which disembark themselves therein by which knowledge he is rendered useful to himself and others and the legacy bequeathed to your petitioner Lucy Ann be lost or of little value to them. They will be torn from their parents, relatives, and friends, and driven in a state of destitution to migrate to a foreign land.*

Free Negroes of Substance

78

A NEGRO CHURCH IN SAVANNAH

Not all free Negroes in the South led lives of desperation. On the contrary, many of them found strength and meaning in their churches. In the South the free Negro's greatest outlet was not the school, the lodge, the literary society, or the reformist organizations. The free Negro poured most of his energies, both emotional and spiritual, into the church, mainly the Baptist and Methodist denominations. Some of the worship services conducted by Negroes were models of propriety, in tone no less than in doctrine. Charles Lyell, the British traveler, was deeply impressed by the service he witnessed at a Baptist church in Savannah.

Next day, I attended afternoon service in a Baptist church at Savannah, in which I found that I was the only white man, the congregation consisting of about 600 negroes, of various shades, most of them very dark. As soon as I entered I was shown to a seat reserved for strangers, near the preacher. First the congregation all joined, both men and women, very harmoniously in a hymn, most of them having evidently good ears for music, and good voices. The singing was followed by prayers, not read, but delivered without notes by a negro of pure African blood, a gray-headed venerable-looking man, with a fine sonorous voice, named Marshall. He, as I learnt afterward, has the reputation of being one of their best preachers, and he concluded by addressing to them a sermon, also without notes, in good style, and for the most part in good English; so much so, as to make me doubt whether a few ungrammatical phrases in the negro idiom might not have been purposely introduced for the sake of bringing the subject home to their family thoughts. He got very successfully

*"Documentary Evidence of the Relations of Indians and Negroes," by James Hugo Johnson from *Journal of Negro History*, XIV, (January 1929), pp. 30–31. Reprinted by permission of The Associated Publishers, Inc.

through one flight about the gloom of the valley of the shadow of death, and, speaking of the probationary state of a pious man left for a while to his own guidance, and when in danger of failing saved by the grace of God, he compared it to an eagle teaching her newly fledged offspring to fly, by carrying it up high into the air, then dropping it, and, if she sees it falling to the earth, darting with the speed of lightning to save it before it reaches the ground. Whether any eagles really teach their young to fly in this manner, I leave the ornithologist to decide; but when described in animated and picturesque language, yet by no means inflated, the imagery was well calculated to keep the attention of his hearers awake. He also inculcated some good practical maxims of morality, and told them they were to look to a future state of rewards and punishments in which God would deal impartially with "the poor and the rich, the black man and the white."

I went afterward, in the evening, to a black Methodist church, where I and two others were the only white men in the whole congregation; but I was less interested, because the service and preaching was performed by a white minister. Nothing in my whole travels gave me a higher idea of the capabilities of the negroes, than the actual progress which they have made, even in a part of a slave state, where they outnumber the whites, than this Baptist meeting. To see a body of African origin, who had joined one of the denominations of Christians, and built a church for themselves—who had elected a pastor of their own race, and secured him an annual salary, from whom they were listening to a good sermon, scarcely, if at all, below the average standard of the compositions of white ministers—to hear the whole service respectably, and the singing admirably performed, surely marks an astonishing step in civilization.*

*Charles Lyell, *A Second Visit to the United States of North America* (2 vols., New York, 1868), II, 14-15.

79

THE NEW ORLEANS NEGRO MILITIA

Some free Negroes possessed considerable worldly goods, including holdings in slaves. A group of Negroes in New Orleans, which was described by Governor William Claiborne as having "extensive connections and much property to defend," had formed itself into a militia. When New Orleans was threatened by the British in the War of 1812, Claiborne wrote to General Andrew Jackson recommending that the Negroes be enrolled. Jackson, badly in need of men and persuaded somewhat by Claiborne's letter, issued a proclamation September 21, 1814, inviting free Negroes to bear arms against the British. Jackson's invitation did not go begging, for the Negro militia was mustered into the service of the United States by the middle of December. Jackson reviewed the Negro troops on December 18, 1814, and sent them an inspiring message immediately thereafter. After the battle, January 8, 1815, was won decisively by the Americans, Jackson's headquarters issued a general order stating that "the two corps of colored volunteers had . . . not disappointed the hopes that were formed of their courage and perseverance." Below is the proclamation Jackson sent inviting enlistment.

PROCLAMATION

TO THE FREE COLORED INHABITANTS OF LOUISIANA

Through a mistaken policy you have heretofore been deprived of a participation in the glorious struggle for national rights in which our country is engaged. This no longer shall exist.

As sons of freedom, you are now called upon to defend our most inestimable blessing. As Americans, your country looks with confidence to her adopted children, for a valorous support, as a faithful return for the advantages enjoyed under her mild and equitable government. As fathers, husbands and brothers, you are summoned to rally round the standard of the Eagle, to defend all which is dear in existence.

Your country, although calling for your exertions, does not wish you to engage in her cause, without amply remunerating you for the services rendered. Your intelligent minds are not to be led away by false representations—Your love of honor would cause you to despise the man who should attempt to deceive you. In the sincerity of a soldier, and the language of truth I address you.

To every noble hearted, generous, freeman of color, volunteering to serve during the present contest with Great Britain, and no longer, there will be paid the same bounty in money and lands, now received by the white soldiers of the U. States, viz. $124 in money, and 160 acres of land. The noncommissioned officers and privates will also be entitled to the same monthly pay and daily rations, and clothes furnished to any American soldier.

On enrolling yourselves in companies, the major-general commanding will select officers for your government, from your white fellow citizens. Your non-commissioned officers will be appointed from among yourselves.

Due regard will be paid to the feelings of freemen and soldiers. You will not, by being associated with white men in the same corps, be exposed to improper comparisons or unjust sarcasm. As a distinct, independent battalion or regiment, pursuing the path of glory, you will, undivided, receive the applause and gratitude of your countrymen.

To assure you of the sincerity of my intentions and my anxiety to engage your invaluable services to our country, I have communicated my wishes to the governor of Louisiana, who is fully informed as to the manner of enrolment, and will give you every necessary information on the subject of this address.
Headquarters, 7th military district,
Mobile, Sept. 21st 1814.

Andrew Jackson,
Maj. gen. commanding.*

The Free Negro in the North

80

A NEGRO CLERGYMAN ON PREJUDICE

In the North, as in the South, strong anti-Negro sentiment was pervasive. Perhaps in the North there were fewer who were openly hostile to the Negro who was not a slave, and doubtless in the North there were more who were fundamentally sympathetic to him than in the South. But few Northerners entertained any uncertainty or raised any question about his innate inferiority. The idea of Negro inferiority was held by all segments of the population. A Negro clergyman, H. Easton of Hartford, Connecticut, commented on the common practice of downgrading the colored populace.

I have no language wherewith to give slavery, and its auxiliaries, an adequate description, as an efficient cause of the miseries it is capable of producing. It seems to possess a kind of omnipresence. It follows its victims in every avenue of life.

The principle assumes still another feature equally destructive. It makes the colored people subserve almost every foul purpose imaginable. Negro or nigger, is an approbrious term, employed to impose contempt upon them as an inferior race, and also to express their deformity of person. Nigger lips, nigger shins, and nigger heels, are phrases universally common among the juvenile class of society, and full well understood by them; they are early learned to think of these expressions, as they are intended to apply to colored people, and as being expressive or descriptive of the odious qualities of their mind and body. These impressions received by the young, grow with their growth, and strengthen with their strength. The term in itself, would be perfectly harmless, were it used only to distinguish one class of society from another; but it is not used with that intent; the practical definition is quite different in England to what it is here, for here, it flows from the fountain of purpose to injure. It is this baneful seed which is sown in the tender soil of youthful minds, and there cultivated by the hand of a corrupt immoral policy.

**Niles' Weekly Register,* December 3, 1814.

The universality of this kind of education is well known to the observing. Children in infancy receive oral instruction from the nurse. The first lessons given are, Johnny, Billy, Mary, Sally, (or whatever the name may be,) go to sleep, if you don't the old *nigger* will care you off; don't you cry—Hark; the old *niggers'* coming—how ugly you are, you are worse than a little *nigger*. This is a specimen of the first lessons given.

The second is generally given in the domestic circle; in some families it is almost the only method of correcting their children. To inspire their half grown misses and masters to improvement, they are told that if they do this or that, or if they do thus and so, they will be poor or ignorant as a *nigger*; or that they will be black as a *nigger;* or have no more credit than a *nigger;* that they will have hair, lips, feet, or something of the kind, like a *nigger*. If doubt is entertained by any, as to the truth of what I write, let them travel twenty miles in any direction in this country, especially in the free States, and his own sense of hearing will convince him of its reality.

See nigger's thick lips—see his flat nose—nigger eye shine—that slick looking nigger—nigger, where you get so much coat?—that's a nigger priest—are sounds emanating from little urchins of Christian villagers, which continually infest the feelings of colored travellers, like the pestiferous breath of young devils; and full grown persons, and sometimes professors of religion, are not unfrequently heard to join in the concert.

A third mode of this kind of instruction is not altogether oral. Higher classes are frequently instructed in school rooms by refering them to the nigger-seat, and are sometimes threatened with being made to sit with the niggers, if they do not behave.*

81

OPPOSITION TO A NEGRO COLLEGE

Since the Negro was regarded as inferior, the mixing of white and colored in the classroom was unpopular in most communities. Oneida Institute of Science and Industry, established at Whitesboro, near Utica, New York, in 1827, welcomed Negroes, but it stood almost alone. The townspeople of Canaan, New Hampshire, irate over the interracial policy of Noyes Academy, used oxen teams to physically transplant the school to another site in 1834. "We view with abhorrence," said the Canaanites in a public meeting, "the attempt to establish in this town a school for the instruction of the sable sons and daughters of Africa, in common with our sons and daughters." In Connecticut there was a similar hostility to mixed schools. When Prudence Crandall admitted a Negro girl, Sarah Harris, to her boarding school in Canterbury, she encountered a bitter protest, eventually forcing her to close the school. Equally strong opposition to separate schools for Negroes was prevalent in the state. A town meeting in New Haven voiced its disapproval of a manual labor school for colored boys by an overwhelming majority. The New Haven Palladium ran an account which mirrored local feeling.

---

*H. Easton, *A Treatise on the Intellectual Character, and the Civil and Political Condition of the Colored People of the United States, and the Prejudices Towards Them* (Boston, 1837), 40-41.

"NEGRO COLLEGE"

Our readers, no doubt, will be surprised at the caption of this paragraph, and will wonder what we mean by "Negro College." We will inform them that we mean, without any jesting, to say that there has been an attempt, a serious attempt, to get up an institution in this place for the education of colored men. The blacks for a few years past have been treated with attention and kindness by the inhabitants of this city. Two or three of our citizens have devoted much time and money for bettering their condition, but the zeal of a few has constantly increased, until a project has been brought forward, which if carried into execution would ruin the prosperity of the city. New Haven was fixed upon, by the convention held in Philadelphia some time since, for the location of a black college. Our citizens called a public meeting to take the subject into consideration, and the following resolutions were advocated by *judge Daggett, N. Smith, R. I. Ingersoll* and *I. H. Townsend*, esqrs. and adopted by about 700 freemen. The rev. *S. S. Jocelyn* and three others opposed, and voted against them.

At a city meeting, duly warned and held at the city hall, in the city of New Haven, on Saturday, the 10th day of September, 1831, to take into consideration a project for the establishment in this city a college for the education of *colored youth*, the following preamble and resolutions were unanimously adopted, viz:

Whereas endeavors are now making to establish a college in this city for the education of the colored population of the United States, the West Indies, and other countries adjacent; and in connection with this establishment the immediate abolition of slavery in the United States is not only recommended and encouraged by the advocates of the proposed college, but demanded as a right; and whereas an omission to notice these measures may be construed as implying either indifference to, or approbation of the same:

Resolved: That it is expedient that the sentiments of our citizens should be expressed on these subjects, and that the calling of this meeting by the mayor and aldermen is warmly approved by the citizens of this place.

Resolved, That in as much as slavery does not exist in Connecticut, and wherever permitted in other states, depends on the municipal laws of the state which allows it, and over which neither any other state nor the congress of the United States has any control, that the propagation of sentiments favorable to the immediate emancipation of slaves, in disregard of the civil institutions of the states in which they belong, and as auxiliary thereto, the cotemperaneous founding of colleges for educating colored people, is an unwarrantable and dangerous interference with the internal concerns of the other states, and ought to be discouraged.

And whereas, in the opinion of this meeting, Yale college, the institutions for the education of females, and the other schools already existing in this city, are important to the community and the general interests of science, and as such have been deservedly patronized by the public, and the establishment of a college in the same place to educate the colored population, is incompatible with the prosperity if not the existence of the present institutions of learning, and will be destructive of the best interests of the city. And believing, as we do, that if the establishment of such a college in any part of the country were deemed expedient, it should never be imposed on any community without their consent:

Therefore, resolved, by the mayor, aldermen, common council, and freemen of the city of New Haven, in city meeting assembled, That we will resist the establishment of the proposed college in this place by every lawful means.

And on motion it was voted that the proceedings of this meeting be signed by the mayor, and countersigned by the clerk, and published in all the newspapers of this city.

Dennis Kimberly, *mayor**

82

THE FIRST ALL-NEGRO CHURCH

Taking its cue from the secular world, the church did not welcome the Negro, as a rule. A dark-skinned person entering a white church was met at the door and ushered to a special reserved section. The unwillingness of Negro worshippers to accept Jim Crow seating arrangements led to the founding of all-Negro churches. The dramatic incident that sparked the withdrawal of Negro Methodists from white congregations took place at St. George's Church in Philadelphia on a November Sunday in 1787. Richard Allen, one of those who walked out, relates the story in the following selection. In 1816 when the Negroes organized a separate branch of Methodism (the African Methodist Episcopal Church) they chose Allen as bishop.

A number of us usually attended St. George's church in Fourth street; and when the colored people began to get numerous in attending the church, they moved us from the seats we usually sat on, and placed us around the wall, and on Sabbath morning we went to church and the sexton stood at the door, and told us to go in the gallery. He told us to go, and we would see where to sit. We expected to take the seats over the ones we formerly occupied below, not knowing any better. We took those seats. Meeting had begun, and they were nearly done singing, and just as we got to the seats, the elder said, "Let us pray." We had not been long upon our knees before I heard considerable scuffling and low talking. I raised my head up and saw one of the trustees, H—— M——, having hold of the Rev. Absalom Jones, pulling him up off of his knees, and saying, "You must get up—you must not kneel here." Mr. Jones replied, "Wait until prayer is over." Mr. H—— M—— said "No, you must get up now, or I will call for aid and force you away." Mr. Jones said, "Wait until prayer is over, and I will get up and trouble you no more." With that he beckoned to one of the other trustees, Mr. L—— S—— to come to his assistance. He came, and went to William White to pull him up. By this time prayer was over, and we all went

---

**Niles Weekly Register*, October 1, 1831.

out of the church in a body, and they were no more plagued with us in the church. This raised a great excitement and inquiry among the citizens, in so much that I believe they were ashamed of their conduct. But my dear Lord was with us, and we were filled with fresh vigor to get a house erected to worship God in. Seeing our forlorn and distressed situation, many of the hearts of our citizens were moved to urge us forward; notwithstanding we had subscribed largely towards finishing St. George's church, in building the gallery and laying new floors, and just as the house was made comfortable, we were turned out from enjoying the comforts of worshipping therein. We then hired a store-room, and held worship by ourselves. Here we were pursued with threats of being disowned, and read publicly out of meeting if we did continue worship in the place we had hired; but we believed the Lord would be our friend. We got subscription papers out to raise money to build the house of the Lord. By this time we had waited on Dr. Rush and Mr. Robert Ralston, and told them of our distressing situation. We considered it a blessing that the Lord had put it into our hearts to wait upon those gentlemen. They pitied our situation, and subscribed largely towards the church, and were very friendly towards us, and advised us how to go on. We appointed Mr. Ralston our treasurer. Dr. Rush did much for us in public by his influence. I hope the name of Dr. Benjamin Rush and Robert Ralston will never be forgotten among us. They were the first two gentlemen who espoused the cause of the oppressed, and aided us in building the house of the Lord for the poor Africans to worship in. Here was the beginning and rise of the first African church in America.*

83

JOB DISCRIMINATION

Some urban Negroes held desirable jobs despite the obstacles. But as a group, Negroes were generally confined to the unskilled jobs—those in which the pay was low and the displacement was high. To break out of this employment strait-jacket Frederick Douglass urged Negroes to seek vocational training in an editorial entitled, "Learn Trades or Starve!" Douglass was an escaped slave who, in 1841, joined the ranks of the reformers. His natural oratorical powers and his facility with words, spoken or written, had made him the most prominent and listened-to Negro of his day. His well-edited weekly (The North Star, *later* Frederick Douglass' Paper) *heightened his influence. Douglass headed an effort in 1854 to establish a manual labor school, but the amount of money raised was woefully inadequate. However, a persuasive case could be made for the idea of training the hand as well as developing the mind, as this editorial by Douglass attests.*

These are the obvious alternatives sternly presented to the free colored people of the United States. It is idle, yea even ruinous, to disguise the matter for a single hour longer; every day begins and ends with the impressive lesson that free negroes must learn trades, or die.

*George A. Singleton, ed., *The Life Experience and Gospel Labors of the Rt. Rev. Richard Allen* (New York, Abingdon Press, 1960), 25-26.

In undesirable areas of work the Negro was able to hold his own. Here the Russian artist Pavel Svinin portrays chimney sweeps and their master being questioned by a passing couple. The year is about 1812, in Philadelphia.

The old avocations, by which colored men obtained a livelihood, are rapidly, unceasingly and inevitably passing into other hands; every hour sees the black man elbowed out of employment by some newly arrived emigrant, whose hunger and whose color are thought to give him a better title to the place; and so we believe it will continue to be until the last prop is levelled beneath us.

As a black man, we say if we cannot stand up, let us fall down. We desire to be a man among men while we do live; and when we cannot, we wish to die. It is evident, painfully evident to every reflecting mind, that the means of living, for colored men, are becoming more and more precarious and limited. Employments and callings, formerly monopolized by us, are so no longer.

White men are becoming house-servants, cooks and stewards on vessels—at hotels.—They are becoming porters, stevedores, wood-sawyers, hod-carriers, brick-makers, white-washers and barbers, so that the blacks can scarcely find the means of subsistence—a few years ago, and a *white* barber would have been a curiosity—now their poles stand on every street. Formerly blacks were almost the exclusive coachmen in wealthy families: this is so no longer; white men are now employed, and for aught we see, they fill their servile station with an obsequiousness as profound as that of the blacks. The readiness and ease with which they adapt themselves to these conditions ought not to be lost sight of by the colored people.

The meaning is very important, and we should learn it. We are taught our insecurity by it. Without the means of living, life is a curse, and leaves us at the mercy of the oppressor to become his debased slaves. Now, colored men, what do you mean to do, for you must do something? The American Colonization Society tells you to go to Liberia. Mr. Bibbs tells you to go to Canada. Others tell you to go to school. We tell you to go to work; and to work you must go or die. Men are not valued in this country, or in any country, for what they *are;* they are valued for what they can *do.* It is in vain that we talk about being men, if we do not the work of men. We must become valuable to society in other departments of industry than those servile ones from which we are rapidly being excluded. We must show that we can *do* as well as *be;* and to this end we must learn trades. When we can build as well as live in houses; when we can *make* as well as *wear* shoes; when we can produce as well as consume wheat, corn and rye—then we shall become valuable to society. Society is a hard-hearted affair.—With it the helpless may expect no higher dignity than that of paupers. The individual must lay society under obligation to him, or society will honor him only as a stranger and sojourner. *How* shall this be done? In this manner: use every means, strain every nerve to master some important mechanical art. At present, the facilities for doing this are few—institutions of learning are more readily opened to you than the work-shop; but the Lord helps them who will help themselves, and we have no doubt that new facilities will be presented as we press forward.

If the alternative were presented to us of learning a trade or of getting an education, we would learn the trade, for the reason, that with the trade we could get the education, while with the education we could not get the trade. What we, as a people, need most, is the means for our own elevation.—An educated colored man, in the United States, unless he has within him the heart of a hero, and is willing to engage in a life-long battle for his rights, as a man, finds few inducements to remain in this country. He is isolated in the land of his birth—debarred by his color from congenial association with whites; he is equally cast out by the ignorance of the *blacks.* The remedy for this must comprehend the elevation of the masses; and this can only be done by putting the mechanic arts within the reach of colored men.

We have now stated pretty strongly the case of our colored countrymen; perhaps some will say, *too* strongly; but we know whereof we affirm.

In view of this state of things, we appeal to the abolitionists, What boss anti-slavery mechanic will take a black boy into his wheelwright's shop, his blacksmith's shop, his joiner's shop, his cabinet shop? Here is something *practical;* where are the whites and where are the blacks that will respond to it? Where are the anti-slavery milliners and seamstresses that will take colored girls and teach them trades, by which they can obtain an honorable living? The fact that we have made good cooks, good waiters, good barbers, and whitewashers, induces the belief that we may excel in higher branches of industry. *One thing is certain: we must find new methods of obtaining a livelihood, for the old ones are failing us very fast.*

We, therefore, call upon the intelligent and thinking ones amongst us, to urge upon the colored people within their reach, in all seriousness, the duty and the necessity of giving their children useful and lucrative trades, by which they may commence the battle of life with weapons commensurate with the exigencies of the conflict.*

Adjustment and Advance

84

NEGRO REJECTION OF COLONIZATION

The discriminations faced by the free Negro were numerous and varied but they do not tell his complete story. A sizable portion of Negroes would not permit Jim Crow "to get them down." As Americans in a booming country with great natural resources, they were optimistic, given to hope that tomorrow would bring a better day. Because of this faith, most Negroes were cool toward schemes to send them out of the country. However, deportation of the Negro population had many ardent supporters in white circles. In December 1816 a group of distinguished citizens, among them Henry Clay, Judge Bushrod Washington, Francis Scott Key, and Senator John Randolph, founded the American Colonization Society. Designed to finance the exportation of free Negroes and to spur the voluntary freeing of slaves, thus swelling the ranks of the colored migrants, the Society received funds from private individuals, church groups, state legislatures, and a donation of $100,000 from the United States Congress. With such substantial support, the Society founded the colony of Liberia on the west coast of Africa in 1822.

The greatest problem of the Society was not money-raising but recruit enlistment—the winning of converts among the potential deportees. The appeal to Negroes to go to Liberia was many-sided, but basically the colonizationalists sought to convince the colored people that their outlook in America was hopeless. But, as the Society discovered, most Negroes by far were not prepared to accept the premise that they could never prosper in the land of their birth. Among those joining in the cry against colonization was Peter Williams, pastor of St. Phillips Episcopal Church in New York. Williams' indictment, soundly reasoned if tinged with impassioned language, was delivered in a Fourth of July oration, well-suited to flag-waving and similar patriotic expression.

Though delivered from the fetters of slavery, we are oppressed by an unreasonable, unrighteous, and cruel prejudice, which aims at nothing less than the forcing away of all the free coloured people of the United States to the distant shores of Africa. Far be it from me to impeach the motives of every member of the African Colonization Society. The civilizing and Christianizing of that vast continent, and the extirpation of the abominable traffic in slaves (which notwithstanding all the laws passed for its suppression is still carried on in all its horrors), are no doubt the principal motives which induce many to give it their support.

But there are those, and those who are most active and most influential in its cause, who hesitate not to say that they wish to

**Frederick Douglass' Paper*, March 4, 1853.

rid the country of the free coloured population, and there is sufficient reason to believe, that with many, this is the principal motive for supporting that society; and that whether Africa is civilized or not, and whether the Slave Trade be suppressed or not, they would wish to see the free coloured people removed from this country to Africa.

Africa could certainly be brought into a state of civil and religious improvement without sending all the free people of colour in the United States there.

How inconsistent are those who say that Africa will be benefited by the removal of the free people of colour of the United States there, while they say they are the *most vile and degraded* people in the world. If we are as vile and degraded as they represent us, and they wish the Africans to be rendered a virtuous, enlightened and happy people, they should not *think* of sending *us* among them, lest we should make them worse instead of better.

The colonies planted by white men on the shores of America, so far from benefiting the aborigines, corrupted their morals, and caused their ruin; and yet those who say *we* are the most vile people in the world would send us to Africa to improve the character and condition of the natives. Such arguments would not be listened to for a moment were not the minds of the community strangely warped by prejudice.

Those who wish that that vast continent should be *compensated* for the injuries done it, by sending thither the light of the gospel and the arts of civilized life, should aid in sending and supporting well-qualified missionaries, who should be wholly devoted to the work of instruction, instead of sending colonists who would be apt to turn the ignorance of the natives to their own advantage, and do them more harm than good.

Much has also been said by Colonizationists about improving the character and condition of the people of colour of this country by sending them to Africa. This is more inconsistent still. We are to be improved by being sent far from civilized society. This is a novel mode of improvement. What is there in the burning sun, the arid plains, and barbarous customs of Africa, that is so peculiarly favourable to our improvement! What hinders our improving here, where schools and colleges abound, where the gospel is preached at every corner, and where all the arts and sciences are verging fast to perfection? Nothing, nothing but prejudice. It requires no large expenditures, no hazardous enterprises to raise the people of colour in the United States to as highly improved a state as any class of the community. All that is necessary is that those who profess to be anxious for it should lay aside their prejudices and act towards them as they do by others.

We are NATIVES of this country, we ask only to be treated as well as FOREIGNERS. Not a few of our fathers suffered and bled to purchase its independence; we ask only to be treated as well as those who fought against it. We have toiled to cultivate it, and to raise it to its present prosperous condition; we ask only to share equal privileges with those who come from distant lands, to enjoy the fruits of our labour. Let these moderate requests be granted, and we need not go to Africa nor anywhere else to be improved and happy. We cannot but doubt the purity of the motives of those persons who deny us these requests, and would send us to Africa to gain what they might give us at home.

But they say the prejudices of the country against us are invincible; and as they cannot be conquered, it is better that we should be removed beyond their influence. This plea should never proceed from the lips of any man who professes to believe that a just God rules in the heavens.

The African Colonization Society is a numerous and influential body. Would they lay aside their *own* prejudices, much of the burden would be at once removed; and their example (especially if they were as anxious to have *justice done us here* as to send us to Africa) would have such an influence upon the community at large as would soon cause prejudice to hide its deformed head.

But, alas! the course which they have pursued has an opposite tendency. By the *scandalous misrepresentations* which they are continually giving of our character and conduct we have sustained much injury, and have reason to apprehend much more.

Without any charge of crime we have been denied all access to places to which we formerly had the most free intercourse; the coloured citizens of other places, on leaving their homes, have been denied the privilege of returning; and others have been absolutely driven out.

Has the Colonization Society had no effect in producing these barbarous measures?

They profess to have no other object in view than the colonizing of the free people of colour on the coast of Africa, with their *own consent;* but if our homes are made so uncomfortable that we cannot continue in them, or, if like our brethren of Ohio and New Orleans, we are driven from them, and no other door is open to receive us but Africa, our removal there will be anything but voluntary.

It is very certain that very few free people of colour *wish* to go to that *land.* The Colonization Society *know* this, and yet they do certainly calculate that in time they will have us all removed there.

How can this be effected but by making our situation worse here, and closing every other door against us?*

85

A NEGRO ON TYRANNY AND REVOLUTION

To bring about the new day for which he hoped, the free Negro followed several courses of action. Many sought ways to undermine slavery. A handful of hardy spirits proposed using physical force to free the bondmen. The best known of these bold calls to direct action was issued in 1829 by David Walker, a self-taught

---

*From *Negro Orators and Their Orations,* by Carter G. Woodson. Reprinted by permission of The Associated Publishers, Inc.

North Carolinian who had settled in Boston where he operated a second-hand clothes store. In bitterness and anger, Walker set down his thoughts in a pamphlet as lengthy as its title suggests, "Walker's Appeal in Four Articles; together with a Preamble, to the Coloured Citizens of the World, but in Particular, and very expressly, to those of the United States of America." Walker's pamphlet angered and frightened many Southerners, causing two states to enact laws barring the distribution of incendiary publications, and prompting the governor of Georgia to send a protest letter to the mayor of Boston. Even some reformers, Benjamin Lundy and William Lloyd Garrison among them, felt that Walker had gone too far. Unquestionably, his tone was militant. Of the four passages that follow, two are addressed to Negroes, and two to whites. Perhaps it might be added that Walker died in June 1830, suddenly if not mysteriously, and that his son, Edwin G. Walker, was elected in 1866 to the Massachusetts House of Representatives, an unprecedented honor for a Negro.

My dearly beloved Brethren and Fellow Citizens.

HAVING travelled over a considerable portion of these United States, and having, in the course of my travels, taken the most accurate observations of things as they exist—the result of my observations has warranted the full and unshaken conviction, that we, (coloured people of these United States,) are the most degraded, wretched, and abject set of beings that ever lived since the world began; and I pray God that none like us ever may live again until time shall be no more. They tell us of the Israelites in Egypt, the Helots in Sparta, and of the Roman Slaves, which last were made up from almost every nation under heaven, whose sufferings under those ancient and heathen nations, were, in comparison with ours, under this enlightened and Christian nation, no more than a cypher —or, in other words, those heathen nations of antiquity, had but little more among them than the name and form of slavery; while wretchedness and endless miseries were reserved, apparently in a phial, to be poured out upon our fathers, ourselves and our children, by *Christian* Americans!

These positions I shall endeavour, by the help of the Lord, to demonstrate in the course of this *Appeal,* to the satisfaction of the most incredulous mind—and may God Almighty, who is the Father of our Lord Jesus Christ, open your hearts to understand and believe the truth.

The *causes,* my brethren, which produce our wretchedness and miseries, are so very numerous and aggravating, that I believe the pen only of a Josephus or a Plutarch, can well enumerate and explain them. Upon subjects, then, of such incomprehensible magnitude, so impenetrable, and so notorious, I shall be obliged to omit a large class of, and content myself with giving you an expostion of a few of those, which do indeed rage to such an alarming pitch, that they cannot but be a perpetual source of terror and dismay to every reflecting mind.

I am fully aware, in making this appeal to my much afflicted and suffering brethren, that I shall not only be assailed by those whose greatest earthly desires are, to keep us in abject ignorance and wretchedness, and who are of the firm conviction that Heaven has designed us and our children to be slaves and *beasts of burden* to them and their children. I say, I do not only expect to be held up to the public as an ignorant, impudent and restless disturber of the public peace, by such avaricious creatures, as well as a mover of insubordination—and perhaps put in prison or to death, for giving a superficial exposition of our miseries, and exposing tyrants. But I am persuaded, that many of my brethren, particularly those who are ignorantly in league with slave-holders or tyrants, who acquire their daily bread by the blood and sweat of their more ignorant brethren—and not a few of those too, who are too ignorant to see an inch beyond their noses, will rise up and call me cursed—Yea, the jealous ones among us will perhaps use more abject subtlety, by affirming that this work is not worth perusing, that we are well situated, and there is no use in trying to better our condition, for we cannot. I will ask one question here.—Can our condition be any worse?—Can it be more mean and abject? If there are any changes, will they not be for the better, though they may appear for the worst at first? Can they get us any lower? Where can they get us? They are afraid to treat us worse, for they know well, the day they do it they are gone.

* * *

Men of colour, who are also of sense, for you particularly is my APPEAL designed. Our more ignorant brethren are not able to penetrate its value. I call upon you therefore to cast your eyes upon the wretchedness of your brethren, and to do your utmost to enlighten them—*go to work and enlighten your brethren!*—Let the Lord see you doing what you can to rescue them and yourselves from degradation. Do any of you say that you and your family are free and happy, and what have you to do with the wretched slaves and other people? So can I say, for I enjoy as much freedom as any of you, if I am not quite as well off as the best of you. Look into our freedom and happiness, and see of what kind they are composed!! They are of the very lowest kind—they are the very *dregs!*—they are the most servile and abject kind, that ever a people was in possession of! If any of you wish to know how FREE you are, let one of you start and go through the southern and western States of this country, and unless you travel as a slave to a white man (a servant is a *slave* to the man whom he serves) or have your free papers, (which if you are not careful they will get from you) if they do not take you up and put you in jail, and if you cannot give good evidence of your freedom, sell you into eternal slavery, I am not a living man: or any man of colour, immaterial who he is, or where he came from, if he is not *the fourth from the negro race!!* (as we are called) the white Christians of America will serve him the same they will sink him into wretchedness and degradation for ever while he lives. And yet some of you have the hardihood to say that you are free and happy! May God have mercy on your freedom and happiness!! I met a coloured man in the street a short time since, with a string of boots on his shoulders; we fell into conversation, and in course of which, I said to him, what a miserable set of people we are! He asked, why?—Said I, we are so subjected under the whites, that we cannot obtain the comforts of life, but by cleaning their boots and shoes, old clothes, waiting on them, shaving them &c. Said he, (with the boots on his shoulders) "I am completely happy!!! I never want to live any better or happier than when I can get a plenty of boots and shoes to clean!!!" Oh! how can those who are actuated by avarice only, but think, that our Creator made us to be an inheritance to them for ever, when they see that our greatest glory is centered in such mean and low objects? Understand me, brethren, I do not mean to speak against the occupations by which we acquire enough and sometimes scarcely that, to render ourselves and families comfortable through life. I am subjected to the same inconvenience, as you all.—My objections are, to our *glorying* and being *happy* in such low employments; for if we are men, we ought to be thankful to the Lord for the past, and for the future. Be looking forward with thankful hearts to higher attainments than *wielding the razor* and *cleaning boots and shoes.* The man whose aspirations are not *above,* and even *below* these, is indeed, ignorant and wretched enough. I advance it therefore to you, not as a *problematical,* but as an unshaken and for ever immoveable *fact,* that your full glory and happiness, as well as all other coloured people under Heaven, shall never be fully consummated, but with the *entire emancipation of your enslaved brethren all over the world.* Your may therefore, go to work and do what you can to rescue, or join in with tyrants to oppress them and yourselves, until the Lord shall come upon you all like a thief in the night. For I believe it is the will of the Lord that our greatest happiness shall consist in working for the salvation of our whole body. When this is accomplished a burst of glory will shine upon you, which will indeed astonish you and the world. Do any of you say this never will be done? I assure you that God will accomplish it—if nothing else will answer, he will hurl tyrants and devils into *atoms* and make way for his people. But O my brethren! I say unto you again, you must go to work and prepare the way of the Lord.

* * *

Americans! notwithstanding you have and do continue to treat us more cruel than any heathen nation ever did a people it had subjected to the same condition that you have us. Now let us reason—I mean you of the United States, whom I believe God designs to save from destruction, if you will hear. For I declare to you, whether you believe it or not, that there are some on the continent of America, who will never be able to repent. God will surely destroy them, to show you his disapprobation of the murders they and you have inflicted on us. I say, let us reason; had you not better take our body, while you have it in your power, and while we are yet ignorant and wretched, not knowing but a little, give us education, and teach us the pure religion of our Lord and Master, which is calculated to make the lion lay down in peace with the lamb, and which millions of you have beaten us nearly to death for trying to obtain since we have been among you, and thus at once, gain our affection while we are ignorant? Remember Americans, that we must and shall be free and enlightened as you are, will you wait until we shall, under God, obtain our liberty by the crushing arm of power? Will it not be dreadful for you? I speak Americans for your good. We must and shall be free I say, in spite of you. You may do your best to keep us in wretchedness and misery, to enrich you and your children, but God will deliver us from under you. And wo, wo, will be to you if we have to obtain our freedom by fighting. Throw away your fears and prejudices then, and enlighten us and treat us like men, and we will like you more than we do now hate you,* and tell us now no more about colonization, for America is as much our country, as it is yours.—Treat us like men, and there is no danger but we will all live in peace and happiness together. For we are not like you, hard hearted, unmerciful, and unforgiving. What a happy country this will be, if the whites will listen. What nation under heaven, will be able to do any thing with us, unless God gives us up into its hand? But Americans, I declare to you, while you keep us and our children in bondage, and treat us like brutes, to make us support you and your families, we cannot be your friends. You do not look for it, do you? Treat us then like men, and we will be your friends. And there is not a doubt in my mind, but that the whole of the past will be sunk into oblivion, and we yet, under God, will become a united and happy people. The whites may say it is impossible, but remember that nothing is impossible with God.

* * *

If any are anxious to ascertain who I am, know the world, that I am one of the oppressed, degraded and wretched sons of Africa, rendered so by the avaricious and unmerciful, among the whites.—If any wish to plunge me into the wretched incapacity of a slave, or murder me for the truth, know ye, that I am in the hand of God, and at your disposal. I count my life not dear unto me, but I am ready to be offered at any moment. For what is the use of living, when in fact I am dead. But remember, Americans, that as miserable, wretched, degraded and abject as you have made us in preceding, and in this generation, to support you and your families, that some of you, (whites) on the continent of America, will yet curse the day that you ever were born. You want slaves, and want us for your slaves!!! My colour will yet, root some of you out of the very face of the earth!!!!!! You may doubt it if you please. I know that thousands will doubt—they think they have us so well secured in wretchedness, to them and their children, that it is impossible for such things to occur. So did the antideluvians doubt Noah, until the day in which the flood came and swept them away. So did the Sodomites doubt, until Lot had got out of the city, and God rained down fire and brimstone from Heaven upon them, and burnt them up. So did the king of Egypt doubt the very existence of a God; he said, "who is the Lord, that I should let Israel go?" Did he not find to his sorrow, who the Lord was, when he and all his mighty men of war, were smothered to death in the Red Sea? So did the Romans doubt, many of them were really so ignorant, that they thought the whole of mankind were made to be slaves to them; just as many of the Americans think now, of my colour. But they got dreadfully deceived. When men got their eyes opened, they

*You are not astonished at my saying we hate you, for if we are men, we cannot but hate you, while you are treating us like dogs.

made the murderers scamper. The way in which they cut their tyrannical throats, was not much inferior to the way the Romans or murderers, served them, when they held them in wretchedness and degradation under their feet.*

86

THE ESCAPE OF HENRY BOX BROWN

Many Negroes struck at slavery by assisting runaways in their dash for Canada or the free states. The most noted of all the guides in the Underground Railroad was Harriet Tubman, called "the Moses of her people," for her brave and resourceful thrusts into slave territory. Herself a former fugitive, Harriet ran a double peril in her dangerous missions. Harriet's zeal, if not her daring, was matched by William Still. Stationed at Philadelphia, Still was the pivotal figure in hundreds of escapes. He was numbered among the trusted few who were present when Henry "Box" Brown completed his hazardous journey from Richmond to Philadelphia encased in a baize-lined container, an exploit that became a classic in Underground Railroad lore. Still himself described the dramatic incident. Of course after Brown's escape, shippers and freight handlers in the South examined odd-shaped boxes and crates more carefully.

HENRY BOX BROWN.

ARRIVED BY ADAMS' EXPRESS.

Although the name of Henry Box Brown has been echoed over the land for a number of years, and the simple facts connected with his marvelous escape from slavery in a box published widely through the medium of anti-slavery papers, nevertheless it is not unreasonable to suppose that very little is generally known in relation to this case.

Briefly, the facts are these, which doubtless have never before been fully published—

Brown was a man of invention as well as a hero. In point of interest, however, his case is no more remarkable than many others. Indeed, neither before nor after escaping did he suffer one-half what many others have experienced.

He was decidedly an unhappy piece of property in the city of Richmond, Va. In the condition of a slave he felt that it would be impossible for him to remain. Full well did he know, however, that it was no holiday task to escape the vigilance of Virginia slave-hunters, or the wrath of an enraged master for committing the unpardonable sin of attempting to escape to a land of liberty. So Brown counted well the cost before venturing upon this hazardous undertaking. Ordinary modes of travel he concluded might prove disastrous to his hopes; he, therefore, hit upon a new invention altogether, which was to have himself boxed up and forwarded to Philadelphia direct by express. The size of the box and how it was to be made to

---

**Walker's Appeal in Four Articles; together with a Preamble, to the Coloured Citizens of the World, but in Particular, and very expressly, to those of the United States of America, Written in Boston, State of Massachusetts, September 28, 1829* (third ed., Boston, 1830), 3-5, 33-35, 78-83.

fit him most comfortably, was of his own ordering. Two feet eight inches deep, two feet wide, and three feet long were the exact dimensions of the box, lined with baize. His resources with regard to food and water consisted of the following: One bladder of water and a few small biscuits. His mechanical implement to meet the death-struggle for fresh air, all told, was one large gimlet. Satisfied that it would be far better to peril his life for freedom in this way than to remain under the galling yoke of Slavery, he entered his box, which was safely nailed up and hooped with five hickory hoops, and was then addressed by his next friend, James A. Smith, a shoe dealer, to Wm. H. Johnson, Arch street, Philadelphia, marked, "This side up with care." In this condition he was sent to Adams' Express office in a dray, and thence by overland express to Philadelphia. It was twenty-six hours from the time he left Richmond until his arrival in the City of Brotherly Love. The notice, "This side up, &c.," did not avail with the different expressmen, who hesitated not to handle the box in the usual rough manner common to this class of men. For a while they actually had the box upside down, and had him on his head for miles. A few days before he was expected, certain intimation was conveyed to a member of the Vigilance Committee that a box might be expected by the three o'clock morning train from the South, which might contain a man. One of the most serious walks he ever took—and they had not been a few—to meet and accompany passengers, he took at half past two o'clock that morning to the depot. Not once, but for more than a score of times, he fancied the slave would be dead. He anxiously looked while the freight was being unloaded from the cars, to see if he could recognize a box that might contain a man; one alone had that appearance, and he confessed it really seemed as if there was the scent of death about it. But on inquiry, he soon learned that it was not the one he was looking after, and he was free to say he experienced a marked sense of relief. That same afternoon, however, he received from Richmond a telegram, which read thus, "Your case of goods is shipped and will arrive to-morrow morning."

At this exciting juncture of affairs, Mr. McKim, who had been engineering this important undertaking, deemed it expedient to change the programme slightly in one particular at least to insure greater safety. Instead of having a member of the Committee go again to the depot for the box, which might excite suspicion, it was decided that it would be safest to have the express bring it direct to the Anti-Slavery Office.

But all apprehension of danger did not now disappear, for there was no room to suppose that Adams' Express office had any sympathy with the Abolitionist or the fugitive, consequently for Mr. McKim to appear personally at the express office to give directions with reference to the coming of a box from Richmond which would be directed to Arch street, and yet not intended for that street, but for the Anti-Slavery office at 107 North Fifth street, it needed of course no great discernment to foresee that a step of this kind was wholly impracticable and that a more indirect and covert method would have to be adopted. In this dreadful crisis Mr. McKim, with his usual good judgment and remarkably quick, strategical mind, especially in matters pertaining to the U. G. R. R., hit upon the following plan, namely, to go to his friend, E. M. Davis, who was then extensively engaged in mercantile business, and relate the circumstances. Having daily intercourse with said Adams' Express office, and being well acquainted with the firm and some of the drivers, Mr. Davis could, as Mr. McKim thought, talk about "boxes, freight, etc.," from any part of the country without risk. Mr. Davis heard Mr. McKim's plan and instantly approved of it, and was heartily at his service.

"Dan, an Irishman, one of Adams' Express drivers, is just the fellow to go to the depot after the box," said Davis. "He drinks a little too much whiskey sometimes, but he will do anything I ask him to do, promptly and obligingly. I'll trust Dan, for I believe he is the very man." The difficulty which Mr. McKim had been so anxious to overcome was thus pretty well settled. It was agreed that Dan should go after the box next morning before daylight and bring it to the Anti-Slavery office direct, and to make it all the more agreeable for Dan to get up out of his warm bed and go on this errand before day, it was decided that he should have a five dollar gold piece for himself. Thus these preliminaries having been satisfactorily arranged, it only remained for Mr. Davis to see Dan and give him instructions accordingly, etc.

Next morning, according to arrangement, the box was at the Anti-Slavery office in due time. The witnesses present to behold the resurrection were J. M. McKim, Professor C. D. Cleveland, Lewis Thompson, and the writer.

Mr. McKim was deeply interested; but having been long identified with the Anti-Slavery cause as one of its oldest and ablest advocates in the darkest days of slavery and mobs, and always found by the side of the fugitive to counsel and succor, he was on this occasion perfectly composed.

Professor Cleveland, however, was greatly moved. His zeal and earnestness in the cause of freedom, especially in rendering aid to passengers, knew no limit. Ordinarily he could not too often visit these travelers, shake them too warmly by the hand, or impart to them too freely of his substance to aid them on their journey. But now his emotion was overpowering.

Mr. Thompson, of the firm of Merrihew & Thompson—about the only printers in the city who for many years dared to print such incendiary documents as anti-slavery papers and pamphlets—one of the truest friends of the slave, was composed and prepared to witness the scene.

All was quiet. The door had been safely locked. The proceedings commenced. Mr. McKim rapped quietly on the lid of the box and called out, "All right!" Instantly came the answer from within, "All right, sir!"

The witnesses will never forget that moment. Saw and hatchet quickly had the five hickory hoops cut and the lid off, and the marvellous resurrection of Brown ensued. Rising up in his box, he reached out his hand, saying, "How do you do, gentlemen?" The little assemblage hardly knew what to think or do at the moment. He was about as wet as if he had come up out of the Delaware. Very soon he remarked that, before leaving Richmond he had selected for his arrival-hymn (if he lived) the Psalm beginning with these words: *"I waited patiently for the Lord, and He heard my prayer."* And most touchingly did he sing the psalm, much to his own relief, as well as to the delight of his small audience.*

87

THE NEW YORK FREE SCHOOL

One way in which the free Negro sought to overcome obstacles was through education. Negroes had faith that the ability to read and write would be their entree to a better life. Generally excluded from the public, tax-supported schools, they responded by raising money to establish schools of their own, while pressing for public funds. The response by state and local authorities was slow and halting, but after 1840 some states began to appropriate dollars for Negro education. Negro children who had the opportunity to attend school made the best of it, as a rule. The pupils in the New York African Free School needed no hickory stick to make them learn their lessons. Founded by the New York Manumission Society just after the Revolutionary War, the school's reputation brought many white visitors to its classrooms. In 1828 the proud principal, Charles C. Andrews, sent samples of his students' work to an abolitionist group, along with the following letter.

Letter and Works Sent to the American Convention for Promoting the Abolition of Slavery

Having at the suggestion of some of the Trustees of the School under my charge, informed my pupils that the American Convention was soon to meet in Baltimore, and intimated its objects and its labours, I proposed to the senior boys the propriety of their attempting something in the form of an Address from them to that body; promising to forward such essay as I should judge to be the most appropriate. I certify that the foregoing communication is the original production of the boy who has signed it, with no other correction or alteration than the *erasure of a few superfluous words.*

Charles C. Andrews

ON SLAVERY

Slavery, oh, thou cruel stain,
Thou dost fill my heart with pain:
See my brother, there he stands
Chained by slavery's cruel bands.

Could we not feel a brother's woes,
Relieve the wants he undergoes,
Snatch him from slavery's cruel smart,
And to him freedom's joy impart?

George R. Allen, aged 12 years

---

*William Still, *The Underground Railroad* (Phil., Peoples Publishing House Co., 1872), 81-85.

ON FREEDOM

Freedom will break the tyrant's chains,
And shatter all his whole domain;
From slavery she will always free
And all her aim is liberty.

Thomas S. Sidney, aged 12 years

GEORGE W. MOORE'S ESSAY

Gentlemen,

Will you suffer a poor little descendant of Africa to address you in behalf of myself and fellow schoolmates? I am but young, but when I consider what great things have been done for our race, and still are doing for them, I feel thankful. In the first place many of us are restored to our liberty, and secondly many are enjoying education. Since I have been in school I have learned considerable of the several branches taught; namely, reading, writing, arithmetic, geography, grammar, &c.

Gentlemen, since the last convention, New York has been freed from slavery. You have the good wishes of myself and fellow schoolmates, hoping that you may prosper in your undertakings.

George W. Moore, aged 15 years

ELIVER REASON'S ESSAY

Gentlemen,

I now address you in behalf of myself and my schoolmates: will you suffer a poor boy of my description, to address you thus:

How many years have our poor Africans been in chains of slavery and perhaps have not seen a day of rest in many years, how likely is it, that they have been stolen from their native country, when they were young, from their dear father and mother; there are so many in the southern States chained in slavery for no other crime, than the color of their skin! I ought to return thanks to the Almighty Being, for putting it into the hearts of such gentlemen as you, to condescend to take notice of us, and, in the second place, I ought to return thanks to the gentlemen that have taken into consideration the condition of our ill-fated people. May the Supreme Being reward you ten fold for the good you do for us, is the desire of an injured African.

Eliver Reason

ISAIAH G. DEGRASS'S ESSAY

Gentlemen,

I feel myself highly honoured by addressing you in behalf of myself and the African race. I am but a poor descendant of that injured people. When I reflect upon the enormities which continue to be practised in many parts of our otherwise favoured country, on the ill-fated Africans, and their descendants, who are torn by the hands of violence from their native country, and sold like brutes to tyrannical slave-holders in different countries, where they are held in slavery and bondage, I ought to return thanks unto Almighty God, for having put it into the hearts of such distinguished men as you, to undertake the cause of Abolishing Slavery; and I ought to feel myself greatly blessed for enjoying the many privileges I do; while there are so many in the southern States chained in slavery, who perhaps, have left mothers, fathers, sisters and brothers, to mourn their loss. I feel myself greatly blessed in belonging to a school which has been established for many years by the Manumission Society. The different branches that are taught in this school, are reading, writing, arithmetic, geography, navigation, astronomy, and map drawing. Our schools which now contain 700 male and female scholars, continue to be conducted on the Lancastarian system, and the improvement of the scholars is such, as to be satisfactory to the trustees, and all visitors who come to the school. Next to the Supreme Being, gentlemen, you deserve the gratitude and thankfulness of our whole race. When I reflect on the great things that you have done for us, I can but with gratitude fall at your feet and thank you. It makes my heart burn within me, when I think of the poor Africans who are torn from their homes and relatives; deprived of the protection and advice of their friends and forced to a distance from the means of proving and defending their rights; these wretched victims of avarice and cruelty languish a long time in bondage before they can procure assistance.

You gentlemen, who are advocates for the abolition of such, deserve the gratitude and thanks of our whole race. May Divine Providence assist you in all your proceedings, is the wish of a descendant of Africa.

Isaiah G. Degrass, aged 15 years*

88

NEGRO COLLEGE GRADUATES

By midcentury a handful of white colleges had opened their doors to Negroes. Oberlin in 1834 was the first to take such a step officially. By 1860 twenty-eight Negroes had earned degrees from recognized colleges. In 1826 Amherst and Bowdoin each had a Negro graduate. At the graduation exercises at Bowdoin College, John B. Russwurm delivered a commencement oration whose militant tone foreshadowed a career as co-editor of the first Negro newspaper, Freedom's Journal, *and later as a notable public figure in Liberia. Here he speaks at Bowdoin's commencement.*

African Eloquence

FROM THE NATIONAL PHILANTHROPIST

John B. Russwurm, a man of colour, was one of the graduates at the late commencement of Bowdoin College. He is said to be a man of excellent character, and much esteemed by his tutor and classmates. The following extract from his Oration, from the Eastern Argus, will be gratifying to our readers.

**Minutes of the Adjourned Session of the Twentieth Biennial American Convention for Promoting the Abolition of Slavery and Improving the Condition of the African Race, Held at Baltimore, November 1828* (Philadelphia, 1828), 64-68.

"It is the irresistable course of events, that all men who have been deprived of their liberty, shall recover this precious portion of their indefeasible inheritance. It is vain to stem the current: degraded man will rise in his native majesty and claim his rights—They may be withheld from him now, but the day will arrive, when they must be surrendered.

"Can we conceive of anything which can cheer the desponding spirit, can reanimate and stimulate it to put everything to the hazard. Liberty can do this. Such were its effects upon the Haytiens—men who in slavery showed neither spirit nor genius—but when Liberty, whence once Freedom struck their astonished ears, they became new creatures—stepped forth like men, and showed to the world, that though slavery may benumb, it cannot entirely destroy our faculties. Such men were Touissant Louverture, Dessalines, and Christophe!

"The Haytiens have adopted the republican form of government: and so firmly is it established that in no country are the rights and privileges of citizens and foreigners more respected, and crimes less frequent.—They are a brave and generous people—if cruelties were inflicted during the Revolutionary war, it was owing to the policy pursued by the French commanders, which compelled them to use retaliatory measures.

"For who shall expostulate with men who have been hunted with blood hounds—who have been threatened with an *Auto de fe*—whose relations and friends have been hung on gibbets before ther eyes—have been sunk by hundreds in the sea—and tell them they ought to exercise kindness towards such mortal enemies? Remind me not of the moral duties of meekness and generosity—show me the man who has exercised them under these trials, and you point to one who is more than human. It is an undisputed fact, that more than sixteen thousand Haytiens perished in the modes above specified. The cruelties inflicted by the French, on the children of Hayti, have exceeded the crimes of Cortez and Pizarro.

"Twenty-two years of their Independence, so gloriously achieved, have effected wonders. No longer are they the same people. They had faculties, yet were these faculties oppressed under the load of servitude and ignorance. With a countenance erect and fixed on heaven, they can now contemplate the works of Divine munificence. Restored to the dignity of man and to society, they have acquired a new existence; their powers have been developed; a career of glory and happiness unfolds itself before them.

"Placed by Divine Providence Amid circumstance more favorable than were their ancestors, the Haytiens can more easily then they, make rapid strides in the career of civilization; they can demonstrate that although the God of nature may have given them a darker complexion, still they are men, alike sensible to all the miseries of slavery, and to all the blessings of freedom.*

**Genius of Universal Emancipation,* Baltimore, October 14, 1826.

89

THE NEW YORK LIBRARY FOR COLORED

To encourage learning outside the classroom, Negroes established libraries. Typical of these was the "Philadelphia Library Company of Colored Persons," organized in 1832 for the purpose of "promoting among our rising youth, a proper cultivation for literary pursuits and improvement of the faculties and powers of their minds." Although the word "colored" appeared in its title, its sponsors pointed out that the library was designed "to embrace the entire population of the city and county of Philadelphia." A year later the Negroes of New York founded a library under the auspices of the Phoenix Society, a self-improvement organization headed by Samuel E. Cornish, co-founder of Freedom's Journal. *In a letter to a New York newspaper, Cornish described the library.*

A LIBRARY FOR THE PEOPLE OF COLOR
(FROM THE NEW YORK OBSERVER)

MESSRS. EDITORS:—Aware that you take a lively interest in the subject of the improvement and elevation of our colored population, I am free to address you in behalf of a Library and Reading Room lately opened by the executive committee of the Phoenex Society, for their benefit.

The institution is located in spacious rooms, second story of the north-west corner of Canal and Mercer streets. Connected with it, is a classic school of ten or twelve promising youth. Much good, it is hoped, will result from the successful prosecution of the purposes of this establishment.

The establishment of schools, of libraries, of reading rooms, and the delivery of public lectures for our benefit, I trust will be seed sown in good ground.

Some among us are poor, and ignorant, and vicious, because we have been neglected. The time has come, in which we sincerely hope our community will not stop to find fault with our oppressed people, but turn their attention to their education, and to the improvement of their condition. Permit me, therefore, through your useful paper, to solicit donations from the favored citizens of New York, in books, maps, papers, money, &c. for the benefit of our feeble institution. And I would beg the benevolent ladies of our city, who are first in every good work, not to forget us. We shall thankfully receive from them any volumes they may have read and laid by, or any useful papers they can dispense with. We hope to be the objects of some of the ten thousand acts of daily benevolence; and we will promise, in return, to bestow on our benefactors the blessing of thousands ready to perish.

The objects of the institution are general improvement, and the training of our youth to habits of reading and reflection.

I need not tell you that, for the want of such institutions, many of the young and unthinking part of our colored citizens are led by those older than themselves to haunts of wickedness and vice. Many young men, yea! and old ones too, spend their evenings in improper places, because they have no public libraries, no reading rooms, nor useful lectures, to attract their attention, and occupy their leisure hours. We hope to save such from ruin, and lead them to habits of virtue and usefulness.

The plans of operation, for the present, will be as follows:

1st. The rooms will be opened Mondays, Wednesdays and Fridays, from 4 to 9 o'clock, P.M.

2dly. There will be a 4, a 6, and an 8 o'clock class of readers. These classes may consist of from 25 to 30 or more—each class having selected its course of reading and appointed its reader, whose duty it shall be to read for one hour. All the class shall note prominent parts, and then retire into the adjacent room to converse on the subjects, together with other occurrences of the day; calculated to cultivate the mind and improve the heart.

3dly. We propose to have a course of lectures delivered, on morals, economy, and the arts and sciences generally, under such arrangements as shall benefit all the classes.

4thly. The Constitutions of the Temperance and Moral Societies will be kept at the Library, and all the readers earnestly solicited to enlist in those causes.

In conclusion, I am happy to state, that the institution will be under the immediate direction of the executive committee of the Society—of which committee, the Rev. Messrs. Peter Williams, of the Episcopal, Christopher Rush, of the Methodist, and Theodore S. Wright, of the Presbyterian churches, are members.

Will you do something for us? Will you urge the call of humanity and religion in our behalf?

As agent of the Society, I shall call on the wise and good of our community—those who are blessed with all the privileges of enlightened civilization and religion, to bestow some of these blessings on the neglected and oppressed, by donations in maps, books, and journals—and I pledge myself, in the name of the Society, and as present Librarian, to make the best use of all the gifts we may receive.

Permit me to subscribe myself,

Respectfully yours, &c.
Samuel E. Cornish*

90

PHILADELPHIA NEGRO MUTUAL AID SOCIETIES

In their efforts to help themselves, Negroes formed mutual aid societies. Faced by the high wall of color in employment, in housing, and in social acceptance generally, the Negro drew from his own resources, acting upon the theory that to be dependent was to be degraded. Hence, a characteristic of the Negro community was the presence of self-help organizations. Like other Americans, the Negro was a "joiner," attracted to group organization although remaining an individualist. But Negro organizations served not only as a social outlet but as a vehicle of group advancement. Thus it is not surprising that in 1849 in Philadelphia alone there were more than one hundred mutual aid societies, as a contemporary report indicates.

**The Colonizationist and Journal of Freedom,* January 1834, pp. 306-307.

BENEFICIAL SOCIETIES.

By the returns it appears that 4904 persons, or nearly one-half the adult population, are members of Mutual Beneficial Societies, the funds of which are appropriated to support the members in sickness, and to bury the dead. Many of these persons belong to two or more Societies at once, with the view of increasing the amount to be received when sick. The names of 106 of these Mutual Beneficial Associations have been received, and particulars of income, &c. of 76 of them. These 76 societies consist of 5187 members. The contributions are from 25 to 37½ cents per month, and paid weekly, monthly, or quarterly. The allowance per week to the sick members varies from $1.50 to 3.00 per week, being generally $2.50 or 3.00. From ten to twenty dollars is usually allowed for funeral expenses. The annual income of these 76 societies is stated to be $16,814.23, and their permanent invested funds, $17,771.83.

Six hundred and eighty-one families are reported to have been assisted by them during the year 1837, and the sums furnished to 517 of these families is reported and stated at $7189.86. On comparing this list with that given in the year 1847, we find that the number of societies is increased from 80 to 106; and that more than one-half of those then reported have disappeared, or have assumed new names. The permanent funds of the 76 societies of which the details have been furnished, exceed those reported in 1837 by upwards of $7,700, while the annual subscription is less by about $2000; although, if the 29 societies whose income is not reported, be supposed to average the same rate as the others, the amount annually subscribed for mutual relief will considerably exceed the amount so contributed in 1837.

It is clear that these charitable funds must very considerably relieve the distress attendant on the sickness of the heads of families, and maintain a large portion of the people of colour, under privations, and in circumstances, which would otherwise throw them upon the public for relief. This is evident from the returns of the Alms-house for 1847. Out of 4303 patients admitted during that year, 523 or 12.15 per cent. were people of colour; and of the 1704, the average number of patients in the house, 196, or 11.5 per cent. were of this description. The proportion of people of colour in the county of Philadelphia was, in 1840, 8.3 per cent. that of the whole population. When we advert to the character of the pauperism of the people of colour during that year, and find that of the 523 patients admitted, considerably more than one-half were cases of fever from adjoining districts of Moyamensing and the city, the small number of ordinary paupers admitted into the Alms-house, must create surprise.

The amount of out-door relief furnished to the people of colour is likewise quite small. The whole number that receive public out-door aid, is stated, in the returns we have received, at 442, a number probably too small.*

---

*_A Statistical Inquiry into the Condition of the People of Colour of Philadelphia,_ pub. by the Society of Friends (Phila., 1849), 22-23.

91

ORGANIZATION OF THE GROUP AS A WHOLE

In addition to forming societies to help the individual in distress, Negroes also formed organizations to advance the group as a whole. They held numerous meetings and conventions designed to improve their general condition. At their national conventions, designed to meet annually, the delegates generally formulated an introductory, platform-like statement which invariably stressed faith in God and devotion to American ideals. Conforming to this practice the Fifth Annual Convention for the Improvement of the Free People of Colour in the United States, meeting at Wesley Church in Philadelphia in June 1835, drew up a "Declaration of Sentiment" embodying these affirmations.

We rejoice that it is our lot to be the inhabitants of a country blest by nature, with a genial climate and fruitful soil, and where the liberty of speech and the press is protected by law.

We rejoice that we are thrown into a revolution where the contest is not for landed territory, but for freedom; the weapons not carnal, but spiritual; where struggle is not for blood, but for right; and where the bow is the power of God, and the arrow the instrument of divine justice; while the victims are the devices of *reason*, and the prejudice of the human heart. It is in this glorious struggle for civil and religious liberty, for the establishment of peace on earth and good will to men, that we are morally bound by all the relative ties we owe to the author of our being, to enter the arena and boldly contend for victory.

Our reliance and only hope is in God. If success attend the effort, the downfall of Africa from her ancient pride and splendour, will have been more than glorious to the establishment of *religion;* every drop of blood spilt by her descendants under the dominion of prejudice and persecution, will have produced peaceful rivers, that shall wash from the soil of the human heart, the mountains of vice and corruption, under which this nation has long withered.

And if our presence in this country will aid in producing such a desirable reform, although we have been reared under a most debasing system of tyranny and oppression, we shall have been born under the most favourable auspices to promote the redemption of the world; for our very sighs and groans, like the blood of martyrs, will prove to have been the seed of the church; for they will freight the air with their voluminous ejaculations, and will be borne upwards by the power of virtue to the great Ruler of Israel, for deliverance from this yoke of merciless bondage. Let us not lament, that under the present constituted powers of this government, we are disfranchised; better far than to be partakers of its guilt. Let us refuse to be allured by the glittering endowments of official stations, or enchanted with the robe of American citizenship. But let us choose like true patriots, rather to be the victims of oppression than the administrators of injustice.

Let no man remove from his native country, for our principles are drawn from the book of divine revelation, and are incorporated in the Declaration of Independence, "that all men are born equal, and endowed by their Creator with certain inalienable rights; that among these are life, liberty, and the pursuit of happiness." Therefore, our only trust is in the agency of divine truth, and the spirit of American liberty; our cause is glorious and must finally triumph. Though the blighting hand of time should sweep us from the stage of action; though other generations should pass away, our principles will live forever; we will teach our children, and our children's children, to hand them down to unborn generations, and to the latest posterity; not merely for the release of the bondman from his chains, nor for the elevation of the free coloured man to the privileges of citizenship; nor for the restoration of the world from infidelity and superstition; but from the more fatal doctrine of *expediency*, without which the true principles of religion can never be established, liberty never secure, or the sacred rights of man remain inviolate.*

92

CONVENTION TRIBUTE TO AN IRISH PATRIOT

At their meetings Negroes often expressed gratitude to their white supporters and champions. For his forthright condemnation of slavery, the great Irish liberator, Daniel O'Connell, was a revered name among colored people and was often the subject of resolutions of praise. One of these tributes came from a convention of Negroes in New York.

MEETING OF THE FREE PEOPLE OF COLOR

Agreeably to public notice, a large and respectable meeting of the free people of color, called by the New York Society, auxiliary to the Convention of the Free People of Color, for their improvement in these United States, assembled in the Abyssinean Baptist Church in Anthony Street, on Wednesday Evening, December 26, 1832.

* * *

Particular interest was excited upon the reading of a part of the speech of the Honorable *Daniel O'Connell*, delivered at the Anniversary meeting of the London Anti-Slavery Society held in Exeter Hall, May 12th, 1832. Some observations on the character of Mr. O'Connell as a philanthropist, were made and the following resolutions offered and unanimously adopted, viz:

Resolved, That we highly appreciate the undeviating exertions of the friends of humanity in these United States, and in Great Britain, in the sacred cause of emancipation, and that they are entitled to our greatest respect and most sincere thanks.

Resolved, That we recognize in the Honorable *Daniel O'Connell*, of Ireland, the champion of religious liberty, the uncompromising advocate of universal emancipation, the friend of the oppressed Africans and their descendants, and of the unadulterated rights of man.

Minutes of the Fifth Annual Convention for the Improvement of the Free People of Colour in the United States, June 1-5, 1835 (Phila., 1835), 22-23.

Resolved, That we regret that we are unable to make suitable returns for the disinterested friendship that he has manifested towards the cause of liberty and equality, to the terror of the traffickers in human flesh and blood; and that we should consider ourselves unworthy the sympathies of the liberals, and traitors to our cause, if we should withhold this public expression of our respectful gratitude.

Resolved, That we tender to the Hon. DANIEL O'CONNELL our sincere thanks and respect for his great exertions in the cause of the oppressed,—hoping that when his labors of benevolence shall be finished on earth,—when the oppressor shall cease from his oppression,—he may receive the heavenly reward of Him who holds in his hands the destinies of nations.

Resolved, That an address be prepared to accompany the above resolutions, and that the same be forwarded to Mr. O'Connell with all convenient dispatch.

Resolved, That the above resolution be published in as many of the papers friendly to the cause of emancipation as practicable, signed by the Chairman and Secretary.

* * *

Samuel Hardenburgh, *Chairman**

93

NEGRO SERVICE IN THE PHILADELPHIA EPIDEMIC

Though Negroes sought their own betterment through their meetings and conventions, they were not insensitive to their broader obligations as citizens. Whenever the chance arose they were as likely as others to shoulder their civic responsibilities. The most dramatic instance of Negro service to the community took place in Philadelphia where a yellow-fever epidemic broke out in the late summer of 1793. As terror and panic gripped the city, an appeal was made to the Negroes to assist in caring for the sick and removing the dead. Under the leadership of the highly respected clergymen, Richard Allen and Absalom Jones, the Negroes responded readily, their conduct winning the commendation of Matthew Clarkson, mayor of the city. For the record, Jones and Allen drew up a narrative statement concerning the role of the Negro, portions of which follow.

IN CONSEQUENCE of a partial representation of the conduct of the people, who were employed to nurse the sick in the calamitous state of the city of Philadelphia, we were solicited by a number of those who felt themselves injured thereby, and by the advice of several respectable citizens, to step forward and declare facts as they really were; and seeing that from our situation, on account of the charge we took upon us, we had it more fully and generally in our power to know and observe the conduct and behavior of those that were so employed.

Early in September, a solicitation appeared in the public papers to the people of color to come forward and assist the distressed,

**The Abolitionist,* February 1833, 28.

perishing and neglected sick; with a kind of assurance, that people of our color were not liable to take the infection; upon which we and a few others met and consulted how to act on so truly alarming and melancholy an occasion. After some conversation, we found a freedom to go forth, confiding in Him who can preserve in the midst of a burning, fiery furnace. Sensible that it was our duty to do all the good we could to our suffering fellow mortals, we set out to see where we could be useful. The first we visited was a man in Elmsley's Alley, who was dying, and his wife lay dead at the time in the house. There were none to assist but two poor, helpless children. We administered what relief we could, and applied to the overseers of the poor to have the woman buried. We visited upwards of twenty families that day —they were scenes of woe indeed! The Lord was pleased to strengthen us and remove all fear from us, and disposed our hearts to be as useful as possible. In order the better to regulate our conduct, we called on the mayor next day, to consult with him how to proceed so as to be most useful. The first object he recommended was a strict attention to the sick and the procuring of nurses. This was attended to by Absalom Jones and William Gray; and in order that the distressed might know where to apply, the mayor advertised the public that upon application to them they would be supplied. Soon after, the mortality increasing, the difficulty of getting a corpse taken away was such, that few were willing to do it when offered great rewards. The colored people were looked to. We then offered our services in the public papers, by advertising that we would remove the dead and procure nurses. Our services were the production of real sensibility; we sought not fee nor reward, until the increase of the disorder rendered our labor so arduous, that we were not adequate to the service we had assumed. The mortality increasing rapidly, obliged us to call in the assistance of five hired men in the awful charge of interring the dead. They, with great reluctance, were prevailing upon to join us. It was very uncommon, at this time, to find any one that would go near, much more handle a sick or dead person.

When the sickness became general, and several of the physicians died, and most of the survivors were exhausted by sickness or fatigue, that good man, Dr. Rush, called us more immediately to attend upon the sick, knowing that we could both bleed. He told us that we could increase our utility by attending to his instructions, and according directed us where to procure medicine duly prepared, with proper directions how to administer them, and at what stages of the disorder to bleed; and when we found ourselves incapable of judging what was proper to be done, to apply to him and he would, if able, attend them himself or send Edward Fisher, his pupil, which he often did: and Mr. Fisher manifested his humanity by an affectionate attention for their relief. This has been no small satisfaction to us; for we think that when a physician was not attainable, we have been the instruments in the hands of God, for saving the lives of some hundreds of our suffering fellow mortals.

* * *

Sarah Bass, a colored widow woman, gave all the assistance she could in several families, for which she did not receive anything;

and when anything was offered her, she left it to the option of those she served.

A colored woman nursed Richard Mason and son. They died. Richard's widow, considering the risk the poor woman had run, and from observing the fears that sometimes rested on her mind, expected she would have demanded something considerable; but upon asking her what she demanded, her reply was, "fifty cents per day." Mrs. Mason intimated it was not sufficient for her attendance. She replied, that it was enough for what she had done, and would take no more. Mrs. Mason's feelings were such, that she settled an annuity of 6£ a year on her for life. Her name was Mary Scott.

An elderly, colored woman nursed——with great diligence and attention. When recovered, he asked what he must give her for her services—she replied, "a dinner, master, on a cold winter's day." And thus she went from place to place, rendering every service in her power, without an eye to reward.

A young colored woman was requested to attend one night upon a white man and his wife, who were very ill. No other person could be had. Great wages were offered her—she replied, "I will not go for money, if I go for money, God will see it and may make me take the disorder and die; but if I go and take no money, he may spare my life. She went about 9 o'clock, and found them both on the floor. She could procure no candle or other light, but stayed with them about two hours, and then left them. They both died that night. She was afterwards very ill with the fever. Her life was spared.

Caesar Cranchal, a man of color, offered his services to attend the sick, and said, "I will not take your money; I will not sell my life for money." It is said he died with the flux.

A colored lad, at the widow Gilpin's, was intrusted with his young master's keys, on his leaving the city, and transacted his business with the greatest honesty and despatch; having unloaded a vessel for him in the time, and loaded it again.

A woman that nursed David Bacon charged with exemplary moderation, and said she would not have any more.

It may be said in vindication of the conduct of those who discovered ignorance or incapacity in nursing, that it is, in itself, a considerable art derived from experience as well as the exercise of the finer feelings of humanity. This experience nine-tenths of those employed, it is probable, were wholly strangers to.*

*Richard Allen, *op. cit.*, 48-50, 56-57.

CHAPTER FIVE

Abolitionism and the Crisis of the Fifties

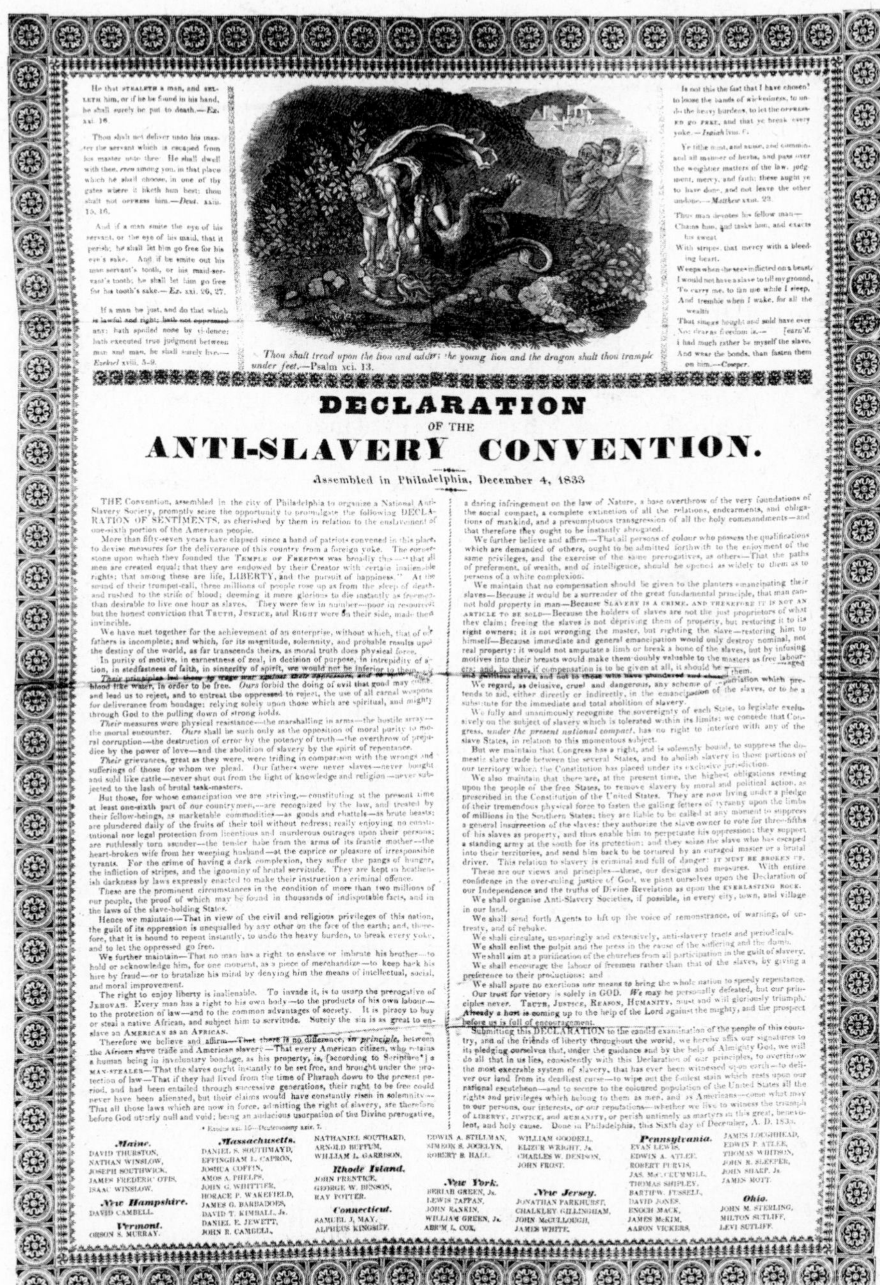

He that STEALETH a man, and SELLETH him, or if he be found in his hand, he shall surely be put to death.—*Ex.* xxi. 16.

Thou shalt not deliver unto his master the servant which is escaped from his master unto thee: He shall dwell with thee, *even* among you, in that place which he shall choose, in one of thy gates where it liketh him best: thou shalt not OPPRESS him.—*Deut.* xxiii. 15, 16.

And if a man smite the eye of his servant, or the eye of his maid, that it perish; he shall let him go free for his eye's sake. And if he smite out his man-servant's tooth, or his maid-servant's tooth; he shall let him go free for his tooth's sake.—*Ex.* xxi. 26, 27.

If a man be just, and do that which is lawful and right; hath not oppressed any; hath spoiled none by violence; hath executed true judgment between man and man, he shall surely live.—*Ezekiel* xviii. 5–9.

Thou shalt tread upon the lion and adder: the young lion and the dragon shalt thou trample under feet.—Psalm xci. 13.

Is not this the fast that I have chosen? to loose the bands of wickedness, to undo the heavy burdens, to let the OPPRESSED GO FREE, and that ye break every yoke.—*Isaiah* lviii. 6.

Ye tithe mint, and anise, and cummin, and all manner of herbs, and pass over the weightier matters of the law, judgment, mercy, and faith: these aught ye to have done, and not leave the other undone.—*Matthew* xxiii. 23.

Thus man devotes his fellow man—
Chains him, and tasks him, and exacts his sweat
With stripes, that mercy with a bleeding heart.
Weeps when she sees inflicted on a beast.
I would not have a slave to till my ground,
To carry me, to fan me while I sleep,
And tremble when I wake, for all the wealth
That sinews bought and sold have ever earn'd.
No: dear as freedom is,—
I had much rather be myself the slave,
And wear the bonds, than fasten them on him.—*Cowper.*

DECLARATION
OF THE
ANTI-SLAVERY CONVENTION.

Assembled in Philadelphia, December 4, 1833

THE Convention, assembled in the city of Philadelphia to organize a National Anti-Slavery Society, promptly seize the opportunity to promulgate the following DECLARATION OF SENTIMENTS, as cherished by them in relation to the enslavement of one-sixth portion of the American people.

More than fifty-seven years have elapsed since a band of patriots convened in this place, to devise measures for the deliverance of this country from a foreign yoke. The cornerstone upon which they founded the TEMPLE OF FREEDOM was broadly this—"that all men are created equal; that they are endowed by their Creator with certain inalienable rights; that among these are life, LIBERTY, and the pursuit of happiness." At the sound of their trumpet-call, three millions of people rose up as from the sleep of death, and rushed to the strife of blood; deeming it more glorious to die instantly as freemen, than desirable to live one hour as slaves. They were few in number—poor in resources; but the honest conviction that TRUTH, JUSTICE, and RIGHT were on their side, made them invincible.

We have met together for the achievement of an enterprise, without which, that of our fathers is incomplete; and which, for its magnitude, solemnity, and probable results upon the destiny of the world, as far transcends theirs, as moral truth does physical force.

In purity of motive, in earnestness of zeal, in decision of purpose, in intrepidity of action, in stedfastness of faith, in sincerity of spirit, we would not be inferior to them.

Their principles led them to wage war against their oppressors, and to spill human blood like water, in order to be free. *Ours* forbid the doing of evil that good may come, and lead us to reject, and to entreat the oppressed to reject, the use of all carnal weapons for deliverance from bondage; relying solely upon those which are spiritual, and mighty through God to the pulling down of strong holds.

Their measures were physical resistance—the marshalling in arms—the hostile array—the mortal encounter. *Ours* shall be such only as the opposition of moral purity to moral corruption—the destruction of error by the potency of truth—the overthrow of prejudice by the power of love—and the abolition of slavery by the spirit of repentance.

Their grievances, great as they were, were trifling in comparison with the wrongs and sufferings of those for whom we plead. Our fathers were never slaves—never bought and sold like cattle—never shut out from the light of knowledge and religion—never subjected to the lash of brutal task-masters.

But those, for whose emancipation we are striving,—constituting at the present time at least one-sixth part of our countrymen,—are recognized by the law, and treated by their fellow-beings, as marketable commodities—as goods and chattels—as brute beasts; are plundered daily of the fruits of their toil without redress; really enjoying no constitutional nor legal protection from licentious and murderous outrages upon their persons; are ruthlessly torn asunder—the tender babe from the arms of its frantic mother—the heart-broken wife from her weeping husband—at the caprice or pleasure of irresponsible tyrants. For the crime of having a dark complexion, they suffer the pangs of hunger, the infliction of stripes, and the ignominy of brutal servitude. They are kept in heathenish darkness by laws expressly enacted to make their instruction a criminal offence.

These are the prominent circumstances in the condition of more than two millions of our people, the proof of which may be found in thousands of indisputable facts, and in the laws of the slave-holding States.

Hence we maintain—That in view of the civil and religious privileges of this nation, the guilt of its oppression is unequalled by any other on the face of the earth; and, therefore, that it is bound to repent instantly, to undo the heavy burden, to break every yoke, and to let the oppressed go free.

We further maintain—That no man has a right to enslave or imbrute his brother—to hold or acknowledge him, for one moment, as a piece of merchandize—to keep back his hire by fraud—or to brutalize his mind by denying him the means of intellectual, social, and moral improvement.

The right to enjoy liberty is inalienable. To invade it, is to usurp the prerogative of JEHOVAH. Every man has a right to his own body—to the products of his own labour—to the protection of law—and to the common advantages of society. It is piracy to buy or steal a native African, and subject him to servitude. Surely the sin is as great to enslave an AMERICAN as an AFRICAN.

Therefore we believe and affirm—That there is no difference, *in principle*, between the African slave trade and American slavery—That every American citizen, who retains a human being in involuntary bondage, as his property, is, [according to Scripture*] a MAN-STEALER—That the slaves ought instantly to be set free, and brought under the protection of law—That if they had lived from the time of Pharaoh down to the present period, and had been entailed through successive generations, their right to be free could never have been alienated, but their claims would have constantly risen in solemnity—That all those laws which are now in force, admitting the right of slavery, are therefore before God utterly null and void; being an audacious usurpation of the Divine prerogative, a daring infringement on the law of Nature, a base overthrow of the very foundations of the social compact, a complete extinction of all the relations, endearments, and obligations of mankind, and a presumptuous transgression of all the holy commandments—and that therefore they ought to be instantly abrogated.

We further believe and affirm—That all persons of colour who possess the qualifications which are demanded of others, ought to be admitted forthwith to the enjoyment of the same privileges, and the exercise of the same prerogatives, as others—That the paths of preferment, of wealth, and of intelligence, should be opened as widely to them as to persons of a white complexion.

We maintain that no compensation should be given to the planters emancipating their slaves—Because it would be a surrender of the great fundamental principle, that man cannot hold property in man—Because SLAVERY IS A CRIME, AND THEREFORE IT IS NOT AN ARTICLE TO BE SOLD—Because the holders of slaves are not the just proprietors of what they claim; freeing the slaves is not depriving them of property, but restoring it to its right owners; it is not wronging the master, but righting the slave—restoring him to himself—Because immediate and general emancipation would only destroy nominal, not real property: it would not amputate a limb or break a bone of the slaves, but by infusing motives into their breasts would make them doubly valuable to the masters as free labourers; and, because, if compensation is to be given at all, it should be given to the outraged and guiltless slaves, and not to those who have plundered and abused them.

We regard, as delusive, cruel and dangerous, any scheme of expatriation which pretends to aid, either directly or indirectly, in the emancipation of the slaves, or to be a substitute for the immediate and total abolition of slavery.

We fully and unanimously recognize the sovereignty of each State, to legislate exclusively on the subject of slavery which is tolerated within its limits: we concede that Congress, *under the present national compact*, has no right to interfere with any of the slave States, in relation to this momentous subject.

But we maintain that Congress has a right, and is solemnly bound, to suppress the domestic slave trade between the several States, and to abolish slavery in those portions of our territory which the Constitution has placed under its exclusive jurisdiction.

We also maintain that there are, at the present time, the highest obligations resting upon the people of the free States, to remove slavery by moral and political action, as prescribed in the Constitution of the United States. They are now living under a pledge of their tremendous physical force to fasten the galling fetters of tyranny upon the limbs of millions in the Southern States; they are liable to be called at any moment to suppress a general insurrection of the slaves: they authorize the slave owner to vote for three-fifths of his slaves as property, and thus enable him to perpetuate his oppression: they support a standing army at the south for its protection: and they seize the slave who has escaped into their territories, and send him back to be tortured by an enraged master or a brutal driver. This relation to slavery is criminal and full of danger: IT MUST BE BROKEN UP.

These are our views and principles—these, our designs and measures. With entire confidence in the over-ruling justice of God, we plant ourselves upon the Declaration of our Independence and the truths of Divine Revelation as upon the EVERLASTING ROCK.

We shall organise Anti-Slavery Societies, if possible, in every city, town, and village in our land.

We shall send forth Agents to lift up the voice of remonstrance, of warning, of entreaty, and of rebuke.

We shall circulate, unsparingly and extensively, anti-slavery tracts and periodicals.

We shall enlist the pulpit and the press in the cause of the suffering and the dumb.

We shall aim at a purification of the churches from all participation in the guilt of slavery.

We shall encourage the labour of freemen rather than that of the slaves, by giving a preference to their productions: and

We shall spare no exertions nor means to bring the whole nation to speedy repentance.

Our trust for victory is solely in GOD. *We* may be personally defeated, but our principles never. TRUTH, JUSTICE, REASON, HUMANITY, must and will gloriously triumph. Already a host is coming up to the help of the Lord against the mighty, and the prospect before us is full of encouragement.

Submitting this DECLARATION to the candid examination of the people of this country, and of the friends of liberty throughout the world, we hereby affix our signatures to it; pledging ourselves that, under the guidance and by the help of Almighty God, we will do all that in us lies, consistently with this Declaration of our principles, to overthrow the most execrable system of slavery, that has ever been witnessed upon earth—to deliver our land from its deadliest curse—to wipe out the foulest stain which rests upon our national escutcheon—and to secure to the coloured population of the United States all the rights and privileges which belong to them as men, and as Americans—come what may to our persons, our interests, or our reputations—whether we live to witness the triumph of LIBERTY, JUSTICE, and HUMANITY, or perish untimely as martyrs in this great, benevolent, and holy cause. Done in Philadelphia, this Sixth day of December, A. D. 1833.

* Exodus xxi. 16—Deuteronomy xxiv. 7.

Maine.
DAVID THURSTON,
NATHAN WINSLOW,
JOSEPH SOUTHWICK,
JAMES FREDERIC OTIS,
ISAAC WINSLOW.

New Hampshire.
DAVID CAMBELL.

Vermont.
ORSON S. MURRAY.

Massachusetts.
DANIEL S. SOUTHMAYD,
EFFINGHAM L. CAPRON,
JOSHUA COFFIN,
AMOS A. PHELPS,
JOHN G. WHITTIER,
HORACE P. WAKEFIELD,
JAMES G. BARBADOES,
DAVID T. KIMBALL, Jr.
DANIEL E. JEWETT,
JOHN R. CAMBELL,
NATHANIEL SOUTHARD,
ARNOLD BUFFUM,
WILLIAM L. GARRISON.

Rhode Island.
JOHN PRENTICE,
GEORGE W. BENSON,
RAY POTTER.

Connecticut.
SAMUEL J. MAY,
ALPHEUS KINGSLEY.

EDWIN A. STILLMAN,
SIMEON S. JOCELYN,
ROBERT B. HALL.

New York.
BERIAH GREEN, Jr.
LEWIS TAPPAN,
JOHN RANKIN,
WILLIAM GREEN, Jr.
ABR'M L. COX,
WILLIAM GOODELL,
ELIZUR WRIGHT, Jr.
CHARLES W. DENISON,
JOHN FROST.

New Jersey.
JONATHAN PARKHURST,
CHALKLEY GILLINGHAM,
JOHN McCULLOUGH,
JAMES WHITE.

Pennsylvania.
EVAN LEWIS,
EDWIN A. ATLEE,
ROBERT PURVIS,
JAS. McCRUMMILL,
THOMAS SHIPLEY,
BARTH'W. FUSSELL,
DAVID JONES,
ENOCH MACK,
JAMES McKIM,
AARON VICKERS,
JAMES LOUGHHEAD,
EDWIN P. ATLEE,
THOMAS WHITSON,
JOHN R. SLEEPER,
JOHN SHARP, Jr.
JAMES MOTT.

Ohio.
JOHN M. STERLING,
MILTON SUTLIFF,
LEVI SUTLIFF.

Published by J. Fleeper, No. 121 North Second Street, Philadelphia.

INTRODUCTION

Abolitionism and the Crisis of the Fifties

Negroes in the North took part in many of the reform movements that left their stamp on pre-Civil War America. In a period characterized by a variety of crusades, temperance and women's rights among them, it was inevitable that some Negroes would join in. In support of the anti-liquor movement Negroes of three states—New York, New Jersey, and Massachusetts—formed the States' Delevan Union Temperance Society of Colored People. Negroes, too, were interested in the struggle for equal rights for women, particularly the right to vote. At the first women's convention held in America, a gathering at Seneca Falls, New York, in July 1848, Frederick Douglass was the only man to take a prominent role in the deliberations and the only man to support the revolutionary proposal of equal suffrage. Negro conventions generally went on record as favoring the political and legal equality of the sexes.

Although Negroes could be numbered in a variety of reform endeavors, it is but natural that their keenest interest would center in the organized movement against slavery. The slaves were Negroes and the pro-slavery argument hinged upon the inferiority of the black man. Hence Negroes sought membership in the many societies formed by the abolitionists, becoming part of the movement to blot human bondage from the land.

If the abolitionists had a common goal, they differed as to method of attack. For one thing, they held varying views as to a militant, aggressive approach. Prior to 1830 the abolitionist societies employed the technique of persuasion and conciliation. In the early abolitionist movement the key figures were quiet-mannered men of property and standing, often prominent laymen in their churches. These early societies sought the gradual, rather than the immediate abolition of slavery. They did not object to compensated emancipation, often themselves paying masters to free their slaves. Many of these early societies viewed colonization of the Negro—deporting him to Africa—as an acceptable, long-range solution.

This conciliatory abolitionist approach was personified in Benjamin Lundy and William Ellery Channing. A self-educated Quaker from New Jersey, Lundy settled in Ohio in 1815, founding the Union Humane Society. Six years later he began publishing a newspaper little in size but most impressive in title, *The Genius of Universal Emancipation.* In this periodical Lundy espoused the doctrines of gradual emancipation and colonization. Although of slight physique, Lundy did much of his traveling by foot, staff in hand and pack on his back, his errand to enlist supporters and to find a territory to which Negroes would migrate. William Ellery Channing, like Lundy, was an olive-branch abolitionist. Channing, whose fame as a scholar and a Unitarian clergyman extended far beyond his Boston parishioners, was opposed to strong language in denouncing slave-owners. In a letter to Daniel Webster (May 14, 1828), Channing suggested that Northerners should allay the fears of Southerners by saying to them, "We consider slavery as your calamity, not your crime, and we will share with you the burden of putting an end to it."

By 1830 the Lundy-Channing approach, and the old-line abolitionist societies that had followed it, were in retreat. Although their accomplishments were far from negligible, it was obvious that slavery was flourishing as never before. In the early decades of the nineteenth century, slavery would not have been measurably slowed down regardless of whatever techniques the abolitionists employed. For at that period the South seemed to be an increasingly dominant force in the life of the nation. With the cotton kingdom expanding toward the Mississippi and beyond, the South regarded slavery as its greatest asset as it readied itself to contest with the North for the greatest prize of all—a West to be won.

But although the early abolitionist societies could not be held derelict because slavery was not dying, it was inevitable that many reformers would be led to question the efficacy of the non-aggressive approach. Thus the stage was set for the emergence of a new breed of abolitionist, ready for ways and means more direct and forceful. By 1830 abolitionism moved into a more militant phase, reflecting something of the revolutionary temper of Nat Turner and the strong language of David Walker, although its leaders would have disowned the one and disavowed the other.

The new abolitionism was formally launched with the founding of the American Anti-Slavery Society at Philadelphia in 1833. Bent on "abolitionizing the country," the Society appointed agents to take the message to the people and turned out tracts and pamphlets by the tens of thousands, having over 20,000 Southerners on its mailing list. If the cause needed a martyr to give it momentum it had one in 1837 in Elijah P. Lovejoy. His tragic fate was given wide coverage in the public newspapers and his name became a symbol to reformers. A clergyman who had become editor of a religious journal, *Observer,* Lovejoy moved to Alton, Illinois, in 1836. Here, as in St. Louis, his anti-slavery views met with determined opposition, his presses being thrown into the river on three separate occasions. On a night in November 1837 Lovejoy was killed as he emerged from a building which the mob, bent on destroying his press, had set on fire.

The personification of the root-and-branch spirit of abolitionism was William Lloyd Garrison, who had been a young journeyman printer in Newburyport, Massachusetts, before moving to Boston. Here on January 1, 1831, he launched *The Liberator,* with its famous manifesto stating that he was in earnest, would not equivocate, excuse or retreat a single inch, and that he would be heard. The dedicated Garrison quickly became a leading abolitionist, founding the New England Anti-Slavery Society in 1832, and serving for twenty-five years as president of the American Anti-Slavery Society. Working closely with Garrison was Wendell Phillips, one of the most effective orators of the nineteenth century. Coming from an old Boston family and a graduate of both the college and law school of Harvard, Phillips sacrificed social standing and a career in politics to work for the slave.

Garrison's *Liberator* in its first, struggling years owed much to the support of its Negro subscribers, and Negroes, in truth, were in the forefront of the revived abolitionism. They took part in many of the organizational meetings, thus muting the sometimes raised question as to the wisdom of admitting Negroes to membership in the movement. To enroll Negroes was important to the success of the cause, not only as a sign that color prejudice did not hold sway, but for the substantial contribution they made. The anti-slavery concert owed much to the efforts of Negro lecturers, agents, clergymen, and journalists. Negro abolitionists ranged from the rich and well-bred Robert Purvis to the unlettered, but deeply moving, Sojourner Truth, whose personality was as striking as the name she assumed.

Negro abolitionists made a distinctive contribution to the progress of abolitionism across the Atlantic. During the two decades preceding the Civil War a procession of Negroes paraded throughout the British Isles, pleading the cause of the chain-burdened slave. Speaking before large and enthusiastic audiences, this impressive roster of visiting Negroes included Frederick Douglass, J. W. C. Pennington (hired in 1851 as a lecturer by the Glasgow Female New Association for the Abolition of Slavery), the scholarly Alexander Crummell, Henry Highland Garnet, Samuel Ringgold Ward, and Martin R. Delany, explorer and colonizationist. Perhaps the best-known of these pre-war visitors was William Wells Brown, who spent over five years in the British Isles, traveling over 12,000 miles and making over a thousand speeches.

Negro reformers might be lionized in London but at home in America the story was different. Abolitionists as a class lived dangerously, often being roughed up, and sometimes being stoned. A Negro abolitionist required a double dose of courage. No reform lecturer was more likely to be set upon by unfriendly hands than a black one, or more likely to receive less assistance from a see-no-evil policeman.

Abolitionists faced danger because many people considered them self-righteous and fanatical, bitter and narrow, being unjust to their opponents. Such views have been shared in part by some later historians who viewed the abolitionists as neurotics afflicted by an inner turmoil and conflict from which they sought escape in befriending the slave. Hence what these not-normal people were really seeking, runs this argument, was not freedom for the slave so much as release from their own private devils.

But such an analysis tends to ignore the fundamental soundness of the views they expressed. As for their strong, denunciatory language, the abolitionists, like revolutionaries before and since, felt that overstatement was necessary: "Brother May, I have need to be all on fire," said Garrison to Samuel J. May, "for I have mountains of ice about me to melt." Moreover to lump all abolitionists together as having the same, peculiar personality is to ignore the extremely wide variations among them in temperament and outlook.

In approach, too, the newer radical abolitionists differed among themselves. Garrison and his followers decried political action, becoming non-voting and non-office-holding abolitionists. Holding that the Constitution of the United States was pro-slavery, the Garrison abolitionists relied on what they termed "moral suasion." But outside of New England, the abolitionists after 1840 turned to politics, founding the Liberty Party and later giving support to its paler successors in pure abolitionism, the Free Soil and Republican parties.

If they differed in approach, abolitionists were alike in their methods of operation. Following the standard procedures of reform groups, they held meetings—weekly, monthly, quarterly, and yearly—at which reports were given, resolutions were passed, and petitions were signed. Between meetings their societies operated through committees, standing and special. Agents were sent out to give speeches, to solicit funds, and to get subscriptions to their periodicals of the societies.

The printing press played a major role in the crusade against slavery. Abolitionist organizations saturated the public with literature, much of it for free distribution. From their offices came prodigious quantities of sermons, speeches, essays, poems, newspapers, excerpts from friendly and hostile sources, and a whole body of materials for juveniles, including spelling jingles patterned after the *New England Primer*. The abolitionists could point to a few gifted poets like John Greenleaf Whittier and James Russell Lowell. Their most successful novelist was Harriet Beecher Stowe, whose *Uncle Tom's Cabin* made a lasting impression on the northern mind. The literary brigade included the Carolina-born aristocrat, Angelina Grimké, who with her sister, Sarah, had left Charleston to live in the North and bear witness against slavery. Angelina became a lecturer and a pamphleteer, eventually marrying a man after her own heart (and mind), Theodore D. Weld. In 1836 Angelina completed a lengthy pamphlet, *Appeal to the Christian Women of the South,* which the American Anti-Slavery Society printed in quantity for nationwide distribution.

Abolitionist literature was sent into the South but most of it went unread because it was not delivered. Citizens of Charleston, South Carolina, set an example in July 1835 by breaking into the post office, seizing abolitionist papers and burning them in the streets. Local officials lent a hand: "Postmasters to ransack the mail is very reprehensible," wrote Elihu Embree, editor and publisher of *The Emancipator*. Postmaster General Amos Kendall, a slaveholder, wished to exclude abolitionist materials from circulating in the South, and he sought President Jackson's advice. Jackson ordered that such mail be delivered to none except subscribers. He followed this up in his message to Congress on December 7, 1835, condemning "incendiary publications, intended to instigate the slaves to insurrection," and recommending a law making it a crime to circulate such materials through the mail. Although Congress did not respond to Jackson's wishes, southern postmasters were left free to use their own judgment as to the distribution of abolitionist mail. However, the charge that freedom of the press was being imperiled became one of the major points in the mounting abolitionist charge that slavery's defenders were sapping fundamental American liberties.

As a force in history, the abolitionist crusade owed much to the dramatic events of the 1850's. For in this fateful decade the slavery issue took on a newer and deeper urgency. The question of slavery in the territories became more pressing than ever with the acquisition of lands resulting from the war with Mexico, ending in 1848. The Compromise Act of 1850 established the principle of popular sovereignty in the territories—a generally accepted solution. But another of the compromise measures, the Fugitive Slave Law, which was designed to make it easier to recapture runaways, aroused deep hostility in the North—a hostility by no means confined to abolitionists.

Sectional animosities, already high, became feverish four years later when a law, the Kansas-Nebraska Act, opened to slavery a portion of the public domain from which it had been barred since 1820. Almost overnight a new party, the Republicans, came into existence to protest the spread of slavery into the territories. The Republicans gained tens of thousands of converts in 1857 when the Supreme Court handed down the Dred Scott decision. The central issue—whether Scott, a slave, was a citizen of the United States—was decided in the negative. But then the Court proceeded to declare that Congress could not prohibit slavery in federal territory.

The Supreme Court's edict aroused a furious debate. In the state of Illinois, two candidates for a seat in the United States Senate, Stephen A. Douglas and Abraham Lincoln, vigorously debated the issue of extending slavery to the territories. But increasingly the rush of events seemed to make all debate and all further talk seem pointless. In October 1859 John Brown and twenty-one men-at-arms, five of them Negroes, seized a government arsenal at Harpers Ferry, Virginia. Brown was captured and put to death. His attempted coup struck a raw and sensitive nerve in the South. But in the North the feeling grew that John Brown had died a martyr's death, making the gallows glorious like the cross, as Ralph Waldo Emerson put it.

The following year brought no easement; indeed it brought a national election which was to signal a parting of the ways between the sections. In the November elections the Republicans won with Abraham Lincoln. Thereupon, South Carolina lost no time in seceding from the Union. Her lead was followed by six other states before Lincoln took office on March 4, 1861. Some five weeks later Fort

Sumter, a federal stronghold in the Charleston harbor, was shelled by South Carolina. Lincoln immediately issued a call for volunteers to put down a rebellion.

War had come—a turn of events that the abolitionists viewed as the fulfillment of their dire prediction that slavery, sooner or later, would lead the country into a bloody clash at arms.

The New Spirit of Abolitionism

94

APPRECIATION FOR THE LIBERATOR

The early abolitionist movement was characterized by a tone of mildness and sweet reasonableness. But the idea of having a "fraternal feeling" for the slaveholder receded after 1830, in part due to the coming of William Lloyd Garrison. The publication of his small, four-page folio, Liberator, *set a new, militant tone. "I will be as harsh as truth, and as uncompromising as justice," wrote Garrison in the first issue, dated January 1, 1831. Counting himself a friend of the Negro, Garrison spoke to colored audiences in half a dozen cities during the first six months of 1831. "I never rise to address a colored audience, without feeling ashamed of my own color," he said, in his standard speech, "ashamed of being identified with a race of men who have done you so much injustice." It is not surprising that Negroes felt drawn to such a man. One day before the* Liberator *made its first appearance, James Forten, a Revolutionary War powder boy who had become a successful sailmaker in Philadelphia, wrote to Garrison expressing appreciation for his efforts and enclosing money for subscriptions. Forten's letter clearly foreshadows the long "love affair" between Garrison and the Negro.*

JAMES FORTEN TO WILLIAM LLOYD GARRISON

Phila.: Dec. 31, 1830

Dear Sir:

I am extremely happy to hear that you are establishing a Paper in Boston. I hope your efforts may not be in vain; and that the "Liberator" be the means of exposing more and more the odious system of Slavery, and of raising up friends to the oppressed and degraded People of Colour throughout the Union. Whilst so much is doing in the world, to ameliorate the condition of mankind, and the spirit of Freedom is marching with rapid strides and causing tyrants to tremble; may America awake from the apathy in which she has long slumbered. She must sooner or later fall in with the irresistible current. Great efforts are now making in the cause of Liberty: the people are becoming more interested and determined on the subject.

Although the Southern States have erected severe laws against the Free People of Colour, they will find it impossible to go in opposition to the Spirit of the times. We have only to hope that with such philanthropists as Mr. Lundy and yourself will come forward to plead our cause; we can never be sufficiently grateful to our long tried, faithful and zealous friend, Mr. Lundy. He had indeed laboured for us, through evil and good reports, and under many disadvantages and hardships; may he hereafter receive his reward. . . . I herewith inclose you the money for twenty-seven subscribers, and their names and places of abode, you will also herewith receive. I would request you to send on a few Extra Papers, that I may hand them to my friends.*

95

THE MAGNA CHARTA OF THE ANTI-SLAVERY MOVEMENT

The new spirit of abolition which Garrison exemplified received a wider expression in the formation of the American Anti-Slavery Society at Philadelphia on December 4, 1833. The sixty-two delegates from eleven states proclaimed as their dual objects "the entire abolition of slavery in the United States," and the elevation of "the character and condition of the people of color." The duty of drafting a manifesto was assigned to a committee, in which the bulk of the work fell on Garrison, assisted by John Greenleaf Whittier, and the Reverend Samuel J. May. The resulting "Declaration of Sentiments," subsequently described by reformer Oliver Johnson as "the Magna Charta of the anti-slavery movement," was a forthright call to action, its closing passages taking on a revolutionary ring.

Therefore we believe and affirm—That there is no difference, in principle, between the African slave trade and American slavery;

That every American citizen, who retains a human being in involuntary bondage as his property, is [according to Scripture†] a MAN-STEALER;

That the slaves ought instantly to be set free, and brought under the protection of law;

That if they had lived from the time of Pharaoh down to the present period, and had been entailed through successive generations, their right to be free could never have been alienated, but their claims would have constantly risen in solemnity;

That all those laws which are now in force, admitting the right of slavery, are therefore before God utterly null and void; being an audacious usurpation of the Divine prerogative, a daring infringement on the law of Nature, a base overthrow of the very foundations of the social compact, a complete extinction of all the relations, endearments, and obligations of mankind, and a presumptuous transgression of all the holy commandments—and that therefore they ought to be instantly abrogated.

We further believe and affirm—That all persons of color who possess the qualifications which are demanded of others, ought to be admitted forthwith to the enjoyment of the same privileges, and the exercise of the same prerogatives, as others; and that the paths of preferment, of wealth, and of intelligence, should be opened as widely to them as to persons of a white complexion.

---

*From "Early Manuscript Letters Written by Negroes," by Dorothy B. Porter, from *Journal of Negro History*, April 1939, pp. 199–200. Reprinted by permission of The Associated Publishers, Inc.

We maintain that no compensation should be given to the planters emancipating their slaves—

Because it would be a surrender of the great fundamental principle, that man cannot hold property in man;

Because SLAVERY IS A CRIME, AND THEREFORE IT IS NOT AN ARTICLE TO BE SOLD;

Because the holders of slaves are not the just proprietors of what they claim; freeing the slaves is not depriving them of property, but restoring it to its right owners; it is not wronging the master, but righting the slave—restoring him to himself;

Because immediate and general emancipation would only destroy nominal, not real property: it would not amputate a limb or break a bone of the slaves, but by infusing motives into their breasts would make them doubly valuable to the masters as free laborers: and

Because if compensation is to be given at all, it should be given to the outraged and guiltless slaves, and not to those who have plundered and abused them.

We regard, as delusive, cruel, and dangerous, any scheme of expatriation which pretends to aid, either directly or indirectly, in the emancipation of the slaves, or to be a substitute for the immediate and total abolition of slavery.

We fully and unanimously recognize the sovereignty of each State to legislate exclusively on the subject of slavery which is tolerated within its limits; we concede that Congress, under the present national compact, has no right to interfere with any of the slave States, in relation to this momentous subject.

But we maintain that Congress has a right, and is solemnly bound, to suppress the domestic slave trade between the several States, and to abolish slavery in those portions of our territory which the Constitution has placed under its exclusive jurisdiction.

We also maintain that there are, at the present time, the highest obligations resting upon the people of the free States, to remove slavery by moral and political action, as prescribed in the Constitution of the United States. They are now living under a pledge of their tremendous physical force to fasten the galling fetters of tyranny upon the limbs of millions in the Southern States; they are liable to be called at any moment to suppress a general insurrection of the slaves: they authorize the slave owner to vote for three-fifths of his slaves as property, and thus enable him to perpetuate his oppression; they support a standing army at the south for its protection; and they seize the slave who has escaped into their territories, and send him back to be tortured by an enraged master or a brutal driver. This relation to slavery is criminal and full of danger: IT MUST BE BROKEN UP.

These are our views and principles—these, our designs and measures. With entire confidence in the over-ruling justice of God, we plant ourselves upon the Declaration of our Independence, and the truths of Divine Revelation, as upon the EVERLASTING ROCK.

We shall organize Anti-Slavery Societies, if possible, in every city, town, and village in our land.

We shall send forth Agents to lift up the voice of remonstrance, of warning, of entreaty and rebuke.

We shall circulate, unsparingly and extensively, anti-slavery tracts and periodicals.

We shall enlist the pulpit and the press in the cause of the suffering and the dumb.

We shall aim at a purification of the churches from all participation in the guilt of slavery.

We shall encourage the labor of freemen rather than that of the slaves, by giving a preference to their productions: and

We shall spare no exertions nor means to bring the whole nation to speedy repentance.

Our trust for victory is *solely* in GOD. We may be personally defeated, but our principles never. TRUTH, JUSTICE, REASON, HUMANITY, must and will gloriously triumph. Already a host is coming up to the help of the Lord against the mighty, and the prospect before us is full of encouragement.

Submitting this DECLARATION to the candid examination of the people of this country, and of the friends of liberty throughout the world, we hereby affix our signatures to it; pledging ourselves that, under the guidance and by the help of Almighty God, we will do all that in us lies, consistently with this Declaration of our principles, to overthrow the most execrable system of slavery, that has ever been witnessed upon earth—to deliver our land from its deadliest curse—to wipe out the foulest stain which rests upon our national escutcheon—and to secure to the colored population of the United States all the rights and privileges which belong to them as men, and as Americans—come what may to our persons, our interests, or our reputations—whether we live to witness the triumph of LIBERTY, JUSTICE, and HUMANITY, or perish untimely as martyrs in this great, benevolent, and holy cause.

*Done in Philadelphia, this sixth day of December, A.D. 1833.**

96

AN ABOLITIONIST POET

One of the most widely quoted authors in the pages of the abolitionist publications was the gifted John Greenleaf Whittier whose anti-slavery poems were copied in paper after paper. A Quaker from Haverhill, Massachusetts, and a close friend of Garrison for a time, Whittier became an active abolitionist in the early 1830's, being numbered among the original members of the American Anti-Slavery Society. An experienced journalist and pamphleteer, Whittier's fame as an abolitionist rested largely on his some ninety poems against slavery. One of the most popular of these was the lament of a Virginia slave mother whose daughters had been sold down the river to the rice-swamps of Louisiana. The separation-of-families theme loomed large in the abolitionist attack on slavery, and in this instance the effect was heightened by Whittier's literary skills.

**Proceedings of the Anti-Slavery Convention Assembled at Philadelphia, December 4, 5, and 6, 1833* (New York, 1833), 14-16.

The Farewell

of a Virginia Slave Mother to Her Daughters, Sold into Southern Bondage.

Gone, gone—sold and gone,
To the rice-swamp dank and lone.
Where the slave-whip ceaseless swings,
Where the noisome insect stings,
Where the fever demon strews
Poison with the falling dews,
Where the sickly sunbeams glare
Through the hot and misty air,—
Gone, gone—sold and gone,
To the rice-swamp dank and lone,
From Virginia's hills and waters,—
Woe is me, my stolen daughters!

Gone, gone—sold and gone,
To the rice-swamp dank and lone.
There no mother's eye is near them,
There no mother's ear can hear them;
Never, when the torturing lash
Seams their back with many a gash,
Shall a mother's kindness bless them,
Or a mother's arms caress them.
Gone, gone—sold and gone,
To the rice-swamp dank and lone,
From Virginia's hills and waters—
Woe is me, my stolen daughters!

Gone, gone—sold and gone,
To the rice-swamp dank and lone.
Oh, when weary, sad, and slow,
From the fields at night they go,
Faint with toil, and racked with pain,
To their cheerless homes again—
There no brother's voice shall greet them—
There no father's welcome meet them.
Gone, gone—sold and gone,
To the rice-swamp dank and lone,
From Virginia's hills and waters—
Woe is me, my stolen daughters!

Gone, gone—sold and gone,
To the rice-swamp dank and lone,
From the tree whose shadow lay
On their childhood's place of play—
From the cool spring where they drank—
Rock, and hill, and rivulet bank—
From the solemn house of prayer,
And the holy counsels there—
Gone, gone—sold and gone,

To the rice-swamp dank and lone,
From Virginia's hills and waters,—
Woe is me, my stolen daughters!

Gone, gone—sold and gone,
To the rice-swamp dank and lone—
Toiling through the weary day,
And at night the spoiler's prey.
Oh, that they had earlier died,
Sleeping calmly, side by side,
Where the tyrant's power is o'er
And the fetter galls no more!
Gone, gone—sold and gone,
To the rice-swamp dank and lone,
From Virginia's hills and waters,—
Woe is me, my stolen daughters!

Gone, gone—sold and gone,
To the rice-swamp dank and lone.
By the holy love He beareth—
By the bruised reed He spareth—
Oh, may He, to whom alone
All their cruel wrongs are known,
Still their hope and refuge prove,
With a more than a mother's love,
Gone, gone—sold and gone,
To the rice-swamp dank and lone,
From Virginia's hills and waters,—
Woe is me, my stolen daughters! *

97

"THE GREATEST OF THE ANTISLAVERY PAMPHLETS"

The most widely distributed single work ever published by an abolitionist society was American Slavery As It Is, *which sold over 100,000 copies within a year after its appearance. Its author-compiler-editor was Theodore D. Weld, an intense, deeply religious man who had been the leading abolitionist organizer in the West, establishing local societies and recruiting young men as agents. Stung by the familiar charge that the abolitionists grossly misrepresented slavery because they had no first-hand information about it, Weld set about to collect testimony from southern sources alone—from speeches, writings, and newspapers. After amassing a great abundance of data, Weld then sifted and checked it. His findings were published in 1839 by the American Anti-Slavery Society. Over two hundred pages in length,* American Slavery As It Is *has been called by the present-day authority, Dwight L. Dumond, "the greatest of the antislavery pamphlets." The portions reproduced below are passages from Weld's "Introduction," followed by three typical "testimonies."*

**The Complete Poetical Works of John Greenleaf Whittier* (Boston, Houghton Mifflin Company, 1892), 177-179.

READER, you are empannelled as a juror to try a plain case and bring in an honest verdict. The question at issue is not one of law, but of fact—" What is the actual condition of the slaves in the United States?" A plainer case never went to a jury. Look at it. TWENTY-SEVEN HUNDRED THOUSAND PERSONS in this country, men, women, and children, are in SLAVERY. Is slavery, as a condition for human beings, good, bad, or indifferent? We submit the question without argument. You have common sense, and conscience, and a human heart;—pronounce upon it. You have a wife, or a husband, a child, a father, a mother, a brother or a sister—make the case your own, make it theirs, and bring in your verdict. The case of Human Rights against Slavery has been adjudicated in the court of conscience times innumerable. The same verdict has always been rendered—"Guilty;" the same sentence has always been pronounced, "Let it be accursed;" and human nature, with her million echoes, has rung it round the world in every language under heaven, "Let it be accursed. Let it be accursed." His heart is false to human nature, who will not say "Amen." There is not a man on earth who does not believe that slavery is a curse. Human beings may be inconsistent, but human *nature* is true to herself. She has uttered her testimony against slavery with a shriek ever since the monster was begotten; and till it perishes amidst the execrations of the universe, she will traverse the world on its track, dealing her bolts upon its head, and dashing against it her condemning brand. We repeat it, every man knows that slavery is a curse. Whoever denies this, his lips libel his heart. Try him; clank the chains in his ears, and tell him they are for *him;* give him an hour to prepare his wife and children for a life of slavery; bid him make haste and get ready their necks for the yoke, and their wrists for the coffle chains, then look at his pale lips and trembling knees, and you have *nature's* testimony against slavery.

* * *

But we will not anticipate topics, the full discussion of which more naturally follows than precedes the inquiry into the actual condition and treatment of slaves in the United States.

As slaveholders and their apologists are volunteer witnesses in their own cause, and are flooding the world with testimony that their slaves are kindly treated; that they are well fed, well clothed, well housed, well lodged, moderately worked, and bountifully provided with all things needful for their comfort, we propose—first, to disprove their assertions by the testimony of a multitude of impartial witnesses, and then to put slaveholders themselves through a course of cross-questioning which shall draw their condemnation out of their own mouths. We will prove that the slaves in the United States are treated with barbarous inhumanity; that they are overworked, underfed, wretchedly clad and lodged, and have insufficient sleep; that they are often made to wear round their necks iron collars armed with prongs, to drag heavy chains and weights at their feet while working in the field, and to wear yokes, and bells, and iron horns; that they are often kept confined in the stocks day and night for weeks together, made to wear gags in their mouths for hours or days, have some of their front teeth torn out or broken off, that they may be easily detected when they run away; that they are frequently flogged with terrible severity, have red pepper rubbed into their lacerated flesh, and hot brine, spirits of turpentine, &c., poured over the gashes to increase the torture; that they are often stripped naked, their backs and limbs cut with knives bruised and mangled by scores and hundreds of blows with the paddle, and terribly torn by the claws of cats, drawn over them by their tormentors; that they are often hunted with bloodhounds and shot down like beasts, or torn in pieces by dogs; that they are often suspended by the arms and whipped and beaten till they faint, and when revived by restoratives, beaten again till they faint, and sometimes till they die; that their ears are often cut off, their eyes knocked out, their bones broken, their flesh branded with red hot irons; that they are maimed, mutilated and burned to death over slow fires. All these things and more, and worse, we shall *prove*. Reader, we know whereof we affirm, we have weighed it well; *more and worse* WE WILL PROVE. Mark these words, and read on; we will establish all these facts by the testimony of *slaveholders* in all parts of the slave states, by slaveholding members of Congress and of state legislatures, by ambassadors to foreign courts, by judges, by doctors of divinity, and clergymen of all denominations, by merchants, mechanics, lawyers and physicians, by presidents and professors in colleges and *professional* seminaries, by planters, overseers and drivers. We shall show, not merely that such deeds are committed, but that they are frequent; not done in corners, but before the sun; not in one of the slave states, but in all of them; not perpetrated by brutal overseers and drivers merely, but by magistrates, by legislators, by professors of religion, by preachers of the gospel, by governors of states, by "gentlemen of property and standing," and by delicate females moving in the "highest circles of society." We know, full well, the outcry that will be made by multitudes at these declarations; the multiform cavils, the flat denials, the charges of "exaggeration" and "falsehood" so often bandied, the sneers of affected contempt at the credulity that can believe such things, and the rage and imprecations against those who give them currency. We know, too, the threadbare sophistries by which slaveholders and their apologists seek to evade such testimony. If they admit that such deeds are committed, they tell us that they are exceedingly rare, and therefore furnish no grounds for judging of the general treatment of slaves; that occasionally a brutal wretch in the *free* states barbarously butchers his wife, but that no one thinks of inferring from that, the general treatment of wives at the North and West.

They tell us, also, that the slaveholders of the South are proverbially hospitable, kind, and generous, and it is incredible that they can perpetrate such enormities upon human beings; further, that it is absurd to suppose that they would thus injure their own property, that self interest would prompt them to treat their slaves with kindness, as none but fools and madmen wantonly destroy their own property; further, that Northern visitors at the South come back testifying to the kind treatment of the slaves, and that the slaves themselves corroborate such representations. All these pleas, and scores of others, are bruited in every corner of the free States; and who that hath eyes to see, has not sickened at the blindness that saw not, at the palsy of heart that felt not, or the cowardice and sycophaney that dared not expose such shallow fallacies. We are not to be turned from our purpose by such vapid babblings. In their appropriate places we propose to consider these objections and various others, and to show their emptiness and folly.

The foregoing declarations touching the inflictions upon slaves, are not hap-hazard assertions, nor the exaggerations of fiction conjured up to carry a point; nor are they the rhapsodies of enthusiasm, nor crude conclusions, jumped at by hasty and imperfect investigation, nor the aimless outpourings either of sympathy or poetry; but they are proclamations of deliberate, well-weighed convictions, produced by accumulations of proof, by affirmations and affidavits, by written testimonies and statements of a cloud of witnesses who speak what they know and testify what they have seen, and all these impregnably fortified by proofs innumerable, in the relation of the slaveholder to his slave, the nature of arbitrary power, and the nature and history of man.

Of the witnesses whose testimony is embodied in the following pages, a majority are slaveholders, many of the remainder have been slaveholders, but now reside in free States.

Another class whose testimony will be given consists of those who have furnished the results of their own observation during periods of residence and travel in the slave States.

* * *

Between the larger divisions of the work, brief personal narratives will be inserted, containing a mass of facts and testimony, both general and specific.*

NARRATIVE OF MR. WILLIAM LEFTWICH, A NATIVE OF VIRGINIA

Mr. Leftwich is a grandson of Gen. Jabez Leftwich, who was for some years a member of Congress from Virginia. Though born in Virginia, he has resided most of his life in Alabama. He now lives in Delhi, Hamilton county, Ohio, near Cincinnati.

As an introduction to his letter, the reader is furnished with the following testimonial to his character, from the Rev. Horace Bushnell, pastor of the Presbyterian church in Delhi. Mr. B. says:

"Mr. Leftwich is a worthy member of this church, and is a young man of sterling integrity and veracity. H. Bushnell."

The following is the letter of Mr. Leftwich, dated Dec. 26, 1838.

"Dear Brother—Though I am not ranked among the abolitionists, yet I cannot, as a friend of humanity, withhold from the public such facts in relation to the condition of the slaves, as have fallen under my own observation. That I am somewhat acquainted with slavery will be seen, as I narrate some incidents of my own life. My

---

*Theodore D. Weld, ed., *American Slavery As It Is: Testimony of a Thousand Witnesses,* New York Anti-Slavery Society (New York, 1839), 7-10.

parents were slaveholders, and moved from Virginia to Madison county, Alabama, during my infancy. My mother soon fell a victim to the climate. Being the youngest of the children, I was left in the care of my aged grandfather, who never held a slave, though his sons owned from 90 to 100 during the time I resided with him. As soon as I could carry a hoe, my uncle by the name of Neely, persuaded my grandfather that I should be placed in his hands, and brought up in habits of industry. I was accordingly placed under his tuition. I left the domestic circle, little dreaming of the horrors that awaited me. My mother's own brother took me to the cotton field, there to learn habits of industry, and to be benefited by his counsels. But the sequel proved, that I was there to feel in my own person, and witness by experience many of the horrors of slavery. Instead of kind admonition, I was to endure the frowns of one, whose sympathies could neither be reached by prayers and cries of his slaves, nor by the entreaties of sufferings of a sister's son. Let those who call slaveholders kind, hospitable and humane, mark the course the slaveholder pursues with one born free, whose ancestors fought and bled for liberty; and then say, if they can without a blush of shame, that he who robs the helpless of every *right*, can be truly kind and hospitable.

"In a short time after I was put upon the plantation, there was but little difference between me and the slaves, except being *white*, I ate at the master's table. The slaves were my companions in misery, and I well learned their condition, both in the house and field. Their dwellings are log huts, from ten to twelve feet square; often without windows, doors or floors. They have neither chairs, tables or bedsteads, these huts are occupied by eight, ten or twelve persons each. Their bedding generally consists of two old blankets. Many of them sleep night after night sitting upon their blocks or stools; others sleep in the open air. Our task was appointed and from dawn till dark all must bend to the work. Their meals were taken without knife or plate, dish or spoon. Their food was corn *pone* prepared in the coarsest manner, with a small allowance of meat. Their meals in the field were taken from the hands of the carrier, wherever he found them, with no more ceremony than in the feeding of swine. My uncle was his own overseer. For punishing in the field, he preferred a large hickory stick; and wo to him whose work was not done to please him, for the hickory was used upon our heads as remorselessly as if we had been mad dogs. I was often the object of his fury, and shall bear the marks of it on my body till I die. Such was my suffering and degradation, that at the end of five years, I hardly dared to say I was *free.* When thinning cotton, we went mostly on our knees. One day, while thus engaged, my uncle found my row behind and, by way of admonition, gave me a few blows with his hickory, the marks of which I carried for weeks. Often I followed the example of the fugitive slaves, and betook myself to the mountains; but hunger and fear drove me back, to share with the wretched slave his toil and stripes. But I have talked enough about my own bondage; I will now relate a few facts, showing the condition of the slaves *generally.*

"My uncle wishing to purchase what is called a good 'house wench,' a *trader* in human flesh soon produced a woman, recommending her as highly as ever a jockey did a horse. She was purchased, but on trial was found wanting in the requisite qualifications. She then fell a victim to the disappointed rage of my uncle; innocent or guilty, she suffered greatly from his fury. He used to tie her to a peach tree in the yard, and whip her till there was no sound place to lay another stroke, and repeat it so often that her back was continually sore. Whipping the females around the legs, was a favorite mode of punishment with him. They must stand and hold up their clothes, while he plied his hickory. He did not, like some of his neighbors, keep a pack of hounds for hunting runaway negroes, but he kept one dog for the purpose, and when he came up with a runaway, it would have been death to attempt to fly, and it was nearly so to stand. Sometimes, when my uncle attempted to whip the slaves, the dog would rush upon them and relieve them of their rags, if not of their flesh. One object of my uncle's special hate was "Jerry," a slave of a proud spirit. He defied all the curses, rage and stripes of his tyrant. Though he was often overpowered—for my uncle would frequently wear out his stick upon his head—yet he would never submit. As he was not expert in picking cotton, he would sometimes run away in the fall, to escape abuse. At one time, after an absence of some months, he was arrested and brought back. As is customary, he was stripped, tied to a log, and the cow-skin applied to his naked body till his master was exhausted. Then a large log chain was fastened around one ankle, passed up his back, over his shoulders, then across his breast, and fastened under his arm. In this condition he was forced to perform his daily task. Add to this he was chained each night, and compelled to chop wood every Sabbath, to make up lost time. After being thus manacled for some months, he was released—but his spirit was unsubdued. Soon after, his master, in a paroxysm of rage, fell upon him, wore out his staff upon his head, loaded him again with chains, and after a month, sold him farther south. Another slave, by the name of Mince, who was a man of great strength, purloined some bacon on a Christmas eve. It was missed in the morning, and he being absent, was of course suspected. On returning home, my uncle commanded him to come to him, but he refused. The master strove in vain to lay hands on him; in vain he ordered his slaves to seize him—they dared not. At length the master hurled a stone at his head sufficient to have felled a bullock—but he did not heed it. At that instant my aunt sprang forward, and presenting the gun to my uncle, exclaimed, 'Shoot him! shoot him!' He made the attempt, but the gun missed fire, and Mince fled. He was taken eight or ten months after that, while crossing the Ohio. When brought back, the master, and an overseer on another plantation, took him to the mountains and punished him to their satisfaction in secret; after which he was loaded with chains and set to his task.

"I have spent nearly all my life in the midst of slavery. From being the son of a slaveholder, I descended to the condition of a slave, and from that condition I rose (if you please to call it so,)

The American Anti-Slavery Society used pictures like these with its pamphlets and separately in their attempt to influence men in both the North and the South.

to the station of a *'driver.'* I have lived in Alabama, Tennessee, and Kentucky; and I *know* the condition of the slaves to be that of unmixed wretchedness and degradation. And on the part of slave-holders, there is cruelty *untold.* The labor of the slave is constant toil, wrung out by fear. Their food is scanty, and taken without comfort. Their clothes answer the purposes neither of comfort nor decency. They are not allowed to read or write. Whether they may worship God or not, depends on the will of the master. The young children, until they can work, often go naked during the warm weather. I could spend months in detailing the sufferings, degradation and cruelty inflicted upon slaves. But my soul sickens at the remembrance of these things."

TESTIMONY OF MR. LEMUEL SAPINGTON,
A NATIVE OF MARYLAND

Mr. Sapington, is a repentant "soul driver" or slave trader, now a citizen of Lancaster, Pa. He gives the following testimony in a letter dated, Jan. 21, 1839.

"I was born in Maryland, afterwards moved to Virginia, where I commenced the business of farming and trafficking in slaves. In my neighborhood the slaves were 'quartered.' The description generally given of negro quarters is correct. The quarters are without floors, and not sufficient to keep off the inclemency of the weather, they are uncomfortable both in summer and winter. The food there consists of potatoes, pork, and corn, which were given to them daily, by weight and measure. The sexes were huddled together promiscuously. Their clothing is made by themselves after night, though sometimes assisted by the old women who are no longer able to do out door work, consequently it is harsh and uncomfortable. I have frequently seen those of both sexes who have not attained the age of twelve go naked. Their punishments are invariable cruel. For the slightest offence, such as taking a hen's egg, I have seen them stripped and suspended by their hands, their feet tied together, a fence rail of ordinary size placed between their ankles, and then most cruelly whipped, until, from head to foot, they were completely lacerated, a pickle made for the purpose of salt and water, would then be applied by a fellow-slave, for the purpose of healing the wounds as well as giving pain. Then taken down and without the least respite sent to work with their hoe.

"Pursuing my assumed right of driving souls, I went to the Southern part of Virginia for the purpose of trafficking in slaves. In that part of the state, the cruelties practised upon the slaves, are far greater than where I lived. The punishments there often resulted in death to the slave. There was no law for the negro, but that of the overseer's whip. In that part of the country, the slaves receive nothing for food, but corn in the ear, which has to be prepared for baking after working hours, by grinding it with a hand-mill. This they take to the fields with them, and prepare it for eating by holding it on their hoes, over a fire made by a stump. Among the gangs, are often young women, who bring their children to the fields, and lay them in a fence corner, while they are at work, only being permitted to nurse them at the option of the overseer. When a child is three weeks old, a woman is considered in working order. I have seen a woman, with her young child strapped to her back, laboring the whole day, beside a man, perhaps the father of the child, and he not being permitted to give her any assistance, himself being under the whip. The uncommon humanity of the driver allowing her the comfort of doing so. I was then selling a drove of slaves, which I had brought by water from Baltimore, my conscience not allowing me to drive, as was generally the case uniting the slaves by collars and chains, and thus driving them under the whip. About that time an unaccountable something, which I now know was an interposition of Providence, prevented me from prosecuting any farther this unholy traffic; but though I had quitted it, I still continued to live in a slave state, witnessing every day its evil effects upon my father beings. Among which was a heart-rending scene that took place in my father's house, which led me to leave a slave state, as well as all the imaginary comforts arising from slavery. On preparing for my removal to the state of Pennsylvania, it became necessary for me to go to Louisville, in Kentucky, where, if possible, I became more horrified with the impositions practiced upon the negro than before. There a slave was sold to go farther south, and was handcuffed for the purpose of keeping him secure. But choosing death rather than slavery, he jumped overboard and was drowned. When I returned four weeks afterwards his body, that had floated three miles below, was yet unburied. One fact; it is impossible for a person to pass through a slave state, if he has eyes open, without beholding every day cruelties repugnant to humanity.

Respectfully Yours,
Lemuel Sapington"

TESTIMONY OF MR. HIRAM WHITE,
A NATIVE OF NORTH CAROLINA.

Mr. White resided thirty-two years in Chatham county, North Carolina, and is now a member of the Baptist Church at Otter Creek Prairie, Illinois.

"About the 20th December, 1830, a report was raised that the slaves in Chatham county, North Carolina, were going to rise on Christmas day, in consequence of which a considerable commotion ensued among the inhabitants; orders were given by the Governor to the militia captains, to appoint patrolling captains in each disrict, and orders were given for every man subject to military duty to patrol as their captains should direct. I went two nights in succession, and after that refused to patrol at all. The reason why I refused was this, orders were given to search every negro house for books or prints of any kind, and *Bibles* and *Hymn* books were particularly mentioned. And should we find any, our orders were to inflict punishment by whipping the slave until he *informed who* gave them to him, or how they came by them.

"As regards the comforts of the slaves in the vicinity of my residence, I can say they had nothing that would bear that name. It is true, the slaves in general, of a good crop year, were tolerably well fed, but of a bad crop year, they were, as a general thing, cut short of their allowance. Their houses were pole cabins, without loft or floor. Their beds were made of what is there called 'broomstraw.' The men more commonly sleep on benches. Their clothing would compare well with their lodging. Whipping was common. It was hardly possible for a man with a common pair of ears, if he was out of his house but a short time on Monday mornings, to miss of hearing the sound of the lash, and the cries of the sufferers pleading with their masters to desist. These scenes were more common throughout the time of my residence there, from 1799 to 1831.

"Mr. Hedding of Chatham county, held a slave woman. I traveled past Heddings as often as once in two weeks during the winter of 1828, and always saw her clad in a single cotton dress sleeves came half way to the elbow, and in order to prevent her running away, a child, supposed to be about seven years of age, was connected with her by a long chain fastened round her neck, and in this situation she was compelled all the day to *grub* up the roots of shrubs and sapplings to prepare ground for the plough. It is not uncommon for slaves to make up on Sundays what they are not able to perform through the week of their tasks.

"At the time of the rumored insurrection above named, Chatham jail was filled with slaves who were said to have been concerned in the plot. Without the least evidence of it, they were punished in divers ways; some were whipped, some had their *thumbs screwed in a vice* to make them confess, but no proof satisfactory was ever obtained that the negroes had ever thought of an insurrection, nor did any so far as I could learn, acknowledge that an insurrection had ever been projected. From this time forth, the slaves were prohibited from assembling together for the worship of God, and many of those who had previously been authorized to preach the gospel were prohibited.

"Amalgamation was common. There was scarce a family of slaves that had females of mature age where there were not some mulatto children.

Hiram White"

Otter Creek Prairie, Jan. 22, 1839*

98

UNCLE TOM'S CABIN

In circulation as in influence, all abolitionist writings yielded to Uncle Tom's Cabin, *almost an event rather than a book. Its author, Harriet Beecher Stowe, was the daughter of a leading Congregational minister, Lyman Beecher, and sister of clergymen Edward Beecher and Henry Ward Beecher.* Uncle Tom's Cabin, *although a projection of the abolitionist view of society, nevertheless had a vitality of its own. Mrs. Stowe had considerable literary skill; moreover, her materials—deathbed scenes, slave pens and auction blocks, fierce dogs and sadistic overseers—tended to move the reader. The book's phenomenal sales and influence were increased by adaptation to the stage; traveling "Tom shows" quickly became a theatrical staple in the North. Mrs. Stowe's book may no longer cause readers to forget important engagements as they wipe away a tear, but those who may be unmoved by it today can understand why it has been characterized as "the novel that awakened the conscience of a nation." The passages that follow deal with three of the book's best-known characters, Topsy, Simon Legree, and Uncle Tom, all classic figures in the literature of propaganda.*

One morning, while Miss Ophelia was busy in some of her domestic cares, St. Clare's voice was heard, calling her at the foot of the stairs.

"Come down here, cousin; I've something to show you."

---

*Theodore D. Weld, ed. *American Slavery As It Is: Testimony of a Thousand Witnesses,* American Anti-Slavery Society (New York, 1839), 49-51.

"What is it?" said Miss Ophelia, coming down, with her sewing in her hand.

"I've made a purchase for your department,—see here," said St. Clare; and, with the word, he pulled along a little negro girl, about eight or nine years of age.

She was one of the blackest of her race; and her round, shining eyes, glittering as glass beads, moved with quick and restless glances over everything in the room. Her mouth, half open with astonishment at the wonders of the new Mas'r's parlor, displayed a white and brilliant set of teeth. Her woolly hair was braided in sundry little tails, which stuck out in every direction. The expression of her face was an odd mixture of shrewdness and cunning, over which was oddly drawn, like a kind of veil, an expression of the most doleful gravity and solemnity. She was dressed in a single filthy, ragged garment, made of bagging; and stood with her hands demurely folded before her. Altogether, there was something odd and goblin-like about her appearance,—something, as Miss Ophelia afterwards said, "so heathenish," as to inspire that good lady with utter dismay; and, turning to St. Clare, she said,—

"Augustine, what in the world have you brought that thing here for?"

* * *

Sitting down before her, she began to question her.

"How old are you, Topsy?"

"Dunno, Missis," said the image, with a grin that showed all her teeth.

"Don't know how old you are? Didn't anybody ever tell you? Who was your mother?"

"Never had none!" said the child, with another grin.

"Never had any mother? What do you mean? Where were you born?"

"Never was born!" persisted Topsy, with another grin, that looked so goblin-like, that, if Miss Ophelia had been at all nervous, she might have fancied that she had got hold of some sooty gnome from the land of Diablerie; but Miss Ophelia was not nervous, but plain and business-like, and she said, with some sternness,—

"You mustn't answer me in that way, child; I'm not playing with you. Tell me where you were born, and who your father and mother were."

"Never was born," reiterated the creature, more emphatically; "never had no father nor mother, nor nothin'. I was raised by a speculator, with lots of others. Old Aunt Sue used to take care of us."

The child was evidently sincere; and Jane, breaking into a short laugh, said,—

"Laws, Missis, there's heaps of 'em. Speculators buys 'em up cheap, when they's little, and gets 'em raised for market."

"How long have you lived with your master and mistress?"

"Dunno, Missis."

"Is it a year, or more, or less?"

"Dunno, Missis."

"Laws, Missis, those low negroes,—they can't tell; they don't know anything about time," said Jane; "they don't know what a year is; they don't know their own ages."

"Have you ever heard anything about God, Topsy?"

The child looked bewildered, but grinned as usual.

"Do you know who made you?"

"Nobody, as I knows on," said the child, with a short laugh.

The idea appeared to amuse her considerably; for her eyes twinkled, and she added,—

"I spect I grow'd. Don't think nobody never made me."

"Do you know how to sew?" said Miss Ophelia, who thought she would turn her inquiries to something more tangible.

"No, Missis."

"What can you do?—what did you do for your master and mistress?"

"Fetch water, and wash dishes, and rub knives, and wait on folks."

"Were they good to you?"

"Spect they was," said the child, scanning Miss Ophelia cunningly.

Miss Ophelia rose from this encouraging colloquy; St. Clare was leaning over the back of her chair.

"You find virgin soil there, cousin; put in your own ideas, —you won't find many to pull up."

* * *

Slowly the weary, dispirited creatures wound their way into the room, and, with crouching reluctance, presented their baskets to be weighed.

Legree noted on a slate, on the side of which was pasted a list of names, the amount.

Tom's basket was weighed and approved; and he looked, with an anxious glance, for the success of the woman he had befriended.

Tottering with weakness, she came forward, and delivered her basket. It was of full weight, as Legree well perceived; but, affecting anger, he said,—

"What, you lazy beast! short again! stand aside, you'll catch it, pretty soon!"

The woman gave a groan of utter despair, and sat down on a board.

The person who had been called Misse Cassy now came forward, and, with a haughty, negligent air, delivered her basket. As she delivered it, Legree looked in her eyes with a sneering yet inquiring glance.

She fixed her black eyes steadily on him, her lips moved slightly, and she said something in French. What it was, no one knew; but Legree's face became perfectly demoniacal in its expression, as she spoke; he half raised his hand, as if to strike,—a gesture which she regarded with fierce disdain, as she turned and walked away.

"And now," said Legree, "come here, you Tom. You see, I telled ye I didn't buy ye jest for the common work; I mean to promote ye, and make a driver of ye; and to-night ye may jest as well begin to get yer hand in. Now, ye jest take this yer gal and flog her; ye've seen enough on't to know how."

"I beg Mas'r's pardon," said Tom; "hopes Mas'r won't set me at that. It's what I an't used to,—never did,—and can't do, no way possible."

"Ye'll larn a pretty smart chance of things ye never did know, before I've done with ye!" said Legree, taking up a cowhide, and striking Tom a heavy blow across the cheek, and following up the infliction by a shower of blows.

"There!" he said, as he stopped to rest; "now will ye tell me ye can't do it?"

"Yes, Mas'r," said Tom, putting up his hand, to wipe the blood, that trickled down his face. "I'm willin' to work night and day, and work while there's life and breath in me; but this yer thing I can't feel it right to do;—and, Mas'r, I *never* shall do it,—*never!*"

Tom had a remarkably smooth, soft voice, and a habitually respectful manner, that had given Legree an idea that he would be cowardly, and easily subdued. When he spoke these last words, a thrill of amazement went through every one; the poor woman clasped her hands, and said, "O Lord!" and every one involuntarily looked at each other and drew in their breath, as if to prepare for the storm that was about to burst.

Legree looked stupefied and confounded; but at last burst forth,—

"What! ye blasted black beast! tell *me* ye don't think it *right* to do what I tell ye! What have any of you cussed cattle to do with thinking what's right? I'll put a stop to it! Why, what do ye think ye are? May be ye think ye'r a gentleman, master Tom, to be a telling your master what's right, and what an't! So you pretend it's wrong to flog the gal!"

"I think so, Mas'r," said Tom; "the poor crittur's sick and feeble; 'twould be downright cruel, and it's what I never will do, nor begin to. Mas'r, if you mean to kill me, kill me; but, as to my raising my hand again any one here, I never shall,—I'll die first!"

Tom spoke in a mild voice, but with a decision that could not be mistaken. Legree shook with anger; his greenish eyes glared fiercely, and his very whiskers seemed to curl with passion; but, like some ferocious beast, that plays with its victim before he devours it, he kept back his strong impulse to proceed to immediate violence, and broke out into bitter raillery.

"Well, here's a pious dog, at last, let down among us sinners!—a saint, a gentleman, and no less, to talk to us sinners about our sins! Powerful holy crittur, he must be! Here, you rascal, you make believe to be so pious,—didn't you never hear, out of yer Bible, 'Servants, obey yer masters'? An't I yer master? Didn't I pay down twelve hundred dollars, cash, for all there is inside yer old cussed black shell? An't yer mine, now, body and soul?" he said, giving Tom a violent kick with his heavy boot; "tell me!"

In the very depth of physical suffering, bowed by brutal oppression, this question shot a gleam of joy and triumph through Tom's soul. He suddenly stretched himself up, and, looking earnestly to heaven, while the tears and blood that flowed down his face mingled, he exclaimed,—

"No! no! no! my soul an't yours, Mas'r! You haven't bought it,—ye can't buy it! It's been bought and paid for, by one that is able to keep it;—no matter, no matter, you can't harm me!"

"I can't! said Legree, with a sneer; "we'll see,—we'll see! Here, Sambo, Quimbo, give this dog such a breakin' in as he won't get over, this month!"

The two gigantic negroes that now laid hold of Tom, with fiendish exultation in their faces, might have formed no unapt personification of the powers of darkness. The poor woman screamed with apprehension, and all rose, as by a general impulse, while they dragged him unresisting from the place.*

The Negro Abolitionist

99

JAMES FORTEN, JR.

From the beginning the Negro took an active role in the militant abolitionist movement. The New England Anti-Slavery Society held its organizational meeting at the African Baptist Church in Boston. Negroes were present at the formation of the American Anti-Slavery Society, Garrison drafting its declaration of sentiments at the home of a Negro, Lewis Evans. The "Declaration" itself bore the signatures of three Negroes, James C. McCrummel, a Philadelphia dentist, Robert Purvis of Byberry, Pennsylvania, and James G. Barbadoes of Boston. On the twelve-man executive committee of the Society, there was always a trio of Negroes. The American and Foreign Anti-Slavery Society, founded in 1840, regularly carried five Negroes on its executive committee. In 1847 Frederick Douglass served as president of the New England Anti-Slavery Society. Purvis, who had attended the founding meeting of the Pennsylvania Anti-Slavery Society in 1837, was elected its president in 1851. As a rule, the various abolitionist groups made it a point to welcome Negroes as members, to invite them to be guest speakers, and to appoint them as agents.

In the spring of 1836 the Ladies' Anti-Slavery Society of Philadelphia invited James Forten, Jr., son of Garrison's friend, to deliver an address. Young Forten's words were not devoid of eloquence or meaning; the style is vigorous and the argument is logical.

My friends, do you ask why I thus speak? It is because I love America; it is my native land; because I feel as one should feel who sees destruction, like a corroding cancer, eating into the very heart of his country, and would make one struggle to save her;—because I love the stars and stripes, emblems of our National Flag—and long to see the day when not a slave shall be found resting under its shadow; when it shall play with the winds pure and unstained by the blood of "captive millions."

---

*Harriet Beecher Stowe, *Uncle Tom's Cabin* (introduction by Dwight L. Dumond, New York, 1962), 294, 297-298, 413-416.

Again, the South most earnestly and respectfully solicits the North to let the question Slavery alone, and leave it to their bountiful honesty and humanity to settle. Why, honesty, I fear has fled from the South, long ago; sincerity has fallen asleep there, pity has hidden herself; justice cannot find the way; helper is not at home; charity lies dangerously ill; benovolence is under arrest; faith is nearly extinguished; truth has long since been buried, and conscience is nailed on the wall. Now, do you think it would be better to leave it to the bountiful honesty and humanity of the South to settle? No, no. Only yield to them in this one particular and they will find you vulnerable in every other. I can tell you, my hearers, if the North once sinks into profound silence on this momentous subject, you may then bid farewell to peace, order and reform; then the condition of your fellow creatures in the southern section of our country will never be ameliorated; then may the poor slave look upon his weighty chains, and exclaim, in the agony of his heart, "To these am I immutably doomed; the glimmering rays of hope are lost to me for ever; robbed of all that is dear to man, I stand a monument of my country's ingratitude. A *husband*, yet separated from the dearest tie which binds me to this earth. A father, yet compelled to stifle the feelings of a father, and witness a helpless offspring torn by a savage hand from its mother's fond embrace, no longer to call her by that endearing title. A wretched slave, I look upon the departing brightness of the setting sun, and when her glorious light revisits the morn, these clanking irons tell me I am that slave still; still am I to linger out a life of ignominious servitude, till death shall unloose these heavy bars—unfetter my body and soul."

* * *

You are called fanatics. Well, what if you are? Ought you to shrink from this name? God forbid. There is an eloquence in such fanaticism, for it whispers hope to the slave; there is sanctity in it, for it contains the consecrated spirit of religion; it is the fanaticism of a Benezet, a Rush, a Franklin, a Jay; the same that animated and inspired the heart of the writer of the Declaration of Independence. Then flinch not from your high duty; continue to warn the South of the awful volcano they are recklessly sleeping over; and bid them remember, too, that the drops of blood which trickle down the lacerated back of the slave, will not sink into the barren soil. No, they will rise to the common God of nature and humanity, and cry aloud for vengeance on his destroyer's head. Bid them think of this, that they may see from what quarter the terrible tempest will come; not from the breakings out of insurrections, so much dreaded, but for which men are indebted to the imagery of their minds more than to fact; not from the fanatics, or the publication of their papers, calculated to spread desolation and blood, and sever the Union, as is now basely asserted, but it will come from HIM who declared "Vengeance is mine, and I will repay."

You are not aiming to injure your southern brethren, but to benefit them; to save them from the impending storm. You are not seeking the destruction of the Union; but to render it still stronger; to link it together in one universal chain of *Justice*, and *Love*, and

Freedom. The Faith you have embraced teaches you to live in bonds of charity with all mankind. It is not by force of arms that Abolitionists expect to remove one of the greatest curses that ever afflicted or disgraced humanity; but by the majesty of moral power. Oh! how callous, how completely destitute of feeling, must that person be, who think of the wrongs done to the innocent and unoffending captive, and not drop one tear of pity—who can look upon slavery and not shudder at its inhuman barbarities? It is a withering blight to the country in which it exists—a deadly poison to the soil on which it is suffered to breathe—and to satiate the cravings of its appetite, it feeds, like a vulture, upon the vitals of its victims. But it is in vain that I attempt to draw a proper likeness of its horrors; it is far beyond the reach of my abilities to describe to you the endless atrocities which characterize the system. Well was it said by Thomas Jefferson, that "God has no attribute which can take sides with such oppression." See what gigantic force is concentrated in these few words—God has no attribute which can take sides with such oppression.

Ladies—I feel that I should have confined my remarks more particularly to your society, and not have extended them to the whole field of Abolition. Pardon me for the digression.

I rejoice to see you engaged in this mighty cause; it befits you; it is your province; your aid and influence is greatly to be desired in this hour of peril; it never was, never can be insignificant. Examine the records of history, and you will find that woman has been called upon in the severest trials of public emergency. That your efforts will stimulate the men to renewed exertion I have not the slightest doubt; for, in general, the pride of man's heart is such, that while he is willing to grant unto woman exclusively, many conspicuous and dignified privileges, he at the same time feels an innate dispostion to check the modest ardour of her zeal and ambition, and revolts at the idea of her managing the reigns of improvement. Therefore, you have only to be constantly exhibiting some new proof of your interest in the cause of the oppressed, and shame, if not duty, will urge our sex on the march. It has often been said by anti-abolitionists that the females have no right to interfere with the question of slavery, or petition for its overthrow; and they had better be at home attending to their domestic affairs, &c. What a gross error—what an anti-christian spirit this bespeaks. Were not the holy commands, "Remember them that are in bonds, as bound with them," and "Do unto others as ye would they should do unto you," intended for woman to obey as well as man? Most assuredly they were.*

---

*James Forten, Jr., *An Address Delivered before the Ladies' Anti-Slavery Society of Philadelphia, April 14, 1836* (Phila., 1836), 10-13.

100

CHARLES LENOX REMOND

Some Negroes served as full-time agents of abolitionist societies. First of these in point of time was Charles Lenox Remond of Salem, Massachusetts, who in 1838 became an agent-lecturer for the Massachusetts Anti-Slavery Society. Two years later Remond was selected by the American Anti-Slavery Society as a delegate to the World Anti-Slavery Convention, meeting in London. British reformers made his two-year sojourn a pleasant experience. As an agent of the Massachusetts abolitionists, Remond spent much of his time in traveling throughout New England. In a letter to Thomas Cole, a Boston reformer, Remond tells of his activities in Maine, in company for a time with Ichabod Codding, a white agent.

Winthrop, Me., July 3d, 1838.

My Dear Friend:—I take advantage of the earliest opportunity to inform you, that on the third day after bidding you farewell, I met my friend Mr. Codding, at Brunswick, at which place, on the following Sunday afternoon, I addressed the friends a short time, and was well received. On Tuesday following, left Brunswick for Alfred, to attend the formation of a County Anti-Slavery Society. There was not much interest taken in the meeting. On the following evening I was invited to address the meeting and complied. On the next day, I was invited to go into the country a short distance. I cut loose from Mr. Codding very reluctantly, and commenced lecturing in my feeble way. Received requests to lecture in four different places on four successive evenings. I consented, and spoke in each place an hour and a half; and although my audiences were generally dark on the subject of prejudice and slavery, I received on every occasion the most marked attention, and assurances of good feeling for the cause, and wishes for the success of our enterprise. At one place, they resolved at the close of the lecture, to form a society and lend their assistance in the great work.

On Wednesday last I went to Saco, to attend the conference meeting of the Congregational denomination. The delegation of ministers was very numerous, and much interest was manifested to every great and good, and benevolent undertaking, save the cause of the poor slave in our own beloved but guilty country. On Thursday evening I was invited to speak on the subject in the Baptist meeting-house. My audience was almost entirely composed of ministers who were attending the conference, and a good number of interesting and intelligent ladies. At this place they have determined to do something forthwith for the slave, by forming a male and female society, and contributing to the cause. On last Sabbath afternoon, I lectured in the meeting-house in Bowdoin. Nothing special occurred.

I am now at the house of our kind and devoted friend, Rev. David Thurston, and the feeling manifested on every occasion by his wife and daughters in behalf of human liberty is indeed such as may well make glad the hearts of our brethren in bonds. It is of no use for me to attempt to give you any thing like a description of the change which I believe is now taking place on the subject of slavery and the

elevation of the nominally free. We have every thing, friend Thomas, to encourage us. Slavery is trembling, prejudice is falling, and I hope will soon be buried—buried beyond resurrection; and we will write over its grave as over Babylon—'Prejudice, the mother of abominations, the liar, the coward, the tyrant, the waster of the poor, the brand of the white man, the bane of the black man, is fallen! is fallen!'
Yours truly,

C. Lenox Remond.*

101

CELEBRATION OF WEST INDIA EMANCIPATION DAY

Negroes joined in the celebrations of the abolitionist holiday, August 1. Abolitionists were not enthusiastic about the Fourth of July, believing that it was a mockery to celebrate independence and freedom as long as slavery existed. Hence, they made it a point to celebrate West India Emancipation Day, August 1, when in 1834 the act abolishing slavery in England's island possessions had gone into effect: In most instances Negroes celebrated August 1 in company with whites—indeed, at Harrisville, Ohio, in 1859, the Negroes made all arrangements and invited whites from three counties. In some instances Negroes held celebrations of their own. The following account of the August 1, 1844, observances in Massachusetts refers twice to Frederick Douglass as a speaker, and to a gathering of Boston Negroes. The speakers referred to as "Messrs. Roberts and Smith" undoubtedly were Benjamin F. Roberts and Thomas Paul Smith, who later took opposite sides on the wisdom of abolishing Jim Crow schools in Boston.

THE FIRST OF AUGUST

The illustrious Anniversary of West Indian Emancipation was celebrated in this State with even unusual demonstrations of festivity and temperate joy. The members and friends of this Society and the public generally were invited to meet at Hingham to solemnize the great day. The celebration took place on the Second of August, in consequence of the inclemency of the First, but it lost nothing of its interest or its prosperity by the delay. Everything was propitious to the success of the occasion. A larger number was assembled than had perhaps ever before met together on any Anti-Slavery occasion. The population of the neighboring towns poured itself upon Hingham in numbers unsurpassed even by the gatherings of political parties. The town wore a holiday aspect. The streets were decorated with flags and appropriate mottoes. The bells were rung. It was a day of general rejoicing. When the Steamboat that conveyed the friends from Boston and the counties of Essex and Middlesex, arrived, a procession was formed and proceeded, "an army with banners," under the direction of Mr. JAIRUS LINCOLN and his aids to Tranquillity Grove, a spot which seemed formed by the hand of Nature for such a meeting. Mr. GARRISON took the chair with some appropriate remarks. The meeting was soon adjourned to give place to the collation, which was furnished by general contribution, but most tastefully and ele-

*From *Mind of the Negro As Reflected in Letters During the Crisis, 1800–1860*, by Carter G. Woodson. Reprinted by permission of The Associated Publishers, Inc.

gantly disposed by the ladies of Hingham. In the afternoon the services were resumed and addresses were made by Messrs. QUINCY, PIERPONT, DOUGLASS, J. F. CLARKE, W. A. WHITE, HOWE, RUSSELL, CLAPP, SPRAGUE and JOHNSON. The company remained together until the approach of evening compelled a reluctant dispersion. It was a day that will be long remembered for its social enjoyment and its inspiriting associations.

The day was also duly celebrated in Boston by the colored citizens. They went in procession with appropriate banners to the Tremont Chapel, where they listened to able and pertinent addresses from Messrs. ROBERTS and SMITH. In the evening a soiree was held in the Infant School Room, where an elegant collation was served and the hours pleasantly and profitably filled up by speech and song.

At Concord a meeting was held in the Court House, as no Meeting House could be obtained for the occasion, where an address of singular beauty and eloquence was delivered to a numerous audience by RALPH WALDO EMERSON. An entertainment was provided, after which addresses were made by Messrs. W. A. WHITE, S. J. MAY, DOUGLASS, CYRUS PIERCE and others. These two celebrations having been held on the First, notwithstanding the weather, the friends who had attended them were able to join in the festivities at Hingham.

The day was also duly kept at New Bedford and doubtless at many other places. It is an anniversary which is fast taking the place of the Fourth of July in the hearts of the true lovers of Liberty. May it continue to commend itself more and more to their hearts until they can supersede it by a more glorious anniversary of their own —a true Declaration of Independence,—which will proclaim Liberty to all the inhabitants of the Land!*

102

YOUNG NEGRO SUPPORTERS OF ABOLITIONISM

Negroes participated in the auxiliary enterprises and activities of the abolitionist organizations, among them the juvenile groups. The reformers were eager to draw youngsters into their ranks. "We attach vast importance to these juvenile meetings and associations," ran an editorial in Pennsylvania Freeman *of May 23, 1839: "The children are, after all, our most important forces." The abolitionist magazine for children,* The Slave's Friend, *was distributed without charge. In Pittsburgh in 1838 a group of young Negroes formed a society. They sent $5.00 to the* Colored American, *a New York weekly, with an accompanying letter, which follows.*

Pittsburg, Nov. 14, '39

Gentlemen,—At a meeting of the Juvenile Anti-Slavery Society, held November 11, it was unanimously resolved that five dollars should be given to the support of the Colored American—a paper which of all others we ought to support. We hope that this small

**Thirteenth Annual Report of the Massachusetts Anti-Slavery Society, January 22, 1845,* (Boston, 1845), 34-35.

donation may be the means of doing good, and we pray you, in the name of the members of the Juvenile Anti-Slavery Society, to accept it as a small token of the esteem we have for your paper. The Juvenile Anti-Slavery Society was formed on the seventh of July, 1838. It is a "cent a week" society, and is the first and only one of the kind formed this side of the mountains. The Society now consists of about forty members; several of whom have addressed the Society, at different times. We conclude by expressing our hope that our little mite may be of some service in the cause, in which you are engaged.

Very respectfully,
Your obdt. servants,
David Peck, Pres. J. A. S. S.

Geo. B. Vashon, Sec.*

On June 1, 1856, Henry Ward Beecher brought before the congregation of the Plymouth Church a young Negro woman, a fugitive from the slave state, Virginia. His savage parody with this unhappy girl of a slave auction had a powerful impact upon his audience.

Abolition's Widening Influence

103

THEODORE PARKER ASSISTS AT A MARRIAGE

The necessity for being concerned about the plight of the Negro was sharply driven home to abolitionists by the Fugitive Slave Law of 1850, a measure designed to make it easier to recapture runaways. It denied the testimony of the alleged fugitive; it provided stiff penalties for anyone obstructing the escape or recovery of a runaway, and it was ex post facto, *reaching back to escaped slaves who had almost forgotten that they had once been chattels. Abolitionists were up in arms, referring to the measure as the "Man Stealing Law" and the "Bloodhound Bill." Preaching at Boston's Melodeon Hall on September 22, six days after the bill became law, Theodore Parker solemnly vowed that he would do all in his power to rescue a fugitive: "What is a fine of a thousand dollars, and jailing*

**The Colored American,* November 23, 1839 (New York and Phila.).

for six months, to the liberty of a man?" The Unitarian pastor proved to be as good as his word. When two agents of a slavemaster came to Boston looking for William and Ellen Craft, who had fled from Georgia in January 1849, Parker housed Ellen for a week while advising the agents that they had better leave the aroused city. On November 7, Parker married the runaways, noting that they had been wedded a long time, but without legal sanction. Parker described the ceremony and his own highly dissimilar gifts to the groom.

I have known them ever since their flight from slavery. After the two slave-hunters had gone, they wished to go to England, and requested me to marry them after the legal and usual form. I told them how to get the certificate of publication according to the new law of Massachusetts. It was done, and at the time appointed I went to the place appointed, a boarding-house for colored people. Before the marriage ceremony I always advise the young couple of the duties of matrimony, making such remarks as suit the peculiar circumstances and character of the parties. I told them what I usually tell all bridegrooms and brides. Then I told Mr. Craft that their position demanded peculiar duties of him. He was an outlaw; there was no law which protected his liberty in the United States; for that, he must depend on the public opinion of Boston, and on himself. If a man attacked him, intending to return him to slavery, he had a right, a natural right, to resist the man unto death; but he might refuse to exercise that right for *himself*, if he saw fit, and suffer himself to be reduced to slavery rather than kill or even hurt the slave-hunter who should attack him. But his *wife* was dependent on him for protection; it was his duty to protect her, a duty which it seemed to me he could not decline. So I charged him, if the worst came to the worst, to defend the life and the liberty of his wife against any slave-hunter at all hazards, though in doing so he dug his own grave and the grave of a thousand men.

Then came the marriage ceremony; then a prayer such as the occasion inspired. Then I noticed a *Bible* lying on one table and a sword on the other; I saw them when I first came into the house and determined what use to make of them. I took the Bible, put it into William's right hand, and told him the use of it. It contained the noblest truths in the possession of the human race, &c., it was an instrument he was to use to help save his own soul, and his wife's soul, and charged him to use it for its purpose, &c. I then took the *sword* (it was a "Californian knife;" I never saw such an one before, and am not well skilled in such things); I put that in his right hand, and told him if the worst came to the worst to use that to save his wife's liberty, or her life, if he could effect it in no other way. I told him that I hated violence, that I reverenced the sacredness of human life, and thought there was seldom a case in which it was justifiable to take it; that if he could save his wife's liberty in no other way, then this would be one of the cases, and as a *minister of religion* I put into his hands these two dissimilar instruments, one for the body, if need were—one for his soul at all events. Then I charged him not to use it except at the last extremity, to bear no harsh and revengeful feelings against those who once held him in bondage, or such as sought to make him and his wife slaves even now. "Nay," I said, "if you cannot use the sword in defence of your wife's liberty without hating the man you strike, then your action will not be without sin."

I gave the same advice I should have given to white men under the like circumstances—as, escaping from slavery in Algiers.*

104

THE TRIAL OF ANTHONY BURNS

On May 24, 1854, Anthony Burns was arrested in Boston as a fugitive slave and put in irons in the courthouse. His counsel, Richard Henry Dana, and Robert Morris, a Negro, secured a three-day adjournment. A public meeting held in Fanueil Hall on May 26 was addressed by Wendell Phillips and Theodore Parker. The latter called attention to the fact that he was a clergyman and a lover of peace:."But there is a means, and there is an end; liberty is the end, and sometimes peace is not the means toward it." An attempt to storm the courthouse was repulsed, one of the defenders of the courthouse being killed. State militia and federal troops were summoned to guard Burns. Feeling ran high during the week, reaching its peak when United States Commissioner Edward G. Loring pronounced a verdict in favor of the owner of Burns. One of those who followed the case with more than ordinary interest was young Charlotte Forten, just sixteen. Her family was strongly abolitionist; her grandfather was James Forten, and her uncle was Robert Purvis. Her father, sailmaker Robert Bridges Forten, had sent Charlotte to Salem, Massachusetts, where she could attend Salem Normal School and live at the home of abolitionist Charles Lenox Remond and his sister, Sarah. Here she met many of the Massachusetts abolitionists who deepened her interest in reformist movements. The serious-minded young miss began to keep a diary in May 1854—the month of the Burns episode. Here are some excerpts concerning it.

Thursday, May 25, 1854. Did not intend to write this evening, but have just heard of something which is worth recording;—something which must ever rouse in the mind of every true friend of liberty and humanity, feelings of the deepest indignation and sorrow. Another fugitive from bondage has been arrested; a poor man, who for two short months has trod the soil and breathed the air of the "Old Bay State," was arrested like a criminal in the streets of her capital, and is now kept strictly guarded,—a double police force is required, the military are in readiness; and all this is done to prevent a man, whom God has created in his own image, from regaining that freedom with which, he, in common with every other human being, is endowed. I can only hope and pray most earnestly that Boston will not again disgrace herself by sending him back to a bondage worse than death; or rather that she will redeem herself from the disgrace which his arrest alone has brought upon her. . . .

---

*John Weiss, *Life and Correspondence of Theodore Parker* (2 vols., New York, 1864), II, 99-100.

Fugitive Slave Bill.

Saturday, May 27. . . . Returned home, read the Anti-Slavery papers, and then went down to the depot to meet father; he had arrived in Boston early in the morning, regretted very much that he had not reached there the evening before to attend the great meeting at Faneuil Hall. He says that the excitement in Boston is very great; the trial of the poor man takes place on Monday. We scarcely dare to think of what may be the result; there seems to be nothing too bad for these Northern tools of slavery to do.

Tuesday, May 30. Rose very early and was busy until nine o'clock; then, at Mrs. Putnam's urgent request, went to keep store for her while she went to Boston to attend the Anti-Slavery Convention. I was very anxious to go, and will certainly do so to-morrow; the arrest of the alleged fugitive will give additional interest to the meetings, I should think. His trial is still going on and I can scarcely think of anything else; read again to-day as most suitable to my feelings and to the times, "The Runaway Slave at Pilgrim's Point," by Elizabeth B. Browning; how powerfully it is written! how earnestly and touchingly does the writer portray the bitter anguish of the poor fugitive as she thinks over all the wrongs and sufferings that she has endured, and of the sin to which tyrants have driven her but which they alone must answer for! It seems as if no one could read this poem without having his sympathies roused to the utmost in behalf of the oppressed.—After a long conversation with my friends on their return, on this all-absorbing subject, we separated for the night, and I went to bed, weary and sad.

Wednesday, May 31. . . . Sarah and I went to Boston in the morning. Everything was much quieter—outwardly than we expected, but still much real indignation and excitement prevail. We walked past the Court-House, which is now lawlessly converted into a prison, and filled with soldiers, some of whom were looking from the windows, with an air of insolent authority which made my blood boil, while I felt the strongest contempt for their cowardice and servility. We went to the meeting, but the best speakers were absent, engaged in the most arduous and untiring efforts in behalf of the poor fugitive; but though we missed the glowing eloquence of Phillips, Garrison, and Parker, still there were excellent speeches made, and our hearts responded to the exalted sentiments of Truth and Liberty which were uttered. The exciting intelligence which occasionally came in relation to the trial, added fresh zeal to the speakers, of whom Stephen Foster and his wife were the principal. The latter addressed, in the most eloquent language, the women present, entreating them to urge their husbands and brothers to action, and also to give their aid on all occasions in our just and holy cause.—I did not see father the whole day; he, of course, was deeply interested in the trial.—Dined at Mr. Garrison's; his wife is one of the loveliest persons I have ever seen, worthy of such a husband. At the table, I watched earnestly the expression of that noble face, as he spoke beautifully in support of the non-resistant principles to which he has kept firm; his is indeed the very highest Christian spirit, to which I cannot hope to reach, however, for I believe in 'resistance to tyrants,' and would fight for liberty until death. We came home in the evening, and felt sick at heart as we passed through the streets of Boston on our way to the depot, seeing the military as they rode along, ready at any time to prove themselves the minions of the South.

Thursday, June 1st. . . . The trial is over at last; the commissioner's decision will be given to-morrow. We are all in the greatest suspense; what will that decision be? Alas! that any one should have the power to decide the right of a fellow being to himself! It is thought by many that he will be acquitted of the *great crime* of leaving a life of bondage, as the legal evidence is not thought sufficient to convict him. But it is only too probable that they will sacrifice him to propitiate the South, since so many at the North dared oppose the passage of the infamous Nebraska Bill.

Friday, June 2. Our worst fears are realized; the decision was against poor Burns, and he has been sent back to a bondage worse, a thousand times worse than death. Even an attempt at rescue was utterly impossible; the prisoner was completely surrounded by soldiers with bayonets fixed, a cannon loaded, ready to be fired at the slightest sign. To-day Massachusetts has again been disgraced; again has she shewed her submission to the Slave Power; and Oh! with what deep sorrow do we think of what will doubtless be the fate of that poor man, when he is again consigned to the horrors of Slavery. With what scorn must that government be regarded, which cowardly assembles thousands of soldiers to satisfy the demands of slaveholders; to deprive of his freedom a man, created in God's own image, whose sole offence is the color of his skin! And if resistance is offered to this outrage, these soldiers are to shoot down American citizens without mercy; and this by the express orders of a government which proudly boasts of being the freeest [*sic*] in the world; this on the very soil where the Revolution of 1776 began; in sight of the battle-field, where thousands of brave men fought and died in opposing British tyranny, which was nothing

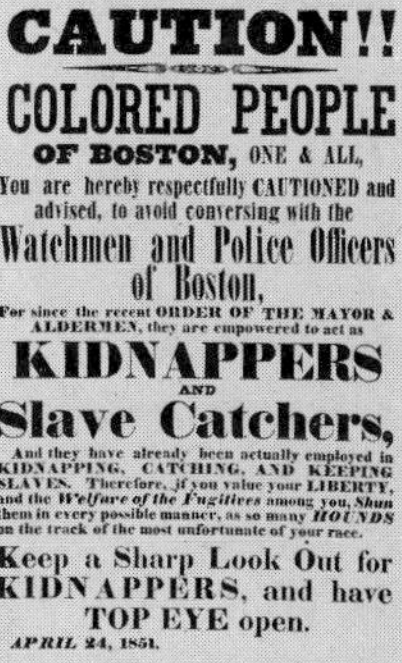

compared with the American oppression of to-day. In looking over my diary, I perceive that I did not mention that there was on the Friday night after the man's arrest, an attempt made to rescue him, but although it failed, on account of there not being men enough engaged in it, all honor should be given to those who bravely made attempt. I can write no more. A cloud seems hanging over me, over all our persecuted race, which nothing can dispel.*

105

DRED SCOTT'S PETITION FOR FREEDOM

The return of runaway slaves aroused deep hostility in northern communities. But by the mid-fifties the main concern of the abolitionists was the spread of slavery into the territories, a threat which became a reality in 1854 with the Kansas-Nebraska Act. This measure created resentment among tens of thousands of Americans who were not abolitionists. Opposition to slavery in the territories steadily mounted, reaching a fever pitch with the Dred Scott decision. Although pronounced in 1857 this history-making ruling by the Supreme Court had been set in motion ten years earlier when Scott filed a suit for freedom in the Missouri courts. His original petition read as follows.

DRED SCOTT
vs.
ALEX. SANDFORD, SAML. RUSSEL, AND IRENE EMERSON

To the Honorable, the Circuit Court within and for the County of St. Louis.

Your petitioner, Dred Scott, a man of color, respectfully represents that sometime in the year 1835 your petitioner was purchased as a slave by one John Emerson, since deceased, who afterwards, to-wit; about the year 1836 or 1837, conveyed your petitioner from the State of Missouri to Fort Snelling, a fort then occupied by the troops of the United States and under the jurisdiction of the United States, situated in the territory ceded by France to the United States under the name of Louisiana, lying north of 36 degrees and 30′ North latitude, now included in the State of Missouri, and resided and continued to reside at Fort Snelling upwards of one year, and held your petitioner in slavery at such Fort during all that time in violation of the Act of Congress of 1806 and 1820, entitled An Act to Authorize the People of Missouri Territory to form a Constitution and State Government, and for the admission of such State into the Union on an equal footing with the original states, and to Prohibit Slavery in Certain Territories.

Your petitioner avers that said Emerson has since departed this life, leaving his widow Irene Emerson and an infant child whose name is unknown to your petitioner; and that one Alexander Sandford administered upon the estate of said Emerson and that your

*Ray Allen Billington, ed., *The Journal of Charlotte Forten* (New York, Dryden Press, 1953), 34-37. Reprinted by permission of Ray A. Billington.

petitioner is now unlawfully held in slavery by said Sandford and by said administrator, and said Irene Emerson claims your petitioner as part of the estate of said Emerson and by one Samuel Russell.

Your petitioner therefore prays your Honorable Court to grant him leave to sue as a poor person, in order to establish his right to freedom, and that the necessary orders may be made in the premises.

Dred Scott

State of Missouri } ss.
County of St. Louis }

This day personally came before me, the undersigned, a Justice of the Peace, Dred Scott, the person whose name is affixed to the foregoing petition, and made oath that the facts set forth in the above petition are true to the best of his knowledge and belief, that he is entitled to his freedom.

Witness my hand this 1st day of July, 1847.

his
Dred X Scott
mark.

Sworn to and subscribed before me this 1st day of July, 1847.

Peter W. Johnstone
Justice of the Peace

Upon reading the above petition this day, it being the opinion of the Judge of the Circuit Court, that the said petition contains sufficient matter to authorize the commencement of a suit for his freedom, it is hereby ordered that the said petitioner Dred Scott be allowed to sue on giving security satisfactory to the Clerk of the Circuit Court for all costs that may be adjudged against him, and that he have reasonable liberty to attend to his counsel and the court as the occasion may require, and that he be not subject to any severity on account of this application for his freedom.

A. Hamilton

July 2d, 1847 Judge of Circuit Court 8th Jd. Cir.*

106

THE DRED SCOTT DECISION

Scott's case left the Missouri tribunals, eventually reaching the United States Supreme Court. Its decision angered Northerners since it struck at the power of Congress over slavery in the territories. The decision was especially repugnant to Negroes inasmuch as it denied their citizenship. Scott himself was soon set free, and the decision itself was to have a short life, its no-Negro-citizenship clause running afoul of a ruling by Attorney General Edward Bates in November 1862, and receiving its death blow with the Fourteenth Amendment in 1868. But no judicial edict of the nineteenth century evoked a more stormy response. The excerpt below is the portion of the ruling which dealt with the citizenship of the Negro.

---

*Albert Bushnell Hart, *American History Told By Contemporaries* (5 vols., New York, Macmillan, 1909), IV, 122-123.

The question is simply this: Can a negro, whose ancestors were imported into this country, and sold as slaves, become a member of the political community formed and brought into existence by the Constitution of the United States, and as such become entitled to all the rights, and privileges, and immunities, guarantied by that instrument to the citizen? One of which rights is the privilege of suing in a court of the United States in the cases specified in the Constitution.

It will be observed, that the plea applies to that class of persons only whose ancestors were negroes of the African race, and imported into this country, and sold and held as slaves. The only matter in issue before the court, therefore, is, whether the descendants of such slaves, when they shall be emancipated, or who are born of parents who had become free before their birth, are citizens of a State, in the sense in which the word citizen is used in the Constitution of the United States. And this being the only matter in dispute on the pleadings, the court must be understood as speaking in this opinion of that class only, that is, of those persons who are the descendants of Africans who were imported into this country, and sold as slaves.

* * *

It becomes necessary, therefore, to determine who were citizens of the several States when the Constitution was adopted. And in order to do this, we must recur to the Governments and institutions of the thirteen colonies, when they separated from Great Britain and formed new sovereignties, and took their places in the family of independent nations. We must inquire who, at that time, were recognised as the people or citizens of a State, whose rights and liberties had been outraged by the English Government; and who declared their independence, and assumed the powers of Government to defend their rights by force of arms.

In the opinion of the court, the legislation and histories of the times, and the language used in the Declaration of Independence, show, that neither the class of persons who had been imported as slaves, nor their descendants, whether they had become free or not, were then acknowledged as a part of the people, nor intended to be included in the general words used in that memorable instrument.

It is difficult at this day to realize the state of public opinion in relation to that unfortunate race, which prevailed in the civilized and enlightened portions of the world at the time of the Declaration of Independence, and when the Constitution of the United States was framed and adopted. But the public history of every European nation displays it in a manner too plain to be mistaken.

They had for more than a century before been regarded as beings of an inferior order, and altogether unfit to associate with the white race, either in social or political relations; and so far inferior, that they had no rights which the white man was bound to respect; and that the negro might justly and lawfully be reduced to slavery for his benefit. He was bought and sold, and treated as an ordinary article of merchandise and traffic, whenever a profit could be made by it. This opinion was at that time fixed and universal in the civilized portion of the white race. It was regarded as an axiom in morals as well as in politics, which no one thought of disputing, or supposed to be open to dispute; and men in every grade and position in society daily and habitually acted upon it in their private pursuits, as well as in matters of public concern, without doubting for a moment the correctness of this opinion.

And in no nation was this opinion more firmly fixed or more uniformly acted upon than by the English Government and English people. They not only seized them on the coast of Africa, and sold them or held them in slavery for their own use; but they took them as ordinary articles of merchandise to every country where they could make a profit on them, and were far more extensively engaged in this commerce than any other nation in the world.

The opinion thus entertained and acted upon in England was naturally impressed upon the colonies they founded on this side of the Atlantic. And, accordingly, a negro of the African race was regarded by them as an article of property, and held, and bought and sold as such, in every one of the thirteen colonies which united in the Declaration of Independence, and afterwards formed the Constitution of the United States. The slaves were more or less numerous in the different colonies, as slave labor was found more or less profitable. But no one seems to have doubted the correctness of the prevailing opinion of the time.

The legislation of the different colonies furnishes positive and indisputable proof of this fact.

* * *

The language of the Declaration of Independence is equally conclusive:

It begins by declaring that, "when in the course of human events it becomes necessary for one people to dissolve the political bands which have connected them with another, and to assume among the powers of the earth the separate and equal station to which the laws of nature and nature's God entitle them, a decent respect for the opinions of mankind requires that they should declare the causes which impel them to the separation."

It then proceeds to say: "We hold these truths to be self-evident: that all men are created equal; that they are endowed by their Creator with certain unalienable rights; that among them is life, liberty, and the pursuit of happiness; that to secure these rights, Governments are instituted, deriving their just powers from the consent of the governed."

The general words above quoted would seem to embrace the whole human family, and if they were used in a similar instrument at this day would be so understood. But it is too clear for dispute, that the enslaved African race were not intended to be included, and formed no part of the people who framed and adopted this declaration; for if the language, as understood in that day, would embrace them, the conduct of the distinguished men who framed the Declaration of Independence would have been utterly and flagrantly inconsistent with the principles they asserted; and instead of the sympathy of mankind, to which they so confidently appealed, they would have deserved and received universal rebuke and reprobation.

Yet the men who framed this declaration were great men—high in literary acquirements—high in their sense of honor, and incapable of asserting principles inconsistent with those on which they were acting. They perfectly understood the meaning of the language they used, and how it would be understood by others; and they knew that it would not in any part of the civilized world be supposed to embrace the negro race, which, by common consent, had been excluded from civilized Governments and the family of nations, and doomed to slavery. They spoke and acted according to the then established doctrines and principles, and in the ordinary language of the day, and no one misunderstood them. The unhappy black race were separated from the white by indelible marks, and laws long before established, and were never thought of or spoken of except as property, and when the claims of the owner or the profit of the trader were supposed to need protection.

This state of public opinion had undergone no change when the Constitution was adopted, as is equally evident from its provisions and language.

The brief preamble sets forth by whom it was formed, for what purposes, and for whose benefit and protection. It declares that it is formed by the *people* of the United States; that is to say, by those who were members of the different political communities in the several States; and its great object is declared to be to secure the blessings of liberty to themselves and their posterity. It speaks in general terms of the *people* of the United States, and of *citizens* of the several States, when it is providing for the exercise of the powers granted or the privileges secured to the citizen. It does not define what description of persons are intended to be included under these terms, or who shall be regarded as a citizen and one of the people. It uses them as terms so well understood, that no further description or definition was necessary.

But there are two clauses in the Constitution which point directly and specifically to the negro race as a separate class of persons, and show clearly that they were not regarded as a portion of the people or citizens of the Government then formed.

One of these clauses reserves to each of the thirteen States the right to import slaves until the year 1808, if it thinks proper. And the importation which it thus sanctions was unquestionably of persons of the race of which we are speaking, as the traffic in slaves in the United States had always been confined to them. And by the other provision the States pledge themselves to each other to maintain the right of property of the master, by delivering up to him any slave who may have escaped from his service, and be found within their respective territories. By the first above-mentioned clause, therefore, the right to purchase and hold this property is directly sanctioned and authorized for twenty years by the people who framed the Constitution. And by the second, they pledge themselves to maintain and uphold the right of the master in the manner specified, as long as the Government they then formed should endure. And these two provisions show, conclusively, that neither the description of persons therein referred to, nor their descendants, were embraced in any of the other provisions of the Constitution; for certainly these two clauses were not intended to confer on them or their posterity the blessings of liberty, or any of the personal rights so carefully provided for the citizen.

* * *

Upon the whole, therefore, it is the judgment of this court, that it appears by the record before us that the plaintiff in error is not a citizen of Missouri, in the sense in which that word is used in the Constitution; and that the Circuit Court of the United States, for that reason, had no jurisdiction in the case, and could give no judgment in it. Its judgment for the defendant must, consequently, be reversed, and a mandate issued, directing the suit to be dismissed for want of jurisdiction.*

107

JOHN BROWN IN HIS OWN DEFENSE

The abolitionist attack on slavery received its most militant expression in John Brown's raid on a government arsenal at Harpers Ferry in 1859. To abolitionists the captured Brown was more than a striking figure in a terrible drama—he was a symbol, if not of freedom, at least of eternal hostility to slavery. While in jail Brown accepted his fate with dignity and fortitude, not flinching in spirit or recanting in doctrine. The speech which follows was made during his imprisonment; it captures something of his spirit and helps to explain the martyrdom which was to crown his death.

JOHN BROWN'S LAST SPEECH [NOV. 2]

"I have, may it please the Court, a few words to say.

"In the first place, I deny everything but what I have all along admitted,—the design on my part to free the slaves. I intended certainly to have made a clean thing of that matter, as I did last winter, when I went into Missouri and there took slaves without the snapping of a gun either side, moved them through the country, and finally left them in Canada. I designed to have done the same thing again, on a larger scale. That was all I intended. I never did intend murder, or treason, or the destruction of property, or to excite or incite slaves to rebellion, or to make insurrection.

"I have another objection: and that is, it is unjust that I should suffer such a penalty. Had I interfered in the manner which I admit, and which I admit has been fairly proved (for I admire the truthfulness and candor of the greater portion of the witnesses who have testified in this case),—had I so interfered in behalf of the rich, the powerful, the intelligent, the so-called great, or in behalf of any of their friends,—either father, mother, brother, sister,

*Benjamin C. Howard, *Report of the Decision of the Supreme Court of the United States in the Case of Dred Scott. . .* (Washington, 1857), 9, 13-14, 15-17, 60.

wife, or children, or any of that class,—and suffered and sacrificed what I have in this interference, it would have been all right; and every man in this court would have deemed it an act worthy of reward rather than punishment. . . .

"This court acknowledges, as I suppose, the validity of the law of God. I see a book kissed here which I suppose to be the Bible, or at least the New Testament. That teaches me that all things whatsoever I would that men should do to me, I should do even so to them. It teaches me, further, to 'remember them that are in bonds, as bound with them.' I endeavored to act up to that instruction. I say, I am yet too young to understand that God is any respecter of persons. I believe that to have interfered as I have done—as I have always freely admitted I have done—in behalf of His despised poor, was not wrong, but right. Now, if it is deemed necessary that I should forfeit my life for the furtherance of the ends of justice, and mingle my blood further with the blood of my children and with the blood of millions in this slave country whose rights are disregarded by wicked, cruel, and unjust enactments,—I submit; so let it be done!

"Let me say one word further.

"I feel entirely satisfied with the treatment I have received on my trial. Considering all the circumstances, it has been more generous than I expected. But I feel no consciousness of guilt. I have stated from the first what was my intention, and what was not. I never had any design against the life of any person, nor any disposition to commit treason, or excite slaves to rebel, or make any general insurrection. I never encouraged any man to do so, but always discouraged any idea of that kind.

"Let me say, also, a word in regard to the statements made by some of those connected with me. I hear it has been stated by some of them that I have induced them to join me. But the contrary is true. I do not say this to injure them but as regretting their weakness. There is not one of them but joined me of his own accord, and the greater part of them at their own expense. A number of them I never saw, and never had a word of conversation with, till the day they came to me; and that was for the purpose I have stated.

"Now I have done."*

108

A LETTER TO JOHN BROWN'S WIDOW

Brown's death stirred Negroes as nothing previously had done. They had counted him as one of their staunchest friends, even though they had not formed branches of the United States League of Gileadites, an organization he had conceived for them. On the night of Brown's hanging, December 2, 1859, Negroes throughout the North held meetings. On that Friday the Negroes in Boston had held all-day church meetings, closing their businesses. In Detroit at the Second Baptist Church, with George H. Parker, president of the Old Captain John Brown Liberty League, in the chair, the assembled Negroes vowed that they would ever venerate Brown's character. In these meetings held by Negroes, resolutions were drafted

*F. B. Sanborn, *The Life and Letters of John Brown* (Boston, 1891), 584-585.

extending sympathy to Brown's family and to the relatives and friends of his raiding party. The selection below is a letter to Mrs. Brown from a young Negro schoolteacher and abolitionist, Frances Ellen Watkins, who had spent two weeks with her at the home of William Still. Miss Watkins had already won some attention as a writer of popular verse, a reputation she would later enhance under her married name, Frances Ellen Watkins Harper.

LETTER TO JOHN BROWN'S WIFE

Farmer Centre, Ohio, Nov. 14th.

My Dear Madam:—In an hour like this the common words of sympathy may seem like idle words, and yet I want to say something to you, the noble wife of the hero of the nineteenth century. Belonging to the race your dear husband reached forth his hand to assist, I need not tell you that my sympathies are with you. I thank you for the brave words you have spoken. A republic that produces such a wife and mother may hope for better days. Our heart may grow more hopeful for humanity when it sees the sublime sacrifice it is about to receive from his hands. Not in vain has your dear husband periled all, if the martyrdom of one hero is worth more than the life of a million cowards. From the prison comes forth a shout of triumph over that power whose ethics are robbery of the feeble and oppression of the weak, the trophies of whose chivalry are a plundered cradle and a scourged and bleeding woman. Dear sister, I thank you for the brave and noble words that you have spoken. Enclosed I send you a few dollars as a token of my gratitude, reverence and love.

Yours respectfully,
Frances Ellen Watkins

Post Office address: care of William Still, 107 Fifth St., Philadelphia, Penn.

May God, our own God, sustain you in the hour of trial. If there is one thing on earth I can do for you or yours, let me be apprized. I am at your service.*

109

THE "HOUSE DIVIDED"

With sectional emotions running high during the winter of 1859-1860, the country moved toward the presidential campaign. The Republicans nominated Abraham Lincoln of Illinois, who had won national prominence in 1858 when he ran for the United States Senate. In seeking this Senate seat, held by Stephen A. Douglas, Lincoln launched his campaign with a speech on June 17, 1858, at Springfield, in which he asserted that a house divided against itself could not stand. Although revolutionary in its implications, the "house divided" phrase was not new. But after Lincoln evoked it in his address at Springfield the American people sensed as never before that the problem he put before them could no longer be brushed aside. In American political expression few figures of speech had a greater effect than "house divided." In the selection that follows Lincoln introduces it and proceeds to make it his central theme as he addresses the closing session of the Republican state convention.

*William Still, *op. cit.*, 762.

Mr. PRESIDENT and Gentlemen of the Convention.

If we could first know *where* we are, and *whither* we are tending, we could then better judge *what* to do, and *how* to do it.

We are now far into the *fifth* year, since a policy was initiated, with the *avowed* object, and *confident* promise, of putting an end to slavery agitation.

Under the operation of that policy, that agitation has not only, *not ceased,* but has *constantly augmented.*

In *my* opinion, it *will* not cease, until a *crisis* shall have been reached, and passed.

"A house divided against itself cannot stand."

I believe this government cannot endure, permanently half *slave* and half *free.*

I do not expect the Union to be *dissolved*—I do not expect the house to *fall*—but I *do* expect it will cease to be divided.

It will become *all* one thing, or *all* the other.

Either the *opponents* of slavery, will arrest the further spread of it, and place it where the public mind shall rest in the belief that it is in course of ultimate extinction; or its *advocates* will push it forward, till it shall become alike lawful in *all* the States, *old* as well as *new*—*North* as well as *South.*

Have we no *tendency* to the latter condition?

Let any one who doubts, carefully contemplate that now almost complete legal combination—piece of *machinery* so to speak—compounded of the Nebraska doctrine, and the Dred Scott decision. Let him consider not only *what work* the machinery is adapted to do, and *how well* adapted; but also, let him study the *history* of its construction, and trace, if he can, or rather *fail,* if he can, to trace the evidences of design, and concert of action, among its chief bosses, from the beginning.

But, so far, *Congress* only, had acted; and an *indorsement* by the people, *real* or apparent, was indispensable, to *save* the point already gained, and give chance for more.

The new year of 1854 found slavery excluded from more than

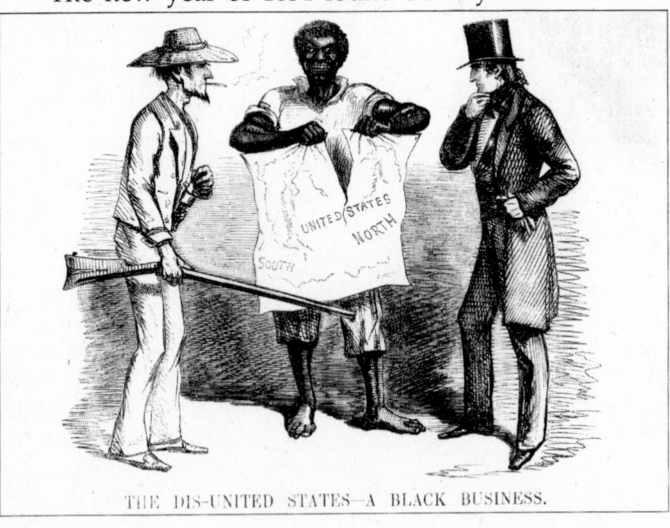

THE DIS-UNITED STATES—A BLACK BUSINESS.

Growing antagonism between Free North and Slave South began to receive attention around the world. This was how Punch, *the English humor magazine, summed up the situation in 1856.*

half the States by State Constitutions, and from most of the national territory by Congressional prohibition.

Four days later, commenced the struggle, which ended in repealing that Congressional prohibition.

This opened all the national territory to slavery; and was the first point gained.

This necessity had not been overlooked; but had been provided for, as well as might be, in the notable argument of *"squatter sovereignty,"* otherwise called *"sacred right of self government,"* which latter phrase, though expressive of the only rightful basis of any government, was so perverted in this attempted use of it as to amount to just this: That if any *one* man, choose to enslave *another,* no *third* man shall be allowed to object.*

110

A NEGRO ABOLITIONIST CRITIC OF LINCOLN

In the presidential campaign of 1860 Negroes and abolitionists preferred Lincoln to the other candidates, but they were not enthusiastic about him, accepting him as the best of a bad lot. Some Negroes were openly critical of the Republican nominee, among them H. Ford Douglas of Illinois. A runaway slave who had become an abolitionist orator, Douglas attacked Lincoln in a series of speeches during the summer of 1860. In the selection that follows, taken from a speech delivered at Framingham, Massachusetts, in early July, Douglas expressed the kind of reservations which abolitionists had about Lincoln.

Every department of the national life—the President' chair, the Senate of the United States, the Supreme Court and the American pulpit—is occupied and controlled by the dark spirit of American slavery. . . .

We have four parties in this country that have marshalled themselves on the highway of American politics, asking for the votes of the American people to place them in possession of the government. We have what is called the Union party, led by Mr. Bell, of Tennessee; we have what is called the Democratic party, led by Stephen A. Douglas, of Illinois; we have the party called the Seceders, or the Slave-Code Democrats, led by John C. Breckinridge, of Kentucky, and then we have the Republican party, led by Abraham Lincoln, of Illinois. All of these parties ask for your support, because they profess to represent some principle. So far as the principles of freedom and the hopes of the black men are concerned, all these parties are barren and unfruitful; neither of them seeks to lift the negro out of his fetters, and rescue this day from odium and disgrace.

Take Abraham Lincoln. I want to know if any man can tell me the difference between the anti-slavery of Abraham Lincoln, and the anti-slavery of the old Whig party, or the anti-slavery of Henry Clay? Why, there is no difference between them. Abraham Lincoln

---

*Roy P. Basler, ed., *The Collected Works of Abraham Lincoln* (9 vols, New Brunswick, New Jersey, Rutgers University Press, 1953), II, 461-462.

is simply a Henry Clay Whig, and he believes just as Henry Clay believed in regard to this question. And Henry Clay was just as odious to the anti-slavery cause and anti-slavery men as ever was John C. Calhoun. In fact, he did as much to perpetuate negro slavery in this country as any other man who has ever lived. Henry Clay once said, "That is property which the law declares to be property," and that "two hundred years of legislation have sanctioned and sanctified property in slaves"! Wherever Henry Clay is today in the universe of God, that atheistic lie is with him, with all its tormenting memories.

I know Abraham Lincoln, and I know something about his anti-slavery. I know the Republicans do not like this kind of talk, because, while they are willing to steal our thunder, they are unwilling to submit to the conditions imposed upon that party that assumes to be anti-slavery. They say that they cannot go as fast as you anti-slavery men go in this matter; that they cannot afford to be uncompromisingly honest, nor so radical as you Garrisonians; that they want to take time; that they want to do the work gradually. They say, "We must not be in too great a hurry to overthrow slavery; at least, we must take half a loaf, if we cannot get the whole." Now, my friends, I believe that the very best way to overthrow slavery in this country is to occupy the highest possible anti-slavery ground. Washington Irving tells a story of a Dutchman, who wanted to jump over a ditch, and he went back three miles in order to get a good start, and when he got up to the ditch, he had to sit down on the wrong side to get his breath. So it is with these political parties; they are compelled, they say, when they get up to the ditch of slavery, to stop and take breath.

* * *

Then, there is another item which I want to bring out in this connection. I am a colored man; I am an American citizen; and I think that I am entitled to exercise the elective franchise. I am about twenty-eight years old, and I would like to vote very much. I think I am old enough to vote, and I think that, if I had a vote to give, I should know enough to place it on the side of freedom. No party, it seems to me, is entitled to the sympathy of anti-slavery men, unless that party is willing to extend to the black man all the rights of a citizen. I care nothing about that anti-slavery which wants to make the Territories free, while it is unwilling to extend to me, as a man, in the free States, all the rights of a man. In the State of Illinois, where I live—my adopted State—I have been laboring to make it a place fit for a decent man to live in. In that State, we have a code of black laws that would disgrace any Barbary State, or any uncivilized people in the far-off islands of the sea. Men of my complexion are not allowed to testify in a court of justice, where a white man is a party. If a white man happens to owe me anything, unless I can prove it by the testimony of a white man, I cannot collect the debt. Now, two years ago, I went through the State of Illinois for the purpose of getting signers to a petition, asking the Legislature to repeal the 'Testimony Law,' so as to permit colored men to testify against white men. I went to prominent Republicans, and among others, to Abraham Lincoln and Lyman Trumbull, and neither of them dared to sign that petition, to give me the right to testify in a court of justice! In the State of Illinois, they tax the colored people for every conceivable purpose. They tax the negro's property to support schools for the education of the white man's children, but the colored people are not permitted to enjoy any of the benefits resulting from that taxation. We are compelled to impose upon ourselves additional taxes, in order to educate our children. The State lays its iron hand upon the negro, holds him down, and puts the other hand into his pocket and steals his hard earnings, to educate the children of white men: and if we sent our children to school, Abraham Lincoln would kick them out, in the name of Republicanism and anti-slavery!

* * *

Hypocrisy is not a growth peculiar to American soil, but it has reached its most hateful development here. . . . God has given us a goodly land in which to build up an empire of thought; it ought also to be an empire of freedom. . . .

All other races are permitted to travel over the wide field of history, and pluck the flowers that blossom there,—to glean up the heroes, philosophers, sages and poets and put them into a galaxy of brilliant genius; but if a black man attempts to do so, he is met at the threshold by the objection, "You have no ancestry behind you." Now, friends, I am proud of the negro race, and I thank God that there does not course in my veins a single drop of Saxon blood. I think that "negro" looks just as well on paper, and sounds as sweetly to the ear as "Saxon"; and I believe that by education, by wealth, and by religion, the negro may make that name as honorable as ever was that of "Saxon. . . ."

I know very well how imperfectly I have said my say. What can I say, then, as a black man, rather than to thank the men and women of New England who have so nobly stood by the rights and liberties of my unfortunate race during the long years of suffering and sorrow, feeling, as their only compensation, that every wrong and every outrage which we suffer

"In the hot conflict of the right, shall be
A token and a pledge of victory"?*

**The Liberator*, July 13, 1860.

CHAPTER SIX

Day of Freedom

INTRODUCTION

Day of Freedom

The Civil War did not start out as a crusade to abolish slavery. Indeed, during the first weeks of the conflict, both Lincoln and Congress denied that they had any intention of overthrowing the established institutions of the South. In the early stages of the war, the Lincoln administration insisted that its sole goal was that of preserving the Union.

But this idea gradually lost much of its force. Its waning influence was signalized on January 1, 1863, when Lincoln issued the Emancipation Proclamation declaring free the slaves in the rebelling states. True enough, Lincoln had originally thought of the proclamation as a military measure rather than as a manifesto of human liberty. But the proclamation, almost in spite of its creator, changed the whole tone and character of the war, becoming a fresh expression of one of man's loftiest aspirations—the quest for freedom. In the space of a few months, Lincoln's edict took on the evocative power reserved only for the half dozen great charter expressions of human liberty in the entire Western tradition.

Ever a growing man, Lincoln was not slow in sensing the new dimensions which his proclamation had taken on. Its more abiding meaning became ever clearer to him, as evidenced by his celebrated Gettysburg Address of November 19, 1863. Asked to make a few remarks at a battlefield which was being dedicated as a national cemetery, Lincoln closed his short speech by urging his countrymen to dedicate themselves to the task of giving to America "a new birth of freedom." Thus did Lincoln reveal that he had fully grasped the great truth that the war had become not an effort to restore the Union as it was, but a crusade to reconstitute America on a broadened base of human liberty.

Lincoln was not alone in sensing that after the proclamation, slavery was doomed in the United States. His countrymen, too, had grown in their concept of the meaning of the war. This new understanding was evidenced in the most popular of the songs sung by the Union soldiers, "John Brown's Body," and "Rally 'Round the Flag, Boys." The first of these affirmed that although John Brown's body was mouldering in the grave, his soul was marching on; the second song urged the soldiers to shout the battle-cry of freedom while rallying around the flag. On the homefront this spirit was caught by Julia Ward Howe's anthem, "The Battle Hymn of the Republic," whose stanzas struck an exalted chord.

In assessing the roots of this enlarged concept of freedom, the active role of the Negro himself must be noted. The Civil War Negro did more than exhort his fellow-Americans to live up to their great ideals of freedom: he proceeded to set an example by his own actions. For one thing, tens of thousands of Negroes freed themselves. The movement began on the night of May 23, 1861, when three fugitives paddled soundlessly up to Fortress Monroe, Union-held although in Virginia, and presented themselves to the picket guard. The next morning they were brought before General Benjamin F. Butler, who put them to work, declaring them to be "contraband of war." Triggered by Butler's history-making decision, a slave exodus was soon underway. Now convinced that if they suc-

Slave fugitives on the trail. Called "contraband" because they were still legally property and yet no longer cowed slaves, Negroes traveled to the Union lines by every means at their disposal.

ceeded in reaching the Stars and Stripes their freedom would be assured, the emboldened slaves began a series of mass migrations which one eyewitness described as being "like the oncoming of cities."

When these fugitives reached the Union lines, they brought with them serious problems of disease and disorder. But they also brought brawny arms, broad backs, and trained skills for labor. Some two hundred thousand such freedmen followed the Union armies, doing the heavy work. Fugitive Negroes also brought with them an unrivaled knowledge of the South's waterways and land configurations. But the greatest military role of the former slave was that of arms-bearer. Former slaves made up three-quarters of the Negroes who were mustered into the Union armies.

As a Union soldier, the Negro made a measurable contribution to the war effort. During the first eighteen months of the war, the Negro was not permitted to join the army. The early offers by Negroes to form military companies had been uniformly turned down by local, state, and federal authorities. The rare attempts by military commanders to enlist Negroes were unsupported in Washington, David Hunter furnishing a case in point. Commander of the Department of the South, Hunter organized the "First South Carolina Volunteer Regiment" in April 1862. Upon urging from a Kentucky congressman, C. A. Wickliffe, the House passed a resolution requesting the Secretary of War to furnish information about Hunter's recruiting activities. Hunter's bold reply enabled him to escape official reprimand, but lack of funds forced him to abandon the experiment.

Opposition to the Negro as a soldier was rooted in fears—fears that he lacked the qualities of a fighting man, fears that arming the Negro would be an admission that white soldiers had not been equal to the job, and the fear that to make the Negro a soldier would be to bring about a change in his position in American life. But the intention to by-pass the Negro had to be abandoned when the war dragged into its second year. With the Union ranks thinning and with white enlistments falling off, the opposition to Negro troops gradually waned. This changing sentiment was reflected in a popular song, "Sambo's Right to be Kilt." Finally by the spring of 1863, both the northern states and the national government were vying for Negro recruits.

In general the Negro's response to invitations to join the army was good. By the end of the war, some 180,000 colored men had enlisted, comprising between nine and ten per cent of the total Union enlistments. These Negro soldiers took part in 499 military engagements, of which 39 were major battles. Their death toll was high, amounting to 68,178, or slightly over 37% of their total number.

The Negro soldier faced a number of special discriminations. His period of enlistment was longer than that of whites; he had little chance of rising to the rank of commissioned officer; his salary was that of a military laborer, and his medical care was inferior. Field service had its special hazards. As a rule the firearms given to the Negro soldier were obsolete or faultily constructed. Worst of all, if he fell into the hands of the enemy, he faced the danger of not being treated as a prisoner of war, but as a runaway slave taking part in an armed rebellion.

Despite the discriminations against him, the morale of the colored soldier was good because he felt the army had something to offer him. It was a step upward in the social scale. It gave him the opportunity to learn to read and write, to make something of himself. Military service would help him to prepare for the responsibilities which awaited him when the guns were stacked. Proof of the high spirits of the Negro soldier was furnished by his conduct on the battlefield. Secretary of War Stanton, in a letter on February 8, 1864, to Lincoln, attested to the valor of Negro troops, writing as follows: "At Milliken's Bend, at Port Hudson, Morris Island and other battlefields, they have proved themselves among the bravest of the brave, performing deeds of daring and shedding their blood with a heroism unsurpassed by soldiers of any other race."

Many southern Negroes were of service to the Union army even though not in uniform. These non-combatants were of great assistance to soldiers who had escaped from Confederate prisons or who had been cut off from their units—feeding them, hiding them and conducting them to places of safety. Other Negroes served as spies and scouts. During the spring of 1862 more than fifty such volunteers were employed in the Department of North Carolina. "They frequently went from thirty to three hundred miles within the enemy's lines; visiting his principal camps and most important posts, and bringing us back important and reliable information," reported Vincent Colyer, Superintendent of the Poor under Major General Ambrose E. Burnside. Also rendering service of a quasi-military nature were Negro nurses like Savannah-born Susie King Taylor in South Carolina's Sea Islands. When Clara Barton, later the moving spirit in the founding of the American Red Cross, made the hospital rounds at Beaufort during the summer of 1863, she was accompanied by young Mrs. Taylor.

Negroes saw service at sea as on land. Always facing a manpower shortage, the navy had signed up Negroes from the beginning of the war. Anxious to attract them and to have them re-enlist, the navy treated Negroes fairly well; they were messed and quartered with other crew members and they had opportunities for promotion. The Negro response was all the navy could have hoped for, 29,000 of them signing up for the service. This comprised one quarter of the total number of men sailing the Union fleet. Four of these Negroes won the Navy Medal of Honor. Perhaps the best known of these was Joachim Pease, loader of the number-one gun on the *Kearsarge*. One of the fifteen Negroes on board this warship when she met the most famous of Confederate raiders, the *Alabama,* in a historic sea duel, off the coast of France, Pease was cited by his superior officer as having shown the utmost in courage and fortitude.

The homefront Negro, South and North, played a role well worth noting. The contribution of the slaves to the Southern cause was incalculable. War industry in the Confederacy had a slave labor base. As the armories and munitions plants tried to increase their output, they sent out appeals for more and more skilled Negro laborers. The Tredegar Iron Works of Richmond had a standing "help wanted" advertisement for one thousand such factory workers. Equally great was the demand for slave blacksmiths, harness makers, shoemakers, carpenters, wheelwrights, and miners.

The plantation Negro was "the stomach of the Confederacy," producing its crops of potatoes, corn, peanuts, oats, barley, and wheat. "Much of our success," wrote Jefferson Davis, president of the Confederacy, "was due to the much-abused institution of African servitude." White men were enabled to go into the army, explained Davis, by leaving to slaves the cultivation of the fields, the care of the livestock, and the protection of the women and children. Sharing this opinion of the role of the slaveworker was General U. S. Grant, who described the whole South as a military camp. Because slaves were required to work in the fields without regard to sex or age, wrote he, "the 4,000,000 of colored non-combatants were equal to more than three times their number in the North, age for age, sex for sex." The support received from its Negroes was one of the factors enabling the Confederacy to withstand the Union forces for four years.

In the North the Negro civilian was chiefly notable for his all-out support of the war effort. Particularly active were Negro women's organizations, such as the "Ladies' Union Bazaar Association" of New York. Some of these groups were devoted to helping the soldiers—sending them boxes, or purchasing flags and banners for the regiments. To raise the money, the women formed sewing circles and then held fairs to sell their needlework and other objects. Some Negro women's organizations had as their primary goal the assistance of the newly arrived slaves, distributing food and clothing to them. Typical of these charitable groups was the Contraband Relief Society, made up of forty women of the District of Columbia, and devoted to helping fugitives who had found their way to the nation's capital. Other women's organizations sent money to assist former slaves still in the South, the Colored Ladies' Sanitary Commission of Boston on one occasion sending $500 for the suffering freedmen of Savannah. Some individual Negro women, including Charlotte Forten, went to teach the three R's in those regions which had come under the Union flag.

Negro men on the home front were active in trying to influence public opinion in support of the war effort. Negroes sensed that the war would bring about an improvement in their lot. Hence their spokesmen prodded mayors, governors, and congressmen to support the war effort and to stand firmly behind the Lincoln administration. To the President himself, Negroes acted as a whip and spur, successively urging him to permit colored volunteers to join the army, to declare the slaves free, and to support equal suffrage.

It was this last issue—the right to vote—that particularly gripped the attention of the Negro during the last year of the war. Colored leaders held the opinion that freedom without the suffrage was somewhat of a sham. To Negroes, political equality was the very basis upon which to build other equalities. Black men had repeatedly let both Lincoln and Congress know of this desire for the ballot—in one instance a group of New Orleans Negroes sent a suffrage petition addressed jointly to the President and Congress, dated March 13, 1864, and bearing exactly 1,000 signatures. Of these petitioners, 27 had borne arms under Andrew Jackson at the Battle of New Orleans in the War of 1812.

The Negro did not get the ballot during the Civil War. But the war brought him much else. Former slaves were learning to read and write, had begun to lease land and sell crops, were giving themselves surnames and contracting legal marriages. They were, for the first time, speaking their own minds—voicing their expectations and hopes.

When the Negro took stock of the things that had come to pass during those four years of war, he felt for the first time that he had a stake in America, that his future was not in leaving this country to settle someplace else. As nothing else, the Civil War deepened the Negro's sense of identity with the land of his birth. It gave him a new sense of belonging, a feeling that the United States was really his country, and a good place for his children.

For all its bloodshed and sorrow, the Civil War was a major step in the direction of human freedom and the dignity of man. This step was symbolized by the Negro, as he made the journey from property to contraband of war, to freedom, and then to citizenship. And contributory to this change in status was the Negro's own readiness to play an active role in the conflict.

111

THE NEGRO'S OPTIMISM

It was with mixed feelings that most Negroes in the North regarded the coming of the Civil War. Like other Americans, they were sobered when they thought of the bloodshed and destruction that war would bring. But they also sensed that the war might furnish an opportunity to strike at slavery and discrimination based on color. Hence the immediate reaction of most Negroes was to view the war primarily as a continuation of the abolitionist crusade by other means. Their attitude was mirrored in a front-page editorial in The Anglo-African Weekly *of May 11, 1861, published in New York, which could not resist taking a sideswipe at prejudice while urging the country to prepare itself for a new day.*

MAKE WAY FOR LIBERTY!

"All roads lead to Rome" was the Roman adage, but it is the reverse with Washington; to it there seems to be only one, whose obstruction isolates the Government from a vast majority of the people. Therefore they are clamorous for the right of way to the capital: but we are anxious for a way to liberty; when slavery is attacked, all roads will lead to freedom.

Dan O'Connell said that "England's difficulty was Ireland's opportunity." Adopting the idea, we can say, with equal truth and greater justice, that the Union's danger is the slave's deliverance. God forbid that we should take pleasure in the distress of our countrymen, or rejoice at their afflictions any further than as they may be instrumental in inducing them "to do justly and to love mercy," as an opportunity of making a way to their hearts and of laying our claims before their awakened consciences.

The idea may appear extravagant, and to the American mind, repulsive, but we say, that no adjustment of the nation's difficulty is possible until the claims of the black man are first met and satisfied: "the judgement is set and the books are opened." His prostrate body forms an impediment over which liberty cannot advance; an impregnable barrier, behind which slavery securely entrenched will "laugh a siege to scorn." His title to life, to liberty and the pursuit of happiness must be acknowledged, or the nation will be forsworn; and being so, incur the dreadful penalty of permanent disunion, unending anarchy, and perpetual strife. Massachusetts may pour out her blood for the Union, and lavish her treasure to restore concord, but so long as her generals stand ready to rivet fetters upon the struggling bondmen, her blood and treasure will be spent in vain. Men of the North away with your Baalam-like proclivities, your trifling with truth and trafficking in principles. Liberty has always lost more by the cowardice of her supporters than by the bravery of her foes. Look upon us not as outcasts, pariahs, slaves, but as men whom the Almighty has endowed with the same faculties as yourselves, but in whom your cruelty has blurred his image and thwarted his intent.

If we are black, remember that your ancestors stole our fathers from their homes to drag out weary lives to bring you wealth. If we are ignorant, it is you that have shut the light of knowledge from our souls and brutalized our instincts. If we are degraded, yours is the disgrace, for you have closed up every avenue whereby we might emerge from degregation and robbed us of all incentive to elevation. The enormity of your guilt, the immensity of the wrong does not appear in contemplating what you have made us, but in the consideration of what you have prevented us from being. God only can estimate its extent and comprehend its consequences. Let no more efforts be made to effect a union between light and darkness, liberty and slavery, heaven and hell. Reason testifies that it is impossible, and your own sad experience verifies her testimony. If you would restore the Union and maintain the government you so fondly cherish, make way for liberty universal and complete. But the day of supplication is past—the hour of action is at hand. The black man, either with cooperation or without it must be ready to strike for liberty whenever the auspicious moment comes.

Let us then concentrate our energies and unite our hearts, by taking counsel with each other how slavery can most speedily be abolished.

Let us prepare ourselves by suitable organizations, to give effective aid to any movement that opens up a way to liberty, either at our country's call or of our own free wills.

> "Then in the name of God and all these rights
> Advance your standards, draw your willing swords."*

112

THE NEGRO'S DESIRE TO SERVE

Holding their views of the war, it was natural that Negroes would offer their services. The War Department received a number of offers from Negroes, among them Jacob Dodson, a Senate attendant. Massachusetts Negroes petitioned the legislature to allow them to serve and also resolved to form themselves into training companies. Below are the series of resolutions by Boston Negroes and an address given by Alfred M. Green at a meeting of Philadelphia Negroes on April 20, 1861.

RESOLUTION BY BOSTON NEGROES

The following Resolutions were adopted at a recent meeting of the colored citizens of Boston:—

Whereas, the traitors of the South have assailed the United States Government, with the intention of overthrowing it for the purpose of perpetuating slavery; and,

Whereas, in such a contest between the North and South—believing, as we do, that it is a contest between liberty and despotism—it is as important for each class of citizens to declare, as it is for

---

**The Anglo-African Weekly*, New York, May 11, 1861.

the rulers of the Government to know, their sentiments and position; therefore,

Resolved, That our feelings urge us to say to our countrymen that we are ready to stand by and defend the Government as the equals of its white defenders—to do so with "our lives, our fortunes, and our sacred honor," for the sake of freedom and as good citizens; and we ask you to modify your laws, that we may enlist—that full scope may be given to the patriotic feelings burning in the colored man's breast—and we pledge ourselves to raise an army in the country of fifty thousand colored men.

Resolved, That more than half of the army which we could raise, being natives of the South, knowing its geography, and being acquainted with the character of the enemy, would be of incalculable service to the Government.

Resolved, That the colored women would go as nurses, seamstresses, and warriors, if need be, to crush rebellion and uphold the Government.

Resolved, That the colored people, almost without an exception, "have their souls in arms, and all eager for the fray," and are ready to go at a moment's warning, if they are allowed to go as soldiers.

Resolved, That we do immediately organize ourselves into drilling companies, to the end of becoming better skilled in the use of fire-arms; so that when we shall be called upon by the country, we shall be better prepared to make a ready and fitting response.*

ALFRED M. GREEN'S ADDRESS

From the *Philadelphia Press*, of April 22, 1861.

A number of prominent colored men are now raising two regiments at the Masonic Hall, in South Eleventh street, and hundreds of brawny ebony men are ready to fill up the ranks if the State will accept their services. Peril and war blot out all distinction of race and rank. These colored soldiers should be attached to the Home Guard. They will make Herculean defenders. Colored men, it will be remembered, fought the glorious battle of Red Bank, when the city was in peril in 1777. The following is the address:

The time has arrived in the history of the great Republic when we may again give evidence to the world of the bravery and patriotism of a race, in whose hearts burns the love of country, of freedom, and of civil and religious toleration. It is these grand principles that enable men, however proscribed, when possessed of true patriotism, to say: "My country, right or wrong, I love thee still!"

It is true, the brave deeds of our fathers, sworn and subscribed to by the immortal Washington of the Revolution of 1776, and of Jackson and others, in the War of 1812, have failed to bring us into recognition as citizens, enjoying those rights so dearly bought by those noble and patriotic sires.

It is true, that our injuries in many respects are great; fugitive-slave laws, Dred Scott decisions, indictments for treason, and long and dreary months of imprisonment. The result of the most unfair

---

*_The Liberator_, May 31, 1861.

rules of judicial investigation has been the pay we have received for our solicitude, sympathy, and aid in the dangers and difficulties of those "days that tried men's souls."

Our duty, brethren, is not to cavil over past grievances. Let us not be derelict to duty in the time of need. While we remember the past, and regret that our present position in the country is not such as to create within us that burning zeal and enthusiasm for the field of battle, which inspires other men in the full enjoyment of every civil and religious emolument, yet let us endeavor to hope for the future, and improve the present auspicious moment for creating anew our claims upon the justice and honor of the Republic; and, above all, let not the honor and glory achieved by our fathers be blasted or sullied by a want of true heroism among their sons. Let us, then, take up the sword, trusting in God, who will defend the right, remembering that these are other days than those of yore—that the world to-day is on the side of freedom and universal political equality.

That the war-cry of the howling leaders of Secession and treason is, let us drive back the advance guard of civil and religious freedom; let us have more slave territory; let us build stronger the tyrant system of slavery in the great American Republic. Remember, too, that your very presence among the troops of the North would inspire your oppressed brethren of the South with zeal for the overthrow of the tyrant system, and confidence in the armies of the living God—the God of truth, justice, and equality to all men.

With a knowledge of your zeal and patriotism, and a hope of its early development, I am yours, for God and humanity.

A. M. Green.

Philadelphia, April 20, 1861.*

A War for Emancipation

113

SAVING THE UNION

The attitude of Negroes that the war was a struggle for humanity was not widely held in the North during the first year of the conflict. Gradually, however, this point of view gained ground, as clergymen, abolitionists, and other reformers kept insisting that the freeing of the slaves be made a paramount war aim. As the war dragged on into the middle of its second year and the death toll rose sharply, there was a growing sentiment in the North to free the slaves of the enemy. With enlistments dwindling and manpower needs becoming more acute, the slaves of the enemy represented a source of strength both as military laborers and as soldiers. Union army commanders urged Lincoln to strike at slavery. Their stand was supported by an influential group of Republicans, holders of the national purse strings and members of Lincoln's own party. Moreover, the freeing of the slaves would strike a popular chord in England and on the Continent, undermining the

*Alfred M. Green, *Letters and Discussions on the Formation of Colored Regiments . . .* (Phila., 1862), 304.

Confederacy's efforts to win diplomatic recognition in the capitals of Europe. Impelled by such considerations, Lincoln made up his mind in the summer of 1862. On June 22, he summoned his cabinet and told them of his intention to proclaim the emancipation of those states which remained in rebellion on January 1, 1863. Lincoln invited the secretaries to make comments. William H. Seward, Secretary of State, pointed out that it would be best to wait for a military success before issuing such a revolutionary document. Lincoln agreed. While waiting for his generals to produce a victory in the field, Lincoln received an open letter from Horace Greeley, editor of the influential New York Tribune, *urging him to abolish slavery and make use of Negro troops. Lincoln's answer to this "Prayer of Twenty Millions," was a clear statement of his attitude as of then.*

Executive Mansion,
Washington, August 22, 1862.

Hon. Horace Greely:
Dear Sir

I have just read yours of the 19th. addressed to myself through the New-York Tribune. If there be in it any statements, or assumptions of fact, which I may know to be erroneous, I do not, now and here, controvert them. If there be in it any inferences which I may believe to be falsely drawn, I do not now and here, argue against them. If there be perceptible in it an impatient and dictatorial tone, I waive it in deference to an old friend, whose heart I have always supposed to be right.

As to the policy I "seem to be pursuing" as you say, I have not meant to leave any one in doubt.

I would save the Union. I would save it the shortest way under the Constitution. The sooner the national authority can be restored; the nearer the Union will be "the Union as it was." If there be those who would not save the Union, unless they could at the same time *save* slavery, I do not agree with them. If there be those who would not save the Union unless they could at the same time *destroy* slavery, I do not agree with them. My paramount object in this struggle *is* to save the Union, and is *not* either to save or to destroy slavery. If I could save the Union without freeing *any* slave I would do it, and if I could save it by freeing *all* the slaves I would do it; and if I could save it by freeing some and leaving others alone I would also do that. What I do about slavery, and the colored race, I do because I believe it helps to save the Union; and what I forbear, I forbear because I do *not* believe it would help to save the Union. I shall do *less* whenever I shall believe what I am doing hurts the cause, and I shall do *more* whenever I shall believe doing more will help the cause. I shall try to correct errors when shown to be errors; and I shall adopt views so fast as they shall appear to be true views.

I have here stated my purpose according to my view of *official* duty; and I intend no modification of my oft-expressed *personal* wish that all men every where could be free. Yours,

A. LINCOLN*

---

*Basler, *op. cit.*, V, 388-389.

114

THE EMANCIPATION PROCLAMATION

Lincoln's answer, clear as it was, did not still the clamor for a proclamation of freedom. The patiently waiting President knew this all too well. Finally on September 17, 1862, the Battle of Antietam gave him the military excuse he needed. Five days later he issued a preliminary proclamation warning the states in rebellion that if they did not lay down their arms by January 1, 1863, their slaves would be declared free. The Confederacy ignored the ultimatum. Nevertheless, in the weeks following September 22, many people held doubts as to whether Lincoln would not back down. When the Congressional elections of November 1862 went against the Republicans, some of the President's advisors laid the blame to the preliminary proclamation and urged him to recall it. But Lincoln's mind was made up. On the appointed day he issued the final Emancipation Proclamation, which in addition to declaring free rebel-owned slaves, asked the former bondmen to abstain from violence, to labor faithfully, and invited them to join the armed forces. Deficient in exalted sentiment and uninspired in language, the Emancipation Proclamation nonetheless was destined to become a rallying cry for freedom.

EMANCIPATION PROCLAMATION
BY THE PRESIDENT OF THE UNITED STATES OF AMERICA: A PROCLAMATION

January 1, 1863

Whereas, on the twenty-second day of September, in the year of our Lord one thousand-eight hundred and sixty two, a proclamation was issued by the President of the United States, containing, among other things, the following, to wit:

"That on the first day of January, in the year of our Lord one thousand eight hundred and sixty-three, all persons held as slaves within any State or designated part of a State, the people whereof shall then be in rebellion against the United States, shall be then, thenceforward, and forever free; and the Executive Government of the United States, including the military and naval authority thereof, will recognize and maintain the freedom of such persons, and will do no act or acts to repress such persons, or any of them, in any efforts they may make for their actual freedom.

"That the Executive will, on the first day of January aforesaid, by proclamation, designate the States and parts of States, if any, in which the people thereof, respectively, shall then be in rebellion against the United States; and the fact that any State, or the people thereof, shall on that day be, in good faith, represented in the Congress of the United States by members chosen thereto at elections wherein a majority of the qualified voters of such State shall have participated, shall, in the absence of strong countervailing testimony, be deemed conclusive evidence that such State, and the people thereof, are not then in rebellion against the United States."

Now, therefore I, Abraham Lincoln, President of the United States, by virtue of the power in me vested as Commander-in-Chief, of the Army and Navy of the United States in time of actual armed rebellion against authority and government of the United States, and as a fit and necessary war measure for suppressing said rebellion, do, on this first day of January, in the year of our Lord one thousand eight hundred and sixty three, and in accordance with my purpose so to do publicly proclaimed for the full period of one hundred days, from the day first above mentioned, order and designate as the States and parts of States wherein the people thereof respectively, are this day in rebellion against the United States, the following, towit:

Arkansas, Texas, Louisiana, (except the Parishes of St. Bernard, Plaquemines, Jefferson, St. Johns, St. Charles, St. James[,] Ascension, Assumption, Terrebonne, Lafourche, St. Mary, St. Martin, and Orleans, including the City of New-Orleans) Mississippi, Alabama, Florida, Georgia, South-Carolina, North-Carolina, and Virginia, (except the fortyeight counties designated as West Virginia, and also the counties of Berkley, Accomac, Northampton, Elizabeth-City, York, Princess Ann, and Norfolk, including the cities of Norfolk & Portsmouth [)]; and which excepted parts are, for the present, left precisely as if this proclamation were not issued.

And by virtue of the power, and for the purpose aforesaid, I do order and declare that all persons held as slaves within said designated States, and parts of States, are, and henceforward shall be free; and that the Executive government of the United States, including the military and naval authorities thereof, will recognize and maintain the freedom of said persons.

And I hereby enjoin upon the people so declared to be free to abstain from all violence, unless in necessary self-defence; and I recommend to them that, in all cases when allowed, they labor faithfully for reasonable wages.

And I further declare and make known, that such persons of suitable condition, will be received into the armed service of the United States to garrison forts, positions, stations, and other places, and to man vessels of all sorts in said service.

And upon this act, sincerely believed to be an act of justice, warranted by the Constitution, upon military necessity, I invoke the considerate judgment of mankind, and the gracious favor of Almighty God.

In witness whereof, I have hereunto set my hand and caused the seal of the United States to be affixed.

Done at the City of Washington, this first day of January, in the year of our Lord one thousand eight hundred and sixty three, and of the Independence of the United States of America the eighty-seventh.

By the President:
Abraham Lincoln

William H. Seward,
Secretary of State *

*Basler, *op. cit.*, VI, 28-30.

115

THE BOSTON CELEBRATION

During the late afternoon and early evening of January 1, 1863, Negroes throughout the country held meetings to celebrate the signing of the proclamation. One such meeting was held at the Tremont Temple in Boston. Frederick Douglass, one of the featured speakers, described the anxiety of the participants as they awaited word that Lincoln had actually signed the measure, and their joy when they learned that he had.

Our ship was on the open sea, tossed by a terrible storm; wave after wave was passing over us, and every hour was fraught with increasing peril. Whether we should survive or perish depended in large measure upon the coming of this proclamation. At least so we felt. Although the conditions on which Mr. Lincoln had promised to withhold it had not been complied with, yet, from many considerations, there was room to doubt and fear. Mr. Lincoln was known to be a man of tender heart, and boundless patience: no man could tell to what length he might go, or might refrain from going, in the direction of peace and reconciliation. Hitherto, he had not shown himself a man of heroic measures, and, properly enough, this step belonged to that class. It must be the end of all compromises with slavery—a declaration that thereafter the war was to be conducted on a new principle, with a new aim. It would be a full and fair assertion that the government would neither trifle, or be trifled with, any longer. But would it come? On the side of doubt, it was said that Mr. Lincoln's kindly nature might cause him to relent at the last moment; that Mrs. Lincoln, coming from an old slaveholding family, would influence him to delay, and to give the slaveholders one other chance.* Every moment of waiting chilled our hopes, and strengthened our fears. A line of messengers was established between the telegraph office and the platform of Tremont Temple, and the time was occupied with brief speeches from Hon. Thomas Russell of Plymouth, Miss Anna E. Dickinson (a lady of marvelous eloquence), Rev. Mr. Grimes, J. Sella Martin, William Wells Brown, and myself. But speaking or listening to speeches was not the thing for which the people had come together. The time for argument was passed. It was not logic, but the trump of jubilee, which everybody wanted to hear. We were waiting and listening as for a bolt from the sky, which should rend the fetters of four millions of slaves; we were watching, as it were, by the dim light of the stars, for the dawn of a new day; we were longing for the answer to the agonizing prayers of centuries. Remembering those in bonds as bound with them, we wanted to join in the shout for freedom, and in the anthem of the redeemed.

Eight, nine, ten o'clock came and went, and still no word. A visible shadow seemed falling on the expecting throng, which the confident utterances of the speakers sought in vain to dispel. At last, when patience was well-nigh exhausted, and suspense was becom-

*I have reason to know that this supposition did Mrs. Lincoln great injustice.

ing agony, a man (I think it was Judge Russell) with hasty step advanced through the crowd, and with a face fairly illumined with the news he bore, exclaimed in tones that thrilled all hearts, "It is coming!" "It is on the wires!!" The effect of this announcement was startling beyond description, and the scene was wild and grand. Joy and gladness exhausted all forms of expression, from shouts of praise to sobs and tears. My old friend Rue, a colored preacher, a man of wonderful vocal power, expressed the heartfelt emotion of the hour, when he led all voices in the anthem, "Sound the loud timbrel o'er Egypt's dark sea, Jehovah hath triumphed, his people are free."

About twelve o'clock, seeing there was no disposition to retire from the hall, which must be vacated, my friend Grimes (of blessed memory), rose and moved that the meeting adjourn to the Twelfth Baptist church, of which he was pastor, and soon that church was packed from doors to pulpit, and this meeting did not break up till near the dawn of day. It was one of the most affecting and thrilling occasions I ever witnessed, and a worthy celebration of the first step on the part of the nation in its departure from the thraldom of ages.*

116

A NEW BIRTH OF FREEDOM

Most Negroes regarded the Emancipation Proclamation as a freedom document, seeing only its anti-slavery side. But if this point of view was wishful thinking on the day Lincoln signed the measure, it became more widely prevalent with the passing of every month. The war for the preservation of the Union had given way to the war as an instrument for the expansion of human freedom. This turn of events, this broader interpretation, was signalized in the Gettysburg Address of November 19, 1863. During the opening days of July 1863, the Confederate Army under Robert E. Lee had been repulsed in its efforts to reach Washington by sweeping through Pennsylvania. At Gettysburg, site of a major battle, the Lincoln administration decided to dedicate the field of combat as a cemetery for the soldiers who fell there. As part of the ceremonial exercises, the President was asked to make a statement. Just as the battle itself marked a military turning point in the war, so Lincoln's brief address marked a new direction in its ideology. Lincoln centered his remarks around the unfolding significance of the war, linking it to America's revolutionary heritage while simultaneously giving to it a new dimension.

Fourscore and seven years ago our fathers brought forth on this continent a new nation, conceived in liberty and dedicated to the proposition that all men are created equal.

Now we are engaged in a great civil war, testing whether that nation or any nation so conceived and so dedicated can long endure. We are met on a great battlefield of that war. We have come to dedicate a portion of that field as a final restingplace of those who here gave their lives that that nation might live. It is altogether fitting and proper that we should do this.

---

*Frederick Douglass, *Life and Times of Frederick Douglass* (Hartford, 1882), 428-430.

But, in a larger sense, we cannot dedicate, we cannot consecrate, we cannot hallow this ground. The brave men, living and dead, who struggled here have consecrated it far above our poor power to add or detract. The world will little note nor long remember what we say here, but it can never forget what they did here. It is for us the living, rather, to be dedicated here to the unfinished work which they who fought here have thus far so nobly advanced. It is rather for us to be here dedicated to the great task remaining before us, that from these honored dead we take increased devotion to that cause for which they gave the last full measure of devotion; that we here highly resolve that these dead shall not have died in vain; that this nation, under God, shall have a new birth of freedom; and that government of the people, by the people, for the people, shall not perish from the earth.*

The Negro Serviceman

117

MEN OF COLOR, TO ARMS!

The sanction of Negro levies by Lincoln in the Emancipation Proclamation marked the beginning of the large-scale tapping of this great reservoir of manpower. Lincoln's go-ahead signal found a ready response in northern state capitals. Many governors, desperately anxious to fill their quotas, now saw a way out. But with a relatively sparse Negro population of their own, northern states had to send agents to Union-held regions of the South. Here, however, these agents found a formidable rival in the national government itself. On March 25, 1863, Secretary Stanton dispatched General Lorenzo Thomas, adjutant general of the Union army, to the Mississippi Valley, with power to organize brigades of Negro soldiers. Two months later, on May 22, a Bureau of Colored Troops was established, being authorized to supervise the organizing of Negro units and to examine candidates seeking commissions in them.

Negro leaders were overjoyed at the change of heart of the Lincoln administration. Some prominent Negroes became recruiting agents, among them William Wells Brown, J. W. Loguen, J. Mercer Langston, and Frederick Douglass. The last named wrote a stirring editorial urging Negroes to join up.

MEN OF COLOR, TO ARMS!

When first the rebel cannon shattered the walls of Sumter and drove away its starving garrison, I predicted that the war then and there inaugurated would not be fought out entirely by white men. Every month's experience during these dreary years has confirmed that opinion. A war undertaken and brazenly carried on for the perpetual enslavement of colored men, calls logically and loudly for colored men to help suppress it. Only a moderate share of sagacity was needed to see that the arm of the slave was the best defense against the arm of the slaveholder. Hence with every reverse to the national arms, with every exulting shout of victory raised by the slaveholding rebels, I have implored the imperiled nation to unchain against her foes, her powerful black hand. Slowly and reluctantly that appeal is beginning to be heeded. Stop not now to complain

*Basler, *op. cit.* VII, 23.

that it was not heeded sooner. It may or it may not have been best that it should not. This is not the time to discuss that question. Leave it to the future. When the war is over, the country is saved, peace is established, and the black man's rights are secured, as they will be, history with an impartial hand will dispose of that and sundry other questions. Action! Action! not cricism, is the plain duty of this hour. Words are now useful only as they stimulate to blows. The office of speech now is only to point out when, where, and how to strike to the best advantage. There is no time to delay. The tide is at its flood that leads on to fortune. From East to West, from North to South, the sky is written all over, "Now or never." Liberty won by white men would lose half its luster. "Who would be free themselves must strike the blow." "Better even die free, than to live slaves." This is the sentiment of every brace colored man amongst us. There are weak and cowardly men in all nations. We have them amongst us. They tell you this is the "white man's war"; that you will be no "better off after than before the war;" that the getting of you into the army is to "sacrifice you on the first opportunity." Believe them not; cowards themselves, they do not wish to have their cowardice shamed by your brave example. Leave them to their timidity, or to whatever motive may hold them back. Ihave not their timidity, or to whatever motive may hold them back. I have not thought lightly of the words I am now addressing you. The counsel I give comes of close observation of the great struggle now in progress, and of the deep conviction that this is your hour and mine. In good earnest then, and after the best deliberation, I now for the first time during this war feel at liberty to call and counsel you to arms. By every consideration which binds you to your enslaved fellow-countrymen, and the peace and welfare of your country; by every

A group portrait of a Negro detachment. Such pictures were used in recruiting efforts throughout the nation.

Courtesy of Chicago Historical Society

aspiration which you cherish for the freedom and equality of yourselves and your children; by all the ties of blood and identity which make us one with the brave black men now fighting our battles in Louisiana and in South Carolina, I urge you to fly to arms, and smite with death the power that would bury the government and your liberty in the same hopeless grave. I wish I could tell you that the State of New York calls you to this high honor. For the moment her constituted authorities are silent on the subject. They will speak by and by, and doubtless on the right side; but we are not compelled to wait for her. We can get at the throat of treason and slavery through the State of Massachusetts. She was first in the War of Independence; first to break the chains of her slaves; first to make the black man equal before the law; first to admit colored children to her common schools, and she was first to answer with her blood the alarm cry of the nation, when its capital was menaced by rebels. You know her patriotic governor, and you know Charles Sumner. I need not add more.

Massachusetts now welcomes you to arms as soldiers. She has but a small colored population from which to recruit. She has full leave of the general government to send one regiment to the war, and she has undertaken to do it. Go quickly and help fill up the first colored regiment from the North. I am authorized to assure you that you will receive the same wages, the same rations, the same equipments, the same protection, the same treatment, and the same bounty, secured to the white soldiers. You will be led by able and skillful officers, men who will take special pride in your efficiency and success. They will be quick to accord to you all the honor you shall merit by your valor, and see that your rights and feelings are respected by other soldiers. I have assured myself on these points, and can speak with authority. More than twenty years of unswerving devotion to our common cause may give me some humble claim to be trusted at this momentous crisis. I will not argue. To do so implies hesitation and doubt, and you do not hesitate. You do not doubt. The day dawns; the morning star is bright upon the horizon! The iron gate of our prison stands half open. One gallant rush from the North will fling it wide open, while four millions of our brothers and sisters shall march out into liberty. The chance is now given you to end in a day the bondage of centuries, and to rise in one bound from social degradation to the plane of common equality with all other varieties of men. Remember Denmark Vesey of Charleston; remember Nathaniel Turner of Southampton; remember Shields Green and Copeland, who followed noble John Brown, and fell as glorious martyrs for the cause of the slave. Remember that in a contest with oppression, the Almighty has no attribute which can take sides with oppressors. The case is before you. This is our golden opportunity. Let us accept it, and forever wipe out the dark reproaches unsparingly hurled against us by our enemies. Let us win for ourselves the gratitude of our country, and the best blessings of our posterity through all time.*

---

*Carter G. Woodson, *Negro Orators and Their Orations* (Associated Publishers, Washington, 1925), 253-255. Reprinted by permission.

118

THE QUALITY OF THE BLACK SOLDIER

Despite the disadvantages he encountered, the morale of the Negro soldier was likely to be above par. "The number of desertions have been few," wrote General Thomas on December 24, 1863, concerning the 20,830 Negroes he had enlisted up to that time. The typical Negro volunteer made a dependable and resolute soldier. He was fighting for the Union, as were his white comrades in arms. But the colored soldier was also fighting to win a new dignity and self-respect, and for an America in which his children would have greater liberties and responsibilities. The Negro as a soldier was analyzed by Thomas Wentworth Higginson, colonel of the First South Carolina Volunteers, in his Army Life in a Black Regiment. *A former abolitionist who had backed John Brown in the Kansas struggle, Higginson was also a man of letters. Hence his study of the Negroes under his command became a literary classic in its moving portrayal of the former slave as a man of war.*

So far as I have seen, the mass of men are naturally courageous up to a certain point. A man seldom runs away from danger which he ought to face, unless others run; and each is apt to keep with the mass, and colored soldiers have more than usual of this gregariousness. In almost every regiment, black or white, there are a score or two of men who are naturally daring, who really hunger after dangerous adventures, and are happiest when allowed to seek them. Every commander gradually finds out who these men are, and habitually uses them; certainly I had such, and I remember with delight their bearing, their coolness, and their dash. Some of them were negroes, some mulattoes. One of them would have passed for white, with brown hair and blue eyes, while others were so black you could hardly see their features. These picked men varied in other respects too; some were neat and well-drilled soldiers, while others were slovenly, heedless fellows,—the despair of their officers at inspection, their pride on a raid. They were the natural scouts and rangers of the regiment; they had the two-o'clock-in-the-morning courage, which Napoleon thought so rare. The mass of the regiment rose to the same level under excitement, and were more excitable, I think, than whites, but neither more nor less courageous.

Perhaps the best proof of a good average of courage among them was in the readiness they always showed for any special enterprise. I do not remember ever to have had the slightest difficulty in obtaining volunteers, but rather in keeping down the number. The previous pages include many illustrations of this, as well as of their endurance of pain and discomfort. For instance, one of my lieutenants, a very daring Irishman, who had served for eight years as a sergeant of regular artillery in Texas, Utah, and South Carolina, said he had never been engaged in anything so risky as our raid up the St. Mary's. But in truth it seems to me a mere absurdity to deliberately argue the question of courage, as applied to men among whom I waked and slept, day and night, for so many months together. As well might he who has been wandering for years upon the desert, with a Bedouin escort, discuss the courage of the men whose tents have been his shelter and whose spears his guard. We, their officers, did not go there to teach lessons, but to receive them. There were more than a hundred men in the ranks who had voluntarily met more dangers in their escape from slavery than any of my young captains had incurred in all their lives.

* * *

The question was often asked, whether the Southern slaves or the Northern free blacks made the best soldiers. It was a compliment to both classes that each officer usually preferred those whom he had personally commanded. I preferred those who had been slaves, for their greater docility and affectionateness, for the powerful stimulus which their new freedom gave, and for the fact that they were fighting, in a manner, for their own homes and firesides. Every one of these considerations afforded a special aid to discipline, and cemented a peculiar tie of sympathy between them and their officers. They seemed like clansmen, and had a more confiding and filial relation to us than seemed to me to exist in the Northern colored regiments.

So far as the mere habits of slavery went, they were a poor preparation for military duty. Inexperienced officers often assumed that, because these men had been slaves before enlistment, they would bear to be treated as such afterwards. Experience proved the contrary. The more strongly we marked the difference between the slave and the soldier, the better for the regiment. One half of military duty lies in obedience, the other half in self-respect. A soldier without self-respect is worthless. Consequently there were no regiments in which it was so important to observe the courtesies and proprieties of military life as in these. I had to caution the officers to be more than usually particular in returning the salutations of the men; to be very careful in their dealings with those on picket or guard-duty; and on no account to omit the titles of the non-commissioned officers. So, in dealing out punishments, we had carefully to avoid all that was brutal and arbitrary, all that savored of the overseer. Any such dealing found them as obstinate and contemptuous as was Topsy when Miss Ophelia undertook to chastise her. A system of light punishments, rigidly administered according to the prescribed military forms, had more weight with them than any amount of angry severity. To make them feel as remote as possible from the plantation, this was essential. By adhering to this, and constantly appealing to their pride as soldiers and their sense of duty, we were able to maintain a high standard of discipline,—so, at least, the inspecting officers said,—and to get rid, almost entirely, of the more degrading class of punishments,—standing on barrels, tying up by the thumbs, and the ball and chain.

In all ways we had to educate their self-respect. For instance, at first they disliked to obey their own non-commissioned officers. "I don't want him to play de white man ober me," was a sincere objection. They had been so impressed with a sense of inferiority that the distinction extended to the very principles of honor. "I ain't got colored-man principles," said Corporal London Simmons, indignantly defending himself from some charge before me. "I'se

The assault of the Louisiana Colored Volunteers on the Confederate defenses at Port Hudson, La., May 27, 1863, was the first major battle in which Negro troops took part.

got white-gemman principles. I'se do my best. If Cap'n tell me to take a man, s'pose de man be as big as a house, I'll clam hold on him till I die, inception [excepting] I'm sick."

But it was plain that this feeling was a bequest of slavery, which military life would wear off. We impressed it upon them that they did not obey their officers because they were white, but because they were their officers, just as the Captain must obey me, and I the General; that we were all subject to military law, and protected by it in turn. Then we taught them to take pride in having good material for non-commissioned officers among themselves, and in obeying them. On my arrival there was one white first sergeant, and it was a question whether to appoint others. This I prevented, but left that one, hoping the men themselves would at least petition for his removal, which at length they did. He was at once detailed on other duty. The picturesqueness of the regiment suffered, for he was very tall and fair, and I liked to see him step forward in the centre when the line of first sergeants came together at dress-parade. But it was a help to discipline to eliminate the Saxon, for it recognized a principle.

Afterward I had excellent battalion-drills without a single white officer, by way of experiment; putting each company under a sergeant, and going through the most difficult movements, such as division-columns and oblique-squares. And as to actual discipline, it is doing no injustice to the line-officers of the regiment to say that none of them received from the men more implicit obedience than Color-Sergeant Rivers. I should have tried to obtain commissions for him and several others before I left the regiment, had their literary education been sufficient; and such an attempt was finally made by Lieutenant-Colonel Trowbridge, my successor in immediate command, but it proved unsuccessful. It always seemed to me an insult to those brave men to have novices put over their heads, on the ground of color alone; and the men felt it the more keenly as they remained longer in service. There were more than seven hundred enlisted men in the regiment, when mustered out after more than three years' service. The ranks had been kept full by enlistment, but there were only fourteen line-officers instead of the full thirty. The men who should have filled those vacancies were doing duty as sergeants in the ranks.

In what respect were the colored troops a source of disappointment? To me in one respect only,—that of health. Their health improved, indeed, as they grew more familiar with military life; but I think that neither their physical nor moral temperament gave them that toughness, that obstinate purpose of living, which sustains the more materialistic Anglo-Saxon. They had not, to be sure, the same predominant diseases, suffering in the pulmonary, not in the digestive organs; but they suffered a good deal. They felt malaria less, but they were more easily choked by dust and made ill by dampness. On the other hand, they submitted more readily to sanitary measures than whites, and, with efficient officers, were more easily kept clean. They were injured throughout the army by an undue share of fatigue duty, which is not only exhausting but demoralizing to a soldier; by the unsuitableness of the rations, which gave them salt meat instead of rice and hominy; and by the lack of good medical attendance. Their childlike constitutions peculiarly needed prompt and efficient surgical care; but almost all the colored troops were enlisted late in the war, when it was hard to get good surgeons for any regiments, and especially for these. In this respect I had nothing to complain of since there were no surgeons in the army for whom I would have exchanged my own.

And this late arrival on the scene affected not only the medical supervision of the colored troops, but their opportunity for a career. It is not my province to write their history, nor to vindicate them, nor to follow them upon those larger fields compared with which the adventures of my regiments appear but a partisan warfare. Yet this, at least, may be said. The operations on the South Atlantic coast, which long seemed a merely subordinate and incidental part of the great contest, proved to be one of the final pivots on which it turned. All now admit that the fate of the Confederacy was decided by Sherman's march to the sea. Port Royal was the objective point to which he marched, and he found the Department of the South, when he reached it, held almost exclusively by colored troops. Next to the merit of those who made the march was that of those who held open the door. That service will always remain among the laurels of the black regiments.*

119

EDUCATION FOR NEGRO SOLDIERS

The army attracted Negroes because it gave them the opportunity to learn to read and write. "In each of the camps of the colored regiments, the best built cabin was a schoolhouse," wrote Colonel James McKaye, a member of the Freedmen's Inquiry Commission, designed to investigate the condition of the newly freed slaves. James Monroe Trotter, lieutenant in the famed Massachusetts Fifty-Fourth Regiment, and later register of deeds under President Cleveland, left a description of what he called, "The School-master in the Army," which follows.

Of the many interesting experiences that attended our colored soldiery during the late war none are more worthy of being recounted than those relating to the rather improvised schools, in which were taught the rudimentary branches. One would naturally think that the tented field, so often suddenly changed to the bloody field of battle, was the last place in the world where would be called into requisition the schoolteacher's services; in fact it would hardly be supposed that such a thing was possible. Yet in our colored American army this became not only possible but really practicable, for in it frequently, in an off-hand manner, schools were established and maintained, not only for teaching the soldiers to read and write but also to sing, nor were debating societies, even, things unheard of in the camp life of these men. And what shall we say of the halls of learning in which were gathered his eager pupils? Well, certainly these would not compare favorably with those of civil life, as may well be imagined. As says Bryant, truly and beautifully, speaking of primitive religious worship:

'The groves were God's first temples.'

So, too, in the groves and fields of their new land of liberty, these men found their first temples of learning, and in spite of all inconveniences these school tents were rendered quite serviceable. Of the text books used there is not much to say, for these were generally 'few and far between.' Books were used at times, of course, but quite as often the instruction given was entirely oral. That these spare facilities did not render the teacher's efforts ineffective was abundantly proven in the service, and has been proven since in civil life.

* * *

It must, of course, be remembered that in our colored regiments a very large percentage of the men were illiterate, especially in those composed of men from the south and so lately escaped from under the iron heel of slavery. Indeed, in many of them there could scarcely be found at the commencement of the service a man who could either

---

*Thomas Wentworth Higginson, *Army Life in a Black Regiment* (Michigan State University Press, 1960), 190–191, 200–203. Reprinted by permission of Michigan State University Press.

read or write. Many an officer can recall his rather novel experience in teaching his first sergeant enough of figures and script letters to enable the latter to make up and sign the company morning report. All honor to those faithful, patient officers, and all honor, too, give to those ambitious sergeants who after awhile conquered great difficulties and became educationally proficient in their lines of duty.

In this connection I readily call to mind one of the most, if not the most, unique figures of all my experience in the army. It was Colonel James Beecher, of the famous Beecher family, and a brother of Henry Ward Beecher. He was in command of the First North Carolina Colored Regiment. In this position it would be hard to overestimate the variety and value of his services, for he became for his soldiers at once a gallant fighter, an eloquent, convincing preacher, and a most indefatigable and successful school-teacher. Preaching had been his vocation before entering the army, and so it was but natural for him to continue in that work. At one time our regiment lay encamped near his in South Carolina, and I well remember how, on one Sabbath morning, the two commands formed a union service, all listening with deep, thrilling interest to the inspiring words of this "fighting parson." That he was indeed a fighting parson we fully learned not long after this Sabbath service. For again we met on the bloody field of battle, where in the very front of the fight we saw him gallantly leading his no less gallant men, even after he had been wounded, and while the blood almost streamed down his face. Seeing him thus was to ever remember him and his noble work with his regiment.

Colonel Beecher when encamped neglected no opportunity to form schools of instruction for his men, in order that they might become not only intelligent, efficient soldiers, but also intelligent, self-respecting citizens, should they survive the perils of war.

But let it not be supposed for a moment that only officers and men of another race were engaged in this noble work of school-teaching in our colored army. Not a few of the best workers were colored chaplains, who wisely divided their time between preaching, administering to the sick by reason of wounds or otherwise, and to teaching the old 'young idea how to shoot;' while many non-commissioned officers and private soldiers cheerfully rendered effective service in the same direction. Nor must we close without expressing warm admiration for those earnest, ambitious soldier pupils who, when finding themselves grown to man's estate, having been debarred by the terrible system of slavery from securing an education, yielded not to what would have been considered only a natural discouragement, but, instead, followed the advice and instruction of their comrade teachers, and, bending themselves to most assiduous study, gained in some cases great proficiency, and in all much that fitted them for usefulness and the proper enjoyment of their well-earned liberty. And so we say, all honor to teachers and taught in the Grand Army that made a free republic, whose safe foundation and perpetuity lies in the general education of its citizens.*

*Joseph T. Wilson, *The Black Phalanx* (Hartford, Conn., 1888), 505-507.

120

DESIRE FOR BLACK RECRUITS

While Negro soldiers were proving their mettle, Negro sailors were also serving the Union cause. From the outbreak of hostilities, the navy had welcomed colored recruits. One of the reasons for this open-arms policy was expressed in an order issued by the Secretary of the Navy, Gideon Welles.

Navy Department, April 30, 1862

Sir—The approach of the hot and sickly season upon the Southern coast of the United States renders it imperative that every precaution should be used by the officers commanding vessels to continue the excellent sanitary condition of their crews. The large number of persons known as 'contrabands' flocking to the protection of the United States flag affords an opportunity to provide in every department of a ship, especially for boats' crews, acclimated labor. The flag-officers are required to obtain the services of these persons for the country by enlisting them freely in the navy, with their consent, rating them as boys, at eight, nine, or ten dollars per month, and one ration. Let a monthly return be made of the number of this class of persons employed on each vessel under your command.

I am respectfully, your obedient servant,

Gideon Welles*

121

A DARING NEGRO PILOT

A Negro naval officer was a rarity, although one former slave attained the rank of captain. This was Robert Smalls, who owed his fame to a spectacular escape from the Charleston harbor aboard the Confederate cotton steamer, Planter. *A slave pilot on the* Planter, *Smalls had impersonated the captain and sailed the boat into the outer harbor where the blockading Union ships were stationed. Requiring careful planning and brilliant execution, Smalls' feat was widely acclaimed in the North. The story is told in a series of letters from high-ranking officers, as published in the government-sponsored compendium, the* Official Records of the Union and Confederate Navies.

ABDUCTION OF THE CONFEDERATE STEAMER PLANTER
FROM CHARLESTON, S.C.,
MAY 13, 1862.

REPORT OF FLAG-OFFICER DU PONT, U.S. NAVY.

Flagship Wabash,
Port Royal Harbor, S.C.,
May 14, 1862.

Sir: I enclose a copy of a report from Commander E. G. Parrott; brought here last night by the late rebel steam tug *Planter,* in charge of an officer and crew from the *Augusta.* She was an armed dispatch

**Appleton's Annual Cyclopedia . . . of the Year 1862* (New York, 1867), 753.

and transportation steamer attached to the engineer department at Charleston, under Brigadier-General Ripley, whose barge, a short time since, was brought out to the blockading fleet by several contrabands.

The bringing out of this steamer, under all the circumstances, would have done credit to anyone. At 4 in the morning, in the absence of the captain, who was on shore, she left her wharf close to the Government office and headquarters, with palmetto and Confederate flag flying, passed the successive forts, saluting as usual by blowing her steam whistle. After getting beyond the range of the last gun she quickly hauled down the rebel flags and hoisted a white one.

The *Onward* was the inside ship of the blockading fleet in the main channel, and was preparing to fire when her commander made out the white flag.

The armament of the steamer is a 32-pounder, on pivot, and a fine 24 pounder howitzer. She had, besides, on her deck, four other guns, one 7-inch rifle, which were to be taken the morning of the escape to the new fort on the middle ground. One of the four belonged to Fort Sumter, and had been struck, in the rebel attack on that fort, on the muzzle.

Robert, the intelligent slave and pilot of the boat, who performed this bold feat so skillfully, informed me of this fact, presuming it would be a matter of interest to us to have possession of this gun.

This man, Robert Smalls, is superior to any who has yet come into the lines, intelligent as many of them have been. His information has been most interesting, and portions of it of the utmost importance.

The steamer is quite a valuable acquisition to the squadron, by her good machinery and very light draft. The officer in charge brought her through St. Helena Sound and by the inland passage down Beaufort River, arriving here at 10 last night.

On board the steamer when she left Charleston were 8 men, 5 women, and 3 children.

I shall continue to employ Robert as a pilot on board the *Planter* for the inland waters, with which he appears to be very familiar.

I do not know whether, in views of the Government, the vessel will be considered a prize; but, if so, I respectfully submit to the Department the claims of this man Robert and his associates.

Very respectfully, your obedient servant,

S. F. Du Pont,
Flag-Officer,
Comdg. South Atlantic Blockading Squadron.

Hon. Gideon Welles,
*Secretary of the Navy, Washington.**

**Official Records of the Union and Confederate Navies*, ser. 1, vol. XII, 820-836.

122

A WASHINGTON NEGRO AID SOCIETY

As the Union forces systematically encircled the Confederacy and penetrated further into it, the tens of thousands of Negroes who had become their own masters were, in the main, overjoyed with their new status. Being free, however, had problems of its own, as they soon found out. Each had to make an adjustment to a new way of life. Fortunately for the newly emancipated slave, his own efforts were generously supplemented by the nearly eighty freedmen's aid societies which, with their auxiliaries, came into existence during the ten years following the outbreak of the war. In essence, particularly in their initial stages, these societies were relief agencies, bent mainly on alleviating the suffering of the freedmen and the white refugees. Although many of these societies were run by religious groups, the winning of denominational converts was not a major motive. Numbered among the relief societies were those organized by Negroes themselves. The city of Washington, for example, had its Contraband Relief Society, headed by the fashionable Elizabeth Keckley, dressmaker and seamstress to Mrs. Lincoln. In the passage below, Mrs. Keckley relates the manner in which the association was founded and financed.

One fair summer evening I was walking the streets of Washington, accompanied by a friend, when a band of music was heard in the distance. We wondered what it could mean, and curiosity prompted us to find out its meaning. We quickened our steps, and discovered that it came from the house of Mrs. Farnham. The yard was brilliantly lighted, ladies and gentlemen were moving about, and the band was playing some of its sweetest airs. We approached the sentinel on duty at the gate, and asked what was going on. He told us that it was a festival given for the benefit of the sick and wounded soldiers in the city. This suggested an idea to me. If the white people can give festivals to raise funds for the relief of suffering soldiers, why should not the well-to-do colored people go to work to do something for the benefit of the suffering blacks? I could not rest. The thought was ever present with me, and the next Sunday I made a suggestion in the colored church, that a society of colored people be formed to labor for the benefit of the unfortunate freedmen. The idea proved popular, and in two weeks "the Contraband Relief Association" was organized, with forty working members.

In September of 1862, Mrs. Lincoln left Washington for New York, and requested me to follow her in a few days, and join her at the Metropolitan Hotel. I was glad of the opportunity to do so, for I thought that in New York I would be able to do something in the interests of our society. Armed with credentials, I took the train for New York, and went to the Metropolitan, where Mrs. Lincoln had secured accommodations for me. The next morning I told Mrs. Lincoln of my project; and she immediately headed my list with a subscription of $200. I circulated among the colored people, and got them thoroughly interested in the subject, when I was called to

Boston by Mrs. Lincoln, who wished to visit her son Robert, attending college in that city. I met Mr. Wendell Phillips, and other Boston philanthropists, who gave me all the assistance in their power. We held a mass meeting at the Colored Baptist Church, Rev. Mr. Grimes, in Boston, raised a sum of money, and organized there a branch society. The society was organized by Mrs. Grimes, wife of the pastor, assisted by Mrs. Martin, wife of Rev. Sella Martin. This branch of the main society, during the war, was able to send us over eighty large boxes of goods, contributed exclusively by the colored people of Boston. Returning to New York, we held a successful meeting at the Shiloh Church, Rev. Henry Highland Garnet, pastor. The Metropolitan Hotel, at that time as now, employed colored help. I suggested the object of my mission to Robert Thompson, Steward of the Hotel, who immediately raised quite a sum of money among the dining-room waiters. Mr. Frederick Douglass contributed $200, besides lecturing for us. Other prominent colored men sent in liberal contributions. From England a large quantity of stores was received. Mrs. Lincoln made frequent contributions, as also did the President.*

123

TYPES OF FREEDMEN

If the goals of these societies were similar, their activities varied according to the population to be served. For the freedmen were a varied lot. In the Mississippi Valley, for example, five classes were noted by John Eaton, the able and dedicated General Superintendent of Freedmen, Department of the Tennessee, as follows.

A rough classification of the freed people will serve to clarify the reader's appreciation of the various groups in whose interests we labored:

First, all new arrivals; with whom were grouped those employed as laborers in military service, as hospital attendants, officers' servants, employees in the commissary and quartermaster's departments, etc.

Second, those resident in cities. Freedmen supplied by far the larger share of industrial pursuits with laborers. They worked as barbers, hackmen, draymen, porters, carpenters, shoemakers, blacksmiths, tailors, seamstresses, nurses, laundresses, waiters in hotels and private families, cooks, etc. Not a few of this second class were well-to-do; many conducted enterprises of their own, either mechanical or commercial. Some were teachers. Properly connected, too, with those resident in cities, were the employees and waiters on steamboats, and stevedores.

A third and large class found employment as woodchoppers, on islands and at points of security along the river, rendering a service absolutely essential to our commercial and military operations.

*Elizabeth Keckley, *Behind the Scenes* (New York, 1868), 112-116.

Fourth, those who labored on plantations. These were subdivided as follows: First, those who were employed by the owners of the lands, or the whites or blacks who leased of the Government; Second, those who were independent planters or gardeners,—either cultivating on shares, or leasing of the owners or of the Government.

Fifth, the sick and those otherwise incapacitated who were distributed among the hospitals or on the "Home Farms" where they contributed what labor they could toward their own support. With these should be classed the hundreds of orphaned or abandoned children for whom, with the help of private benevolence, orphanages were established as soon as practicable.*

124

THE DEMANDS OF LOUISIANA

"What do you people want?" This was the question invariably put to the former slaves by freedmen's aid officials, army commanders, and journalists. The answers they got were, as a rule, clear and direct, the freedmen leaving no doubts as to their desires and hopes. Their attitude was described in a letter to James McKaye from General Nathaniel P. Banks, written from Alexandria, Louisiana, on March 28, 1864.

I entertain no doubt whatever of the capabilities of the emancipated colored people to meet and discharge the duties incident to the great change in their condition. I have seen them in all situations, within the last year and a half, and it is with much pleasure I say, as I stated to you in person, that they seem to me to have a clearer comprehension of their position, and the duties which rest upon them, than any other class of our people, accepting the necessity of labor which rests upon them as upon others. The conditions they uniformly impose show the good sense with which they approach the change in their condition.

They demand, in the first instance, that to whatever punishment they may be subjected, they shall not be flogged.

2d. That they shall labor only when they are well treated.

3d. That families should not be separated.

4th. That their children shall be educated.

With these stipulations I have never found any person of that race who did not readily accept the necessity of continuous and faithful labor at just rates of compensation, which they seem willing to leave to the Government. As far as the experiment goes in this department, they have justified in the fullest degree this conclusion, and, subject to the conditions which they impose, they are willing to and have rendered faithful labor.

There were in this department, when I assumed command, many thousands of colored persons without employment or home, who

---

*John Eaton, *Grant, Lincoln and the Freedmen* (New York, 1907), 132-133.

were decimated by disease and death of the most frightful character. To these, natives of the plantations in the department, have been added many thousand fugitives from the surrounding States, of every age and condition. There are not, at this time, 500 persons that are not self-supporting, and there has not been in the last year, any day when we would not have gladly accepted ten or twenty thousand, irrespective of their condition, in addition to those we have of our own. Except that the negro understood the necessities of his position, and was able, in the language of your letter, "to meet and discharge the duties incident to the great change in his condition," this result would have been physically impossible.

Wherever, in the department, they have been well treated, and reasonably compensated, they have invariably rendered faithful service to their employers.

From many persons who manage plantations, I have received the information that there is no difficulty whatever in keeping them at work, if the conditions to which I have above referred are complied with.*

When a Virginia slave owner fled at the advance of the Union forces in May 1862, he left his "family" behind.

*James A. McKaye, *The Mastership and Its Fruits* (New York, 1864), 16-17.

125

IMPRESSMENT OF SLAVES

The Negroes who remained in the Confederacy contributed greatly to its war effort. So great was the need for slaves in constructing fortifications and embattlements that the Confederacy resorted to impressment. The army was authorized to impress slaves, and six states gave a similar power to their governors. The most comprehensive of these measures was a Congressional act of February 17, 1864, which provided for the hiring of up to 20,000 slaves for service in war factories and military hospitals and in erecting fortifications. Slave owners were to be paid $25 a month for each slave, plus compensation for those lost through death or flight. Below is a typical impressment request, one submitted to the Governor of Virginia, John Letcher, from the President of the Confederacy.

Richmond, Va., *March 11, 1863.*

Governor Letcher,
Richmond, Va.:

SIR: I have the honor to call upon Your Excellency, in accordance with an act passed by the Legislature of Virginia October 3, 1862, for 2,832 negroes to labor for sixty days on the fortifications in this State. A letter from the Secretary of War, transmitting a communication from Col. J. F. Gilmer, chief of Engineer Bureau, explaining the necessity for the call, enumerating the counties upon which it is suggested the draft be made, is herewith transmitted.

Jefferson Davis

Engineer Bureau,
Richmond, Va., March 4, 1863.

Hon. James A. Seddon,
Secretary of War:

SIR: An additional supply of labor for the fortifications in Virginia is absolutely necessary to complete the works within the time desired by General R. E. Lee. A list of the counties is herewith transmitted, upon which it is recommended that the call for slaves be made. It is proper to state that each number in this list (with three exceptions, which are marked) when added to the aggregate of all the slaves actually furnished by each county heretofore, whether called for by officers of the army or under the act of the Virginia Legislature passed October 3, 1862, makes 5 per cent. of the slave population. Moreover, this requisition is not wholly a new one, for a large proportion of each number submitted consists of deficiencies on the part of the counties to meet the calls made upon them in October and November last. It is therefore respectfully recommended that His Excellency the President of the Confederates States be requested to submit to His Excellency the Governor of Virginia a call on said counties for the number of slaves placed opposite their respective names, to labor for sixty days on the public defenses.

I have the honor to be, &c.,

J. F. Gilmer,
*Colonel of Engineers and Chief of Bureau**

COUNTY	NUMBER OF SLAVES	COUNTY	NUMBER OF SLAVES
Albermarle	164	Henry	57
Amherst	54	Louisa	130[a]
Appomattox	35	Lunenburg	90
Augusta	49	Mocklenburg	89
Bedford	233	Montgomery	30
Bototourt	41	Nelson	126
Brunswick	222	Orange	50[a]
Buckingham	142	Patrick	24
Campbell	231	Pittsylvania	307
Charlotte	103	Prince Edward	51
Cumberland	20	Pulaski	33
Fluvanna	63	Roanoke	48
Franklin	28	Rockbridge	64
Greene	31	Rockingham	75[a]
Halifax	242	TOTAL	2,833

[a]The calls on Louisa, Orange, and Rockingham are reduced from 199, 158, and 119, respectively, because of known losses from inroads of the enemy.

126

IMPRESSMENT OF FREE NEGROES

Impressment of slaves was very unpopular with their owners, who feared that their impressed bondmen might run away or be overworked or underfed. One way to get a labor supply without incurring the resentment of the powerful slaveholding class was to impress the free Negro. In February 1863 the Virginia legislature passed such a measure. In the passage below, General Lee is asked to sign a requisition for some 1000 free Negroes from twenty-four Virginia counties.

Engineer Bureau
Richmond, Va., March 9, 1863.

General R. E. Lee,
Commanding Army of Northern Virginia:

GENERAL: There is still a great want of labor to complete the defenses of this city and Petersburg; and to avoid as far as possible additional calls on the slave force of the country, so much needed in the agricultural operations of the approaching season, I respectfully suggest that a requisition, suitably apportioned, be made on the free-negro population of the counties and corporations not heretofore called on. A requisition of this kind is authorized by an act of the Virginia Legislature, passed February 12, 1863, "to amend and re-enact an ordinance to provide for the enrollment and employment of free negroes in the public service, passed by the convention July 1,

**Official Records*, ser. 1, vol. 51, pt. 2, p. 682-683.

1861." In accordance with the second section of this act, which directs "that upon the requisition of the commanding officer of any post or department of the State or Confederate forces for labor in erecting batteries, intrenchments, or other necessities of the military service, addressed to the presiding justice of any county, or mayor or senior alderman of any corporation as aforesaid, he shall proceed forthwith," &c. I inclose for your signature drafts of requisitions on twenty-four counties and corporations for free-negro labor. The act prescribes the pay and term of service. Should these papers meet your approval you are respectfully requested to sign them, and if returned to this bureau they will be issued to the respective presiding justices and mayors.

I have the honor to be, &c.,

J. F. Gilmer,
*Colonel of Engineers and Chief of Bureau.**

PROPOSED REQUISITION FOR FREE NEGROES

COUNTIES AND CORPORATIONS	NUMBER	COUNTIES AND CORPORATIONS	NUMBER
Bath	9	King William	20
Brunswick	58	Louisa	22
Charles City	100	Madison	7
Charlotte	23	Nelson	9
Chesterfield	59	New Kent	20
Dinwiddie	54	Nottoway	12
Essex	50	Petersburg City	100
Fluvanna	31	Powhatan	63
Goorbland	62	Prince Edward	52
Greensville	12	Prince George	50
Hanover	10	Southhampton	142
Henrico	25		
King and Queen	40	TOTAL	1,029

While their master hides behind the door—pistol in hand—one of his slaves points the Union troops in a false direction.

**Official Records*, ser. 1, vol. 51, pt. 2, pp. 683-684.

127

A PROPOSAL TO ENLIST FREED SLAVES

The Confederate armies were accompanied by Negroes. These latter, as a rule, were orderlies, cooks, teamsters, and laborers. In some instances they were armed and, to all outward appearances, soldiers, such a contingent being noted by a Union medical officer in September 1862 in western Maryland. But although Negroes were used extensively as military laborers, and might even be given arms in unusual circumstances, to make them full-fledged soldiers was a most painful thought to the Confederate authorities, being in essence a repudiation of the traditions of the South. But proposals to arm the slave multiplied with the passing months, and by the autumn of 1863 open debate on the subject had become common. Later that year a high-ranking officer, Patrick R. Cleburne, a divisional commander of the Army of Tennessee, wrote out a lengthy report recommending the enlistment of Negroes. During 1864, with the ranks growing thinner and thinner, the Confederate Congress, center of the opposition, began to waver. Its final approval, which came in March 1865—far too late to be effective—was given only after the step had been recommended by the highly respected Robert E. Lee. His reasons were given in a reply to a letter from a member of Congress.

Headquarters Confederate States Armies,
February 18th, 1865.

HON. E. BARKSDALE, HOUSE OF REPRESENTATIVES, RICHMOND.

SIR:—I have the honor to acknowledge the receipt of your letter of the 12th inst., with reference to the employment of negroes as soldiers. I think the measure not only expedient, but necessary. The enemy will certainly use them against us if he can get possession of them; and as his present numerical superiority will enable him to penetrate many parts of the country, I cannot see the wisdom of the policy of holding them to await his arrival, when we may by timely action and judicious management, use them to arrest his progress. I do not think that our white population can supply the necessities of a long war without overtaxing its capacity and imposing great suffering upon our people; and I believe we should provide resources for a protracted struggle—not merely for a battle or a campaign.

In answer to your second question, I can only say that, in my opinion, the negroes, under proper circumstances, will make efficient soldiers. I think we could at least do as well with them as the enemy, and he attaches great importance to their assistance. Under good officers, and good instructions, I do not see why they should not become soldiers. They possess all the physical qualifications, and their habits of obedience constitute a good foundation for discipline. They furnish a more promising material than many armies of which we read in history, which owed their efficiency to discipline alone. I think those who are employed should be freed. It would be neither just nor wise, in my opinion, to require them to serve as slaves. The best course to pursue, it seems to me, would be to call for such as are willing to come with the consent of their owners. An impressment or draft would not be likely to bring out the best class, and the use of coercion would make the measure distasteful to them and to their owners.

I have no doubt that if Congress would authorize their reception into service, and empower the President to call upon individuals or States for such as they are willing to contribute, with the conditon of emancipation to all enrolled, a sufficient number would be forthcoming to enable us to try the experiment. If it proved successful, most of the objections to the measure would disappear, and if individuals still remained unwilling to send their negroes to the army, the force of public opinion in the States would soon bring about such legislation as would remove all obstacles. I think the matter should be left, as far as possible, to the people and to the States, which alone can legislate as the necessities of this particular service may require. As to the mode of organizing them, it should be left as free from restraint as possible. Experience will suggest the best course, and it would be inexpedient to trammel the subject with provisions that might, in the end, prevent the adoption of reforms suggested by actual trial.

With great respect,

Your obedient servant,
R. E. Lee, *General**

The Negro's Lincoln

128

ATTITUDE OF A FORMER SLAVE

The overwhelming mass of Negroes of Lincoln's day viewed him with an admiration mixed with reverence. They were ready to forget his tardiness in issuing an emancipation proclamation, and to overlook his fetish for colonization (especially since the results of the latter were so meagre). The Negro rank and file saw in Lincoln a humanitarian who was ever growing in knowledge and wisdom. They loved him because he was approachable, lacking in pretense or false pride. For the first time in history, Negroes attended the public receptions given by the First Family. Colored men and women could be numbered among the visitors who daily thronged the White House corridors, bent on a private word with the Chief Executive. To former slaves, Lincoln took on a father image, filling in for the male parent they had never known, or known but little.

Lincoln was destined to live in history because he was a man the people loved. No other group exemplified this deep affection as did the colored Americans of his day. Well before Booth's bullet found its mark, the Negro people had fixed the mould for the historical Lincoln—the Lincoln who would be proclaimed by generations to come as the greatest of American public servants, a towering figure whose pervasive spirit was confined to no one period, to no one country.

Something of the attitude of the former slave toward Lincoln was reflected in a report in 1863 of the Freedmen's Inquiry Commission.

Our Chief Magistrate would probably be surprised to learn with what reverence, bordering on superstition, he is regarded by these

*J. B. Jones, *A Rebel War Clerk's Diary* (2 vols., Phila., 1866), II, 432-433.

poor people. Recently at Beaufort a gang of colored men, in the service of the quartermaster, at work on the wharf, were discussing the qualifications of the President, his wonderful power, how he had dispersed their masters, and what he would undoubtedly do hereafter for the colored race, when an aged, white headed negro, a "praise man" (as the phrase is) amongst them, with all the solemnity and earnestness of an old prophet, broke forth:

What do you know 'bout Massa Linkum? Massa Linkum be ebrewhere. He walk de earth like de Lord.*

Courtesy of Chicago Historical Society

129

ATTITUDE OF NEGRO SOLDIERS

To Negro soldiers Lincoln was not only Commander-in-Chief. He was a friend, a benefactor, the man who gave to the war its meaning and purpose. When Lincoln made a one-day visit to City Point, Virginia, on June 21, 1864, the Negro troops stationed there had an opportunity to demonstrate their regard for him. Horace Porter, a lieutenant colonel on General Grant's staff, witnessed the scene, and recorded it.

After a while General Grant said: "Mr. President, let us ride on and see the colored troops, who behaved so handsomely in Smith's attack on the works in front of Petersburg last week." "Oh, yes," replied Mr. Lincoln; "I want to take a look at those boys. I read with the greatest delight the account given in Mr. Dana's despatch to the

**Official Records*, ser. 3, vol. III, 436.

Secretary of War of how gallantly they behaved. He said they took six out of the sixteen guns captured that day. I was opposed on nearly every side when I first favored the raising of colored regiments; but they have proved their efficiency, and I am glad they have kept pace with the white troops in the recent assaults. When we wanted every able-bodied man who could be spared to go to the front, and my opposers kept objecting to the negroes, I used to tell them that at such times it was just as well to be a little color-blind. I think, general, we can say of the black boys what a country fellow who was an old-time abolitionist in Illinois said when he went to a theater in Chicago and saw Forrest playing *Othello*. He was not very well up in Shakspere, and didn't know that the tragedian was a white man who had blacked up for the purpose. After the play was over the folks who had invited him to go to the show wanted to know what he thought of the actors, and he said: 'Waal, layin' aside all sectional prejudices and any partiality I may have for the race, derned ef I don't think the nigger held his own with any on 'em.'" The Western dialect employed in this story was perfect.

The camp of the colored troops of the Eighteenth Corps was soon reached, and a scene now occurred which defies description. They beheld for the first time the liberator of their race—the man who by a stroke of his pen had struck the shackles from the limbs of their fellow-bondmen and proclaimed liberty to the enslaved. Always impressionable, the enthusiasm of the blacks now knew no limits. They cheered, laughed, cried, sang hymns of praise, and shouted in their negro dialect, "God bress Massa Linkum!" "De Lord save Fader Abraham!" "De day ob jubilee am come, shuah." They crowded about him and fondled his horse; some of them kissed his hands, while others ran off crying in triumph to their comrades that they had touched his clothes. The President rode with bared head; the tears had started to his eyes, and his voice was so broken by emotion that he could scarcely articulate the words of thanks and congratulation which he tried to speak to the humble and devoted men through whose ranks he rode. The scene was affecting in the extreme, and no one could have witnessed it unmoved.*

130

NEGROES PRESENT A BIBLE TO LINCOLN

The most elaborate expression by Negroes of their regard for Lincoln was a Bible given to him by a group of Baltimore Negroes. Costing $580.75, it was a pulpit-sized volume bound in royal purple, with two heavy gold clasps. The front cover bore an engraving which depicted Lincoln in the act of striking the bonds from the wrists of a slave. The back cover bore an inscription expressing respect and admiration for Lincoln. From the 519 Negroes who contributed to

*Wayne C. Temple, ed., Horace Porter, *Campaigning with Grant* (Bloomington, Ind., 1961), 218-220.

the purchase price, four were selected to go to the White House and formally present the gift. The address to the President by one of these delegates, the Reverend S. W. Chase, at the brief but impressive ceremony on September 7, 1864, and Lincoln's reply, read as follows.

MR. PRESIDENT: The loyal colored people of Baltimore have entrusted us with authority to present this Bible as a testimonial of their appreciation of your humane conduct towards the people of our race. While all others of this nation are offering their tribute of respect to you, we cannot omit suitable manifestation of ours. Since our incorporation into the American family we have been true and loyal, and we are now ready to aid in defending the country, to be armed and trained in military matters, in order to assist in protecting and defending the star-spangled banner.

Towards you, sir, our hearts will ever be warm with gratitude. We come to present to you this copy of the Holy Scriptures, as a token of respect for your active participation in furtherance of the cause of the emancipation of our race. This great event will be a matter of history. Hereafter, when our children shall ask what mean these tokens, they will be told of your worthy deeds, and will rise up and call you blessed.

The loyal colored people of this country everywhere will remember you at the Throne of Divine Grace. May the King Eternal, an all-wise, Providence protect and keep you, and when you pass from this world to that of eternity, may you be borne to the bosom of your Saviour and your God.*

REPLY TO LOYAL COLORED PEOPLE OF BALTIMORE UPON PRESENTATION OF A BIBLE

September 7, 1864

This occasion would seem fitting for a lengthy response to the address which you have just made. I would make one, if prepared; but I am not. I would promise to respond in writing, had not experience taught me that business will not allow me to do so. I can only now say, as I have often before said, it has always been a sentiment with me that all mankind should be free. So far as able, within my sphere, I have always acted as I believed to be right and just; and I have done all I could for the good of mankind generally. In letters and documents sent from this office I have expressed myself better than I now can. In regard to this Great Book, I have but to say, it is the best gift God has given to man.

All the good the Saviour gave to the world was communicated through this book. But for it we could not know right from wrong. All things most desirable for man's welfare, here and hereafter, are to be found portrayed in it. To you I return my most sincere thanks for the very elegant copy of the great Book of God which you present.†

---

*Basler, *op. cit.*, VII, 543.
†*Ibid.*, 542.

131

NEGRO REACTION TO LINCOLN'S DEATH

As might have been expected, Lincoln's death stunned and saddened Negroes beyond measure. "It was the gloomiest day I ever saw," wrote the Negro soldier-surgeon, John H. Napier. On that bleak mid-April morning, when Lincoln died, the inconsolable Mrs. Lincoln sent for Elizabeth Keckley, her mulatto modiste. More than dressmaker to the First Lady, Mrs. Keckley had taken on the additional roles of personal maid, traveling companion, and trusted confidante.

At the approximate hour that Mrs. Keckley was gazing upon the lifeless form of the President, the forty-eighth annual conference of the African Methodist Episcopal Church, which had been in session in Baltimore since the preceding Thursday, listened to the sad news from the lips of its presiding officer, Bishop Daniel A. Payne. Thereupon the delegates drafted a series of appropriate resolutions, the first of the thousands of such resolutions throughout the country.

Among those who mourned the loss of Lincoln, perhaps no tears were more sincere than those of the former slaves. To them he was the personification of the freedom for which they had prayed. At St. Helena Island in South Carolina, schoolmistress Laura M. Towne took note of the deep grief of the people among whom she would spend the thirty-five remaining years of her life of dedication.

MRS. KECKLEY VIEWS THE BODY

Morning came at last, and a sad morning was it. The flags that floated so gayly yesterday now were draped in black, and hung in silent folds at halfmast. The President was dead, and a nation was mourning for him. Every house was draped in black, and every face wore a solemn look. People spoke in subdued tones, and glided whisperingly, wonderingly, silently about the streets.

About eleven o'clock on Saturday morning a carriage drove up to the door, and a messenger asked for "Elizabeth Keckley."

"Who wants her?" I asked.

"I come from Mrs. Lincoln. If you are Mrs. Keckley, come with me immediately to the White House."

I hastily put on my shawl and bonnet, and was driven at a rapid rate to the White House. Everything about the building was sad and solemn. I was quickly shown to Mrs. Lincoln's room, and on entering, saw Mrs. L. tossing uneasily about upon a bed. The room was darkened, and the only person in it besides the widow of the President was Mrs. Secretary Welles, who had spent the night with her. Bowing to Mrs. Welles, I went to the bedside.

"Why did you not come to me last night, Elizabeth—I sent for you?" Mrs. Lincoln asked in a low whisper.

"I did try to come to you, but I could not find you," I answered, as I laid my hand upon her hot brow.

I afterwards learned, that when she had partially recovered from the first shock of the terrible tragedy in the theatre, Mrs. Welles asked:

"Is there no one, Mrs. Lincoln, that you desire to have with you in this terrible affliction?"

"Yes, send for Elizabeth Keckley. I want her just as soon as she can be brought here."

Three messengers, it appears, were successively despatched for me, but all of them mistook the number and failed to find me.

Shortly after entering the room on Saturday morning, Mrs. Welles excused herself, as she said she must go to her own family, and I was left alone with Mrs. Lincoln.

She was nearly exhausted with grief, and when she became a little quiet, I asked and received permission to go into the Guests' Room, where the body of the President lay in state. When I crossed the threshold of the room, I could not help recalling the day on which I had seen little Willie lying in his coffin where the body of his father now lay. I remembered how the President had wept over the pale beautiful face of his gifted boy, and now the President himself was dead. The last time I saw him he spoke kindly to me, but alas! the lips would never move again. The light had faded from his eyes, and when the light went out the soul went with it! What a noble soul was his—noble in all the noble attributes of God. Never did I enter the solemn chamber of death with such palpitating heart and trembling footsteps as I entered it that day. No common mortal had died. The Moses of my people had fallen in the hour of his triumph. Fame had woven her choicest chaplet for his brow. Though the brow was cold and pale in death, the chaplet should not fade, for God had studded it with the glory of the eternal stars.

When I entered the room, the members of the Cabinet and many distinguished officers of the army were grouped around the body of their fallen chief. They made room for me, and, approaching the body, I lifted the white cloth from the white face of the man that I had worshipped as an idol—looked upon as a demi-god. Notwithstanding the violence of the death of the President, there was something beautiful as well as grandly solemn in the expression of the placid face. There lurked the sweetness and gentleness of childhood, and the stately grandeur of godlike intellect. I gazed long at the face, and turned away with tears in my eyes and a choking sensation in my throat. Ah! never was man so widely mourned before. The whole world bowed their heads in grief when Abraham Lincoln died.*

A RESOLUTION OF MOURNING

Proceedings of the Forty-Eighth Annual Session of the African Methodist Episcopal Church, April 13th, 1865.

April 15, 1865

Conference met. Bishop Payne in the chair.

Bishop Payne here arose and gave notice of the terrible assassination of President Lincoln. He said it was a most painful duty, and the pain was increased from knowing he fell by the hand of a cowardly assassin, and not rather by a magnificent foe. He advised the appointment of a committee to draft resolutions expressive of the sentiments of the Conference.

The committee withdrew, and in a few minutes reported the following:—

---

*Keckley, *op. cit.*, 187-191.

Whereas, We the members of the Baltimore Annual Conference of the African M. E. Church have heard with most profound regret, and not unmingled with indignation, of the cowardly assassination on the 14th day of April, in the City of Washington, of the Chief Magistrate of the Republic, the great and good Abraham Lincoln, therefore,

Resolved, by the Baltimore Annual Conference of the African M. E. Church, in Conference assembled, that while we bow in submission to the event that has transpired, we can but shed tears at the cruel act of the assassin.

Resolved, That while the blood of John Brown was shed to inaugurate the meting out of justice to those who had long oppressed the Savior in the person of the bondsmen, the death of the great President will be made the occasion of continuing the work until the divine mandate which awards death to men-stealers, be fully and literally accomplished.

Resolved, That we extend to his successor, President Johnson, our hands and hearts, together with the two hundred thousand muskets in the hands of our brethren to protect the flag of our country.

Resolved, That we tender to the estimable Lady of the White House our profoundest condolence. And be it further

Resolved, That we tender our sympathies to the Hon. W. H. Seward, Secretary of State, who has been inhumanly assaulted.*

MOURNING OF SOUTH CAROLINA FREEDMAN

Saturday, April 29, 1865

It was a frightful blow at first. The people have refused to believe he was dead. Last Sunday the black minister of Frogmore said that if they knew the President were dead they would mourn for him, but they could not think that was the truth, and they would wait and see. We are going to-morrow to hear what further they say. One man came for clothing and seemed very indifferent about them —different from most of the people. I expressed some surprise. "Oh," he said, "I have lost a friend. I don't care much now about anything." "What friend?" I asked, not really thinking for a moment. "They call him Sam," he said; "Uncle Sam, the best friend ever I had." Another asked me in a whisper if it were true that the "Government was dead." Rina says she can't sleep for thinking how sorry she is to lose "Pa Linkum." You know they call their elders in the church—or the particular one who converted and received them in—their spiritual father, and he has the most absolute power over them. These fathers are addressed with fear and awe as "Pa Marcus," "Pa Demas," etc. One man said to me, "Lincoln died for we, Christ died for we, and me believe him de same mans," that is, they are the same person.

We dressed our school-house in what black we could get, and gave a shred of crape to some our children, who wear it sacredly. Fanny's bonnet supplied the whole school.†

---

*John E. Washington, *They Knew Lincoln* (New York, 1942), appendix, 10.

†Rupert Sargent Holland, ed., *Letters and Diary of Laura M. Towne* (Cambridge, Mass., 1912), 102.

132

THE THIRTEENTH AMENDMENT

In Lincoln's death the colored people lost a friend and the nation lost a leader. But the legacy of the war still abided. Negroes could look to the future with some measure of hope. Congress had established a Bureau of Refugees, Freedmen and Abandoned Lands, which threw the weight of the federal government in the work of assisting the former slaves to stand on their own feet. Congress, too, had passed an act abolishing slavery, which later that year would become the Thirteenth Amendment. To commemorate the adoption of this historic measure by Congress, the chaplain of the House of Representatives, William H. Channing, and a group of Republican Congressmen, requested Henry Highland Garnet to deliver a memorial sermon in the House chambers. This in itself was no mean sign of a new day. Still militant, although mellowed by time and circumstance, Garnet delivered a discourse, on Sunday, February 12, 1865, which was an eloquent restatement of the American doctrine of equal opportunity in a land of infinite promise.

It is often asked when and where will the demands of the reformers of this and coming ages end? It is a fair question, and I will answer.

When all unjust and heavy burdens shall be removed from every man in the land. When all invidious and proscriptive distinctions shall be blotted out from our laws, whether they be constitutional, statute, or municipal laws. When emancipation shall be followed by enfranchisement, and all men holding allegiance to the government shall enjoy every right of American citizenship. When our brave and gallant soldiers shall have justice done unto them. When the men who endure the sufferings and perils of the battle-field in the defence of their country, and in order to keep our rulers in their places, shall enjoy the well-earned privilege of voting for them. When in the army and navy, and in every legitimate and honorable occupation, promotion shall smile upon merit without the slightest regard to the complexion of a man's face. When there shall be no more class-legislation, and no more trouble concerning the black man and his rights, than there is in regard to other American citizens. When, in every respect, he shall be equal before the law, and shall be left to make his own way in the social walks of life.

We ask, and only ask, that when our poor frail barks are launched on life's ocean—

> "Bound on a voyage of awful length
> And dangers little known,"

that, in common with others, we may be furnished with rudder, helm, and sails, and charts, and compass. Give us good pilots to conduct us to the open seas; lift no false lights along the dangerous coasts, and if it shall please God to send us propitious winds, or fearful gales, we shall survive or perish as our energies or neglect shall determine. We ask no special favors, but we plead for justice.

While we scorn unmanly dependence; in the name of God, the universal Father, we demand the right to live, and labor, and to enjoy the fruits of our toil. The good work which God has assigned for the ages to come, will be finished, when our national literature shall be so purified as to reflect a faithful and a just light upon the character and social habits of our race, and the brush, and pencil, and chisel, and Lyre of Art, shall refuse to lend their aid to scoff at the afflictions of the poor, or to caricature, or ridicule a long-suffering people. When caste and prejudice in Christian churches shall be utterly destroyed, and shall be regarded as totally unworthy of Christians, and at variance with the principles of the gospel. When the blessings of the Christian religion, and of sound, religious education, shall be freely offered to all, then, and not till then, shall the effectual labors of God's people and God's instruments cease.

If slavery has been destroyed merely from *necessity,* let every class be enfranchised at the dictation of *justice.* Then we shall have a Constitution that shall be reverenced by all: rulers who shall be honored, and revered, and a Union that shall be sincerely loved by a brave and patriotic people, and which can never be severed.

* * *

Honorable Senators and Representatives! illustrious rulers of this great nation! I cannot refrain this day from invoking upon you, in God's name, the blessings of millions who were ready to perish, but to whom a new and better life has been opened by your humanity, justice, and patriotism. You have said, "Let the Constitution of the country be so amended that slavery and involuntary servitude shall no longer exist in the United States, except in punishment for crime." Surely, an act so sublime could not escape Divine notice; and doubtless the deed has been recorded in the archives of heaven. Volumes may be appropriated to your praise and renown in the history of the world. Genius and art may perpetuate the glorious act on canvass and in marble, but certain and more lasting monuments in commemoration of your decision are already erected in the hearts and memories of a grateful people.

The nation has begun its exodus from worse than Egyptian bondage; and I beseech you that you say to the people, "*that they go forward.*" With the assurance of God's favor in all things done in obedience to his righteous will, and guided by day and by night by the pillars of cloud and fire, let us not pause until we have reached the other and safe side of the stormy and crimson sea. Let freemen and patriots mete out complete and equal justice to all men, and thus prove to mankind the superiority of our Democratic, Republican Government.*

**A Memorial Discourse by Rev. Henry Highland Garnet, delivered in the Hall of the House of Representatives, Washington, D.C., on Sabbath, February 12, 1865* (Phila., 1865), 85-87, 88-89.

CHAPTER SEVEN

The Burdens of Reconstruction

The burdens of reconstruction cannot take away from the achievement of those southern Negroes who went from their states and districts to sit in Congress. Controversy surrounds many of the Negroes who were elected to office, both in their states and in the national government. But, for the short time they sat in office, they were a force to be heard. While they were heard, not only Negroes but all Americans were represented by their fight for justice and advancement. Below are some of the members of the 41st and 42d Congress of the United States. Standing are Representatives Robert C. De Large of South Carolina and Jefferson H. Long of Georgia. Sitting, from left to right: Senator of the United States, H. R. Revels of Mississippi, and four other representatives, Benjamin S. Turner of Alabama; Josiah T. Walls of Florida; Joseph H. Rainy of South Carolina; and R. Brown Elliot of South Carolina.

INTRODUCTION

The Burdens of Reconstruction

Appomattox, the crossroads village where General Robert E. Lee surrendered to General U. S. Grant, and Ford Theater, where Abraham Lincoln was assassinated, symbolize the close of an era in American life. From that time forward, the United States faced new problems or grappled with new forms of old problems. Paramount among these was, and is, the problem of the position and the role of the Negroes in the United States. "The negro question," Carl Schurz reported to President Andrew Johnson late in 1865, "[is] an integral part of the question of union in general, and the question of reconstruction in particular."

The legacy of slavery was real; "I do not like the negro as well free as I did a slave," testified a loyal Virginian and his words echoed the sentiment of the nation. The Negro as a freeman was an unknown quantity, largely uneducated, grossly stereotyped, crudely visible, practically untried in a free society, and a potential threat to the existing political, economic, and social alignments. If allowed to vote, which party would he support? If allowed to compete in a free market, whose jobs would he take? If permitted to intermix with whites, what social complications would follow?

These questions reflected the basic doubts which greeted the emancipated Negro at the beginning of Reconstruction and, to some extent, continued to dog his progress in the decades that followed. During the first fifteen years after the Civil War, the questions are important primarily because they were raised at all, reflecting the established and significant fact that the Negro after almost 250 years in America had finally begun to be viewed as an individual. His rights as a citizen, if not immediately granted, were to be openly discussed.

The discussion of these rights characterized the Reconstruction period more than any other single issue. The Joint Committee on Reconstruction was established by the Congress in December 1865, to lay out the lines of a Reconstruction policy. Recent scholarship has questioned whether the Committee was dominated by the so-called Radical Republicans, but it is clear that the Committee's purpose was to offset the President's leadership with a Congressional program of Reconstruction. The attention which both witnesses and majority and minority committee members paid to the Negro suggests the significance of the colored people in the Reconstruction process. President Johnson's views coincided more closely with those of the minority report and in his one famous confrontation with a group of Negroes, he was curt and condescending, losing for himself the respect of Negro leaders and the possibility of winning their support.

While the Negro was a problem of national scope, he had his own related problems. "The negro knows," a ranking Union officer in Tennessee reported early in 1866, "that without his rights . . . secured, and his life and property secured, he is not safe from the poor whites." It was a question of survival and Negro leaders realized that the protection of life, property, and civil rights for the race were a *sine qua non*.

Politically, the Negroes had no choice but to support the Republican Party during these years and, with Johnson taking a narrow

A political meeting of southern Negroes. The drawing, by W. L. Sheppard, was for a Harper's Weekly *article on the first presidential election by men who were now citizens (1868) but who only a short time before had been slaves.*

view of Negro claims, race leaders gravitated to the Radical wing of the party. At every opportunity, through their newspapers like the *Loyal Georgian* or the *Colored American* (Washington, D.C.), they spoke to their own people in terms of the Republican Party. The game of politics was the central focus of Negro leadership in this period. In part, this stemmed from the Reconstruction process itself which dominated the period and was totally a political movement. If Negroes were to participate they had to play the same game. In part, too, their strength was a lever most useful in politics: numbers. By 1870 there were 4,900,000 Negroes in the United States, of whom 3,800,000 were in the ex-Confederate South. Properly voted, these numbers could bring rewards to the whole race.

On paper the results were of some consequence. The constitutional amendments on the abolition of slavery (13th), the extension of civil rights (14th), and the right of suffrage (15th) were directly concerned with the Negro. Two congressional statutes elaborated more specifically on civil rights (1866 and 1875); two others established and continued the Freedmen's Bureau (1865 and 1866) and two others were passed to prevent southern whites from interfering with the Reconstruction process (Force Act of 1870 and the Ku Klux Klan Act of 1871). While Negroes did not specifically shape this legislation, their testimony and voting strength provided some of the impetus.

Negro leaders did not sit high in the councils of the dominant Republican party. They worked on lower levels, trying to establish communication between their race and white leaders. Late in 1865, as the thirty-ninth Congress convened, a group of prominent Negroes, led by Frederick Douglass and George T. Downing, gathered in Washington "charged with the duty to look after the best interests of the recently emancipated." This was probably the first Negro lobby and they were paid for their work. Douglass was the preëminent man of his race and symbolized Negro leadership. An enthusiastic Republican, he could remind backsliders in 1871 of "the vast and wonderful strides we have as a class taken during the last ten years and under Republican rule. . . ." Yet Douglass was not above reflecting to white leaders the needs of his people. "We are not free," he wrote in 1872. "Congress has neglected to do its full duty," in failing to implement by statute the constitutional amendments.

Along with Douglass were less prominent Negro leaders who served the same causes. George T. Downing, a Rhode Island politician, was a close friend of Charles Sumner, Massachusetts' senior senator, and worked hard for the Civil Rights bill. John Mercer Lanston was another leader who served in many capacities, including a term in Congress and as dean of the law school of Howard University.

The southern states sent before 1900 seventeen Negroes to both Houses of Congress, two of whom served in the Senate. The quality of their service varied but none of them entered the higher circles of Congressional leadership. Blanche K. Bruce of Mississippi was the only Negro to serve a full term in the Senate and for several sessions he was known as the "silent Senator." He was active politically but without great influence. In the House of Representatives, Negro congressmen worked hard for the Civil Rights Act which finally passed in 1875. Their spoken testimony in its behalf and their ability to counteract the taunts of the opposition during floor debate marked their major contributions.

The Negroes' political achievements during these years were more impressive at the state and local level. The Georgia constitutional convention of 1868 numbered 31 Negro delegates and the document they produced, according to a native observer, "was a credit to the ideal of a growing and expanding democracy." Lotteries and imprisonment for debt were abolished. The poll tax was restricted, Negroes were enfranchised, the idea of public education endorsed, and the legislature apportioned on "a fairer basis than any which had existed since 1843," and some which succeeded it. In Georgia's chief city, Negro councilmen were elected for a one-year term in 1871. One of them, William Finch, worked to inaugurate a public school system while in office and, after his term, successfully pressured the city to include schools for Negro children.

The famous South Carolina legislature, controlled by Negroes, was described by a New England journalist after a visit in early 1873. James S. Pike's book, *The Prostrate State: South Carolina Under Negro Government* is a severe indictment of the Negro as incompetent, inferior, and corrupt. Recent scholarship has shown that Pike's evaluation was based on preconception, inadequate documentation, and a highly selective technique of using evidence. Before Pike traveled to South Carolina, he had written about the state and its Negro government in precisely the same terms as appeared in his book. When he did visit the state to gather evidence for his book, his journal records conversations with very few persons, including only one Negro and no white Radical leaders. A comparison of his book with his journal suggests that he molded the data he had collected to fit what he wanted to say rather than what he had seen and heard. Since *The Prostrate South* has influenced generations of observers and historians to conclude that the Negro's political role in Reconstruction was marked with corruption and incompetence, it is important to reappraise the book itself, which betrays its own inadequacies. The Negro legislature of South Carolina was no better or worse than white political bodies during a period of turmoil and upheaval.

In the North, Negroes were fewer in number but equally active. Occasionally candidates for minor offices, they exerted most of their energies before 1870 to winning the right to vote. At the end of the Civil War, only six states permitted colored men to cast a ballot (Maine, New Hampshire, Vermont, Massachusetts, Rhode Island, and New York). The campaign to convert other states was waged on a state-by-state basis as the issue came up in referenda or the legislature. Supported by newspapers and politicians of the Radical Republican persuasion, Negroes stumped the North, met in convention, and published pamphlets and newspapers in behalf of equal suffrage. Their effort was not successful, as state after state registered disapproval. Only 3 states (Iowa, Minnesota, Wisconsin) changed their stand before the passage of the Fifteenth Amendment.

While the Negroes' concern for life and liberty in this period created events of dramatic magnetism, their basic concern for property, the right to make a living, was equally important. In economic matters, as in other areas, the Negro became for the first time an individual, struggling for the right to do more than exist. Untrained in all but the crudest skills, the freedman stayed with the land, trying to farm and hoping to own. A few were successful. The vast majority toiled without the opportunity to become landowners or even self-sufficient tenants. These "houseless, half-clad people," as the *Arkansas State Gazette* put it in 1869, were an important element in the South's prosperity, but like so many poor whites, were unable to share in the wealth.

Urban Negroes, most of whom resided in the North, were restricted primarily to the unskilled trades and menial service. A few, like George T. Downing, became eminently successful, but the larger majority of Negroes remained as waiters, servants, barbers, washerwomen, or hodcarriers. The lure of the city proved to be more glitter than gold and colored people suffered from low wages and high costs of living. Their efforts to join trade unions were without success; even the short-lived National Labor Union was unable to hold Negro laborers, most of whom withdrew to form their own abortive Colored Labor Union in 1870.

Toward the end of the 1870's, economic desperation led some Negroes to one solution: migration. By 1878, migration talk was in the air. How many thousands of Negroes moved from the South to Kansas and other mid-western states will never be documented, but the number is undoubtedly less than the estimates, which run into the hundreds of thousands. While destitution and poverty followed these migrants, as twin crosses of every migration of any people, the fact that the Exodus did take place, in a somewhat organized fashion, is a credit to the Negro which is sometimes overlooked. And again while some white groups did assist the impoverished migrants, Negroes in the North and East organized to help their own unfortunates. The most impressive moral of the Exodus, however, is motivation. Negroes wanted a better life than the white South would permit.

One of the elements of the better life, North and South, was education. Freedmen of all ages flocked to schools which missionary groups and the Freedmen's Bureau began to open up after the War. Negro colleges were established, for example, Howard University in Washington, Fisk University in Tennessee, and Hampton Institute in Virginia. However, they could be little more than vocational schools during their early years. Public school systems for whites were created for the first time in the South during Reconstruction, followed in some cases by segregated Negro schools, as in the Atlanta of William Finch. In the North where the public school movement was firmly rooted, the issue in some states was whether the Negro should be educated, too. "It is the opprobrium of our school laws," the Illinois Superintendent of Public Instruction wrote in 1868, "that they in no manner recognize or provide for the education of the children of persons of color." In states like New York and Ohio, Negroes and whites generally attended separate schools, although the practice sometimes varied from city to city. New York City had a completely segregated system while Rochester, New York, had integrated schools.

The educational barriers of this period did not discourage a race which had grown accustomed to them. Indeed enthusiasm for education could almost be called a legacy of slavery. "The history of our fathers will show," the Charleston *Missionary Record* remarked in 1873, "that in the days when darkness brooded over our race and hung as a mighty pall . . . , they were not unmindful that education was a priceless boon. . . . " Like their fathers, the sons of the postwar period not only viewed education as a "priceless boon," but created evidence which demonstrated that the race could use the tools of knowledge. Negro newspapers from New York to New Orleans flourished sporadically in this period; speeches and addresses, however stilted they sound today, set high standards for the time; published convention proceedings were informative and persuasive. Negro leaders in and out of Congress spoke and were heard by an enlarging circle of alert, literate, cultured people. "the *Citizen* finds its way to my family every week and is always a welcome visitor," an Iowa Negro wrote to a Kansas editor. "We get some larger journals, but I notice the *Citizen* is always perused first of all."

The first fifteen years after the Civil War contained the elements for the struggle which was to engage the Negro for the next century. Severe problems of civil rights, segregation, education, political power, and race unity faced the Negro and none of them were to be solved in a decade. But in this period they had begun to attack all of these problems and had tasted success. One problem, embracing and transcending all others, still eluded a solution: the whites. When the white man recognized the Negro as a man and not as a black man, this problem would yield to solution.

The Southern View of the Freedman and the Negro Response

133

A MODERATE, THOUGH SKEPTICAL, VIEW

The Joint Committee on Reconstruction was the Congressional weapon by which the Radical Republicans hoped first to persuade President Andrew Johnson to join in a restrictive Reconstruction policy and, when that hope flickered out, to spearhead the Radical program over against the President's. One of the earliest Congressional investigating committees, the Joint Committee, authorized its various subcommittees to hear evidence in Washington and elsewhere bearing on the progress of Reconstruction and the status of race relations in the former Confederacy.

The Joint Committee was preponderantly Republican, of both the moderate and Radical variety. The evidence which the hearings piled up was calculated to demonstrate that more rigorous controls were needed than President Johnson had instituted. Nevertheless, the testimony can stand as a fair picture of the troubles brewing in the South and, in particular, of the difficulties which Negroes encountered as they tried to establish themselves as a free people. General Robert E. Lee's answers are reflective of a moderate clear-thinking Southerner.

Question. How do the people in Virginia, the secessionists more particularly, feel toward the freedmen?

Answer. Every one with whom I associate expresses kind feelings towards the freedmen. They wish to see them get on in the world, and particularly to take up some occupation for a living and to turn their hands to some work. I know that efforts have been made among the farmers, near where I live, to induce them to engage for the year at regular wages.

Question. Do you think there is a willingness on the part of their old masters to give them fair, living wages for their labor?

Answer. I believe it is so. The farmers generally prefer those servants who have been living with them before. I have heard them express their preference for the men whom they know, who had lived with them before, and their wish to get them to return to work.

Question. Are you aware of the existence of any combination among the whites to keep down the wages of the negroes?

Answer. I am not. I have heard that, in several counties, land owners have met in order to establish a uniform rate of wages; but I never heard, nor do I know, of any combination to keep down wages, or establish any rate which they did not think fair. The means of paying wages in Virginia are very limited now, and there is a difference of opinion as to how much each person is able to pay.

Question. General, you are very competent to judge of the capacity of black men for acquiring knowledge: I want your opinion on that capacity, as compared with the capacity of white men?

Answer. I do not know that I am particularly qualified to speak on that subject, as you seem to intimate; but I do not think that he is as capable of acquiring knowledge as the white man is. There are some more apt than others. I have known some to acquire knowledge and skill in their trade or profession. I have had servants of my own who learned to read and write very well.

Question. Do they show a capacity to obtain knowledge of mathematics and the exact sciences?

Answer. I have no knowledge on that subject. I am merely acquainted with those who have learned the common rudiments of education.

Question. General, are you aware of the existence among the blacks of Virginia, anywhere within the limits of the State, of combinations having in view the disturbance of the peace, or any improper and unlawful acts?

Answer. I am not. I have seen no evidence of it, and have heard of none. Wherever I have been they have been quiet and orderly, not disposed to work, or rather not disposed to any continuous engagement to work, but just very short jobs, to provide them with the immediate means of subsistence.

Question. Has the colored race generally as great a love of money and property as the white race possesses?

Answer. I do not think it has. The blacks with whom I am acquainted look more to the present time than to the future.

Question. Does that absence of a lust of money and property arise more from the nature of the negro than from his former servile condition?

Answer. Well, it may be, in some measure, attributable to his former condition. They are an amiable, social race. They like their ease and comfort, and, I think, look more to their present than to their future condition.

Question. What is the position of the colored men in Virginia with reference to the persons they work for? Do you think they would prefer to work for northern men or for southern men?

Answer. I think it very probable that they would prefer the northern man, although I have no facts to go upon.

Question. That having been stated very frequently in reference to the cotton States, does it result from a fear of bad treatment on the part of the resident population, or from the idea that they will be more fairly treated by the new-comers? What is your observation in that respect in regard to Virginia?

Answer. I have no means of forming an opinion; I do not know any such case in Virginia; I know of numbers of the blacks engaging with their old masters, and I know of a good many who prefer to go off and look for new homes. Whether it is from any dislike of their former masters, or from a desire of change, or that they feel more free and independent, I do not know.

Question. How would an amendment to the Constitution be

received by the secessionists, or by the people at large, allowing the colored people or certain classes of them to exercise the right of voting at elections?

Answer. I think, so far as I can form an opinion, in such an event they would object.

Question. They would object to such an amendment?

Answer. Yes, sir.

Question. Suppose an amendment should, nevertheless, be adopted, conferring on the blacks the right of suffrage, would that, in your opinion, lead to scenes of violence and breaches of the peace between the two races in Virginia?

Answer. I think it would excite unfriendly feelings between the two races. I cannot pretend to say to what extent it would go, but that would be the result.

Question. Are you acquainted with the proposed amendment now pending in the Senate of the United States?

Answer. No, sir; I am not. I scarcely ever read a paper. [The substance of the proposed amendment was here explained to the witness by Mr. CONKLING.] So far as I can see, I do not think the State of Virginia would object to it.

Question. Would she consent, under any circumstances, to allow the black people to vote even if she were to gain a larger number of representatives in Congress?

Answer. That would depend upon her interests. If she had the right of determining that, I do not see why she should object. If it were to her interest to admit these people to vote, that might overrule any other objection that she had to it.

Question. What, in your opinion, would be the practical result? Do you think that Virginia would consent to allow the negro to vote?

Answer. I think that, at present, she would accept the smaller representation. I do not know what the future may develop. If it should be plain to her that these persons will vote properly and understandingly, she might admit them to vote.

Question. Do you think it would turn a good deal, in the cotton States, upon the value of the labor of the black people—upon the amount which they produce?

Answer. In a good many States in the south, and in a good many counties in Virginia, if the black people now were allowed to vote, it would, I think, exclude proper representation; that is, proper, intelligent people would not be elected; and rather than suffer that injury they would not let them vote at all.

Question. Do you not think that the question, as to whether any southern State would allow the colored people the right of suffrage in order to increase representation, would depend a good deal on the amount which the colored people might contribute to the wealth of the State in order to secure two things: first, the larger representation, and, second, the influence derived from these persons voting?

Answer. I think they would determine the question more in reference to their opinion as to the manner in which those votes would be exercised, whether they consider those people qualified to vote. My own opinion is, that, at this time, they cannot vote intelligently, and that giving them the right of suffrage would open the door to a great deal of demagogism, and lead to embarrassments in various ways. What the future may prove, how intelligent they may become, with what eyes they may look upon the interests of the State in which they may reside, I cannot say more than you can.

Question. Do you not think that Virginia would be better off if the colored population were to go to Alabama, Louisiana, and the other southern States?

Answer. I think it would be better for Virginia if she could get rid of them. That is no new opinion with me. I have always thought so, and have always been in favor of emancipation—gradual emancipation.

Question. As a question of labor alone, do you think that the labor which would flow into Virginia, if the negroes left it for the cotton States, would be far more advantageous to the State and to its future prosperity?

Answer. I think it would be for the benefit of Virginia, and I believe that everybody there would be willing to aid it.

Question. Do you not think that the State of Virginia is absolutely injured and its future impaired by the presence of the black population there?

Answer. I think it is.

Question. And do you not think it is peculiarly adapted to the quality of labor which would flow into it, from its great natural resources, in case it was made more attractive by the absence of the colored race?

Answer. I do.*

134

FREEDOM BUT NO FURTHER

Individuals who testified before members of the Joint Committee gave the proponents of more rigorous controls all the ammunition they needed. Thomas Conway, a former Freedmen's Bureau official, testifies on the basis of his experience in dealing with both Negro and white in the South. The testimony of the Reverend William Thornton, ex-slave, and Madison Newby, Negro farmer, follows that of Thomas Conway.

THOMAS CONWAY

Question. What, in your judgment, would be the effect of the withdrawal of the Freedmen's Bureau or some organization or system like that from Louisiana?

---

*Testimony of General Robert E. Lee of Virginia, Washington, D.C., February 17, 1866. Questions by Senator Jacob M. Howard of Michigan and Representative Henry T. Blow of Missouri, of the Subcommittee on Virginia, North Carolina, and South Carolina of the Joint Committee on Reconstruction. Joint Committee on Reconstruction, *Report,* 39th Congress, 1st Session, Part II, 130, 132, 134, 136.

Answer. I should expect in Louisiana, as in the whole southern country, that the withdrawal of the Freedmen's Bureau would be followed by a condition of anarchy and bloodshed, and I say that much in the light of as large an experience upon the subject as any man in the country. I have been in the army since the 19th of April, 1861; I have been over the whole country, almost from Baltimore to the Gulf. I was one of the first who held any official position in regard to the freedmen, and I am pained at the conviction I have in my own mind that if the Freedmen's Bureau is withdrawn the result will be fearful in the extreme. What it has already done and is now doing in shielding these people, only incites the bitterness of their foes. They will be murdered by wholesale, and they in their turn will defend themselves. It will not be persecution merely; it will be slaughter; and I doubt whether the world has ever known the like. These southern rebels, when the power is once in their hands, will stop with nothing short of extermination. Governor Wells himself told me that he expected in ten years to see the whole colored race exterminated, and that conviction is shared very largely among the white people of the south. It has been threatened by leading men there that they would exterminate the freedmen. They have said so in my hearing. In reply I said that they could not drive the freedmen out of the nation, because, in the first place, they would not go; and for another reason, that they had no authority to drive them out; and for a third reason, that they were wanted in the south as laborers. To that they replied, that, if necessary, they would get their laborers from Europe; that white laborers would be more agreeable to them; that the negro must be gotten rid of in some way, and that, too, as speedily as possible. I have heard it so many times, and from so many different quarters, that I believe it is a fixed determination, and that they are looking anxiously to the extermination of the whole negro race from the country. There is an agent here now, with letters from the governor of Louisiana to parties in New York, with a view of entering at once upon negotiations to secure laborers from various parts of Europe. There are other parties endeavoring to get coolies into the south, and in various places there are immense efforts made to obtain white labor to supplant that of the negro. It is a part of the immense and desperate programme which they have adopted and expect to carry out within ten years. It is the same determination to which I referred in my report. I said the negro race would be exterminated unless protected by the strong arm of the government; no weak arm will do. The very strongest arm of the government is needed to shield them. The wicked work has already commenced, and it could be shown that the policy pursued by the government is construed by the rebels as not being opposed to it.

Question. State, if you please, what you know as to the views and feelings of the white people in that region of country—those who have heretofore been rebels—as to the authority of the general government, and also as to whether any change in their views and feelings are manifest since hostilities ceased; if so, what that change is, and what has been the occasion of it, in your opinion.

Answer. In the neighborhood of New Orleans, comprising about

In New Orleans, Negroes being arrested for vagrancy by the Provost Guard, from Frank Leslie's Illustrated Newspaper, *May 21, 1864.*

twenty parishes in Louisiana, which we have mostly controlled since the time of General Butler's arrival, there has been, to my knowledge, a considerable loyal element—not an element which became loyal since the occupation of the district by our troops, but men who were loyal previously. With those who sympathized with and participated in the rebellion, (and I think I know them all.) I was brought in contact, and with nearly every propertyholder in the State. My communication with them, and my knowledge of their actions, convinced me that at heart they were not changed, but were opposed to us and opposed to our government—not willing to make their opposition physical, but secret and quiet. They do now, and always have thrown every possible obstacle in the way of our work—men, too, with whom I had expected better things. Some of the leading officers of the State down there—men who do much to form and control the opinions of the masses—instead of doing as they promised, and quietly submitting to the authority of the government are engaged in issuing slave codes and in promulgating them to their subordinates, ordering them to carry them into execution, and this to the knowledge of State officials of a higher character, the governor and others. And the men who issued them were not punished except as the military authorities punish them. The governor inflicted no punishment on them while I was there, and I don't know that, up to this day, he has ever punished one of them. These rules were simply the old black code of the State, with the word "slave" expunged and "negro" substituted. The most odious features of slavery were preserved in them.

* * *

Question. Are the people there disposed to resort to personal violence or chastisement to compel the negroes to work now?

Answer. They are so disposed in nearly every instance. A resort to violence is the first thought that I have seen exhibited when freedmen did not act exactly to suit the employer. The planters frequently came to me with requests (in fact, it was almost daily) to be allowed to correct the laborers on their own plantations. It is the universal conviction, and the universal purpose with them, too, to do that so far as they are allowed to do it; and, so far as they can, they will do it. The only constraint put upon them in regard to it is through the agency of the Freedmen's Bureau. Without that, I am satisfied, they would very rapidly return to the old system of slavery. In some portions of the State of Louisiana, now, they have organized patrols of militiamen, who go up and down the roads the same as if they were scouting in time of war, to prevent the negroes from going from one place to another. I am satisfied, from the most reliable reports, that under the most strict rules of evidence it could be proved that in portions of the State these acts are being done the same as under the old system; that, except as regards buying and selling, the old system of slavery is being carried on in all its essential features, and that there is a deep-rooted determination, arising from the old habits of treating the negro, to continue the same treatment and the same restrictions that existed prior to the war. The Freedmen's Bureau was regarded by the planters in Louisiana in the language of one of their leaders, as a "conservative machine." This arose from the conduct of General Fullerton, whom the President sent to relieve me.

Question. What is your opinion as to the extent of general knowledge among the freedmen; and what is their capacity for understanding their rights and the questions that are being agitated in the country?

Answer. I have taken a great deal of pains to secure, for my own satisfaction, accurate information on that subject, and I have ques-

A drawing from Frank Leslie's Illustrated Newspaper, *Feb 2, 1867. The scene shows an office of the Freedmen's Bureau, one of the strongest champions of the Negro's rights.*

tioned the lowest and meanest of them as to their ideas of liberty and their duty as citizens; and I have never yet found any view expressed by them, or any evidence through their answers or conduct, which led me to think they were any lower or more ignorant than the lower order of the white people who live down there or that they had any less accurate knowledge of government and duty toward it than the lower class of white people. I have seen very ignorant white people there who had all the privileges of citizenship. I have seen them go to the polls and vote, when they had no better idea of the questions at issue in the election, or the importance of the act they were performing, than the lowest negro I ever saw. The great majority of colored people understand very well and have a very accurate idea of what their personal liberty is, and how far it is to be regulated in order to be a blessing to them, and a very good idea of their duty as citizens. They have one idea which underlies every other, and that is, that notwithstanding the treatment they receive at the hands of the government, and the want of complete protection and complete liberty the government has so far caused them to suffer, they believe that it will yet secure them full protection, full liberty, and a full enjoyment of all their rights as citizens and as men; and they are working very energetically in Louisiana for the attainment of that purpose. They have their societies and clubs, in which they canvass very carefully every act of the government in regard to them, and in regard to the rebels who live all around them. They read the newspapers pretty generally. I believe two-thirds of the negroes in Louisiana can read. They publish a newspaper there, read it, and sustain it. With the use of schools, and the diligence in learning among them, which arises partly from the suddenness of the opportunity presented, and in part from a desire to ascertain precisely what the government is doing for them, and how they can best live as men and citizens ought to live. These reasons, I think, mainly explain the causes of the desire they manifest in this regard, and the result will, I think, be their nearly all becoming quite intelligent in a short time.

Question. What, in your opinion, would be the effect upon whites, blacks, and all concerned, of giving the negro the right to vote?

Answer. I do not think the effect would be to inaugurate a war of races there, for this reason: The negroes are so numerous, and they would be so intensely determined to enjoy what rights they have in that respect, that the whites would submit, seeing the impossibility of preventing it, and for the purpose of avoiding collisions and bloodshed in the country. The lives and safety of loyal white men require the protection and assistance that would grow from the negro's vote. I think the troops should be retained, and that small squads of them should be stationed all through the country, so as to shield the freedmen in the enjoyment of this right till the whites have become familiar with it. The militia forces should not be organized in the south during this generation. These things being done, my judgment is that there would be no trouble at all. On the contrary, it would, in a more speedy and thorough manner than any other, secure permanent peace and prosperity to the country. In the present condition of things there they cannot hope for peace or prosperity, because loyal men cannot remain without the protection of the government, and the negroes have no safety in the protection of their white foes. When the negroes come to see that their own life and liberty are to be sacrificed, they will struggle manfully against such a result, and they will importune the government, and call upon mankind to be their witness, until liberty and safety are insured them; they will persevere devotedly until their rights are accomplished. There are so many of them, and so many white people to help them, I don't see how the government can resist giving them every protection warranted by the Constitution.*

REVEREND WILLIAM THORNTON

Question. Were you ever a slave?

Answer. Yes, sir.

Question. When were you made free?

Answer. I was made free under the proclamation.

Question. Where do you reside?

Answer. Hampton, Elizabeth City county, Virginia.

Question. How do the old rebel masters down there feel toward your race?

Answer. The feeling existing there now is quite disagreeable.

Question. Do they not treat the colored race with kindness down there?

Answer. No, sir.

Question. What acts of unkindness can you mention?

Answer. I was asked the other day if I did not know I was violating the law in celebrating marriages. I did not know that that was the case, and I went up the clerk's office to inquire; I said nothing out of the way to the clerk of the court; I only asked him if there had been any provision for colored people to be lawfully married. Said he, "I do not know whether there is or not, and if they are granting licenses you can't have any; that is my business, not yours." After I found I was violating the law, I went to the Freedmen's Bureau and stated the case. A provision was afterwards made in the bureau granting licenses, and authorizing me to marry. Some days after that an old gentleman named Houghton, a white man living in the neighborhood of my church, was in the church. In my sermon I mentioned the assassination of Mr. Lincoln. Next day I happened to meet Houghton, who said to me, "Sir, as soon as we can get these Yankees off the ground and move that bureau, we will put you to rights; we will break up your church, and not one of you shall have a church here." Said I, "For what? I think it is for the safety of the country to have religious meetings, and for your safety as well as everybody else's." "We will not have it, sir," said he, and then he

---

*Testimony of Thomas Conway of New York, Washington, D.C., February 22, 1866. Questions by Senator George H. Williams of Oregon of the Subcommittee on Florida, Louisiana, and Texas of the Joint Committee on Reconstruction. Joint Committee on Reconstruction, *Report*, 39th Congress, 1st Session, Part IV, 78-79, 82-83, 83-84.

commenced talking about two classes of people whom they intended to put to rights, the colored people and the loyal white men. I asked him in what respect he was going to put them to rights; said he, "That is for myself."

Question. Is he a man of standing and condition in the neighborhood?

Answer. He owns property there.

Question. Is he a rebel?

Answer. Oh, yes.

Question. Can you speak of any acts of violence committed by the whites upon the blacks?

Answer. Yes, sir; about three weeks ago a colored man got another one to cut some wood for him, and sent him into the woods adjoining the property of a Mr. Britner, a white man. The colored man, not knowing the line between the two farms, cut down a tree on Britner's land, when Britner went into the woods and deliberately shot him as he would shoot a bird.

Question. Was he not indicted and punished for that?

Answer. They had him in prison.

Question. Is he not in prison now?

Answer. I heard that they had let him out last Sunday morning.

Question. Do you know any other instances of cruelty?

Answer. I have church once a month in Matthews county, Virginia, the other side of the bay. The last time I was over there an intelligent man told me that just below his house a lady and her husband, who had been at the meeting, received thirty-nine lashes for being there, according to the old law of Virginia, as if they had been slaves. This was simply because they were told not to go to hear a Yankee darkey talk. They said he was not a Yankee but was a man born in Virginia, in Hampton.

Question. Why did they not resist being flogged?

Answer. They are that much down.

Question. Did they not know that they had a right to resist?

Answer. They dare not do it.

Question. Why?

Answer. I do not know. On the 1st of January we had a public meeting there, at which I spoke. The next night when I was coming from the church, which is about a mile and a half from my house, I met a colored man who told me that there was a plot laid for me; I went back to the church and got five of my church members to come with me. I afterwards learned that a fellow named Mahon, a white man, had determined, for my speech that day, to murder me the first chance.

Question. Did that come to you in so authentic a form as to leave no doubt upon your mind?

Answer. I believe he made the threat. The next day he said to me, "We hope the time will come that these Yankees will be away from here, and then we will settle with you preachers." That gave me to understand that the threat was made.

Question. Do you wish to state any other instances?

Answer. These are as many as I care to speak of.

Question. Do you stand in fear of the rebel white men?

Answer. Yes, sir, I do. If all the Union men that are down there would protect us we would not be so much afraid. I went down there to pay my taxes upon my land, but I could not see any person to pay them to; I didn't want to pay any but the United States government; and finally, they told me at the court-house that I had better let it alone until I could see further about it.

Question. What is your land worth?

Answer. I gave $700 for it.

Question. Is there a house on it?

Answer. Yes.

Question. Do the colored people down there love to work?

Answer. They work if they can get anything for it; but the rebel people down there who have got lands will not let the colored people work unless they work for their prices, and they drive them away. They expect colored people down there to work for ten or eighteen cents a day. Six or eight dollars a month is the highest a colored man can get; of course he gets his board, but he may have a family of six to support on these wages, and of course he cannot do it.

Question. Now that the blacks are made free, will they not, if left to themselves with the protection of the whites, become strollers and rovers about the country and live in idleness, and pilfer and misbehave generally?

Answer. No, sir.

Question. Why not?

Answer. Because they have all been used to work, and will work if they can get anything to do.

Question. Do they not want to go away from the old places where they have been accustomed to live and go off west somewhere?

Answer. No, sir; we want to stay in our old neighborhoods, but those of us who have gone away are not allowed to go back. In Surrey county they are taking the colored people and tying them up by the thumbs if they do not agree to work for six dollars a month; they tie them up until they agree to work for that price, and then they make them put their mark to a contract.

Question. What other bad treatment do they practice on the blacks? do they whip them?

Answer. Yes, sir; just as they did before the war; I see no difference.

Question. Have you seen them whipped since the war?

Answer. Several times.

Question. By their old masters?

Answer. By the old people around the neighborhood; the old masters got other people to do it.

Question. Do they whip them just as much as they did before the war?

Answer. Just the same; I do not see any alteration in that. There are no colored schools down in Surrey county; they would kill any one who would go down there and establish colored schools. There have been no meetings or anything of that kind. They patrol our houses just as formerly.

Question. What do you mean by patrolling your houses?

Answer. A party of twelve or fifteen men go around at night searching the houses of colored people, turning them out and beating them. I was sent here as a delegate to find out whether the colored people down there cannot have protection. They are willing to work for a living; all they want is some protection and to know what their rights are; they do not know their rights; they do not know whether they are free or not, there are so many different stories told them.

Question. Where did you learn to read?

Answer. I first picked up a word from one and then from another.

Question. Have you ever been at school?

Answer. Never in my life.

Question. Are the black people there anxious for education and to go to school?

Answer. Generally they are; but down in my neighborhood they are afraid to be caught with a book.*

135

NEGROES DEMAND A POLITICAL ROLE

Frederick Douglass

The interview, February 7, 1866, which a group of prominent Negroes had with President Johnson was the first of its kind, patterned after many similar interviews in which special interest groups approached the chief executive. In this instance, President Johnson had already demonstrated his increasing distrust of Negro participation in government and was under attack from the Radical wing of the Republican party. He undoubtedly recognized that the Negro group, in speaking for itself, was speaking also for that politically potent Republican segment.

The President's inability to come to grips with the issues raised by Frederick Douglass and George Downing, and his bluntness, bordering on the intemperate, foreshadowed his famous "Swing around the Circle" before the elections later in the year. In contrast, Douglass' and Downing's pointed firmness and controlled emotion made this first Negro effort a tactical victory. Given the opportunity, Negro leaders could express themselves clearly on the issue of greatest concern to them.

Mr. George T. Downing then addressed the President as follows:

We present ourselves to your Excellency, to make known with pleasure the respect which we are glad to cherish for you—a respect which is your due, as our Chief Magistrate. It is our desire for you to know that we come feeling that we are friends meeting a friend. We should, however, have manifested our friendship by not coming to further tax your already much burdened and valuable time; but we

*Testimony of various Negroes from Norfolk, Virginia, Washington, D.C., February 3, 1866. Questions by Senator Jacob M. Howard of Michigan of the Subcommittee on Virginia, North Carolina, and South Carolina of the Joint Committee on Reconstruction. Joint Committee on Reconstruction, *Report,* 39th Congress, 1st Session, Part II, 52-53, 54, 55, 56, 59.

have another object in calling. We are in a passage to equality before the law. God hath made it by opening a Red Sea. We would have your assistance through the same. We come to you in the name of the colored people of the United States. We are delegated to come by some who have unjustly worn iron manacles on their bodies—by some whose minds have been manacled by class legislation in States called free. The colored people of the States of Illinois, Wisconsin, Alabama, Mississippi, Florida, South Carolina, North Carolina, Virginia, Maryland, Pennsylvania, New York, New England States, and District of Columbia have specially delegated us to come.

Our coming is a marked circumstance, noting determined hope that we are not satisfied with an amendment prohibiting slavery, but that we wish it enforced with appropriate legislation. This is our desire. We ask for it intelligently, with the knowledge and conviction that the fathers of the Revolution intended freedom for every American; that they should be protected in their rights as citizens, and be equal before the law. We are Americans, native born Americans. We are citizens; we are glad to have it known to the world that you bear no doubtful record on this point. On this fact, and with confidence in the triumph of justice, we base our hope. We see no recognition of color or race in the organic law of the land. It knows no privileged class, and therefore we cherish the hope that we may be fully enfranchised, not only here in this District, but throughout the land. We respectfully submit that rendering anything less than this will be rendering to us less than our just due; that granting anything less than our full rights will be a disregard of our just rights and of due respect for our feelings. If the powers that be do so it will be used as a license, as it were, or an apology, for any community, or for individuals thus disposed, to outrage our rights and feelings. It has been shown in the present war that the Government may justly reach its strong arm into States, and demand for them, from those who owe it allegiance, their assistance and support. May it not reach out a like arm to secure and protect its subjects upon whom it has a claim?

Following upon Mr. Downing, Mr. Fred. Douglass advanced and addressed the President, saying:

Mr. President, we are not here to enlighten you, sir, as to your duties as the Chief Magistrate of this Republic, but to show our respect, and to present in brief the claims of our race to your favorable consideration. In the order of Divine Providence you are placed in a position where you have the power to save or destroy us, to bless or blast us—I mean our whole race. Your noble and humane predecessor placed in our hands the sword to assist in saving the nation, and we do hope that you, his able successor, will favorably regard the placing in our hands the ballot with which to save ourselves.

We shall submit no argument on that point. The fact that we are the subjects of Government, and subject to taxation, subject to volunteer in the service of the country, subject to being drafted, subject to bear the burdens of the State, makes it not improper that we should ask to share in the privileges of this condition.

I have no speech to make on this occasion. I simply submit these observations as a limited expression of the views and feelings of the delegation with which I have come.

Response of the President:

In reply to some of your inquiries, not to make a speech about this thing, for it is always best to talk plainly and distinctly about such matters, I will say that if I have not given evidence in my course that I am a friend of humanity, and to that portion of it which constitutes the colored population, I can give no evidence here. Everything that I have had, both as regards life and property, has been perilled in that cause, and I feel and think that I understand—not to be egotistic—what should be the true direction of this question, and what course of policy would result in the melioration and ultimate elevation, not only of the colored, but of the great mass of the people of the United States. I say that if I have not given evidence that I am a friend of humanity, and especially the friend of the colored man, in my past conduct, there is nothing that I can now do that would. I repeat, all that I possessed, life, liberty, and property, have been put up in connection with that question, when I had every inducement held out to take the other course, by adopting which I would have accomplished perhaps all that the most ambitious might have desired. If I know myself, and the feelings of my own heart, they have been for the colored man. I have owned slaves and bought slaves, but I never sold one. I might say, however, that practically, so far as my connection with slaves has gone, I have been their slave instead of their being mine. Some have even followed me here, while others are occupying and enjoying my property with my consent. For the colored race my means, my time, my all has been perilled; and now at this late day, after giving evidence that is tangible, that is practical, I am free to say to you that I do not like to be arraigned by some who can get up handsomely-rounded periods and deal in rhetoric, and talk about abstract ideas of liberty, who never perilled life, liberty, or property. This kind of theoretical, hollow, unpractical friendship amounts to but very little. While I say that I am a friend of the colored man, I do not want to adopt a policy that I believe will end in a contest between the races, which if persisted in will result in the extermination of one or the other. God forbid that I should be engaged in such a work!

Now, it is always best to talk about things practically and in a common sense way. Yes, I have said, and I repeat here, that if the colored man in the United States could find no other Moses, or any Moses that would be more able and efficient than myself, I would be his Moses to lead him from bondage to freedom; that I would pass him from a land where he had lived in slavery to a land (if it were in our reach) of freedom. Yes, I would be willing to pass with him through the Red sea to the Land of Promise, to the land of liberty; but I am not willing, under either circumstance, to adopt a policy which I believe will only result in the sacrifice of his life and the shedding of his blood. I think I know what I say. I feel what I say;

and I feel well assured that if the policy urged by some be persisted in, it will result in great injury to the white as well as to the colored man. There is a great deal of talk about the sword in one hand accomplishing an end, and the ballot accomplishing another at the ballot-box.

* * *

Now, we are talking about where we are going to begin. We have got at the hate that existed between the two races. The query comes up, whether these two races, situated as they were before, without preparation, without time for passion and excitement to be appeased, and without time for the slightest improvement, whether the one should be turned loose upon the other, and be thrown together at the ballot-box with this enmity and hate existing between them. The query comes up right there, whether we don't commence a war of races. I think I understand this thing, and especially is this the case when you force it upon a people without their consent.

You have spoken about government. Where is power derived from? We say it is derived from the people. Let us take it so, and refer to the District of Columbia by way of illustration. Suppose, for instance, here, in this political community, which, to a certain extent, must have government, must have laws, and putting it now upon the broadest basis you can put it—take into consideration the relation which the white has heretofore borne to the colored race—is it proper to force upon this community, without their consent, the elective franchise, without regard to color, making it universal?

Now, where do you begin? Government must have a controlling power—must have a lodgment. For instance, suppose Congress should pass a law authorizing an election to be held at which all over twenty-one years of age, without regard to color, should be allowed to vote, and a majority should decide at such election that the elective franchise should not be universal; what would you do about it? Who would settle it? Do you deny that first great principle of the right of the people to govern themselves? Will you resort to an arbitrary power, and say a majority of the people shall receive a state of things they are opposed to?

Mr. Douglass: That was said before the war.

The President: I am now talking about a principle; not what somebody else said.

Mr. Downing: Apply what you have said, Mr. President, to South Carolina, for instance, where a majority of the inhabitants are colored.

The President: Suppose you go to South Carolina; suppose you go to Ohio. That doesn't change the principle at all. The query to which I have referred still comes up when government is undergoing a fundamental change. Government commenced upon this principle; it has existed upon it; and you propose now to incorporate into it an element that didn't exist before. I say the query comes up in undertaking this thing whether we have a right to make a change in regard to the elective franchise in Ohio, for instance: whether we shall not let the people in that State decide the matter for themselves.

Each community is better prepared to determine the depositary of its political power than anybody else, and it is for the Legislature, for the people of Ohio to say who shall vote, and not for the Congress of the United States. I might go down here to the ballot-box tomorrow and vote directly for universal suffrage; but if a great majority of the people said no, I should consider it would be tyrannical in me to attempt to force such upon them without their will. It is a fundamental tenet in my creed that the will of the people must be obeyed. Is there anything wrong or unfair in that?

Mr. Douglass (smiling): A great deal that is wrong, Mr. President, with all respect.

The President: It is the people of the States that must for themselves determine this thing. I do not want to be engaged in a work that will commence a war of races. I want to begin the work of preparation, and the States, or the people in each community, if a man demeans himself well, and shows evidence that this new state of affairs will operate, will protect him in all his rights, and give him every possible advantage when they become reconciled socially and politically to this state of things. Then will this new order of things work harmoniously; but forced upon the people before they are prepared for it, it will be resisted, and work inharmoniously. I feel a conviction that driving this matter upon the people, upon the community, will result in the injury of both races, and the ruin of one or the other. God knows I have no desire but the good of the whole human race. I would it were so that all you advocate could be done in the twinkling of any eye; but it is not in the nature of things, and I do not assume or pretend to be wiser than Providence, or stronger than the laws of nature.

Let us now seek to discover the laws governing this thing. There is a great law controlling it; let us endeavor to find out what that law is, and conform our actions to it. All the details will then properly adjust themselves and work out well in the end.

God knows that anything I can do I will do. In the mighty process by which the great end is to be reached, anything I can do to elevate the races, to soften and ameliorate their condition I will do, and to be able to do so is the sincere desire of my heart.

I am glad to have met you, and thank you for the compliment you have paid me.

Mr. Douglass: I have to return to you our thanks, Mr. President, for so kindly granting us this interview. We did not come here expecting to argue this question with your excellency, but simply to state what were our views and wishes in the premises. If we were disposed to argue the question, and you would grant us permission, of course we would endeavor to controvert some of the positions you have assumed.

Mr. Downing: Mr. Douglass, I take it that the President, by his kind expressions and his very full treatment of the subject, must have contemplated some reply to the views which he has advanced, and in which we certainly do not concur, and I say this with due respect.

The President: I thought you expected me to indicate to some extent what my views were on the subjects touched upon in your statement.

Mr. Downing: We are very happy, indeed, to have heard them.

Mr. Douglass: If the President will allow me, I would like to say one or two words in reply. You enfranchise your enemies and disfranchise your friends.

The President: All I have done is simply to indicate what my views are, as I supposed you expected me to, from your address.

Mr. Douglass: My own impression is that the very thing that your excellency would avoid in the southern States can only be avoided by the very measure that we propose, and I would state to my brother delegates that because I perceive the President has taken strong grounds in favor of a given policy, and distrusting my own ability to remove any of those impressions which he has expressed, I thought we had better end the interview with the expression of thanks. (Addressing the President.) But if your excellency will be pleased to hear, I would like to say a word or two in regard to that one matter of the enfranchisement of the blacks as a means of preventing the very thing which your excellency seems to apprehend —that is a conflict of races.

The President: I repeat, I merely wanted to indicate my views in reply to your address, and not to enter into any general controversy, as I could not well do so under the circumstances.

Your statement was a very frank one, and I thought it was due to you to meet in the same spirit.

Mr. Douglass: Thank you, sir.

The President: I think you will find, so far as the South is concerned, that if you will all inculcate there the idea in connection with the one you urge, that the colored people can live and advance in civilization to better advantage elsewhere than crowded right down there in the South, it would be better for them.

Mr. Douglass: But the masters have the making of the laws, and we cannot get away from the plantation.

The President: What prevents you?

Mr. Douglass: We have not the single right of locomotion through the Southern States now.

The President: Why not; the government furnishes you with every facility.

Mr. Douglass: There are six days in the year that the Negro is free in the South now, and his master then decides for him where he shall go, where he shall work, how much he shall work—in fact, he is divested of all political power. He is absolutely in the hands of those men.

The President: If the master now controls him or his action, would he not control him in his vote?

Mr. Douglass: Let the Negro once understand that he has an organic right to vote, and he will raise up a party in the Southern States among the poor, who will rally with him. There is this conflict that you speak of between the wealthy slaveholder and the poor man.

The President: You touch right upon the point there. There is this conflict, and hence I suggest emigration. If he cannot get employment in the South, he has it in his power to go where he can get it.

* * *

Mr. Douglass, on turning to leave, remarked to his fellow delegates: "The President sends us to the people, and we go to the people."

The President: Yes, sir; I have great faith in the people. I believe they will do what is right.*

Reconstruction: A Black Page?

136

A RECONSTRUCTED STATE GOVERNMENT—MISSISSIPPI

No southern state under Reconstruction was typical, but Mississippi can serve as an adequate example of Negro participation in state government. Between 1868 and 1874, Mississippi established the framework for an effectively democratic, reform-oriented state government.

The constitutional convention of 1868, consisting of 84 white men and 16 Negroes, drew up a document which prohibited racial distinctions and property qualifications for voting and jury duty. It enhanced the powers of the governor, expanded the judiciary, and increased the number of elected state officers to include, among others, a commissioner for immigration and agriculture and a state superintendent of public education.

The first legislature under the new constitution convened in 1870 with 35 Negroes out of a total of 140 men in both houses. This body and its successor in 1872, which had approximately the same proportion of Negro members, enacted a series of laws which, given more favorable conditions, could have created a creditably governed state.

In the space of four years, the legislature established the credit of the state and passed a stiff tax measure to substantiate it. It reorganized the state university, created and financed a bi-racial educational system, including two Negro normal schools and a Negro university. It rehabilitated old state buildings and constructed new facilities for the mentally and physically disabled. The legislators repealed all laws based on race and affirmed the right of all citizens to use places of public accommodation, without distinction of color.

This was a substantial achievement, but its potential for sound government was shattered by the political venality and physical violence which made a shambles of Mississippi after 1873. In his testimony before a Congressional subcommittee investigating the Ku Klux Klan in November, 1871, Alexander K. Davis, a Negro politician, revealed some of the early fruits of Mississippi's achievements as well as the latent reaction and disorder which was to follow.

Question. Do you know, or have you been informed, of any influence being brought to bear on the colored voters, to deter them from voting, or to influence their political action at the polls?

---

*Interview with the President of the United States, Andrew Johnson, by a delegation of Negroes, headed by Frederick Douglass and George T. Downing, February 7, 1866. Quoted from Philip S. Foner, *The Life and Writings of Frederick Douglass* (New York, 1955), IV, 182-193.

Answer. No, sir; I have not since last spring. There was, last spring, a great many threats made about colored people voting, and this organization was threatening a great many colored people, by men that claimed to have nothing to do with it.

* * *

Question. What was the character of those threats you speak of?

Answer. The character of them was about this: I will not say that I know of them—threats being made of that kind, but I have heard of threats being made that this Klan would see to the negroes voting, or how they voted. I have had gentlemen to tell me, right on the streets here, that we would not be able to carry this county; though we had a majority of two thousand in the county, that we would never be able to carry it again. That was last spring. Since the investigation of some of these outrages, I have heard of no threats at all of men. Since this canvass opened I have heard of no threats. I have been through the county as much as anybody in it, I reckon.

* * *

Question. The census, I observe, states the white population to be, I believe, 5,107, and the black population 15,798. Is that about the population, according to your knowledge and information?

Answer. Yes, sir; about it, sir.

Question. Do you know of any colored churches or school-houses being burned in this county?

Answer. There have been one or two colored school-houses burned in the county; there was one at Shuqualak, and one was burned within the last ten days at Brooksville. That is about all the colored school-houses burned. There have been one or two white school-houses, out here in the southwest corner of the county, burned. Three of them were burned during the year 1870 and the spring of 1871.

Question. What information have you of the burning of the colored school at Shuqualak?

Answer. I have none, sir. All the burnings have been wrapped up in mystery. Nobody knew anything about them.

* * *

Question. What is the sentiment of the whites in this county as to the colored schools?

Answer. Well, sir, in a portion of the county the majority of the whites, I think, are favorable; in all the northeast portion of the county, and Macon here, and probably Shuqualak and that district down there, the majority of the whites, I think, are favorable to the free schools; but in the southeast corner, and southwest corner, and the northwest corner of the county, and all the west part of the county, the most of the whites are opposed to free schools for anybody, white or black. I have met a great many persons and talked with them. I met a leading man in the northwest corner of the county who keeps a store up there, a wealthy man, and he told me he thought it an outrage. He thought the principle was wrong that he should be taxed to educate other people's children; he said he had to educate his own, and he did not think it was right. It is generally said that what he says is the sentiment of his whole community. He is a very quiet man, though, and I have never heard of his participating in the disturbances. That is pretty generally the feeling.

Question. Is that the sole objection made to the free schools, the expense it entails in the shape of taxes?

Answer. That is the only public objection they make. What their private views are I do not pretend to say at all. The only objection I have heard of their making to any of the friends of the system is that they did not think they ought to be taxed to support them.

Question. Do you hear any opposition to colored suffrage?

Answer. Well, no, sir; there is no open opposition in this county, scarcely; our paper here opposes it; it has at its head a motto, "All the time in opposition to negro suffrage," that is, it raised it after the election of 1869, and pulled it down a few weeks ago. I presume they will raise it again after this election is over; everybody that is a candidate now for every party claims to be a friend to universal suffrage. We have three or four tickets in the field, all claiming to be friends to negro suffrage.

Question. Have you heard any considerable number of democrats denounce that motto as not representing the sentiments of the democratic party in this county?

Answer. No, sir; I have heard some few. I have heard it myself, that motto, and I have heard one or two say that it did not represent the sentiments of their party. The most prominent democrats here now claim that there is no opposition to universal suffrage or free schools, and that they are not opposed to radicalism.

Question. Do you believe them to be sincere in the sentiments they express?

Answer. No, sir; I don't believe them.

Question. Have there been any cases in which any white men, implicated in the various outrages you have detailed, have ever been brought to justice and punished?

Answer. None; I never have heard of one yet being punished. I have heard of several attempts to investigate, but they have never succeeded. I have had witnesses tell me that they have gone before grand juries here—I know witnesses that told me they were going before grand juries to report certain parties that they recognized that had committed outrages, and they went before the grand juries and have seen parties on that grand jury that they knew were connected with the Klan, or were members of the bands that had committed these outrages; and they then and there stated that they didn't know anything about it—just heard of it. They said they didn't think it was safe to do so, and I know it was so. There are white men in this town, I know a man that has lived here always, and probably has at stake as much as anybody in this county; he told me this morning that he wouldn't testify what he knew before the committee, because, he said, it would be published; he said he didn't intend to be slaughtered. There are plenty of men here, sir, that will not do it. They don't believe that there will be any effort made—that their testimony before this committee will simply amount to informing the outside world as to these outrages, and that is about all; and that they will not lend any aid at all to bring these parties to justice, and it will only place them in the position of being more obnoxious to these men and more liable to be killed.*

Southerners sought to re-establish their power over the Negro. The freedmen, all too aware of the white threat, resisted. The result was conflict. This drawing shows the police beating down a Negro mob in New Orleans, in 1874.

137

THE CIVIL RIGHTS ACT OF 1875

The Civil Rights Act of 1875 became law after an extended debate which began in the previous session of Congress. Championed by Senator Charles Sumner of Massachusetts, who did not live to see its enactment, the bill contained several clauses which were struck before passage, including those which called for integrated schools and cemeteries. In general it barred segregated facilities in public transportation, accommodation, and amusement.

At a time when control of the former Confederate states was rapidly slipping away, the act was a final Republican effort to tie the Negro vote to that party by means of national legislation. The act was rarely enforced and its key sections were declared unconstitutional by the Supreme Court in 1883.

R. H. Cain was a leading Negro South Carolinian during the Reconstruction period, an able politician, and minister of one of the largest churches in the South, the Emmanuel AME Church of Charleston.

Mr. Speaker, there are periods in the history of nations and of peoples when it is necessary that men belonging to a race or races whose rights and interests are at stake should lay aside all feelings of delicacy and hesitation and vindicate their rights, their character, and their nationality. I have listened with some surprise to the speech of the gentleman who has just taken his seat, [Mr. White-

Testimony Taken by the Joint Select Committee to Inquire into the Condition of Affairs in the Late Insurrectionary States. Mississippi, v. I, 42nd Cong., 2nd sess., Senate Report 41, pt. 11 (Washington, 1872), 477-478.

HEAD] I have been surprised at his attempt to ridicule and cast a slur upon a race of men whose labor has enabled him and his for two hundred years to feed, and drink, and thrive, and fatten.

I have sat in this House nearly nine months, and I have listened to gentlemen recognized as the leaders on the other side attempting to demonstrate as they supposed the inferiority of a race of men whom they have so long outraged, and to cast a slur upon them because they have been helpless. But revolutions never go backward. The mills of the gods grind slowly, but surely and exceeding fine. The times have changed. The wheels have rolled up different circumstances from those that were rolled up in the days of the old *régime*.

The gentleman from Virginia calls in question the propriety of passing the civil-rights bill. I cannot agree with him, and for this reason; my understanding of human rights, of democracy if you please, is all rights to all men, the government of the people by the people, and for the people's interest, without regard to sections, complexions, or anything else.

Why not pass the civil-rights bill? Are there not five millions of men, women, and children in this country, a larger number than inhabited this country when the fathers made the tea party in Boston harbor, five millions whose rights are as dear and sacred to them, humble though they be, as are the rights of the thirty-odd millions of white people in this land? I am at a loss to understand the philosophy which these gentlemen have learned; how they can arrogate to themselves all rights, all liberty, all law, all government, all progress, all science, all arts, all literature, and deny them to other men formed of God equally as they are formed, clothed with the same humanity, and endowed with the same intellectual powers, but robbed by their connivance of the means of development. I say I am at a loss to understand how they can deny to us these privileges and claim them for themselves.

The civil-rights bill simply declares this: that there shall be no discriminations between citizens of this land so far as the laws of the land are concerned. I can find no fault with that. The great living principle of the American Government is that all men are free. We admit from every land and every nationality men to come here and under the folds of that noble flag repose in peace and protection. We assume that, whatever education his mind may have received, each man may aspire to and acquire all the rights of citizenship. Yet because, forsooth, God Almighty made the face of the negro black, these gentlemen would deny him that right though he be a man. Born on your soil, reared here amid the toils and sorrows and griefs of the land, producing by his long years of toil the products which have made your country great, earnestly laboring to develop the resources of this land, docile though outraged, yet when the gentlemen who held them in bondage—sir, I will not repeat the dark scenes that transpired under the benign influence and direction of that class of men.

He tells you that since the liberation of the negro the people of the North want to stir up strife. Why, sir, you of the South stir up the strife. When the Government of the United States had made the black man free; when Congress, in the greatness of its magnanimity prepared to give to every class of men their rights, and in reconstructing the Southern States guaranteed to all the people their liberties, you refused to acquiesce in the laws enacted by Congress; you refused to "accept the situation," to recognize the rights of that class of men in the land. You sought to make the reconstruction acts a nullity, if possible. You sought to re-enslave the black man by every means in your power. You denied the validity of those reconstruction acts which undertook to protect him in his liberty. It is because you thus refused to accept the situation as it ought to have been accepted that there is now strife in the land. And I will tell you further that there will be strife all over this land as long as five millions of black men, women, and children are deprived of their rights. There will be no real and enduring peace so long as the rights of any class of men are trampled under foot, North or South, East or West.

Gentlemen say that the republican party is keeping up a continual strife among classes. Why, sir, it is not the republican party that is keeping up strife. The republican party is seeking to maintain peace. It is the southern men that make the strife, because they will not let us have our liberties, because they seek to thwart the designs of the Government. No man can read the tales of horror now being brought out by the investigating committees in the South, without realizing the fact that it is not the northern people or the republican party that makes this strife in the country.

I regard it as essential to the peace of the country that there shall be no discrimination between citizens; and the civil-rights bill I regard as a just and righteous measure which this Government must adopt in order to guarantee to all citizens equal rights.

And, Mr. Speaker, I am astonished that there is an apparent disposition in some quarters to give this question the go-by. "O," gentlemen say, "you will stir up strife in the country"—"bad blood," the gentleman from Virginia said. Well, I think there has been a good deal of "bad blood" in the South already. It seems to me that a few years ago they had some "bad blood" in the South—very bad blood. And if any one will read the transactions in the South during the last few months, he will find that the "bad blood" has not all got out of the South—bad blood stirred up, not by the northern people, but by the southern people themselves.

Now, I do not think there is so much bad blood between the blacks and whites. The gentleman tells us in the next breath that they have the best laborers in the country. Well, if the labor is so good why do you not treat your laborers well? If they are the best class of laborers, if they do so much, why not guarantee to them their rights? If they are good laborers, if they produce your corn and your rice, if they give you such grand products, is it not proper and just that you should accord to them the rights that belong to them in common with other men?

The gentleman said that the slaves lived better than their masters. That is susceptible of grave doubt. I think there is a great difference between hog and hominy in the log cabin and all the luxuries of life in the richly-carpeted mansion. It seems to me there is a great difference when one class bear all the labor and produce all the crops, while the other class ride in their carriages, do all the buying and selling, and pocket all the money.

The gentleman says he wishes to defend "old Virginny." Now, I do not think that Virginia is any better than the rest of the States in this respect. My colleague has already stated that they do not allow colored people to ride in the cars except in cars labeled "Colored people allowed in this car." "Old Virginny never tires!" In this connection let me bring another fact to the gentleman's notice. Eight or ten months ago a lady acquaintance of mine was traveling from South Carolina to Washington; she had ridden in a first-class car through North Carolina, having paid a first-class fare; but when she got to the gentleman's noble State of "old Virginny," she was rudely taken and pushed out of the first-class car into the smoking-car, where she was obliged to remain until she passed out of "old Virginny." It is in this way that they give colored people all their rights and privileges in "old Virginny." It seems to me that such things as this must make "bad blood" for somebody.

But, Mr. Speaker, the gentleman says that this measure is merely an attempt on the part of the people at the North to continue agitation and strife. Sir, I believe that if Congress had boldly passed the civil-rights bill a year ago; if it had let the nation know that the mandates of the highest authority of the land must be obeyed, there would be no trouble to-day about the civil-rights bill, nor about "mixed schools," &c. The laws of the country would be obeyed. The trouble is merely that there has been a disposition to some extent on the part of some republicans to minister to the prejudices of southern men. Why is it that southern men make all this ado about schools? I think, Mr. Speaker, you will find that of all the men who have voted against the civil-rights bill in the contest that has been going on, there have been more men from the South than from the North on the republican side. The trouble arises in that direction.

But gentlemen speak about "bad blood." Sir, the statistics show—I want to illustrate the manner in which some of the southern people feel about the "bad blood"—the statistics show that there are 1,728,000 mulattoes in the South. One would naturally think there was a good deal of "bad blood" between the two classes—a great deal of unkind feeling!

Mr. Speaker, I regard the civil-rights bill as among the best measures that ever came before Congress. Why, sir, it is at the very foundation of good government. I take a higher view of the question than that of prejudice between the two classes. I regard this five million of men, women and children in the country as an integral part of the country, interwoven with all its interests. The laboring class of the South are as much a part of the population of this country as any other laboring class. The gentleman says that the South has its laborers. So they have. Very well; why should you not keep those laborers there? Why are the gentleman's friends desirous of killing them off? Why do you drive them from the fields? Why do you drive them from their homes? A committee of this House tells us the testimony taken before them shows there are two or three thousand men, women, and children who have been driven from plantations simply because the men voted the republican ticket. That is all. The bad blood of the South comes because the negroes are republicans. If they would only cease to be republicans, and vote the straight-out democratic ticket there would be no trouble. Then the bad blood would sink entirely out of sight.

* * *

Drawing from Harper's Weekly, *June 4, 1870, showing the registration of colored voters for the first municipal election in Richmond, Virginia, since the end of the Civil War.*

But, Mr. Speaker, this question of civil rights is one which ought to be met plainly and fully. It ought to be made clear and plain to the whole country. What are you going to do with these people? They are here and here they are going to stay. We are going to fight it out on this line if it takes the whole summer. Here we are, part and parcel of this Union, born here and here we expect to die.

But, sir, I have no fear for the future. I believe the time will come when the sense of justice of this nation, when the enlightenment of this century, when the wisdom of our legislators, when the good feeling of the whole people will complete this grand work by lifting up out of degradation a race of men which has served long and faithfully by placing it, so far as the laws are concerned, upon an equal footing with all other classes. I have faith in this country. My ideas are progressive. I recognize the fact that there has been a constant progress in the development of ideas in this country. The great principle which underlies our Government, of liberty, of justice, of right, will eventually prevail in this land and we shall enjoy equal rights under the laws. I regret exceedingly gentlemen talk of social equality. That seems to be their great bugaboo. O, if you put colored men upon an equality before the law they will want social equality! I do not believe a word of it. Do you suppose I would introduce into my family a class of white men I see in this country? Do you suppose for one moment I would do it? No, sir; There are men even who have positions upon this floor, and for whom I have respect, but of whom I should be careful how I introduced them into my family. I should be afraid indeed their old habits acquired beyond Mason and Dixon's line might return. No, Mr. Speaker, it is a damnable prejudice, the result of the old cursed system of slavery. It is that which brought about this prejudice and has caused it to overshadow the whole land. Slavery has left the poison still in their minds. Slavery and its effects have nearly expired. It is, to be sure, in its last dying throes. The rude hand of war opened a cavern into which ran much of the bad blood spoken of. The stamp of Phil Sheridan's gallant troopers let much more of it out. Before this Congress closes it will pass the civil-rights bill, giving equal rights and protection to all classes throughout the country. Then indeed, thank God, the last vestige of that old barbarism will have disappeared, and peace shall spread her wings over a united, prosperous, and happy people.

Mr. Speaker, I possibly owe an apology to the House for these remarks, because I entered the House only twenty minutes before the gentleman from Virginia [MR. WHITEHEAD] stopped speaking; but I felt it was a duty I owed to myself and to the race to which I belong to hurl back his aspersions against the people with whom I am identified, and whom I have endeavored to vindicate here to-night.

There has been a great cry, Mr. Speaker, about schools. Let me give you some statistics bearing upon that part of the case. I have been at some pains to look over the statistics of education in the South, the East, the West, and the North. And in the returns of the last census I find these figures: The number of whites who read throughout the Union was 6,412,246. The number of colored who read was 172,779; the difference being 6,239,467. Number of whites who cannot write, 2,842,062. Colored who cannot write, 2,778,515. I think, so far as the educational clause of the civil-rights bill is concerned, we shall not lose anything if it is struck out.

* * *

We could afford for the sake of peace in the republican ranks, if for nothing else—not as a matter of principle—to except the school clause.

So far as the grave-yards are concerned, why, we are not much troubled where we shall be buried. We know very well we shall be buried somewhere if we die. We are certain of that; somebody will get us out of the way.

Mr. Speaker, I regard it as essential, therefore, that this bill should pass. These five millions of people for whom I speak are waiting for its passage. Their hopes, their prospects, their lives to a certain extent depend upon it. And I think this country owes it to them. Having lifted them out of slavery, having emancipated them, having given them manhood in a sense, I regard it as essential to the interests of this country that they shall make them citizens of this country, with all that that word imports, and that they shall guarantee to them the protection necessary for their lives and for their property.

It is also necessary, Mr. Speaker, that this bill should pass that we may go through the length and breadth of this country without lot or hinderance. I know there are prejudices; but we must expect that these will exist. Let the laws of the country be just; let the laws of the country be equitable; that is all we ask, and we will take our chances under the laws in this land. We do not want the laws of this country to make discriminations between us. Place all citizens upon one broad platform; and if the negro is not qualified to hoe his row in this contest of life, then let him go down. All we ask of this country is to put no barriers between us, to lay no stumbling blocks in our way, to give us freedom to accomplish our destiny, that we may thus acquire all that is necessary to our interest and welfare in this country. Do this, sir, and we shall ask nothing more.*

138

THE EXODUS OF 1879

The exodus of Negroes from the South in 1879 has never been fully explained nor have the statistical dimensions of the movement been accurately determined. It was as close to a grass roots upheaval as any movement in American history, before or since.

The exodus was concentrated in the Mississippi Valley from Louisiana and Mississippi to Missouri and Kansas, but other states, both southern and western, were also affected. Self-styled Negro leaders rose up to claim credit for the movement, as charitable northern organizations formed to assist the sufferers.

The exodus can be viewed as a protest against the tightening post-Reconstruction conditions in the South and as an early example of power of the organized Negro, however loosely the knots of organization were tied. The failure of the migrants to establish themselves securely in their new communities and the inability of those communities to provide adequately for the newcomers discouraged future mass migrations until the twentieth century. The failure, however, should not detract from their heroic efforts. An impoverished and hitherto immobile people had ventured on their own for unfamiliar lands in a migration reminiscent of previous westward movements.

A LETTER OF ROBERT KIMBROUGH

Dear Sir,

I avail myself of the opportunity of addressing you a few lines in order to get your views on the greatest question of the day with us in the West and South. That is the migration of the Negros / sic / from the South. I think we have forwarded on from this City about 15 or 16 hundred mostly from Miss. and La. Some from our old stamping grounds in Miss. We are heartily in sympathy with them and render them all the assistance in our power. Nearly all of them that are coming are in destitute conditions but we have managed to furnish them Transportation. We have not yet received any material assistance from the White people but they seem to be willing to assist us. We have not received any aid from any place other than here at home. The newspapers stated that the old anti-slavery party had forwarded to us means and clothing but such is not the case; for up to this time we have not received anything of the kind. We have done and will continue to do all in our power to forward them on their

*Speech of Representative R. H. Cain of South Carolina, February 3, 1875, *Congressional Record*, 43rd Congress, 2nd Session, 956-957.

journey and if I live I expect to join them in Kansas soon. I cannot get anything in this section to earn a living at. I have writen to Senator Windom and will say to you that if there is any appointments to be made to look after the interest of our people in Kansas. You will do me a great favor by using your influence in my interest. Mr. C. H. Tandy will be at the Capitol in a few days and he will explain the matters more fully.

I have the honor to remain very Truly yours &c.

Robt. Kimbrough
Secretary Transportation Committee*

THE NORTH AROUSED

It is quite evident from the tone of the leading papers of the North, that the people of that portion of our country are getting warmly interested in the condition of the colored people of the South.

Many times, since emancipation was proclaimed, have the people of that part of the Union been made to feel, that the colored people were only free in name, but still there was apparently a doubt always in the minds of the very best men as to what ought to be or, as to what could be done about it, but the developments of the last few months; are showing quite plainly what can be done, and the temper of the people is getting worked up to the point of decided action in behalf of those poor unfortunate sons of toil who have suffered so long and so terribly. While the mere politician brought the stories of wrong, of persecution, and of outrage to notice, the people doubted, but when it came to pass that being no longer able to bear up under the wrongs in their own land, and thousands of the freedmen began to leave home on their own account, to seek shelter, protection, and liberty in the free states, the eyes of all friends of humanity began to open to a full realization of the fact that the time had at length arrived when they could with propriety take hold of the matter and lend a helping hand to this long abused people, and to that end money is being subscribed and clothing and other necessaries are being sent to such of the people as have succeeded in reaching the free states, and efforts to help all out of the South that desire to get out are being successfully made. The planters are getting uneaisey and are doing what they can to prevent the exodus of their laborers. They have so influenced the owners of the steamboats as to prevent them from taking on board the anxious migrationist and hence hundreds have been left on the river banks unable to get to a land of freedom, but all this is to be remedid. Boats in abundance can be had and they will be sent down the river and all that desire to get on them will be allowed to do so, and they will be landed wherever they wish to be, and then the cruel monsters of the South who have persecuted them as no other people in this country were ever persecuted, will be made to realize that though the "mills of the gods may grind slowly they certainly grind surely." The planters may send their agents

*Robert Kimbrough, St. Louis, Missouri, to Senator Blanche K. Bruce, Washington, D.C., April 3, 1879. From the Blanche K. Bruce Papers, Historical Society of Pennsylvania, Philadelphia.

among the refugees to persuade them to return, and may make all kinds of offers to them, as they have been doing through Dr. Nagle of New Orleans, but they will find that where they induce one to return South, they will meet a hundred on their way North. The people of the North, thank God, are at last aroused, and their great hearts are beating in full sympathy with the poor blacks who after their tortures of the past two centuries have determined to strike a blow for their own freedom. To the free states the colored people of the South are bound to make their way. Some will come to Kansas, and we would advise all that are prepared to go to farming to come west, and the thousands who desire to work by the day or month will bend their steps to Indiania, Illinois, Ohio, Iowa, and many others will go even further North; for the idea that the black man cannot flourish in the most extreme Northern states is all bosh, and to prove this it is only necessary in the language of John Brown Jr., to look for a moment at the hundreds of fugitives who went to Canada before emancipation and to see how well they have got along, to get that foolish notion out of the heads of all who say the black man can't stand cold.

Joseph Cook, (who, by the way is one of the noblest types of New England philanthropist, struck the key note last Sabbath in the park in this city, when he declaired that the free states all over this Union were ready to give the black man a chance, to work out his own destiny, and in that work the white people were ready to help, and to prove what he said he drew from his pocket ONE HUNDRED DOLLARS and put it into the hands of Gov, St. John with the injunction that he should use it to help the poor and needy runaways from Southern persecution. Mr. Cook, "God bless him") will return to the East and tell such a story concerning these people as will fire up not only the old abolishionist, but as will wake up the later friends of humanity and the people, the poor, downcast, and down trodden people of the South will find that with the arousing of the people of the North, will come to them such assistence as will enable them to begin a life of independence in those parts of our country where God is known, and where Jesus his son is worshiped as the Savior of all men. Thank God the North is getting aroused, which means salvation to the *black* man of America.*

AN APPEAL FOR HELP IN BEHALF
OF THE COLORED REFUGEES IN KANSAS.

One year ago this month we published a statement from Mrs. Elizabeth L. Comstock, of Topeka, setting forth the destitution of the Refugees in Kansas, asking for your contribution of money, clothing and bedding. The response was generous. We received several carloads of goods, and forwarded them to Topeka, met the demand, and saved much suffering. Then we reported 20,000 arrivals in the new State. To-day comes a similar appeal from Mrs. Comstock, saying the number has increased to over 60,000, and still they come. Our supplies are very short, extreme cold weather and exposure have induced much sickness, multitudes are suffering for fuel

*Editorial "The North Aroused," *Topeka Colored Citizen*, May 31, 1879.

and shelter and the necessaries of life, and again we ask your contribution.

Below we give extracts from letters received from our agents in Kansas, whom the Association depends upon to distribute supplies, thinking this may be the best form of appeal we can use:

"Our people (refugees) here number from 700 to 800, principally Texans, poor, simple, field hands, the poorest of the exodites, those who came overland with Texas teams, trusting hearts, no money, large families, and devout Christians, about nine-tenths of them requiring aid. Fifty sick. During the cold weather many were frostbitten, some disabled. Coughs, pneumonia, ague, are the common sickness. This cold weather the people suffer much. I am out of funds, and twenty-five dollars behind. Two poor creatures from Texas just called on me for a bed-quilt to cover them to-night, and dress each, *mothers;* I had none to give them. What we need most is medicine for the sick and help for the aged widows, then warm bedding and clothing."

Oswego, Dec. 23, '80.

W. S. Newlon

"It has been a very cold winter so far, and severe on our poor folks. Quite a number have just come from Texas. I wish I had some funds to relieve them. Great need of lumber for shelter."

Parsons, Kas. Milton W. Reynolds, Pres't Labette Co. F.R.A.

* * *

Daniel Votaw, Independence, Kas., Dec. 25, 1880: "2,500 refugees in our part of the work, 1,500 of whom need assistance, so many came too late to make crops this year. Many of them are sick. They sleep so cold at night it is killing them. Fifty of them are not able to leave their rooms or tents."

* * *

Baxter Springs, 1000 refugees; 300 the age for going to school. Not much sickness. No color prejudice. School needed. Population of whites, 1,500. Too poor to sustain a school. Bedding, warm clothing, bed ticks, shoes, greatly needed.

* * *

Chetopa, 1,000 refugees; Pneumonia, colds, &c., result of exposure. School greatly needed. Children's clothing, nourishing food for sick and aged. This village is the most direct point they reach in Kansas by railroad from Texas.

* * *

A. B. Whiting, Topeka, Kas., says, Dec. 31: "The very old and physically helpless, the widows with large families of young children, 'the lame, halt and blind' among our exodites, can be counted by hundreds. These are, and such as these always will be, objects of charity, and many children are needing clothing to fit them for school."

* * *

While we invite your contributions again for our less fortunate countrymen, we urge again that, in sending, you be careful and follow this direction. Direct them to "H. N. RUST & CO., CENTRAL WAREHOUSE, CHICAGO."

Mark each Package "RELIEF GOODS," also mark *on each package* the sender's name and address. Only in this way can we know from whom the goods come, and acknowledge the receipt of them. We are constantly in receipt of packages without the shipper's name, and as frequently the shipper wonders that we do not acknowledge the receipt of the goods. Be careful and do this and we will be prompt to acknowledge the same. Send cash contribution to WM. PENN NIXON, *Inter-Ocean*.

The principal Railroads coming into Chicago have generously brought relief goods free, and will continue so to do. The Express Companies also bring *small parcels* free, which courtesy is duly appreciated by their patrons along the different routes, and by all friends of the cause.

Respectfully yours,

Horatio N. Rust
*Secretary Southern Refugee Relief Association**

Reconstruction: A National Problem

139

THE STRUGGLE FOR EQUAL RIGHTS: EDUCATION

The education of Negro children following the Civil War was a problem in the North as well as in the South. While northeastern states generally provided schools for colored children before the war, the states of the Middle West were laggard. When the issue arose after the war, the basic decision to educate all children regardless of color came relatively quickly, leaving only the tenacious problem of whether to maintain segregated or integrated facilities. States such as Pennsylvania or Illinois which bordered on the South carried pockets of segregated schools for decades after Reconstruction. Isolated cities such as Indianapolis and New York were reluctant to move toward integration.

In 1870 the Republican-dominated Illinois state constitutional convention incorporated in the constitution a provision calling for the education of all children. The state superintendent of public instruction, who had agitated for such a provision, quickly spotted the thorns awaiting the unwary who would grasp at this new constitutional injunction. His observations clarify the dilemma of midwestern states, which was to a lesser degree matched in eastern states.

While Illinois communities gradually complied with the new constitution, it required a court case and additional pressures to persuade them that schools should be integrated. Even so, a few instances of segregation remained in Illinois, as in other northern states, well into the twentieth century.

The principle, then, is established by this first Section of the 8th Article of the supreme law of the State, that hereafter all the school-going children in Illinois, shall be equally entitled to the benefits of the free public schools, without exception or discrimination.

---

*Leaflet prepared by the Southern Refugee Relief Association (Chicago, Illinois), January 22, 1881.

All the youth of the State are, and henceforth shall be, equal before the law, in respect to their claims to a good common school education. Whatever laws the General Assembly may pass in relation to public education, whatever system of common schools may be adopted, must be in harmony with this fundamental principle. And whatever inhibitive or restrictive provisions there may be in any existing school laws, in relation to free schools; whatever therein is incompatible or in conflict with this broad and catholic rule of the fundamental law, is already abrogated by the supreme authority of the Constitution itself, and the school system, in all its parts and operations, must be administered in accordance with the letter and spirit of the new Constitution, which recognizes no distinctions or disabilities among the youth of the State.

* * *

Having long waited and watched for this great consummation, and having done what little I could to hasten its coming, I hail it now with unspeakable satisfaction. Of all the wise and noble provisions of the new organic law under which Illinois is henceforth to work out her destiny as a commonwealth, not one is wiser or nobler than that which drops the ballot alike into every hand, and, with impartial justice, dispenses to all alike, the priceless blessings of intellectual improvement and culture. God will smile upon the State that thus remembers the children of a poor and despised race, reaching out to them the helping hand.

But what is the immediate, present effect of this declaration of the supreme law, upon the *status* of those most concerned, in respect to education, and upon the powers and duties of school officers?

In my judgment, the right to a good common school education is conferred upon colored children, equally with others, by this section of the 8th Article, *ipso facto;* that the right fully accrued and attached, when the new Constitution went into effect, on the 8th of August, 1870; and that since that date, now, and henceforth, school directors, and other boards of education working under the general law, may and should provide for the free education of colored children, as efficiently and thoroughly as for the education of white children. It is not a case for labored interpretation or construction; the language of the supreme law is too explicit to need any studied interpretation, and it is as peremptory as it is clear: "Shall provide a thorough and efficient system of free schools, whereby *all the children* of this state may receive a good common school education." There is no white, no black, no exception, distinction or discrimination in this language. Its scope is co-extensive with the territorial limits of the State and the boon which it provides is for every child in the State. The only question, touching the matter of eligibility, will hereafter be: Is this youth one of the "children of this State," and of lawful school age?

* * *

I am glad to be able to say that there is a general disposition throughout the State, to recognize and give effect to the organic law, at once, in advance of any supplementary or compulsory legislation, in respect to the rights of people of color to the benefits of the system of common schools. Boards of directors have, for the most part, already included colored children in their school arrangements and provisions for the current year, and many hundreds of them are now for the first time in the public schools of the State—either in separate schools or in co-attendance with other children.

* * *

The question whether separate schools shall be provided for colored children, or whether there shall be the same schools for all, is one of very secondary importance, and should never be permitted to disturb the peace and harmony of any school district or community. It was regarded as too trivial a matter for mention, even, in the new Constitution, and, in my estimation, the Legislature would do well to be equally silent on the subject. It is one of those matters which involve no *principle* worth striving about, and which are best left to regulate themselves. All experience demonstrates the folly and futility of undertaking to control a matter of that kind by legislative enactments. The result has always been more mischief than good.

The just principle is established, the franchise is conferred, beyond the reach of even the law-making power, that all the children of the State shall receive a good common school education. The strong arm of the supreme authority is pledged to secure this for every child in the State, white or black. This is the one great fact, the one vital point, in comparison with which all else is trivial and unworthy of contention. What our colored citizens need, what they and their friends have been struggling for, is the means of educating their children; the solid boon of *knowledge-culture;* not the paltry privilege, (if it be such,) the empty name, of sitting in the same seats, or in the same house, with white children. This great right to free education they now enjoy, this inestimable boon has been conferred upon them. Let them make the most of it, and become an upright, intelligent, educated people, and all other questions and consequences will take care of themselves. I do not think that our colored citizens can *afford* to make a noise about this thing; it is unworthy of them, and of that honorable pride and self-respect which should animate them in their efforts to advance their race in the higher elements of civilization and power. I know, furthermore, that these are the views entertained by the leading minds among them, many of whom have said to me that they preferred separate schools; that they did not desire, and indeed would not permit their children to go where they were not wanted, and where they would be exposed to unfeeling taunts and insults; that in all places where the old prejudices exist, it would be better, in all respects, for their children to attend separate schools; that they were not beggars for social favors, but merely, as citizens, demanded an equal chance with others to educate their children, having no fears that *when educated* they would be able to get on in the world and take care of themselves.

* * *

With prudence and common sense, this problem will gradually and safely work out its own solution. *Prejudice* and *cost,* will be the two antagonistic forces involved in most instances, and sooner or later the *latter* will be likely to prevail. When the continued indulgence of a mere prejudice is found to be expensive, it is not probable that it will be very long persisted in. The conflict of these two opposing elements will especially appear in districts where there are but a few colored children—not enough for a separate school of reasonable size. There are a great many such districts in the State, having less than half a score, each, of colored children of school age. Now, when it is understood that these *must be provided for*—that they cannot be neglected or ignored—that there is room for them in the schools already established, where they can be educated without a dollar of additional expense, while the opening of separate schools would involve heavy outlays, for sites, buildings, teachers, fuel and all the other necessary accessories, greatly increasing the burdens of taxation, and making the cost, *per capita,* of educating this handful of colored children from five to ten times greater than that of the others—when all this comes to be perceived and reflected upon, and it is considered that the same state of things must continue from year to year, the net value of the caste-feeling that lies at the bottom of it all, will be apt to be very thoughtfully reviewed, and most likely given up. The taxpayers will be comforted by the reflection that it cannot, after all, be a very fearful degradation for them to imitate the example of the Congress of the United States, in each chamber of which a colored man now sits daily side by side with the white members of those august bodies.

In districts having colored children in sufficient numbers for separate schools of economical size, this argument will, of course, be without force, or of very little force, since, in such cases, additional school accommodations must be provided at any rate. In these cases it will be for the directors and people, both white and colored, to decide what course to pursue, and should the preference be for separate schools, such preference, whether wise or otherwise, can at least be indulged without adding to the burdens of taxation. In many such cases it may be that, for the present at least, separate schools will be advisable. They will certainly be advisable where the schools of a district would be broken up or imperilled by pursuing the other course. Wiser counsels are sure to prevail in the end.*

140

INTEGRATED SCHOOLS IN THE DISTRICT OF COLUMBIA

In 1871 the District of Columbia received a completely new statutory charter, but the section on education was brief and called for additional legislation. One bill, detailing the educational system for the district, never left the Senate. Still, a brief debate on one of the provisions relating to integrated schools permitted the Mississippi senator, Hiram R. Revels, to talk about a subject he knew at first

---

*Newton Bateman, Superintendent of Public Instruction, *Eighth Biennial Report* of the Supt. of Public Instruction of the State of Illinois, 1869-70 (Springfield, 1870), 25-29.

hand. Revels was the first of two Negroes to serve in the Senate, although his term was an abbreviated one.

Then, as now, Congressional control over the District of Columbia and the District's favored position as the site of the nation's capital made any issue there of more than local importance. So it was with the debate over segregated schools. If the amendment passed, the District would have local control and segregation would ensue. If the amendment failed, the District would have to admit all children without reference to color.

Revels' speech is unremarkable and his illustrations somewhat varnished, but he was trying by circumspection to point out that the Negro wanted the opportunity to go to school and to ride the trains and streetcars as others did—in short, the opportunity to live without special restrictions.

In regard to the wishes of the colored people of this city I will simply say that the trustees of colored schools and some of the most intelligent colored men of this place have said to me that they would have before asked for a bill abolishing the separate colored schools and putting all children on an equality in the common schools if they had thought they could obtain it. They feared they could not; and this is the only reason why they did not ask for it before.

I find that the prejudice in this country to color is very great, and I sometimes fear that it is on the increase. For example, let me remark that it matters not how colored people act, it matters not how well they behave themselves, how well they deport themselves, how intelligent they may be, how refined they may be—for there are some colored persons who are persons of refinement; this must be admitted—the prejudice against them is equally as great as it is against the most low and degraded colored man you can find in the streets of this city or in any other place.

* * *

Mr. President, let me here remark that if this amendment is rejected, so that the schools will be left open for all children to be entered into them, irrespective of race, color, or previous condition, I do not believe the colored people will act imprudently. I know that in one or two of the late insurrectionary States the Legislatures passed laws establishing mixed schools, and the colored people did not hurriedly shove their children into those schools; they were very slow about it. In some localities where there was but little prejudice or opposition to it they entered them immediately; in others they did not do so. I do not believe that it is in the colored people to act rashly and unwisely in a matter of this kind.

But, sir, let me say that it is the wish of the colored people of this District, and of the colored people over this land, that this Congress shall not do anything which will increase that prejudice which is now fearfully great against them. If this amendment be adopted you will encourage that prejudice; you will increase that prejudice; and, perhaps, after the encouragement thus given, the next step may be to ask Congress to prevent them from riding in the street cars, or something like that. I repeat, let no encouragement be given to a prejudice against those who have done nothing to justify it, who are poor and perfectly innocent, as innocent as infants. Let nothing be done to encourage that prejudice. I say the adoption of this amendment will do so.

* * *

Sir, during the canvass in the State of Mississippi I traveled into different parts of that State, and this is the doctrine that I everywhere uttered: that while I was in favor of building up the colored race I was not in favor of tearing down the white race. Sir, the white race need not be harmed in order to build up the colored race. The colored race can be built up and assisted as I before remarked, in acquiring property, in becoming intelligent, valuable, useful citizens, without one hair upon the head of any white man being harmed.

Let me ask, will establishing such schools as I am now advocating in this District harm our white friends? Let us consider this question for a few minutes. By some it is contended that if we establish mixed schools here a great insult will be given to the white citizens, and that the white schools will be seriously damaged. All that I ask those who assume this position to do is to go with me to Massachusetts, to go with me to some other New England States where they have mixed schools, and there they will find schools in as prosperous and flourishing a condition as any to be found in any part of the world. They will find such schools there; and they will find between the white and colored citizens friendship, peace, and harmony.

When I was on a lecturing tour in the State of Ohio, I went to a town, the name of which I forget. The question whether it would be proper or not to establish mixed schools had been raised there. One of the leading gentlemen connected with the schools in that town came to see me and conversed with me on the subject. He asked me, "Have you been to New England, where they have mixed schools?" I replied, "I have, sir." "Well," said he, "please tell me this: does not social equality result from mixed schools?" "No, sir; very far from it," I responded. "Why;" said he, "how can it be otherwise?" I replied, "I will tell you how it can be otherwise, and how it is otherwise. Go to the schools and you see there white children and colored children seated side by side, studying their lessons, standing side by side, and reciting their lessons, and perhaps, in walking to school, they may walk along together; but that is the last of it. The white children go to their homes; the colored children go to theirs; and on the Lord's day you will see those colored children in colored churches, and the white children in white churches. . . .

Then, Mr. President, I hold that establishing mixed schools will not harm the white race. I am their friend. I said in Mississippi, and I say here, and I say everywhere, that I would abandon the Republican party if it went into any measures of legislation really damaging to any portion of the white race; but it is not in the Republican party to do that.*

---

*Speech of Senator Hiram Revels of Mississippi, Feb. 8, 1871, *Congressional Globe,* 41st Congress, 3rd Session, Part II, pp. 1059-1060.

141

AN UNRECONSTRUCTED NATION

The Louisville Convention was called in 1883 to assert the political independence of the Negro at a time when the Republican party was discarding the issues on which it had based its Reconstruction policies. The Democratic party, not yet dominated by the South, had made consequential inroads into northern state governments and, though oriented toward a neutral or hostile policy on race questions, was not yet committed. Many of the old-line race leaders who were tied to the Republican cause by office or promise of office absented themselves and even worked to stop the Convention before the delegates gathered.

The Convention leaders did not want to compromise the spirit of independence which marked the idea of a convention. They undoubtedly believed that a strong show of race unity, without reference to party, would open the hearts and coffers of one of the parties, presumably the Republicans, to support a strong stand on issues concerning Negroes. In this they were eventually disappointed.

The Convention drew delegates from both sides of the Mason-Dixon line. The Convention appointed committees to seek Congressional assistance, to seek court action in cases involving the violation of the rights of citizenship, and to call another convention when necessary. This did not occur.

Frederick Douglass gave the keynote speech in the form of an address to the people of the United States. It was intended not only for the Convention delegates but for all citizens, Negro and white, who were or could be in some way concerned about the relations between the races in 1883.

Born on American soil in common with yourselves, deriving our bodies and our minds from its dust, centuries having passed away since our ancestors were torn from the shores of Africa, we, like yourselves, hold ourselves to be in every sense Americans, and that we may, therefore, venture to speak to you in a tone not lower than that which becomes earnest men and American citizens. Having watered your soil with our tears, enriched it with our blood, performed its roughest labor in time of peace, defended it against enemies in time of war, and at all times been loyal and true to its best interests, we deem it no arrogance or presumption to manifest now a common concern with you for its welfare, prosperity, honor and glory.

If the claim thus set up by us be admitted, as we think it ought to be, it may be asked, what propriety or necessity can there be for the Convention, of which we are members? and why are we now addressing you in some sense as suppliants asking for justice and fair play? These questions are not new to us. From the day the call for this Convention went forth this seeming incongruity and contradiction has been brought to our attention. From one quarter or another, sometimes with argument and sometimes without argument, sometimes with seeming pity for our ignorance, and at other times with fierce censure for our depravity, these questions have met us. With apparent surprise, astonishment, and impatience, we have been asked: "What more can the colored people of this country want than they now have, and what more is possible to them?" It is said they were once slaves, they are now free; they were once subjects, they are now sovereigns; they were once outside of all American institutions, they are now inside of all and are a recognized part of the whole American people. Why, then, do they hold Colored National Conventions and thus insist upon keeping up the color line between themselves and their white fellow-countrymen?

* * *

Why are we here in this National Convention? To this we answer, first, because there is a power in numbers and in union; because the many are more than the few; because the voice of a whole people, oppressed by a common injustice, is far more likely to command attention and exert an influence on the public mind than the voice of single individuals and isolated organizations; because, coming together from all parts of the country, the members of a National convention have the means of a more comprehensive knowledge of the general situation, and may, therefore, fairly be presumed to conceive more clearly and express more fully and wisely the policy it may be necessary for them to pursue in the premises. Because conventions of the people are in themselves harmless, and when made the means of setting forth grievances, whether real or fancied, they are the safety-valves of the Republic, a wise and safe substitute for violence, dynamite, and all sorts of revolutionary action against the peace and good order of society.

* * *

Our resort to this measure has been treated by many as if there were something radically wrong in the very idea of a convention. It has been treated as if it were some ghastly, secret conclave, sitting in darkness to devise strife and mischief. The fact is, the only serious feature in the argument against us is the one which respects color. We are asked not only why hold a convention, but, with emphasis, why hold a *colored* convention? Why keep up this odious distinction between citizens of a common country and thus give countenance to the color line? It is argued that, if colored men hold conventions, based upon color, white men may hold white conventions based upon color, and thus keep open the chasm between one and the other class of citizens, and keep alive a prejudice which we profess to deplore. We state the argument against us fairly and forcibly, and will answer it candidly and we hope conclusively. By that answer it will be seen that the force of the objection is, after all, more in sound than in substance. No reasonable man will ever object to white men holding conventions in their own interests, when they are once in our condition and we in theirs, when they are the oppressed and we the oppressors. In point of fact, however, white men are already in convention against us in various ways and at many important points. The practical construction of American life is a convention against us. Human law may know no distinction among men in respect of rights, but human practice may. Examples are painfully abundant.

* * *

It is our lot to live among a people whose laws, traditions, and prejudices have been against us for centuries, and from these they are not yet free. To assume that they are free from these evils simply because they have changed their laws is to assume what is utterly unreasonable and contrary to facts. Large bodies move slowly. Individuals may be converted on the instant and change their whole course of life. Nations never. Time and events are required for the conversion of nations. Not even the character of a great political organization can be changed by a new platform. It will be the same old snake though in a new skin. Though we have had war, reconstruction and abolition as a nation, we still linger in the shadow and blight of an extinct institution. Though the colored man is no longer subject to be bought and sold, he is still surrounded by an adverse sentiment which fetters all his movements. In his downward course he meets with no resistance, but his course upward is resented and resisted at every step of his progress. If he comes in ignorance, rags, and wretchedness, he conforms to the popular belief of his character, and in that character he is welcome. But if he shall come as a gentleman, a scholar, and a statesman, he is hailed as a contradiction to the national faith concerning his race, and his coming is resented as impudence. In the one case he may provoke contempt and derision, but in the other he is an affront to pride, and provokes malice. Let him do what he will, there is at present, therefore, no escape for him. The color line meets him everywhere, and in a measure shuts him out from all respectable and profitable trades and callings. In spite of all your religion and laws he is a rejected man.

He is rejected by trade unions, of every trade, and refused work while he lives, and burial when he dies, and yet he is asked to forget his color, and forget that which everybody else remembers. If he offers himself to a builder as a mechanic, to a client as a lawyer, to a patient as a physician, to a college as a professor, to a firm as a clerk; to a Government Department as an agent, or an officer, he is sternly met on the color line, and his claim to consideration in some way is disputed on the ground of color.

Not even our churches, whose members profess to follow the despised Nazarene, whose home, when on earth, was among the lowly and despised, have yet conquered this feeling of color madness, and what is true of our churches is also true of our courts of law. Neither is free from this all-pervading atmosphere of color hate. The one describes the Deity as impartial, no respecter of persons, and the other the Goddess of Justice as blindfolded, with sword by her side and scales in her hand held evenly between high and low, rich and poor, white and black, but both are the images of American imagination, rather than American practices.

Taking advantage of the general disposition in this country to impute crime to color, white men *color* their faces to commit crime and wash off the hated color to escape punishment. In many places where the commission of crime is alleged against one of our color, the ordinary processes of the law are set aside as too slow for the impetuous justice of the infuriated populace. They take the law into their own bloody hands and proceed to whip, stab, shoot, hang, or burn the alleged culprit, without the intervention of courts, counsel, judges, juries, or witnesses. In such cases it is not the business of the accusers to prove guilt, but it is for the accused to prove his innocence, a thing hard for any man to do, even in a court of law, and utterly impossible for him to do in these infernal Lynch courts. A man accused, surprised, frightened and captured by a motley crowd, dragged with a rope about his neck in midnight-darkness to the nearest tree, and told in the coarsest terms of profanity to prepare for death, would be more than human if he did not, in his terror-stricken appearance, more confirm suspicion of guilt than the contrary. Worse still, in the presence of such hell-black outrages, the pulpit is usually dumb, and the press in the neighborhood is silent or openly takes side with the mob. There are occasional cases in which white men are lynched, but one sparrow does not make a summer. Every one knows that what is called Lynch law is peculiarly the law for colored people and for nobody else. If there were no other grievance than this horrible and barbarous Lynch law custom, we should be justified in assembling, as we have now done, to expose and denounce it. But this is not all. Even now, after twenty years of so-called emancipation, we are subject to lawless raids of midnight riders, who, with blackened faces, invade our homes and perpetrate the foulest of crimes upon us and our families. This condition of things is too flagrant and notorious to require specifications or proof. Thus in all the relations of life and death we are met by the color line. We cannot ignore it if we would, and ought not if we could. It hunts us at midnight, it denies us accommodation in hotels and justice in the courts; excludes our children from schools, refuses our sons the chance to learn trades, and compels us to pursue only such labor as will bring the least reward. While we recognize the color line as a hurtful force, a mountain barrier to our progress, wounding our bleeding feet with its flinty rocks at every step, we do not despair. We are a hopeful people. This convention is a proof of our faith in you, in reason, in truth and justice—our belief that prejudice, with all its malign accompaniments, may yet be removed by peaceful means; that, assisted by time and events and the growing enlightenment of both races, the color line will ultimately become harmless. When this shall come it will then only be used, as it should be, to distinguish one variety of the human family from another. It will cease to have any civil, political, or moral significance, and colored conventions will then be dispensed with as anachronisms, wholly out of place, but not till then. Do not marvel that we are discouraged. The faith within us has a rational basis, and is confirmed by facts. When we consider how deep-seated this feeling against us is; the long centuries it has been forming; the forces of avarice which have been marshaled to sustain it; how the language and literature of the country have been pervaded with it; how the church, the press, the play-house, and other influences of the country have been arrayed in its support, the progress toward its extinction must be considered vast and wonderful.

If liberty, with us, is yet but a name, our citizenship is but a sham, and our suffrage thus far only a cruel mockery, we may yet congratulate ourselves upon the fact that the laws and institutions of the country are sound, just and liberal. There is hope for a people when their laws are righteous whether for the moment they conform to their requirements or not. But until this nation shall make its practice accord with its Constitution and its righteous laws, it will not do to reproach the colored people of this country with keeping up the color line—for that people would prove themselves scarcely worthy of even theoretical freedom, to say nothing of practical freedom, if they settled down in silent, servile and cowardly submission to their wrongs, from fear of making their color visible. They are bound by every element of manhood to hold conventions in their own name and on their own behalf, to keep their grievances before the people and make every organized protest against the wrongs inflicted upon them within their power. They should scorn the counsels of cowards, and hang their banner on the outer wall. Who would be free, themselves must strike the blow. We do not believe, as we are often told, that the Negro is the ugly child of the national family, and the more he is kept out of sight the better it will be for him. You know that liberty given is never so precious as liberty sought for and fought for. The man outraged is the man to make the outcry. Depend upon it, men will not care much for a people who do not care for themselves. Our meeting here was opposed by some of our members, because it would disturb the peace of the Republican party. The suggestion came from coward lips and misapprehended the character of that party. If the Republican party cannot stand a demand for injustice and fair play, it ought to go down. We were men before that party was born, and our manhood is more sacred than any party can be. Parties were made for men, not men for parties.

* * *

The colored people of the South are the laboring people of the South. The labor of a country is the source of its wealth; without the colored laborer to-day the South would be a howling wilderness, given up to bats, owls, wolves, and bears. He was the source of its wealth before the war, and has been the source of its prosperity since the war. He almost alone is visible in her fields, with implements of toil in his hands, and laboriously using them to-day.

Let us look candidly at the matter. While we see and hear that the South is more prosperous than it ever was before and rapidly recovering from the waste of war, while we read that it raises more cotton, sugar, rice, tobacco, corn, and other valuable products than it ever produced before, how happens it, we sternly ask, that the houses of its laborers are miserable huts, that their clothes are rags, and their food the coarsest and scantiest? How happens it that the land-owner is becoming richer and the laborer poorer?

The implication is irresistible—that where the landlord is prosperous the laborer ought to share his prosperity, and whenever and wherever we find this is not the case there is manifestly wrong somewhere.

* * *

The trouble is not that the colored people of the South are indolent, but that no matter how hard or how persistent may be their industry, they get barely enough for their labor to support life at the very low point at which we find them. We therefore throw off the burden of disgrace and reproach from the laborer where Mr. Calhoun and others of his class would place it, and put it on the land-owner where it belongs. It is the old case over again. The black man does the work and the white man gets the money.

* * *

Nor is it to be wondered at that the standard of morals is not higher among us, that respect for the rights of property is not stronger. The power of life and death held over labor which says you shall work for me on my own terms or starve, is a source of crime, as well as poverty.

* * *

No more crafty and effective device for defrauding the southern laborers could be adopted than the one that substitutes orders upon shopkeepers for currency in payment of wages. It has the merit of a show of honesty, while it puts the laborer completely at the mercy of the land-owner and the shopkeeper. He is between the upper and the nether millstones, and is hence ground to dust. It gives the shopkeeper a customer who can trade with no other storekeeper, and thus leaves the latter no motive for fair dealing except his own moral sense, which is never too strong. While the laborer holding the orders is tempted by their worthlessness, as a circulating medium, to get rid of them at any sacrifice, and hence is led into extravagance and consequent destitution.

The merchant puts him off with his poorest commodities at highest prices, and can say to him take these or nothing. Worse still. By this means the laborer is brought into debt, and hence is kept always in the power of the land-owner. When this system is not pursued and land is rented to the freedman, he is charged more for the use of an acre of land for a single year than the land would bring in the market if offered for sale. On such a system of fraud and wrong one might well invoke a bolt from heaven—red with uncommon wrath.

It is said if the colored people do not like the conditions upon which their labor is demanded and secured, let them leave and go elsewhere. A more heartless suggestion never emanated from an oppressor. Having for years paid them in shop orders, utterly worthless outside the shop to which they are directed, without a dollar in their pockets, brought by this crafty process into bondage to the land-owners, who can and would arrest them if they should attempt to leave when they are told to go.

We commend the whole subject to the Senate Committee of Labor and Education, and urge upon that committee the duty to call before it not only the land-owners, but the landless laborers of the South, and thus get at the whole truth concerning the labor question of that section.

* * *

Flagrant as have been the outrages committed upon colored citizens in respect to their civil rights, more flagrant, shocking, and scandalous still have been the outrages committed upon our political rights by means of bull-dozing and Kukluxing, Mississippi plans, fraudulent counts, tissue ballots, and the like devices. Three States in which the colored people outnumber the white population are without colored representation and their political voice suppressed. The colored citizens in those States are virtually disfranchised, the Constitution held in utter contempt and its provisions nullified. This has been done in the face of the Republican party and successive Republican administrations.

* * *

This is no question of party. It is a question of law and government. It is a question whether men shall be protected by law, or be left to the mercy of cyclones of anarchy and bloodshed. It is whether the Government or the mob shall rule this land; whether the promises solemnly made to us in the Constitution be manfully kept or meanly and flagrantly broken. Upon this vital point we ask the whole people of the United States to take notice that whatever of political power we have shall be exerted for no man of any party who will not, in advance of election, promise to use every power given him by the Government, State or National, to make the black man's path to the ballot-box as straight, smooth and safe as that of any other American citizen.

We are as a people often reproached with ambition for political offices and honors. We are not ashamed of this alleged ambition. Our destitution of such ambition would be our real shame. If the six millions and a half of people whom we represent could develop no aspirants to political office and honor under this Government, their mental indifference, barrenness and stolidity might well enough be taken as proof of their unfitness for American citizenship.

It is no crime to seek or hold office. If it were it would take a larger space than that of Noah's Ark to hold the white criminals.

* * *

We are far from affirming that there may not be too much zeal among colored men in pursuit of political preferment; but the fault is not wholly theirs. They have young men among them noble and true, who are educated and intelligent—fit to engage in enterprise of "pith and moment"—who find themselves shut out from nearly all the avenues of wealth and respectability, and hence they turn their attention to politics. They do so because they can find nothing else. The best cure for the evil is to throw open other avenues and activities to them.

We shall never cease to be a despised and persecuted class while we are known to be excluded by our color from all important positions under the Government.

* * *

We hold it to be self-evident that no class or color should be the exclusive rulers of this country. If there is such a ruling class, there must of course be a subject class, and when this condition is once established this Government of the people, by the people, and for the people, will have perished from the earth.*

---

*"Address to the People of the United States," by Frederick Douglass from *The Life and Writings of Frederick Douglass*, Vol. IV, edited by Philip S. Foner.

CHAPTER EIGHT

A Time of Transition

By the 1890's the southern Negro was reacting to both traditional and new forces in the South, and indeed the nation. Traditional areas of employment still maintained their hold. The Negro domestic often enjoyed an honored position in the white Southerner's household, both after as well as before the Civil War. Certainly the sight of Negroes picking cotton was one that had not changed in a hundred years. But there were new forces at work. The long row of women stemming tobacco shows one of the many developments of southern industry. Industry had begun to awaken the South, and employment in growing industry was to provide one of the keys the Negro would use to open new opportunities for himself. Another major force was education. The picture shows a Virginia one-room schoolhouse where both young and old acquired skills that would unlock for them the twentieth century.

INTRODUCTION

A Time of Transition

For Negroes, the last two decades of the nineteenth century posed questions more penetrating and far-reaching than any since emancipation. Because of the termination of northern Reconstruction policies and the crystallizing desire on the part of southern states to control the southern Negro, colored leaders were forced to construct new organizations with a new rationale, to seek new white friends, new sources of funds, and new techniques for combatting the new pressures. Their dilemma is summed up in a report of an interview between a white trustee of Howard University and a Negro teacher. As the Negro teacher began to tell of his difficulties, the white trustee interrupted to remark, "It is very unfortunate, but still true that your people are not united, you don't act together." When the teacher went on to say that in this instance all of the Negro teachers were on one side and all of the whites on the other, the trustee quickly observed, "Now that will never do. You must never allow a color line to be drawn."

This was a period of rising race consciousness, called by some "race nationalism," during which Negroes first utilized their mark of distinction as a proud call for unity. During this period the word "Negro" came back into use along with some short-lived alternatives like "Afro-American." Negroes, generally, came to realize that whatever they did, they had to do it in terms of their race, whether at home, at work, in school, in church, or in public places. They became aware that their objectives were race objectives and set to work to accomplish them. Their efforts along this line, some of which are documented in this chapter, were faltering and faulty, yet these laid the essential groundwork for the organizations which were to come shortly after the new century began.

And so the lines were drawn between black and white, southern whites successfully fighting to gain northern acquiescence to their management of Negroes on their own terms, Negro leaders fighting with less success to organize themselves to the point where they could demand those rights which had slipped away since Reconstruction. Most of these organizational efforts were exclusively Negro; a few, notably the work of Booker T. Washington, were established in cooperation with whites. While almost all of them eschewed politics, at base the movements were political, since the Negro realized as well as the white man that his rise would be measured by his vote.

The movements manifested greater race consciousness, too. Negroes began to realize that they had a substantive stake in protecting and expanding their rights. The Louisville Convention of Colored Men, meeting in the fall of 1883, symbolized the new era in which Negroes found themselves. Politics in the old sense of whipping up enthusiasm for the Republican party was missing. Instead, the Convention, highly representative of Negroes north and south, concentrated on larger issues of political, as distinct from partisan, rights, education, civil rights, and economic problems. The Convention reflected the rise of a new generation of Negro leadership. "Many of the old leaders were not present . . . ," the Negro reporter remarked. "They were from the first opposed to the call." Frederick

Douglass, the keynoter, was suspect to the younger generation because he was a staunch Republican partisan and officeholder, but in this instance "he soared above party."

The Civil Rights Act of 1875 was the final Congressional bulwark for the protection of Negroes to fall. In a decision announced in the fall of 1883, the United States Supreme Court declared that it was unconstitutional, in spite of a ringing dissent by Justice John Marshall Harlan. Like the Louisville Convention just a month earlier, this decision was symbolic of the new era, since it removed the protection of the federal government from areas where Negroes and whites might come together and left the jurisdiction up to the several states. Railroads, inns, restaurants, and similar places of public accommodation could be and were segregated, as education had long been, in the South and certain areas of the North. Gone was the last legal resort of the race to achieve parity. The "party" was changing its face for the Negro and resentment stirred.

Old line Negroes remained firm in their commitment to the Grand Old Party, but some of the younger ones wavered, attracted by President Grover Cleveland's efforts to appoint colored men to office and by the sympathy which he evidenced for the Negro's plight. These moved into the Democratic camp but they did not stay very long, as the southern wing of the party proved that it was dominant and adamant on racial issues. By the end of the 1880's, the national political structure seemed to exclude the Negro almost entirely.

In the South there arose one last political hope. In the middle of the decade, disgruntled southern farmers organized alliances which came together in late 1888 in a national federation. Negro farmers had organized separately in the Colored Farmers Alliance and Cooperative Union and rapidly spread into nine states and the Indian Territory (Oklahoma). Its leader, the Reverend R. M. Humphrey, and most of its organizers were white, but it was reputed to have over a million members.

The Colored Alliance grew restive under the conservative leadership which controlled their white counterpart in 1890, endorsing more radical third-party programs and the Lodge federal elections bill which the white Alliance denounced. After 1890, southern Negroes found themselves involved in a political free-for-all in which Republicans, Democrats, and the Alliance-supported Populist Party contested for their votes. The southern Populists' first tactic was to bring the Negro into party councils on an equal basis and incorporate in state platforms some measures aimed at alleviating the convict lease system and protecting the Negro's political rights. The Negro "is a citizen as much as we are," the white president of a Texas Populist convention told the delegates in 1891, "and the party that acts on that fact will gain the colored vote." However upright the desire, expediency dictated that the Populists abandon this position. Faced with epithet, violence, and fraud, the Populists replied in kind. The elections of 1892 saw their defeat in the South and the end of any political effort to work with the Negro on an equitable basis.

National politics during the 1880's staged its swan song on a race issue in the decade-long debate in Congress on the Blair bills. The focus was education, a primary race objective. The bills, sponsored by Republican Senatory Henry W. Blair of New Hampshire, called for sizable grants from the federal government to the states and fixed national attention on illiteracy and the lack of educational facilities in the South. The evidence which the bills' proponents introduced demonstrated clearly that the South was spending too little for education and the implication was just as clear that state moneys below the Mason-Dixon line were not equitably allocated between the races. This was a divisive issue in the Senate. In spite of this danger, southern Negroes in particular were strongly in favor of the bills.

As the North retreated before the southern attitude of local control, Negro race consciousness was aroused and their position strengthened by several forces the significance of which reached beyond the decade of the 1880's. Much of the thrust was concentrated in education. Even while the debate over the Blair bill raged, the Negro's rate of illiteracy declined rapidly. In terms of Negro population over ten years of age, approximately 80% were illiterate in 1870 and 70% in 1880. By 1890, the percentage had dropped to less than 60% and by 1900 to less than 45%.

Southern Negroes began to see education as their sole salvation. "We need education," the *Huntsville* (Ala.) *Gazette* admonished in 1889. Individual northern philanthropists were particularly attracted to industrial education. As Hampton Institute, the patron saint of industrial education, prospered, its doctrine became a favored one, North and South. Booker T. Washington's Tuskegee Institute, modeled after Hampton where Washington was trained, came into being in 1881. Negroes began to condemn classical education as unsuited to the needs of the race. "The moralist and the missionary are no equals for the man whose ideas of honest toil are supplemented by a common school training and an educated hand," T. Thomas Fortune wrote in 1884. Negro colleges in the South established industrial departments. Southern whites, anxious to have a trained labor supply and fearful that higher education would feed Negro resistance, fell in with the emphasis on industrial education and many states made small continuing legislative grants to these Negro institutions. "There is nothing that the young negroes of this country need to be taught," said Senator John T. Morgan of Alabama, "so much as industrial and technical education of certain descriptions. They are not calculated to become scholars; their condition in life does not warrant it."

The success with which northern Negroes confronted civil rights was another manifestation of growing race consciousness and developing strength. Their reaction to the Supreme Court's decision in the Civil Rights cases was one of dismay and outrage. They felt instinctively that they had been betrayed and they saw clearly the pattern of disabilities which was being imposed upon them. Equal Rights groups sprang up in northern states and cities and some of these took the lead in persuading state legislatures to pass civil rights acts. In Ohio, a watered-down act emerged from an acrid partisan quarrel and left the Negroes dissatisfied. In Connecticut, the legislature responded to a petition for such an act drawn up by a state-wide Negro convention. By the end of 1884, four states had enacted civil rights acts, and seven followed in 1885.

The 1880's witnessed the beginning of a flow of articles on the subject of the race question such as had never been seen before. Southerners like Senator John T. Morgan of Alabama, Henry W. Grady of Georgia, and Henry Watterson of Kentucky and others authored persuasive articles in the leading journals of the day: *Nation, Century, Forum,* and the *North American Review.* Their argument was simply that the South could take care of its own and should be left alone to do the job. Some implied that the race was dying out, an implication that would be set forth in more sophisticated statistical form in the next decade and which was demonstrably false. Taken together these articles represented the South's desire to localize and control the Negro question.

Negro spokesmen like Frederick Douglass and, later, William S. Scarborough, in national journals, and T. Thomas Fortune, John P. Green, and the Reverend Francis J. Grimke in race circles maintained a continuing rebuttal. In this decade, the race for the first time produced spokesmen whose fluency and perceptiveness marked them as mature by any standard, without regard to race. In private, many of them were discouraged, but in public they were resolute. For the most part, they were not offered an opportunity to write for national journals, and the chief burden of answering the South fell on the shoulders of George W. Cable, a former Confederate soldier living in the North, whose logic and eloquence gave the Negro group a great boost.

The debate in national magazines paralleled a growing sectional division among Negroes. When Fortune introduced the idea of a national organization for independent action in May of 1887, he got race support in the North and a mixed reception in the South. Booker T. Washington extended his "hearty and thorough endorsement" from Tuskegee, but the colored newspaper in Atlanta more cautiously asked for "the most careful thought" on it, pointing out that although the idea was advanced from the North, "it must be developed and put into practise by Southerners."

Fortune bided his time. The Republican party in 1887 was looking forward to the campaign of 1888. Out of power, it was in a position to make promises to the race which undercut any real effort for independent race action. When the promises did not materialize after the 1888 elections, Fortune raised the idea again in the fall of 1889. This time the call was answered and the race began to organize nationally in what was to be an abortive but precedent-making effort.

The first Afro-American League convention met in Chicago in January 1890. The representation from the South was scanty, reflecting the widening sectional gap. The League's importance as a race movement stemmed from several sources. It was a federation, with local branches in various states, a format which its constitution refined and which would be adapted successfully by Negroes in the early twentieth century. Its purposes were large and nonpartisan and its constitution required that its officers resign if they were elected or appointed to political office. Its local branches in the North in the next decade were active and achieved some success in working for civil rights in their localities.

What distinguished the League from previous organizations and identified it most closely with later ones was its stress on legal redress of grievances. Its constitution designated the office of attorney and spelled out objectives which repeatedly emphasized an appeal to courts of law. For the first time, an organized Negro group turned to law rather than party for justice. In concept and in statement, the Afro-American League was further testimony to the race's increased self-awareness and self-reliance. Its inability to sustain itself for more than a few years bespoke the weight of the odds.

The next decade began disastrously for the Negro; 1890 was a symbolic year. The last Blair bill was beaten in Congress. The Negro was disfranchised in Mississippi, segregated by law in Louisiana, and boldly attacked by the new Governor of South Carolina. During the decade lynching and violence increased in intensity and race riots dotted the South. Virginia, Alabama, and Georgia restricted suffrage by statute in 1892 and thereafter, one by one, the southern states fell into line. The popularity of American imperialism, carrying with it the direct implication of white supremacy, was further evidence of the nation's acquiescence in the South's racial policies.

The U. S. Supreme Court's decision in the case of *Plessy* v *Ferguson* (1895) symbolically placed the nation's blessing on the South's victory. With Justice John Marshall Harlan again in the minority, crying that "our Constitution is color-blind," the majority of the court found that separate facilities for Negroes were and could be equal. With this case, the nation relegated its "Negro Problem" to the states, to local communities and their citizens.

In a decade of despondency, one of the less well-known achievements was the emergence of the Negro woman. The voice of Ida Wells-Barnett had long been admired by the race in recognition of her shrill defiance of white supremacy; the work of Fanny Jackson Coppin as principal of Philadelphia's Institute for Colored Youth had long been respected. In 1893, however, after attempts to gain prominence for the race at the Chicago World's Fair had fizzled, the Congress of Representative Women invited a local resident to participate in a session along with recognized leaders of her race. Mrs. Fannie Barrier Williams delivered an eloquent speech on the Negro woman and the resulting publicity cultivated a widespread demand for her on the speaker's platform. She toured the country urging women to organize to effect reforms in education, home life, religion, and employment. In Memphis, she chastised the women of the race for "living below our opportunities" and wherever she spoke or wrote, she stressed the importance of women's clubs. Mrs. Williams was more of a publicist than an organization woman and left to other activists, notably Mrs. Booker T. Washington and Mrs. Mary Church Terrell, the role of organizational leadership. A National Federation of Afro-American Women was established in 1895 and merged with another group the following year to form the National Association of Colored Women, which still thrives.

The northern Negro laboring man was not able to channel his frustrations quite as easily. The trend which began in the previous decade accentuated in the 1890's, and Negroes found themselves losing out to white immigrants in job areas like barbering and domestic service, which had earlier been their domain. The Knights of Labor had made overtures to the Negro worker in the 1880's and recruited members, but local unions frequently stopped at the color line. The American Railway Union in 1893 ignored the urging of its leader, Eugene V. Debs, and kept Negroes out. The newly organized American Federation of Labor adopted an intergration policy in 1890, but only a few of its member unions followed suit. Some colored workers formed their own organizations, but these were without strength. By and large, the Negro protest in the 1890's took the form of agitation and strikebreaking. In plant after plant, the Negro accepted the role of strikebreaker because he was rejected as a union man. Meat-packing, iron and steel, textiles, railroads, and mining were some of the industries which the Negro penetrated as strikebreaker, often retaining his foothold after the strike was over. While the Negro laborer's success was measured, he was learning rapidly to move in an industrial society.

In 1886, Frederick Douglass had privately confessed the hope that "a great man" would emerge as race leader. This private hope became for some race spokesmen a public expression in the early 1890's. The erratic editor of the *Washington Bee* asserted that the new leadership would have to come from the South. The astute editor of the *Cleveland Gazette* predicted that "whoever the white people recognize in the United States will be duly enthralled by the colored people and recognized as their leader." These qualifications characterized Booker T. Washington, especially after his Atlanta Exposition address in September, 1895. Northern and southern whites alike were quick to praise the speech's tone and message and express confidence in the man. Negroes at first were split, but Negro leaders fell into line as Washington cemented his relationships with white political leaders and philanthropists.

Washington's leadership in the last years of the century was firmly established. He increased his associations with whites and engaged in political lobbying in state houses and in Washington through trusted agents. He became the dispenser of white dollars to Negro institutions; he established control, through financial arrangements, over Negro journalists like T. Thomas Fortune and Negro journals like the *Colored American*. By 1900, Washington had brought some order to the Negro group, albeit on white terms.

Viewed from this perspective, his immediate success is no mystery. Whites and Negroes alike were waiting for his kind of leadership, however much Negroes fretted under it after it arrived. A man of great charm and poise, with a knack for speaking and writing with ease and simplicity, he appealed to the vast majority of both races. His unique affirmation that he was not interested in personal political preferment moved him apart from most of his race contemporaries. On the other hand, he was jealous of his power and relentlessly guarded its sources, white and black, political and philanthropic.

The doctrine of industrial education was unpalatable to many northern Negro leaders, as much because it seemed to apply only to Negroes, as distinct from other ethnic minorities, as because it was so heavily supported by whites. The opposition began to speak out in the 1890's, still without threatening the power structure which Washington erected. The polarization between Washington's supporters and critics like W. E. B. DuBois was to become crucial in the first years of the new century.

By 1900, the Negro had made substantial progress against insuperable odds. White domination was king in the South and violence a cruel first minister. Segregation was enshrined into law, and education was a weak supplicant for funds. In the North, prejudice was virile and discrimination a reality. Yet in spite of these weighty burdens, the Negro had cut illiteracy almost in half in these twenty years and had established a modus operandi in politics and education in the South. Northern Negroes had chewed away at segregation by state law. More Negroes were attending northern colleges and universities, more Negroes were teaching in integrated public schools, more Negroes were established in professions.

Thrown back on their own resources, southern Negroes more than held their own as an increasing percentage of the population, as wage-earner, farm owner, and small business proprietor. More conscious than ever of race and more desirous than ever for race unity, the southern Negro had come a long way since the day of emancipation and the end of Reconstruction.

Perhaps most significantly, the Negro in 1900 received an invitation to return to politics, through the back door. Shortly after Theodore Roosevelt accepted the Republican vice-presidential nomination, he wrote to a Harvard-trained Negro attorney: "I wish I could meet Booker Washington and you, with Paul Dunbar, and talk the matter over at length." The "matter" in this instance was "to help the race in every way on the upward path [and to] work for them." For the Negro, the blue dawn of the new century was streaked with light.

The Negro Speaks and Acts

142

THE CIVIL RIGHTS DECISION

On October 15, 1883, the Supreme Court handed down its decision in a group of cases which are together known as the Civil Rights cases. The cases tested the constitutionality of the federal Civil Rights Act of 1875 which penalized discrimination on account of race, color, or previous condition of servitude on railroads, in inns and restaurants, and other places of public accommodation. The Court pointed out that the statute could rest only on the first section of the Fourteenth Amendment, which prohibited states from abridging the privileges and immunities of or denying equal protection of the laws to United States citizens or from depriving any person of life, liberty, or property without due process of law. The majority opinion held that the Fourteenth Amendment prohibited states from restricting the rights of citizens but that it did not give Congress the right to legislate in this area. The court dismissed as irrelevant the argument that the Thirteenth Amendment was a constitutional source for the federal statute.

Justice John M. Harlan was the lone dissenter. He argued that slavery rested upon an assumed inferiority and that the deprivations which the federal statute prohibited maintained the stigma of inferiority and slavery. Both the Thirteenth and Fourteenth Amendments, he pointed out, specifically empowered Congress to pass laws to enforce them. The Fourteenth Amendment, in particular, was relevant, since many of the private institutions which discriminated against the Negro were recognized or licensed by the state and were therefore an instrumentality of the state. The actions of these institutions were in effect actions of the state, he asserted, and the statute was constitutionally proper in prohibiting these state actions. He recognized that citizens of a state were also citizens of the United States and argued that the federal government has the obligation to enforce the rights of its citizens.

Although the Civil Rights Act of 1875 was not enforced, the Court's decision was a blow to Negro hopes. Their reaction, exemplified in this editorial, was one of bitterness and bewilderment. The editorial was written by T. Thomas Fortune, then in his early thirties, a man of considerable though erratic ability.

THE CIVIL RIGHTS DECISION

The colored people of the United States feel to-day as if they had been baptized in ice water. From Maine to Florida they are earnestly discussing the decision of the Supreme Court declaring the Civil Rights law to be unconstitutional. Public meetings are being projected far and wide to give expression to the common feeling of disappointment and apprehension for the future.

The Republican party has carried the war into Africa, and Africa is accordingly stirred to its centre.

We need not at this time review the legal aspects of the law or the decision. In times past we have done so.

It was only a few months ago that the Supreme Court declared that the Ku Klux law was unconstitutional—that the United States was powerless to protect its citizens in the enjoyment of life, liberty and the pursuit of happiness. What sort of Government is that which openly declares it has no power to protect its citizens from ruffianism, intimidation and murder! Is such a Government worthy of the respect and loyalty of honest men? It certainly does not enjoy our respect and our loyalty to it is the cheapest possession we have.

Having declared that colored men have no protection from the government in their political rights, the Supreme Court now declares that we have no civil rights—declares that railroad corporations are free to force us into smoking cars or cattle cars; that hotel keepers are free to make us walk the streets at night; that theatre managers can refuse us admittance to their exhibitions for the amusement of the public—it has reaffirmed the infamous decision of the infamous Chief Justice Taney that a "black man has no rights that a white man is bound to respect."

We look facts squarely in the face; we are not given to dodging and hedging—we believe in striking squarely from the shoulder. Then, what is the position in which the Supreme Court has left us? Simply this—we have the ballot without any law to protect us in the enjoyment of it; we are declared to be created equal, and entitled to certain rights, among them life, liberty and the pursuit of happiness, but there is no law to protect us in the enjoyment of them. We are aliens in our native land; we are denied an equal measure of that protection which flows from citizenship, and which is denied to no other class of American citizens—denied to us because the position we hold to the American people is a decidedly new and peculiar one. The colored people have been told emphatically that they have the ballot, and if they cannot use it it can't be helped. We are placed at the mercy of every lawless ruffian; we are declared to be the victims of infamous injustice without redress; we are told that we can expect nothing from the United States government, which we have always regarded as the football of the States—an expensive thing that could just as well be lopped off as not.

The Republican party has certainly tried the faith of the colored man. It has gradually stripped him of all the rights which had been given to him for his valor in the field and his patriotism in time of peace. We maintain that the Republican party has made an infamous use of the power which our votes aided to bestow upon it; we maintain that it has betrayed us at every point, and that it stands to-day denuded of its successful hypocrisy, a mean, cunning, treacherous organization.

We should not misinterpret the signs of the times; we should not be deceived by men and parties; we should not hide it from ourselves that there are huge breakers ahead. The Democratic party is a fraud—a narrowminded, corrupt, bloody fraud; the Republican party has grown to be but little better. We do not any longer know where to put our hands upon it; we are no longer able to say whether it is a friend or a foe.

We are disgusted with the Democratic party.

Our faith in the Republican party hangs upon the frailest thread.

The Government of the United States is the puppet of the States—a thing without power to protect the citizens of its own creation.*

143

FEDERAL AID TO EDUCATION

One of the most persistent debates throughout the 1880's revolved around the question of whether the federal government should grant public aid to education. From the first introduction of his bill to grant aid to common schools in 1876 until its final defeat in 1890, the leading advocate was Henry W. Blair, Republican senator from New Hampshire. Three of Blair's bills passed the Senate with diminishing majorities in 1884, 1886, and 1888, only to be kept off the House

*New York *Globe*, Oct. 20, 1883.

calendar each time. In 1890 it was defeated in the Senate by a 42-36 vote. In an effort to find a workable compromise, Blair modified his proposal slightly during the decade-long debate. By 1884 the bill gave virtually complete control over the funds to state officials rather than joint control by federal and state officials.

Because the bill proposed aiding the states on the basis of illiteracy, the states of the Old Confederacy stood to receive almost two-thirds of the total. The poorer southern states were unable to support the type of educational system which their citizens and northern philanthropists felt was necessary to cut down their illiteracy rates, which ranged from 13% in Missouri to 55% in South Carolina, and included eight states over 40%. Many southern politicians were naturally interested in having the Blair Bill pass.

Sectional overtones were everywhere present during the debates. If Northerners were going to grant such a large subsidy to the South, they wanted some guarantee that Negroes would benefit as much from it as whites. Senator Matthew C. Butler of South Carolina put this dilemma well when he observed that "as the Senator from Ohio [John Sherman] said . . . that he could not trust the South to disburse this money owing to our prejudice against the colored people, . . . in the same spirit . . . I would not trust him to control it." Eventually, Republicans wearied of efforts to support the southern Negro, and the Blair Bill formed a good index of this. In 1884, 80% of the Senate Republicans supported it; in 1890 only 59% could be found in the ranks.

But Blair never wavered from his conviction that federal aid to education was the best answer to the plight of the southern Negro. This speech was his first one, offered in support of the bill as he presented it in 1882, and affords a good summary of his views.

It is proper to observe that in the rebel States, where slavery existed in 1860, the valuation then aggregated $2,289,029,642, of which $842,927,400 was in slaves, and proper allowance must be made for this fact in estimating present power to bear taxation. The negroes were then taxed; they were productive as property. Now they require to be educated; then education would have destroyed them as property. They are now doing little more as a totality than to support themselves. Their taxable property is thus far very slight. It has been stated as a matter of pride on this floor that in Georgia colored people are taxed for $6,000,000 of property. The assessed valuation of Georgia is by the last census $239,472,559. What, then, must be the general poverty of the colored people of Georgia, even when of her total population (which is 1,542,180) 725,274 have accumulated $6,000,000, or eight dollars each, of taxable property. And if these things be so in Georgia, what must be the destitution of the colored race elsewhere throughout the South, and how idle to be talking of their educating themselves.

* * *

I speak now of the general fact, and I believe that this state of things is but temporary. It will, however, become permanent unless the proper remedy of increased intelligence and well-directed industry is applied. And to this end the means must come largely from without, for they do not exist within these States. In Kentucky and Delaware the negro child is educated only from the taxation of his own race. As a rule he can have no school at all unless from charity.

The country was held together by the strong and bloody embrace of war, but that which the nation might and did do to retain the integrity of its territory and of its laws by the expenditure of brute force will all be lost if for the subjection of seven millions of men by the statutes of the States is to be substituted the thralldom of ignorance and tyranny of an irresponsible suffrage. Secession, and a confederacy founded upon slavery as its chief corner-stone, would be better than the future of the Southern States—better for both races, too—if the nation is to permit one-third, and that the fairest portion of its domain, to become the spawning ground of ignorance, vice, anarchy, and of every crime. The nation as such abolished slavery as a legal institution; but ignorance is slavery, and no matter what is written in your constitutions and your laws slavery will continue until intelligence, the handmaid of liberty, shall have illuminated the whole land with the light of her smile.

Before the war the Southern States were aristocracies, highly educated and disciplined in the science of politics. Hence they preserved order and flourished at home, while they imposed their will upon the nation at large. Now all is changed. The suffrage is universal, and that means universal ruin unless the capacity to use it intelligently is created by universal education. Until the republican constitutions, framed in accordance with the Congressional reconstruction which supplanted the governments initiated by President Johnson, common-school systems, like universal suffrage, were unknown. Hence in a special manner the nation is responsible for the existence and support of those systems as well as for the order of things which made them necessary. That remarkable progress has been made under their influence is true, and that the common school is fast becoming as dear to the masses of the people at the South as elsewhere is also evident.

The nation, through the Freedmen's Bureau, and perhaps to a limited extent in other ways, has expended $5,000,000 for the education of negroes and refugees in the earlier days of reconstruction, while religious charities have founded many special schools which have thus far cost some ten millions more. The Peabody fund has distilled the dews of heaven all over the South; but heavy rains are needed; without them every green thing must wither away.

* * *

I have had the honor to introduce a bill (Senate bill 151) appropriating fifteen millions of dollars the first year, fourteen millions the second year, and afterward a sum diminishing one million yearly, until there shall have been ten annual distributions, the last of which would be six millions—it being thought probable that State systems could by that time maintain themselves, or that from the perpetual-fund bill, should that fortunately become a law, all the aid necessary could thereafter be derived. This bill has been reported by the Senate Committee on Education and Labor with its unanimous support so far as the amount appropriated is concerned. I believe that to give a larger sum would induce the people of the States where most of it would be expended to depend too largely upon the national Treasury for the support of their schools, and the result would be waste and inefficiency.

The community must pay to the extent of its ability, or it will lose interest in its schools and its children will not be properly educated, no matter how much money may be received, the burden of raising which the people do not feel. Besides it will be difficult for those portions of the country which are comparatively unused to the practical administration of school systems at once economically and profitably to absorb the full amount which is really needed, and which will be required as greater accommodations, competent teachers in sufficient numbers, and larger attendance of pupils are secured. The proportion of $15,000,000 which this bill would give to the Southern States would prolong their existing schools for at least three months, with present accommodations and teachers, and, in addition, would secure the extension of the school system to such districts and children as are now absolutely without the pale of any educational privileges whatever. In my belief no less sum can possibly do this.*

144

INDUSTRIAL EDUCATION FOR THE NEGRO

This description of Hampton Institute was written by a Negro attorney, T. McCants Stewart, who, at the time of its writing in 1883, was on the faculty of the Liberia (West Africa) College, and was visiting the United States to study Negro educational institutions.

Hampton Institute, in Hampton, Virginia, opened its doors in 1868. Its founder, Samuel Chapman Armstrong, was born and raised in Hawaii and graduated from Williams College. During the Civil War he commanded various regiments of colored troops and after the war he offered his services to the Freedman's Bureau. He was placed in charge of one of the eight districts for Virginia, with headquarters at Fort Monroe, soon to be moved to Hampton. His work with the Freedman's Bureau convinced him that the only hope for the freedman's future lay in industrial education.

Early in 1867 Armstrong began a long and successful crusade to locate funds to buy a 159-acre estate in Hampton and to build a major vocational school there. On April 1, 1868, the school opened with fifteen students and a temporary building. The next year Hampton Institute erected its first permanent building at a cost of $33,000, and three years later added the impressive Virginia Hall, at a cost of $76,000. A combination of Hampton's Jubilee Singers and Armstrong's prodigious labors soon opened the pocketbooks of northern philanthropists until it became the institution which Stewart described. With Armstrong as its earliest effective advocate, "the idea of industrial education," Booker T. Washington once said, "beginning for our people at Hampton, has gradually spread until . . . it has permeated the whole race in every section of the country."

The day after my arrival, I was put into the hands of an excellent New England gentleman, who was to show me through the Institute. He took me first to the barn, a large and substantial building in which are stored the products of the farm, and in which the

**Congressional Record*, 47th Congress, 1st Session, June 13, 1882, 4830-4831.

stock have their shelter. We ascended a winding staircase, reached the top, and looked down upon the Institute grounds with their wide shell-paved walls, grassplots, flower-beds, orchards, groves and many buildings—the whole full of life, and giving evidence of abundant prosperity, and surrounded by a beautiful and charming country.

* * *

We went into the shoe-making department. It is in the upper part of a two-story brick building. On the first floor the harness-making department is located. We were told that Frederick Douglass has his harness made here. One certainly gets good material and honest work; and reasonable prices are charged. In the shoe department several Indian boys and youths were at work. There were also three or four colored boys. They make annually for the United States government two thousand pairs of shoes for the Indians. They also look after outside orders, and do all the repairing, etc., of boots and shoes for the faculty, officers, and students—making fully five thousand pairs of shoes a year, if we include the repairing in this estimate. At the head of this department is a practical shoemaker from Boston. Each department has a practical man at its head. We visited, not all the first day, the blacksmith, wheelwright and tin shops, and looked through the printing office, and the knitting-room, in which young men are engaged manufacturing thousands of mittens annually for a firm in Boston. These two departments are in a commodious brick edifice, called the "Stone Building." It is the gift of Mrs. Valeria Stone.

One of the most interesting departments is located also in the "Stone Building"—the sewing-room. In it are nearly a score, perhaps more, of cheerful, busy girls. The rapid ticking of the machine is heard, and the merry laugh followed by gentle whispers gives life to the room. These young girls are the future wives and mothers; and the large majority of them will be married to poor men. In the kitchen, the laundry, and the sewing-room, they are acquiring a knowledge and habits of industry that will save their husbands' pennies, and thus keep them from living from hand to mouth, making an everlasting struggle to save their nose from the grindstone. In the schoolroom, they are gathering up those intellectual treasures, which will make them in a double sense helpmeets unto their husbands.

Standing in the carpenter and paint shops, and in the saw mill, and seeing Negro youths engaged in the most delicate kind of work, learning valuable and useful trades, I could not help from feeling that this is an excellent institution, and that I would like to have my boys spend three years here, from fourteen to seventeen, grow strong in the love for work, and educated to feel the dignity of labor, and get a trade: then if they have the capacity and desire to qualify for a "top round in the ladder," for leadership in the "world's broad field of battle," it will be time enough to think of Harvard and Yale and Edinburgh, or perhaps similar African institutions.

Mr. George H. Corliss, of Rhode Island, presented to the school in 1879 a sixty-horse power Corliss engine. Soon after Mr. C.P.

Huntington, of the Missouri & Pacific R.R., gave a saw mill, and as a result of these gifts large industrial operations were begun. The saw mill is certainly an extensive enterprise. Logs are brought up from the Carolinas, and boards are sawn out, and in the turning department fancy fixtures are made for houses, piazzas, etc.

There are two farms. The Normal School farm, and the Hemenway farm, which is four miles from the Institute. On the former seventy tons of hay and about one hundred and twenty tons of ensilaged fodder-corn were raised last year, besides potatoes, corn, rye, oats, asparagus, and early vegetables. Five hundred thousand bricks were also made. The Hemenway farm, of five hundred acres, is in charge of a graduate and his wife. Its receipts reach nearly three thousand dollars a year, and the farm promises to do invaluable service in time towards sustaining this gigantic work. All of the industries do not pay. For example, the deficit in the printing office last year was about seven hundred dollars. This is due to the employment and training of student labor. The primary aim is not the making of money but the advancement of the student. After they learn, they are good, profitable workmen; but they then leave the Institute to engage in the outside world in the battle of life. On the farm is a large number of stock, milch cows and calves, beef cattle, horses and colts, mules, oxen, sheep and hogs—in all nearly five hundred heads.

In these various industries, the farm, saw mill, machine shop, knitting, carpentering, harness making, tinsmithing, blacksmithing, shoe-making, wheelwrighting, tailoring, sewing, printing, etc., over five hundred students are engaged in 1883. They earned over thirty thousand dollars—an average of seventy dollars each. There is no question about the fact that this is a "bee-hive" into which a bee can enter, if accepted, with nothing but his soul and his muscle, and get a good education!*

145

A PLEA TO REPUBLICANS

In May, 1884, seventy-five delegates from twelve states convened in Pittsburgh in an almost exclusively northern convention. Frederick Douglass was present, representing the District of Columbia, but considerable opposition developed to his active participation. The convention was calculated to strengthen the Republican party's backbone on race issues and to hold wavering Negro leaders in the party fold.

John P. Green was an Ohio legislator who was born in North Carolina in 1845 and moved to Cleveland at the age of twelve years. A high school graduate, he studied law and then spent a brief period in South Carolina during Reconstruction. Returning to Cleveland, he was elected Justice of the Peace for three successive terms and, in 1881, to the lower house of the state legislature. He was the first Negro to serve in the state Senate. As a legislator, he was

*T. Thomas Fortune, *Black and White: Land, Labor, and Politics in the South* (New York; Fords, Howard, & Hulbert, 1884), pp. 87-90.

known for his advocacy of civil rights and as the "Daddy of Labor Day" since he introduced the state Labor Day bill which became law in 1890. Under Presidents William McKinley and Theodore Roosevelt he had a patronage position in the Post Office Department in Washington.

MR. CHAIRMAN AND GENTLEMEN: The Negro-hating class of the United States, not satisfied that they robbed us of our liberties, and for two hundred and fifty years subjected us to bondage worse than death, which prostituted our manhood, and denied us all the essentials to the pursuit of happiness, have to-day, like their Attic prototype, prepared for us a procrustean bed, to which we must conform, or lie in torture on it. If too short, they would stretch us to its dimensions, and if we overreach, curtail our fair proportions. Such an emergency as this, my friends, we are here to ponder over, and how we best may meet it.

It is a sad reflection for the young colored men of this day and generation that, though they are nominally free, they are as a matter of fact so proscribed and hampered by class legislation, unjust decisions and caste distinctions, as almost to produce in their mind the conviction that the term citizen is a delusion and a snare—meaning one thing in the North, and another in the South—everywhere varying in its signification, according to the color of the person to whom it is applied. Turn where he may, he is confronted with a discouraging paradox. In Ohio, Indiana, and other States of the North, for instance, the colored man is a citizen, and by implication the equal of every other citizen; yet if he has in his veins "a distinct and visible admixture of African blood," he is not, according to law, the equal of the white citizen. In South Carolina, Georgia and all Southern States, he has the right of suffrage, nominally, but he finds that custom has made "a scarecrow of the law" and he has neither a "free ballot nor a fair count." At every point, although to the manor born, at home, and in the midst of friends (?) he is none the less an alien and an outcast—hated, shunned and despised.

* * *

What can be more hateful than a law like the following, found upon the pages of the revised statutes of Ohio, and to the same effect in other Northern states: "A person of pure white blood who intermarries, or has illicit carnal intercourse with any Negro, or person having a distinct and visible admixture of African blood; or any Negro, or person having a distinct and visible admixture of African blood, who intermarries, or has illicit carnal intercourse with any person of pure white blood, shall be fined not less than one hundred dollars, or imprisoned not more than three months, or both." (R. S. 6987). Here then is a statute that prescribes and limits our social status, and makes criminal in us an act which is permitted to every other race under the sun, and to-day, unless he has been pardoned, a colored man languishes in prison in the city of Toledo, Ohio, for marrying a white woman, an act which is not denied to any man in the State of Ohio, except to those of African descent. Far be it for me, or any other colored man, so far as my knowledge goes, to entertain a desire to trespass on the society of any person, or force our company on one who does not desire it, be she white or colored; for our social domain is sufficiently broad and varied to satisfy the most exacting, embracing, as it does, ladies of all shades of color to be found on the habitable globe. But to sit still, in this progressive age, with an obnoxious law, which discriminates against us on account of our racial affinity, staring us in the face, and menacing our future welfare, would be not only unwise, but criminal.

* * *

Laws passed ostensibly for the punishment and suppression of crime, but in reality to entrap and enslave the ignorant and too-confiding freedmen, are seized upon as a sure and never failing source for the supply of labor for the coal mines of Alabama, and the construction of public works in most of the Southern States. Speaking of this system, a committee of the Mississippi Legislature says: "Crimes have been committed under the guise of law, more cruel and offensive than in the Fleet and Marshalsea under the English system;" and in regard to the subletting system the report says: "It is so horrible that the committee deem it improper to make public its horrors." Some one may say, "These laws are of a general nature, and hence bear equally upon persons of both races." There might be some ground on which to base such a statement, were it not for the glaring facts, that in those States where these systems are in vogue, the laboring and lower classes are composed almost exclusively of colored people, and the juries, judges and witnesses are nearly all white men, who believe that the natural estate of the Negro is to labor for them and for the additional reason that the convicts so sentenced and ill-treated are almost exclusively colored.

* * *

These evils call loudly for redress, and woe betide us if we heed not the cry! But listen, my friends, and I will speak to you of another monster of evil, whose Gargantuan proportions, restricted to no particular section of this country, cast a baleful shadow, to dwarf and blight the energies of every colored American. I refer to caste prejudice; an influence as widespread as it is obnoxious to its victims; which defies all statutory enactments, yields to no physical pressure, and will, I fear, succumb only to the stern logic of events. It is so thoroughly woven in the texture of our social fabric, that it confronts a colored man wheresoever he may turn. Is there a youth of African descent born in this land of liberty, in the full blaze of our boasted civilization, whose hopes beat high, and whose aspirations would lead him up the mount of fame! Then let him not imagine that any laudable ambition, profound learning, suavity of manner, or correctness of deportment, can open for him the doors which caste has closed against him, or make for him a place at the fireside of the dominant race. If he would keep alive the precious germ and make it bear perennial fruit, let him stop this bane as he would the deadly simoom and seek for strength and encouragement from that source from which all blessings flow. However, the worst phase of this iniquity does not consist in the fact that the colored American is, at home, a social pariah, whose very touch is shunned; it lies deeper than this, and becomes oppressive, when met in the commercial world, obstructing our progress and keeping us poor. The road to clerical positions is nearly blocked by it; the doors of school houses are closed against us asking positions as teachers, unless it be in schools for colored children exclusively, and our ministers are remanded to the pulpits of colored organizations. The doors to lodges and benevolent associations refuse to open to us knocking, while barber-shops, restaurants, hotels and common carriers, either refuse flatly to accommodate us, or else make us to feel that we are of the despised race by insulting us. Recognizing the fact that matters of a strictly social nature will regulate themselves, and that every man has a right to select his own company, no gentleman or lady of color demands or expects any legislation in this behalf, for to do so, would be superlative nonsense. But while the foregoing is true, it is none the less a fact that, where this prejudice intervenes to rob us of the means necessary to the enjoyment of our civil rights, we do complain, and look to the government to protest and shield us by direct legal enactment. And, here, again, we are confronted by another paradox, as enunciated by our model Supreme Court; that is to say, the constitution has created us citizens, but except in the territories, has conferred upon us no rights which Congress can protect us in.

* * *

It will hardly be disputed that in the past, when we were bound down in grief and sorrow, that grand organization known as the Republican party, like a white winged angel of mercy, came to our rescue, and pulled us out of the slough of despond, placed our feet upon the rock of liberty, threw about our shoulders the mantle of citizenship, and placing in our hands improved arms and the ballot as our shield of defense, if properly used, bade us advance and protect ourselves in the rights of life, liberty and the pursuit of happiness. For all this we are grateful, and say "God bless the grand old party!" But this is not sufficient; it must do more ere its noble mission will be fulfilled. In its platforms, and by the utterances of some of its most conspicuous standard bearers, it has declared in favor of the equality of all men before the law. Nay, more; we have been taught to believe by the platforms and declarations of that party in the past, that it stood for just such a centralized form of government as could and would protect the humblest citizen in all the fundamental rights implied in the term, and would merit and gain the dignified term "nation." Will it longer stand by in silence, while good men and true are denied their citizenship in sections of this country, and murdered while quietly attempting to maintain them? Is it ready now to admit that this government has not the power under the law to protect the humblest citizen in the enjoyment of his civil liberties? That its only power is to tax and draft for war, giving nothing in return? or will it stand by the doctrine that this government is of the people and for the people, having in its organism those essential inherent qualities which will perpetuate its own existence, and gain the respect and love of the citizen? If the former, we would none of it; but if the latter, then are we willing to once again rally to its support, and contribute of our votes and influence, and of our blood if need be, as we have done many another time in the past, to the end that it may maintain its position of proud eminence. There is one danger, however, incident to this age of magic that we must guard against. I refer to the danger of being too easily discouraged. Our progress during the last two decades has been of such a phenomenal nature, that we are apt to become discouraged if we do not see the results of our labor speedily appear. This should not be; for though the picture disclosed to our view is a sad one in many respects, when compared with that which confronted us twenty years ago it is full of encouragement. From every section of this glorious land come encouraging reports as to the progress of the colored Americans. In the South, where his name is legion, he only needs protection and a little encouragement, to enable him to become a strong tower of defense. Thoroughly American in all his feelings and sympathies, with a willing heart and strong arm, the United States may well be proud of him as a reliable source of strength in a time of need. He is accumulating wealth and heeping up stores of knowledge, and his influence is destined to be felt for good for all time to come.*

146

THE AFRO-AMERICAN LEAGUE

The Afro-American League was the first real effort to establish a continuing Negro association. The ante-bellum convention movement was largely local or sectional. The post-Civil War conventions were largely political and unconnected. The structure and objectives of the Afro-American League had considerable influence on the later Niagara Movement and the National Association for the Advancement of Colored People.

The first call for the League came in 1887 but was ignored because of the impending campaign and election of 1888. The second call came in October 1889, at which time, the originator of the League idea, T. Thomas Fortune, reprinted the earlier call and suggested constitution, asserting that the time had come. The League was scheduled to meet in Louisville, but the location was changed to Chicago which could offer more adequate and less segregated facilities. This change may have reduced somewhat the representation from the deep South.

Southern representation was a vital concern of the League which was heralded by its supporters as a national organization. Fortune withdrew as a candidate for the presidency of the League in favor of a well-known North Carolina educator, J. C. Price. The permanent chairman was a Georgian, W. A. Pledger, who had had the same position in the Louisville Convention seven years earlier. In spite of these earnest efforts, northern Negroes predominated.

In keynoting the convention, Fortune advanced some novel proposals. He urged the formation of an Afro-American bank, a lobbying committee in Washington, and an emigration bureau to assist internal migration. In one form or another, each of these was to become a reality after 1900. Urban Negroes established banks in their own cities, national Negro organizations supported lobbyists, and the National Urban League performed some of the services of an emigration bureau.

---

*New York *Globe*, May 3, 1884.

CONSTITUTION OF THE AFRO-AMERICAN NATIONAL LEAGUE

Article II.

The objects of the League are to protest against taxation without representation; to secure a more equitable distribution of school funds in those sections where separate schools exist; to insist upon a fair and impartial trial by a judge and jury of peers in all causes of law wherein we may be party; to resist by all legal and reasonable means mob and lynch law whereof we are made the victims and to insist upon the arrest and punishment of all such offenders against our legal rights; to resist the tyrannical usages of all railroad, steamboat and other corporations, and the violent or unlawful conduct of their employees in all cases where we are concerned, by prosecution of all such corporations and their employees, in State and Federal Courts; to labor for the reformation of all penal institutions where barbarous, cruel and unchristian treatment of convicts is practiced and assist healthy immigration from terror-ridden sections to other and more law-abiding sections. The objects of the League are to encourage State and local leagues in their efforts to break down color bars, and in obtaining for the Afro-American an equal chance with others in the avocations of life, and to unite with such branch leagues for organized and effective work in securing the full privileges of citizenship.

* * *

ADDRESS OF THE AFRO-AMERICAN LEAGUE

To the Citizens of the Republic: We feel it to be our solemn duty to state the reasons which impel us to meet in national convention, to form an organization of such a character as the Afro-American League is designed to be.

In all times it has been the custom of mankind to give reasons for the inauguration of any movement having for its objects the reformation of great abuses which threaten the sacred liberties of those who take such a step.

We are citizens of the great Republic. We are not aliens. In war and peace, in the avenues of industry, and upon the fields of carnage where the soldiers of the Nation battled for the perpetuation of the Republic, we have not shirked any duty. We have been true to the Constitution, true to the best traditions of the Republic, and we feel that the Nation will adjudge our contention just and the course we have deemed it wise to pursue manly and patriotic. It has become patent to all candid men that the results of the war of the rebellion are not such as the people anticipated when the slave was manumitted and the freeman was enfranchised. It cannot be denied that although slavery had been abolished by the supreme voice of the people an industrial system had been established upon it in certain sections as unjust, grinding, and as inhuman as that which it has replaced.

* * *

In the organization of the Afro-American League we hope to secure, by non-partisan action, by submitting our cause to the entire people, the co-operation of all lovers of justice and fair play, even as in the days before the war, of whatever party, in our contention. We hope to stimulate among the Afro-Americans more thrift, more economy and a higher morality.

We hope to lead the Afro-American into ways of more correct education, the better to meet the present requirements of the age. To this end we rely more upon the wisdom of establishing agricultural, mechanical and business schools, together with the academical and professional schools, rather than maintaining exclusive schools for mental training. We hope, and earnestly expect, that each State in which large numbers of Afro-Americans are congregated will supplement the appropriations now made for the maintenance of public schools, by liberal appropriations for the establishment and maintenance of such agricultural, mechanical and business schools, which can be easily made self-sustaining. We also favor the principle of National aid for the education of the people.

* * *

The unsuspected number of atrocities committed in many of the Southern States within the past year, together with the fact that such outrages have from time to time disgraced the majesty of the law in those States and brought the entire Nation into disrepute in the eyes of the civilized world, convinced us that an abnormal condition, from whatever cause, prevails in those States in so far that it is commonly understood and believed that the law in the South is not expected to be observed by white citizens, and that they are considered above the law.

We firmly believe that many of our white fellow-citizens of the South, as well as in other sections of the country, deplore and condemn this fearful conditions of affairs, and are anxious for the credit of their States, that the law shall be impartially administered. We hope to enlist the co-operation of this element of our fellow-citizens in creating a healthier public opinion, and in securing the enforcement of the laws without fear or favor, and without regard to race, and in condemning and bringing to justice all offenders against the majesty of the law.

To enable us to secure the ends of the Afro-American League, we urge upon the people the establishment of the Afro-American banks; we urge them to engage in co-operative industry; we urge them to educate their hands as well as their heads, and, while acknowledging the efficiency and wisdom of well directed migration within the United States, we urge upon the people the necessity of a more equal distribution of the Afro-American population throughout the country; we urge them to co-operate with us in the work of the league in creating an opinion in the Nation by which we shall ultimately, with the providence of God, work out the great destiny of which we feel we share in common with our fellow citizens of all other nations.*

* * *

---

*Constitution and Address to the Nation of the Afro-American National League, New York, Jan. 25, 1890.

147

A SOUTHERN EXECUTIVE VIEWS THE NEGRO

During the late nineteenth century a new group of politicians came to power in the South. Supported by the back-country poor whites, they sought to wrest control of their states from the aristocratic and pro-business Redeemers, who had, during the 1870's, overturned the Radical regimes. Their programs varied from state to state, but generally they favored greater political representation for the poor whites, a more equally distributed tax burden, an end to the corrupt alliances between corporations and politicians, regulation of railroads, and disfranchisement of those Negroes who still had the ballot.

For Benjamin R. Tillman this meant a headlong battle with the economic conservatives who ran the Democratic party, men like Wade Hampton of his own South Carolina, and President Grover Cleveland, whom Tillman once threatened to stab with a pitchfork, thus earning for himself the nickname Pitchfork Ben. Long an enemy of the Negro, Tillman had been a leading instigator of the bloody Hamburg, S. C., riot in 1876, and had organized the vigilante Red Shirts to prevent Negroes from voting in that election. After two unsuccessful attempts to dictate the Democratic nomination for governor in 1886 and 1888, Tillman decided to capture that office for himself. He had built up a solid reputation as a reformer during his two previous attempts, and with a program of over-turning the influence of corporations in the legislature and broader white participation in education, he won the governorship in 1890.

After two reform terms as governor, Tillman was elected to the Senate in 1894, and there he served for the rest of his life. It was in Washington that he made a national reputation as his generation's most vitriolic opponent of the Negro. In 1895, before assuming his Senate seat, he led the South Carolina constitutional convention which took away the Negro's last vestige of participation in the political process of South Carolina.

The crowd which assembled to hear his inaugural speech in 1890 was the largest one to gather at Columbia since the Redeemers had defeated the reconstruction regime in 1876. "We come as reformers," Tillman said, and most of his address was given over to the specific reforms he pledged to enact, but his brief discourse on the Negro was a succinct statement of his views.

INAUGURAL ADDRESS

Gentlemen of the General Assembly:

It is seldom in the history of politics that a man is so honored as I am. It is not customary to perform the ceremony of inauguration in public, and only once before, that I am aware, has it been necessary in South Carolina to hold it in the open air in order to let the people see. To the large number of my fellow citizens who have done me the honor to come as witnesses of this impressive ceremonial, I can only say in simple words, "I thank you." To the people I owe my election after a most memorable canvass. To the people only I owe allegiance, and to the people I pledge loyal service.

* * *

Before I proceed to discuss in plain straightforward fashion the legislation I shall ask you to consider, I desire to congratulate you upon the signal victory achieved by the people at the recent election.

Democracy, the rule of the people, has won a victory unparalleled in its magnitude and importance; and those whose hearts were troubled as they watched the trend of National legislation in its unblushing usurpation of authority, its centralizing grasp upon the throat of the States, its abject surrender to the power of corporate money and class interests—all such must lift up joyful hearts of praise to the All-Ruler, and feel their faith in the stability of our republican institutions strengthened. In our own State the triumph of Democracy and white supremacy over mongrelism and anarchy, of civilization over barbarism, has been most complete. And it is gratifying to note the fact that this was attended by political phenomena which was a surprise to all of us. Our colored fellow citizens absolutely refused to be led to the polls by their bosses. The opportunity of having their votes freely cast and honestly counted, which it has been claimed is denied the negroes, caused scarcely a ripple of excitement among them. They quietly pursued their avocations and left the conduct of the election to the whites. Many who voted cast their ballots for the regular Democratic ticket, and the consequence is that today there is less race prejudice and race feeling between white men and black men of South Carolina than has existed at any time since 1868.

The dismal experiment of universal negro suffrage, inspired by hate and a cowardly desire for revenge; the rotten government built upon it and propped with bayonets; the race antagonism which blazed up and is still alive; the robbery under the forms of taxation; the riot and debauchery in our legislative halls and in our Capitol; the prostitution and impotence of our Courts of justice, while rape, arson and murder stalked abroad in open daylight; the paralysis of trade; the stagnation of agriculture; the demoralization of society; the ignorance, the apathy, the despair which followed and brooded over the land—all these things have we endured and survived. Nearly a quarter of a century has passed since the two peoples who occupy our territory were taught to hate each other. The carpet-bag vampires and native base traitors who brought it about and kept it alive for their own sinister purposes are nearly all gone. There never was any just reason why the white and black men of Carolina should not live together in peace and harmony. Our interests are the same, and our future, whether for weal or woe, cannot be divorced. The negro was a staunch friend and faithful servant during the war, when there was every opportunity to glut upon our wives and children any hatred or desire for revenge. He had none. There is not a single instance on record of any disloyalty to his master's family during that trying and bloody period. The recollection of this fact should make us charitable towards him for the excesses to which he was excited by the opportunity, example and instigation of his white leaders during the dark days I have just depicted. His conduct in the recent political campaign shows that he has begun to think for himself, and realizes at last that his best friends and safest advisers are the white men who own the land and give him employment. When it is clearly shown that a majority of our colored voters are no longer imbued with the Republican idea, then the vexed negro problem will be solved, and the nightmare of a return to negro domination will haunt us no more. Cannot I appeal to the magnanimity of the dominant race? Cannot I pledge in your behalf that we white men of South Carolina stand ready and willing to listen kindly to all reasonable complaints? To grant all just, right and safe privileges to these colored people? That they shall have equal protection under the law and a guarantee of fair treatment at our hands?

That the colored people have grievances, it is idle to deny. That the memory of the wrongs and insults heaped upon the whites by the blacks during their eight years' rule, has provoked retaliation, and often injustice, is true. It was natural and inevitable. But we owe it to ourselves as a Christian people; we owe it to the good name of our State, which has been blackened thereby, and its prosperity retarded, that these things should be stopped. The whites have absolute control of the State government, and we intend at any and all hazards to retain it. The intelligent exercise of the right of suffrage, at once the highest privilege and most sacred duty of the citizen, is as yet beyond the capacity of the vast majority of colored men. We deny, without regard to color, that "all men are created equal"; it is not true now, and was not true when Jefferson wrote it. But we cannot deny, and it is our duty as the governing power in South Carolina to ensure to every individual, black and white, the "right to life, liberty and the pursuit of happiness."

With all the machinery of the law in our hands; with every department of the government, Executive, Legislative, and Judical held by white men; with white juries, white Solicitors, white Sheriffs, it is simply infamous that resort should be had to lynch law, and that prisoners should be murdered because the people have grown weary of the law's delay and its inefficient administration. Negroes have nearly always been the victims; and the confession is a blot on our civilization. Let us see to it that the finger of scorn no longer be pointed at our State because of this deplorable condition of affairs. Let us hunt out the defects in our laws; let us make plain and simple the rules of Court which have outraged justice by granting continuances and new trials upon technicalities. Let us insist that only intelligent, sober, virtuous citizens sit on our juries. Let punishment for crime, by whomsoever committed, be prompt and sure, and with the removal of the cause the effect will disappear. And as a last desperate remedy, to be used only when others fail, grant the Executive the power of absolute removal of any Sheriff who fails to prevent any such act of violence in his County after the law has taken control of the prisoner.*

---

*Benjamin R. Tillman's First Inaugural Address in *Journal of the House of Representatives of the General Assembly of the State of South Carolina . . . 1890* (Columbia, 1891), pp. 130-133.

148

HELPING THE NEGRO TO HELP HIMSELF

The Lake Mohonk Conference on the Negro Question met on June 4, 5, and 6, 1890. Although ex-President Rutherford B. Hayes was disappointed that more Southerners did not accept the invitation, he was pleased that at least seventeen Southerners did. The Conference agreed on a six-point program for the Negro's future, underlining the need for industrial education and repeating the Christian virtues of thrift, temperance, self-reliance, and the importance of the Christian home and family. They concluded with a "fraternal" invitation to all Americans "to the unselfish service of helping the Negro to help himself." This platform pretty well reflected the tone of the Conference.

Almost the sole dissenting view to the majority approach was that offered by Judge Albion W. Tourgée. Where the other participants were deliberative, Tourgée was, in the words of Hayes, "an orator—pungent, dramatic, original, and daring." For a generation before the conference he had been an outspoken defender of the southern Negro. Raised in Ohio, he moved to North Carolina in the fall of 1865, and there he developed a reputation as one of the most brilliant Northerners to serve any Reconstruction regime. His novels attempted to humanize the southern Negro to his generation, and to show the evil influence of many white institutions.

Tourgée demonstrated that he did not subscribe to the Conference view of industrial education. Now he rose to state his general observations on the role of the Negro in the United States. That Tourgée's speech should have been controverted by three such different men as a scholar, a banker, and a southern businessman showed the extent to which whites had reached a consensus by 1890. Andrew D. White was a graduate of Yale who attended many European universities. Trained as a historian, White became president of Cornell in 1868, and transformed that struggling college into a respectable university. Roeliff Brinkerhoff was a Union general during the Civil War. After the war he became a banker in Ohio, and took a deep interest in prison reform. Of Mr. Glenn little is known except that he was a Baltimore businessman.

ALBION W. TOURGEE

I have not always been quite sure that the teaching we are giving the Negro is the very best, either for him or for ourselves. It has occurred to me that God and Mammon are queerly mixed in the ideal we commend to him. Praise God and make money seems to me a fair paraphrase of the advice given him even here. I doubt the good results of the prescription. Remember, he may take us literally. There is danger that such an education may produce hypocrites and misers. Men are needed, I think, more than ministers; example rather than exhortation. I may be wrong, but I have thought wise expenditure a more important lesson for the race to-day than rigid economy. To my mind, every rich Negro is an evidence of bad teaching. No Negro has a right to be rich while so many of his people are ignorant and unformed. But what can we expect? They are black and "inferior." Freedom did not make them wise and perfect, as it no doubt would if they had been white. They have taken us at our word. They are better economists than we ourselves. They live with less expenditure than any equal number of white people. A larger proportion of them have become land-owners than of any equally impoverished and unprepared class of whites in a like period, a smaller proportion of them are supported by public charity, a larger number of them have become rich, and their aggregate possessions are greater than any equal number of illiterate, landless whites without inheritance or fortuitous discovery ever accumulated in twenty-five years. Not a single white teacher who preaches the gospel of economy to the colored man can begin to live on what the majority of his hearers deem abundance. It is the lesson of wise and fruitful expenditure that should be most earnestly enforced. The race needs heroes and patriots and martyrs rather than millionaires. And they will have heroes and patriots—men who will joyfully live and die for their fellows—when they have learned to honor devotion to the right, and when individual self-sacrifice for the collective good is accounted a better thing than successful accumulation.

So far as the peaceful and Christian solution of the race problem is concerned, indeed, I am inclined to think that the only education required is that of the *white* race. The hate, the oppression, the injustice, are all on our side; and every Negro who wins the honors of his class in a Northern college, becomes a cashier in a national bank at Topeka, writes a story which New England people read, publishes a newspaper which white people are compelled to peruse, wins a membership in the Boston Press Club, becomes a dry-goods clerk in Chicago, or so good a ball-player that a crack club has to secure his services lest another should—each and every one of these colored men is a missionary sent of God to the white people of the United States, to teach them the fundamental truth of Christianity.

There are three elements of the race problem in the United States,—the white man of the North, the white man of the South, and the Negro. The problem itself consists chiefly of the views which these three elements take of the Negro and his relation to the others. The Northern white man's view of the Negro is easily stated. He regards him either with complete indifference or as a mere object of compassion,—one of those "weaklings" whom Dr. Harris informed us we were not required to treat with justice,—who is to be supplied with a nursing-bottle, and encouraged to suck it as peaceably as may be. He is at best only an object of charity. Such a thing as duty or a bond of reciprocal interest and obligation existing between them is hardly thought of. Some go so far as to say, and sometimes, perhaps, even to *believe,* that there is no race problem,—nothing to be done to wipe out the memory of past wrong or give assurance of future opportunity.

With few exceptions, the white man of the South regards the colored man as a predestinate inferior, to be governed, controlled, and treated as such, to be educated and trained for a secondary and subordinate position. This does not necessarily imply unkindness or intended injustice. It only means the assertion of inherent superiority, and by inference the right to prescribe what constitutes justice to the Negro, what privileges shall be granted to him, and what degree of subserviency shall be demanded of him. This was the hypothesis on which slavery rested. It is the view which colored all our past civilization. It overthrew the presumptions of the common law and in the name of Jesus Christ pronounced, by the authority of the churches, the ban of eternal subjection against the superstitious child of Ham. . . .Whitefield urged the introduction of slavery into Georgia as a Christian duty, and advocated the importation of Negroes in order that they might be Christianized with the same fervor that their deportation is now urged, that they may be reheathenized.

* * *

Instead of treating the man of dusky skin as we *know* we would wish him to treat us in like conditions, we simply make it the measure of our duty that we shall treat him as well as we can afford to do, without interfering with our own comfort or prejudices, or as well as *we* think he ought to be treated. Even we who are met here to discuss the Negro, to deplore his infirmities, to magnify our charity, to extol our own excellences and determine what ought to be done with and for him, do not regard his opinion about the matter as at all important. We do not ask him what he thinks of his conditions. Not one in all this assembly has put the question, "In his condition, how would we wish the residue of the American people to treat us?"

* * *

We congratulate ourselves on what we have contributed for his mental and religious development, but quite ignore the fact that for every dollar we have given for his enlightenment he had before given a thousand for our enrichment. We boast of the public school system of the States of the South, in which so many colored children are being educated; but we forget to acknowledge the fact that the public school system was planted in every Southern State by the vote of the Negro, in direct opposition to an overwhelming majority of the whites, and that two white children enjoy its benefits to one colored one. We extol the public spirit which divides the public school fund of the States of the South between the schools of both races, though the Negro pays but a small proportion of the taxes, but are as silent as the grave in regard to the equally important fact that it is the unrequited labor of the colored man which created the major part of the valuation on which the white man pays taxes.

To the Negro in the United States the race question is one of color only. He is what he is, and all his conditions are what they are merely because a white Christian people have prescribed such conditions for him because he has more or less colored blood in his veins. That is why he was imported. That is the reason he was held to service without recompense. That is the reason he was not allowed to marry or have a family. Because of this he was prohibited by law from learning to read or write. Because of this he was prevented from taking or holding property. Because of this every obstacle was put in the way of his progress from barbarism to civilization. *We* do not, *we* cannot, realize this fact of color. We have even been told here that "there *is* no race problem"! I wonder if the man who made the statement ever tried to apply the Christ-rule to the relation of the races in this Christian land. Did he ever think what it would mean to have in his veins even a few drops of that blood which Christianity for centuries taught was the indelible mark of the Divine curse? Did you ever think, sir, how much it would take to hire any one in this audience to assume the burden of a black skin for a lifetime? Where would have been your career of honor, sir, if your cheek had shown a trace of African bronze?

* * *

In all the prayers that have been offered at this Conference I have not heard one word of thankfulness that *we* are white. I do not suppose any man here dare utter such a prayer in public; yet, excepting only life and the hope of salvation, this is the most priceless blessing we enjoy.

* * *

Let us never forget to thank God that we are white, even if we are ashamed to go before him on our knees and thank him that we are his favorite children, the pets of his mercy, and the superiors of those to whom he gave darker skins! Especially let us never forget that this is the prime factor in the Negro's view of the race question, and will continue to grow more important to him as he increases in knowledge, refinement, wealth, and sensibility, unless we make some radical improvement in our white Christianity.

Another fact that must continue to affect the Negro's view of the race question and of the relations he sustains to the white man in the United States is the character of his past. It is easy for us to excuse *ourselves* for the wrongs of slavery, but, day by day, it is growing harder for the colored man to do so; and it is simply to state a universal fact of human nature to declare that a great and lasting wrong like slavery done to a whole people because of race or creed grows blacker and darker for generations and ages as they go away from it. The educated grandchild of the slave who looks back into the black pit of slavery will find little excuse for the white Christian civilization which forbade marriage, crushed aspiration, and after two centuries and a half offered the world as the fruits of Christian endeavor five millions of bastard sons and daughters, —the product of a promiscuity *enforced by law and upheld by Christian teaching!*

* * *

We say—perhaps we sometimes even *think*—that, because slavery no longer exists as a legalized form of society, we may dismiss it from our thought, and no longer consider it as a factor of our civilization. In truth, the conditions it bequeathed are far more difficult and delicate than those attending its existence. It is a living force in the white man's thought and in the colored man's life. The lessons it taught to both races are ineradicable by law, and are beyond the control of mere reason. The white man of the South thinks he would rather perish from the earth than be accounted only the equal of the colored man; while the Negro is fast coming to an appreciation of the fact that subordination is only a longer name for subjection. He dare not yield his claim to equality of right and opportunity, even if he would. These irrepressible conflicting tendencies are the heritage of slavery, and the American people who planted and protected this upas-tree must see to it that they do not bring a still greater evil. What ought *we* to do? Let us try to imagine ourselves colored men, with dusky wives and children, and then answer with the fear of God before our eyes!

A good deal has been said here about the character and quality of the Negro's religion. I always wonder that a white Christian dare cast any imputation on the Negro's faith. For one, I am glad that he has *any* faith at all. To me, the fact that the American Negro is *ever* a Christian is the greatest of miracles that has been wrought since the grave yielded up its dead. Remember in what school he was taught Christian truth! Look at his surroundings as he must view them! Think that his first religious lessons were that God had created him to serve the will of his white Christian brother; that the earth and its fulness belonged to the white man, and that the Negro was added merely to promote his pleasure and advantage; that the white man was allowed to own, occupy, and possess all he could acquire, but it was a sin for the colored man to assume control of his own body and brain; that marriage was a holy ordinance to the white man, but a forbidden privilege to the Negro; that home and family were sacred to his white brother, but forbidden by Christian law to the slave; that the white man was expected to die in defence of the virtue of his wife and daughter, but that the Negro's cabin stood forever open to the ravisher; that knowledge was the key-stone of the white man's religion, progress, and liberty, but that Christian laws forbade the colored man to learn to read the word of God!

* * *

Nay, if you wish a lesson in Christian devotion and self-sacrifice, read the story of the African Methodist Church, every one of the half million members of which is the child of a slave,—who twenty-five years ago were not worth twenty-five cents apiece outside of the clothes they wore,—and see the reported aggregate of more than $2,000,000 paid by them for religious and charitable purposes in one year. No other church has ever begun to equal that under like conditions of poverty and difficulty. Strike off half, and it still remains a miracle. Halve it again, and the Christians of the Catacombs may well hail them across the intervening ages as their closest exemplars!

* * *

For two centuries, Christian civilization encouraged and compelled mere promiscuity among the slaves. As soon as they became free, this unhallowed relation became offensive to our eyes, and men and women who had previously "taken up with each other," as the courts phrased it, were required to register themselves as man and wife, or abandon their previous relations. For this registration they were also required to pay a good round fee. In several counties embraced in my judicial district, I investigated the proportion of those who assumed and those who renounced the old relation. The former was surprisingly large, ranging from 94 to 97 per cent., according to the estimates of the best informed parties. I suppose in the whole eight counties it would have reached 90 per cent. at least. Let the marriage bonds be dissolved throughout the State of New York to-day, and it may be doubted if as large a proportion of her intelligent white citizens would choose again their old partners.

* * *

I have not wished by these remarks to give offence or disturb the harmony of this meeting; but I could not consent that he who fought with me for the land we love should be without one to speak for him in a council where the wise men of another race have met to consider *his* welfare, condemn *his* faults, and determine what duty the white Christians of America owe to eight millions of people who served faithfully for two centuries, paying in advance the tuition of their children in the school of civilization.*

ANDREW D. WHITE

There is an old theory that the first thing a speaker should do is to get the sympathy of his audience. My friends, I feel that I ought to have your sympathy; for I come forward, "no orator as Brutus is," succeeding this outburst of eloquence, of wit, of humor, of pathos, with which my distinguished friend has enchained you, and which will make it, I fear, very difficult for me to bring you back into what seems to me the true line of our deliberations.

Carried away, as I have been, by his eloquence, as he has depicted to us the horrors of the past, the wrongs of the black race, the crimes in which North and South have shared, I have remembered one great text, "Forgetting those things which are behind, and reaching forth unto those things which are before, I press forward toward the mark." I trust that he will forgive me if I say that, while I recognize in his speech much which should incite us all to more earnest effort, I must still insist that the first and only question at a meeting like this should be, "What is to be done, and how can we do it?" This is no time for crimination and recrimination. We know that we have been miserable sinners: let us press forward, and see if the future cannot be made to atone for the past.

* * *

There is, indeed, an evolution by a simple natural process, a process which is comparatively easy and peaceful, but there is far more frequent evolution by catastrophe, by cataclysm; and I feel now that we are at the parting of the ways between these two. The question is, In this evolution of a better future for the South, for the black man, for the white man, for the whole country, for humanity, are we to have progress by growth or progress by catastrophe? Is it to be a great cataclysm,—races projected against each other, destroying each other, with the survival of the fittest, in the worst sense in which that phrase can be brought home to us, or a steady progress by education?

* * *

Here is a great question to be settled. It is not to be settled, and I trust my friend will pardon me for saying so, even by such

---

*Albion W. Tourgée, in *First Mohonk Conference on the Negro Question,* June 4-6, 1890 (Boston, George H. Ellis, 1890), 108-114.

magnificent and thrilling denunciations as his. I believe that it is far more likely to be settled by these young women who have given us the simple story of their teaching in the South. Far more effective than all charges and counter-charges will be the work of the various Christian bodies in settling these questions. All peaceful agencies must be pressed into the service, individual, State, and national. Whatever minor injustice may have been involved in the Blair bill, which my friend has so eloquently denounced, I confess to a deep regret that it or some other adequate measure did not pass. We cannot always have all that we would have; but we can at any rate press on to something that is better. I say it deliberately, Anything is better than bringing this question to a bloody issue.

* * *

All that we can do is to prepare the way for a peaceful evolution, to smooth the path toward a time when the black man shall have peaceably become what Providence determines that he may and ought to become. I am not in favor of forcing any question whatever, least of all any social question. Give the black man a fair chance, give him simple aid where he has a right to it, and then leave him to develop a better future.

MR. GLENN, OF BALTIMORE

In rising to address so distinguished an audience as this, and after the eloquent addresses which it has been my pleasure and privilege to listen to, I must confess that I feel somewhat appalled. I am no orator. I am a simple business man, and the ideas which I shall advance are only from the practical side.

* * *

These days have to me been a revelation. It is the first time that I have ever felt that I could speak with perfect freedom with Northern men, and that, notwithstanding our divergence of views, it was possible for us to interchange ideas with that mutual consideration without which the solution of any problem would be impossible. After the course which these discussions have taken, I can say, without hesitation, that, if the mind of the North and the mind of the South can be brought together outside of this parlor as they have come together within it, the Negro problem would be solved. With harmony, I do not believe that any problem can present itself to the consideration of the Anglo-Saxon mind which will not be easy of solution. Without harmony, you have lately tried to solve a problem; and it has convulsed the life of the nation to its very centre. But, to bring about this harmony, the attitude of both the South and the North must be changed. I was brought up to believe that a man who was able to hold a slave and would refuse to do so was guilty of moral cowardice in rejecting the responsibility. This idea I cannot expect you to accept. On the other hand, you must not expect me to believe that slavery was sin, and that the slaveholder was a moral reprobate, to be saved, not by grace, but only by the uncovenanted mercies of the Almighty. You will have to learn to regard the institution as a step in the hands of Providence in the progress of the race, and to look at it, not from a sentimental, but from an historical point of view. We all know the part that the feudal system has played in the progress of civilization. We would not wish it back again. There are many things connected with it which we would not repeat to-day. But the feudal system was as far in advance of the Roman slavery which it replaced as it was behind the liberty of the eighteenth century, which supplanted it. And so with slavery: it was a step in the civilization of the race, and as far ahead of the African barbarism, whose place it took, as it was behind the freedom for which it made way.

* * *

This question, in my opinion, is in its essence not national, but local. The Indian question is a national one. It is a national heritage and a national obligation. It presses upon all parts alike, and presses upon no section. This is not the case with the Negro problem. The responsibility of their presence has been placed upon the South, and they should manage it. I do not mean that we do not want your help. We need your money to help us to build the schools which our insufficiency of means does not enable us to supply; for on the education of the Negro depends his regeneration. For this reason I am sorry the Blair bill did not pass, although I could not indorse all of its provisions. Your system of education is more complete than ours; and we want your noble women, who are willing to sacrifice their comfort and their lives, to help us in this best of all missionary work. But, when you have done your best, you have only, as General Brinkerhoff says, touched us in spots; while the Negro problem and the race are throughout our Southern country from one end to the other. They touch us at every point, and we touch them. We understand them better than you, and to us should be left their management. The government should never interfere in behalf of the black man where it would not and could not interfere on behalf of the white man, and should never interfere to protect the black man of South Carolina when it would not interfere for the same reason to protect the white man of Ohio. The political salvation of the South depends much upon the solution of this problem; and the easy solution of it, in my opinion, depends upon whether this solution is or is not left to those who are the natural friends of the Negro, who best understand him, and to whom his development and education, or the contrary, mean a people's progress or a people's decay.

* * *

When you bring the colored man to believe that the Southern men are his friends, and then confer upon him the widest liberty possible,—in that way, I believe, is his salvation to come.

GEN. BRINKERHOFF

I am delighted with the spirit of this convention. I agree in the main with all the efforts that are attempted; but, when I look in the face of this problem, and know that there are eight millions of people in almost utter darkness, who have come up out of bondage without a moral sense, a mass of ignorance, and contrast with this the efforts we are making, I am conscious how limited they are. I know that we are reaching out, and must, in the nature of things, continue to reach out, from the North at arm's length to do this work; but we reach only small spots of the darkness of this continent. Now, I want this Conference and these Northern people somehow, and in some way, to look at this question from the standpoint of the white men of the South. Let us remember that the white people of the South are a noble people, that there is nowhere in the United States a purer strain of American blood than in the Old South. Remember that the white men and women of the South are as religious a people as we have on the American continent. More than that, they are a profoundly religious people. So far as I know them, and I know them pretty thoroughly, they believe in God, in immortality, and in the Christian religion. In the South you find no agnosticism, no anarchism, no atheism. The Southern white people are more thoroughly Christian than any similar body of people upon the continent, in my judgment.*

149

SEPARATE BUT EQUAL

After the collapse of Reconstruction governments, southern whites began gradually to legalize the informal practices of segregation which obtained in the South. One such law was passed by the Louisiana legislature in 1890 and provided that "all railway companies carrying passengers . . . in this State shall provide separate but equal accommodations for the white and colored races."

Plessy *vs.* Ferguson *tested the constitutionality of this recent trend in southern legislation. Plessy was a mulatto who, on June 7, 1892, bought a first-class ticket on the East Louisiana Railway for a trip from New Orleans to Covington, La., and sought to be seated in the "white" coach. Upon conviction of a violation of the 1890 statute, he appealed to the Supreme Court of Louisiana, which upheld his conviction, and finally to the U.S. Supreme Court, which pronounced the Louisiana law constitutional, on May 18, 1896. The defense of Plessy and attack on the Louisiana statute was in the hands of four men, the most famous of whom was Albion W. Tourgée. M. J. Cunningham, Attorney General of Louisiana, was assisted by two other lawyers in defending the statute. The majority opinion of the Court was delivered by Justice Henry B. Brown. John Marshall Harlan dissented and Justice David J. Brewer did not participate, making it a 7-1 decision.*

In his dissent to this decision Harlan asserted that "Our Constitution is color-blind, and neither knows nor tolerates classes among citizens. In respect of civil rights, all citizens are equal before the law." He offered the prophecy that "the judgment rendered this day will, in time, prove to be quite as pernicious as the decision made by this tribunal in the Dred Scott case."

The constitutionality of this act is attacked upon the ground that it conflicts both with the Thirteenth Amendment of the Constitution, abolishing slavery, and the Fourteenth Amendment, which prohibits certain restrictive legislation on the part of the States.

---

*Mr. Glenn, Gen. Brinkerhoff, Andrew D. White, in *First Mohonk Conference on the Negro Question,* June 4-6, 1890 (Boston, George H. Ellis, 1890), pp. 117-124.

1. That it does not conflict with the Thirteenth Amendment, which abolished slavery and involuntary servitude, except as a punishment for crime, is too clear for argument. Slavery implies involuntary servitude—a state of bondage: the ownership of mankind as a chattel, or at least the control of the labor and services of one man for the benefit of another, and the absence of a legal right to the disposal of his own person, property and services.

* * *

A statute which implies merely a legal distinction between the white and colored races—a distinction which is founded in the color of the two races, and which must always exist so long as white men are distinguished from the other race by color—has no tendency to destroy the legal equality of the two races, or reestablish a state of involuntary servitude. Indeed, we do not understand that the Thirteenth Amendment is strenuously relied upon by the plaintiff in error in this connection.

2. By the Fourteenth Amendment, all persons born or naturalized in the United States, and subject to the jurisdiction thereof, are made citizens of the United States and of the State wherein they reside; and the States are forbidden from making or enforcing any law which shall abridge the privileges or immunities of citizens of the United States, or shall deprive any person of life, liberty or property without due process of law, or deny to any person within their jurisdiction the equal protection of the laws.

* * *

The object of the amendment was undoubtedly to enforce the absolute equality of the two races before the law, but in the nature of things it could not have been intended to abolish distinctions based upon color, or to enforce social, as distinguished from political equality, or a commingling of the two races upon terms unsatisfactory to either. Laws permitting, and even requiring, their separation in places where they are liable to be brought into contact do not necessarily imply the inferiority of either race to the other, and have been generally, if not universally, recognized as within the competency of the state legislatures in the exercise of their police power. The most common instance of this is connected with the establishment of separate schools for white and colored children, which has been held to be a valid exercise of the legislative power even by courts of States where the political rights of the colored race have been longest and most earnestly enforced.

* * *

While we think the enforced separation of the races, as applied to the internal commerce of the State, neither abridges the privileges or immunities of the colored man, deprives him of his property without due process of law, nor denies him the equal protection of the laws, within the meaning of the Fourteenth Amendment, we are not prepared to say that the conductor, in assigning passengers to the coaches according to their race, does not act at his peril, or that the provision of the second section of the act, that denies to the passenger compensation in damages for a refusal to receive him into the coach in which he properly belongs, is a valid exercise of the legislative power. Indeed, we understand it to be conceded by the State's attorney, that such part of the act as exempts from liability the railway company and its officers is unconstitutional. The power to assign to a particular coach obviously implies the power to determine to which race the passenger belongs, as well as the power to determine who, under the laws of the particular State, is to be deemed a white, and who a colored person.

* * *

It is claimed by the plaintiff in error that, in any mixed community, the reputation of belonging to the dominant race, in this instance the white race, is *property,* in the same sense that a right of action, or of inheritance, is property. Conceding this to be so, for the purposes of this case, we are unable to see how this statute deprives him of, or in any way affects his right to, such property. If he be a white man and assigned to a colored coach, he may have his action for damages against the company for being deprived of his so called property. Upon the other hand, if he be a colored man and be so assigned, he has been deprived of no property, since he is not lawfully entitled to the reputation of being a white man.

In this connection, it is also suggested by the learned counsel for the plaintiff in error that the same argument that will justify the state legislature in requiring railways to provide separate accommodations for the two races will also authorize them to require separate cars to be provided for the people whose hair is of a certain color, or who are aliens, or who belong to certain nationalities, or to enact laws requiring colored people to walk upon one side of the street, and white people upon the other, or requiring white men's houses to be painted white, and colored men's black, or their vehicles or business signs to be of different colors, upon the theory that one side of the street is as good as the other, or that a house or vehicle of one color is as good as one of another color. The reply to all this is that every exercise of the police power must be reasonable, and extend only to such laws as are enacted in good faith for the promotion for the public good, and not for the annoyance or oppression of a particular class.

* * *

We consider the underlying fallacy of the plaintiff's argument to consist in the assumption that the enforced separation of the two races stamps the colored race with a badge of inferiority. If this be so, it is not by reason of anything found in the act, but solely because the colored race chooses to put that construction upon it. The argument necessarily assumes that if, as has been more than once the case, and is not unlikely to be so again, the colored race should become the dominant power in the state legislature, and should enact a law in precisely similar terms, it would thereby relegate the white race to an inferior position. We imagine that the white race, at least, would not acquiesce in this assumption. The argument also assumes that social prejudices may be overcome by legislation, and that equal rights cannot be secured to the negro except by an enforced commingling of the two races. We cannot accept this proposition. If the two races are to meet upon terms of social equality, it must be the result of natural affinities, a mutual appreciation of each other's merits and a voluntary consent of individuals.*

150

A MODERATE NEGRO VIEW

Booker T. Washington

The Atlanta Cotton States and International Exposition was in a sense the response of the New South to the Midwest's Columbian Exposition two years earlier. Booker T. Washington had received favorable notice on both sides of the Mason-Dixon line for the moderate, non-inflammatory contents of his public statements and was invited to appear before a Congressional committee in the spring of 1895 along with white Southerners who were requesting federal financial assistance for their Exposition. The biracial quality of the Exposition was to be emphasized by a Negro building, designed and constructed entirely by Negroes and containing only exhibits relating to the progress of the race. To carry this theme further, the Exposition Board of Directors decided to have a Negro participate in the opening ceremonies and selected Washington as the man who could best manifest the amicable and cooperative relationships existing between white and black in the South. From President Grover Cleveland down, the white reaction to Washington's speech was enthusiastic and laudatory, a kind of national sigh of relief that a Negro spokesman could recognize the limits of the race question. The speech is a consummate statement of what whites wanted to hear and what Washington believed was best for Negroes at that time.

Mr. President and Gentlemen of the Board of Directors and Citizens.

One-third of the population of the South is of the Negro race. No enterprise seeking the material, civil, or moral welfare of this section can disregard this element of our population and reach the highest success. I but convey to you, Mr. President and Directors, the sentiment of the masses of my race when I say that in no way have the value and manhood of the American Negro been more fittingly and generously recognized than by the managers of this magnificent Exposition at every stage of its progress. It is a recognition that will do more to cement the friendship of the two races than any occurrence since the dawn of our freedom.

Not only this, but the opportunity here afforded will awaken among us a new era of industrial progress. Ignorant and inexperienced, it is not strange that in the first years of our new life we began at the top instead of at the bottom; that a seat in Congress or the state legislature was more sought than real estate or industrial skill; that the political convention or stump speaking had more attractions than starting a dairy farm or truck garden.

A ship lost at sea for many days suddenly sighted a friendly vessel. From the mast of the unfortunate vessel was seen a signal, "Water, water; we die of thirst!" The answer from the friendly vessel at once came back, "Cast down your bucket where you are." A second time the signal, "Water, water; send us water!" ran up from the distressed vessel, and was answered, "Cast down your bucket

---

**Plessy* vs. *Ferguson*, 163 U.S. 537 *United States Reports: Cases Adjudged in the Supreme Court* (New York, Banks & Brothers, 1896).

where you are." The captain of the distressed vessel, at last heeding the injunction, cast down his bucket, and it came up full of fresh, sparkling water from the mouth of the Amazon River. To those of my race who depend on bettering their condition in a foreign land or who underestimate the importance of cultivating friendly relations with the Southern white man, who is their next-door neighbour, I would say: "Cast down your bucket where you are"—cast it down in making friends in every manly way of the people of all races by whom we are surrounded.

Cast it down in agriculture, mechanics, in commerce, in domestic service, and in the professions. And in this connection it is well to bear in mind that whatever other sins the South may be called to bear, when it comes to business, pure and simple, it is in the South that the Negro is given a man's chance in the commercial world, and in nothing is this Exposition more eloquent than in emphasizing this chance. Our greatest danger is that in the great leap from slavery to freedom we may overlook the fact that the masses of us are to live by the productions of our hands, and fail to keep in mind that we shall prosper in proportion as we learn to dignify and glorify common labour and put brains and skill into the common occupations of life; shall prosper in proportion as we learn to draw the line between the superficial and the substantial, the ornamental gewgaws of life and the useful. No race can prosper till it learns that there is as much dignity in tilling a field as in writing a poem. It is at the bottom of life we must begin, and not at the top. Nor should we permit our grievances to overshadow our opportunities.

To those of the white race who look to the incoming of those of foreign birth and strange tongue and habits for the prosperity of the South, were I permitted I would repeat what I say to my own race, "Cast down your bucket where you are." Cast it down among the eight millions of Negroes whose habits you know, whose fidelity and love you have tested in days when to have proved treacherous meant the ruin of your firesides. Cast down your bucket among these people who have, without strikes and labour wars, tilled your fields, cleared your forests, builded your railroads and cities, and brought forth treasures from the bowels of the earth, and helped make possible this magnificent representation of the progress of the South. Casting down your bucket among my people, helping and encouraging them as you are doing on these grounds, and to education of head, hand, and heart, you will find that they will buy your surplus land, make blossom the waste places in your fields, and run your factories. While doing this, you can be sure in the future, as in the past, that you and your families will be surrounded by the most patient, faithful, law-abiding, and unresentful people that the world has seen. As we have proved our loyalty to you in the past, in nursing your children, watching by the sick-bed of your mothers and fathers, and often following them with tear-dimmed eyes to their graves, so in the future, in our humble way, we shall stand by you with a devotion that no foreigner can approach, ready to lay down our lives, if need be, in defence of yours, interlacing our industrial, commercial, civil, and religious life with yours in a way that shall make the interests of both races one. In all things that are purely social we can be as separate as the fingers, yet one as the hand in all things essential to mutual progress.

There is no defence or security for any of us except in the highest intelligence and development of all. If anywhere there are efforts tending to curtail the fullest growth of the Negro, let these efforts be turned into stimulating, encouraging, and making him the most useful and intelligent citizen. Effort or means so invested will pay a thousand per cent interest. These efforts will be twice blessed—"blessing him that gives and him that takes."

* * *

Nearly sixteen millions of hands will aid you in pulling the load upward, or they will pull against you the load downward. We shall constitute one-third and more of the ignorance and crime of the South, or one-third its intelligence and progress; we shall contribute one-third to the business and industrial prosperity of the South, or we shall prove a veritable body of death, stagnating, depressing, retarding every effort to advance the body politic.

Gentlemen of the Exposition, as we present to you our humble effort at an exhibition of our progress, you must not expect overmuch. Starting thirty years ago with ownership here and there in a few quilts and pumpkins and chickens (gathered from miscellaneous sources), remember the path that has led from these to the inventions and production of agricultural implements, buggies, steam-engines, newspapers, books, statuary, carving, paintings, the man-

The Negro Mammy. Nurse and often mother-figure for southern children of well-to-do families, the Mammy exercised a strong but almost undefinable influence upon the Southerner's outlook on the world around him.

agement of drug-stores and banks, has not been trodden without contact with thorns and thistles. While we take pride in what we exhibit as a result of our independent efforts, we do not for a moment forget that our part in this exhibition would fall far short of your expectations but for the constant help that has come to our educational life, not only from the Southern states, but especially from Northern philanthropists, who have made their gifts a constant stream of blessing and encourgement.

The wisest among my race understand that the agitation of questions of social equality is the extremest folly, and that progress in the enjoyment of all the privileges that will come to us must be the result of severe and constant struggle rather than of artificial forcing. No race that has anything to contribute to the markets of the world is long in any degree ostracized. It is important and right all privileges of the law be ours, but it is vastly more important that we be prepared for the exercises of these privileges. The opportunity to earn a dollar in a factory just now is worth infinitely more than the opportunity to spend a dollar in an opera-house.

In conclusion, may I repeat that nothing in thirty years has given us more hope and encouragement, and drawn us so near to you of the white race, as this opportunity offered by the Exposition; and here bending, as it were, over the altar that represents the results of the struggles of your race and mine, both starting practically empty-handed three decades ago, I pledge that in your effort to work out the great and intricate problem which God has laid at the doors of the South, you shall have at all times the patient, sympathetic help of my race; only let this be constantly in mind, that, while from representations in these buildings of the product of field, of forest, of mine, of factory, letters, and art, much good will come, yet far above and beyond material benefits will be that higher good, that, let us pray God, will come, in a blotting out of sectional differences and racial animosities and suspicions, in a determination to administer absolute justice, in a willing obedience among all classes to the mandates of law. This, this, coupled with our material prosperity, will bring into our beloved South a new heaven and a new earth.*

151

NEGRO BUSINESSMEN

The National Negro Business League was organized by Booker T. Washington in 1900 to provide a vehicle for exchanging information and inspiration among Negro businessmen and to establish and support local leagues. The League thrived until America's entrance into World War I, supported most of that time by Andrew Carnegie and managed by Washington and his Tuskegee aids. Significantly, it was the first race organization to acknowledge and honor the businessman as distinct from the politician, minister, or newspaperman, and would

---

*Booker T. Washington, "The Atlanta Exposition Address," Sept. 18, 1895, in Washington, *Up From Slavery: An Autobiography* (1900; Garden City, New York, Doubleday, Page & Co., 1910 ed.), 218-225.

be followed by race organizations of lawyers, doctors, retail merchants, funeral directors, and bankers.

The League emphasis rested on the accepted virtues of the ninteenth century: honesty, self-reliance, hard work, and thrift—at a time when reformers were beginning to plead for government aid in controlling aggressive monopoly, finance capitalism, exploitation of labor, and slums. In holding up the small businessman as a prototype, Washington and the League obscured from race vision some other legal means by which white businessmen forged ahead. With understandable pride, Negroes arose to tell of their own or of their community's business success without fully comprehending that this kind of success, in white America, was already outdated.

The first National Negro Business League convention was held in Boston in August, 1900. Approximately 400 delegates gathered, 80% of whom were from the deep South. One-third of the northern delegates came from the host state of Massachusetts. Booker T. Washington was elected President and stayed on the platform to assist the chairman. The convention was enthusiastic and orderly.

REMARKS OF DR. A. J. LOVE OF CHATTANOOGA, TENN.

Chattanooga, Tenn., is a town that will represent ancient Pompeii, though not sleeping, at the foot of Lookout Mountain, which raises its head above the clouds, where was fought that famous battle, in as beautiful a piece of country as the eye wishes to behold. Verdure there is ravished by nature. We have about fifteen thousand inhabitants, eight thousand of whom are colored, five thousand of which number labor in the manufactories, ranging all the way from boiler making, file manufacturing, stove furnaces, sawmills, henneries and every form of ware which the hardware world knows anything about. There the Negro is in his acme as to being a "maker." He understands his business there. He is one of the originators as to conception, as to plans, as to patterns. He helps to manufacture; and it is there where the manufacturer himself knows the value of the man in ebony.

There are about one hundred "homes," in round numbers, valued at about $150,000. We have men in business, about thirty-five; representing grocers, fifteen; saloon men, about six; one undertaker, who is not at home now. He happens to be here. One money lender and men in other minor businesses, representing about $65,000 invested, the entire capital being about $243,000. I promised not to take much of your time and I shall not; and last, but not least, we are in the iron manufacturing business ourselves. We have two foundries there, owned, operated, controlled and worked and run by colored men, capitalized to-day at $25,000. These foundries have passed the stage of experimentation; they are now certainties; they are paying institutions. Everything they manufacture they have orders for. Their work is in demand. They have not as much capital as they need and as they wish, but with that amount of capital they have succeeded in the manufacture of stoves and cooking utensils and skillets, and grates for furnaces and foundries; and right there in Chattanooga they have a great demand for that work.

Now, I want to say that I feel that the Negroes in Chattanooga are doing a great work; I feel that they are doing a work which the race, if they knew about it, might be proud of; but I want to say, with the environment in Chattanooga, as in other places in the South, the habits of the Negro might be bettered immensely, so that in a few years they might have money they have not now.

REMARKS OF MR. DUNGEE OF MONTGOMERY, ALA.

I am sent here to you as the representative of the Citizens' Commercial Union of Montgomery, Ala., an organization composed of nearly every colored business man in that city and its suburbs, and numbering also among its members many individuals of both sexes, who while not actually engaged in mercantile or business pursuits, yet feel a personal and lively interest in everything that pertains to the material advancement of their race.

About three years ago this institution was conceived in the minds of some eight or ten colored business and professional men in Montgomery, and entered into existence under its present name, with a president, two vice-presidents, a secretary, treasurer and five members; a striking contrast to a present membership of over two hundred, a majority of whom are *business* men who *mean business* and do business. I have the honor to be the treasurer of this organization, which possibly may in some measure and manner account for the present privilege of being their delegate, and through them the representative of the business element of Montgomery, although as yet I have never been directly charged with embezzlement, misfeasance or malfeasance in office. At any rate, I regard it as a decided honor to come from them, and a positive pleasure to come to you in such a capacity and on such an occasion as this. And they have instructed me to bring to you not only greetings hearty and as warm as the climate from which I come, but to assure you of the earnest, the intensely earnest interest we, by anticipation, feel in your deliberations here, and of our heartfelt and soulful desire and determination to coöperate with you in whatever means or measures you may see fit to adopt to enhance the business interests which are the vital interests of the colored citizens of this country.

To begin with, we have a beautiful Southern city down there—not half so beautiful, however, nor quite so large as your city of Boston, but it is growing in both respects, and with the characteristic optimism of the Southern sons of Ham we have great hopes for the future. We have a population of about 2,000 Negroes, owning over 1,500 homes; we have representatives in 85 per cent of the business pursuits followed in that city by white men and women; we have twenty-three grocery stores, several of which combine general merchandise with their regular lines. The aggregate amount of the stock carried by these stores approximates $5,000. One alone, of which I shall speak later, carries a stock worth $1,000. We have three drug stores owned and operated by colored men, each one doing a successful and increasing business. One of these stores, beginning fifteen months ago with a cash capital of $200, now carries a stock worth $1,000, and employs one clerk and one apprentice at an aggregate salary of $75 per month. One other started in business five years ago with a capital of about $300. This store has done a business since that time amounting to over $20,000, and has on its files

Above: the executive committee of the National Negro Business League, headed by Booker T. Washington (seated, second from left). These men, community leaders from both the North and the South, worked to improve the Negro's position during the period of transition.

47,000 prescriptions compounded during that time, 99 per cent of which were written by one colored physician. We have twenty restaurants, the greater number of which are making money; several are doing well, and one in particular is doing remarkably well. This one, owned and controlled by a colored woman, does a monthly business of $600, 25 per cent of which is net. This lady also owns two public carriages and four horses, which bring her a net profit each month of $30. We have one dry goods and clothing store, with a millinery department attached, and just here you will allow me to give more than a passing notice to this particular business institution, as it reflects unbounded credit not only on the owner, but on the race he represents. This young man, who, by the way, is one of the trustees of the Tuskegee Normal and Industrial Institute, served his apprenticeship in the dry goods business, first as porter and general man of all work, subsequently as clerk at the counter in a white clothing store. About five years ago he conceived the idea of entering into business for himself, and with a partner and $350 in cash he began in a modest way the first, and so far as I know, the only, venture of the kind in Alabama. By dint of persistent effort, strict attention to business details and sterling principles of honesty and honor, he was soon able to buy his partner out, add to his stock and business facilities, until this year, with a continually increasing trade, he has been compelled to secure an adjoining building to find space to store a stock which is invoiced at $18,000, with yearly sales amounting to $35,000.

These individual cases represent a type of business men and women that is not by any means uncommon in Montgomery. We have dozens of others, men who take front rank in their various vocations and quietly but steadily are forging ahead. We have a harness maker who in this particular business is the acknowledged superior of any other in town. We have thirty shoemakers conducting shops of their own and doing good work. We have a dozen contractors and builders, one of whom superintended the construction of that magnificent chapel at Tuskegee; another has risen in twelve or fourteen years from buggy boy to be the owner of five houses and lots, one on the principal residential street of the city, all told valued at $7,000. We have fifteen blacksmith shops owned by colored men, three wood and coal yards, seven butcher stalls, five green grocers, seventeen draymen, twelve men who own and handle public carriages; one dairyman, who milks and owns fifteen cows, and whose dairy product has never stood below third in an official chemical test among twenty white competitors. He has on several occasions stood first. We have several insurance agents, one pension claim agent, several real estate agents, one lawyer, one jeweller, one dentist, five pharmacists, four hundred preachers, five physicians and two undertakers, all doing well.

* * *

Among the women we have seven professional nurses, one matron at the Hale Infirmary, an institution erected and donated to his race by a Negro, James Hale, at a cost of nearly $5,000, and for the past twelve years conducted by colored people for the benefit of their race. We have two milliners, as proficient as any in the city, both employed by our colored dry goods merchant, J. N. Adams. We have over sixty competent seamstresses and dressmakers, two confectioners and candy makers, several music teachers, both vocal and instrumental.

But I shall not tire you with a further account of our business efforts, but ask you to consider these instances as illustrations of the whole and tell me what they mean. To my mind they mean that the Negro has at last awakened to the idea of self-help; he has felt himself too long (though of necessity) the white man's burden, and is making a most strenuous effort to share it and finally shoulder it alone. But though many of us feel that manly sense of independence which comes with self-reliance, we have to look with sorrowing eyes upon the struggling masses left behind us; and my people have sent me here to tell you how deeply we feel our indebtedness to you for your part in assisting us thus far; and for this we entreat you to stay yet awhile longer, till with the strength developed by self-help and helping others, we can carry the entire load ourselves. And with your help, with Booker T. Washington's help and with God's help we shall succeed.

REMARKS OF MR. GEORGE C. JONES OF LITTLE ROCK, ARK.

I come from a city of 50,000 inhabitants—16,000 colored. Ten years ago was the introduction of a colored undertaker establishment in that city; your humble servant attempted to open such a place of business. The first thought that struck me at that time was, where shall I open it? The next thought was, go out on the main street and be a competitor right. I came out on the main street of that city, I opened a business for my people, and the first of the kind in the state, beside an establishment of twenty years, a man of large means. I began in an humble way, and in five years from the day I opened that business there were three other undertakers in the city. I control more business than all the undertakers in the city put together. There is but one undertaker in my city who does business on his own account, using his own outfit, and that is your humble servant.

* * *

Let me say to you first, you hear much of the South, what hard times they have down there. That is all right. It has never been as hard as we want it down there. The harder the times the closer the Negroes will get together. When you come to Little Rock we will hire no hall, open no park except what is owned by Negroes of the city and of the state; and when we give you a reception in Little Rock, we will give it to you in our own carriages, drawn by our own horses and driven by our own Negroes.

I think this is the right meeting for our people. I think the time has come that such a convention is needed, but it is not needed for one year; it is needed for many years. It is the only convention that I ever attended by my people—and I make it a rule to try to attend most of them—where I have seen them trying to do something and meaning something.*

152

RACIAL PRIDE

William Edward Burghardt DuBois was the first Negro to earn a Ph.D. from Harvard and his dissertation on the African slave trade was the first publication of the Harvard Historical Series. He spent a year of study in Germany with the help of a grant from the Slater Fund before returning to take up professorial posts at Wilberforce University in Ohio and Atlanta University. DuBois in the 1890's turned his attention to contemporary race problems. DuBois brought a freshness to his race that ranged from rank discourtesy and brutal candor to imaginative scholarship and a brilliant literary style. He had a condescending air which alienated Negroes and whites alike, but his was the best-trained and most facile mind which had yet engaged race problems, and he began to apply the new discipline of sociology and the refined art of history to them. Prior to 1900, he was still in lesser positions of authority, but his leadership and organizational abilities would be tried shortly after the twentieth century began.

THE CONSERVATION OF THE RACES

Here, then, is the dilemma, and it is a puzzling one, I admit. No Negro who has given earnest thought to the situation of his people in America has failed, at some time in life, to find himself at these cross-roads; has failed to ask himself at some time: What, after all, am I? Am I an American or am I a Negro? Can I be both? Or is it my duty to cease to be a Negro as soon as possible and be an American? If I strive as a Negro, am I not perpetuating

---

*Dr. A. J. Love of Chattanooga, *Proceedings of the National Negro Business League, 1st Meeting, Boston, August 23-24, 1900* (Boston, 1901), 52-53.

the very cleft that threatens and separates Black and White America? Is not my only possible practical aim the subduction of all that is Negro in me to the American? Does my black blood place upon me any more obligation to assert my nationality than German, or Irish or Italian blood would?

It is such incessant self-questioning and the hesitation that arises from it, that is making the present period a time of vacillation and contradiction for the American Negro; combined race action is stifled, race responsibility is shirked, race enterprises languish, and the best blood, the best talent, the best energy of the Negro people cannot be marshalled to do the bidding of the race. They stand back to make room for every rascal and demagogue who chooses to cloak his selfish deviltry under the veil of race pride.

* * *

If we carefully consider what race prejudice really is, we find it, historically, to be nothing but the friction between different groups of people; it is the difference in aim, in feeling, in ideals of two different races; if, now, this difference exists touching territory, laws, language, or even religion, it is manifest that these people cannot live in the same territory without fatal collision; but if, on the other hand, there is substantial agreement in laws, language and religion; if there is a satisfactory adjustment of economic life, then there is no reason why, in the same country and on the same street, two or three great national ideals might not thrive and develop, that men of different races might not strive together for their race ideals as well, perhaps even better, than in isolation. Here, it seems to me, is the reading of the riddle that puzzles so many of us. We are Americans, not only by birth and by citizenship, but by our political ideals, our language, our religion. Farther than that, our Americanism does not go. At that point, we are Negroes, members of a vast historic race that from the very dawn of creation has slept, but half awakening in the dark forests of its African fatherland. We are the first fruits of this new nation, the harbinger of that black to-morrow which is yet destined to soften the whiteness of the Teutonic to-day. We are that people whose subtle sense of song has given America its only American music, its only American fairy tales, its only touch of pathos and humor amid its mad money-getting plutocracy. As such, it is our duty to conserve our physical powers, our intellectual endowments, our spiritual ideals; as a race we must strive by race organization, by race solidarity, by race unity to the realization of that broader humanity which freely recognizes differences in men, but sternly deprecates inequality in their opportunities of development.*

---

*W. E. B. DuBois, *The Conservation of the Races* (Washington: Occasional Papers, No. 2, American Negro Academy, 1897), pp. 11-12.

153

NEGRO INTELLECTUAL NEEDS

Alexander Crummell was an Episcopalian minister who struggled to be allowed to take his vows and then found himself confined to a poor church in New York City. He studied in England and became a leading figure in Liberia after 1853.

Returning to his pulpit after the Civil War, Crummell was already well known to American Negroes because of his Liberian service. He moved to a church in Washington and served the cause of the church and the race. "He simply worked," wrote W. E. B. DuBois, "inspiring the young, rebuking the old, helping the weak, guiding the strong." His voice was a clear call to independence of mind, an exhortation to develop the total talent of the race. Crummell did not become involved in acrimonious dispute or leadership squabbles. In a sense during the last decades of his life, he was the elder statesman, but one who had never known gutter partisanship.

THE ATTITUDE OF THE AMERICAN MIND TOWARD THE NEGRO INTELLECT

The American mind has refused to foster and to cultivate the Negro intellect. Join to this a kindred fact, of which there is the fullest evidence. Impelled, at times, by pity, a modicum of schooling and training has been given the Negro; but even this almost universally, with reluctance, with cold criticism, with microscopic scrutiny, with icy reservation, and at times, with ludicrous limitations.

Cheapness characterizes almost all the donations of the American people to the Negro:—Cheapness, in all the past, has been the regimen provided for the Negro in every line of his intellectual, as well as his lower life. And so, cheapness is to be the rule in the future, as well for his higher, as for his lower life:—cheap wages and cheap food, cheap and rotten huts; cheap and dilapidated schools; cheap and stinted weeks of schooling; cheap meeting houses for worship; cheap and ignorant ministers; cheap theological training; and now, cheap learning, culture and civilization!

Noble expectations are found in the grand literary circles in which Mr. Howells moves—manifest in his generous editing of our own Paul Dunbar's poems. But this generosity is not general, even in the world of American letters.

You can easily see this in the attempt, now-a-days, to sidetrack the Negro intellect, and to place it under limitations never laid upon any other class.

The elevation of the Negro has been a moot question for a generation past. But even to-day what do we find the general reliance of the American mind in determinating this question? Almost universally the resort is to material agencies! The ordinary, and sometimes the *extraordinary* American is unable to see that the struggle of a degraded people for elevation is, in its very nature, a warfare, and that its main weapon is the cultivated and scientific mind.

Ask the great men of the land how this Negro problem is to be solved, and then listen to the answers that come from divers classes of our white fellow-citizens. The merchants and traders of our great cities tell us—"The Negro must be taught to work;" and they will pour out their moneys by thousands to train him to toil. The clergy in large numbers, cry out—"Industrialism is the only hope of the Negro;" for this is the bed-rock, in their opinion, of Negro evangelization! "Send him to Manual Labor Schools," cries out another set of philanthropists. "Hic haec, hoc, is going to prove the ruin of the Negro" says the Rev. Steele, an erudite Southern Savan. "You must begin at the bottom with the Negro," says another eminent authority—as though the Negro had been living in the clouds, and had never reached the bottom. Says the Honorable George T. Barnes, of Georgia—"The kind of education the Negro should receive should not be very refined nor classical, but adapted to his present condition:" as though there is to be no future for the Negro.

And so you see that even now, late in the 19th century, in this land of learning and science, the creed is—"Thus far and no farther," *i.e.* for the American black man.

One would suppose from the universal demand for the mere industrialism for this race of ours, that the Negro had been going daily to dinner parties, eating terrapin and indulging in champagne; and returning home at night, sleeping on beds of eiderdown; breakfasting in the morning in his bed, and then having his valet to clothe him daily in purple and fine linen—all these 250 years of his sojourn in this land. And then, just now, the American people, tired of all this Negro luxury, was calling him, for the first time, to blister his hands with the hoe, and to learn to supply his needs by sweatful toil in the cotton fields.

Listen a moment, to the wisdom of a great theologian, and withal as great philanthropist, the Rev. Dr. Wayland, of Philadelphia. Speaking, not long since, of the "Higher Education" of the colored people of the South, he said "that this subject concerned about 8,000,000 of our fellow-citizens, among whom are probably 1,500,000 voters. The education suited to these people is that which should be suited to white people under the same circumstances. These people are bearing the impress which was left on them by two centuries of slavery and several centuries of barbarism. This education must begin at the bottom. It must first of all produce the power of self-support to assist them to better their condition. It should teach them good citizenship and should build them up morally. It should be, first, a good English education. They should be imbued with the knowledge of the Bible. They should have an industrial education. An industrial education leads to self-support and to the elevation of their condition. Industry is itself largely an education, intellectually and morally, and, above all, an education of character. Thus we should make these people self-dependent. This education will do away with pupils being taught Latin and Greek, while they do not know the rudiments of English."

Just notice the cautious, restrictive, limiting nature of this advice! Observe the lack of largeness, freedom and generosity in it. Dr. Wayland, I am sure, has never specialized just such a regimen for the poor Italians, Hungarians or Irish, who swarm, in lowly degradation, in immigrant ships to our shores. No! for them he wants, all Americans want, the widest, largest culture of the land;

the instant opening, not simply of the common schools; and then an easy passage to the bar, the legislature, and even the judgeships of the nation. And they oft times get there.

But how different the policy with the Negro. *He* must have "an education which begins at the bottom." "He should have an industrial education," &c. His education must, first of all, produce the power of self-support, &c.

Now, all this thought of Dr. Wayland is all true. But, my friends it is all false, too; and for the simple reason that it is only half truth. Dr. Wayland seems unable to rise above the plane of burden-bearing for the Negro. He seems unable to gauge the idea of the Negro becoming a thinker. He seems to forget that a race of thoughtless toilers are destined to be forever a race of senseless *boys;* for only beings who think are men.

How pitiable it is to see a great good men be-fuddled by a half truth. For to allege "Industrialism" to be the grand agency in the elevation of a race of already degraded labourers, is as much a mere platitude as to say, "they must eat and drink and sleep;" for man cannot live without these habits. But they never civilize man; and *civilization* is the objective point in the movement for Negro elevation. Labor, just like eating and drinking, is one of the inevitabilities of life, one of its positive necessities. And the Negro has had it for centuries; but it has never given him manhood. It does not *now,* in wide areas of population, lift him up to moral and social elevation. Hence the need of a new factor in his life. The Negro needs light: . . . the light of civilization.

* * *

George Washington Carver teaching a class on soil chemistry at Tuskegee Institute. The world famous chemist, born in 1864, discovered hundreds of uses for the peanut, sweet potato, and soy bean. Director of the Department of Agricultural Research at Tuskegee Institute, Carver conducted research that revitalized the economy of the South.

The Negro Race in this land must repudiate this absurd notion which is stealing on the American mind. The Race must declare that it is not to be put into a single groove; and for the simple reason (1) that *man* was made by his Maker to traverse the whole circle of existence, above as well as below; and that universality is the kernel of all true civilization, of all race elevation. And (2) that the Negro mind, imprisoned for nigh three hundred years, needs breadth and freedom, largeness, altitude, and elasticity; not stint nor rigidity, nor contractedness.

But the "Gradgrinds" are in evidence on all sides, telling us that the colleges and scholarships given us since emancipation, are all a mistake: and that the whole system must be reversed. The conviction is widespread that the Negro has no business in the higher walks of scholarship; that, for instance, Prof. Scarborough has no right to labor in philosophy; Professor Kelly Miller in mathematics; Professor DuBois, in history; Dr. Bowen, in theology; Professor Turner, in science; nor Mr. Tanner in art. There is no repugnance to the Negro buffoon, and the Negro scullion; but so soon as the Negro stands forth as an intellectual being, this toad of American prejudice, as at the touch of Ithuriel's spear, starts up a devil!

It is this attitude, this repellant, this forbidding attitude of the American mind, which forces the Negro in this land, to both recognize and to foster the talent and capacity of his own race, and to strive to put that capacity and talent to use for the race. I have detailed the dark and dreadful attempt to stamp that intellect out of existence. It is not only a past, it is also, modified indeed, a present fact; and out of it springs the need of just such an organization as the Negro Academy.*

---

*Alexander Crummell, *The Attitude of the American Mind Toward the Negro Intellect* (Washington, Occasional Papers, No. 3, American Negro Academy, 1898), 12-16.

CHAPTER NINE

The Negro Stands Up

The twentieth century was acclaimed as the "dawn of a new age." The previous hundred years had seen almost unbelievable advances in science, technology, and the rise of cities. It is not surprising, therefore, that during this era the Negro "stood up." The slave generation had passed away, their sons stood in their place. The meeting of President Theodore Roosevelt and Booker T. Washington was symbolic of the new status of the Negro. Roosevelt's personal feelings may have combined an aristocratic condescension with a politician's smile, but Washington did *stand by his side. The President* did *publicly accord Washington his respect, his esteem. Behind this polite veneer of two men, one white, and one black, existed the racial hatred, bitterness, and violence of a nation still divided. But a new Negro is arising, and he will not be content with the old ways.*

INTRODUCTION

The Negro Stands Up

At the turn of the century as the Negro race grasped for a power lever which would return an equal measure of justice, the ligaments of race leadership tightened. Booker T. Washington seemed to be everywhere, traveling incessantly in and out of the South, seeking donors, spreading his industrial education gospel and listening to the pulse-beat of his people. He followed closely the ebb and flow of the race in journalism, philanthropy, political appointments, and railroad segregation laws. He nursed the various organizations which had his blessing like the National Negro Business League and never lost track of those which sprang up in opposition to him. His opponents "would have felt less bitter toward" him, a white reformer commented years later, "if he had been able to delegate authority; but like most self-made men, he took details upon himself."

The opposition among Negroes to Washington was primarily northern as the century began, although one of the acknowledged spokesmen, W. E. B. DuBois, was still at Atlanta University, continuing his sociological studies and refining his ideological position. DuBois placed his emphasis on the race's need for leadership and the discovery of talent within the race.

Washington's concern over the growing polarization was based on his fear that a more aggressive policy would alienate white support of Negro institutions and seriously curtail the flow of money and the acceleration of educational and organizational efforts. Washington was also concerned about his own leadership role and the challenge which the opposition—he called it the enemy—was mounting. His strategy, based in part upon information which his friends or agents in the North sent him, was to call a conference which would establish himself and his ideas as dominant, leaving room for the dissidents to preach and practice under the watchful eye of the Tuskegee organization.

Washington's sensitivity to this opposition led him to miscalculate its force. The conference which met in New York City in January 1904 was a failure, in spite of his and the opposition's careful planning. The Committee of Twelve which emerged to carry on its work was so tightly controlled from Tuskegee that the opposition abandoned all attempts to work within the Washington orbit. After casting about unsuccessfully for financial support for some of his own projects, DuBois resolved to call a conference of his own.

Aside from the ideological and internecine struggles between Washington and DuBois, the Tuskegee opponents were enraged and bewildered by the inflexible white supremacy doctrine of southern spokesmen who were becoming less defensive and more unequivocal in their assertions that they could handle the "Negro problem." Their method, it seemed to DuBois, was lynching, convict labor, disfranchisement, segregation, and brutality. If Tuskegee could not stand up to defy this doctrine and its methods, another group should shoulder the responsibility.

DuBois sent out his call from Atlanta in June 1905 for a conference "to oppose firmly the present methods of strangling honest criticism; to organize intelligent and honest Negroes; and to support organs of news and public opinion." The Niagara Movement was designed at the meeting which responded to the call the following month and organized early the next year. It leaned on a small interracial group, The Constitution League, headed by a New York industrialist, John Milholland, and it attracted the critical attention of Washington who tried to undermine its efforts. Its significance was manifold; not only did its emphases coincide generally with its successor organization, the National Association for the Advancement of Colored People (NAACP), but it provided a springboard on which Negro leaders opposed to Washington could test their efforts. The Movement sponsored a publication which was succeeded by the NAACP's *The Crisis.* It drew in and spoke for the enlarging group of Negroes who deplored the narrow platform on which Booker T. Washington stood. It tested and tasted the wrath of northern and southern whites who believed with Washington that political and civil rights and education for leadership were postponable race objectives.

Violence had been a constant companion of Negroes, particularly since the Civil War. The Reconstruction process included the use of federal troops and the rise of the Ku Klux Klan; the dissipation of Reconstruction was accompanied by election violence and a high rate of lynching. In the fifteen years before 1900, over 1500 Negroes were lynched. Between 1900 and 1910, inclusive, almost 900 Negroes were lynched. The sickening brutality of the act of lynching was matched only by its lawlessness and, in too many cases, the innocence of its victims.

The urban response to these public and private postures was race riot. Just before the turn of the century, Wilmington, N.C., exploded in the first race riot of consequence since Reconstruction as a kind of symbolic precedent for twentieth-century cities on both sides of the Mason-Dixon line. The Wilmington riot followed an impassioned election campaign in which the twin tools of intimidation and fraud brought in a white supremacist government. Plans were drawn up before the election to coerce the Negro voter and the Negro worker, and to expel the editor of the Negro paper. Two days after the election, as whites began to execute their plan, the riot flamed.

The Brownsville, Texas, affair (1906) involved three companies of the all-Negro Twenty-fifth Regiment and President Theodore Roosevelt took excessive punitive action against the soldiers, to the astonished dismay of the race. The punishment was later modified by an act of Congress. Two years later, in the city where Abraham Lincoln established his home, a race riot erupted with such virulence that it sensitized a country which had grown accustomed to race violence. The report of William English Walling in the liberal *Independent* galvanized a few northern whites and Negroes to mobilize what would become the NAACP.

The South's posture throughout the early twentieth century placed an inviolable aura around race violence. Deploring the results and attributing the causes to Negroid tendencies toward crime and rape, Southerners preached the doctrine of the Negro's

This cartoon appeared in the Raleigh News and Observer, *on July 4, 1900. Drawn by Norman E. Jennette, it was designed to shock and repulse: The Negro demon should not be allowed to vote! Such propaganda proved to be effective, and in August, 1900, North Carolina had an amendment to the Constitution which amounted to Negro disenfranchisement.*

inferiority and limited capacity with such frequency that even the Senate itself became surfeited. To Senator James K. Vardaman of Mississippi the Negro was a black mammy or trusted servant; the Negro was a black brute or a lascivious ape. Whatever the approach, it hammered home the doctrine that the Negro did not deserve the equal treatment he was not getting and did deserve the unequal treatment he was getting. The South, their partisans repeated, knew the Negro and how to handle him.

The wall which separated the races barred from the South the currents of constructive change which were sweeping the North. The Progressive spirit was marked by a deep wellspring of concern for the individual in a growing society and, after an abortive marriage with Southern Populism before the turn of the century, was largely confined to the North and West. Before 1900, too, it developed an abiding nonpolitical character which sought out the forgotten nooks and crannies in society's structure, studied them, exposed them to light and tried to cleanse them.

Inevitably, the Progressive reformers found the nook and cranny marked "black." As Upton Sinclair exposed the meatpackers and Lincoln Steffens city government, Ray Stannard Baker followed the color line, North and South, to reveal its strength and injustice. As social scientists began to investigate the new science of society, Negro and white scholars turned their attention to the Negro population with serious studies of Ohio, Pennsylvania, Boston, Philadelphia, New York City, Chicago, and St. Louis. As the depersonalized life of the city called for Hull House (1889) in Chicago and the Henry Street Settlement House (1893) in New York to care for individuals whom society had cut adrift, so too did whites and Negroes establish institutions expressly for the helpless urban Negroes.

Negroes and whites alike joined to alleviate some of the distress caused by urbanization. Settlement houses sprang up in major northern cities; in New York, Victoria Earle Matthews founded the White Rose Industrial Association in 1897, an outgrowth of her concern for unemployed women of her race. William L. Bulkley, the first Negro principal of a New York City school, opened a night industrial school for industrial and commercial training in 1903. Three years later, he was instrumental in founding the interracial Committee for Improving the Industrial Conditions of Negroes in New York City.

The nonpolitical Progressives did not stop with social welfare agencies. William English Walling's article on the Springfield, Illinois, riots in 1908 brought an immediate reaction from New York City reformers. Mary White Ovington read it and "within the hour" wrote Walling in appreciation and in answer to his "appeal to citizens to come to the Negro's aid." Others, notably Oswald Garrison Villard, joined and a call was drafted for publication on February 12, 1909. The signers included men and women of both races, primarily from the North and some of the leading nonpolitical Progressives like Jane Addams, John Haynes Holmes, Florence Kelley, Lincoln Steffens, and Lillian D. Wald. Negro leaders were mostly of the anti-Booker Washington stamp: Ida Wells Barnett, William L. Bulkley, Rev. Francis J. Grimké, and DuBois.

The national conference met in New York in the late spring. After listening to prepared papers and speeches from representatives of both races, the conference wrestled with resolutions at great length. The Negroes in attendance were anxious to have the conference's public statement condemn the oppressive conditions in which the race lived as an antidote to the acknowledged Tuskegee position. A committee on permanent organization was established and the conference met again in 1910, this time to recommend the establishment of the NAACP, with a professional staff, a bureau for investigations, a legal aid committee and a publicity department. To those who called this "an unwise movement," the *Nation* replied that equal justice demanded action; "agitation is precisely what is needed."

The early years of the organization were not easy. *The Crisis*, its monthly publication, began in 1910 under the editorship of W. E. B. Dubois, who resigned from Atlanta University to undertake the job. "My career as a scientist," he remembered, "was to be swallowed up in my role as master of propaganda." Local branches sprang up and survived, helping to fight bills in state legislatures which threatened to introduce or extend discrimination. The national office began to investigate lynchings and publicize the record. It fought bills which Southerners introduced into Congress designed further to constrict the Negro in the District of Columbia, in the armed services, and in the federal government. With only a trickle of funds, an enlarging membership and a rainbow of causes, the NAACP shakily but firmly commenced the fight for equality.

It was readily apparent that the NAACP would not directly affect several sensitive areas of discrimination, notably housing and health, employment and industrial education, and the family. The Committee for Improving the Industrial Condition of Negroes in

New York City was too small to undertake a responsibility that was essentially national in scope. The National League for Protection of Colored Women (1906) had branches in several cities to help Negro girls without jobs or funds, but the problems were larger than its capabilities.

Negro leaders and white philanthropists and social workers, many of whom were already engaged with the Committee and the National League, launched a third local group, the Committee on Urban Conditions Among Negroes in New York City. This was to serve as a coordinator for the existing committees. For this effort came money from John D. Rockefeller, Julius Rosenwald and others which enabled the still-separate but consolidating group to federate as the National League on Urban Conditions Among Negroes, soon shortened to National Urban League, employ George Edmund Haynes as an executive secretary and, early in 1911, hire Eugene Kinckle Jones of Louisville as a field secretary. Haynes, who was on the faculty of Fisk University and particularly interested in training Negro social workers, soon exchanged positions with Jones who was to serve the National Urban League as its executive for over forty years.

The Urban League was launched out of the same Progressive spirit which created the NAACP. A predominantly northern movement, it made its way South slowly but more easily because it eschewed agitation for persuasion, but it was no less militant within its defined limits of service. It had a broader acceptance among whites than the NAACP since its humanitarian appeal softened race distinctions, yet it was unflinchingly interracial. "White people," Haynes later recalled "were asked to work *with* Negroes for their mutual advantage and advancement rather than work *for* them as a problem."

The nonpolitical thrust of Progressivism deposited more fruitful seeds in pre-World War I America than did its political arm. The midwestern Progressives who came to Congress, beginning with Wisconsin's Robert M. LaFollette, readily included the Negro in their struggle to utilize the weight of the federal and state governments to equalize opportunity in economic and political matters. Time and again, Albert Cummins of Iowa, Wesley Jones of Washington, and Moses Clapp of Minnesota engaged their southern colleagues on the Senate floor on the "Negro question," not always to their own advantage. Mrs. LaFollette was an untiring friend of the Negro in the District of Columbia, reflecting her husband's views. But when it came to legislation, the Insurgents had to cope with a coalition of Democrats and conservative Republicans which undercut any efforts on their part to create favorable laws.

When Theodore Roosevelt bolted the Republican party, he found himself in the middle of a race dilemma. Should he recognize those Republicans from the South who voted, the lily-whites, or should he recognize those who were disfranchised, the Negroes. He chose the first course and defended himself in the *Outlook.* His Negro support divided. Some attacked his course of action while others defended it, but there was no doubt that he had alienated the vast majority of Negro voters. Seven months after the election, he advised an associate to "pay heed to the Negro in the Northern States," since he himself had failed to do so.

The election of Wilson was marked by a higher percentage of Negro support, up to 20 per cent of the Negro vote according to one observer, than the Democratic party had ever achieved. As a consequence of this and Wilson's own humanitarian leanings, the race had high expectations after his inauguration. These were soon shattered. The Wilson administration lost no time in introducing segregation into such federal agencies as the Post Office and the Treasury Departments. Federal posts which traditionally had gone to Negroes were given to whites, in a calculated policy which opened no other posts to qualified candidates.

The frustrations of politics seasoned the steady diet of circumscription at work and at home. Unions and employers yielded ever so slowly to appeals to accept skilled Negro workers in industry. Professional organizations enforced total or, like the American Bar Association in 1912, qualified bans on Negro members. Southern and border cities passed ordinances to segregate residential districts; when St. Louis voted in a similar ordinance by referendum in 1916, the national reaction made it appear as if a flood level had been reached. Yet many northern cities had separate Negro districts. "They are somewhat segregated by their own motion," read a 1912 Davenport, Iowa, report, and so it was in Syracuse, New York, and St. Paul, Minnesota, Cambridge, Massachusetts, and Lancaster, Pennsylvania, to name a few. Generally, Negro quarters were "worse than white," or their "sanitary conditions are bad," but in some cities, Negroes lived in conditions comparable to whites of the same economic level.

Futility, circumscription, and isolation were the winds which carried what Ray Stannard Baker called in 1916 the "gathering clouds along the color line." Negro education, he pointed out, was still a stepchild in the South. Though colored children were 40 per cent of the school population in eleven southern states, they only received 12 per cent of the school funds. In some states, he added, "the colored people do not even get back all the money for their schools that they themselves actually pay in taxes." Lynching was still a major cause for impatience and the racial taint of news stories a major cause of irritation. The anti-Negro film "Birth of a Nation," portraying Negroes as ignorant rogues and Ku Klux Klansmen as virtuous crusaders during Reconstruction, was one of a number of such popular documents which added to the Negro's indignation and bolstered his stereotype among whites.

The storm which Baker sensed broke the year before the United States entered the World War, taking a form which few had anticipated. Initiated by the U.S. Department of Labor, a scattered movement of colored persons and groups moved North in 1916 to fill industrial jobs made available by the cessation of foreign immigration and the expansion of war industries. The Erie and Pennsylvania Railroads fell in immediately with the plans, followed by a variety of industries, some of which sent agents South to encourage the migration. The movement gathered force and swept thousands of Negroes of both sexes and all ages out of the South. Southerners reacted in alarm. "Our very solvency is being sucked out from underneath," the Jackson (Miss.) *Daily News* declared, while "we go about our affairs as usual." A few cities prohibited or inhibited the enticement of labor from their limits.

While the migration was in full swing, President Wilson asked Congress to declare war on Germany and the country responded with patriotic fervor. The regular army included several regiments of Negro troops and there was a sprinkling of colored National Guard units. There was only one Negro graduate of West Point on active duty, but, for reasons of health, he was unable to serve during the war. The National Guard had a few colored officers, but the Regular Army had none. War fever rose quickly among Negroes, as among whites, and the race clamored for more Negro units and officers. The War Department's response was the creation of two Negro divisions, the 92nd and the 93rd, both of which saw service overseas, although the 93rd Division fought with the French and not as a unit. The Department established a training center for Negro officers in Des Moines, Iowa, but no Negro, outside of a band officer or chaplain, was promoted beyond the rank of Captain.

Three-quarters of the approximately 200,000 Negro troops overseas were in noncombatant labor battalions. In general they and the combat troops suffered discriminatory treatment in recreation, allocation of duties, leaves and passes, and promotion. Colored troops serving in this country suffered comparable indignities; in Houston in August, 1917, members of the Twenty-fourth Infantry rioted in reaction to police brutality. Seventeen whites were killed and thirteen soldiers executed. Alarmed by the charges of discrimination and low morale, the Federal Council of Churches investigated the treatment of Negro soldiers and made its recommendations public in 1918.

Negroes were torn between the desire for race justice and service to the nation. In July, 1917, thousands of Negroes marched silently down Fifth Avenue in New York protesting the violence in East St. Louis and the South. "Mr. President," one banner asked, "why not make America safe for democracy?" Public statements, like Kelly Miller's impassioned open letter to President Wilson, stressed patriotism and the rights of the race. *The Crisis* urged the race to serve its country and unceasingly kept up a drumbeat of protest against injustice.

The Wilson administration was not able to ignore the race protest and made several concessions to secure colored support of the war effort. Secretary of War Newton D. Baker asked Emmett J. Scott, former private secretary to Booker T. Washington, to come to Washington as his special assistant in the fall of 1917. Secretary of Labor William B. Wilson called George E. Haynes to Washington to serve as Director of the Division of Negro Economics in June, 1918. Ralph W. Tyler became a correspondent for the Committee on Public Information, a federal war agency, and such Negro leaders as R. R. Moton, Washington's successor at Tuskegee, and W. E. B. DuBois were invited to tour American encampments abroad immediately after the war.

By mass migration, war service, and organized protest, the Negro abandoned his position as a sectional stepchild to take his place as a national integer. His increasing numbers in the North meant more colored voters, more colored factory workers, and potentially, better-educated Negroes ready to assume leadership in every area of American life, racial and nonracial. His was service gave him another irrevocable claim to be recognized fully as a citizen. "The American Negro, with the freedom and rights of a man, has arrived," wrote a white Methodist bishop from New Orleans, just before the Armistice.

Contrasting Positions and a New Militancy

154

THE VIRTUE OF INDUSTRIAL EDUCATION

In 1903, the book The Negro Problem: A Series of Articles by Representative American Negroes of To-Day *was published in New York. No editor signed his name and the publisher was practically unknown. Nevertheless, the book contains some very forceful statements on the Negro's place in American society by such men as Charles W. Chesnutt, a very successful writer living in Cleveland, Paul Lawrence Dunbar, the poet, and T. Thomas Fortune. The essays by Booker T. Washington and W. E. B. DuBois appear as the first two contributions and are a rare instance of the two men presenting their viewpoints back-to-back in print. The book came out just prior to the January 1904 conference which marked the irrevocable split between the two men and their ideological positions.*

INDUSTRIAL EDUCATION FOR
THE NEGRO

For two hundred and fifty years, I believe the way for the redemption of the Negro was being prepared through industrial development. Through all those years the Southern white man did business with the Negro in a way that no one else has done business with him. In most cases if a Southern white man wanted a house built he consulted a Negro mechanic about the plan and about the actual building of the structure. If he wanted a suit of clothes made he went to a Negro tailor, and for shoes he went to a shoemaker of the same race. In a certain way every slave plantation in the South was an industrial school. On these plantations young colored men and women were constantly being trained not only as farmers but as carpenters, blacksmiths, wheelwrights, brick masons, engineers, cooks, laundresses, sewing women and housekeepers.

I do not mean in any way to apologize for the curse of slavery, which was a curse to both races, but in what I say about industrial training in slavery I am simply stating facts. This training was crude, and was given for selfish purposes. It did not answer the highest ends, because there was an absence of mental training in connection with the training of the hand. To a large degree, though, this business contact with the Southern white man, and the industrial training on the plantations, left the Negro at the close of the war in possession of nearly all the common and skilled labor in the South.

* * *

In most of the industries, though, what happened? For nearly twenty years after the war, except in a few instances, the value of the industrial training given by the plantations was overlooked. Negro men and women were educated in literature, in mathematics and in the sciences, with little thought of what had been taking place during the preceding two hundred and fifty years, except, perhaps, as something to be escaped, to be got as far away from as possible. As a generation began to pass, those who had been trained as mechanics in slavery began to disappear by death, and gradually it began to be realized that there were few to take their places.

* * *

Some years ago, when we decided to make tailoring a part of our training at the Tuskegee Institute, I was amazed to find that it was almost impossible to find in the whole country an educated colored man who could teach the making of clothing. We could find numbers of them who could teach astronomy, theology, Latin or grammar, but almost none who could instruct in the making of clothing, something that has to be used by every one of us every day in the year. How often have I been discouraged as I have gone through the South, and into the homes of the people of my race, and have found women who could converse intelligently upon abstruse subjects, and yet could not tell how to improve the condition of the poorly cooked and still more poorly served bread and meat which they and their families were eating three times a day.

* * *

I would not confine the race to industrial life, not even to agriculture, for example, although I believe that by far the greater part of the Negro race is best off in the country districts and must and should continue to live there, but I would teach the race that in industry the foundation must be laid—that the very best service which any one can render to what is called the higher education is to teach the present generation to provide a material or industrial foundation. On such a foundation as this will grow habits of thrift, a love of work, economy, ownership of property, bank accounts. Out of it in the future will grow practical education, professional education, positions of public responsibility. Out of it will grow moral and religious strength. Out of it will grow wealth from which alone can come leisure and the opportunity for the enjoyment of literature and the fine arts.

* * *

I would set no limits to the attainments of the Negro in arts, in letters or statesmanship, but I believe the surest way to reach those ends is by laying the foundation in the little things of life that lie immediately about one's door. I plead for industrial education and development for the Negro not because I want to cramp him, but because I want to free him. I want to see him enter the all-powerful business and commercial world.

* * *

Almost from the first Tuskegee has kept in mind—and this I think should be the policy of all industrial schools—fitting students for occupations which would be open to them in their home communities. Some years ago we noted the fact that there was beginning to be a demand in the South for men to operate dairies in a skillful, modern manner. We opened a dairy department in connection with the school, where a number of young men could have instruction in the latest and most scientific methods of dairy work. At present we have calls—mainly from Southern white men—for twice as many dairymen as we are able to supply.

* * *

Many seem to think that industrial education is meant to make the Negro work as he worked in the days of slavery. This is far from my conception of industrial education. If this training is worth anything to the Negro, it consists in teaching him how not to work, but how to make the forces of nature—air, steam, water, horse-power and electricity—work for him. If it has any value it is in lifting labor up out of toil and drudgery into the plane of the dignified and the beautiful. The Negro in the South works and works hard; but too often his ignorance and lack of skill causes him to do his work in the most costly and shiftless manner, and this keeps him near the bottom of the ladder in the economic world.

* * *

I close, then, as I began, by saying that as a slave the Negro was worked, and that as a freeman he must learn to work. There is still doubt in many quarters as to the ability of the Negro unguided, unsupported, to hew his own path and put into visible, tangible, indisputable form, products and signs of civilization. This doubt cannot be much affected by abstract arguments, no matter how delicately and convincingly woven together. Patiently, quietly, doggedly, persistently, through summer and winter, sunshine and shadow, by self-sacrifice, by foresight, by honesty and industry, we must re-enforce argument with results. One farm bought, one house built, one home sweetly and intelligently kept, one man who is the largest tax payer or has the largest bank account, one school or church maintained, one factory running successfully, one truck garden profitably cultivated, one patient cured by a Negro doctor, one sermon well preached, one office well filled, one life cleanly lived—these will tell more in our favor than all the abstract eloquence that can be summoned to plead our cause. Our pathway must be up through the soil, up through swamps, up through forests, up through the streams, the rocks, up through commerce, education and religion!*

---

*Booker T. Washington, "Industrial Education for Negroes," in *The Negro Problem: A Series of Articles by Representative American Negroes of To-day* (New York: James Pott & Co., 1903), 10-29.

155

LEADERSHIP EDUCATION

In his defense of educating the Talented Tenth, that ten per cent of the Negro race with leadership potential, W. E. B. DuBois began with a long historical introduction. He called to mind past Negro leaders from Phyllis Wheatley and Paul Cuffee to the post-Civil War generation of Blanche K. Bruce and Bishop Daniel Payne. He defended the recently established Negro universities and their graduates, while admitting their deficiencies, and offered statistical evidence of the occupations which Negro college graduates filled. The evidence, he maintained, demonstrated that Negro college graduates were in leadership positions, including the most important responsibility of training Negro youth.

THE TALENTED TENTH

The problem of training the Negro is to-day immensely complicated by the fact that the whole question of the efficiency and appropriateness of our present systems of education, for any kind of child, is a matter of active debate, in which final settlement seems still afar off. Consequently it often happens that persons arguing for or against certain systems of education for Negroes, have these controversies in mind and miss the real question at issue. The main question, so far as the Southern Negro is concerned, is: What under the present circumstance, must a system of education do in order to raise the Negro as quickly as possible in the scale of civilization? The answer to this question seems to me clear: It must strengthen the Negro's character, increase his knowledge and teach him to earn a living. Now it goes without saying, that it is hard to do all these things simultaneously or suddenly, and that at the same time it will not do to give all the attention to one and neglect the others; we could give black boys trades, but that alone will not civilize a race of ex-slaves; we might simply increase their knowledge of the world, but this would not necessarily make them wish to use this knowledge honestly; we might seek to strengthen character and purpose, but to what end if this people have nothing to eat or to wear? A system of education is not one thing, nor does it have a single definite object, nor is it a mere matter of schools. Education is that whole system of human training within and without the school house walls, which molds and develops men. If then we start out to train an ignorant and unskilled people with a heritage of bad habits, our system of training must set before itself two great aims—the one dealing with knowledge and character, the other part seeking to give the child the technical knowledge necessary for him to earn a living under the present circumstances. These objects are accomplished in part by the opening of the common schools on the one, and of the industrial schools on the other. But only in part, for there must also be trained those who are to teach these schools—men and women of knowledge and culture and technical skill who understand modern civilization, and have the training and aptitude to impart it to the children under them. There must be teachers, and teachers of teachers, and to attempt to establish any sort of a system of common and industrial school training, without *first* (and I say *first* advisedly) without *first* providing for the higher training of the very best teachers, is simply throwing your money to the winds. School houses do not teach themselves—piles of brick and mortar and machinery do not send out *men*. It is the trained, living human soul, cultivated and strengthened by long study and thought, that breathes the real breath of life into boys and girls and makes them human, whether they be black or white, Greek, Russian or American. Nothing, in these latter days, has so dampened the faith of thinking Negroes in recent educational movements, as the fact that such movements have been accompanied by ridicule and denouncement and decrying of those very institutions of higher training which made the Negro public school possible, and make Negro industrial schools thinkable. It was Fisk, Atlanta, Howard and Straight, those colleges born of the faith and sacrifice of the abolitionists, that placed in the black schools of the South the 30,000 teachers and more, which some, who depreciate the work of these higher schools, are using to teach their own new experiments. If Hampton, Tuskegee and the hundred other industrial schools prove in the future to be as successful as they deserve to be, then their success in training black artisans for the South, will be due primarily to the white colleges of the North and the black colleges of the South, which trained the teachers who to-day conduct these institutions. There was a time when the American people believed pretty devoutly that a log of wood with a boy at one end and Mark Hopkins at the other, represented the highest ideal of human training. But in these eager days it would seem that we have changed all that and think it necessary to add a couple of saw-mills and a hammer to this outfit, and, at a pinch, to dispense with the services of Mark Hopkins.

I would not deny, or for a moment seem to deny, the paramount necessity of teaching the Negro to work, and to work steadily and skillfully; or seem to depreciate in the slightest degree the important part industrial schools must play in the accomplishment of these ends, but I *do* say, and insist upon it, that it is industrialism drunk with its vision of success, to imagine that its own work can be accomplished without providing for the training of broadly cultured men and women to teach its own teachers, and to teach the teachers of the public schools.

* * *

It is coming to be seen, however, in the education of the Negro, as clearly as it has been in the education of the youths the world over, that it is the *boy* and not the material product, that is the true object of education. Consequently the object of the industrial school came to be the thorough training of boys regardless of the cost of the training, so long as it was thoroughly well done.

Thus, again, in the manning of trade schools we are thrown back upon the higher training as its source and chief support. What is the chief need for the building up of the Negro public school in the South? The Negro race in the South needs teachers to-day above all else. This is the concurrent testimony of all who know the situation. For the supply of this great demand two things are needed—institutions of higher education and money for school houses and salaries.

It is usually assumed that a hundred or more institutions for Negro training are to-day turning out so many teachers and college-bred men that the race is threatened with an over-supply. This is sheer nonsense. There are to-day less than 3,000 living Negro college graduates in the United States, and less than 1,000 Negroes in college. Moreover, in the 164 schools for Negroes, 95 per cent of their students are doing elementary and secondary work, work which should be done in the public schools. Over half the remaining 2,157 students are taking high school studies. The mass of so-called "normal" schools for the Negro, are simply doing elementary common school work, or, at most, high school work, with a little instruction in methods. The Negro colleges and the post-graduate courses at other institutions are the only agencies for the broader and more careful training of teachers. The work of these institutions is hampered for lack of funds. It is getting increasingly difficult to get funds for training teachers in the best modern methods, and yet all over the South, from State Superintendents, county officials, city boards and school principals comes the wail, "We need TEACHERS!" and teachers must be trained. .

* * *

There was a time when any aged and wornout carpenter could teach in a trade school. But not so to-day. Indeed the demand for college-bred men by a school like Tuskegee, ought to make Mr. Booker T. Washington the firmest friend of higher training. Here he has as helpers the son of a Negro senator, trained in Greek and the humanities, and graduated at Harvard; the son of a Negro congressman and lawyer, trained in Latin and mathematics, and graduated at Oberlin; he has as his wife, a woman who read Virgil and Homer in the same class room with me; he has as college chaplain, a classical graduate of Atlanta University; as teacher of science, a graduate of Fisk; as teacher of history, a graduate of Smith,—indeed some thirty of his chief teachers are college graduates, and instead of studying French grammars in the midst of weeds, or buying pianos for dirty cabins, they are at Mr. Washington's right hand helping him in a noble work. And yet one of the effects of Mr. Washington's propaganda has been to throw doubt upon the expediency of such training for Negroes, as these persons have had.

Men of America, the problem is plain before you. Here is a race transplanted through the criminal foolishness of your fathers. Whether you like it or not the millions are here, and here they will remain. If you do not lift them up, they will pull you down. Education and work are the levers to uplift a people. Work alone will not do it unless inspired by the right ideals and guided by intelligence. Education must not simply teach work—it must teach Life. The Talented Tenth of the Negro race must be made leaders of thought and missionaries of culture among their people. No others can do this work and Negro colleges must train men for it. The Negro race, like all other races, is going to be saved by its exceptional men.*

---

*W. E. B. DuBois, "The Talented Tenth," in *The Negro Problem: A Series of Articles by Representative American Negroes of To-day* (New York: James Pott & Co., 1903), 56-75.

The conference of January 1904 followed almost a year of planning and preparation by both the Washington and DuBois factions. The Tuskegee group took the initiative and Washington secured funds, probably from Andrew Carnegie, to finance the meeting. The leading activists from both factions were present, although the absence of William Monroe Trotter was noticeable. Whites in attendance included Andrew Carnegie, W. H. Baldwin, Jr., a trustee of Tuskegee, Oswald Garrison Villard, editor of the New York Evening Post, *William Hayes Ward, editor of the* Independent, *George F. Peabody, associated with the Peabody Fund, and Carl Schurz.*

At Washington's request, the proceedings of the conference were confidential. He and DuBois addressed the conference briefly and Washington was asked some spirited questions about his stands on suffrage, higher education, and civil rights. At the conclusion of the conference, according to information leaked to the anti-Washington newspaper, The Washington Bee, *the principal of Tuskegee arose to acknowledge his support for higher education and "peaceful and rational methods" to abolish segregation and he promised to speak out on these points. DuBois expressed his satisfaction with Washington's statement and the conference ended.*

Actually, the agreement was more apparent than real, for Washington did not alter his public position, nor did he relinquish control of the machinery set up to carry out the wishes of the conference. As a result, the conference served to harden the gap between the two factions and marked a convenient point from which the polarization can be observed.

LETTER OF INVITATION TO DELEGATES

November 19th, 1903
Hotel Manhattan, New York City

Dear Sir:

More than a year ago, after consultation with Dr. DuBois and others, it was determined to hold in New York City a private conference, to last three days, and to consist of from eighteen to twenty members of the race, who should represent, so far as possible, its leading thought and achievements in all directions, and seek to devise, if possible, through free and frank discussion, such measures as would improve conditions among our people.

New York was selected as the place of meeting for the reason that it is possibly the only city in the country in which so large a number of colored men could assemble without attracting the attention of the Newspapers, and other agents of publicity. It was also felt that persons coming to this city could be free there from other responsibilities, and be able to devote three quiet days to serious study of the needs and conditions of the Negro.

As the funds necessary to pay the expenses of the conference could not be collected in time to hold it last year, it has been decided that the conference will meet in the city of New York, during January 6th, 7th, and 8th, 1904. I am asked to invite you to be present, and to participate in our deliberations.

In case you so desire, all your expenses of travel and board will be defrayed, and the money for this purpose has been so provided that no member of the conference can feel under obligations to any individual or organization.

I greatly hope that you can see your way toward accepting this invitation. Should you desire it, I will send you the names of the other men who have received invitations to the meeting. I feel that our present condition as a race in this country demands that we should make every sacrifice, and put forth every effort, to attend this conference, as the matters to be discussed are of the greatest importance to our future. I do not believe that there has ever been a race gathering so fraught with seriousness and value as the one will be concerning which I am writing.

I hardly need add, since I have said that the conference is to be private, that the whole matter should be held absolutely confidential. Each one who has been asked to attend, has been requested to speak on the subject to no one else.

Very truly yours,

Booker T. Washington

DuBois (Confidential.) Memoranda on the Washington Meeting

Those invited to the meeting may be roughly classified as follows:

Unscrupulously for Washington (Lewis, Fortune, Stewart, McKinley, Smith, Knox, and Washington)

Without enthusiasm or with scruples (Moton, Anderson, Walker, Proctor, Napier, Grant, H. C. Morris)

Uncertain, leaning to Washington (Walters, Hayes, Trower)

Uncertain, possibly against Washington (Kealing, Scott, Lyons)

Anti-Washington (Miller)

Uncompromisingly Anti-Washington (Morgan, E. H. Morris, McGhee, Grimké, DuBois)

Principles of Anti-Washington men

1. Opposition to any organization or person which does not stand for:
   a. The right of Negroes to vote on exactly the same terms as other citizens vote.
   b. Equal civil rights.
   c. Educational opportunities according to ability, including college, normal industrial and common school training.
2. Full, candid and open criticism of Mr. Washington's attitude on:
   a. The suffrage and office holding.
   b. Civil rights.
   c. College and industrial training.
3. Refusal to take part in this meeting or any meeting or any organization where the right of free discussion of Mr. Washington's attitude and the attitude of other influential men is not allowed.

Notes

1. The tactics of the pro-Washington men will take one or more of the following forms:

a. Conciliation and compromise.
b. Irritation and brow-beating.
c. Silent shutting off of discussion by closure methods.

2. Come prepared therefore, in case of
   a. to be firm and hammer at the principles and Washington's record.
   b. to keep good temper and insist on free speech.
   c. to protest against closure or underhand methods even to the extent of leaving the meeting.

Bring every speech or letter or record of Washington you can lay hands on so that he can face his record in print.

The main issue of this meeting is *Washington*, refuse to be side-tracked.

Anti-Washington men will please be in New York Tuesday night. Arrangements will be made for a supper and conference in a private dining room during the hours of 7-10 or later. Kindly write Mr. DuBois immediately as to your presence.*

157

THE NIAGARA MOVEMENT

The Niagara Movement's first general meeting was convened on the Canadian side of Niagara Falls to dramatize its protest against American inequities. It continued this practice of meeting in places with meaningful overtones by gathering in Harpers Ferry (1906), Boston (1907), and Oberlin (1908). The Movement functioned through various committees. The Health Committee, for example, urged a national campaign to wipe out tuberculosis, and the Education Committee recommended a pamphlet on southern Negro education for legislators and the general public. The state and local branches were handicapped for lack of funds although the Chicago and Massachusetts branches, in cooperation with other organizations, were credited with some successes.

Time and money ran out on the Movement. Its addresses became more impassioned and shrill. Booker T. Washington successfully persuaded the Negro and white press to ignore the Movement after 1907. Its political position—hostile to both parties in 1908—left it without a political base and cut it off from the mass of Negroes who were Taft Republicans. Its branches grew impotent and inactive. After 1909, with the exception of William Monroe Trotter, its advocates supported the National Association for the Advancement of Colored People.

THE NIAGARA MOVEMENT ADDRESS, JULY, 1905

We believe that [Negro] American citizens should protest emphatically and continually against the curtailment of their political rights. We believe in manhood sufferage: we believe that no man is so good, intelligent or wealthy as to be entrusted wholly with the welfare of his neighbor.

---

*Carter G. Woodson, ed., *The Works of Francis J. Grimké*, vol. IV (Washington, D.C., Associated Publishers, 1942), 88-90. Reprinted by permission.

We believe also in protest against the curtailment of our civil rights. All American citizens have the right to equal treatment in places of public entertainment according to their behavior and deserts.

We especially complain against the denial of equal opportunities to us in economic life; in the rural districts of the south this amounts to peonage and virtual slavery; all over the south it tends to crush labor and small business enterprises: and everywhere American prejudice, helped often by iniquitous laws, is making it more difficult for Negro-Americans to earn a decent living.

Common school education should be free to all American children and compulsory. High school training should be adequately provided for all, and college training should be the monopoly of no class or race in any section of our common country. We believe that in defense of its own institutions, the United States should aid common school education, particularly in the south, and we especially recommend concerted agitation to this end. We urge an increase in public high school facilities in the south, where the Negro-Americans are almost wholly without such provisions. We favor well-equipped trade and technical schools for the training of artisans, and the need of adequate and liberal endowment for a few institutions of higher education must be patent to sincere well-wishers of the race.

We demand upright judges in courts, juries selected without discrimination on account of color and the same measure of punishment, and the same efforts at reformation for black as for white offenders. We need orphanages and farm schools for dependent children, juvenile reformatories for delinquents, and the abolition of the dehumanizing convict-lease system.

* * *

We plead for health—for an opportunity to live in decent houses and localities, for a chance to rear our children in physical and moral cleanliness.

We hold up for public execration the conduct of two opposite classes of men; the practice among employers of importing ignorant Negro-American laborers in emergencies, and then affording them neither protection nor permanent employment; and the practice of labor unions of proscribing and boycotting and oppressing thousands of their fellow-toilers, simply because they are black. These methods have accentuated and will accentuate the war of labor and capital, and they are disgraceful to both sides.

We refuse to allow the impression to remain that the Negro-American assents to inferiority, is submissive under oppression and apologetic before insults. Through helplessness we may submit, but the voice of protest of ten million Americans must never cease to assail the ears of their fellows, so long as America is unjust.

* * *

We regret that this nation has never seen fit adequately to reward the black soldiers who in its five wars, have defended their country with their blood, and yet have been systematically denied the promotions which their abilities deserve. And we regard as unjust, the exclusion of black boys from the military and navy training schools.

* * *

We repudiate the monstrous doctrine that the oppressor should be the sole authority as to the rights of the oppressed.

The Negro race in America stolen, ravished and degraded, struggling up through difficulties and oppression, needs sympathy and receives criticism; needs help and is given hinderance, needs protection and is given mob-violence, needs justice and is given charity, needs leadership and is given cowardice and apology, needs bread and is given a stone. This nation will never stand justified before God until these things are changed.

Especially are we surprised and astonished at the recent attitude of the church of Christ—on the increase of a desire to bow to racial prejudice, to narrow the bounds of human brotherhood, and to segregate black men in some outer sanctuary. This is wrong, unchristian and disgraceful to the twentieth century civilization.

* * *

And while we are demanding, and ought to demand, and will continue to demand the rights enumerated above, God forbid that we should ever forget to urge corresponding duties upon our people.

The duty to vote.
The duty to respect the rights of others.
The duty to work.
The duty to obey the laws.
The duty to be clean and orderly.
The duty to send our children to school.
The duty to respect ourselves, even as we respect others.*

The Nadir of Race Relations

158

THE LYNCHING OF SAMUEL PETTY

The lynching of Samuel Petty in Leland, Mississippi, on the night of February 24, 1914, was one of three Mississippi lynchings during the same week. Petty was accused of having killed a Deputy Sheriff, Charles W. Kirkland. When news of Kirkland's death reached the river town of Leland, the mob advanced on Petty's cabin and took its revenge.

Lynchings of this kind were so common that its account in the daily press was limited to a brief mention. This description was taken from the letter of an anonymous witness to the editor of The Crisis. *Newspaper accounts differed from his only in their estimates of the size of the mob, which they placed at closer to 300.*

Petty's lynching was the immediate stimulus for a reaction. Many young Negroes met in secret and were reported in the northern Negro newspapers to be forming vigilante groups which would put an end to southern lynchings by the use of the shotgun. Their attempt was abortive.

---

*Cleveland *Gazette*, July 22, 1905.

The news spread like wildfire and in twenty minutes the entire white population was armed and headed for the cabin which was situated about a half mile from the depot, which is in the center of the town. I looked in every direction and could see men and mere boys, some not over 12 years old, carrying rifles, shotguns, pistols and, in fact, every imaginable thing that would shoot. They were acting as though there was an entire army of Negroes to be taken. The man who had killed the officer submitted to arrest by the mob, which by this time numbered about 400. Placing a rope around his neck he was led to the center of the town and in the presence of women and children they proceeded to hold a conference as to the kind of death that should be meted out to him. Some yelled to hang him; some to burn him alive. It was decided in a few minutes. Willing hands brought a large dry-goods box, placed it in the center of the street; in it was straw on which was poured a tub of oil; then the man was lifted with a rope around his neck and placed in this box head down, and then another tub of oil was poured over him. A man from the crowd deliberately lit a match and set fire to the living man. While in this position the flames shot up at great height. The crowd began to yell as the flames shot upward. In an instant the poor creature managed to lift himself out of the box, a mass of flames. He was fighting the flames with his hands in an effort to shield his face and eyes, and in this condition attempted to run. The crowd allowed him to run to the length of the rope, which was held by willing hands, until he reached a distance of about twenty feet; then a yell went up from the crowd to shoot. In an instant there were several hundred shots and the creature fell in his tracks. The crowd deliberately walked up to the prostrate form and shot the remainder of their guns into his lifeless body. With the flames still leaping into the air, he was pulled back into the fire that was now roaring with boxes and oil brought out of the different stores by men and boys. Every time they would throw on more oil and boxes the crowd would yell as though they were at a bull fight. Standing about fifty or seventy-five feet from the scene I could actually smell the flesh of the poor man as it was being burned. Not a voice was raised in the defense of the man. No one attempted to hide their identity. I looked into the faces of men whom I knew to be officers of the town lending a willing hand in the burning of this man. No wonder the coroner who held the inquest returned a verdict that the Negro came to his death "at the hands of an enraged mob unknown to the jury," because to get a jury in that town they had to get some who participated in the burning. I can never feel toward the white man as I have felt after seeing what I have attempted to describe. After burning the body into ashes the burned bones and ashes were buried in the edge of the street in front of a colored barber shop.

May God forbid that any other living man will ever see a sight as I witnessed; this is the third Negro who has been killed in this vicinity in the last three weeks. The man burned was named Sam Pettie, known by everybody to be quiet and inoffensive. I write this hoping you may get enough out of what I have tried to describe to tell your great number of readers what we are up against. To mention my name in connection with this would be equivalent to committing suicide.*

Compiled by the Tuskegee Institute, these figures must be considered conservative. Statistics gathered by other groups, such as the NAACP, run slightly higher. The annual incidence of Negro lynchings continued high through 1922, declined in the late 1920's and early 1930's, but did not drop below 10 consistently until 1935.

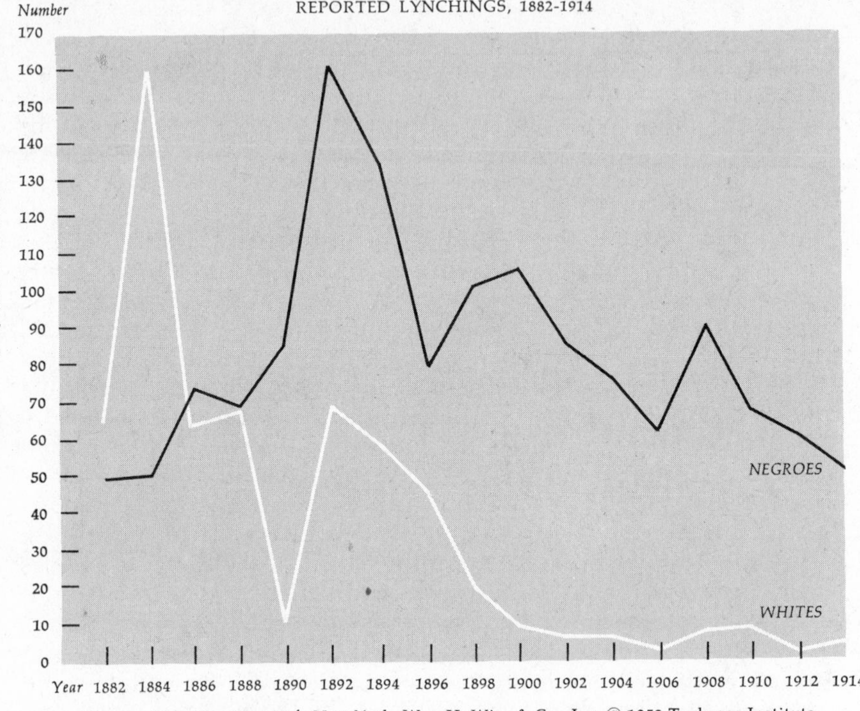

Source: *1952 Negro Year Book*, New York, Wm. H. Wise & Co., Inc. © 1952 Tuskegee Institute.

159

THE SPRINGFIELD RIOT

William English Walling was typical of the intellectuals who carried a great deal of weight during the Progressive era. Walling was cofounder of the Intercollegiate Socialist Society, of the Women's Trade Union League, and of the NAACP. He was one of the few socialists to support America's entrance into World War I.

Throughout his entire life Walling evinced considerable sympathy for the underdog, whether the worker, the woman, or the Negro. Visiting his parents in Chicago at the time of the Springfield riot of August 1908, Walling boarded the first train for Abraham Lincoln's old home town. His description of that riot, in the September 3, 1908, issue of the Independent, *precipitated the previously vague and scattered demands for an organization which could halt the steady deterioration of the Negro's place in American life. Walling directed the maneuverings which led to the call for the NAACP in 1909, and he was chosen its first head.*

**The Crisis*, VIII (May 1914), 20. Reprinted with permission of *The Crisis* Magazine, official publication of the NAACP.

On the morning after the first riot I was in Chicago and took the night train for Springfield, where I have often visited and am almost at home. On arriving in the town I found that the rioting had been continued thruout the night, and was even feared for the coming evening, in spite of the presence of nearly the whole militia of the State. Altho we visited the Mayor, military headquarters, the leading newspaper, and some prominent citizens, my wife and I gave most of our attention to the hospital, the negro quarters and the jail.

We at once discovered, to our amazement, that Springfield had no shame. She stood for the action of the mob. She hoped the rest of the negroes might flee. She threatened that the movement to drive them out would continue. I do not speak of the leading citizens, but of the masses of the people, of workingmen in the shops, the store-keepers in the stores, the drivers, the men on the street, the wounded in the hospitals and even the notorious "Joan of Arc" of the mob, Kate Howard, who had just been released from arrest on $4,000 bail. [She has since committed suicide.—*Editor.*] The *Illinois State Journal* of Springfield exprest the prevailing feeling even on its editorial page:

"While all good citizens deplore the consequences of this out-burst of the mob spirit, many even of these consider the outburst was *inevitable,* at some time, from existing conditions, needing only an overt act, such as that of Thursday night, to bring it from latent existence into active operation. The implication is clear that conditions, not the populace, were to blame and that many good citizens could find no other remedy than that applied by the mob. It was not the fact of the whites' hatred toward the negroes, but of the negroes' own misconduct, general inferiority or unfitness for free institutions that were at fault."

On Sunday, August 16th, the day after the second lynching, a leading white minister recommended the Southern disfranchisement scheme as a remedy for *negro* (!) lawlessness, while all four ministers who were quoted in the press proposed swift "justice" for *the negroes,* rather than recommending true Christianity, democracy and brotherhood to the whites.

* * *

Besides suggestions in high places of the negro's brutality, criminality and unfitness for the ballot we heard in lower ranks all the opinions that pervade the South—that the negro does not need much education, that his present education even has been a mistake, that whites cannot live in the same community with negroes except where the latter have been taught their inferiority, that lynching is the only way to teach them, etc. In fact, this went so far that we were led to suspect the existence of a Southern element in the town, and this is indeed the case. Many of the older citizens are from Kentucky or the southern part of Illinois. Moreover, many of the street railway employees are from the South. It was a street railway man's wife that was assaulted the night before the riots, and they were street railway employees, among others, that led the mob to the jail.

* * *

It was, in fact, only three days after the first disturbance when they fully realized that the lenient public opinion of Springfield was not the public opinion of Illinois or the North, that the rioters began to tremble. Still this did not prevent them later from insulting the militia, repeatedly firing at their outposts and almost openly organizing a political and business boycott to drive the remaining negroes out. Negro employers continue to receive threatening letters and are dismissing employees every day, while the stores, even the groceries, so fear to sell the negroes goods that the State has been compelled to intervene and purchase $10,000 worth in their behalf.

The menace is that if this thing continues it will offer *automatic rewards* to riotous elements and negro haters in Springfield, make the reign of terror permanent there, and offer every temptation to similar white elements in other towns to imitate Springfield's example.

* * *

Either the spirit of the abolitionists, of Lincoln and of Lovejoy must be revived and we must come to treat the negro on a plane of absolute political and social equality, or Vardaman and Tillman will soon have transferred the race war to the North.

Already Vardaman boasts "that such sad experiences as Springfield is undergoing will doubtless cause the people of the North to look with more toleration upon the methods employed by the Southern people."

The day these methods become general in the North every hope of political democracy will be dead, other weaker races and classes will be persecuted in the North as in the South, public education will undergo an eclipse, and American civilization will await either a rapid degeneration or another profounder and more revolutionary civil war, which shall obliterate not only the remains of slavery but all the other obstacles to a free democratic evolution that have grown up in its wake.

Yet who realizes the seriousness of the situation, and what large and powerful body of citizens is ready to come to their aid?*

160

A RACIST STATEMENT

A group of southern politicians who had seized control of their states in the name of the poor whites during the 1890's and 1900's had moved on to the Senate by the time Woodrow Wilson became President. As Pitchfork Ben Tillman of South Carolina had defended southern disfranchisement during the late 1890's and 1900's, so by the 1910's James K. Vardaman of Mississippi took over the burden of that defense. To secure his Populist-inspired program and his election, Vardaman sought the support of the rural areas by ferocious tirades against Negroes, whom, he felt, received too much of the state's educational budget. His enemies charged that he openly countenanced lynching. In 1911 he was elected to take his radical economic and racial ideas to the Senate, where he

*The *Independent*, vol. 65 (Sept. 3, 1908), 530-534.

served until 1919, when his opposition to World War I cost him his support in Mississippi.

Vardaman's speeches drew heavily from many of the scientific theories which were widely accepted during the 1910's. Northern publishers and readers applauded The Negro, A Menace to American Civilization *(1907), written by Robert W. Shufeldt, a popular biologist associated with the Smithsonian Institution, and* The Color Life: A Brief in Behalf of the Unborn *(1905), authored by William B. Smith, a philosophy and mathematics professor at Tulane University. Upon these and dozens of similar books Vardaman rested his frank racism.*

But the door of hope might have remained closed so far as the progress the negro was to make for himself was concerned. He has never created for himself any civilization. He has never risen above the government of a club. He has never written a language. His achievements in architecture are limited to the thatched-roofed hut or a hole in the ground. No monuments have been builded by him to body forth and perpetuate in the memory posterity the virtues of his ancestors.

For countless ages he has looked upon the rolling sea and never dreamed of a sail. In truth, he has never progressed, save and except when under the influence and absolute control of a superior race.

* * *

He is living in Africa to-day, in the land where he sprang, indigenous, in substantially the same condition, occupying the same rude hut, governed by the same club, worshiping the same fetish that he did when the Pharaohs ruled in Egypt. He has never had any civilization except that which has been inculcated by a superior race. And it is a lamentable fact that his civilization lasts only so long as he is in the hands of the white man who inculcates it. When left to himself he has universally gone back to the barbarism of the jungle.

* * *

Now, I know the negro has made a certain order of progress in the South. He has acquired property. He is acquiring book learning. I am advised that there is a decrease of illiteracy of something like 12 per cent in every decade. There is no doubt about that. But I am going to make a statement which, I dare say, will astonish some of the gentlemen who have shown such honest and sincere interest in the negro's advancement. While he has progressed mentally, he has deteriorated morally and physically. It is a lamentable fact that as a race the negro in America is more criminal to-day than he was in 1861. And certain diseases which were unknown among them before the war are decimating their ranks, filling the hospitals with incurables and the asylums with lunatics. I predict that these diseases will cause a marked falling off in the birth rate in the next decade.

* * *

Now, Mr. President and Senators, I do not want to do anything that will arrest the negro's progress. I would not raise my hand against his material advancement. I believe that I am his real friend. I know him; I understand him in all the relations of life. I have lived with him from my infancy. I was nursed by an old black mammy, the recollection of whose tender ministrations to me are among the sweetest assets of my life. A dear old negro woman nursed every one of our babies. A most faithful, trustworthy, devoted servant and friend was this good old woman. I never permit an opportunity to pass to pay the tribute of my love and respect for her memory. As governor of my State I am sure that I exerted myself as much to protect the negro in the enjoyment of his life, his liberty, the pursuit of happiness, and the products of his own toil as any executive in America has ever done. He does not vote much in Mississippi, but I really think that he votes more than he ought to vote, if he votes at all. I do not think it was ever intended by the Creator that the two races should live together upon equal terms—enjoy equal political and social advantages. One or the other must rule. The people of the South tried to share with the negro in the government of the country after the war, but the negro declined to share with the white man. Black heels rested cruelly upon white necks for many years after the close of the war. The white man endured the negro's misrule, his insolence, impudence, and infamy. He suffered his criminal incapacity to govern until the public domain had been well-nigh squandered and the public treasury looted. We saw the civilization reared by the genius of our fathers, glorified and cemented by their sacred blood, vanishing from the earth, and by means, I will not say in this presence, fair, but by means sufficient, we invoked the law of self-preservation; we arose in the might of an outraged race and as the Savior scourged the money changers from the temple, so the southern white man drove from power the scalawag, the carpetbagger, and the incompetent negro.

* * *

God Almighty never intended that the negro should share with the white man in the government of this country; and you can not improve upon the plans of God Almighty or defeat His purposes, either, by legislative enactments. Do not forget that. It matters not what I may say or others may think; it matters not what constitutions may contain or statutes provide, wherever the negro is in sufficient numbers to imperil the white man's civilization or question the white man's supremacy the white man is going to find some way around the difficulty. And that is just as true in the North as it is in the South. You need not deceive yourselves about that. The feeling against the negro in Illinois when he gets in the white man's way is quite as strong, more bitter, less regardful of the negro's feelings and conditions than it is in Mississippi. And that is true of every other Northern State. I have been all over the States of Illinois, Ohio, Iowa, Indiana, some of the Western States, and New England States. I know the temper of the white people on this question. I had the pleasure of speaking in the city of Springfield soon after they had had a lynching fest. A negro was thought to have committed an unmentionable crime. The mob got after him. The sheriff and his friend carried the negro away in his friend's automobile. They returned, and the mob found the negro had made his escape. To wreak their vengeance upon those who undertook to uphold the law they proceeded to destroy the automobile, and they demolished the restaurant belonging to the man who had carried the negro away. A thing of that kind could hardly happen in the South.

The difference between the southern man's conduct in a matter of this character and that of the people of Illinois is this: The southern mob sometimes gets the guilty man and hangs him. In the North, if the mob finds itself unable to punish the beast who committed the outrage, they proceed to destroy property and kill everything of a dark color. Mr. President, I am not the negro's enemy. I know what is best for him. I think I can measure his productive capacity. I know the influences that move him. I am familiar with the currents of passion which sweep through his savage blood. I understand his hates, his jealousies, and his attachments. In a word, I think I know him as he really is. And knowing him, I believe I know what is best for him. You can not measure the negro by the standard you would measure accurately the white man. He is different from the white man physically, morally, and mentally. The pure-blooded negro is without gratitude. He does not harbor revenge. He is not immoral—he is unmoral. I have never known one who ever felt the guilt of sin, the goading of an outraged conscience, or the binding force of a moral obligation. The pure-blooded negro reaches mental maturity soon after he passes the period of puberty. The cranial sutures become ossified by the time he reaches 20 years of age, and it is not uncommon to find one who reads fluently at 15 years of age not to know a letter in the book at the age of 25 or 30.

No; I am not an enemy to the negro; I want to educate him—or rather train him—along proper lines; I want to train him in a way that we may improve his hand and educate his heart; I want to build, if possible, a moral substratum upon which to rear this mental superstructure; but if that is not done, with his ideas of morality, or as Froude, the historian, would put it, his ideas of "unmorality"—when you enhance his mentality without building this moral substratum, upon which it is to rest, you simply increase his capacity for harm. Your education will only serve to make a less desirable citizen.

I want, first, to build the foundation. The white man and the negro of the South are not enemies. They may be made so if you continue to insist on trying to bring them into abnormal relationship. The relations that existed between them before and immediately succeeding the war was akin to that of father and son. My recollections of the black folk on the farm during my boyhood are among the pleasant memories of my life. The negroes in Mississippi know that I am not their enemy. I would not permit them to vote, but I would protect them in the enjoyment of their life, liberty, and the pursuit of happiness and the product of their toil. And if the white people of the South are permitted to proceed along proper rational lines, knowing and recognizing the negro's inferiority, desiring, however, his betterment; if they are permitted to work out, although handicapped, as they are, with laws which were conceived in hatred and brought forth in a spasm of venom and revenge—if they are permitted to do it, Mr. President, in their own proper way, very much more progress will be made for the negro's uplifting, for the negro's improvement than will be made if it shall be directed by men who do not know any more about it personally than I do about the political economy of the planet Mars.*

Organized Response

161

THE FOUNDING OF THE N.A.A.C.P., 1909

The letter from William English Walling to Hamilton Holt is clear evidence of the manner in which Walling and his associates were following up the momentum generated by his article on the Springfield, Illinois, riot. Hamilton Holt was the managing editor of The Independent. *Brooklyn-born and a graduate of Yale College, Holt was involved in a number of "causes," particularly those concerned with strengthening the League of Nations after World War I.*

The "call" was a brief document, probably the work of Oswald Garrison Villard. To those who drafted and signed the call, the Berea College case was important since the U.S. Supreme Court had decided in 1908 (Berea College *v.* Kentucky) *that the Kentucky statute prohibiting domestic corporations from teaching white and Negro students in the same institution was valid and this was construed as an attack on the principle of higher education for Negroes.*

New York, Feb. 1, 1909

My dear Mr. Holt:

In view of your radical criticism of the first draft of our "appeal", I am all the more gratified that you have decided positively to be with us. The first draft was only a very rough draft anyway, and was sent out for the precise purpose of getting criticism. However, you have been more generous to us than everybody else put together in this respect. Mr. Villard said that he did not like it altogether, but his chief criticism seemed to be that it was too long. In view of his importance to us and the position he took, I asked that the committee would doubtless be more pleased to act on such a draft than on the previous one. However, I do not believe that Mr. Villard or any of those interested in the movement share in any way your extreme optimism. I do not think this phrase is too strong a one for the position you take. Seeing that you demand the same thing for the negro as we do, and are ready to do as much in that direction as anybody in the country, this is certainly no personal reflection. But I do believe that you are very seriously mistaken indeed.

It may be that lynchings are decreasing, just as executions are decreasing in Russia—that is, that "order is being restored"; in other words, that the negro is thoroughly terrorized and everywhere in the South in constant fear of murder. Indeed, such a moderate portrayal of the situation as that of Ray Stannard Baker thoroughly bears me out in this position.

As to the vote of the negro, it is true that the disfranchising laws passed a few years ago are only beginning to go into effect. You may

Congressional Record, 63rd Cong., 2nd Sess. (Feb. 6, 1914), 3036, 3038, 3040.

be literally right as to the negro vote up to the present, but if there has not been a big decrease in this campaign, the next elections are bound to show it. I understand that the negroes voted for the last time in Atlanta in this election and that it was their vote that elected the right candidate. The Post has always made a fearless and correct statement of this situation and it has been a very pessimistic one indeed. . . .

As to your next point, that the oligarchy is not attempting the subjugation of the poor whites, I do not know from what point of view you are observing Southern politics. The Labor Unions, for instance, have received worse treatment in Alabama than they ever had in Colorado. I have this from a long personal statement of President Lewis, of the great Miners' Union, who knows both situations. Thousands of poor whites are disfranchised everywhere; very many by running behind the obsolete poll-tax, which was enacted undoubtedly partly for this purpose. Also it is scarcely possible that the peonage systems of the South could be reproduced anywhere in the country, unless in West Virginia, which is a half Southern state.

* * *

The "call" did not put in such close juxtaposition as you did the reference to "the most respectable elements of the present ruling class in the South" and "the inflaming of the worst passions of the human heart". I had quoted Hoke Smith and Swanson only as typifying many others. If Hoke Smith has been succeeded by Brown, the latter is scarcely less hostile to the negro. Of course you know I am Southern born myself and know a little not only of the position of public men but of the average private respectable citizen—perhaps the word "most" respectable should be dropped, as there are certainly a few exceptions. Do you not think that the statement that we will treat the negro well as long as he keeps to the position God made him for, in view of the present situation of the South, is inflaming the worst passions of the human heart?

I must apologize for speaking with so much feeling to you on this matter since I have always believed that nobody has higher motives than yours, especially on this question. But I must feel that you have not followed the situation so closely in the past few months as have many other equally cautious and responsible persons as yourself, with whom I have discussed it. However, this is all my personal feeling and has nothing to do with the meeting, which will be delighted to have your frank and full opinion—all the more if it does not happen to be the same as some of the others.

Very sincerely yours,

William E. Walling*

CALL FOR A NATIONAL NEGRO CONFERENCE
FEBRUARY 12, 1909

The celebration of the centennial of the birth of Abraham Lincoln, widespread and grateful as it may be, will fail to justify itself

*William English Walling to Hamilton Holt, Feb. 1, 1909, in Walling Papers, State Historical Society of Wisconsin.

if it takes no note of and makes no recognition of the colored men and women to whom the great emancipator labored to assure freedom. Besides a day of rejoicing, Lincoln's birthday in 1909 should be one of taking stock of the nation's progress since 1865.

How far has it lived up to the obligations imposed upon it by the Emancipation Proclamation? How far has it gone in assuring to each and every citizen, irrespective of color, the equality of opportunity and equality before the law, which underlie our American institutions and are guaranteed by the Constitution?

If Mr. Lincoln could revisit this country in the flesh, he would be disheartened and discouraged. He would learn that on January 1, 1909, Georgia had rounded out a new confederacy by disfranchising the negro, after the manner of all the other Southern States. He would learn that the Supreme Court of the United States, supposedly a bulwark of American liberties, had refused every opportunity to pass squarely upon this disfranchisement of millions, by laws avowedly discriminatory and openly enforced in such manner that the white men may vote and black men be without a vote in their government; he would discover, therefore, that taxation without representation is the lot of millions of wealth-producing American citizens, in whose hands rests the economic progress and welfare of an entire section of the country.

He would learn that the Supreme Court, according to the official statement of one of its own judges in the Berea College case, has laid down the principle that if an individual State chooses, it may "make it a crime for white and colored persons to frequent the same market place at the same time, or appear in an assemblage of citizens convened to consider questions of a public or political nature in which all citizens, without regard to race, are equally interested."

In many States Lincoln would find justice enforced, if at all, by judges elected by one element in a community to pass upon the liberties and lives of another. He would see the black men and women, for whose freedom a hundred thousand of soldiers gave their lives, set apart in trains, in which they pay first-class fares for third-class service, and segregated in railway stations and in places of entertainment; he would observe that State after State declines to do its elementary duty in preparing the negro through education for the best exercise of citizenship.

Added to this, the spread of lawless attacks upon the negro, North, South, and West—even in the Springfield made famous by Lincoln—often accompanied by revolting brutalities, sparing neither sex nor age nor youth, could but shock the author of the sentiment that "government of the people, by the people, for the people, shall not perish from the earth."

Silence under these conditions means tacit approval. The indifference of the North is already responsible for more than one assault upon democracy, and every such attack reacts as unfavorably upon whites as upon blacks. Discrimination once permitted cannot be bridled; recent history in the South shows that in forging chains for the negroes the white voters are forging chains for themselves. "A house divided against itself cannot stand"; this government cannot exist half-slave and half-free any better to-day than it could in 1861.

Hence we call upon all the believers in democracy to join in a national conference for the discussion of present evils, the voicing of protests, and the renewal of the struggle for civil and political liberty.*

Editorial offices of The Crisis, *official publication of the NAACP. The man standing in the foreground is W. E. B. DuBois, editor of what was going to be one of the most important organs of Negro expression in the United States.*

162

THE FOUNDING OF THE NATIONAL URBAN LEAGUE, 1910

The National League on Urban Conditions Among Negroes, soon to be known as the National Urban League, was in some ways coordinate with the NAACP but eventually each charted its own line of activity and developed a friendly spirit of competition. The Urban League introduced a novel concept to social welfare agencies, that of a coordinating committee among agencies. After the northward migration, the Urban League through its various branches became deeply involved with the problem of housing and employment which the migrants brought to northern cities.

The rapid growth of the Urban League as a national organization with active branches placed an additional strain on it, since the branches were dependent for advice on the national office. Since the League was founded in New York City, this became its center of operations and, as this article suggests, the prototype of the kinds of activities in which the League engaged before the First World War.

NATIONAL LEAGUE ON URBAN CONDITIONS AMONG NEGROES

When, during the spring of 1910, Mrs. William H. Baldwin, Jr., called representatives of the many social-welfare organizations working among Negroes to a conference at her New York City home, to consider means of preventing duplication of effort and overlapping

*New York *Evening Post,* February 13, 1909.

The seal of the National Urban League from its founding until 1947.

of work, of promoting cooperation among the agencies and of establishing new organizations to improve neglected conditions, a new era was reached in the handling of the city problem as it affected the Negroes.

From this meeting resulted the National League on Urban Conditions Among Negroes, whose work of uplift is now being felt in ten cities, viz.: New York, Philadelphia, Pa., Norfolk, Va., Richmond, Va., Nashville, Tenn., Louisville, Ky., St. Louis, Mo., Savannah, Ga., Augusta, Ga., and Atlanta, Ga., whose budget has increased from $2,000 to $18,000 per year and whose staff of paid employees has increased from one full-time and three part-time employees to sixteen salaried persons in New York City, three in Nashville and two in Norfolk.

* * *

The problem of the city Negro is but the accentuated counterpart of the problem of all urban inhabitants. Segregation and the consequence congestion, the evils of bad housing conditions with their inevitable accompaniment of dangerous sanitation and loose morals, the lack of facilities for wholesome recreation and the ill-regulated picture shows and dance halls combine to make conditions which demand instant relief. Add to this a population constantly augmented by Negroes from small towns or rural districts of the South, and the problem of the league is before you.

* * *

The league has sought to establish agencies for uplift where needed. If no committee could be found ready to take over and conduct the particular undertaking, the league has handled the movement through its local office staff.

The Sojourner Truth house committee, with Mrs. George W. Seligman as chairman, has undertaken the task of establishing a home for delinquent colored girls under 16 years of age, because of the failure of the State and private institutions to care adequately for these unfortunates. The league made an investigation of this need and formed a temporary committee from which developed the present organization.

The league also inaugurated the movement for the training of colored nursery maids. A committee, of which Mr. Franck W. Barber is chairman, has worked out the details for courses of study in hospital training in care of infants, kindergarten training, child study and household arts.

During the summer of 1911 the league conducted, in Harlem, a playground for boys, for the purpose of demonstrating the need of recreational facilities for the children of Harlem. As a result of this movement, and a continuous agitation for more adequate play facilities, the city has practically committed itself to the operation of a model playground on any plot of ground in the Harlem district, the use of which is donated to the City Parks Department.

The travelers' aid work, in charge of Miss Eva G. Burleigh, has consisted principally in the meeting of the coastwise steamers bringing large numbers of women and girls from Southern ports to New York City, who are without acquaintance with methods of meeting the competition of city life, and who are frequently sent to New York to be exploited by unreliable employment agents or questionable men. The league supports two travelers' aid workers in Norfolk, Va., which is the gateway to the North for hundreds of women and girls from Virginia and the Carolinas.

The preventive or protective work of the league consists of the visiting in the homes of school children who have become incorrigibles or truants, for the purpose of removing the causes of these irregularities. This work is in charge of Mrs. Hallie B. Craigwell and Mr. Leslie L. Pollard.

Probation work with adults from the court of general sessions is done by Mr. Chas. C. Allison, Jr. In connection with this work with delinquents the Big Brother and Big Sister movements are conducted. The league seeks to furnish to each boy or girl passing through the courts the helpful influence and guidance of a man or woman of high moral character.

The league conducts a housing bureau for the purpose of improving the moral and physical conditions among the tenement houses in Negro districts. It seeks principally to prevent the indiscriminate mixing of the good and bad by furnishing to the public a list of houses certified to be tenanted by respectable people. It also seeks to get prompt action of agents and owners or the city departments whenever there is need for correcting certain housing abuses.

* * *

No human movement can move with appreciative success without the propelling impetus of a forceful personality. Social work among Negroes has suffered not so much from the lack of movements as from the lack of conscientious, enthusiastic, trained workers. This fact was emphasized by Dr. George Edmund Haynes when, shortly following Mrs. Baldwin's meeting, he was employed as director of the organization. The result was the establishment of two annual fellowships at the New York School of Philanthropy and Columbia University, and scholarships at Fisk University, where Dr. Haynes holds the chair of social science, and from which he seeks to influence other Southern Negro colleges to standardize their courses in sociology and economics and to encourage promising students to take up social work as a profession.*

Political Impotence

163

WARNING AGAINST THEODORE ROOSEVELT

Theodore Roosevelt's decision to exclude southern Negroes from the Progressive party convention in 1912 made a great impression on northern voting Negroes. W. H. Lewis was a graduate of Amherst College where he was a star football player and held a law degree from Harvard. Lewis was one of the Negroes whom

---

**The Crisis*, VIII (September 1914), 243, 246. Reprinted with permission of *The Crisis* Magazine, official publication of the NAACP

Roosevelt consulted in 1900 after his nomination as the Republican vice-presidential candidate. In spite of his political obligations to Roosevelt, Lewis came out in opposition to the Progressive party and defended the Taft administration. At the time of this speech, he was an assistant attorney general of the United States, a post to which he had been appointed by Taft in 1911. He retired to private practice in Boston soon after the Wilson administration took office.

The party that made this day memorable in history, the great Republican party that achieved our freedom and our citizenship, stands today face to face with the most serious crisis in its history. A new party has arisen which not only claims to be fighting for the principles of the great Emancipator, but to be wearing his mantle. A favorite son of the Republican party who has twice received at its hands the highest honors in the Republic, is leading the fight against it. You are to decide whether you will follow the old party that enfranchised you, or the new party which has disfranchised your fathers and brothers, sisters and mothers in the South. You are to decide whether you will stand by the old party which has maintained inviolate your party representation against every and all assaults made upon it, or whether you will follow the new party which has yielded to the clamor for a lily-white party in the South and a policy of complete elimination of the Negro from politics. The Negro citizen today is upon trial.

I believe today, after sober reflection, you will refuse to go into the new party movement. As a great and good friend of our race, Horace Greeley once tried to lead us into a party which had always stood for slavery and disfranchisement, so today our great and good friend, Colonel Roosevelt, is trying to lead us into a party which in its very beginning, while declaring for the equal rights of all men, excludes us from party representation in a section of the country where it is most vital, and where our safety and happiness depend upon party representation at least. I yield to no man in admiration for Colonel Roosevelt. He was my friend and my idol. He appointed me assistant United States attorney in Massachusetts, and in return I defended the discharge of the Brownsville soldiers, a thing which no other colored Federal office-holder did. He introduced me to President Taft, and wanted me to second Mr. Taft's nomination at Chicago. I have found President Taft all that Mr. Roosevelt represented him to be—a good friend, lovable, absolutely sincere, fearless and just. You will recall that he appointed me to this office in the face of a storm of hostile criticism. He saw to it that I was given not only the empty title but that I was confirmed. The appointment was not personal to myself; it was meant, as he himself has said, as an honor to the colored race in recognition of its progress, and encouragement for the future. The Attorney General, Mr. Wickersham, has not only given me all the official support and courtesy to which I was entitled, but he has gone out of his way, at the sacrifice of his personal time and the expenditure of his personal means, to prevent my expulsion, as well as that of two other members, from the American Bar Association on the ground of color. I do not know what my future is to be. If I had the promise of the highest office in the gift of the nation, or if before my eyes there was a threat of the degradation of the lowest place imaginable, I could not bring myself to agree to the policy of the new Progressive party towards our race. It would not only be suicide, but it would be political murder—base betrayal of my own race and kindred in the South. The issue in this campaign, broadly stated, is, Will the Republicans stand by the nominee of the old party, or by following the new party elect a Democrat President of the United States? A vote for the new party is a vote for the Democratic party because the progressives are Republicans.

* * *

I sat in the gallery of the Coliseum at the birth of the new party. I saw men and women work themselves into a frenzy of enthusiasm. I heard the magnificent keynote of Senator Beveridge. I listened to the strains of the music of 'John Brown's Body' and the 'Battle Hymn of the Republic.' My heart sank within me when I thought that there were men outside clamoring for admission who were denied admission on account of their race and color. Since all men did not include Southern Negroes I could not feel that John Brown's soul was marching there. When that vast audience sang the 'Battle Hymn of the Republic,' 'as Christ died to make men holy, let us die to make men free,' I felt that human cant and hypocrisy could go no further; it had reached its final climax. I made my way back to the great hall the second day to listen to my old friend's confession of faith. Again I saw the waving of banners, the unfurling of standards, the marching of the army of freedom. I heard men and women shout themselves hoarse for the leader of the new party. I was sick at heart that the confession of faith did not include all men, and that men of our race were to be excluded wherever other men objected.

* * *

On the other hand, the Republican party, nationally and locally in the States, has been and is the most progressive party in the nation's history. The distinctive policies of the Progressive party, in the main, are local, not national. Mr. Roosevelt has said that the initiative, the referendum and the recall are not applicable to the Federal Government. His social and industrial programme comes within the police power of the States. The power of the Federal Government to enact this legislation is limited to the District of Columbia, to Government employees and those engaged in Interstate Commerce. Judged by what the Federal Government can do, the Administration of President Taft has been one of the most progressive in the history of the country. All that it needs is a good advertising agent. I seriously fear that there will be little left for the next Administration to do but to carry out the policies of President Taft, and I believe that President Taft is the best man to carry out these policies. This is no time to swap horses, while crossing the stream of discontent and unrest. There never was a President, since Lincoln, more eager to find the real wishes of the people and to follow them.*

*Boston *Evening Transcript,* Sept. 25, 1912.

164

A COLORED MINISTER TO WOODROW WILSON

More Negroes probably supported Woodrow Wilson in 1912 than had ever voted for a Democratic presidential candidate. As the two letters of the Reverend Francis J. Grimké, a prominent Negro minister in Washington, show, the attitude of Wilson's Negro backers changed from eager anticipation to dismay and bitterness as they watched the new President's policies unfold. Their disappointment with Taft, who had either appointed or retained only 31 Negroes, had led to support for Wilson. But by the time Wilson's appointments were confirmed, only nine Negroes were in office, and eight of these were Republican holdovers.

Even more galling than his appointment policy was Wilson's acceptance and defense of cruel forms of segregation in the civil service. Toilet facilities were suddenly segregated and employees of the Post Office, Treasury, and Navy departments were forced to use inconvenient and inferior washrooms. Screens were built to segregate Negroes from whites working in the same office. A nongovernmental group, the National Democratic Fair Play Association, was created in Washington to campaign for further segregation.

FRANCIS J. GRIMKÉ TO WOODROW WILSON

Washington, D.C.,
November 20, 1912

Dear Sir:

I am a colored man. I am a graduate of the Princeton Theological Seminary. I am pastor of the Fifteenth Street Presbyterian Church of Washington City where I came immediately after my graduation in 1878.

You may not know it, but the triumph of the Democratic Party has always been attended, more or less, with a sense of uneasiness on the part of the colored people for fear lest their rights might be interfered with. It is unfortunate that the ascendency of any party in this country should seem to any class of citizens to imperil their rights. But such, unquestionably, is the feeling on the part of the great majority of the colored people, induced by what has been the general attitude of the Democratic Party towards their rights as citizens. I have shared, somewhat, this feeling myself. I have just finished reading, however, an address by you, made, I should judge, to a body of Sunday school teachers, on the "Importance of Bible Study", and printed in the November number of the *Expositor,* and cannot tell you how greatly it has relieved my mind as to the treatment which the colored people are likely to receive from you and your Administration. I said to myself, No American citizen, white or black, need have any reasonable grounds of fear from the Administration of a man who feels as he does, who believes as he does in the Word of God, and who accepts as he does, without any reservation, the great, eternal, and immutable principles of righteousness for which that Word stands.

This impression, in the light of that address, was so strongly borne in upon my mind, that I felt that I would like to have you know it. The simple fact is, the only hope which the colored man has of fair treatment in this country, is to be found in men, who like yourself, believe in God and in his Son, Jesus Christ, and who feel that the greatest service they can render to their fellow men is to square their lives with the principles of the Christian religion, and to bear about with them ever the noble and beautiful spirit of the Man of Nazareth.

With a man of your known Christian character at the head of affairs, I am sure that the race with which I am identified will have no just grounds for complaint. It is a comforting thought, especially, to those who are struggling against great odds, to know that the God of Abraham, of Isaac, and of Jacob—the God that the Bible reveals, is on the throne, and that under Him, as His vice-regent, will be a man who has the courage of his convictions, and who will not falter where duty calls.

You have my best wishes, and the earnest prayer that you may be guided by Divine wisdom in the arduous duties and responsibilities that are so soon to devolve upon you as the Chief Executive of this great nation.

I am, Very truly yours,

Francis J. Grimké

Washington, D.C., September 5, 1913

Dear Sir:

As an American citizen I desire to enter my earnest protest against the disposition, under your Administration, to segregate colored people in the various departments of the Government. To do so is undemocratic, is un-American, is un-Christian, is needlessly to offend the self-respect of the loyal black citizens of the Republic. We constitute one tenth of the population, and, under the Constitution, have the same rights and are entitled to the same consideration as other citizens. We had every reason to hope, from your high Christian character, and from your avowal of lofty principles prior to your election, that your accession to power would act as a check upon the brutal and insane spirit of race hatred that characterizes certain portions of the white people of the country. As American citizens we have a right to expect the President of the United States to stand between us and those who are bent on forcing us into a position of inferiority. Under the Constitution, resting upon the broad foundation of democratic principles as embodied in the Declaration of Independence, there are no superiors and inferiors. Before the law all citizens are equal, and are entitled to the same consideration. May we not expect,—have we not the right to expect, that your personal influence, as well as the great influence which comes from your commanding official position, will be thrown against what is clearly, is distinctly not in accordance with the spirit of free institutions? All class distinctions among citizens are un-American, and the sooner every vestige of it is stamped out the better it will be for the Republic.

Yours truly,

Francis J. Grimké*

*From *The Works of Francis J. Grimké*, edited by Carter G. Woodson, pp. 88–90, 129–130, 133–134. Reprinted by permission of The Associated Publishers, Inc.

165

PROTEST AGAINST PRESIDENT WILSON

Interracial delegations petitioned and visited the White House many times in 1913 and 1914 to request Wilson to modify his position. The most famous of these was the one led by William Monroe Trotter, editor of the Boston Guardian, *which called on the President on November 12, 1914. Massachusetts-bred and a Phi Beta Kappa from Harvard, the brilliant and erratic Trotter had long been an advocate of equal rights. In 1912 he had visited Wilson at Trenton, New Jersey, where he received promises from the Democratic candidate that he would practice fair play toward Negroes. Trotter became one of Wilson's most prominent Negro supporters in the campaign, and he might have expected to receive an appointment himself. His visit in 1914 was front-page news. Protest rallies followed Trotter's shabby treatment by the President. The Administration's leading newspaper supporter, the New York* World, *joined most of the northern white press in denouncing Wilson's attitude, but to no avail.*

Washington, D.C., Nov. 20—Thursday afternoon of last week President Wilson became indignant when William Monroe Trotter, editor of the Boston *Guardian,* as chairman of a committee of protest from the National Independence Equal Rights League against the segregation of Afro-American employees in the government departments in Washington, plainly told the nation's chief executive about it.

The committee met the president by appointment, after waiting a year for a personal interview with him. Mr. Trotter was the spokesman, and in the fervor of his plea for equal rights for his people he forgot the servile manner and speech once characteristic of the Afro-American and he talked to the president as man to man, addressing the head of the government as any American citizen should, especially when discussing a serious matter. But the president did not like Mr. Trotter's attitude and told the committee that if it called on him again it would have to get a new chairman. The president added he had not been addressed in such a manner since he entered the White House.

The delegation charged that Secretary McAdoo and Comptroller Williams in the treasury and Postmaster General Burleson had enforced segregation rules in their offices. The president replied that he had investigated the question and had been assured there had been no discrimination in the comforts and surroundings given to the Afro-American workers. He added he had been informed by officials that the segregation had been started to avoid friction between the races and not with the object of injuring the Afro-American employees.

The president said he was deeply interested in the race and greatly admired its progress. He declared the thing to be sought by the Afro-American people was complete independence of white people, and that he felt the white race was willing to do everything possible to assist them.

Mr. Trotter and other members at once took issue with the president, declaring the Afro-American people did not seek charity or assistance, but that they took the position that they had equal rights with whites and that those rights should be respected. They denied there had been any friction between the two races before segregation was begun.

The president listened to what they had to say, and then told the delegation that Mr. Trotter was losing control of his temper, and that he (the president) would not discuss the matter further with him.

The president said he thought his colleagues in the government departments were not trying to put the employees at a disadvantage, but simply to make arrangements which would prevent friction. He added that the question involved was not a question of intrinsic qualities, because all had human souls and were equal in that respect, but that for the present it was a question of economic policy whether the Afro-American race could do the same things that the white race could do with equal efficiency. He said he thought the Afro-American people were proving that they could, and that everyone wished to help them and that their conditions of labor would be bettered. The entire matter, however, should be treated with a recognition of its difficulties. The president said he was anxious to do what was just, and asked for more memoranda from the committee as to instances of segregation about which they complained.

Mr. Trotter said in his address that his committee did not come "as wards looking for charity, but as full-fledged American citizens, vouchsafed equality of citizenship by the federal constitution."

"Two years ago," said Mr. Trotter, "You were thought to be a second Abraham Lincoln." The president tried to interrupt, asking that personalities be left out of the discussion. Mr. Trotter continued to speak and the president finally told him that if the organization he represented wished to approach him again it must choose another spokesman.

* * *

The spokesman continued to argue that he was merely trying to show how the Afro-American people felt, and asserted that he and others were now being branded as traitors to the race because they advised the people "to support the ticket."

This mention of votes caused the president to say politics must be left out, because it was a form of blackmail. He said he would resent it as quickly from one set of men as from another, and that his auditors could vote as they pleased, it mattered little to him.*

**Chicago Daily Defender* (November 21, 1914), 1–2. Reprinted with permission from the *Chicago Daily Defender.*

166

THE WARTIME NEGRO EXODUS

In the summer of 1916, the Secretary of Labor, William B. Wilson, asked two of his staff members to make a preliminary study of the northward migration of Negroes which was then beginning in some numbers. While this study was sufficient at the time, the Secretary needed fuller information the next year and, in April 1917 he asked Dr. James H. Dillard, the director of the Jeanes and Slater Funds for Negro education in the South, to plan and direct the project.

The Dillard study was a more intensive investigation than its predecessor because the migration had grown in flow and intensity after the United States had become a participant in the war. Dillard hired several special investigators and their work was done during the summer of 1917. W. T. B. Williams, the author of the extract printed here, was the only Negro among Dillard's investigators. While the other investigators restricted themselves to particular regions of the South, Williams had a general assignment, and viewed the migration from a less particularized base.

From the average white man one hears only of the attractive wages offered the Negro in the North and the work of labor agents in the South as the causes of the exodus of Negroes. Both have had their effect, but there are other significant, underlying causes. The North needed labor sorely and sought it where it was available. The South has done little to meet this competition except to complain and to argue that from 50 cents to $1 a day is worth as much to the Negro in the South as the pay of from $2 to $4 and over per day is worth to him in the North. The Negro, however, seems not to be convinced. He appears to be interested in having some experience with from four to six times as much pay as he has ever had before, whatever the conditions. This increased wage, to many almost fabulous sums, has without doubt been the immediately impelling influence that has taken the Negro suddenly into the North in such large numbers. "Better wages" has been the universal response from black and white alike to my inquiry as to why the Negroes are leaving the South.

* * *

The treatment accorded the Negro always stood second, when not first, among the reasons given by Negroes for leaving the South. I talked with all classes of colored people from Virginia to Louisiana—farm hands, tenants, farmers, hack drivers, porters, mechanics, barbers, merchants, insurance men, teachers, heads of schools, ministers, druggists, physicians, and lawyers—and in every instance the matter of treatment came to the front voluntarily. This is the all-absorbing, burning question among Negroes. For years no group of the thoughtful, intelligent class of Negroes, at any rate, have met for any purpose without finally drifting into some discussion of their treatment at the hands of white people.

* * *

Because Negroes have made few public complaints about their condition in the South, the average white man has assumed that they are satisfied; but there is a vast amount of dissatisfaction among them over their lot. There seemed to be no escape and little remedy for it, so there was no point in stirring up trouble for themselves by publicly railing about their plight. The easiest way was the best way. The opportunity to make a living in the North, where hitherto no considerable number of Negroes were wanted, gave them the chance long looked for to move out and to better their condition. Nevertheless these migrants love the South; many of them write back longingly of their homes; still they break their old ties and face a new life in a strange land for the sake of the larger, freer life which they believe awaits them and, particularly, their children. It has taken something more than money to move these masses of people, though money is a necessary condition for the movement and is the immediate occasion of the exodus; but the Negro's list of grievances that have prepared him for this migration is a long one.

The effect of the Negro press in making the Negro actively conscious of his condition is little known outside of the Negro race. At least two of these publications have exercised a tremendous influence in arousing Negroes to this movement from the South. One of these Negro newspapers in Chicago makes its lurid appeal to the lowly class of Negroes. It has increased its circulation in the South manyfold during the last year. In some sections it has probably been more effective in carrying off Negroes than all the labor agents put together. It sums up the Negro's troubles and keeps them constantly before him, and it points out to him in terms he can understand the way of escape. It neglects to mention the new troubles he is likely to meet, but plays up the advantages open to him in most inviting style.

* * *

As tenant [in the South], the Negro works under varying conditions from State to State and in different sections of the same State. In typical portions of South Carolina, the tenant furnishes the stock, plants, cultivates, and gathers the crop for one-half of everything except the cotton seed of which he gets none; or, if he merely furnishes his labor, he gets one-third of everything except the cotton seed.

Similar conditions for tenant farming obtain in the sections of eastern Mississippi which I visited. But many of the Negro tenants feel that it makes little difference what part of the crop is promised them, for the white man gets it all anyway. In the portions of Alabama and Georgia which I visited conditions are apparently easier, for there the tenants get half of the cotton seed as well as half of everything else.

* * *

In certain parts of Mississippi, at any rate, Negro renters fare but little better than tenants. They are subject to the overseer's driving and directions, and must respond to the landlord's bell, just as the other hands do; and when the renter has made his cotton crop he can not sell it. According to the law of the State, only the landlord can give a clear title to the cotton sold. This gives rise to the frequently deferred settlements of which the colored people complain bitterly. Apparently, in order to secure his labor, the landlord often will not settle for the year's work till late in the spring when the next crop has been "pitched." The Negro is then bound hand and foot and must accept the landlord's terms. It usually means that it is impossible for him to get out of the landlord's clutches, no matter how he is being treated. In many cases the Negro does not dare ask for a settlement. Planters often regard it an insult to be required, even by the courts, "to go to their books." A lawyer and planter cited to me the planters' typical excuse: "It is unnecessary to make a settlement, when the tenant is in debt." As to the facts in the case the landlord's word must suffice. It is not easy to get capable lawyers to take Negroes' cases against landlords, even when it is quite apparent injustice is being done. It not infrequently happens that the Negro who obviously makes money and gets out of debt is dismissed from the plantation, a common expression being that as soon as a Negro begins to make money he is no longer any account.

Another form of injustice that has long been preparing the Negro to escape at his first opportunity is the charging of exorbitant prices by the merchants and planters for the "advances" to the Negroes, and the practice of usury in lending money to them. For example, the tenant contracts for his money advances from the 1st of January. He usually receives no money, however, till the 1st of March and none after the 1st of August. But he must pay interest on the whole amount for a year, and sometimes even for the extra months up to the time of the deferred settlement.

* * *

The broadening intelligence of the Negroes makes them more restive under these unfavorable conditions than they have been in the past. Even the masses of them feel vaguely something of the great world movement for democracy. They bear unwillingly the treatment usually given them in the South, and they are making use of this first great opportunity to escape from it. To assume that the Negro has been blind and insensible to all his limitations, proscriptions, and persecutions, as so many whites appear to do, is to ascribe to the Negro less sense than is required to earn the money which alone the South seems to think is taking him away. Money, of course, he must have to live in the South, to say nothing of the North; but the Negro really cares very little for money as such. Cupidity is hardly a Negro vice. There is a good deal in the statement of a leading colored woman of Florida: "Negroes are not so greatly disturbed about wages. They are tired of being treated as children; they want to be men." So they are going where the conditions are more promising in that direction; and the mass of the migrants will in all probability not come back, as the whites generally think they will. Even if they do come back they will be very different people. From a good deal of evidence that is available, it seems that most of the migrants are making good in the North, where they plan to stay.*

---

*W. T. B. Williams, "The Negro Exodus from the South," in U.S. Department of Labor, Division of Negro Economics, *Negro Migration in 1916-1917* (Washington, 1919).

167

NEGROES EXPLAIN THE EXODUS

Emmett J. Scott, for many years private secretary to Booker T. Washington, was called to Washington during the war to become special assistant to the Secretary of War. In this capacity he attempted to ease the hostile conditions under which the colored people were serving the war effort as soldiers and civilians. In this capacity, too, he had an opportunity to collect letters which Negroes in the South wrote to inquire about joining the exodus. These letters were addressed to a variety of individuals and organizations, including Scott himself and the Chicago Defender. *Scott was able to locate a few letters written by Negro migrants to the South, but these were much more scarce.*

Mobile, Ala., Jan. 8, 1917

Dear Sir: I am writing you to see if you can furnish me with any information in regards to colored men securing employment. I would like to know if you could put me in touch with some manufacturing company either some corporation that is employing or in of colored men. My reason is there are a number of young men in this city of good moral and can furnish good reference—that is anxious to leave this section of the country and go where conditions are better. I taken this matter up with Mr. —— of Boston and he referred me to you. I myself is anxious to leave this part of the country and be where a negro man can appreshate beaing a man at the present time I am working as office man for a large corporation which position I have had for the past 11 years, having a very smart boy in his studies I wish to locate where he could recive a good education. I could at a few days notice place 200 good able bodied young men that is anxious to leave this city. these men I refer to is men of good morals and would prove a credit to the community. If you can furnish me with the desired information it will be gladly received. it makes little or no difference as to what state they can go to just so they cross the Mason and Dixie line. trusting you will furnish me with any information you have at hand at an early date, I await your reply.

Dapne, Ala., 4/20/17

Sir: I am writing you to let you know that there is 15 or 20 familys wants to come up there at once but cant come on account of money to come with and we cant phone you here we will be killed they dont want us to leave here & say if we dont go to war and fight for our country they are going to kill us and wants to get away if we can if you send 20 passes there is no doubt that every one of us will com at once. we are not doing any thing here we cant get a living out of what we do now some of these people are farmers and som are cooks barbers and black smiths but the greater part are farmers & good worker & honest people & up to date the trash pile dont want to go no where These are nice people and respectable find a place like that & send passes & we all will come at once we all wants to leave here out of this hard luck place if you cant use us find some place that does need this kind of people we are called Negroes here. I am a reader of the Defender and am delighted to know how times are there & was to glad to, know if we could get some one to pass us away from here to a better land. We work but cant get scarcely any thing for it & they dont want us to go away & there is not much of anything here to do & nothing for it Please find some one that need this kind of a people & send at once for us. We dont want anything but our wareing and bed clothes & have not got no money to get away from here with & beging to get away before we are killed and hope to here from you at once. We cant talk to you over the phone here we are afraid to they dont want to hear one say that he or she wants to leave here if we do we are apt to be killed. They say if we dont go to war they are not going to let us stay here with their folks and it is not any thing that we have done to them.

Cleveland, Ohio, Aug. 28, 1917

hollow Dr. my old friend how are you to day i am well and is doing fine plenty to eat and drink and is making good money in fact i am not in the best of health i have not had good health sence i ben here. i thought once i would hefter be operrated on But i dont no. i were indeed glad to recieve that paper from Union Springs.

* * *

i have seval nochants of coming back, yet i am doing well no trouble what ever except i can not raise my children here like they should be this is one of the worst places in principle you ever look on in your life but it is a fine place to make money all nattions is here, and let me tell you this place is crowded with the lowest negroes you ever meet. when i first come here i cold hardly ever see a Negro but no this is as meny here is they is thir all kinds of loffers. gamblers pockit pickers you are not safe here to walk on the streets at night you are libble to get kill at eny time thir have ben men kill her jest because he want allow stragglers in his family. yet i have not had no trouble no way. and we are making good money here. i have made as hight at 7.50 per day and my wife $4 Sundays my sun 7.50 and my 2 oldes girls 1.25 but my regler wegers is 3.60 fore 8 hours work. me and my family makes one hundred three darlers and 60 cents every ten days. it don cost no more to live here than it do thir, except house rent i pay 12 a month fore rent sence i have rote you everything look closely and tell me what you think is best. i am able to farm without asking any man fore enything on a credit i can not injoy this place let me tell you this is a large place Say Jef thornton, and William Penn taken dinner with us last Sunday and we taken a car ride over the city in the evening we taken the town in and all so the great lake era. they left Sunday night for Akron. Allso Juf griear spent the day with me few days ago give my love to all the Surounding friends

Philadelphia, Pa., Oct. 7, 1917

Dear Sir: I take this method of thanking you for yours early responding and the glorious effect of the treatment. Oh. I do feel so fine. Dr. the treatment reach me almost ready to move I am now housekeeping again I like it so much better than rooming. Well Dr. with the aid of God I am making very good I make $75 per month. I am carrying enough insurance to pay me $20 per week if I am not able to be on duty. I don't have to work hard. dont have to mister every little white boy comes along I havent heard a white man call a colored a nigger you no now—since I been in the state of Pa. I can ride in the electric street and steam cars any where I get a seat. I dont care to mix with white what I mean I am not crazy about being with white folks, but if I have to pay the same fare I have learn to want the same acomidation. and if you are first in a place here shoping you dont have to wait until the white folks get thro tradeing yet amid all this I shall ever love the good old South and I am praying that God may give every well wisher a chance to be a man regardless of his color, and if my going to the front would bring about such conditions I am ready any day—well Dr. I dont want to worry you but read between lines; and maybe you can see a little sense in my weak statement the kids are in school every day I have only two and I guess that all. Dr. when you find time I would be delighted to have a word from the good old home state. Wife join me in sending love you and yours.*

168

DISCRIMINATION IN THE ARMED SERVICES

War mobilization meant more than the enlargement of the military services in 1917, and many non-military groups in America organized their resources to increase their effectiveness during wartime. The Federal Council of Churches of Christ in America created its General Wartime Commission for this purpose, and the Commission, in 1917, established as one of its arms a committee to study the conditions under which Negro soldiers were serving and to call the attention of appropriate authorities to its findings. The committee chairman was the Methodist Bishop of New Orleans, Wilbur P. Thirkield, and his committee was composed of a small interracial group of distinguished clergymen and laymen.

THE NEGRO SOLDIER

If America is to have an army of 12,000,000 men, at least 1,000,000 will be Negroes. Already the number of colored soldiers exceeds 100,000, many of whom have rendered such notable service as to receive mention in the official reports not only of American commanders, but of the Germans as well. The racial discriminations which so largely prevail in civil life have reappeared in the camps, resulting in criticism and irritation on the part of the "race-conscious" Negroes who feel that the army should at least live up to the principles of human equality which are inscribed on its banners.

Bishops W. P. Thirkield, of New Orleans, has prepared a report on the Welfare of Negro Troops, which seeks to discover the grounds

*From *Letters of Negro Migrants of 1916–1918*, by Emmett J. Scott. Reprinted by permission of The Associated Publishers, Inc.

of irritation, and to suggest remedies for evils whose very existence is a reproach to the United States, and whose continuance menaces the strength of the nation's effort to deliver its united power against the German. The report represents the work of a committee of General War Time Commission of the Federal Council of the Churches of Christ. It presents four subjects to the attention of the War Department.

1. In the combatant regiments of Negroes the morale is high, the relation between white officers and colored men is good, and the effect of military training upon the men is conducive to wholesome results in civil life after the war. In non-combatant units, however, the situation appears to be far from satisfactory. The failure to give military training to service battalions and stevedore regiments has stood in the way of their attaining to the feeling both of self-respect and full loyalty that characterize the combatant units. Further, many of the white officers in the non-combatant units have carried over into the army old traditions and prejudices acquired in connection with managing gangs of Negroes on plantations, turpentine farms or construction of public works, and have not had, therefore, toward the men under them the attitude of sympathetic interest that officers take toward fighting men. The fact that in the majority of cases the non-commissioned officers in the service battalions and stevedore regiments have also been whites, who have taken a condescending attitude toward the Negroes and intensified a feeling of discontent. The inevitable result has been to make it more difficult to sustain among the colored people as a

Returning soldiers of the 369th Infantry Regiment aboard the S.S. Stockholm, February, 1919. No man of this regiment was ever captured, and the unit never retreated. Eleven times the 369th was cited for bravery, and the entire regiment received the French Croix de Guerre for gallantry under fire.

whole an adequate recognition of our democratic ideals in the war and the largest devotion to our cause.

2. Information has come that in certain draft boards an unfair and discriminating attitude has been taken toward Negroes, resulting in inducting into the army large numbers, who, if white, would have been exempted in accordance with the provisions of the draft law. To what extent such irregularities prevail it is impossible to say without further investigation, but certain it is that thoughtful Negroes are convinced that this is very frequently the case.

3. Although the number of illiterates among the Negro troops is exceedingly large, little provision is made for instruction. A military order requires all non-English speaking people in our army to be taught, but because even the most illiterate Negroes can understand orders of command it has not been deemed necessary to provide for their instruction. Such instruction would, however, be of great value not only in increasing the usefulness of the Negro in civilian life afterward but also in securing a finer morale during the war through his enhanced recognition of our concern for his welfare and his appreciation of our national ideals.

4. In the case of Negro regiments, particularly non-combatant units, little or no systematic provision has been made for organized athletics, and consequently the colored soldiers have been deprived of the valuable training that comes therefrom, and which is generally more needed by colored soldiers than by white.

By way of relief the committee suggests (1) that a small commission of prominent Negroes proceed overseas to examine and report conditions to the government; (2) that alleged draft board discriminations be investigated and eliminated; (3) that all colored battalions have military training; (4) that white officers for colored units be selected with a view to their sympathetic interest in their men; (5) that new service units have Negro non-commissioned officers; (6) that qualified Negroes be trained for officers in larger numbers; and (7) that directors of athletics be provided for all camps of colored troops.

The War Department has many vast undertakings under its direction, and its brilliant work along many lines is heartily appreciated. It has had few tasks beset with more perplexities than those which relate to the military employment of Negro citizens. These findings of Bishop Thirkield's committee deserve Secretary Baker's most serious consideration. They are not the captious criticisms of political opponents, or the expression of racial self-assertiveness. They are based upon the principles of human equality which lie at the basis of America's participation in the War for Freedom.*

---

*_Christian Advocate_, vol. 93, pt. 2 (September 12, 1918), 1146-1147.

CHAPTER TEN

Reaction and Renaissance

It was, in part, the Negro reaction to white prejudice and violence that sparked the Negro Renaissance. Young intellectuals in the ghettos of the North were forced to question their race, their environment, their nation. The Harlem Negro began to give expression to his inner feeling, to his sense of self. In the endlessly rising tenements, as in this street scene of Harlem, the Negro achieved full stature. It was in New York in 1923 that Paul Robeson began his career on the stage as a voodoo king in Taboo. *And it was in 1925 that Countee Cullen, a Harlem Negro, published his volume of poems* Color. *And it was in 1926 that another young man in Harlem, Langston Hughes, finished his first book of poems,* The Weary Blues.

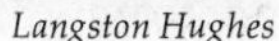

Langston Hughes

Countee Cullen

Paul Robeson

INTRODUCTION

Reaction and Renaissance

1919 was explosive for all Americans, a year almost beyond belief. For Negroes from the late spring until the end of the year it was a nightmare. Serious race riots broke out in Longview, Texas, and Washington, D.C., in June and July; in Chicago, and Knoxville, Tennessee, in August; in Omaha, Nebraska, in September. In that same month, a steel strike erupted and the companies imported Negro strikebreakers. The Department of Justice, investigating radical and seditious activities, included the Negro in its report in the fall of 1919, charging that some Negro leaders were taking the race down the road of Socialism and Communism. The Lusk Committee in New York State reported approximately the same thing a few months later. Seventy-six Negroes were lynched in 1919, the highest annual figure in eleven years. The white national secretary of the NAACP was badly beaten on the streets of Austin, Texas. In all earnestness did a Hampton, Va., Negro confess to a friend, "The alarming conditions all over the country are frightful. . . ."

The race riots stemmed from a variety of local causes, but they had some common features. Newpapers generally treated Negroes with a minimum of respect and frequently headlined allegations of assault and petty crime where a Negro was the accused, with little regard to the substance of the allegation. Economic exploitation of colored people in urban and rural areas became a way of life for white landlords and merchants. In the city, overcrowding bred insanitary housing, exorbitant rents, and high prices from which the Negro could not escape because of residential segregation. In rural areas, sharecroppers and tenants were at the mercy of the white farmer-owner who kept the accounts with his own brand of arithmetic. The inability of Negro factory workers to get a fair shake from unions further agitated the relations between the races. "Every man I spoke to," reported an investigator who spent two months as a laborer in the midwest in the fall of 1919, "talked of warfare between the races." The Negroes were prepared to fight back, and they did. "Shoot Back to Stop Riots" was the

Boston *Herald*'s capsule of the advice given the race by one of its leaders, and the summary of whites killed and wounded in the race riots was testimony to its effectiveness. Planned riots in Memphis, Tennessee, and Montgomery, Alabama, were called off when whites learned that Negroes were armed.

The fear of armed Negroes defending their persons and their homes was a surface manifestation of a deeper, more wraithlike apprehension which grew out of the complex changes wrought by the war. By 1920 more than half of the total population of the country lived in cities, and the Negro was in the van of the movement. Between 1910 and 1920, Negro urban residents increased by one-third while the colored rural population decreased slightly. By 1930, one out of every four Negroes had left the state of his birth, and the direction was generally North. Between 1910 and 1930, the southern Negro dropped from 30% to 25% of the rural population and from 28% to 23% of the urban population. In the North, the urban Negro became a larger fraction, increasing from 2.5% to 4% of city populations. Nine out of every ten northern Negroes lived in cities by 1930.

Negro leadership spoke out more forcefully, even from Tuskegee. R. R. Moton, Tuskegee's principal, asserted in 1929 that "any Negro, every Negro burns with indignation" at railroad discrimination, "and if you tell him the South is the best place for the Negro, and that the southern white man is his best friend, he looks to see whether you really expect him to believe it." Colored newspapers and magazines increased their circulation and their influence, and colored organizations stiffened their programs in defense of the rights of the race. The word "docile," a legacy from slavery which had so often been used to describe the race, was inapplicable. "I feel no desire to apologize to the world because I am a colored woman," wrote an interviewee in response to a questionnaire.

This was the New Negro, a name which grew in popularity among the race during the 1920's, particularly as Negro writers and artists developed national and international reputations. The Negro was changing as he adjusted to these new conditions and new demands, Negro spokesmen claimed, but whites did not recognize the difference largely because whites had increasingly insulated themselves from colored people. Channels of communication had been cut even at the household servant level and new channels between the educated classes of both races were slow to develop. The New Negro, ever more conscious of his race, his environment, his disabilities, and his potential, was determined to break down racial barriers for his own good and that of the country.

One of these barriers, an increasing flow of racist ideology, fed the resurgent Ku Klux Klan which sprang up during the war. The Klan attacked Catholics, Jews, and the foreign-born, as well as Negroes, with equal fervor, burning crosses, sponsoring lynching parties, and publishing shrill calls for purity. "Keep Caucasian blood, society, politics, and civilization PURE," the KKK's blue book proclaimed. The Klan was strong enough, North and South, to become openly a social organization, sponsoring picnics to which the public was invited and supporting political candidates who endorsed its viewpoint. Yet tragic as its violent activities were, and they are well documented, the Klan was easily ridiculed. The New York *World* published a long exposé in 1921 and *Opportunity* quoted with evident approval a comment of the Chicago *Defender:* "As soon as this country retrieves its momentarily mislaid sense of humor, it will laugh the Klan to death." And though this was an oversimplification, the Klan with its outlandish costumes and ritual was laughed into impotency. The Klan's ideology, however, was not as easily disposed of.

Cognizant of the currents of opinion which were abroad in the nation, the NAACP decided to intensify its efforts to prevent lynching. James Weldon Johnson took on the responsibility of lobbying for the NAACP and spent the better part of two years in Washington working for the Dyer Anti-Lynching bill, which was first introduced into Congress in 1919. In 1921, it was reintroduced and passed the House of Representatives but failed in the Senate when Senator William E. Borah of Idaho, a leading figure in the Senate, remained doubtful about its constitutionality. The NAACP had supplied its Congressional supporters with data demonstrating that rape was a cause in only 17% of the lynchings of record and that in thirty-three years, 64 of the lynch victims were women! The experience of a public debate on lynching was a catharsis and Johnson himself believed that "it served to awaken the people of the southern states to the necessity of taking steps themselves to wipe out the crime." That the number of lynchings dropped steadily during the 1920's was testimony enough.

In a negative sense, the decline in lynchings was a sign of progress, but there were other more positive signs, although each was tinged with a touch of despair. Statistics provide a rough index of the road Negroes were trodding. Between 1910 and 1930, Negro school attendance jumped from 45% to 60% of the eligible school population, although school attendance for colored children still lagged that of whites. While racists and some scientists were deriding the Negro's intelligence, other scholars, Negro and white, were demonstrating that the measurable achievement of colored children was equivalent to that of white children when environmental factors were similar. Negro inferiority is a "myth," claimed a Howard University scholar, adding that "the mental and scholastic achievements of Negro children, as with white children, are, in the main, a direct function of their environmental and school opportunities."

Negro students in the North had no legal barrier to an elementary and high-school education. Segregation was forbidden in all northern states and the state departments of education maintained uniform standards for all schools. In many states, Negro and white teachers were assigned without regard to the racial composition of their classes; in almost all states, salaries for Negro and white teachers were based on factors other than race. But legal fact was often supplanted by physical actuality. *De facto* residential segregation in many large cities led to segregated schools. In areas of southern New Jersey, Ohio, Illinois, and Indiana, schools were segregated on principle, without regard to law or residence. Where school systems were flooded with southern migrants, the educational process was slowed because migrant children were irregular in attendance and had more serious health problems, lower motivation, and a higher incidence of mental retardation than non-migrants.

For all of the educational problems which the northern migration created, it had the merit of introducing Negro labor into northern industry. Before the war, one third of the Negro steelworkers were in Alabama. By 1920, the number of Negro steelworkers had more than tripled and less than a quarter were in Alabama; the balance were employed in steel plants from Maryland to Illinois. As the Negro steelworker moved out of the South, he accelerated his progression from unskilled to semi-skilled labor. This pattern was repeated with minor variations in other major industries, but the picture had its dark side, too. Negroes in steel were excluded from the skilled crafts like pipefitting, electrical work, and carpentry. Generally they were given jobs, as one Negro steelworker put it, "that whites won't touch," and were blocked from supervisory and administrative positions. The industrial cities to which they came set Negroes apart in segregated communities, with the connivance of company management. Clairton, Pennsylvania, built a community swimming pool with the help of funds deducted from the pay of every steel worker, but Negroes were not permitted to use the pool. "We will have to work something for them, give them a day or something like that," the plant superintendent remarked.

The general policy of labor unions to ignore or discourage prospective Negro members did not go unnoticed. The National Urban League tried to work with unions and, as early as 1918, publicly asked the American Federation of Labor to take substantive action to get Negro workers into trade unions. Several years later, the NAACP proposed that the A.F.L., the Railway Brotherhoods, and any other acceptable unions join with it to form an Interracial Labor Commission to determine what was "the exact attitude and practice of national labor bodies and local unions toward Negroes and of Negro labor toward unions," and to act upon this information. There was no reply from the unions.

While unions and colored workers sparred intermittently, a quiet counterpoise developed among the writers and artists of Harlem and suddenly flared into a Movement, with a capital "M." James Weldon Johnson, poet, novelist, anthologist, politician, educator, and a national secretary of the NAACP, remarked in 1925 that "no race can ever become great that has not produced a literature," and the Movement of the 1920's was called the Harlem Renaissance. With its roots reaching back before the war, the Renaissance was a lively composite of race music, poetry, short stories, learned articles, novels, and art which penetrated the race barrier and spoke eloquently to peoples of all colors and tongues. Race consciousness in literary and artistic form became a saleable item and whites flocked to Harlem for the new jazz, the blues, the Lindy Hop, and the Charleston.

At root, three major forces dominated the Renaissance. The first was essentially pragmatic: In a little more than fifty years of freedom, the race had produced an intelligentsia, a class of men and women who could work with ideas and express them cogently and provocatively. The Talented Tenth of W. E. B. DuBois became a reality. On a less mundane but equally pragmatic level, the Renaissance was a protest movement using art and literary expressions. "We run / we run," sang the poet Langston Hughes. "We cannot stand these shadows. / Give us the sun." The suffocating oppressiveness which was part of Negro life in America sparked an explosive outcry. Hughes' poem continues: "We were not made / for shade / for heavy shade, / And narrow space of stifling air / That these white things have made." Whether in lament or in bombast, in intricate plot or feathery outline, the Negro artist exposed the hurt of the race.

To the combination of an intelligentsia and a spirit of protest was added the awareness of race. As early as the 1880's, race consciousness had been an evocative concept, but its thrust was never so clearly impacted as in the Renaissance. Where earlier race leaders emphasized pride in race and laid out objectives for the race to bargain for white acceptance, the Renaissance stressed that race was precious and not to be bargained away. The earlier position implied that the Negro should be accepted because he was like the white man; the Renaissance position was that the Negro should be accepted because, as a Negro, he had something to give. In effect, the Negro during the Renaissance came to grips with himself, through his artistic spokesmen. This was to have been, a Negro writer explained thirty years later, "a new technique . . . for solving the race problem in the United States. Art was the golden key."

From the perspective of segregation and the burdens it placed on the race, the South seemed monolithic in its inflexibility, yet beneath the surface, on college campuses and in urban communities, stirred currents of change. A citizens' group in Richmond, Virginia, launched an extensive survey of the Negro's condition in that city in 1928 and its report was an indictment of the controlling policies. A few leading newspapers in the South often counseled cooperation and restraint, though they were in a minority. The Federal Council of Churches established a Commission on the Church and Race Relations in 1922 to assist local ministers with information and to work for the Dyer Anti-Lynching bill. Beginning in 1926 it sponsored biennial interracial conferences of church women and two years later formed a special committee to work with local groups, North and South, on interracial economic problems in industry and agriculture.

In these activities, the Federal Council cooperated with a southern agency which had been established in 1919 by southern whites in conjunction with Negroes. The Commission on Interracial Cooperation quickly organized state commissions in thirteen southern states which in turn created county commissions in two thirds of the 1300 counties. Much of the work of the Commission was accomplished at local levels, lobbying for higher appropriations for Negro schools and trying to prevent extreme discrimination in employment. The Commission utilized two national interracial conferences to highlight race progress and problems. The second, in December, 1928, was a milestone for race relations and the Commission. "Never before in the history of the United States," commented the usually acerb W. E. B. DuBois, "have so many organizations, representing so diverse points of view and methods of approach, come together in a spirit of tolerance and inquiry to seek out the facts which underlie the relations of races in the United States." This was high praise for a commission which was more often pilloried by the militants of both races for trying to fill a vital communications void which white racism and black aspirations had formed.

However fluid the southern attitude on race appeared to be, it was nowhere more adamant than on the suffrage question. To the limit of its power, the NAACP maintained pressure on the South, largely through the instrument of the courts. Twice in five years, the NAACP challenged Texas legislation which permitted segregation by political parties in primary elections and in both cases the Supreme Court struck down the laws. The Fourteenth Amendment, Justice Benjamin Cardozo observed in the 1932 case (*Nixon* v. *Gondon*) "lays a duty upon the court to level by its judgement these barriers of color."

The significance of the voting Negro in the 1920's must be measured in two ways. The tendency to break away from the Republican party was important because it accurately forecast what was to come, a major shift by Negro voters into the Democratic party in the 1930's. Of equal moment was a political commonplace which aroused little contemporary comment: The ability of city political machines to organize the Negro to their own ends. In New York City, Tammany Hall held swav while in Chicago it was the Republican machine of "Big Bill" Thompson. The party affiliation had less importance at local levels than the existence of the machine and, whatever the debits of machine politics, Negroes profited. Philadelphia, Baltimore, St. Louis, Detroit, Boston, Pittsburgh, Cleveland, and smaller cities like Kansas City, New Haven, and Wilmington all had Negroes serving in elective or appointive city offices. In the South, where the Negro vote was scarce, it became important on the rare occasions in cities when the white vote split. Taken with the tendency to vote selectively, the active participation of Negroes in urban political machines held forth the promise of greater political potency.

The political promise of the urban North with its machine-like organization was matched, in the early 1920's, by a different kind of organization with an unusual non-political promise. The Universal Negro Improvement Association offered a vision of uplift and unity for Negroes of the world which was bold and breathtaking. Proudly segregationist—for blacks only, loud and blatant as befit the times, the U.N.I.A. was akin to the white Ku Klux Klan, even down to highsounding titles. Jamaica-born Marcus Garvey, the President General and guiding genius of U.N.I.A., arrived in the United States in 1916 to carry its message to the mainland. Before he was imprisoned for mail fraud in 1925 and deported in 1927, Garvey's organization had operated two steamship lines, created a nurse's corps, a manufacturing corporation, and an unarmed African Legion, and published a respectable newspaper and several lesser publications. On its face, this represented a monumental achievement, attracting hundreds of thousands of Negroes and hundreds of thousands of dollars. While the masses were encouraged and even inspired by Garvey's message, whites scoffed and Negro leadership carped at the U.N.I.A. as an opera bouffe. The Black Star Line was a pathetic failure, the nurse corps and the African Legion untrained, and the corporation existed only on paper. To the solemn and solid white citizenry, Garvey was a ludicrous symbol of a fanciful and fatuous race. But to the Negro, even those who carped, the undertones of Garvey's message of a new day for colored people were pertinent. When he said that black was beautiful, he thrilled a race which had not dared to believe it. The results of the Garvey movement are not measurable, but the Negro could not help but admire the way in which one man built so quickly a movement for and of the race.

There were other movements organized for the Negro with equal zeal but considerably less popular support. The efforts of the Communists to attract the Negro were an unqualified failure. Negroes soon discovered that white American Communists shared the same prejudices as their less disciplined compatriots and that for all the Communists talked about the evils of racism, they drew the same color line. Communism was suspect because it was foreign in origin, anti-Christian, and so class-conscious that it wanted to abolish class distinctions. While militant left-wingers like A. Philip Randolph and Chandler Owen flirted openly with the Socialists, the Communist thrust into the Negro group shattered against a wall of indifference and distaste.

The fabric of Negro life from Garveyism to Communism, from farm tenancy to scab labor, from Harlem Renaissance to residential segregation was stretched close to the breaking point by the depression, which followed the stock market crash in the fall of 1929. As the months rolled on, Negroes suffered layoffs or lower wages, stood in breadlines, employment lines, and even picket lines. Negro farmers saw their cash income plummet and in many cases they themselves were reduced in status and earning power from renter to sharecropper, from sharecropper to wage hand. A movement which began in Chicago before the crash gathered momentum and even some jobs for Negroes. The "don't buy where you can't work" campaign spread to other northern cities, aimed primarily at small retail merchants who occasionally capitulated. Another movement, larger in concept and backed by the National Negro Business League, hoped to weld Negro merchants together to improve their buying power and increase the available jobs for colored people.

In a sense, the depression was easier on Negroes than on whites, since the colored people were, as a whole, more used to poverty and a lower standard of living. Tightening belts was a commonplace occupation and, though no less hungry and heartsick, Negroes were better able to adjust to their situation. Their enforced clannishness was a benefit as families, friends, benevolent societies, and neighborhoods shared their resources to provide the bare essentials of existence. In the long run, though, the depression wore down this meager fellowship and took the starch out of almost everybody. Negroes with seniority lost their jobs to whites, and in too many places whites got job preference on the sole basis of color. Racial hostility tightened, but there was no major outbreak undoubtedly because food, shelter, and family care were more important than racial warfare. While the symbol of the New Negro, the Harlem Renaissance, faded before more pressing needs, the *literati* continued to write and to paint and a few followed the extremists' path into Marxism. The Communists were active among the disadvantaged, including Negroes, but they received little sustained support. In a presidential poll among Negroes taken in the spring of 1932, the Communist candidate received only slightly over 1% of the total votes cast.

The fall election which followed was a landslide for Franklin D. Roosevelt, and Negro voters moved wholesale into the Democratic party, subordinating their memory of the Wilson administration and their fear of the Democratic South to "the desire for change." Since race relations had not been an important part of the campaign, Roosevelt was accepted as a lesser evil rather than a messiah. Since he had shown himself to be liberal in political and economic matters, the *Opportunity* editors rationalized, he "might well be expected to be a liberal in race relations," but they were content to wait and see.

Urbanization and Race Violence

169

A CALL FOR DEMOCRACY AFTER THE WAR

World War I developed an intense patriotic fervor, which embraced a resurgence of democratic feeling, a belief in the equality of men, and its consequent application to government—rule by majority. Since Negroes participated in the war effort as soldiers and on the home front, they too were caught up in the swells of patriotism, which many believed would carry over after the war and break down racial barriers. The more critical observers, like W. E. B. DuBois, editor of The Crisis, *were less sanguine, and in a burst of militant rhetoric sounded the tocsin for a continuation of the struggle against racial inequality. This editorial was cited by the Department of Justice as one example of the unrest and potential subversion among Negro leaders, but its major import was to arouse the Negroes in the country to stand up and strike back when attacked. In some measure, the fighting posture of Negroes in the many race riots during 1919 is attributable to the DuBois editorial.*

RETURNING SOLDIERS

We are returning from war! The Crisis and tens of thousands of black men were drafted into a great struggle. For bleeding France and what she means and has meant and will mean to us and humanity and against the threat of German race arrogance, we fought gladly and to the last drop of blood; for America and her highest ideals, we fought in far-off hope; for the dominant southern oligarchy entrenched in Washington, we fought in bitter resignation. For the America that represents and gloats in lynching, disfranchisement, caste, brutality and devilish insult—for this, in the hateful upturning and mixing of things, we were forced by vindictive fate to fight also.

But today we return! We return from the slavery of uniform which the world's madness demanded us to don to the freedom of civil garb. We stand again to look America squarely in the face and call a spade a spade. We sing: This country of ours, despite all its better souls have done and dreamed, is yet a shameful land.

It *lynches.*

And lynching is barbarism of a degree of contemptible nastiness unparalleled in human history. Yet for fifty years we have lynched two Negroes a week, and we have kept this up right through the war.

It *disfranchises* its own citizens.

Disfranchisement is the deliberate theft and robbery of the only protection of poor against rich and black against white. The land that disfranchises its citizens and calls itself a democracy lies and knows it lies.

It encourages *ignorance.*

It has never really tried to educate the Negro. A dominant minority does not want Negroes educated. It wants servants, dogs, whores and monkeys. And when this land allows a reactionary group by its stolen political power to force as many black folk into these categories as it possibly can, it cries in contemptible hypocrisy: "They threaten us with degeneracy; they cannot be educated."

It *steals* from us.

It organizes industry to cheat us. It cheats us out of our land; it cheats us out of our labor. It confiscates our savings. It reduces our wages. It raises our rent. It steals our profit. It taxes us without representation. It keeps us consistently and universally poor, and then feeds us on charity and derides our poverty.

It *insults* us.

It has organized a nation-wide and latterly a world-wide propaganda of deliberate and continuous insult and defamation of black blood wherever found. It decrees that it shall not be possible in travel nor residence, work nor play, education nor instruction for a black man to exist without tacit or open acknowledgment of his inferiority to the dirtiest white dog. And it looks upon any attempt to question or even discuss this dogma as arrogance, unwarranted assumption and treason.

This is the country to which we Soldiers of Democracy return. This is the fatherland for which we fought! But it is *our* fatherland. It was right for us to fight. The faults of *our* country are *our* faults. Under similar circumstances, we would fight again. But by the God of Heaven, we are cowards and jackasses if now that that war is over, we do not marshal every ounce of our brain and brawn to fight a sterner, longer, more unbending battle against the forces of hell in our own land.

We return.
We return from fighting.
We return fighting.

Make way for Democracy! We saved it in France, and by the Great Jehovah, we will save it in the United States of America, or know the reason why.*

170

THE CHICAGO RACE RIOT OF 1919

No postwar race riot made a deeper impression than the one at Chicago which measured thirty-eight dead and 537 injured over one entire week from July 27 to August 2, 1919. Because the riot laid bare deep wounds in Chicago, interested parties began to demand an impartial investigation of the causes of and responsibilities for the conflict. Even before the smoke had cleared, on August 1, disturbed Negro and white civic leaders representing forty-eight groups met at the Union League Club and unanimously passed a resolution urging Governor Frank O. Lowden to "study the psychological, social, and economic causes underlying the conditions resulting in the present race riots." Three weeks later Lowden appointed the Chicago Commission on Race Relations, composed of six white and six Negro Chicagoans. With the aid of thirty trained social scientists, the Commission began a two-year effort to explore all the facets of racial tensions. Although pressured by those like Governor Lowden, who wanted the report to assert that Negroes were not the intellectual equals of whites, the Commission produced a perceptive and objective study, The Negro in Chicago. *It concluded with fifty-eight recommendations to Chicagoans to avoid repeated violence and to improve the quality of race relations. To this day* The Negro in Chicago *remains a model of how sociological techniques can be used to evaluate mob action.*

The Chicago Riot

Background

In July, 1919, a race riot involving whites and Negroes occurred in Chicago. For some time thoughtful citizens, white and Negro, had sensed increasing tension, but, having no local precedent of riot and wholesale bloodshed, had neither prepared themselves for it nor taken steps to prevent it. The collecting of arms by members of both races was known to the authorities, and it was evident that this was in preparation for aggression as well as for self-defense.

Several minor clashes preceded the riot. On July 3, 1917, a white saloon-keeper who, according to the coroner's physician, died of heart trouble, was incorrectly reported in the press to have been killed by a Negro. That evening a party of young white men riding in an automobile fired upon a group of Negroes at Fifty-third and Federal Streets. In July and August of the same year recruits from the Great Lakes Naval Training Station clashed frequently with Negroes, each side accusing the other of being the aggressor.

Gangs of white "toughs," made up largely of the membership of so-called "athletic clubs" from the neighborhood between Roosevelt

**The Crisis*, XVIII (May 1919), 13–14. Reprinted with permission of *The Crisis* Magazine, official publication of the NAACP.

Road and Sixty-third Street, Wentworth Avenue and the city limits—a district contiguous to the neighborhood of the largest Negro settlement—were a constant menace to Negroes who traversed sections of the territory going to and returning from work. The activities of these gangs and "athletic clubs" became bolder in the spring of 1919, and on the night of June 21, five weeks before the riot, two wanton murders of Negroes occurred, those of Sanford Harris and Joseph Robinson. Harris, returning to his home on Dearborn Street about 11:30 at night, passed a group of young white men. They threatened him and he ran. He had gone but a short distance when one of the group shot him. He died soon afterward. Policemen who came on the scene made no arrests, even when the assailant was pointed out by a white woman witness of the murder. On the same evening Robinson, a Negro laborer, forty-seven years of age, was attacked while returning from work by a gang of white "roughs" at Fifty-fifth Street and Princeton Avenue, apparently without provocation, and stabbed to death.

Negroes were greatly incensed over these murders, but their leaders, joined by many friendly whites, tried to allay their fears and counseled patience.

After the killing of Harris and Robinson notices were conspicuously posted on the South Side that an effort would be made to "get all the niggers on July 4th." The notices called for help from sympathizers. Negroes in turn whispered around the warning to prepare for a riot; and they did prepare.

* * *

Aside from general lawlessness and disastrous riots that preceded the riot here discussed, there were other factors which may be mentioned briefly here. In Chicago considerable unrest had been occasioned in industry by increasing competition between white and Negro laborers following a sudden increase in the Negro population due to the migration of Negroes from the South. This increase developed a housing crisis. The Negroes overran the hitherto recognized area of Negro residence, and when they took houses in adjoining neighborhoods friction ensued. In the two years just preceding the riot, twenty-seven Negro dwellings were wrecked by bombs thrown by unidentified persons.

Story of the Riot

Sunday afternoon, July 27, 1919, hundreds of white and Negro bathers crowded the lake-front beaches at Twenty-sixth and Twenty-ninth Streets. This is the eastern boundary of the thickest Negro residence area. At Twenty-sixth Street Negroes were in great majority; at Twenty-ninth Street there were more whites. An imaginary line in the water separating the two beaches had been generally observed by the two races. Under the prevailing relations, aided by wild rumors and reports, this line served virtually as a challenge to either side to cross. Four Negroes who attempted to enter the water from the "white" side were driven away by the whites. They returned with more Negroes, and there followed a series of attacks with stones, first one side gaining the advantage, then the other.

Eugene Williams, a Negro boy of seventeen, entered the water from the side used by Negroes and drifted across the line supported by a railroad tie. He was observed by the crowd on the beach and promptly became a target for stones. He suddenly released the tie, and went down and was drowned. Guilt was immediately placed on Stauber, a young white man, by Negro witnesses who declared that he threw the fatal stone.

White and Negro dived for the boy without result. Negroes demanded that the policeman present arrest Stauber. He refused, and at this crucial moment arrested a Negro on a white man's complaint. Negroes than attacked the officer. These two facts, the drowning and the refusal of the policeman to arrest Stauber, together marked the beginning of the riot.

Two hours after the drowning, a Negro, James Crawford, fired into a group of officers summoned by the policeman at the beach and was killed by a Negro policeman. Reports and rumors circulated rapidly, and new crowds began to gather. Five white men were injured in clashes near the beach. As darkness came Negroes in white districts to the west suffered severely. Between 9:00 P.M. and 3:00 A.M. twenty-seven Negroes were beaten, seven stabbed, and four shot. Monday morning was quiet, and Negroes went to work as usual.

Returning from work in the afternoon many Negroes were attacked by white ruffians. Street-car routes, especially at transfer points, were the centers of lawlessness. Trolleys were pulled from the wires, and Negro passengers were dragged into the street, beaten, stabbed, and shot. The police were powerless to cope with these numerous assaults. During Monday, four Negro men and one white assailant were killed, and thirty Negroes were severely beaten in street-car clashes. Four white men were killed, six stabbed, five shot, and nine severely beaten. It was rumored that the white occupants of the Angelus Building at Thirty-fifth Street and Wabash Avenue had shot a Negro. Negroes gathered about the building. The white tenants sought police protection, and one hundred policemen, mounted and on foot responded. In a clash with the mob the police killed four Negroes and injured many.

Raids into the Negro residence area then began. Automobiles sped through the streets, the occupants shooting at random. Negroes retaliated by "sniping" from ambush. At midnight, surface and elevated car service was discontinued because of a strike for wage increases, and thousands of employees were cut off from work.

On Tuesday, July 29, Negro men enroute on foot to their jobs through hostile territory were killed. White soldiers and sailors in uniform, aided by civilians, raided the "Loop" business section, killing two Negroes and beating and robbing several others. Negroes living among white neighbors in Englewood, far to the south, were driven from their homes, their household goods were stolen, and their houses were burned or wrecked. On the West Side an Italian mob, excited by a false rumor that an Italian girl had been shot by a Negro, killed Joseph Lovings, a Negro.

Wednesday night at 10:30 Mayor Thompson yielded to pressure and asked the help of three regiments of militia which had been stationed in nearby armories during the most severe rioting, awaiting the call. They immediately took up positions throughout the South Side. A rainfall Wednesday night and Thursday kept many people in their homes, and by Friday the rioting had abated. On Saturday incendiary fires burned forty-nines houses in the immigrant neighborhood west of the Stock Yards. Nine hundred and forty-eight people, mostly Lithuanians, were made homeless, and the property loss was about $250,000. Responsibility for the fires was never fixed.

The total casualties of this reign of terror were thirty-eight deaths—fifteen white, twenty-three Negro—and 537 people injured. Forty-one per cent of the reported clashes occurred in the white neighborhood near the Stock Yards between the south branch of the Chicago River and Fifty-fifth Street, Wentworth Avenue and the city limits, and 34 per cent in the "Black Belt" between Twenty-second and Thirty-ninth Streets, Wentworth Avenue and Lake Michigan. Others were scattered.

Responsibility for many attacks was definitely placed by many witnesses upon the "athletic clubs," including "Ragen's Colts," the "Hamburgers," "Aylwards," "Our Flag," the "Standard," the "Sparklers," and several others. The mobs were made up for the most part of boys between fifteen and twenty-two. Older persons participated, but the youth of the rioters was conspicuous in every clash. Little children witnessed the brutalities and frequently pointed out the injured when the police arrived.

Despite the community's failure to deal firmly with those who disturbed its peace and contributed to the reign of lawlessness that shamed Chicago before the world, there is evidence that the riot aroused many citizens of both races to a quickened sense of the suffering and disgrace which had come and might again come to the city, and developed a determination to prevent a recurrence of so disastrous an outbreak of race hatred. This was manifest on at least three occasions in 1920 when, confronted suddenly with events out of which serious riots might easily have grown, people of both races acted with such courage and promptness as to end the trouble early. One of these was the murder of two innocent white men and the wounding of a Negro policeman by a band of Negro fanatics who styled themselves "Abyssinians"; another was the killing of a white man by a Negro whom he had attacked while returning from work; and still another was the riotous attacks of sailors from the Great Lakes Naval Training Station on Negroes in Waukegan, Illinois.*

171

THE NEGRO IN INDUSTRY

One of the major services which the National Urban League performed after the first World War and well into the post-World War II period was a series

*Chicago Commission on Race Relations, *The Negro in Chicago; A Study of Race Relations and a Race Riot* (Chicago, 1922), 595-601.

of studies of urban communities and their Negro population. This study of Baltimore was confined to industrial problems, and was one of the early efforts of the League. Later investigations were more sophisticated, utilizing the techniques of the social sciences. Not only did these studies reveal important information about the Negro in cities, but they provided an insight into the workings of the cities themselves.

The early studies, such as this survey of Baltimore, did a great deal to boost the morale of Negroes who were pleased to be "investigated," and who took special pride in the fact that Negroes were doing the investigating. The League's stress on labor problems in Baltimore grew out of the larger labor problems which confronted Negroes as they sought better jobs, better working conditions, and union membership. On the basis of evidence such as this survey produced, the League was able to formulate its own policies in regard to industry and labor. Two years after this study was published, the League established its own department to concentrate in this area.

Charles S. Johnson was the first editor of Opportunity, *the League's magazine in which the survey was published. A social scientist of distinction, he left* Opportunity *for Fisk University in 1928. To make this survey, he selected 300 industrial plants as representative, employing approximately half of the industrial workers in the city. Of the 120 labor organizations in Baltimore, 40 cooperated in the survey.*

There were plants employing Negroes for certain grades of work and others refusing to employ them on the similar processes for reasons adequate and sufficient to each respectively. Some of the plants have what they call "labor policies" which summarily exclude all Negroes as below the standard for workers; others with the identical processes regard them as best fitted for their work. No standard appears to be observed; no objective basis for selecting a labor supply seems to exist. Generally speaking the following factors are important in influencing the use of Negroes:

1. Tradition, or the fixed custom of using Negroes in certain portions because they are supposed to be by nature better equipped for it; or because they are popularly regarded as "Negro jobs."
2. The unavailability of white labor.
3. The relatively cheaper cost of Negro labor.
4. The nature of the work which because of its general disagreeableness atracts only the worst class of white labor, and those only temporarily.
5. The nature of the industry making necessary a large proportion of unskilled labor capable of sustained physical exertion.
6. The seasonal character of the industry requiring a ready, fluid labor supply available in need.

Throughout the city the plants that employ Negroes, with a very few exceptions, may readily be pointed out by holding in mind one or more of the considerations listed above. The Baltimore industries, it will be recalled, are highly diversified. This fact militates strongly against any uniformity in proportions of persons, especially Negroes, employed. Again, its industries in many instances are developed and frequently controlled by outsiders who seek this locality for certain outstanding advantages. This fact further militates against uniformity of policy.

* * *

The history of the Negro laborer and the Trade Union Movement is but another aspect of his struggle for status in the industries of Baltimore. Essentially he is a buffer between the employers and the unions. This is an unfortunate position, for there is no security in either stronghold. His relation to his job takes on the nature of a vicious circle. In the unionized crafts he may not work unless he belongs to a union, and the most frequent, specious argument advanced by the unions is that he cannot become a member unless he is already employed. The result is frequently that he neither gets a job nor joins a union. The labor union movement, although recognizing the necessity for removing the menace of strike-breakers through unionization, with most astonishing inconsistency (a few instances excepted) deliberately opposes the organization of Negroes as a menace to the trade.

On the other hand, employers recognize in Negroes a most powerful weapon of opposition to the excessive demands of the unions. The impending shadow of Negroes as strike-breakers has staved off many strikes and lost for the strikers many others. As a further complication of an already bad situation, the most common procedure of the employers is to dismiss their Negro workers as soon as their purposes have been served. Bitterness of feeling between the white and Negro workers as a result of these tactics is inevitable.

The situation at present is one that admits little light. Employers may with generous grace pass the responsibility for exclusion to the unions, while the unions with equal grace pass it back to employers. However, it is a fact that in the "open" shops there is an almost complete exclusion of Negroes from the skilled positions and many of the semi-skilled ones for which the unions are in no sense responsible; and in practically all of the independent crafts, such as carpentry, brick masonry, plumbing and steam-fitting, there is an almost total exclusion for which the employers are not responsible. For in the former case union organizations are not tolerated, and in the latter employers willing to use Negroes have been definitely prohibited by the unions.*

172

THE NEGRO AND ORGANIZED LABOR

The attempts of Negro organizations to get more than a formal acknowledgement of the problem of Negro union membership from the American Federation of Labor were unceasing. The A.F.L.'s tactic was galling to both the NAACP and the National Urban League, not to mention A. Philip Randolph, the founder of the Pullman Porters' union. The League, with its Department of Industrial

**Opportunity*, I (June 1923), 12, 15, 19. Reprinted with permission of the National Urban League.

Relations and its traditional assistance in the area of employment, moved heaven and earth to gain recognition and a chance to sit down and examine the problem with the unions in a constructive way. The editorial printed below was another effort to bring the A.F.L. out into the open and pave the way for joint talks and cooperative action.

One of the barriers which separated the League and the NAACP from a successful assault on trade unionism was their own industrial inexperience. Neither organization had ever tried to work directly with Negro workers; they were non-participants. Moreover, the leadership of the two organizations was, relative to union workers, middle and upper class, and trade unionism was still imbued with a non-Marxist sense of class which made it difficult for it to cooperate with the NAACP and the League.

THE A.F.L. AND THE NEGRO

It is often asserted that black workers have been slow in accepting the doctrines and methods of organized labor. The most exploited workers in the United States, they have remained the least organized and therefore the most feeble in achieving either security in their employment or living wages and decent working conditions. This apparent indifference of the black worker to the benefits of trade unionism has served to draw the fire of various officials of the American Federation of Labor who, when accused of apathy to the fate of Negro labor, have replied from time to time that the Negro worker was unorganizable, and was as yet incapable of appreciating the necessity of identifying himself with the American Labor Movement.

The recent convention of the American Federation of Labor in Toronto lacked much of being able to convince observers that it is the pillar of flame by night and a cloud by day to lead the black worker, or for that matter the white worker, out of the wilderness. Out of the thirty million workers in America less than three million are enrolled in the American Federation. And the number of accessions this year of our Lord, which was to see a great drive in the South, even as reported, was a scanty 35,000.

The American Federation of Labor then not only has failed to unionize the black worker; it has failed to unionize the white worker. It is the citadel not of labor in the large sense but of crafts, and as a craft organization it necessarily has failed to embrace that great mass of unskilled labor with which the bulk of the black workers is identified.

Only in those occupations, generally semi-skilled or unskilled, which attract large numbers of Negroes, such as longshoremen, hod-carriers, common building laborers, or those in which Negroes enjoy a comparative monopoly, such as dining-car waiters and Pullman porters; or those in which Negro competition is able to cope successfully with the competition of white workers, as in the coal mining industry, only in these has American organized labor made any real effort to enlist the black worker in its ranks. The Negro, contrary to general opinion, is not slow to organize. There are approximately 100,000 Negro workers who are affiliated with some form of labor organization, a remarkable number when one considers that the Negro not only is outside of the pale of the skilled craft organizations, but also is compelled oft times to face the opposition of white labor, organized and unorganized, in order to gain a foothold in industry.

It is true that the American Federation of Labor has issued several lofty pronouncements to the effect that no discrimination because of race or color should govern admission to unions. It is also true that only eleven unions affiliated with the Federation specifically deny Negroes membership. But, so far, even when racial prejudice does not operate effectively to keep Negroes out, craft limitations and restrictions achieve the same result.

The statesmanship of the American Federation of Labor has failed to meet the problem of the unskilled worker, therefore it has been inadequate in so far as black workers are concerned. And there will be but little hope for the black worker in the American Federation as long as it is the so-called "aristocracy of labor," as long as it remains structurally a craft organization. And there will not be much hope for the unskilled white worker either in those great industries where crafts give way before the introduction of machinery and the increasing specialization of tasks. Where this has occurred to a considerable degree, the American Federation of Labor has made but little progress; the automobile industry; the packing industry; the rising rayon industries, these three are significant and striking examples of the failure of the Federation to keep pace with modern industrial trends.

In the South, where the Federation contemplates a mighty effort to organize the worker, a higher type of statesmanship will have to be evolved than has hitherto been revealed by the guiding geniuses of the Federation. Any attempt to organize the workers which ignores the presence of the two million black workers will be fraught with disaster. It will take more than official pronouncements of policy. It will demand the resolute facing of the fact that the problems of white labor and the problems of black labor are identical.*

Flood Tide of Racism

173

THE HIGH COST OF PREJUDICE

The idea of the superiority of the white race has a long history, but its modern American intensification began just before the turn of the century, strengthened by the popularizations of Darwinism and America's entrance into the international race for colonies. Southerners before World War I gratefully accepted and used the evidence which the racists published, asserting the inferiority and lack of stamina of the Negro race and boasting of the virtues inherent in the white race. The war dramatized, for racists, the dangers of continuing to permit hundreds of thousands of immigrants into the United States, polluting native Anglo-

**Opportunity*, VII (November 1929), 335–336. Reprinted with permission of the National Urban League.

Saxon stock. Madison Grant took this position in his The Passing of a Great Race *(1916) and again in his introduction to Lothrop Stoddard's* The Rising Tide of Color *(1920).*

The success of the Harlem Renaissance gave new spirit to Negroes. One of their spokesmen stepped forward to lock horns with Stoddard. The Forum *published the discussion entitled, "Should the Negro Be Encouraged to Cultural Equality?" in October 1927, and permitted the Negro author, Alain Locke, a brief rebuttal by letter two months later. Without striking at the pseudoscience on which the Stoddard hypotheses rested, Locke postulated the case of the Talented Tenth.*

THE HIGH COST OF PREJUDICE

The continuance of the present attitude toward the Negro is in fact possible only as long as it is possible to take as most representative of the Negro his worst rather than his best. His greatest disadvantage is not that of inequality of condition but inequality of comparison. For successful peoples are rated, and rate themselves, in terms of their best. Racial and national prestige is, after all, the product of the exceptional few. So when Negro life begins to produce poets, artists, thinkers and to make creative contributions that must be recognized not only as outstanding but as nationally representative, the old attitudes become untenable. In American music and poetry and drama it is impossible to name the foremost talents without including some Negroes; and the promise of the rapid developments of this aspect of Negro achievement, especially as centered in the younger New York group, make the same very probable in the next few years for fiction and the fine arts generally. A Roland Hayes, a Paul Robeson, a Countee Cullen, a Langston Hughes or a Weldon Johnson shift the burden of proof from 'Rastus Jones and the general average; and the crux of the matter becomes the question of what position and recognition must be accorded the cultured and culture producing Negro in American society.

* * *

The cultural recognition of the Negro, I admit, has its costs. But so also has non-recognition, and the situation should be pragmatically balanced in terms of these two costs. It merely fogs the issue when the creed of the slavocracy is sentimentally extended to classes and sections and situations that have no practical reason for holding to it, beyond the fact that it is the traditional way to think and feel. Even in circles that are so representative and stable that they should have no hysteria on the subject of race amalgamation, "no social equality,"—in short, "White Supremacy,"—is held to be the one reservation every typical White man is supposed to make and every typical Negro is expected to concede.

Cultural recognition, on the other hand, means the removal of wholesale social proscription and, therefore, the conscious scrapping of the mood and creed of "White Supremacy". It means an open society instead of a closed ethnic shop. For what? For making possible free and unbiased contacts between the races on the selective basis of common interests and mutual consent, in contrast with what prevails at present,—dictated relations of inequality based on caste psychology and class exploitation. It is predicated on new sorts of social contact,—less intimate in fact, however, than those it means to supplant. Indeed, instead of leaving society open at the bottom, as it now is, for the economic and sex exploitation of the weaker and less desirable elements of Negro life, it means the opening of society at the top for equal and self-respecting intercourse as warranted by mutual gain and common interests.

* * *

In the light of this active contradiction of its own social creed by its own social practice, White orthodoxy on the race question becomes not a consistent creed of race superiority and inner conviction, but the social self-defense of a bad conscience, the hysterical ruse of a self-defeatist vice. It fumes about keeping society closed at the top and insists on keeping it viciously open at the bottom. It claims to eliminate social contact between the races, but actually promotes race mixing. Under conditions and habits such as these contradictions have bred, a rabidly "White America" can not refuse to recognize the Negro and long remain White. For it is pride rather than prejudice that keeps social groups intact; and normally with the Negro there would be more sentimental and practical motives for group cohesion under conditions of social recognition than under those of social proscription, and less intermarriage under free association than miscegenation under forced social subserviency. The enlightened New South may be expected to see this. They already do. For these reasons as well as in the interest of general community reform and progress, they are gradually seeing the necessity for helping reestablish the group morale of the Negro.

* * *

Apart, however, from this broad question that creative genius is the hardest and costliest thing to refuse to recognize, in a suppressed minority group it is the most dangerous thing to deny it free play and recognition. The balked intelligence of such a group, thrown back upon the repressed masses, invariably comes forward within another generation's time in the uglier form of radical leadership. Behind it rally the aroused masses and their harsh demands. As with the Jewish intellectuals of Russia, subverted social light may readily become revolutionary fire. I am not an alarmist; but I can see danger ahead in this persistent American lumping of the best with the worst in Negro life. Race war? Not exactly. Class war, more likely,—with the Negro group temper profoundly changed from its present patient amiability to social desperation, having in its ultimate disillusionment discovered that it has so little to lose.

* * *

For the younger Negro artists and leaders of to-day are proudly race-conscious, and their work is in many cases frankly based on a conscious interpretation of their race life. They have, so to speak, two audiences, and are in many cases strained to know upon which to concentrate. As artists, it would be best for them to face America and humanity at large. Otherwise, two alternatives, each entailing heavy and general social loss, would confront the talented Negro:

either to march off to foreign fields and repeat for the whole American situation what has already tragically happened in the South, where the best and sturdiest have moved off and left an inert and almost leaderless mass to constitute a still heavier social drag and danger; or else to turn in narrowed and vindictive vision to the only course that will give him a chance and swing the hammer of mass action behind the cutting edge of genius.*

174

THE IMPASSE AT THE COLOR-LINE

In his essay in The Forum *Stoddard focused almost exclusively on the American Negro, reducing his global ideas to the American scene. Working within the premise that the American Negro is* different *Stoddard sought to persuade that this difference would be inimical to the "American Way."*

THE IMPASSE AT THE COLOR-LINE

Until recent years the Northern Negroes had little to encourage their aspirations. They remained a very small element scattered widely through our Northern cities and towns. But for more than a decade the mass influx from the South, together with a lesser immigrant influx from the West Indies, has vastly increased their numbers and has quickened them to a new ferment. Also, changed economic conditions have brought them a larger measure of material well-being. An educated class has arisen, some of whose members display literary and artistic talent. This Negro intelligentsia rejects the biracial system of the South, inveighs against the color-line, and threatens our social order with their embittered enmity unless White America admits them to full equality, with its logical implication,—racial amalgamation.

Of this insurgent Negro intelligentsia, Alain Locke,—the writer of the preceding paper,—is a good example. Mr. Locke's line of argument is not novel; it is the thesis to-day expounded by the entire group which he typifies. In many Negro minds a new hope is being born,—a hope more alluring than any which has arisen since the ill founded aspirations of half a century ago. Therefore, for the Negro's own sake, as well as in the interests of social peace, he ought to be told,—tolerantly yet unequivocally,—that this new hope is a delusion, which, if persisted in, will lead to unnecessary disappointments and misfortunes.

For let there be no mistake: White America will not abolish the color-line, will not admit the Negro to social equality, will not open the door to racial amalgamation. That is the meat of the matter. If this spells trouble, then trouble there must be. But the best way to minimize the trouble is to speak frankly at the start, thus checking the spread of false hopes and limiting the resultant bitterness of disillusion.

* * *

Forum, LVIII (October 1927), 501-510.

Even a general knowledge of historical and scientific facts suffices to show the need for a racial basis to our national life,—as it has been, and as we intend that it shall be. We know that *our* America is a *White* America. "America," in the traditional sense of the word, was founded by White men, who evolved institutions, ideals, and cultural manifestations which were spontaneous expressions of their racial temperament and tendencies. And the overwhelming weight of both historical and scientific evidence shows that only so long as the American people remains White will its institutions, ideals, and culture continue to fit the temperament of its inhabitants,—and hence continue to endure.

* * *

Let us probe yet more deeply into the matter. Even if we entirely disregard the weight of scientific evidence which clearly tends to show that crosses between White and Negro are biologically undesirable, we must be guided by one fact which has been scientifically determined beyond all doubt,—the fact that such crosses produce highly disruptive effects. And similar disruptive effects are produced by crosses between Whites and members of non-White races other than Negroes.

A moment's reflection will reveal why this is so. The great racial divisions of mankind are very old and well established. Each race, despite wide internal variation, forms a generalized type possessing a complex pattern of closely linked physical, mental, and temperamental characteristics, which have evolved through long ages of natural selection that have eliminated disharmonic variations and have produced a relatively smooth working psychophysical whole.

Now the interbreeding of such widely differentiated racial types disrupts both patterns and produces hybrid offspring who are more or less disharmonic. Again, the subsequent interbreeding of these first hybrids disrupts still further, breaks apart more and more of the linked characteristics, and ends in a population which displays an almost infinite range of variation instead of the relatively restricted, harmonious range which occurred in the original racial types. To be sure, some of these new variants may theoretically be desirable, as others are undesirable. But one thing is certain: stability and harmony are hopelessly gone, and in their place reign bewildering variety and uncertainty.

* * *

Here are the plain facts of the case: Since the Negroes form nearly one-tenth of the population of the United States, we are *statistically* light mulattos. In the last analysis, the only thing which keeps us from being *biologically* mulattos is the color-line. Therefore, once the principle of the color-line is abandoned, White America is doomed, and a mulatto America stands on the threshold. Under Mr. Locke's formula it might take several generations. Yet it would be inevitable in the long run.

Such is the road which Mr. Locke would have us travel. But it can not be too promptly or emphatically stated that athwart that road we plant the sign: *No Thoroughfare!* White America intends at all costs to remain White, and every attack on the color-line will merely cause it to be applied more strictly and will hinder any feasible adjustment of race relations based upon a recognition of existing realities.

Another point should be clearly understood. If Mr. Locke's arguments do not convince us, still less do his threats intimidate us. For Mr. Locke does threaten in no uncertain voice. He tells us that unless we accede to his demands, the insurgent Negro intelligentsia which he represents will either quit the country or will remain here as apostles of race war and social revolution. That is not a pleasant prospect, but it will not make us "capitulate",—gracefully or otherwise. For we White Americans are quite ready to risk possible ills from racial strife or revolutionary agitation, rather than endure the certain ills that would ensue from the loss of our race identity.

* * *

The polemics of the militant Negro intelligentsia of our Northern cities should not blind us to the genuine progress toward racial adjustment which has already been made, especially in the South, and which promises even better for the future. Over thirty years ago, Booker Washington blazed the trail for the forward looking members of his race when he uttered the memorable phrase: "In all things purely social we can be as separate as the fingers, yet one as the hand in all things essential to mutual progress."

Thanks largely to Booker Washington's frank facing of realities and insistence upon good interracial relations, Southern Negrodom has evolved a group life of its own, with the encouragement and support of the best elements of the White South. Perhaps the most hopeful aspect of the present situation is the well known Commission on Interracial Cooperation, composed of representative Whites and Negroes. This organization functions throughout the South in a constant endeavor to remedy abuses, allay friction, and promote good relations between the races. The solid results attained by the Commission are due to its practical, level headed spirit. The system of racial segregation is tacitly accepted by both sides as axiomatic, their joint efforts being directed to a bettering of conditions within the bounds of the existing social order.

The basis of interracial cooperation has been so soundly laid that it seems as though the time were ripe for a further step. Why should not the best minds of both races attempt to arrive at a frank understanding about the fundamentals of racial relations and try to formulate a definite policy which will have their mutual assent and support?

To the writer, such an attempt seems highly desirable,—even urgently necessary. Furthermore, it seems to me that the only policy which will have a real chance of success is that which may best be termed biracialism,—a parallel evolution of White and Negro race lives, biologically distinct, yet linked by mutual interests and cooperating for common ends. To enlist the support of the best elements of both races for an equitable biracial system, mutual concessions will be needed. Yet, provided the two groups agree on the basic principle of racial separation, such a system can be worked out with substantial fairness to both.*

175

THE RISING TIDE OF COLOR—A CRITICISM

Stoddard's book The Rising Tide of Color *(1920), though its animadversions about American Negroes were subdued compared to the emphasis it placed on other colored stocks, roused scientists and Negro publicists to counteract its message. Franz Boas, an anthropologist who pioneered investigations of race in the interest of science, continually sought to repudiate the Stoddard mystique. His review of Stoddard's book was the most concise and direct statement of this period.*

Mr. Stoddard's book is one of the long series of publications devoted to the self-admiration of the white race, which begins with Gobineau and comes down to us through Chamberlain and, with increasingly passionate appeal, through Madison Grant to Mr. Stoddard. The newer books of this type try to bolster up their unscientific theories by an amateurish appeal to misunderstood discoveries relating to heredity and give in this manner a scientific guise to their dogmatic statements which misleads the public. For this reason the books must be characterized as vicious propaganda, and deserve an attention not warranted by any intrinsic merit in their learning or their logic.

The fundamental weakness of all books of this type, and eminently so of Mr. Stoddard's book, is a complete lack of understanding of the hereditary characteristics of a race as against the hereditary characteristics of a particular strain or line of descent. Each race is exceedingly variable in all its features, and we find in the white race, as well as in all other races, all grades of intellectual capacity from the imbecile to the man of high intellectual power. It is true that intellectual power is hereditary in the individual, and that the healthy, the physically and mentally developed individuals of a race, if they marry among themselves, are liable to have offspring of a similar excellence; but it is equally true that the inferior individuals in a race will also have inferior offspring. If, therefore, it were entirely a question of the eugenic development of humanity, then the aim of the eugenist would be to suppress not the gifted strains of other races, but rather the inferior strains of our own race. A selection of the intelligent, energetic, and highly endowed individuals from all over the world would not by any means leave the white race as the only survivors, but would leave an assembly of individuals who would probably represent all the different races of man now in existence.

It is, therefore, entirely inadmissible to speak of the hereditary traits of a race, as though one race were the sole possessor of desirable mental qualities. The hereditary characteristics of a race include the whole range of varying forms that belong to it and,

**Forum*, LVIII (October 1927), 510-519.

for this reason, the hereditary characteristics of different races show very slight differences only. It is quite impossible to tell how much of the existing differences is due to hereditary and how much to social environment.

The whole basis of the theories developed in Mr. Stoddard's book is contradictory to the fundamental teachings of anthropology. An author who claims that "civilization is the body and the race is the soul," who considers civilization as the result of "the creative urge of a superior germplasm," who refuses to recognize that civilization is the outcome of historical conditions that act favorably on one race at one time, and unfavorably on other occasions, and whose own race consciousness, owing to the environment in which he has grown up, is highstrung, must be led to the abject fear of an equal development of all the members of mankind, without, however, being able to give any kind of convincing proof of the correctness of his theories.*

176

REVIVAL OF THE KU KLUX KLAN

The Ku Klux Klan was revived in 1915 as a fraternal and social organization near Atlanta, Georgia, by a small group of men headed by William Joseph Simmons. Until 1919, little was heard or known about it, but it began in that year to attract attention. In June 1920, Imperial Wizard Simmons invited Edward Y. Clarke and Mrs. Elizabeth Tyler to join him, and the Klan began to grow. In a year, it had 100,000 members in all sections of the country and its expansion was accompanied by a wave of violence, generally directed at individuals for the purpose of cleaning up communities by floggings, tar-and-feather parties, and leave-town warnings. Congress investigated the Klan in the fall of 1921, and the New York World *carried its exposé a month earlier, but neither did more than advertise the Klan without cost to it. At its height, Klan membership may have reached two or even three million, including sympathizers as well as actual members. Clarke and Mrs. Tyler made the Klan a profitable venture with steep membership dues, hood and gown rentals, and other promotional schemes.*

The Klan delighted in using the letter "K" in making up names. The Kloran was their book of ritual, the Kleagle their promotion manager, the Kludd their chaplain, and so on. The Ku Klux Kreed was one of many statements of purpose and belief.

THE KU KLUX KREED

We, *The Order* of the Knights of the Ku Klux Klan, reverentially acknowledge the majesty and supremacy of the Divine Being, and recognize the goodness and providence of the same.

We Recognize our relation to the Government of the United States of America, the Supremacy of its Constitution, the Union of States thereunder, and the Constitutional Laws thereof, and we shall be ever devoted to the sublime principles of a pure Americanism and valiant in the defense of its ideals and institutions.

**The Nation*, CXI (December 8, 1920), 656.

We Avow The distinction between the races of mankind as same has been decreed by the Creator, and shall ever be true in the faithful maintenance of White Supremacy and will strenuously oppose any compromise thereof in any and all things.

We Appreciate the intrinsic value of a real practical fraternal relationship among men of kindred thought, purpose and ideals and the infinite benefits accruable therefrom, and shall faithfully devote ourselves to the practice of an honorable Klanishness that the life and living of each may be a constant blessing to others.*

177

THE ANTI-LYNCHING BILL

Between 1890 and 1920, more men were lynched than were executed by all the courts in the land. This statistic symbolized the telling data which the NAACP had collected on the crime of lynching and, taken with political and race pressures, led to the NAACP decision immediately following the war to put an anti-lynching law at the top of its priorities.

In 1919 three congressmen introduced bills to halt lynching, but their advocates soon agreed on the one submitted by Leonidas C. Dyer, a Republican from East St. Louis. On January 26, 1922, the advocates of the Dyer bill won a Pyrrhic victory when the House voted by almost a two-thirds majority to pass the bill. Although briefly debated in the Senate, the bill was buried by southern Democrats and northern Republicans and never came to a vote. In 1924 the House Judiciary Committee approved the bill, but Dyer failed to persuade the Rules Committee to allow it to reach the floor of the House. After that failure, the supporters of antilynching legislation gave up until the mid-1930's when they regrouped their forces for another battle.

During the 1922 House debate, Dyer was the main spokesman for the bill while Hatton W. Sumners, a Democrat from Dallas, led its opponents. Both were seasoned by almost a decade in the House. Dyer was a veteran of the Spanish-American War, and Sumners had made his reputation as a leader of the men who reformed Texas criminal laws. Opponents of the bill found it unconstitutional because it transferred local police power to the federal government, and, in the words of a Kansas congressman, deprived citizens of the states "of that 'last vestige of their right' to burn each other without a trial." The southern position in defense of states rights had sufficient merit to make constitutional lawyers and some politicians uneasy.

Mr. Dyer. Mr. Chairman and gentlemen of the committee, my interest in this legislation comes from lynchings that have occurred in my own State. My special attention to this matter came five years ago when at the very doors of my home occurred one of the most disgraceful lynchings and riots known to civilization. That occurred in the city of East St. Louis, Ill. I introduced a resolution at that time asking that the House of Representatives investigate that lynching and ascertain the cause and see if there was something we might do to make such disgraceful events scarce and impossible for

---

**Papers Read at the Meeting of Grand Dragons, Knights of the Ku Klux Klan at their First Annual Meeting held at Asheville, North Carolina, July 1923* (n.p., n.d.), 133-134.

the future. In that lynching and in that mob riot there were 100 and more people injured and killed—innocent men and innocent women.

Some of the most outrageous murders known to humanity took place at this time. Little children were taken away from their mother's arms and thrown into the fire.

This affair grew out of a killing that occurred in East St. Louis. There had been race feeling in that city, and there was an automobile containing police officers driven through sections of East. St. Louis that were populated largely by colored people, and while they were doing this they were fired upon—fired upon by somebody, presumably, although I do not think it was ever ascertained as a fact, by some Negroes. A man was killed; another was wounded, and this lynching, this murder of more than 100 people, innocent as you and I of any connection with that affair, took place. Some people started out to find the people who had killed this man for the purpose of lynching them.

This legislation, if enacted into law, will cover cases of that kind, notwithstanding the statement made by some gentleman previous to the holiday recess that this legislation is aimed only at the Southern States, where lynchings have been promiscuous. Mr. Chairman, I may say in this connection that that thought never entered my mind in what I have done to secure this legislation. I want to make it so that lynchings of the kind that happened in East St. Louis, Ill., will not go unpunished to the fullest extent possible.

* * *

Lynchings have been going on in this country for these many years without any special effort apparently being made to prosecute or to punish the guilty. It is true that some few of those who participated in that East. St. Louis lynching were convicted; some whites and some blacks were convicted and sent to the penitentiary. But that is one of the few instances to my knowledge where there has ever been any conviction.

The charge has been made here, Mr. Chairman, that these lynchings are caused by attacks upon women, that they are the result of rape. That is as far from the truth as many of the other extravagant statements that have been made.

I have taken pains to obtain the best possible information regarding lynchings in the last 35 years or more, and I have here a statement prepared by the president of the Tuskegee Institute of Alabama, under date of December 31, 1921. In a word, it says that in this 36-year period, from 1885 to 1921, there has been 4,096 lynchings. Of this number 810 were charged with rape or attempted rape. In other words, of the total number of 4,096, only 810 were even charged with this horrible crime or its attempt. I have taken pains to have other statements compiled. I have one here prepared by the National Association for the Advancement and Protection of Colored People stating that during the period from 1889 up until December, 1919, there were 3,434 known lynchings in the United States. Of that number 570 have been charged with rape or attempted rape—570 out of 3,434.

It is especially emphasized in this connection that there have been many lynchings where the victim was not even accused of rape

THE SHAME OF AMERICA

Do you know that the United States is the Only Land on Earth where human beings are BURNED AT THE STAKE?

In Four Years 1918-1921, Twenty-Eight People were publicly BURNED BY AMERICAN MOBS

3436 People Lynched, 1889-1921

Is Rape the "Cause" of Lynching?

83 WOMEN HAVE BEEN LYNCHED IN THE UNITED STATES

AND THE LYNCHERS GO UNPUNISHED

THE REMEDY

The Dyer Anti-Lynching Bill Is Now Before the United States Senate

THE DYER ANTI-LYNCHING BILL IS NOW BEFORE THE SENATE
TELEGRAPH YOUR SENATORS TODAY YOU WANT IT ENACTED

NATIONAL ASSOCIATION FOR THE ADVANCEMENT OF COLORED PEOPLE

Gumby Collection, Columbia University

In support of the Dyer Anti-Lynching Bill, the NAACP ran this full-page advertisement in The New York Times *and other daily papers in November 1922.*

but in which cases the lynchers gave rape as the cause in order to justify their action. They did this, of course, because they felt that a great majority of the American public would not censure them for lynching under those circumstances; and that is, I take it, why some of the gentlemen rise in their seats and say that this bill should be labeled a bill to legalize rape.

* * *

Mr. Sumners of Texas. Mr. Chairman and gentlemen of the committee, I assume that there is no difference of opinion among men representing the different sections of the country in reference to the fact that the crime of lynching is a crime which nobody can defend, a crime which must be suppressed. The question is how best to proceed to do the thing that ought to be done. Before beginning a discussion of this bill I want to challenge the slanders which have been heaped upon the South by a lot of these hired Negro agitators and white negroettes that have been going over the country falsely representing my people. I received the other day a statement from the Tuskegee Institute. The gentleman who has just taken his seat quoted practically all of his statistics and gave practically all his information from that source. Under the date of December 31, 1921, they sent out broadcast, with release for publication dated January 1, "The lynch record for 1921," from which I quote, "there were 63 persons lynched in 1921. Of those 62 were in the South and one in the North." I do not know how I happened to clip this out, but the Washington Post of July 16, 1921, carried a statement under these headlines, which I quote: "Three Negroes hanged by mob in Duluth; 5,000 seize prisoners at police headquarters; troops ordered out. Attack on young white girl rouses crowd's fury." These Negroes were connected with a circus. They took a white girl into the circus grounds and ravished her. This Duluth, Minn., mob hung them all to a telephone pole in the middle of the city. Three at once in one place. And yet we are told that only one person was lynched in the entire North during all of the year 1921. The gentleman who has just taken his seat told you of a killing in East St. Louis of 100 people at one time.

* * *

Let me tell you something. Suppose this other thing happens —and you can do it under this bill—suppose that a black man takes a little white child and drags her off into seclusion where no voice can hear and no hand can help, and rapes that child, and the father of that child and the brothers of the child come up on him and kill him, and the Federal Government takes them away in the face of public sentiment and places them in the Federal penitentiary, and then has a tax of $10,000 levied against the county for the benefit of the rapist's family, a part of which sum might go to buy that family an automobile to ride by the home of the innocent victim, do you think, as a matter of common sense, with such a policy you could long prevent a condition in that country like those which developed in East St. Louis, Omaha, and Chicago?

* * *

Mr. Chairman, I am opposed to mob violence, to the crimes which provoke mob violence, and to the conditions which permit those crimes to result in mob violence. I am opposed to this bill because it would increase mob violence by encouraging the crimes which are the most provocative of mob violence and which more than all things else combined create the condition out of which mob violence as a punishment for other offenses arises. I am opposed to this bill because the interposition of Federal power would lessen the sense of local responsibility and retard the growth of local purpose to suppress mob violence. I am opposed to this bill because it is unconstitutional and appeals for its support to the very spirit which it denounces—the spirit of disregard for law and for the sacredness of the official oath. This bill can not pass this House unless it is put through by that same spirit which inspires the mob when, backed by the courage of numbers, excused in conscience by the law's delays and alleged miscarriage of justice, they crush through by the sheer weight of numbers the legal barriers which deny the right to proceed in the manner undertaken and do an unlawful thing.

You are asked to do a thing contrary to the supreme law of the land in order to make certain and quick a punishment alleged to be deserved. Gentlemen, that is the identical appeal of the leader of the mob. This bill has incorporated therein provisions which no lawyer in this House or elsewhere can defend and but few, if any, have reputations so poor or so well established that they will hazard them in the attempt. Yet you will be asked to pass the bill. They whisper in your ears "political expediency" and ask you to yield to it. That is the same whisper which comes to the ear of the sherriff when the mob is battering at the jail door. Wonderful example they ask you to set to the constabulary of this country.

I am opposed to lynching. If I were at home and I heard that an effort was being made to arouse the mob spirit, I would oppose it.

If I had been in Omaha when they were about to mob the mayor because he had stood beween the mob and its intended victim, I would have opposed that. To-day the Constitution of the United States stands at the door, guarding the governmental integrity of the States, the plan and the philosophy of our system of government, and the gentleman from Missouri, rope in hand, is appealing to you to help him lynch the Constitution. I am opposed to that. If it were not for the tragic possibilities which are involved and the duty imposed, if I were actuated by political considerations, I would merely register a general protest and hope for favorable action. But, gentlemen, this is not a matter with regard to which either side can afford to play politics.

* * *

This bill, as I say, challenges the efficiency of the government of the States, and here is the difference between this bill and the other bills that we have been enacting here expanding the Federal power: This bill, challenging as it does the relative governmental efficiency of the States and the integrity of purpose of their governmental agencies, placing the Federal Government, as it does, in the attitude of an arbitrary dictator assuming coercive powers over the States, their officers, and their citizens in matters of local police control, would do incomparable injury to the spirit of mutual respect and trustful cooperation between the Federal Government and the States essential to the efficiency of government. As a precedent, this bill, establishing the principles which it embodies and the congressional powers which it assumes to obtain, would strip the States of every element of sovereign power, control, and final responsibility for the personal and property protection of its citizens, and would all but complete the reduction of the States to a condition of governmental vassalage awaiting only the full exercise of the congressional power.

Gentlemen, I do not excuse the sixty-odd lynchings that occurred in the South in a year, but when you consider the millions of black people who live in that country, and when you consider the fact that we do have white men there who are not law-abiding, just as we do have the black men there who are not law-abiding, and you measure what occurs there by what occurred in East St. Louis, Chicago, and Omaha, it shows that the people in that great section of the country are doing the best they can.

* * *

We are tired of it. We know it is not right. The conscience of the country is revolting against these conditions, and if we could get a little more help from you people, exerted with the black people, to encourage them to run out the criminal element from among them while we work on the criminal element of the white people, instead of sending these Negro agitators down there to preach social equality among my people, you would aid more than you are aiding now. We might just as well understand ourselves, gentlemen. That day never will come—there is no necessity for anybody mistaking it—that day never will come when the black man and the white man will stand upon a plane of social equality in this country, and that day never will come in any section of the United States when you will put a black man in office above the white man. That never will happen. It never can happen on the face of God Almighty's earth. It has not happened in 4,000 years and never will. Oh, you can elect one here and there in communities where you have them in control. You can give him a little recognition to keep the boys lined up, but he is under white control, and you never will surrender the control of your government in any community to the black race. It can not happen.

* * *

And it is a rather interesting thing, too, that as society has established legislatures and courts, men in mv part of the country have never yielded to the courts established by legislatures or to laws established by legislatures the protection of their women. There is just one thing they will not litigate. Nowhere under God Almighty's sky will they yet litigate the issue of a foul wrong committed against their women. They have not yielded that yet. You see, they had that jurisdiction first. They delegated authority to the courts after the courts got there, but they were there first. That will change as pioneer influences and ideals give way. It is changing now. There is another thing that makes the situation more difficult in the South. I do not know why, but somewhere in the great purpose of God Almighty He has determined to preserve, for a while yet, at least, these lines of racial cleavage that He has drawn among the races of men.

* * *

When a white woman is raped by a black man the call to the man is from his two strongest, most primitive instincts. No doubt when men lived in caves the strongest instinct of the man was to protect his woman. The next strongest instinct is to protect the blood. When the call comes from the woman, crying out from the depths of her outraged chastity, there comes to the man a call which reaches back to the days when he was a savage in the cave, and he goes. When that call comes from the woman who has been raped by a man of alien blood, woman, who in every age of the world has been the faithful guardian of the purity of the race—when that call comes it is the call of his woman and the call of his blood, and he goes. It is not an easy situation to deal with. He goes not alone. His neighbors, whose women live under the same danger, go with him. The impulse is to kill, to kill as a wild beast would be killed.*

Congressional Record—House (67 Cong., 2 Ses.), January 4, 1922.

178

BLACK RACISM

Marcus Garvey, founder and leader of the Universal Negro Improvement Association, was an enigma to America. Few whites could understand either the man or the movement. Negro leaders, themselves members of the middle class and the intelligentsia, were aghast that Garvey's appeal should be so widespread. The Negro masses to whom he addressed himself did not stop to analyze him; the very magnetism of his person and his message was sufficient to attract them. For Garvey spoke of an uplifted race, not in terms of mere equivalence with whites, but in terms of independence and superiority. His was a nationalism of race lifted above nationalities to continents, and while few Negroes wanted to leave the United States for Africa, the idea of supporting and identifying with a free and independent Africa, moving as a giant among nations of the world, touched their hearts.

Garvey touched their purses, too, and although he himself was innocent of fraud, some of his associates were less pure. His conceptions of black corporations and organizations which would make Negroes economically self-sufficient fired the imagination of men and women whose dependence was their cross. And though Garvey's corporations shriveled under mismanagement and the U.N.I.A. was wracked with internal dissension, what he represented was, for the Negro masses, worth giving to.

Charles S. Johnson's analysis of the Garvey movement was written before Garvey was imprisoned and deported. It is a superb contemporary evaluation, perhaps overgenerous in estimating the number of Garvey supporters, but keen and objective in trying to determine what Garvey meant to Negro America.

AFTER GARVEY—WHAT?

A man who in five years could attach to himself the confidence and loyalty of four million persons, however gullible they might be, who could make his views, even tho absurd, the keystone of a philosophy worthy of elevation to the dignity of a "wing of Negro thot", who could call an international convention and actually get delegates from over forty foreign countries, however futile their deliberations might have been, who could lead a German society to send a petition to him to use his influence against the use of black troops on the Rhine, whether he could do anything about it or not—such a man can scarcely be treated as a joke. Marcus Garvey, picturesquely labeled by himself the "Provisional President of Africa", and by others, variously, as the "Black Moses", the "Emperor Jones of Finance", the "Savior of the Black Race", "Black Ponzi", the "West Indian Wallingford", and in more intimate persiflage as "liar", "martyr", "dreamer", and "thief", has been halted in a most spectacular career by the government of the United States.

* * *

Garvey is a symbol—a symptom. The "Garvey Movement" is just another name for the new psychology of the American Negro peasantry—for the surge of race consciousness felt by Negroes thruout the world, the intelligent as well as the ignorant. It is a black version of that same 100 per cent mania that now afflicts white America, that emboldens the prophets of a "Nordic blood renaissance", that picked up and carried the cry of "self-determination

Marcus Manesseh Garvey, wearing his helmet of feathers "tall as Guinea grass" and his uniform of purple and gold. "Up you mighty race," Garvey was to preach, over and over again, "you can accomplish what you will."

for all people", "India for the Indians", "A Free Ireland". The personal characteristics that make him obnoxious to his critics are precisely those that made him a strong leader. His extravagant self-esteem could have been taken for dignity, his hard-headedness as self-reliance, his ignorance of law as transcendency, his blunders as persecution, his stupidity as silent deliberation, his churlishness and irascibility as the eccentricity of genius.

* * *

The gigantic phantom of a Universal Negro Improvement Association, stretching a protective arm around the 400,000,000 dark peoples of the world was floated by the dues, assessments and contributions of hundreds of thousands of Negroes—vainly? To have succeeded would have been as great a catastrophe to the interest of the white world as failure could have been to the Negroes.

But against this testy element there was at stake unquestionably the hopes and aspirations of a million Negroes. They may have been fleeced, but they were not resentful—nor even shaken in their loyalty.

It is this phase of psychology that is most interesting—that outshadows the personal traits and vicissitudes of Marcus Garvey. For the "Back to Africa Movement", tho visionary and perhaps utterly impossible of accomplishment, afforded a mental relaxation for the long submerged Negro peasantry. It was a dream—but the new psychology has taught us the utility, the compensatory value, of dreams. These might be expected to increase in intensity in direct proportion to the impossibility of conscious realization. Assuming, as we now must, the increased desires and aspirations of Negroes and the correspondingly increased racial consciousness among white groups, what other mode of escape is possible? Balked desires, repressed longings, must have an outlet. This was an outlet.

Essentially this is a movement of pure blood Negroes. It is their revanche. Mixed bloods—mulattoes—have received a shade more consideration at the hands of white America. This is partly a question of kinship, partly the caprice of scientific theory, partly physical similarity, partly traditional advantage in wage opportunities.

The full blood Negroes are at more serious disadvantage against the culture of this country, with its standard of beauty based on angularity and absence of color. They are the children of the soil—the descendants of plantation hands, without voice, without leadership, and with little basis for self pride.

Bad as it is in the United States, it is worst in the West Indies. There the relatively small number of whites has made it necessary to create a distinct middle-color class—the mulattoes, those whose white blood exceeds the black. This hierarchy amounts almost to caste,—the whites superior to the mulattoes but in association with them; the mulattoes superior to the blacks and aggressively so; the blacks at the bottom,—smoldering, resentful.

Out of this last class came Garvey, hating intensely things white and more intensely things near white.

* * *

Addressing his international congress in August 1921, he said: "We are willing to form an alliance with the white people, only we say, 'What is good for you is good for me.' Hand in hand the colored race and the white can accomplish much that is desirable, but there must be equality or the Negro will not join with his ancient master."

Or, again: "If I can interpret correctly the spirit of the Negro, it is for me to say that Negroes everywhere are determined to be free—determined to be liberated—liberated from mob rule, liberated from segregation, liberated from Jimcrowism, liberated from injustices of all kinds. Let the world understand that 400,000,000 Negroes are determined to die for their liberty and that if we must die, we shall die nobly, we shall die gallantly, fighting up the battle heights of Africa to plant there the standard which represents liberty."

* * *

The side-show of Africa for Africans thus devoured the circus of a steamship line plying between this country and Africa. The innumerable branches of the Universal Negro Improvement Association, in which these submerged Negroes got their first taste of authority and importance, were like so many little principalities. The shower of grandiose titles and ceremonial costumes gave added prestige. Supported by the naturally aggressive enthusiasm of West Indian compatriots and by a well paid staff of propagandists and writers, the American Negro peasantry was aroused to the point that "Garvey himself," as one enthusiast remarked, "could not stop the movement."

Around this developed a race philosophy original only in the sense that it was an inversion of white standards—a typical revolt. God is to be thought of as black; instead of Red Cross nurses, there are black cross nurses; the White Star Line becomes the Black Star Line. As the movement grew, other convenient arrangements were taken over. Just prior to the first international convention, DeValera was elected Provisional President of Ireland. Garvey then became Provisional President of Africa. There were Supreme

Highnesses, Presidents General, Knight Commanders of the Order of the Nile, of the Distinguished Service Order of Ethiopia.

* * *

There has been more criticism of Garvey than of the movement. This is misleading. Everybody knows that the roots of the unrest so manifest in the behavior of these Negroes are utterly unaffected by the clamor for the leader's head. It is perhaps good that he has been put away. Certainly there will be less exploitation of the character described in the charges against him. But it must also be remembered that this restlessness will express itself in some way. Dreaming was, to say the least, a harmless substitute for adventure and the satisfaction of long cherished but repressed desires, altho the cost of such a pasttime seemed an intolerable waste to practical men of affairs. The sources of this discontent must be remedied effectively and now, or this accumulating energy and unrest, blocked off from its dreams, will take another direction. Perhaps this also will be harmless. But who knows?*

The Negro Renaissance

179

AN EVALUATION OF THE NEW NEGRO

The height of the Renaissance in Harlem was its acknowledgment by a leading journal of the American intelligentsia, The Survey Graphic. *For its March 1925 issue, the editors invited Alain Locke, professor of philosophy at Howard University, to guest edit a Harlem number as a manifestation of the wealth and variety of literary and artistic talent which fed the Renaissance. The issue was successful enough that Locke and others determined to make it a book, and* The New Negro: An Interpretation *was published late in 1925.*

The excerpt below is taken from Locke's first essay in the book and stands as the most perceptive contemporary analysis and evaluation of the New Negro and his artistic expressions. More than just an example of domestic talent, Locke saw the Renaissance as comparable to "those nascent movements of folk-expression and self-determination" which were surging to the surface all over the globe. "There is a fresh spiritual and cultural focusing," he wrote, "from India to Ireland, from China to Mexico, and home to Harlem."

In the last decade something beyond the watch and guard of statistics has happened in the life of the American Negro and the three norns who have traditionally presided over the Negro problem have a changeling in their laps. The Sociologist, the Philanthropist, the Race-leader are not unaware of the New Negro, but they are at a loss to account for him. He simply cannot be swathed in their formulae. For the younger generation is vibrant with a new psychology; the new spirit is awake in the masses, and under the very eyes of the professional observers is transforming what has been a perennial problem into the progressive phases of contemporary Negro life.

**Opportunity*, I (August 1923), 231, 232, 233. Reprinted with permission of the National Urban League.

Could such a metamorphosis have taken place as suddenly as it has appeared to? The answer is no; not because the New Negro is not here, but because the Old Negro had long become more of a myth than a man. The Old Negro, we must remember, was a creature of moral debate and historical controversy. His has been a stock figure perpetuated as an historical fiction partly in innocent sentimentalism, partly in deliberate reactionism. The Negro himself has contributed his share to this through a sort of protective social mimicry forced upon him by the adverse circumstances of dependence. So for generations in the mind of America, the Negro has been more of a formula than a human being—a something to be argued about, condemned or defended, to be "kept down," or "in his place," or "helped up," to be worried with or worried over, harassed or patronized, a social bogey or a social burden. The thinking Negro even has been induced to share this same general attitude, to focus his attention on controversial issues, to see himself in the distorted perspective of a social problem. His shadow, so to speak, has been more real to him than his personality.

The day of "aunties," "uncles" and "mammies" is equally gone. Uncle Tom and Sambo have passed on, and even the "Colonel" and "George" play barnstorm rôles from which they escape with relief when the public spotlight is off. The popular melodrama has about played itself out, and it is time to scrap the fictions, garret the bogeys and settle down to a realistic facing of facts.

First we must observe some of the changes which since the traditional lines of opinion were drawn have rendered these quite obsolete. A main change has been, of course, that shifting of the Negro population which has made the Negro problem no longer exclusively or even predominantly Southern. Why should our minds remain sectionalized, when the problem itself no longer is? Then the trend of migration has not only been toward the North and the Central Midwest, but city-ward and to the great centers of industry—the problems of adjustment are new, practical, local and not peculiarly racial. Rather they are an integral part of the large industrial and social problems of our present-day democracy. And finally, with the Negro rapidly in process of class differentiation, if it ever was warrantable to regard and treat the Negro *en masse* it is becoming with every day less possible, more unjust and more ridiculous.

* * *

No sane observer, however sympathetic to the new trend, would contend that the great masses are articulate as yet, but they stir, they move, they are more than physically restless. The challenge of the new intellectuals among them is clear enough—the "race radicals" and realists who have broken with the old epoch of philanthropic guidance, sentimental appeal and protest. But are we after all only reading into the stirrings of a sleeping giant the dreams of an agitator? The answer is in the migrating peasant. It is the "man farthest down" who is most active in getting up. One of the most characteristic symptoms of this is the professional man himself migrating to recapture his constituency after a vain effort to maintain in some Southern corner what for years back seemed an established living and clientele. The clergyman following his errant flock, the physician or lawyer trailing his clients, supply the true clues. In a real sense it is the rank and file who are leading, and the leaders who are following. A transformed and transforming psychology permeates the masses.

When the racial leaders of twenty years ago spoke of developing race-pride and stimulating race-consciousness, and of the desirability of race solidarity, they could not in any accurate degree have anticipated the abrupt feeling that has surged up and now pervades the awakened centers. Some of the recognized Negro leaders and a powerful section of white opinion identified with "race work" of the older order have indeed attempted to discount this feeling as a "passing phase," an attack of "race nerves" so to speak, an "aftermath of the war," and the like. It has not abated, however, if we are to gauge by the present tone and temper of the Negro press, or by the shift in popular support from the officially recognized and orthodox spokesmen to those of the independent, popular, and often radical type who are unmistakable symptoms of a new order. It is a social disservice to blunt the fact that the Negro of the Northern centers has reached a stage where tutelage, even of the most interested and well-intentioned sort, must give place to new relationships, where positive self-direction must be reckoned with in ever increasing measure. The American mind must reckon with a fundamentally changed Negro.

* * *

To all of this the New Negro is keenly responsive as an augury of a new democracy in American culture. He is contributing his share to the new social understanding. But the desire to be understood would never in itself have been sufficient to have opened so completely the protectively closed portals of the thinking Negro's mind. There is still too much possibility of being snubbed or patronized for that. It was rather the necessity for fuller, truer self-expression, the realization of the unwisdom of allowing social discrimination to segregate him mentally, and a counter-attitude to cramp and fetter his own living—and so the "spite-wall" that the intellectuals built over the "color-line" has happily been taken down. Much of this reopening of intellectual contacts has centered in New York and has been richly fruitful not merely in the enlarging of personal experience, but in the definite enrichment of American art and letters and in the clarifying of our common vision of the social tasks ahead.

* * *

Each generation, however, will have its creed, and that of the present is the belief in the efficacy of collective effort, in race co-operation. This deep feeling of race is at present the mainspring of Negro life. It seems to be the outcome of the reaction to proscription and prejudice; an attempt, fairly successful on the whole, to convert a defensive into an offensive position, a handicap into an incentive. It is radical in tone, but not in purpose and only the most stupid forms of opposition, misunderstanding or persecution could make it otherwise. Of course, the thinking Negro has shifted a little toward the left with the world-trend, and there is an increasing group who affiliate with radical and liberal movements. But fundamentally for the present the Negro is radical on race matters, conservative on others, in other words, a "forced radical," a social protestant rather than genuine radical. Yet under further pressure and injustice iconoclastic thought and motives will inevitably increase. Harlem's quixotic radicalisms call for their ounce of democracy to-day lest to-morrow they be beyond cure.

The Negro mind reaches out as yet to nothing but American wants, American ideas. But this forced attempt to build his Americanism on race values is a unique social experiment, and its ultimate success is impossible except through the fullest sharing of American culture and institutions. There should be no delusion about this. American nerves in sections unstrung with race hysteria are often fed the opiate that the trend of Negro advance is wholly separatist, and that the effect of its operation will be to encyst the Negro as a benign foreign body in the body politic. This cannot be—even if it were desirable. The racialism of the Negro is no limitation or reservation with respect to American life; it is only a constructive effort to build the obstructions in the stream of his progress into an efficient dam of social energy and power. Democracy itself is obstructed and stagnated to the extent that any of its channels are closed. Indeed they cannot be selectively closed. So the choice is not between one way for the Negro and another way for the rest, but between American institutions frustrated on the one hand and American ideals progressively fulfilled and realized on the other.

* * *

As a world phenomenon this wider race consciousness is a different thing from the much asserted rising tide of color. Its inevitable causes are not of our making. The consequences are not necessarily damaging to the best interests of civilization. Whether it actually brings into being new Armadas of conflict or argosies of cultural exchange and enlightenment can only be decided by the attitude of the dominant races in an era of critical change. With the American Negro, his new internationalism is primarily an effort to recapture contact with the scattered peoples of African derivation. Garveyism may be a transient, if spectacular, phenomenon, but the possible rôle of the American Negro in the future development of Africa is one of the most constructive and universally helpful missions that any modern people can lay claim to.

* * *

For generations the Negro has been the peasant matrix of that section of America which has most undervalued him, and here he has contributed not only materially in labor and in social patience, but spiritually as well. The South has unconsciously absorbed the gift of his folk-temperament. In less than half a generation it will be easier to recognize this, but the fact remains that a leaven of humor, sentiment, imagination and tropic nonchalance has gone into the making of the South from a humble, unacknowledged source. A second crop of the Negro's gifts promises still more largely. He now becomes a conscious contributor and lays aside the status of a beneficiary and ward for that of a collaborator and participant in American civilization. The great social gain in this is the releasing of our talented group from the arid fields of controversy and debate to the productive fields of creative expression. The especially cultural recognition they win should in turn prove the key to that revaluation of the Negro which must precede or accompany any considerable further betterment of race relationships.*

180

THE LITERARY NEGRO

These samples of literary art must speak for themselves. Together they represent, as well as any molecule of art can, the spirit, the tone, the mood, the drive, and the talent of the New Negro in the Renaissance.

Countee Cullen was educated at New York University and Harvard University. His first book of poetry was published in 1925, when he was only twenty-two years old. He was awarded a Guggenheim Fellowship shortly thereafter and continued to write, up until his death in 1946. He earned his living as a teacher in New York City's public schools.

HERITAGE

What is Africa to me:
Copper sun or scarlet sea,
Jungle star or jungle track,
Strong bronzed men, or regal black
Women from whose loins I sprang
When the birds of Eden sang?
One three centuries removed
From the scenes his fathers loved,
Spicy grove, cinnamon tree,
What is Africa to me?

* * *

Africa? A book one thumbs
Listlessly, till slumber comes.
Unremembered are her bats
Circling through the night, her cats
Crouching in the river reeds,
Stalking gentle flesh that feeds
By the river brink; no more
Does the bugle-throated roar
Cry that monarch claws have leapt
From the scabbards where they slept.
Silver snakes that once a year
Doff the lovely coats you wear,
Seek no covert in your fear

*Alain Locke, ed., *The New Negro: An Interpretation* (N. Y., 1925), 3-16.

Lest a mortal eye should see;
What's your nakedness to me?
Here no leprous flowers rear
Fierce corollas in the air;
Here no bodies sleek and wet,
Dripping mingled rain and sweat,
Tread the savage measures of
Jungle boys and girls in love.
What is last year's snow to me,
Last year's anything? The tree
Budding yearly must forget
How its past arose or set—
Bough and blossom, flower, fruit,
Even what shy bird with mute
Wonder at her travail there,
Meekly labored in its hair.
One three centuries removed
From the scenes his father loved,
Spicy grove, cinnamon tree,
What is Africa to me?

* * *

Quaint, outlandish heathen gods
Black men fashion out of rods,
Clay, and brittle bits of stone,
In a likeness like their own,
My conversion came high-priced;
I belong to Jesus Christ,
Preacher of humility;
Heathen gods are naught to me.

Father, Son, and Holy Ghost,
So I make an idle boast;
Jesus of the twice-turned cheek,
Lamb of God, although I speak
With my mouth thus, in my heart
Do I play a double part?
Ever at Thy glowing altar
Must my heart grow sick and falter,
Wishing He I served were black,
Thinking then it would not lack
Precedent of pain to guide it,
Let who would or might deride it;
Surely then this flesh would know
Yours had borne a kindred woe.
Lord, I fashion dark gods, too,
Daring even to give You
Dark despairing features where,
Crowned with dark rebellious hair
Patience wavers just so much as
Mortal grief compels, while touches

Quick and hot, of anger, rise
To smitten cheek and weary eyes.
Lord, forgive me if my need
Sometimes shapes a human creed.
All day long and all night through,
One thing only must I do:
Quench my pride and cool my blood,
Lest I perish in the flood.
Lest a hidden ember set
Timber that I thought was wet
Burning like the dryest flax,
Melting like the merest wax,
Lest the grave restore its dead.
Not yet has my heart or head
In the least way realized
*They and I are civilized.**

181

RUDOLPH FISHER

Rudolph Fisher was a physician, educated at Brown and Howard universities. He wrote a number of short stories and at least one novel before his early death in 1931.

DUST

The long, low, black-and-silver roadster overtook a small clutter of cars waiting at a town crossing, snorted impatiently once or twice, and settled into a grumbling, disgusted purr. The people in the other cars stared, conferred among themselves, and stared again.

Pard grinned at the girl beside him. "Kills 'em to see us in a car like this. Know what they're saying?"

Billie smiled back. "Of course. 'Why, my *dear*, they're *colored*.'"

"No," said Pard. "One word: 'Niggers!' Leaves 'em speechless.—Look at that barmaid in the flivver—can't get her mouth shut."

The signal changed, the cars moved forward. Pard said:

"Now, damn it, eat niggers' dust."

Easily the mighty motor swept them in and out past car after car till they were far in the lead.

"Too bad," said Billie.

"What?"

"There isn't any dust."

With open country and a rolling straightaway they settled down to an even forty. A warm breeze sang round the windshield, ruffling

---

*From *On These I Stand* by Countee Cullen. Copyright 1925 by Harper & Row, Publishers, Inc.; renewed 1953 by Ida M. Cullen. Reprinted by permission of the publishers.

the brown girl's hair with gentle fingers—glossy black hair which the low sun touched to a glow. She looked thoughtfully out over the Connecticut landscape. Wide meadows swept past or stretched gently away, lifting into distant hills; the hills dodged behind one another, and the sun dodged behind the high hills. She looked at the proud dark face of her companion, still grim with the joy of outstripping white folks.

"Horrible thing, prejudice," she said. "Does you all up. Puffs you all out of shape."

"Not if you have a safety-valve. This buggy's mine. Take anything on the road. Only fun fays give me."

"It's such bitter fun."

"Deep, though. Satisfying. If hating's their game, I can hate right along with 'em. They hate me—sure. But I out-hate 'em. I hate 'em so much I like it."

"No. You like covering them with dust."

"Sure."

"Even when there isn't any dust."

A sudden, loud, almost articulate warning cried startlingly out behind them. Pard instinctively swung over, and a bright yellow sport coupe, of a make as powerful as his own roadster, eased effortlessly past. The interval between the two cars widened rapidly; the other motor's abrupt guffaw dwindled to a receding chuckle.

"Billie, did you see that?"

"He's doing sixty."

"The license-plate, I mean."

"Green and white."

"Georgia."

"Georgia?"

"Georgia—the dirty—"

"Lord protect us now," prayed Billie, knowing what was coming.

"Lord protect him," Pard corrected, his face again grimly bitter. "Hold fast."

His foot went down on the gas; the roadster jumped forward like a cruelly spurred horse, then laid back its ears and flattened itself out in a wild, headlong, heedless run.

Already the car ahead was lost around a left bend in the road. Pard took the bend blindly on its inside margin at fifty miles an hour, while Billie closed her eyes. When she looked again the yellow machine was vanishing to the right at the end of a half-mile straightaway. This they clipped off at seventy, taking the next curve, which was luckily shallow, at fifty-five.

The other car re-appeared; the interval had merely been maintained, not diminished. But the road now chose to climb the low ground rises rather than side-step them so that, save for occasional depressions, it was now visible straight ahead for two miles. And it was clear.

The yellow sport coupe, unaware of pursuit, maintained its even sixty. Pard's speedometer passed seventy-five. As his fifteen-mile-an-hour advantage devoured the stretch between him and his object, his lips formed rancorous words:

"No damn cracker—do that to me . . . die first. . . ."

Billie yelled, "If you mean that, let me out!"

"Lyncher. . . . Atta baby—go get 'im—Red-necked hill-billy. . . . Ought to run him off the road anyhow—every cracker less is a nigger more. . . . Listen. . . ."

As they drew nearer, the other engine's voice came back to them no longer a derisive chuckle but a deepening, desperate snarl.

"Holler, damn it. Holler and burn—like a black man down in Georgia—"

"Let up, Pard! Sharp curve ahead—"

The Georgia car, now a mere hundred yards in the lead, was slowing around the turn. Pard took the limit of approach before his foot sought the brake; his tires screeched in a straight skid, protesting the sudden change.

The sound seemed definitely to warn the yellow coupe of hostile approach from behind, whereupon it flung off the turn and engaged the next stretch in deadly earnest. This again was long straight highway, flatter than the other and flanked on either side by low, broad pasture-lands level with the road.

"Here we go," said Pard. Billie hung on, praying. The engine roared insanely, the wind whipped harshly past, swiftly, steadily the lead diminished. Perhaps three-quarters of a mile remained of the stretch when Pard, looking beyond the Georgia car ahead, saw the road split in a fork.

"Got to beat him to that fork. Next town's coming."

"And some cars, maybe," said Billie, thanking God for clear roads thus far.

"Come on, baby!" Pard jammed his foot down and held hard with both hands.

Billie squeezed her lids together. The stridor of the yellow car grew, beat painfully in her ears. "Bye-bye, cracker!" An irresistible impulse forced the girl's eyes open to observe impending disaster: Either car was flinging itself precipitately at the fork, Pard's roadster now a length ahead, to the left; both took the left bend of the fork; when, fifty yards ahead, a third car came out of a blind left intersection and stopped dead halfway across the road, startled to a standstill by the mad onrushing pair.

Both jammed on brakes, Pard bearing right, directly into his competitor's path. The latter swung off the road with a crash into the grassy triangle between the two bends of the fork, managing by the grace of heaven and consummate skill not to flip upside down. Either car came to a standstill, Pard's fifty yards up the highway, the other in the middle of the field.

"Billie was trembling. "Pard—go back—he must be hurt—"

No question now of hatred. Pard wheeled and drove back through the grass to the coupe. As they stopped, the yellow door opened, the driver backed stiffly out, and turned to present to their astonished eyes as black a face as ever came out of Georgia.

A deep breath all around. Then, "Are you—hurt?" Billie managed; and, "I'm sorry," from Pard—"I'll pay for any damage—"

A far hill covered the face of the sun, like a hand concealing a grin.*

182

LANGSTON HUGHES

Langston Hughes was born in Missouri and grew up in Cleveland, Ohio. He began publishing poems in The Crisis *almost as soon as he graduated from high school and never stopped writing. In 1925, at the age of twenty-three, he won a first prize for poetry in an* Opportunity*-sponsored contest. Since then, he has published poetry, prose, drama, autobiography, and history.*

I, TOO

I, too, sing America.

I am the darker brother.
They send me to eat in the kitchen
When company comes,
But I laugh,
And eat well,
And grow strong.
Tomorrow,
I'll sit at the table
When company comes.
Nobody'll dare
Say to me,
"Eat in the kitchen,"
Then.
Besides,
They'll see how beautiful I am
And be ashamed,—

I, too, am America.†

---

*"Dust," by Rudolph Fisher, from *Opportunity*, IX (February, 1931), 46–47. Reprinted with permission of the National Urban League.

†From *The Weary Blues* by Langston Hughes. Copyright 1926 and renewed 1954 by Langston Hughes. Reprinted from *Selected Poems*, by Langston Hughes, by permission of Alfred A. Knopf, Inc.

CHAPTER ELEVEN

The Negro in a Time of Democratic Crisis

The nineteen-thirties brought the Depression, social upheaval, race riots, and bread lines. The end of the decade saw a war in Europe that would explode into World War II. It was a time of new forces, a time of change. Millions of men were drafted into the military to fight. Millions more were drawn into the factories to turn out the munitions of war. Sharecroppers left their farms in the South, heading North, drawn by the high wages of a war economy. When the war was over, millions of Negroes found themselves living in the great industrial centers, still involved in change. The Depression and World War II were times of great events, of new problems, of continual change. The stresses of change brought the Negro, and all Americans, into a time of crisis. But out of this crisis came the social legislation of the thirties, and the Civil Rights laws of a later day.

The Negro in a Time of Democratic Crisis

President Franklin D. Roosevelt's consummate ability to personalize his understanding of human exploitation and underprivilege made him the most attractive President, for Negro citizens, since the Civil War. Robert Vann, publisher of the Negro weekly Pittsburgh *Courier,* who was brought into the 1932 campaign by some of Roosevelt's lieutenants, advised his race to "go home and turn Lincoln's picture to the wall. The debt has been paid in full." Yet, like Lincoln, Roosevelt's actual commitments to the American Negro were slim. He was more a symbol than an activist in his own right. His compassion, though real, was tempered by his own background, by the enormity of the decisions which came up to him, and by political considerations. An enthusiastic politician, he used political weights and measures on a political scale to judge the evidence, and the Negro was often found wanting. When Walter White, the executive secretary of the NAACP, obtained an audience through the good graces of Mrs. Eleanor Roosevelt to plead for the President's public support of the antilynching bill, FDR demurred because he needed southern votes in Congress on other matters.

Roosevelt did not publicly associate himself with Negro projects or Negro leaders before 1935, but his programs and some of his associates were more aggressive. Early in 1933, he approved of a suggestion that someone in his administration assume the responsibility for fair treatment of the Negroes, and he asked Harold Ickes to make the appointment. A young white Georgian, Clark Foreman, came to Washington at Ickes' request to handle the task, and brought in as his assistant an even younger Negro of great promise, Robert C. Weaver. Foreman successfully made his way through the burgeoning maze of new agencies which were springing up and did a respectable job of calling to the attention of agency heads and their assistants an awareness of the special problems of Negroes. Along with Ickes, Daniel Roper, the Secretary of Commerce; Harry Hopkins, FDR's relief administrator; and Aubrey Williams, a Hopkins deputy, were sympathetic to committing the New Deal to work more generously with and for Negroes.

From the first, the various New Deal agencies carried the major burden of this emphasis, since they translated words into bread and butter, shelter, and schooling. For the Negro, the most significant were the Federal Employment Relief Administration (FERA), the National Recovery Administration (NRA), the Works Progress Administration, later called the Work Projects Administration (WPA), the Agricultural Adjustment Administration (AAA), the Tennessee Valley Authority (TVA), the National Youth Administration (NYA), the Civilian Conservation Corps (CCC), and the public housing efforts of several agencies. There were others in the alphabetical jungle which assisted Negroes, as whites, in more specialized ways, such as the Federal Writers' Project, and the Office of Education studies. The very number of agencies added credence to the emergent fact that, for the first time, the federal government had engaged and was grappling with some of the fundamental barriers to race progress.

It was one thing to engage and grapple with a problem at the federal level, and another thing to implement it at lower levels. Most of the New Deal agency programs ran afoul of local laws and customs and most of them capitulated on very practical grounds. As a consequence, Negroes vigorously attacked the inequities, even while they appreciated the limited benefits. FERA, the first New Deal agency to work directly to alleviate the plight of the destitute, tried by locally administered dole and work-projects to pump more money into circulation. Until the end of 1935, when it was abolished, it administered most of the direct relief and work relief programs which the New Dealers initiated, distributing about four billion dollars. Its progress was dogged by racial discrimination, since the design of projects and allocation of funds remained in local hands.

If the relief program raised questions of discrimination, the NRA brought howls of indignation. In the words of a Negro labor specialist, the NRA administrator, General Hugh A. Johnson, was "a complete failure" for not properly recognizing the Negro. The industrial codes established under NRA deferred to geographic wage and employment consideration so that the Negro worker generally earned less money for equal time and was frozen out of skilled jobs. A young Negro lawyer, John P. Davis, organized the Joint Committee on National Recovery in the fall of 1933 to persuade federal authorities to rectify these policies. "It has filed briefs, made appearances at public hearings," he wrote, and "buttonholed administrative officers relative to the elimination of unfair clauses in the codes," but to little avail. In self-defense, NRA officials explained the difficulty in bucking local customs, pointing out also that the NRA was responsible only for industrial workers. Agricultural laborers, domestic servants, and the service trades were not included, and most of the unskilled workers were exempted by statute from wage and hour minimums. "It is not fair," wrote an NRA administrator in a Negro journal, "to blame the NRA for not curing all these ills, if such they be, within a year." Until the Supreme Court decreed its demise in the spring of 1935, the NRA was a favored whipping boy for Negroes, as well as for others. "The Blue Eagle," a Virginia newspaper observed, "may be [for Negroes] a predatory bird instead of a feathered messenger of happiness."

The debit side of the New Deal's efforts to assist Negroes fell far short of its material and psychological credits. Never before had Negro leaders participated in government affairs as freely and as frequently. The Department of Commerce had E. K. Jones, on leave from the National Urban League; the NYA had Mary McLeod Bethune; Interior had William H. Hastie and Weaver; the Social Security Board had Ira DeA. Reid; Labor had Lawrence W. Oxley; the Office of Education had Ambrose Caliver, to mention a few. Never before had there been so great a stress on improving the education of Negroes. Many relief programs included elementary education and training classes as part of the regimen. Negro colleges and universities received funds for buildings. The Office of Education, along with other agencies, began an important study of the status of Negro education.

Professional opportunities opened up in government, although not at the rate at which Negroes were graduating from college. For the first time, Negroes were employed as architects, lawyers, engineers, economists, statisticians, interviewers, office managers, case aids, and librarians. Nonprofessional white-collar jobs, which had rarely been within reach of the race, now became available to trained stenographers, clerks, and secretaries. While many of these jobs centered around programs for Negroes within the government, such as Negro slum clearance projects, Negro NYA offices, and the like, they broke the dam which had hitherto kept Negroes out of these kinds of positions.

Harold Ickes, a former president of the Chicago chapter of the NAACP, was the first New Dealer to be recognized as a tried friend. He quickly ended discrimination in his department and set the example by placing professionally trained Negroes in responsible positions. He first drew FDR's attention to Hastie as a candidate for the federal judge vacancy in the Virgin Islands, and Roosevelt made the appointment in 1937. While Ickes could not breach established segregation patterns in housing, one-eighth of the federal housing projects planned before the end of 1935 were in mixed neighborhoods. Approximately one-half of them were in Negro slum areas and, thanks to the negotiating skill of Ickes' assistant, Robert C. Weaver, the contracts for a substantial portion of these called for the employment of both skilled and unskilled Negro workers.

Eleanor Roosevelt, the New Deal's conscience, made it her business to reaffirm by word and deed her faith in the equality of opportunity for all. She included Negro and mixed organizations on her itineraries, welcomed mixed groups of adults and children to the White House, and spoke up for the race at critical times. In 1936, as part of a long memo on political strategy in the presidential campaign, she urged party leaders to ask respected Negroes like Mrs. Bethune to participate among Negro groups.

Eleanor Roosevelt was more than a symbol of the New Deal's conscience; she was a vehicle for approaching and influencing the President. She performed this service for Walter White when the antilynching bill was before Congress. When Marian Anderson was not permitted to sing in Constitution Hall, Mrs. Roosevelt was the intermediary who secured permission to use the Lincoln Memorial for the concert. It was useful for the President to have his wife serve in these varying capacities, absorbing some of the criticism, supplying him with information he could get from no other source, and sparking his conscience, when that was needed. This relieved the President from having to punctuate his speeches and press conferences with references to the Negro. Before 1935, these were almost nonexistent; after 1935, they increased in frequency and directness, but Roosevelt did not directly commit himself, as his wife did, until his famous Executive Order 8802 of June, 1941, established a Fair Employment Practice Committee to supervise all defense-contract industries.

The labor movement strengthened by New Deal legislation and internal reorganization, confronted, as one of its problems, the question of Negro members. Older unions such as the United Mine Workers and the International Ladies Garment Workers Union welcomed Negroes without distinction. When the CIO broke from the A.F.L., its nucleus of unions including the new and somewhat fragile organizations in the automobile, rubber, and steel industries accepted Negroes on an equal basis, except in those localities where race friction was high. The United Textile Workers attempted to do the same, but the existence of textile plants in southern states made this task more onerous. It was not enough for a union to resolve, as the CIO did, to accept members without regard to race, creed, or color, or even, as the UAW and the organizing committees of the steelworkers did, to offer Negro workers a chance to join up. Negroes still hung back, alternately tempted and frightened by management's offers and threats. The wave of the future was with the industrial unions, and *Opportunity*'s declaration to Negro steelworkers that it would be "the apotheosis of stupidity" for them to stay out of the union battling for recognizance in 1937, was prophetic. The success of the Brotherhood of Sleeping Car Porters, under the leadership of A. Philip Randolph, in gaining recognition as the bargaining agent with the Pullman Company after a twelve-year struggle, marked the beginning of the race's influence in national labor circles and on national labor policy. After his union was recognized, Randolph prodded the A.F.L. to grant it an international charter, making it an equal with other member unions, and he never eased up his fight to liberalize the A.F.L.'s racial policies. Even though he was not persuasive enough to break down these craft and railway-union prejudices, Randolph emerged before World War II as a dominant voice in Negro circles and a power to be reckoned with in American unionism.

With the exception of the church, the major Negro organizations felt the sting of mass apathy. "We recognize our lack of skill at mass appeal," NAACP's Roy Wilkins admitted in 1941. The national office of NAACP attracted men and women of an intellectual bent whose convictions on race matters had not changed with the seasons, since the organization was still dedicated to the abolition of segregation and discrimination. But the spark which had sent John Shillady, Walter White, and James Weldon Johnson into race-hatred areas, North and South, burned low. On the national level, the NAACP fought its battles in court, in Congress, and in the press, but not in communities where racism flourished. At local levels, it depended upon its branches, many of which were woefully weak in finances and leadership, to seek out and rectify racial problems of every description. Its base was too narrow for its superstructure, and its bones creaked from inaction at the community level; yet it thrived because it learned to speak the language of influence in political circles and because it chose wisely the cases of discrimination and segregation which it pursued through the courts. Indeed, the road to the 1954 desegregation decisions was charted, bulldozed, paved, and landscaped by the NAACP.

The National Urban League was tested during the depression and not found wanting. Its leadership was similar to that of the

NAACP, except that to the extent that its goals were more specific, framed in terms of employment, family welfare, health, and education, it was accused of being more timid, dominated by white liberals, and hostile to trade unionism. Its chief executive, E. K. Jones, replied to these criticisms in a private memo in 1941. The League, he said, was not a Negro but "truly an interracial movement. . . . Any movement of this character which advocates understanding through conference and discussion must necessarily refrain from advocating mass action of one race calculated to force the other group to make concessions." Gunnar Mydral, the Swedish sociologist whose monumental study of the Negro in America was published during World War II, found that the League worked actively with unions and held "the lead as a pro-union force among the Negro people." Urban League branches were beginning to receive local support from Community Funds, which gave them greater strength and a source for independent leadership.

The sudden shock of the surprise attack which drew the United States into World War II served more to expose sore spots than to blanket them in loyalty. In the First World War, the protests against unequal treatment were slow to develop and not widely heard, but the Second World War was different. Even before Pearl Harbor, clamors arose from the South warning that the Negro was not going to "come out of this war on top of the heap as he did in the last one." However distorted the comparison, the attitude was clear, and it influenced the government's decision to extend pre-Pearl Harbor patterns into the war period.

The Negro soldier remained separate in the armed services, and not always welcome. Judge William L. Hastie resigned as civilian aide to the Secretary of War in protest against the dissembling tactics of the Army Air Corps to keep the Negro on the ground. *The Crisis,* returning to a World War I cry, criticized the appointment of Southern white officers for Negro troops and the explanation that they could handle them better. When FDR queried Walter White about the carelessness of the Negro press and the consistency of its attack on the war effort, White replied that better treatment for Negroes in the armed services and the invitation of Negro editors to presidential press conferences and top briefings would clear the problem.

The prosperity of war industry and the proscriptive southern mores once again attracted thousands of Negroes to northern cities. The consequent overcrowding and war tension heated racism to the boiling point, as the riots in New York, Detroit, and Los Angeles demonstrated. For the Negro, racism was the same wherever it appeared. In Roy Wilkins' words, "it sounds pretty foolish to be *against* park benches marked 'Jude' in Berlin, but to be *for* park benches marked 'Colored' in Tallahassee, Florida." Negroes could not understand why whites drew distinctions between the Nazi ideology of Aryan supremacy and the American ideology of white supremacy.

The death of Roosevelt and the end of the war in 1945 terminated an era. The office of the Presidency now symbolized a concern for justice and equality for all Americans, including Negroes. The White House had taken a stand in favor of the principle of equal rights, although the practice had lagged. The new President, Harry S. Truman, a man of lesser parts, was to take the next practical step and declare in specifics his belief in the equality of men of whatever race under the law. Where Roosevelt concealed the particular in the general principle, Truman spoke out without check. Where Roosevelt used the excuse of war to delay integration, Truman used the excuse of peace to accelerate it. Where Roosevelt used the federal government to increase economic opportunities for all, Truman used the federal government to increase economic opportunities for Negroes. While the Truman Fair Deal never approximated the energy and the excitement of the Roosevelt New Deal, it was the former which capitalized on the Negro's readiness to take an equal place in American democracy.

Three major strands marked the period between the end of the war and the Supreme Court's 1954 desegregation decision. One related to the improving economic condition of the Negro, a second to the reports of the three Presidential committees, and the third to the increasingly significant role of the United States Supreme Court in racial matters. The Negro's improving economic condition stemmed from a variety of causes. In microcosm, the successful introduction of Jackie Robinson into baseball's National League in 1947 is exemplary, since his breakthrough eventually opened the gates in almost every professional sport. In like manner, the appointment of Ira DeA. Reid to the faculty of New York University was a breakthrough in higher education of lesser quantity but equal quality. Other major universities and colleges eventually followed suit. The forceful policy of the CIO, led by the United Auto Workers, brought the A.F.L. into line. The Negro, Walter Reuther warned in late 1945, "should not allow his painful experiences with many of the old craft unions of the American Federation of Labor to embitter him against all labor unions." Both the Negro and the A.F.L. took the hint. Some craft unions still held out, generally by subterfuge, but the weight of the major unions and their two national federations swung unequivocally to the side of equal opportunity without regard to race.

The *Report* of the President's Civil Rights Committee in 1947 had immediate and far-reaching repercussions. The President's Executive Order 9980 established a fair employment procedure within the government structure. Executive Order 9981 was even more significant since it, in effect, abolished discrimination in the armed services. The committee established by this order to study the situation and make recommendations published its report, *Freedom to Serve,* in 1950, by which time all three of the service branches had abolished the quota system of enlistment and segregation in any form, including separate units and limited opportunities. The Navy was first in its implementation, having started even before the President's order, and although the Army dragged its feet, the committee was satisfied that the order and its execution were effective. A year later, a third Executive Order, 10308, established a President's Committee to insure compliance by government contractors with contractual regulations prohibiting discrimination because of race, creed, color, or national origin. The committee's report was filed early in 1953.

The political reverberations to these dramatic steps by President Truman echoed in the halls of Congress and almost split the Democratic party asunder. In 1948, the Dixiecrats walked out of the Democratic convention in protest to the strong civil rights plank which the young junior Senator from Minnesota, Hubert Humphrey, had pushed through. Truman's election victory that year, in the face of the walkout and the left-wing Progressive Party, was convincing evidence that civil rights had attracted voter support. In Congress, this message from the electorate went unheeded; southern Democrats and conservative Republicans, whose constituencies sent different messages to them, blocked all efforts to write civil rights into statute.

Negroes in general and the NAACP in particular could take some satisfaction in knowing that the Supreme Court was slowly opening basic rights, but in the area of education the progress was even more marked. The NAACP invested heavily of its time and funds in widening educational opportunities by court action. The University of Maryland in 1935 had capitulated at the graduate-school level without taking the case to the Supreme Court. Three years later Missouri was instructed to educate a Negro law student, but its subterfuge worked so well that it tried it again in 1942 by establishing a two-room graduate school in journalism for one qualified Negro graduate student. The University of Oklahoma followed suit when the Supreme Court allowed Missouri's effort to stand, but the end was in sight. In 1950 Texas was told by the Court that its Negro law school had to be equal to that of the white University of Texas Law School, and the doors of the latter were duly opened to Negroes. In a parallel case, Oklahoma was rebuked for permitting a Negro student to be segregated within its state university, and the practice ceased. With a Supreme Court which read the Constitution as a document protecting the rights of all citizens and with the opening of universities at the graduate level, the time was ripe for an all-inclusive appeal for educational opportunities.

The twenty years between the inauguration of Franklin D. Roosevelt and the eve of the Supreme Court desegregation decision were the most revolutionary two decades in the history of the American Negro up to that time. In part, the elemental movements had little to do with race matters; depression, war, prosperity—these were not issues of black and white. Yet they determined a basic posture change: that whites and Negroes would work closely together on matters of national and international importance which had nothing to do with race. Perhaps the most startling development to emerge from these decades was that prominent Negroes began to assume responsibilities in government, business, labor, athletics, education, and the social services which had no connection with race. Negroes, finally, were working in critical jobs because they were needed, and not simply because they were Negroes.

183

HOPE FOR LABOR

Frances Perkins was the first woman cabinet member and her appointment was greeted with some surprise in labor and business circles, but she was a woman of large experience in labor matters, having served in a similar capacity under Roosevelt while he was Governor of New York. Quiet yet firm, Miss Perkins managed her department effectively and won the confidence of labor and the Negro.

This letter is a response to a special memorandum prepared for the President by the National Urban League on the social adjustment of Negroes in the United States. It is one of the earliest statements to and about the race by a highly placed New Dealer.

Department of Labor
Office of the Secretary
Washington
April 27, 1933

Mr. Eugene Kinckle Jones,
Executive Secretary, National Urban League,
1133 Broadway, New York, N. Y.
My dear Mr. Jones:

May I congratulate you on the Special Memorandum for the President on "The Social Adjustment of Negroes in the United States." He has asked me to tell you that he is very glad indeed to have this factual summary. He realizes the unfavorable economic position of the Negro, and the tremendous suffering which the present depression has brought to them and to other unskilled as well as skilled workers. But in spite of the discouragements of the immediate past, he finds great hope for the Negro race in the enormous progress it has made in the last 30 years. Gradually Negro workers have succeeded in securing more skilled and responsible jobs, have made their way in professions and in business. There is also great encouragement in the progress that has been made in the reduction of illiteracy, of infant mortality, and of the general death rate among Negroes.

I can assure you that as this Administration undertakes the problems of relief administration of providing work opportunities, of raising basic wage levels, etc., etc., we shall not forget the special problems of the more than ten million people who belong to your race.

I note that you refer specifically to certain abuses or discriminations in connection with the Mississippi flood control and the Boulder dam project under the past Administration. I am sure that as far as it is legally possible under the contracts already made the President will leave nothing undone which will prevent or stop the exploitation of workmen, whether white or colored, by Federal contractors. I am personally at work on the problem of making sure that labor standards will be more fully provided for in future government undertakings.

As for the Employment Service, this is my own immediate responsibility. You have perhaps seen from the papers that a complete reorganization of the Service is under way. It will take some time to put the cooperative Federal and State system on the kind of basis which will insure real service for working men and women. I can assure you, however, that I shall be glad to have any suggestions you may have from time to time as to how the Service may serve more efficiently all classes of labor.

Sincerely yours,

Frances Perkins,
*Secretary**

184

UNEQUAL WAGES

Negro critics of the New Deal were probably more agitated by the maintenance of the wage differential between white and black workers than by any other government policy in the early years of the Roosevelt administration. Not only did this policy admit the strength of the white supremacist South, but it emphasized distinctions which were both an insult and a financial disability to Negroes. By permitting federal projects to pay Negroes less than whites for approximately equal work, the New Deal invited rebuke and unrest.

The problem, as this article by Robert C. Weaver points out, was not an easy one to solve and the critics were sometimes overhasty in their judgments. Some New Deal administrators, like Harry Hopkins and Aubrey Williams, exerted themselves to mitigate the differences, only to run up against local political pressures. Others, like General Hugh Johnson, merely ignored the problem.

No issue affecting Negroes under the recovery program is of more importance than that of wage policy under the NRA. There is no other question arising out of the new deal which has excited more discussion among enlightened Negroes. Like most important controversies, this is a complicated matter. To discuss it intelligently, one must consider the philosophy of the recovery program and the implications of the Negro's position in American life.

There are two observations which are fundamental. In the first place, Southern industrial life is personal and paternalistic. The employers like to keep in touch with the workers. This paternalism is especially present in the relationship between the white employer and his Negro workers. A manufacturer of the deep South explained why he preferred Negro workers saying that he could handle them easier—they felt close to the boss and he felt close to them. On the other hand, the philosophy behind minimum wage provisions (and all social legislation) is that of an impersonal and highly developed industrial life. Thus there is a fundamental conflict between the Southern system and the labor provisions of the NRA.

**Opportunity*, XI (June 1933), 169. Reprinted with permission of the National Urban League.

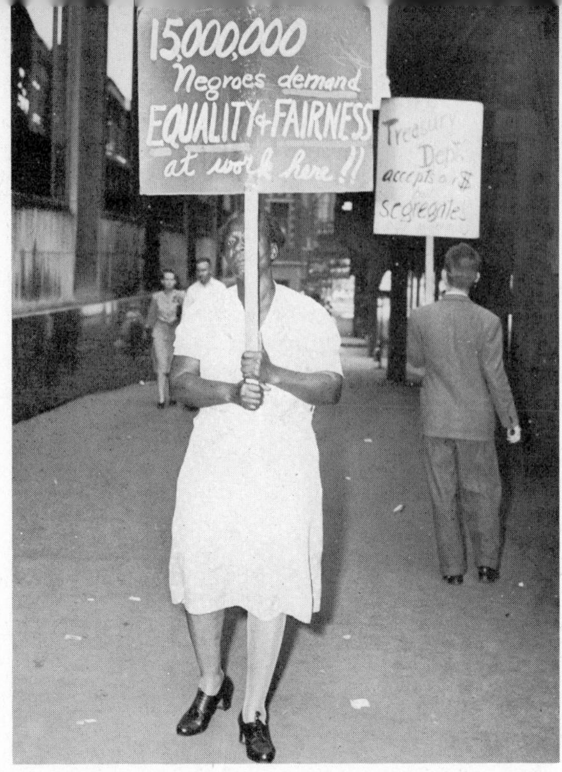

The very idea of a sub-marginal minimum for Negro workers is an expression of the second important feature of the situation—the tendency to lump all Negroes together and judge them by the least desirable and the least able in the group. This tendency is, of course, the most arbitrary and pernicious feature of race prejudice.

Since the inauguration of the NRA there has been a series of attempts to establish lower minimum rates of wages for Negro workers. First it was said that Negroes have a lower standard of living. Then, lower wages were defended on the basis of the Negro's lower efficiency. Lastly, it was pointed out that lower wages for Negroes were traditional and should be incorporated as a feature of the New Deal. However, the most telling and important argument for a lower minimum wage for Negroes was the fact that they were being displaced from industry as a result of the operation of the labor provision of the NRA.

Long before the New Deal was thought of, there was a constant displacement of Negroes by white workers. Certain cities in the South replaced their colored workers with whites; in other places organizations were initiated to foster the substitution of white for black laborers in all positions. The minimum wage regulations of the NRA accelerated this tendency. Indeed, it resulted in wholesale discharges in certain areas. More recently, the tendency has been arrested.

There are many causes for the failure of the program to be carried further. In the first place, there is reason to believe that employers resorted to the discharge of colored workers as a means of forcing the NRA to grant a racial differential. They declared that if a man had to be paid as much as twelve dollars a week, they would pay a white worker that wage. Then, too, there are many instances where it is impossible to discharge a whole working force. Even modern industry with its automatic machinery requires workers of some training, and training is a time and money consuming process. Thus, where Negroes formed a large percentage of the total working force, it was often impracticable to displace them and hire a new all-white labor force.

Nevertheless, there have been many displacements of Negroes. All the available evidence seems to indicate, as one would expect, that perhaps the greater part of this substitution of white for Negro workers has occurred in small enterprises where the Negro is often the marginal worker. In such plants, the separation of Negro workers presented no important question of organizational integrity or of training.

Out of these developments a movement for a racial differential has arisen. The motivating force for such a campaign has come from the Southern employers who have, for the most part, shifted their emphasis from standard of living and tradition to efficiency and displacement. The latter feature—the loss of job opportunities to Negroes—has been made much of in recent months. Appeals have been made to Negro leaders to endorse a lower minimum wage for Negroes on the ground that such action is necessary if Negroes are not to be forced out of industry. The colored leaders have been careful in their championing of this cause. A few have been convinced that it is the only possible way out; some have supported the policy because of local pressure in the South but most have tried to keep out of the discussion. Many are almost convinced that it is the proper choice but fear a loss of prestige among Negroes if they speak in favor of such a measure.

Briefly, the only possible argument for a racial wage differential is one based upon a *de facto* situation. Negroes have lost jobs as a result of the NRA, and a lower wage for them would counteract this tendency. It would assure Negroes of retaining their old jobs and perhaps it would lead to a few additional ones. It may be observed that this reasoning is correct as far as it goes. Certainly, a racial differential would do much to arrest and, perchance, offset the displacement of Negro workers. But there is more involved in this question than the arresting of Negro displacement. In it are the elements which combine to establish the whole industrial position of colored Americans.

The establishment of a lower minimum wage for Negroes would have far reaching effects. It would brand black workers as a less efficient and sub-marginal group. It would increase the ill-will and friction between white and colored workers. It would destroy much of the advance Negroes have made in the industrial North. It would destroy any possibility of ever forming a strong and effective labor movement in the nation. The ultimate effect would be to relegate Negroes into a low wage caste and place the federal stamp of approval upon their being in such a position.

It was pointed out above that the most damnable feature of racial prejudice in America is the tendency to judge all Negroes by the least able colored persons. Obviously, a racial minimum is an expression of such an attitude. Were this not true, why should Negroes be singled out for a special—and lower—rate of pay? There have been no satisfactory or convincing studies of racial efficiency. (Efforts along this line are even more crude than the measures we have which have been set up to gauge intelligence.) Indeed, it is absurd to talk about racial efficiency since Negroes, like every other group of human beings, vary in their effectiveness. The efficiency of a worker depends upon his native ability, environment and specific training. These factors differ between individuals rather than between races. A racial differential on the other hand would say, in effect, that efficiency is based on race and the individual black worker—because he is a Negro—is less efficient.

Now, there is still another phase of this matter. The very attitude which dictates a racial differential would make such a provision most discriminatory against colored workers. Any minimum wage tends to become a maximum. In the case of Negro workers this tendency would be accentuated. Since all Negroes are usually considered the same regardless of their ability, a lower minimum for black labor would in fact, mean that practically all Negroes would receive wages lower than their white prototypes. Not only would this be manifestly unfair, but in certain areas it would undermine the race's industrial progress of the last twenty years. During the period, Negroes have entered the industries of the North and the West as never before. They came from the South, where they were treated with mercy (as opposed to justice), and faced a situation which was new to them. Standards of efficiency were higher and they had to measure up to these new standards. Some failed but the recent data on Negro participation in Northern industry show that many succeeded. It has been a difficult process of adaptation. The fruits have been higher wages and less racial discrimination in rates of pay. To establish a differential based on race, would be, in effect, to take away the fruits of this hard-won victory.

Nor would the white worker respond favorably to the notion of a lower minimum for Negro workers. His first response in the South would be favorable because his ego would be flattered. But when the lower minimum destroyed the effectiveness of the higher minimum, the white recipient of the latter would blame the Negro. The black worker, North and South, would be regarded as the force which rendered it impossible for workers to demand a decent wage and find employment. This would occasion no end of misunderstanding and hatred between the white and black worker.

It is clear that the unity of all labor into an organized body would be impossible if there were a racial differential. The essence of collective bargaining is an impersonal and standard wage. Unionism rests upon the cooperation of all workers. A racial wage differential prevents both of these developments. It would, therefore, destroy the possibility of *a real labor movement* in this country.*

**The Crisis*, XLI (August 1934), 236–238. Reprinted with permission of *The Crisis* Magazine, official publication of the NAACP.

185

INEQUALITIES IN NEW DEAL RELIEF PROGRAMS

An administrator of a government agency sees his projects in a slightly different manner from those who are the beneficiaries. Whatever the federal relief policies, these letters from semiliterate, impoverished southern Negroes document the human and prejudicial inequalities of the execution of New Deal relief programs.

Alabama
April 27, 1934

N.A.A.C.P. Dear Sir:—Please allow me to present a question to you which with myself is very important because I am one of the persons of families that is in very bad need of aid an up to this date have been denied so it have retch the stage that something must be did. It is a well known fact that one cannot live without food and clothes so a friend and myself being among the unemployed and is not getting any aid so far from the public welfare of this county is asking for aid or information about aid from some sorce. Will you see after this matter at once. We get a small order some time and for months can't get anything. Its awful bad to wait for someone who does not care to give you food. Is not there some way or some sorce that we colored people can overcome being shadowed by starvation and depending on something that will not give you food. Please inform me at once if there is any other sorce of getting any relief. We are depending on you for relief or information as to where we might get food. We must have something at once. Please let me know at once.

We will be waiting an answer from you.

Very truly yours,

____

P.S. We are men of families.

Georgia
Jan. 24, 1934

Dear Sir:—Sometime ago about 6 or 7 weeks ago my boy went up in town to sign to get on the releaf work to get some of the govnor money he was out of a job and I am a poor widder woman with a house full of little childrens and a cripple girl to take ceare of they woulden let him sign the white peoples knocked him down run him out of town woulden let him com back to town he went back to town in about 5 weakes they got after him agin about a hundred head of white mens with knives and they run him all ove town they cout him they throwed him in the back of a truck hog fashon he got out som way they put a Bulldog on him then he ran in a stor then som of the collord mens beg the cheef police to put him in jale to keepe the mob from killing him the cheaff say let them kill him just so they dont mobb him heare in town the night marshell put him in jale for safe keeping and I hade to pay him $5.00 to get him out and he had to leave town dont be see heare no more if they see him enny more they will sure kill him he left in the night walking with no money I wont able to gavė him nothing and I want him to help me that is my sun he is just 17 years old.

Just write to help me if you all please take up far me and help me I am his mother my name is ________________

Mississippi
April 30, 1934

Dear Sir: This is ________________ asking for help for my mother her name is ________________ So she says that her age is 84. She says that she was 9 years old when Peace declaired you can tell from that just how ole she is she was large enough to carry water in the time of the War & now she is here sick in bed & has been since February the 25. & I have ben to the Red Cross & also the Relief ofice asking for help & they would not help me with a Dr & neither did they fill a medical prescription for me after the Dr. come to my call she is yet sick & haven got shoes or close & a very little to eat & I am her daughter I haven got work to do to help my self out in paying house rent & nothing in my house to eat & no close to wear The relief has never give me one yrd of cloth & neither a pair of shoes since they started this work up here in ________________.

I have 3 in family my mother & myself & one child & the child only makes $1.50c one dollar & fifty cts (a week) & you knows without me telling you that will not pay rent & get close & make Grocery we are sufering here I will speak the truth. I haven got bread in my home to eat & nothing to buy it with. The relief give me 3 days work last week for the first time & no Grocery at all & I had to gave that to the rent man I ows him this morning $12.00 twelve dollars & he is telling me today if I can not pay the rent to give him his house what must I do I am renting from a man by the name of ________________ Please help me & famely at once.*

186

ENCOURAGEMENT

When the National Urban League celebrated its twenty-fifth anniversary, it was only natural that Eleanor Roosevelt be invited to participate, since she had in two short and busy years as First Lady made clear her conviction that the Negro, too, needed a new deal.

This speech was delivered at the Baltimore, Maryland, observance of the anniversary and was broadcast over a national network on December 12, 1935. While Mrs. Roosevelt spoke only for herself, it was generally assumed that she reflected her husband's views on race relations and that she could say what he, for political reasons, was unable to say.

THE NEGRO AND SOCIAL CHANGE

We have a great responsibility here in the United States because we offer the best example that exists perhaps today throughout the

**The Crisis*, XLI (November 1934), 330–331. Reprinted with permission of *The Crisis* Magazine, official publication of the NAACP.

world, of the fact that if different races know each other they may live peacefully together. On the whole, we in this country live peacefully together though we have many different races making up the citizenry of the United States. The fact that we have achieved as much as we have in understanding of each other, is no reason for feeling that our situation and our relationship are so perfect that we need not concern ourselves about making them better. In fact we know that many grave injustices are done throughout our land to people who are citizens and who have an equal right under the laws of our country, but who are handicapped because of their race. I feel strongly that in order to wipe out these inequalities and injustices, we must all of us work together; but naturally those who suffer the injustices are most sensitive of them, and are therefore bearing the brunt of carrying through whatever plans are made to wipe out undesirable conditions.

Therefore in talking to you tonight, I would like to urge first of all that you concentrate your effort on obtaining better opportunities for education for the Negro people throughout the country. You *must* be able to understand the economic condition and the changes which are coming, not only in our own country, but throughout the world, and this, without better education than the great majority of the Negro people have an *opportunity* to obtain today, is not possible. And without an improvement which will allow better work and better understanding, it will be difficult to remove the handicaps under which some of you suffer.

* * *

I believe, of course, that for our own good in this country, the Negro race as a whole must improve its standards of living, and become both economically and intellectually of higher calibre. The fact that the colored people, not only in the South, but in the North as well, have been economically at a low level, has meant that they have also been physically and intellectually at a low level. Economic conditions are responsible for poor health in children. And the fact that tuberculosis and pneumonia and many other diseases have taken a heavier toll amongst our colored groups, can be attributed primarily to economic conditions. It is undoubtedly true that with an improvement in economic condition it will still be necessary not only to improve our educational conditions for children, but to pay special attention to adult education along the line of better living. For you cannot expect people to change over night, when they have had poor conditions, and adjust themselves to all that we expect of people living as they *should* live today throughout our country.

* * *

One thing I want to speak about tonight because I have had a number of people tell me that they felt the Government in its new efforts and programs was not always fair to the Negro race. And I want to say that though this undoubtedly is so quite often, it is not the intention of those at the top, and as far as possible I hope that we may work together to eliminate any real injustice.

No right-thinking person in this country today, who picks up a paper and reads that in some part of the country the people have not been willing to wait for the due processes of law, but have gone back to the rule of force, blind and unjust as force and fear usually are; can help but be ashamed that we have shown such a lack of faith in our own institutions. It is a horrible thing which grows out of weakness and fear, and not out of strength and courage; and the sooner we as a nation unite to stamp out any such action, the sooner and the better will we be able to face the other nations of the world and to uphold our real ideals here and abroad.

We have long held in this country that ability should be the criterion on which all people are judged. It seems to me that we must come to recognize this criterion in dealing with all human beings, and not place any limitations upon their achievements except such as may be imposed by their own character and intelligence.

This is what we work for as an ideal for the relationship that must exist between all the citizens of our country. There is no reason why all of the races in this country should not live together each of them giving from their particular gift something to the other, and contributing an example to the world of peace on earth, good-will toward men.*

187

A VIEW OF PRESIDENT ROOSEVELT

Franklin Roosevelt was a tempting target for analysis as a person and as President. This editorial summary on the eve of the 1940 presidential election is as comprehensive and objective a statement about Roosevelt's Negro policies as can be found.

THE ROOSEVELT RECORD

On the subject of the Negro, the Roosevelt record is spotty, as might be expected in an administration where so much power is in the hands of the southern wing of the Democratic party. And yet Mr. Roosevelt, hobbled as he has been by the Dixie die-hards, has managed to include Negro citizens in practically every phase of the administration program. In this respect, no matter how far behind the ideal he may be, he is far ahead of any other Democratic president, and of recent Republican ones.

The best proof that Mr. Roosevelt has not catered always to the South and has insisted on carrying the Negro along with his program is to be found in the smearing, race-hating propaganda used against him in the 1936 campaign by southern white groups. Both he and Mrs. Roosevelt were targets of filthy mud-slinging simply because they did not see eye to eye with the South on the Negro.

This does not mean that the Roosevelt administration has done all that it could have done for the race. Its policies in many instances have done Negroes great injustice and have helped to build more secure walls of segregation.

---

*Eleanor Roosevelt, "The Negro and Social Change," *Opportunity*, XIV (January 1936), 22–23. Reprinted with permission of the National Urban League.

On the anti-lynching bill Mr. Roosevelt has said not a mumbling word. His failure to endorse this legislation, to bring pressure to break the filibuster, is a black mark against him. It does no good to say that the White House could not pass down some word on this bill. The White House spoke on many bills. Mr. Roosevelt might have pressed the anti-lynching bill to a vote, especially during January and February, 1938, when there was tremendous public opinion supporting the bill. His failure to act, or even speak, on the anti-lynching bill was the more glaring because, while mobs in America were visiting inhumanities upon Negroes, Mr. Roosevelt periodically was rebuking some foreign government for inhumanity, and enunciating high sentiments of liberty, tolerance, justice, etc.

To declare that the Roosevelt administration has tried to include the Negro in nearly every phase of its program for the people of the nation is not to ignore the instances where government policies have harmed the race.

At Boulder dam, for example, the administration continued the shameful policy begun by Hoover of forbidding Negroes to live in Boulder City, the government-built town. And in its own pet project, the TVA, the administration forbade Negroes to live in Norris, another government-built town at Norris dam.

Full credit must go to the administration for its program of low-cost housing, so sorely needed by low-income families. No one pretends that the American housing program is more than a beginning, but Negroes have shared in it in the most equitable manner. However, there were, outside the slum-clearance program, some damaging practices. The FHA, which insures mortgages for home buyers, has enforced a regulation which puts the power

During the Presidential election campaign of 1940, the Republicans issued a series of cartoons aimed at the Negro. The blasts were aimed at every aspect of the New Deal. Distributed throughout Harlem, and other communities, they had one message: Roosevelt is the Negro's enemy.

and approval of the government on ghetto life. No Negro family which sought a home outside the so-called "Negro" neighborhood could get a FHA-insured loan.

The vast program for youth, the CCC and the NYA, has included our young people, but in the CCC a justifiable complaint has been that Negro instructors, advisers, and reserve army officers were not appointed in any but the tiniest proportion.

There is little need to mention relief and the WPA. Mr. Roosevelt's critics concede what his administration has done in these two branches of his program by concentrating their attack upon the relief that the New Deal has given Negroes. In relief the government set the tone. That tone was so much higher than the city, county and state standards for Negroes in certain areas that, even though differentials existed, the net result was more than it would have been without government supervision. Collective bargaining and the Wages and Hours act have aided Negro workers in private industry.

The farm program has not been ideally administered, but colored people have shared in the benefits. More than 50,000 families have been assisted by the Farm Security administration.

Mr. Roosevelt had the courage to appoint a Negro to a federal judgeship, the first in the history of the country. His nominee was confirmed by a Democratic senate without a murmur. Complaint has been made that in naming about a score of colored administrative assistants and advisers, Mr. Roosevelt has kept Negroes out of any real posts in the government. If it be true that Mr. Roosevelt has created Negro appendages to various bureaus, it cannot be denied that colored people know more about their government and have penetrated nearer to policy-making desks than ever before.

Heavily on the debit side is Mr. Roosevelt's approval of the War department's notorious jim crow in the armed services.

Most important contribution of the Roosevelt administration to the age-old color line problem in America has been its doctrine that Negroes are a part of the country and must be considered in any program for the country as a whole. The inevitable discriminations notwithstanding, this thought has been driven home in thousands of communities ,by a thousand specific acts. For the first time in their lives, government has taken on meaning and substance for the Negro masses.

* * *

Negro voters are posed a question on November 5: Do they believe that in spite of admitted mistakes and failures (both as to them and to government generally) the Roosevelt administration is tending toward the kind of government that is best for the majority of the people; or has the Roosevelt record on the Negro specifically and on the government generally been such that a new administration should be voted into power?*

---

*"The Roosevelt Record," *The Crisis*, XLVII (November, 1940), 343. Reprinted with permission of *The Crisis* Magazine, official publication of the NAACP.

188

THE NEGRO NOT YET LABOR CONSCIOUS

The Negro worker's position relative to labor unions underwent a transformation as a result both of the New Deal legislation recognizing labor's right to bargain and as a result of the emergence of the industrial union concept. The transformation was not simple and easy; it involved massive changes in traditional attitudes by black and white workers alike.

This document from 1937 reflects the various difficulties which surrounded the change. T. Arnold Hill was for many years the Director of the National Urban League's Department of Industrial Relations. Hill wrote his story after on-the-spot survey of conditions.

The Negro and the CIO

Is the Negro being influenced by the CIO? This is a question frequently propounded by laymen concerned with the established reputation of Negroes for law and order over and against the assumed irregularity and revolutionary tactics of the Committee for Industrial Organization. Recently, the writer visited the strike area in the Ohio Valley and in Johnstown, Pennsylvania, where since the latter part of May the independent steel companies have been in constant conflict with protesting workers.

It is essential to point out that Negroes form a very small proportion of the workers in the Republic and Youngstown Sheet and Tube Company plants. In this particular area seldom does the Negro form more than three per cent of the total working population in any one plant. These Negro workers are for the most part confined to the wire mills and the coke ovens. They do semiskilled and a few skilled jobs at some of the plants but never reach a job higher than that of shearer which under normal circumstances pays approximately $110 to $130 every two weeks for a normal eight-hour day. When they work overtime and under strike conditions, as was true recently, they might easily average $150 to $175 every two weeks.

From the standpoint of union workers, Negroes form, therefore, so small a percentage of the total that it makes very little difference whether Negroes go in or stay out of the unions. From the standpoint of the Negro worker, it has been regarded as an immediate personal financial advantage if he did not join the union. Not only was he assured a higher strike wage and longer hours but the loyalty of plant managers who have always regarded Negroes more or less an anti-toxin against labor union uprisings. As a consequence, few of the Negro workers in Johnstown, Warren, Youngstown, or Canton were joining the unions of the Steel Workers' Organization or the CIO. Union organizers offered Negroes the opportunity to join their membership but treated them roughly if they caught them going into a plant at the time of the strike. A number of cases are on record of fights between non-union Negro workers and union white workers, though these appear not to have been the result of racial feeling but purely the result of differences arising over the dispute.

This situation, however, is not universal. In Cleveland, a much larger percentage of Negroes joined the labor union than in the other cities mentioned. In Canton, when one company signed up with the unions, the Negroes saw that it was advantageous for them to join and went in almost 100 per cent with the other CIO members. In Massillon, quite a few were listed among the strikers. In these cities, Negroes were on the picket lines as well as whites.

In contrast to the situation in the Ohio Valley, there is the Pittsburgh area where the U.S. Steel Company controls steel production. Here the percentage of Negroes working in the industry was larger than that in the Ohio area and it was to the advantage of whites to concentrate on Negro membership and to bring it in line with the forces of the CIO. The net result of this was a sizeable number of Negro steel workers included in the organized group that entered into contract with the United States Steel Corporation.

A fair answer, then, to the query—Is the Negro being influenced by the CIO?—is that he is joining the steel workers' organizations when the number of Negroes in an industry being organized is sufficiently large to warrant special efforts on the part of the labor union to get Negroes to join. The Negro is able to see that the larger the number of them employed, the greater is the menace of their unemployment should they not join up with their fellow white workers when demands are pressed and strikes are called. There is a plant in Ohio where 640 odd Negro workers are employed out of a total of 1,000. Efforts are now being made to organize this plant under the banner of the CIO. Should it happen that a large majority of Negroes refuse to sign up for union membership and the union ultimately succeeded in its fight for recognition, not only would it be possible for the union members to bring about the elimination of Negroes, but the likelihood of racial conflict would be quite imminent.

It is well to keep in mind that the larger the percentage of Negroes employed in a plant, the poorer the working conditions and the smaller the wage. Also that Negroes working almost entirely as common laborers and unorganized have little or no chance to increase greatly their wage rate or work upward into skilled levels. If the CIO form of labor union should become the bargaining agent in the places where Negroes work, they would be taken into membership in the same local and under the same union privileges that skilled workers enjoy, whereas today in the conventional craft union organization, unskilled laborers are usually unorganized and the skilled trades object to Negro members, even if they are working in the trades.

My visit to the strike area convinces me that the Negro is not yet labor conscious; that he is not ready to join either the A.F. of L. or the CIO or any other union for fear that the slight gain he has made in industry will be lost. He has not yet sensed the possibility of exclusion if he fails to join a labor union which subsequently becomes the bargaining union group. It should be recognized by white unions that Negro workers can destroy the standards which they set up as long as these Negro workers are not members of the trade union movement. The likelihood of this, however, has diminished since the Wagner Labor Act became law. It is now possible for the bargaining group which represents the majority to so work against the unorganized minority or even an organized minority to the end that better jobs will go to the workers who are members of this dominant trade union bargaining agency. If, in addition, closed shop agreements are effective as we now have them in a number of trades and industries, it will be well nigh impossible for Negroes to go in as new workers when once the closed shop agreements have been entered into. With unemployment as heavy as it is, trade unions are loath to accept new members until their members can find employment.

The observations made in Pennsylvania and Ohio are convincing as to the shortsightedness of Negroes in not cooperating with their fellow white workers. It is a matter of record that in the United Mine Workers, the Ladies' Garment Workers, the Longshoremen's Organization and others, membership in the trade union has been of inestimable good to Negro workers. As the trade union movement goes forward with the help of legislation and liberal public opinion, it would be suicide for the Negro to be swayed by temporary and immediate benefits rather than to be guided by the protection that will come from joining hands with other workers in their common struggle for independence and equality.*

Discrimination in the Thirties and Forties

189

FUNDS FOR EDUCATION IN A SOUTHERN STATE

In 1933, the NAACP learned of a qualified young graduate of the North Carolina State College for Negroes who was blocked from the School of Pharmacy of the University of North Carolina because of his color. The organization went to court in behalf of the student, Thomas Hocutt, and enlisted as lawyers, William H. Hastie, then just a few years out of law school, and two local Durham attorneys. The appearance of three colored lawyers shocked the town and the opposition counsel which included the state's attorney-general, a leading white member of the state bar, and the dean of the University Law School.

The NAACP lost the case on a technicality—the failure of the president of the Negro college to supply a transcript for Hocutt's application because he did not want to be involved in or responsible for an interracial situation. But the judge recognized the quality of the colored attorney's brief and argument and forthrightly said in his opinion that Hocutt had been denied admission only because he was a Negro.

In the excerpt below, Walter White, the then executive secretary of the NAACP, describes some of the reactions to the Hocutt case, including a brief exchange on the floor of the North Carolina legislature.

---

*T. Arnold Hill, "The Negro and the CIO," *Opportunity*, XV (August, 1937), 243–244. Reprinted with permission of the National Urban League.

* * *

Although we lost the case legally, we won it in extraordinary fashion in the court of public opinion. Students of the University of North Carolina were polled by *The Daily Tarheel,* and a surprisingly large percentage favored immediate admission of qualified Negroes at least to the graduate schools of the University. Even those students who favored continuation of segregation voted their belief that nonsegregated tax-supported schools were inevitable. The state legislature was asked to appropriate funds for education of Negro students in professional schools "where they may be lawfully admitted," but the state senate killed the bill after it had been passed by the house of representatives. But even in that development a new South made its appearance.

Angered by the Hocutt suit, some of the legislators, particularly those from the more backward rural areas, demanded decrease instead of increase in funds for the education of Negroes.

One legislator, Deacon Barden of Craven, was so stirred by the proposal that he was moved to declare, as quoted in the *Greensboro Daily News* of March 18, 1933:

"Mr. Speaker, I have sat here and watched this house today. I know there is nothing I can say that will stop what you are doing. But I tremble when I think of its consequences. Here you have voted to decrease all the appropriations and God knows they are small enough, at best, to the Negro institutions, and you give the Cherokee Indian school nearly fifty percent more than the gentleman from Ashe had allowed it. Mr. Speaker, I wonder by what process you increase the appropriation to the Indians who scalped our forefathers and take from the Negroes who slaved for us?

"I came to this general assembly as honestly and as reverently as I went to my church. I wanted to do the fair thing by everybody in North Carolina. This thing affects me deeply. I am a freshman here, and maybe I am not yet callous to such injustice as this. I am apprehensive of what is going on here. I know it's pleasant to be in the majority but there are things that ring louder in my ears than the shouts of majorities. Mr. Speaker, the gentleman from Durham introduced an amendment here to lift the appropriations of the North Carolina College for Negroes from $18,130 to $24,170 recommended by the Appropriations Committee. I would like to know why you voted this down."

Mr. Cherry replied: "Because we thought they could live on it."

Mr. Barden went back at him. "Does the gentleman mean then, that in making other recommendations for increases, or decreases, he did not know what he was doing? . . . The original appropriation in all conscience is small enough."

Mr. Bowie, who had kept still nearly all the day, rose to enlighten Judge Barden.

"Doesn't the gentleman know that this Negro college in Durham is doing classical work?" Mr. Bowie asked.

"I do, and hasn't it the right to do that kind of work?" Mr. Barden replied spiritedly.

"Well, at a time like this I don't think so," Mr. Bowie continued.

"Your son got a classical education, didn't he?" Mr. Barden asked.

"Yes, but my son and a Negro are different," Mr. Bowie said with manifest resentment.

"They are both citizens of North Carolina, aren't they?" Mr. Barden shot back.

Chairman Murphy rapped for order, but said: "The chair wishes to say that its agrees heartily with the gentleman from Craven."*

190

THE PRAGMATISM OF A SOUTHERN SENATOR

Huey Long came up the hard way in Louisiana politics and chose a course totally unlike any Southerner of recent vintage. After establishing himself firmly as Governor, he had himself elected to the Senate from Louisiana. This interview reveals Long as he was shortly before his assassination. It was written by Roy Wilkins, then editor of The Crisis *and destined to be the executive secretary of the NAACP about twenty years later. It was probably the only personal interview to a Negro reporter for a Negro publication which Long gave.*

AN INTERVIEW WITH LOUISIANA'S KINGFISH

Contrary to my expectations, I had no difficulty getting an interview with Senator Huey P. Long, the Kingfish, Dictator of the State of Louisiana, aspirant to the Presidency in 1936. I reasoned that nothing more serious could happen than a refusal to see me, especially since the location was New York and not Baton Rouge or New Orleans, so up to the twenty-fifth floor of the Hotel New Yorker I took myself.

Two things I wanted to know, if the Kingfish would talk: what was he going to do about the lynching which had been staged the day before in Franklinton, La.: and what hope did his "share-the-wealth" program hold out for Negro Americans?

It is a certainty that I am not as important as a German naval captain and since Huey had received that worthy some years ago in green pajamas, I could not complain when he received me in maroon silk pajamas.

It developed that in calling at 9:30 I had arrived just about as the senator was rising. After a bit he came into the room barefooted and bawling for breakfast to be ordered. He shook hands with all of us present, hesitating not a bit when he came to the only Negro. The dictator's hair was tousled; sleep was in his eyes; the pajamas added the only bright note. All men, I thought, dictators or not, look pretty much the same in the morning. After an hour and a quarter of waiting my turn came.

Through a sitting room, past a bathroom and into the bedroom of the "Dictator of the Delta." There he was, barefoot still, in pajamas

*Walter F. White, *A Man Called White* (N.Y., Viking Press, 1948), 159-160. Copyright 1948 by Walter White. Reprinted by permission of The Viking Press, Inc.

still, bending over his bed on which were spread nine or ten shirts from which he was trying to make a selection.

"Sit down," he invited, plunging right in, "you know I came up here to see a show, to get a little fun away from the senate, but I haven't done a thing but see newspapermen."

"Well, Senator, I would like to ask you just a few questions," I began.

"Sure. Let me tell you about the nigras," he interrupted. In the first two minutes I found out Huey does all the talking and that he uses "nigger," "nigra," and occasionally "colored," but mostly "nigger."

"One of them newspapers (he hates newspapers) yesterday tried to put me on the spot about niggers voting. You saw it? Why, say, I ain't gonna get into that fight. They don't vote in the South—you from the South?—well, they don't vote down there, so why should I go into that? I have been able to do a hell of a lot of things down there because I am Huey Long—they know I'm square; a lot of guys would have been murdered politically for what I've been able to do quietly for the niggers. But do you think I could get away with niggers voting? No sirree! These newspapers are trying to jam me!"

"But, Senator—" I tried to edge in. No use. The flood continued while he shook out some tooth powder and hunted his toothbrush:

"Lissen here. My educational program is for everybody, whites and blacks. I can't have my people ignorant. Louisiana had a high illiteracy rate, couldn't read or write. I mean whites couldn't either, but there were more among the niggers. (I thought of the figures for education in Louisiana and thought to say a word, but no one could stem that tide of words from him; anyway I was here for an interview, not for an argument.) When I became governor I said 'this has gotta stop.' I gave 'em school books free at the state's expense. I started free schools, day and night, so they could learn to read and write and figger.

"Maybe you think that was easy in the case of the niggers. There are plenty of ignorant white people with hatred in their hearts from the war between the states. They did not want the niggers to go to school. That was tough on me. They said their niggers had to work. So what did I do? I opened night schools. They kept on hollering and I simply had to put my foot down. I said (beating his breast) 'I'm the governor and I say the ignorant in this state have to learn, blacks as well as whites.' And they learned."

"Yes, but—" I made another effort. He merely took another swipe with his toothbrush and drove on, cocking a shrewd eye at me as I stood at the door of the green and black bathroom:

"Now, young man, you can see some things without me writing them down. I'm not working for equality or anything like that. I figger when you teach niggers to read and write and figger they can kinda look out for themselves—you know, people can't cheat them like they did before. You know they cheat them, don't you? (Did I?) Why, (and here he grew confidential, drawing a diagram

The plantation overseer and his field hands. Taken in the Mississippi Delta in 1936, the scene reflects what must have seemed, to all six men present, a society that would never change.

on the dresser with his toothbrush handle) down home we have plantations ten miles long and five miles wide. They have a system that's lawful but bad for the niggers. Maybe when a nigger tenant got through working at the end of the year he had enough to buy the baby a rattle for Christmas and maybe not. That ain't right. I taught 'em to figger. They got to look out for themselves. Maybe you think it didn't raise hell among the landlords. . . ."

He paused to read a telegram and answer the telephone (incidentally in very correct English) and I managed to get in a question:

"How about lynching, Senator? About the Costigan-Wagner bill in congress and that lynching down there yesterday in—"

He ducked the Costigan-Wagner bill, but of course, everyone knows he is against it. He cut me off on the Franklinton lynching and hastened in with his "pat" explanation:

"You mean down in Washington parish (county)? Oh, that? That one slipped up on us. Too bad, but those slips will happen. You know while I was governor there were no lynchings and since this man (Gov. Allen) has been in he hasn't had any. (There have been 7 lynchings in Louisiana in the last two years.) This one slipped up. I can't do nothing about it. No sir. Can't do the dead nigra no good. Why, if I tried to go after those lynchers it might cause a hundred more niggers to be killed. You wouldn't want that, would you?"

"But you control Louisiana," I persisted, "you could—"

"Yeah, but it's not that simple. I told you there are some things even Huey Long can't get away with. We'll just have to watch out for the next one. Anyway that nigger was guilty of coldblooded murder."

"But your own supreme court had just granted him a new trial."

"Sure we got a law which allows a reversal on technical points. This nigger got hold of a smart lawyer somewhere and proved a technicality. He was guilty as hell. But we'll catch the next lynching."

Quickly and positively changing the subject he ran on:

"Now about 'the share-the-wealth.' I say niggers have got to have homes and security like anybody else. (I thought: security and lynching?) I stand on that. They say to me: 'Do you mean niggers have to have a home?' I say: 'yes, a nigger is entitled to a home.' Who'll disagree with that? It's fair."

Sitting down opposite me now with his legs crossed, wriggling his toes, talking now quietly, now oratorically, but always amiably, the senator switched to another topic. He was courtesy itself (except for that word "nigger" which he certainly does not regard as offensive) and he was evidently trying earnestly to put over what he considered his "good points" on the Negro question.

"Why down in Louisiana," he continued, "the whites have decided nigras have got to have public health care. Got to give 'em clinics and hospitals. Got to keep 'em healthy. That's fair and it's good sense. I said to them: 'you wouldn't want a colored woman (one of his few uses of the word "colored") watching over your children if she had pyorrhea, would you?' They see the point. The same goes for other diseases. We got hospitals and clinics down there to care for niggers just like everybody else."

"In your article," he concluded, as he called for a long distance call to New Orleans and moved to select some underwear, "don't say I'm working for niggers. I'm not. I'm for the poor man—all poor men. Black and white, they all gotta have a chance. They gotta have a home, a job and a decent education for their children. 'Every Man a King'—that's my slogan. That means every man, niggers long with the rest, but not specially for niggers. . . .

"Come to see me in Washington. Drop in any time. Share the wealth, yessir—Hello, New Orleans? Goodday—hello, hello. . . ."

With a wave of his naked arm in farewell (he had taken off his pajama coat) the Kingfish sent me on my way.

In the hall his secretary said a little proudly, as if to prove something:

"Well, you got your interview, didn't you?"

What about Kingfish Long and Negroes? What can they expect from him? Draw your own conclusions from the above. I have not attempted to polish it off. It is pretty much as he said it. No smooth, Ph.D. language. No oily phrases like: "I admire the Negro race because it has made the greatest progress, etc., etc." No special promises.

He dodges the hard questions on lynching and the vote, and is vague on the easy ones.

My guess is that Huey is a hard, ambitious, practical politician. He is far shrewder than he is given credit for being. My further guess is that he wouldn't hesitate to throw Negroes to the wolves if it became necessary; neither would he hesitate to carry them along if the good they did him was greater than the harm. He will walk a tight rope and go along as far as he can. He told New York newspapermen he welcomed Negroes in the share-the-wealth clubs in the North where they could vote, but down South? Down South they can't vote: they are no good to him. So he lets them strictly alone. After all, Huey comes first.

Anyway, menace or benefactor, he is the most colorful character I have interviewed in the twelve years I've been in the business.*

191

THE NEGRO IN THE ARMED FORCES IN WORLD WAR II

Although the federal government took definite steps to halt racial discrimination in war industries, segregation held firm in the armed forces. The Navy continued to use Negroes only in menial capacities and accepted few volunteers. Only with the greatest reluctance did the Army Air Force agree to train Negroes as pilots and navigators, and early in the war veteran Negro pilots, even ones with combat experience in the Spanish Civil War, were rejected. Since most training camps were located in the South, Negro servicemen were subjected to humiliation both on and off duty, and many training officers were southern whites with ingrained prejudice.

In 1940, prominent Negro dean of the Howard University School of Law and former federal judge William H. Hastie was appointed as civilian aide to the Secretary of War to assist in solving problems arising from large numbers of Negroes in the armed forces. In this capacity, Hastie was repeatedly frustrated in his attempts to abolish segregation and to secure equal treatment for Negroes in uniform. Hostility and opposition to his policies, as he explains in this article, led to his resignation in January 1943.

Reactionary policies and discriminatory practices of the Army Air Forces in matters affecting Negroes were the immediate cause of my resignation as Civilian Aide to the Secretary of War.

The Army Air Forces are growing in importance and independence. In the post war period they may become the greatest single component of the armed services. Biased policies and harmful practices established in this branch of the army can all too easily infect other branches as well. The situation had become critical. Yet, the whole course of my dealings with the Army Air Forces convinced

The Crisis, XLII (February 1935), 41–52. Reprinted with permission of *The Crisis* Magazine, official publication of the NAACP.

me that further expression of my views in the form of recommendations within the department would be futile. I, therefore, took the only course which can, I believe, bring results. Public opinion is still the strongest force in American life.

To the Negro soldier and those who influence his thinking, I say with all the force and sincerity at my command that the man in uniform must grit his teeth, square his shoulders and do his best as a soldier, confident that there are millions of Americans outside of the armed services, and more persons than he knows in high places within the military establishment, who will never cease fighting to remove every racial barrier and every humiliating practice which now confront him. But only by being at all times a first class soldier can the man in uniform help in this battle which shall be fought and won.

When I took office, the Secretary of War directed that all questions of policy and important proposals relating to Negroes should be referred to my office for comment or approval before final action. In December, 1940, the Air Forces referred to me a plan for a segregated training center for Negro pursuit pilots at Tuskegee. I expressed my entire disagreement with the plan, giving my reasons in detail. My views were disregarded. Since then, the Air Command has never on its own initiative submitted any plan or project to me for comment or recommendation. What information I obtained, I had to seek out. Where I made proposals or recommendations, I volunteered them.

This situation reached its climax in late December, 1942, when I learned through army press releases sent out from St. Louis and from the War Department in Washington that the Air Command was about to establish a segregated officer candidate school at Jefferson Barracks, Mo., to train Negro officers for ground duty with the Army Air Forces. Here was a proposal for a radical departure from present army practice, since the officer candidate training program is the one large field where the army is eliminating racial segregation.

Moreover, I had actually written to the Air Command several weeks earlier in an attempt to find out what was brewing at Jefferson Barracks. The Air Command replied as late as December 17, 1942, giving not even the slightest hint of any plan for a segregated officer candidate school. It is inconceivable to me that consideration of such a project had not then advanced far enough for my office to have been consulted, even if I had not made specific inquiry. The conclusion is inescapable that the Air Command does not propose to inform, much less counsel with, this office about its plans for Negroes.

* * *

To date, all Negro applicants, a number of them well and fully qualified, for appointment as army service pilots have been rejected. Two applicants were actually instructed to report for training. They did so but were sent home as soon as it was discovered that they were Negroes. I am advised that this matter is receiving further study. The simple fact is that the Air Command does not want Negro pilots flying in and out of various fields, eating, sleeping and mingling with other personnel, as a service pilot must do in carrying out his various missions.

Negro medical officers in the Air Forces are getting only part of the special training in aviation medicine which is available. They are not admitted to the principal school of aviation medicine at Randolph Field.

Even the branch school program in which it is represented that Negro officers share without discrimination is in fact discriminatory. Many white officers enrolled at branch schools of aviation medicine have the opportunity of full time resident study. The Negro officer is permitted to commute periodically from his home station at Tuskegee for work at the Maxwell Field branch school. Such grudging partial tender of makeshift schemes may be expected to continue unless a genuine change of racial attitude and policy occurs in the Air Command.

While Negro trainees and cadets at the Tuskegee Air Base have done well from a strictly technical point of view, they have suffered such demoralizing discrimination and segregation that, in my judgment, the entire future of the Negro in combat aviation is in danger. Men cannot be humiliated over a long period of time without a loss of combat efficiency.

Specifically, Negro and white officers serving at Tuskegee in the common enterprise of training Negroes for the combat have separate messes. They are not permitted to have quarters in the same building. Separate toilet facilities have been provided. If the group of white officers at Tuskegee insist upon this and I have no evidence that they do—they are psychologically unsuited to train Negroes for combat. If they do not insist, the racial attitude of the local commands, or of higher authority is all the more apparent.

Despite original design to advance Negro officers and to place them in posts of administrative responsibility at Tuskegee as rapidly as they should qualify, that design is not being carried out in the post administration, except in the station hospital.

Early in the history of the Tuskegee project, a Negro soldier guarding a warehouse was disarmed and arrested by civilian authorities because he had challenged a white civilian. From then on friction continued. A new commander was appointed. He disarmed Negro military policemen assigned to patrol duty in the town of Tuskegee. A recent member of the Alabama state police force was assigned to Tuskegee as an army officer with duties related to his civilian experience. The Negro soldier was embittered, but the prejudiced community was somewhat mollified.

Fundamentally, it seems to me the Air Command has either failed to comprehend or failed to care that its policies and prejudices are tending to tear down rather than build up the pride, dignity and self respect which Negro soldiers like all other soldiers must possess if they are to achieve maximum combat efficiency.

Military men agree that a soldier should be made to feel that he is the best man, in the best unit in the best army in the world. When the Air Command shall direct its policies and practices so as to help rather than hinder the development of such spirit among its Negro soldiers, it will be on the right road.*

192

A PRESIDENTIAL NEWS CONFERENCE

Acting in part on the advice of Walter White, President Franklin D. Roosevelt agreed to a special conference for Negro newspaper publishers in February 1944. White had told the President that the exclusion of Negro reporters from White House and major federal agency news conferences was one reason why the Negro press was hostile and inaccurate in its reporting.

The excerpts reprinted here show Roosevelt in a characteristic manner, taking a question and spinning out a series of stories in reply to it which do not actually engage the original question, yet which relate sufficiently to it to avoid a direct charge of evasion.

Mr. Ira Lewis (Pittsburgh *Courier):* There is one very pressing question that is causing the colored people lots of concern. I think that we represent here perhaps five or six million readers, and that question is posed to us at all times. It is a grievous and vexing one. It has to do with the treatment of our boys in the armed services. They haven't been treated right by civilian police, and by the M.P.'s. We know of instances where soldiers on furlough have come home and taken off their uniform, on account of intimidation.

And they think, Mr. President, that that is your responsibility. They think that you alone can correct that. I think you can put your hand right on the question, which will do more towards strengthening morale and making more for unity and making the Negro citizen believe that he is a part of this great commonwealth. Just one word from you, we all feel, would do that.

Thank you.

The President: I am glad you brought that up, because I have been in touch with it. It is perfectly true, there is definite discrimination in the actual treatment of the colored engineer troops, and others. And you are up against it, as you know perfectly well. I have talked about it—I had the Secretary of War and the Assistant—everybody in on it. The trouble lies fundamentally in the attitude of certain white people—officers down the line who haven't got very much more education, many of them, than the colored troops and the Seabees and the engineers, for example. And well, you know the kind of person it is. We all do. We don't have to do more than think of a great many people that we know. And it has become not a question of orders—they are repeated fairly often, I think, in all the camps of colored troops—it's a question of the personality of the individual. And we are up against it, absolutely up against it. I always think of the fact that it probably is improving. I like to think that mere association helps things along.

*William H. Hastie, "Why I Resigned," *Chicago Daily Defender*, February 6, 1943, 1–2. Reprinted with permission from the *Chicago Daily Defender*.

I always think of two or three years ago—not an election trip—I was down in Chattanooga. A very interesting thing happened. I was going all around to the points of interest in Chattanooga—I think I dedicated one of the dams—and I drove with Governor Cooper through the streets, the southern end of Chattanooga, through the Negro section.

And there was tremendous enthusiasm to see the President. And suddenly we came onto this broad avenue that was running south, we came to a place where all the enthusiasm quit and stopped; and there were a good many colored people on the streets, but they just stood there, they were completely apathetic.

And I turned to Governor Cooper. I said, "What's the matter with these people?"

He said, "You are not in Tennessee any longer, you are in Georgia." (*Laughter*)

That is a very interesting thing.

Now in Tennessee the great majority of Negroes in Chattanooga are voting; they can take part in the life of the community. You get across this invisible line, you pop over into the State of Georgia, not one of them can vote. Now that is just a plain fact. It's an interesting fact. Just, as I said, hands down—*(demonstrating)*—no enthusiasm at all; and a block further back everybody saying, "Hello, Mr. President," and so forth and so on. They are all right in Tennessee. People in Tennessee are just as well off as before. I don't know what they are kicking about in Georgia, which is my State, unfortunately.

And there is just one thing in here—*(indicating a prepared statement presented by the Negro Newspaper Publishers Association)*—the only thing I didn't agree with, and that is a thing which vour Association, I think, could do something about. You talk about people in other countries. We all know that they are very different from Americans in every way. I will give you one example—something has got to be done about it in time.

Last year I went to a place called Gambia in Africa, at the mouth of the Gambia River. Bathurst is the capital. I think there are about three million inhabitants, of whom one hundred and fifty are white. And it's the most horrible thing I have ever seen in my life. I was there twice. The natives are five thousand years back of us. Disease is rampant, absolutely. It's a terrible place for disease.

And I looked it up, with a little study, and I got to the point of view that for every dollar that the British, who have been there for two hundred years, have put into Gambia, they have taken out ten. It's just plain exploitation of those people. There is no education whatsoever.

* * *

Now, as I say, we have got to realize that in a country like Gambia—and there are a lot of them down there—the people, who are in the overwhelming majority, have no possibility of self-government for a long time. But we have got to move, the way we did in the Philippines, to teach them self-government. That means education, it means sanitation, it means all those things. And that would be just as good for every white American to know as every colored American; but we don't know.

Now, because of your traditional, historic Association, it would be a perfectly grand thing if your Association could send two or three people out there, as a committee, to write stories about what is needed.

I am taking up with Prime Minister Winston Churchill at the present time—I think he will see the point—the general thought that the United Nations ought to have an inspection committee of all these colonies that are way, way down the line, that are not ready to have anything to say yet because the owning country has given them no facilities.

And if we sent a committee from the United Nations, and I used the example of Gambia, to go down to Gambia, "If you Britishers don't come up to scratch—toe the mark—then we will let all the world know."

Well, the Prime Minister doesn't like that idea. And his comeback was, "All right, the United Nations will send an inspection committee to your own South in America."
(Laughter)

He thought he had me.

I said, "Winston, that's all right with me. Go ahead and do it. Tell the world. We call it freedom of the press, and you also call it 'pitiless publicity'—you can right a lot of wrongs with 'pitiless publicity.'"

It would be a grand thing. I wouldn't mind if we had a committee of the United Nations come here and make a report on us. Why not? We have got some things to be ashamed of, and other things that are not as bad as they are painted. It wouldn't hurt at all—bring it all out.

So, if your Association could do something like that—teach us a little bit more about the world. . . .*

The Truman Administration

193

A SIGNIFICANT CONTRIBUTION TO PUBLIC OPINION

President Harry S. Truman issued four Executive Orders of major importance to Negroes and to the country during his administration. The first created the President's Committee on Civil Rights in December 1946. The Committee was instructed to investigate existing statutes and law enforcement measures at all levels of government and recommend how each might be strengthened. Its report entitled To Secure These Rights *was given wide distribution. Many of its recommendations were incorporated into Truman's ten-point civil rights message to Congress in February 1948. In a general sense, this was the first governmental*

---

*FDR, *The Public Papers and Addresses of Franklin D. Roosevelt, 1944-1945*, S. I. Rosenman, comp. (N.Y., Harper, 1950), Vol. XIII, 66-70.

attempt to determine the status of the Negro and his relationship to government in the United States and it made a significant contribution to public opinion on race matters.

The Condition of Our Rights

The Crime of Lynching

In 1946 at least six persons in the United States were lynched by mobs. Three of them had not been charged, either by the police or anyone else, with an offense. Of the three that had been charged, one had been accused of stealing a saddle. (The real thieves were discovered after the lynching.) Another was said to have broken into a house. A third was charged with stabbing a man. All were Negroes.

* * *

While available statistics show that, decade by decade, lynchings have decreased, this Committee has found that in the year 1947 lynching remains one of the most serious threats to the civil rights of Americans. It is still possible for a mob to abduct and murder a person in some sections of the country with almost certain assurance of escaping punishment for the crime. The decade from 1936 through 1946 saw at least 43 lynchings. No person received the death penalty, and the majority of the guilty persons were not even prosecuted.

The communities in which lynchings occur tend to condone the crime. Punishment of lynchers is not accepted as the responsibility of state or local governments in these communities. Frequently, state officials participate in the crime, actively or passively. Federal efforts to punish the crime are resisted. Condonation of lynching is indicated by the failure of some local law enforcement officials to make adequate efforts to break up a mob. It is further shown by failure in most cases to make any real effort to apprehend or try those guilty. If the federal government enters a case, local officials sometimes actively resist the federal investigation.

* * *

Police Brutality

We have reported the failure of some public officials to fulfill their most elementary duty—the protection of persons against mob violence. We must also report more widespread and varied forms of official misconduct. These include violent physical attacks by police officers on members of minority groups, the use of third degree methods to extort confessions, and brutality against prisoners. Civil rights violations of this kind are by no means universal and many law enforcement agencies have gone far in recent years toward stamping out these evils.

* * *

Much of the illegal official action which has been brought to the attention of the Committee is centered in the South. There is evidence of lawless police action against whites and Negroes alike, but the dominant pattern is that of race prejudice. J. Edgar Hoover referred, in his testimony before the Committee, to a particular jail where "it was seldom that a Negro man or women was incarcerated who was not given a severe beating, which started off with a pistol whipping and ended with a rubber hose."

* * *

There are other cases in the files of the Department of Justice of officers who seem to be "trigger-happy" where weak or poor persons are concerned. In a number of instances, Negroes have been shot, supposedly in self-defense, under circumstances indicating, at best, unsatisfactory police work in the handling of criminals, and, at worst, a callous willingness to kill.

* * *

The total picture—adding the connivance of some police officials in lynchings to their record of brutality against Negroes. In other situations—is, in the opinion of this Committee, a serious reflection on American justice. We know that Americans everywhere deplore this violence. We recognize further that there are many law enforcement officers in the South and the North who do not commit violent acts against Negroes or other friendless culprits. We are convinced, however, that the incidence of police brutality against Negroes is disturbingly high.

* * *

The Right to Vote

The right of all qualified citizens to vote is today considered axiomatic by most Americans. To achieve universal adult suffrage we have carried on vigorous political crusades since the earliest days of the Republic. In theory the aim has been achieved, but in fact there are many backwaters in our political life where the right to vote is not assured to every qualified citizen. The franchise is barred to some citizens because of race; to others by institutions or procedures which impede free access to the polls. Still other Americans are in substance disfranchised whenever electoral irregularities or corrupt practices dissipate their votes or distort their intended purpose. Some citizens—permanent residents of the District of Columbia—are excluded from political representation and the right to vote as a result of outmoded national traditions. As a result of such restrictions, all of these citizens are limited, in varying degrees, in their opportunities to seek office and to influence the conduct of government on an equal plane with other American citizens.

The denial of the suffrage on account of race is the most serious present interference with the right to vote. Until very recently, American Negro citizens in most southern states found it difficult to vote. Some Negroes have voted in parts of the upper South for the last twenty years. In recent years the situation in the deep South has changed to the point where it can be said that Negroes are beginning to exercise the political rights of free Americans. In the light of history, this represents progress, limited and precarious, but nevertheless progress.

* * *

Discriminatory Hiring Practices

Discrimination is most acutely felt by minority group members in their inability to get a job suited to their qualifications. Exclusions of Negroes, Jews, or Mexicans in the process of hiring is effected in various ways—by newspaper advertisements requesting only whites or gentiles to apply, by registration or application blanks on which a space is reserved for "race" or "religion," by discriminatory job orders placed with employment agencies, or by the arbitrary policy of a company official in charge of hiring.

A survey conducted by the United States Employment Service and contained in the Final Report of the Fair Employment Practice Committee reveals that of the total job orders received by USES offices in 11 selected areas during the period of February 1-15, 1946, 24 percent of the orders were discriminatory. Of 38,195 orders received, 9,171 included specifications with regard to race, citizenship, religion, or some combination of these factors.

* * *

On-the-Job Discrimination

If he can get himself hired, the minority worker often finds that he is being paid less than other workers. This wage discrimination is sharply evident in studies made of individual cities and is especially exaggerated in the South. A survey, conducted by the Research and Information Department of the American Federation of Labor, shows that the average weekly income of white veterans ranges from 30 to 78 percent above the average income of Negro veterans in 26 communities, 25 of them in the South. In Houston, for example, 36,000 white veterans had a weekly income of $49 and 4,000 Negro veterans had average incomes of $30—a difference of 63 percent. These differences are not caused solely by the relegation of the Negroes to lower types of work, but reflect wage discriminations between whites and Negroes for the same type of work. The Final Report of the FEPC states that the hourly wage rates for Negro common laborers averaged 47.4 cents in July, 1942, as compared with 65.3 cents for white laborers.

* * *

In presenting this evidence, the Committee is not ignoring the fact that an individual Negro worker may be less efficient than an individual white worker or vice versa. Nor does it suggest that wage differences which reflect actual differences in the competence of workers are unjustifiable. What is indefensible is a wage discrimination based, not on the worker's ability, but on his race.

While private business provided almost 70 percent of all cases docketed by the FEPC for the fiscal year 1943-44, about a fourth of the complaints were against the federal government itself. This at once calls to question the effectiveness of the Civil Service Commission rules against such discrimination, and the various departments' directives and executive orders that have restated this policy on non-discrimination from time to time.

* * *

Finally, labor unions are guilty of discriminatory labor practices. Six percent of the complaints received by the FEPC were made against unions, and the FEPC states that when challenged, private industry eliminated discrimination much more readily than did unions. On the other hand, it should be noted that great strides have been made in the admission of minorities to unions. Both the American Federation of Labor and the Congress of Industrial Organizations have repeatedly condemned discriminatory union practices. But the national organizations have not yet fully attained their goals. Some railway unions have "Jim Crow" auxiliaries into which Negroes, Mexicans, or Orientals are shunted, with little or no voice in union affairs. Furthermore, there is a rigid upper limit on the type of job on which these members can be employed.

Government's Responsibility: Securing the Rights

* * *

The national government should assume leadership in our American civil rights program because there is much in the field of civil rights that it is squarely responsible for in its own direct dealings with millions of persons. It is the largest single employer of labor in the country. More than two million persons are on its payroll. The freedom of opinion and expression enjoyed by these people is in many ways dependent upon the attitudes and practices of the government. By not restricting this freedom beyond a point necessary to insure the efficiency and loyalty of its workers, the government, itself, can make a very large contribution to the effort to achieve true freedom of thought in America. By scrupulously following fair employment practices, it not only sets a model for other employers to follow, but also directly protects the rights of more than two million workers to fair employment.

* * *

Leadership by the federal government in safeguarding civil rights does not mean exclusive action by that government. There is much that the states and local communities can do in this field, and much that they alone can do. The Committee believes that Justice Holmes' view of the states as 48 laboratories for social and economic experimentation is still valid. The very complexity of the civil rights problem calls for much experimental, remedial action which may be better undertaken by the states than by the national government. Parallel state and local action supporting the national program is highly desirable. It is obvious that even though the federal government should take steps to stamp out the crime of lynching, the states cannot escape the responsibility to employ all of the powers and resources available to them for the same end. Or again, the enactment of a federal fair employment practice act will not render similar state legislation unnecessary.

In certain areas the states must do far more than parallel federal action. Either for constitutional or administrative reasons, they must remain the primary protectors of civil rights. This is true of governmental efforts to control or outlaw racial or religious discrimination practiced by privately supported public-service institutions such as schools and hospitals, and of places of public accommodation such as hotels, restaurants, theaters, and stores.

Furthermore, government action alone, whether federal, state, local, or all combined, cannot provide complete protection of civil rights. Everything that government does stems from and is conditioned by the state of public opinion. Civil rights in this country will never be adequately protected until the intelligent will of the American people approves and demands that protection. Great responsibility, therefore, will always rest upon private organizations and private individuals who are in a position to educate and shape public opinion. The argument is sometimes made that because prejudice and intolerance cannot be eliminated through legislation and government control we should abandon that action in favor of the long, slow, evolutionary effects of education and voluntary private efforts. We believe that this argument misses the point and that the choice it poses between legislation and education as to the means of improving civil rights is an unnecessary one. In our opinion, both approaches to the goal are valid, and are, moreover, essential to each other.*

194

EQUALITY IN THE ARMED SERVICES

President Truman issued two Executive Orders in July 1948. One dealt with discrimination in employment within the government and the other created a second Presidential Committee, this time to study the problem of "equality of treatment and opportunity" in the armed services. Since the World Wars had sensitized Negroes to the military's predisposition to segregate and discriminate, this Committee was a most welcome one for Negroes. It, too, was a representative committee and it recognized the delicacy of its task in working with the branches of the armed forces. Its report, Freedom to Serve, *was submitted to President Truman in 1950 and was a major force in effecting the abolition of segregation and the reduction of discrimination in the service branches.*

The Course of the Inquiry

* * *

The scope of the executive order required that there be equality of treatment and opportunity for all persons in the armed services without regard to race, color, religion, or national origin. Members of various minority groups have asserted the existence of discrimination on these grounds, but no evidence was presented to the Committee and no specific facts were found indicating formally defined service policies denying equality of treatment and opportunity except with respect to Negroes. In their case practices resulting in inequality of treatment and opportunity had the sanction of official policy and were embodied in regulations.

The Committee felt, therefore, that its examination should leave room for gathering facts and developing conclusions affecting all minorities, but that it should proceed with the material on hand concerning the specific status of Negroes in the services. Once this racial factor should be satisfactorily disposed of, the Committee believed, a formula would be evolved applicable to all minorities. For this reason specific mention is limited throughout the report to recommendations and changes affecting Negroes.

**To Secure These Rights: The Report of the President's Committee on Civil Rights* (New York, 1947), ix, x-xi, 20-103.

There follows a summary account of the extent to which the President's executive order presently is being implemented, with an indication of the policy changes that have been put into effect by the services since the order was issued in July 1948.

The Navy

All jobs and ratings in the naval general service now are open to all enlisted men without regard to race or color. Negroes are currently serving in every job classification in general service.

All courses in Navy technical schools are open to qualified personnel without regard to race or color and without racial quotas. Negroes are attending the most advanced technical schools and are serving in their ratings both in the fleet and at shore installations.

Negroes in general service are completely integrated with whites in basic training, technical schools, on the job, in messes and sleeping quarters, ashore and afloat.

Chief, first-, second-, and third-class stewards now have the rate of chief, first-, second-, and third-class petty officers. (Policy change adopted June 7, 1949.)

Stewards who qualify for general ratings now can transfer to general service.

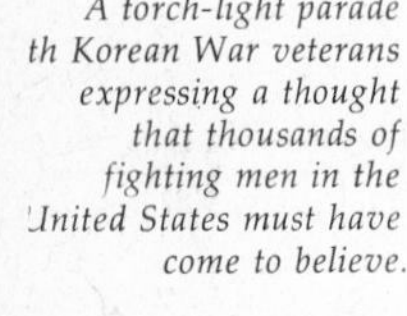

A torch-light parade th Korean War veterans expressing a thought that thousands of fighting men in the Jnited States must have come to believe.

The Marine Corps, which as a part of the Navy is subject to Navy policy, has abolished its segregated Negro training units. (Policy change adopted June 7, 1949.) Marine Corps training is now integrated, although some Negro marines are still assigned to separate units after basic training. In this respect the effectuation of Navy policy in the Marine Corps is yet to be completed.

The Air Force

The Air Force announced its new racial policy on May 11, 1949. As a result of this policy, the all-Negro 332d Fighter Wing at Lockbourne Field, Ohio, has been broken up, and its personnel either sent to school for further training, transferred to white units in other commands, or separated under current regulations.

A majority of other Negro units has also been abolished. As of January 31, 1950, only 59 Negro units remained, and 1,301 units were racially integrated, as compared with 106 Negro units and only 167 mixed units on June 1, 1949, when the Air Force policy went into effect.

Approximately 74 percent of the 25,000 Negroes in the Air Force on January 31, 1950, were serving in integrated units; and 26 percent still were serving in Negro units. This integration process is continuing.

All Air Force jobs and schools are open to qualified personnel without racial restriction or quotas. Six percent of the total personnel attending technical training schools in January 1950 were Negro.

Negroes serving in mixed units and attending service schools are integrated with whites in living conditions.

The Army

All Army jobs now are open to Negroes. (Policy change adopted September 30, 1949.)

All Army school courses are open to Negroes without restriction or quota. (Policy change adopted September 30, 1949.)

For the first time Negroes no longer are limited in assignment to Negro and overhead (housekeeping) units, but are to be assigned according to their qualifications to any unit, including formerly white units. (Policy change adopted January 16, 1950.)

Negroes serving in mixed units will be integrated on the job, in barracks and messes. (Policy change adopted January 16, 1950.)

The 10 percent limitation on Negro strength in the Army has been abolished, and there no longer are Negro quotas for enlistment. (Policy change adopted March 27, 1950.)*

**Freedom to Serve: A Report of the President's Committee on Equality of Treatment and Opportunity in the Armed Services* (Washington, 1950).

195

PROGRESS IN NEGRO EMPLOYMENT

The developments in the employment of Negroes at all levels were of sufficient interest for the prestigious Fortune *magazine to publish an article on the subject. Some of the material in the article was referred to in the majority report of the Senate Committee on Labor and Public Welfare on Senate bill S. 3368, but this article had a wider audience with a substantial proportion of business executives. Its publication in* Fortune *is in itself worthy of note.*

John A. Davis was a professor of political science at Lincoln University in Pennsylvania who had a Ford Foundation fellowship to work in the field of civil rights. He had previously been associated with the New York State Committee on Discrimination and the federal FEPC.

Negro Employment: A Progress Report

The history of Negro employment in the last decade shows an uneven but advancing line of progress. More than that, it is, strikingly, a history of unrealized fears. In that fact lies the hope for continued progress.

* * *

In the North, Negroes found acceptance on professional levels as chemists and engineers. As early as 1942, such firms as Western Electric in Kearny, New Jersey, General Electric in Schenectady, Curtiss-Wright and Bell Aircraft in Buffalo, Lockheed in Los Angeles, and International Harvester in Chicago were employing Negroes fairly and affording unsegregated access to eating, locker, toilet, and recreational facilities.

These advances were not always easy, and often required careful and even expensive preparation. A pioneer has been International Harvester Co., which since 1919 has followed a no-discrimination policy. Long ago International Harvester learned that the key to successful introduction of Negro personnel was the cooperation of its supervisors. In its Central Training School, International Harvester began an experiment in educating this middle-management group. In the classes company policy was stated not on a high moral tone but as an effort simply to hire the best-qualified persons regardless of race or color. Situations regarding the introduction of Negroes into work groups, problems of racial frictions, upgrading, etc., were frankly discussed. International Harvester deserves full credit for its intelligent approach, its forthright declarations, and its willingness to share its findings with other employers and the public.

It is in the South, however, that management faces the acid test. As the South goes through a new industrial boom, new plants by the hundreds are springing up along the Atlantic coast and in the Delta. If industry has the courage, it can lead a sociological revolution comparable to the breakup by the factory of the caste system in India. What is required is a simple declaration and practice of fair employment for all regardless of reprisal by bigots. During the last war examples of integrated work groups could be found in many places, such as Ingalls Shipbuilding in Georgia, Rheem

Manufacturing Co. and Higgins, Inc. (shipbuilding), in New Orleans, Bibb Manufacturing Co. in Columbus, Georgia, the Norfolk Navy Yard in Virginia, etc.

In opening new southern plants International Harvester again has shown the way. In 1948, when its Memphis works was opened, Fowler McCormick, then chairman of the board, announced that the company would hire Negroes at equal pay with whites and in equal work. Since it was a new plant, and no vested interests of prestige and status had been established, the move was possible. The plant today employs 2,400 production and maintenance workers, of whom about 650 are Negroes. All workers are paid equally and advanced on ability. Because of the upgrading of Negroes, several minor wildcat walkouts occurred at the start but there have been none since 1950.

Other corporations settling in Memphis have followed the example. Firestone Tire & Rubber, in its Memphis plant, today has about 600 Negroes of a total of 3,000 production workers. In fact, Negro workers at this plant became so secure that when the company at one time refused to rescind the suspension of several Negroes, they were able to start a wildcat walkout in which they were joined by white fellow workers.

The principal barrier to the spread of Negro employment in the South is, of course, the taboo of segregation. Yet the custom no longer has the strong legal and community sanction it once had. Segregation in industry as to eating, drinking, and toilet facilities is common only in the middle and Deep South. Segregation as to place of work is not required except in South Carolina, where a state law of doubtful constitutionality requires separate entrances, exits, and pay windows in textile plants.

At present "checkerboard" employment patterns (no segregation in work areas) exist in New Orleans at Haspel Brothers, Flintkote Co., Swift & Co., Chrysler, and International Harvester. Checkerboard policies can also be found at International Harvester in Louisville and Memphis, at Glenn Martin in Baltimore, and to a lesser degree at many other southern plants.

The employment of a growing number of Negroes at higher wages has meant a considerable boost to the economy of the South. Negroes have begun building better homes, buying cars, radios, televisions, better clothes, etc., so that southern merchants, some of whom had once sought to keep the Negro down, today are benefiting from this new prosperity.

* * *

In all, state FEPCs have investigated over 5,000 complaints (of which 70 per cent involved race, 16 per cent religion, 8 per cent national origin, and 6 per cent other causes), and yet public acceptance has been so high and conciliation so effective that only five public hearings against employers have been held to force compliance. Limited court action has been resorted to only four times; in one case *Railway Mail Association v. Corsi* the constitutionality of FEPC legislation was upheld by the Supreme Court as an exercise of the police power of the state.

In addition to state legislation, twenty-two municipalities (eleven in Ohio alone) have antidiscrimination ordinances, ranging from mere declarations of public policy as in Akron, to comprehensive laws establishing administrative bodies and providing penalties for violations, as in Minneapolis, Philadelphia, and Cleveland.

One measure of success is the praise that has come from business leaders representing forty-five U.S. corporations that have lived with the law. Such statements have been made public by the FEPC authorities in Connecticut, New Jersey, Philadelphia, Minneapolis and New York.

In the face of such testimonials the opposition to FEPC by such business organizations as the National Association of Manufacturers in Pennsylvania, the Chamber of Commerce in Ohio, and General Motors (which has a good record of fair employment) in Michigan, based on their contention that legislation would interfere with management's rights, appears as a "cultural lag." The basis of the free-enterprise system in America is the concept of free opportunity. It would appear to be good business to support the concept.

Some 1,200,000 Negroes belong to labor unions. In twenty-three unions, Negroes are national officers. The C.I.O. as a whole, the left-wing unions, and the United Mine Workers of America have excellent records on fair employment. C.I.O. has a national committee against discrimination, while several unions, such as the auto workers, steelworkers, and packing-house workers, maintain staffs on discrimination. The record of many A.F. of L. unions is distinctly bad, but some, like the ladies' garment workers, the plasterers and cement finishers, the painters, the hod carriers and common laborers' union, and in spots the longshoremen, are doing a better-than-average job.

A large number of labor unions do restrict job opportunities for Negroes. Eighteen unions (eleven A.F. of L. and seven independent) exclude Negroes by constitutional provisions, bylaws, or tacit consent. Nine others (seven A.F. of L. and two independent) organize Negroes in Jim Crow locals.

The worst offenders are the four railway brotherhoods and the switchmen's union. Almost as bad are the electrical workers, boilermakers, plumbers and pipe fitters, sheet-metal workers, and asbestos workers (all A.F. of L.), who not only have excluded Negroes but often have overtly prevented them from working in building crafts. The skilled building-trades unions have used their control of apprenticeship to restrict or bar Negroes. The electrical workers and the plumbers have used their control of municipal licensing boards to keep Negro mechanics out of their trade. (In some industrial work situations the electrical workers, the machinists, and the boilermakers have admitted Negroes.)

Clearly, management cannot hire Negroes who are prevented from qualifying in a trade, nor can it reform labor. The task of revising labor-union policies is one for labor and for government, especially where government protects rights of organization.

* * *

Negro resentment against present conditions in defense plants is mounting, principally because this defense expansion is taking place in the South. New plants, such as Lockheed's at Marietta, Georgia, re-establish old patterns. Discrimination is in force at the Atomic Energy Commission sites at Oak Ridge, Paducah, Savannah River, and the Tri-City area of Washington. These charges have been documented in a memorandum to the President by the Urban League and the National Association for the Advancement of Colored People.

In education (by which we hope to solve the race problem in America), the Negro teacher finds it hard to obtain a position above the grade-school level in the North and West. No great American university, with the exception of the University of Chicago, has for any significant period hired Negroes with professional status and tenure. Apart from the city colleges of New York, only two important American colleges, Oberlin and Haverford, have followed the example of Chicago. In fact there are more Negro professors in North Carolina than in all the colleges of the North and West; but they are, of course, in Negro colleges.

In the sales, clerical, and white-collar jobs, Negroes still find it extremely difficult to obtain jobs equal to their talents; only 5.7 per cent of non-farm colored persons work as clerks or salespersons while the corresponding percentage for white workers is 22.4 per cent. In aviation, the caste barrier on skilled jobs stands firm. Negro officers who flew Air Force and Navy planes are not allowed to fly U.S. commercial planes.

These are some of the tasks of a free America. Ours is a democratic and a resilient society. It has shown fundamental respect for human rights, and it has absorbed change in response to the will of the majority. Because America has demonstrated these capacities, the Negro has demonstrated overwhelming loyalty to his country and turned a deaf ear, as various studies have shown, to the wiles of the Communists. Yet we have to move forward on the employment job ahead. An enlightened management has the responsibility and an opportunity to lead the way.*

---

*John A. Davis, "Negro Employment: A Progress Report," *Fortune*, XLVI (July 1952), 102-162. Reprinted from *Fortune* magazine by special permission; © 1952 Time, Inc.

CHAPTER TWELVE

New Peaks of Confrontation

A demonstration in Selma, Alabama, before the famous Selma-to-Montgomery march of 1965. The demonstration became an increasingly effective tool in the hands of disciplined men and women, North and South, who sought to dramatize the plight of blacks in America, the oppressive effects of segregation, and the power of love. Demonstrators were not always successful in achieving their more immediate, specific goals, but they did awaken the conscience of the nation.

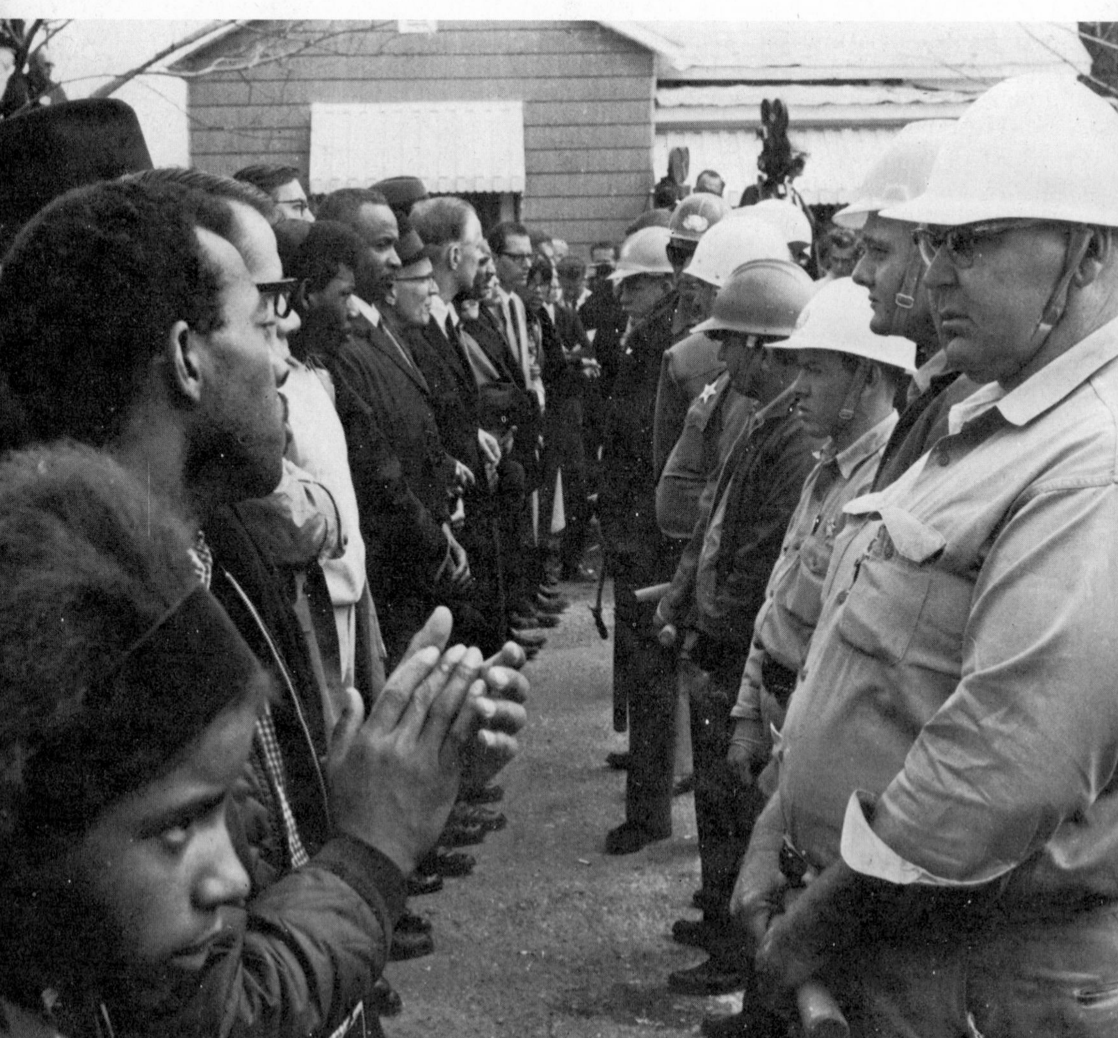

New Peaks of Confrontation

Inevitably, recent events appear to move with greater speed than those in the distant past. This was particularly true in judging the Negro's role in American history after 1954, yet in this instance the appearance and the reality coincided. The changes in attitudes and the incidence of significant events tended to accelerate with a swiftness that approached revolution. Louis Lomax, an experienced black journalist, called this the Negro revolt and the phrase invites comparison with the earlier revolution which shaped the United States from the thirteen colonies. There were differences: the eighteenth-century rebels sought separation while their twentieth-century counterparts have sought integration, but there were more important similarities. Negroes rejected white domination; the colonists British domination. Negroes wanted equal economic opportunities; so did the colonists. Negroes wanted full citizenship; so did the colonists. Negroes wanted relief from arbitrary law and arbitrary interpretation of law; so did the colonists. And the colonists produced a document which simply and eloquently expressed their principles. For blacks the Declaration of Independence was still a credo.

The events and attitude changes after 1954 were not without direction and purpose, although the very complexity of change sometimes made these obscure. A number of identifiable forces provided the thrust which brought about significant change, a revolution within the limits of law. It is not enough to identify institutional and mass forces, however, because change begins in the intellect and emotions, the minds and hearts of individuals communicating and communing together.

Beneath the accumulation of individual and group reactions to civil rights activity between 1954 and 1970, the momentum of history worked a ferment. Six forces can be isolated, but all are interconnected. The initial force was the Constitution itself as the Supreme Court began to read it in 1954. The desegregation decision of that year was a watershed which not only marked the actual beginning of the revolution in the Negro's assimilation, but delineated the path-breaking role which the Court was going to play in the process.

The next year the Court began to lay the groundwork for desegregation in education. It held fast to the determination that its decree would not be undermined by state postures like Virginia's "massive resistance," a phrase based on the doctrine of interposition, which held that a state could insert its sovereignty between the federal government and state citizens. By instructions to lower courts to maintain jurisdiction, the Court erected constitutional safeguards around the rights of all citizens to equal protection. When the Little Rock imbroglio reached the impasse brought on by the governor of Arkansas, the Court in a unanimous and moving decision (*Cooper* v. *Aaron,* 1958) made clear its dedication to the equal protection of the laws. The supreme law of the land, the Court concluded, presupposes "active support by state and local authorities" for compliance. "To withhold it, and indeed to use political power to try to paralyze the supreme Law, precludes the maintenance of our federal system as we have known and cherished it for one hundred and seventy years."

A second force was political in nature and form. Before 1954, two Democratic Presidents had in their own ways demonstrated concern and used the weight of their office for Negro rights as citizens. When Dwight D. Eisenhower was elected, Negroes questioned whether this concern and influence followed the office or the party and man. In Eisenhower the country had a pleasant, congenial President who chose not to confront the integration and equal opportunity issues until they were forced upon him. In the Little Rock explosion he was something less than forceful. Although he created two presidential equal rights committees, one on government contracts and one on government employment, they lacked sufficient authority to exercise their responsibilities adequately. The two civil rights bills which were passed during the Eisenhower administration received little support from the White House. The 1957 act created the Civil Rights Commission with limited authority to investigate and study deprivations of the right to vote, and the 1960 act strengthened the federal government's right to take into court certain abrogations of voting rights and made property destruction by fire or explosive a federal crime under specified conditions. This provision was an effort to stem the rash of bombings and fires which spread over the South and in northern cities in resistance to civil rights agitation.

The Kennedy years were brief in measured time, but within their span the President compacted an ineluctable policy. Soon after he entered the White House, he established the President's Committee on Equal Economic Opportunity, combining the two Eisenhower committees into one, and gave it sufficient authority for it to become an alert and persuasive instrument in opening up employment opportunities for Negroes. As chairman, Vice-President Lyndon B. Johnson gave it direction and spark. In another critical area, Kennedy had promised to prohibit housing discrimination by executive order, but the political balance of power in Congress caused him, like FDR before him, to delay it to the dismay of black leaders. Finally, in November 1962, he signed Executive Order #11063 prohibiting discrimination in all government-owned and operated housing as well as that for which there was to be government financing. In still another political stratagem, Kennedy designated Robert C. Weaver as the probable Secretary of Urban Affairs and Housing, but Congress rejected the new Cabinet post and its designee.

The total Kennedy commitment can be seen in many ways. He was the first President to address a special message to Congress in behalf of civil rights. During the Congressional debate over the civil rights bill in 1963, he encouraged Negro leaders in their plans to organize a march on Washington, met with them during that historic day, and issued a statement complimenting the marchers for their peaceful, disciplined performance. Without vacillation, Kennedy enforced the Supreme Court's desegregation decisions. After fruitless discussions and in the face of blatant opposition from the governors of Mississippi (1962) and Alabama (1963), he insisted upon the entrance of black students into state universities in compliance with court orders. Kennedy's legacy was the involvement of the entire Executive branch of the government in the pursuit of equal rights.

The tragedy of Kennedy's assassination served as a spur to his civil rights program, and President Johnson immediately and unequivocally dedicated himself to its implementation. Using skills which his long Congressional leadership had honed to a fine edge, Johnson fought the civil rights bill through the Congress and signed it in early July 1964. In the Senate, the fight was led by his own Vice-President-to-be, Hubert H. Humphrey, and the 1964 election campaign which followed hinged in some part upon their leadership in civil rights. The response of the electorate, with hardly a trace of white backlash, made it clear as of November 1964 that the majority of Americans endorsed the principles of civil rights and the obligation of the federal government to enforce them. The firm executive posture developed by Kennedy and enlarged by Johnson, taken with the four federal civil rights laws enacted between 1957 and 1965, created the second major force which propelled the mid-century Negro revolution.

The third force represented as much a break with the past as did the others. The Negro church had been less than dynamic in its participation in interracial activities, but within its walls ferment had been at work. Some of its younger ministers received their training in integrated northern universities and seminaries and returned to speak in measured tones about the church's responsibility for freedom. Some of its younger educated laypersons, especially in cities, were groping for some instrument of organization to take the lead in relieving the pressures of segregation. Older church members who had been passive but not unmoved did not obstruct the rising of the yeast.

The first outward sign came in 1955 from Montgomery, Alabama, where the Negro community organized in one short December weekend. The church was the catalyst and Martin Luther King, Jr., the agent in the bus boycott protesting segregated seating. The moral leadership of King and his ministerial colleagues in Montgomery symbolized the resurgence of the Negro church as a factor in the Negro revolution, a term which King himself was to use in describing the events between 1955 and 1963. The movement which King led grew out of the bedrock from which the church itself had sprung and took the name Southern Christian Leadership Conference (SCLC). By 1963 it represented some 85 organizations dedicated to purposeful Christian action for the abolition of segregation and discrimination. Its cornerstone, laid down with loving hands by King, was nonviolent action.

The renaissance of the Negro church as a channel for protest had repercussions which echoed in the sanctuaries of the white churches. White southern ministers who tried to extend the hand of fellowship to Negro brethren were peremptorily fired or insistently excused from their pulpits. Northern ministers began to speak up bravely and a few joined the marchers and the riders and the sitters-in to demonstrate their Christian convictions. The Catholic Church in Louisiana and elsewhere forthrightly desegregated its schools in the face of raucous opposition. But the greater impact of the Negro church's awakening fell on its young people and those of other churches around the land.

A revolution requires almost by definition young leadership and young followers and the Negro revolution was no exception. The young people who sprang to action as leaders and followers made up the fourth force which generated this mid-century revolution. Many who had toiled in the ranks for decades were pushed or gently moved aside as young men like King, James Farmer of the Congress of Racial Equality (CORE), and others formulated activist plans. The black young people fired the revolution with zeal and energy and hope.

The impetus which Negro youth gave the movement burst into the public eye in Greensboro, North Carolina, early in 1960 when college students there staged a sit-in at lunch counters in the town. Not only was this movement successful in Greensboro, but it set off a series of demonstrations at stores and shopping centers, beaches and swimming pools, restaurants, motels, and other places which accommodated the public. Presidential candidate Kennedy called the sit-in movement a sign that "the American spirit is coming alive again." Out of the sit-in movement came the Freedom Rides, church demonstrations, the silent marches, and eventually, in August 1963, the March on Washington.

These events were significant for several interrelated reasons. Most of the demonstrations were nonviolent, following the teachings of Martin Luther King. The participants were trained neither to flinch nor to strike back, no matter the violence that their presence encouraged. As a result, some of the demonstrators were subjected to merciless beatings and crude torment as they sat or marched or rode. Nonviolence exposed as never before the ineffectiveness and indisposition of local police authorities to handle crowds and protect their victims.

Of even greater importance than nonviolence, these demonstrations were channels for high-principled, enthusiastic young people who had heretofore had few opportunities to make their feelings known. Long before Greensboro, young Negroes had nervously and restlessly protested their inability to express themselves constructively and collectively. Individual expressions were not enough and Negro organizations were controlled by older men and women. The Greensboro incident loosed the bonds and students of both races soon joined the battle. The Student Non-Violent Coordinating Committee (SNCC) was quickly formed to coordinate demonstrations in the South and North. Interracial groups of students from northern colleges and universities traveled South to help the civil rights cause by instructing Negroes in voter registration procedures and explaining their rights under the law. Training centers for these students sprang up in various parts of the country to make sure that they would be prepared for their responsibilities. In 1963 several black organizations, consolidated as the Council of Federated Organizations (COFO), planned a statewide Mississippi campaign in

1964 with centers in various key cities. The objective was to create a broad base of interest and experience in local Negro groups from which stronger civil rights demands could be launched. In Meridian, there were classes in remedial reading, arithmetic, and sewing. The small library had books not generally available to rural southern Negroes, and all blacks were encouraged to try to register to vote. The COFO experiment, largely run by men and women in their twenties, reflected the important hold which the youth of both races had attained in a few short years. There were dangers; three young men who were working in Meridian were brutally murdered in June and others were harassed, arrested, threatened, and injured.

The rise of activism, generated in some part by black youths and their white counterparts, was in itself a force which forwarded the Negro revolution. Beginning with the Montgomery bus boycott, activism penetrated into almost every area of civil rights contention. The organized efforts by citizens and parents to implement the school desegregation decisions, as in Little Rock, were one part of the activist thrust. The Birmingham demonstrations of 1963 to break down lunch counter and job discrimination were still another. Black and white citizens in New York City, Cleveland, Milwaukee, Chicago, and points west protested by demonstration the murder of Medgar Evers, de facto segregation in education and housing, and, in the March on Washington, Congress's reluctance to pass a strong civil rights bill. Sitters-in embarrassed merchants, corporations, public officials, religious denominations, and educational institutions by their insistent demands for equal rights. Not all of the protests were well organized or well founded, but activism proved to be a powerful method to dramatize an issue, mobilize public support, and press a resisting group to accept an equal rights solution.

The sixth force in the Negro revolution was less conspicuous on the firing line or in the public press. Every revolutionary movement needs an intellectual rationale, reasoned expositions of aims and objectives which reach deep into history, logic, societal relations, psychology, and economics. The Negro revolution had its intelligentsia, too, and their works were an important construct in the accelerated movement toward equal rights. The NAACP brief on which the Supreme Court depended for its *Brown* v. *Board of Education* decision was a composite document, but it was not widely known. Individual statements which preceded and followed the decision were more instructive and more penetrating in their delineations. The literary form, particularly the novel, was the most pliant form by which black intellectuals could develop their positions. Chester Himes, Ralph Ellison, and James Baldwin exposed some of the most tender roots of interracial and intraracial relationships. Lorraine Hansberry and Baldwin used dramatic form for the same purpose. Essayists like Saunders Redding, Baldwin, and E. Franklin Frazier probed the deeper ramifications of segregation. Psychologists like Kenneth Clark and historians like John Hope Franklin, in more dispassionate form, revealed the blight of second-class citizenship. Journalists like Louis Lomax, ministers like King, and educators like Benjamin E. Mays seared the secular and spiritual soul of white and black America as they sought out truth in an interrelated but separate society.

The generalized consequence of these literary and scholarly efforts was an almost invulnerable argument favoring equal opportunity and equal rights. For the first time, Negro intellectuals were able to make a case that was at one with the historic principles and contemporary values of American society. Ellison admitted to confusion and contempt, Baldwin confessed hatred without vengeance, Clark's scientific explorations demonstrated the disability of segregation, Lomax examined activism, King preached loving strength, and Redding looked back at fear. The message was one of measured hope, but its expression varied from dark anger to frustrated optimism. As important as the message was the tone. All of the Negro intellectuals, with the exception of the Black Muslim leaders, grappled with racial and interracial dilemmas as American problems, the solutions to which lay within the democratic process. All of them in varying degrees urged both races to take more active roles, to stand up and be counted.

A few whites joined black intellectuals in their efforts to establish a basic rationale and the number increased with the years. Some, like Harry Ashmore of Little Rock, had been touched by the bitterness of battle, while others were sensitized by their own study and experience. Lillian Smith, Robert Penn Warren, Harry Golden, and Ralph McGill—Southerners all—stood head and shoulders above northern white liberals in their understanding exposition of interracial problems. Yet it was characteristic of black intellectuals to eschew close relationships with white liberals and even to castigate them for failures to take stronger positions and actions. This strain of suspicion ran through their literary efforts and became generalized throughout the Negro revolutionary movement, to the consternation and concern of the whites.

In sum, the black intellectuals provided a thoughtful base from which action groups operated in the years after the Supreme Court's 1954 decision. Theirs was an eyeball-to-eyeball confrontation with elemental human drives and frustrations explored through a wide variety of channels without a unanimity of conclusions. Their impact on America came not only from what they said, but from the highly respected ways in which they said it. Their leverage grew out of their command of their material. The literati enlarged their literary reputations because of their skill with the novel, essay, or dramatic form. The scholars earned tribute because of the integrity and quality of their work. In short, their talents transcended their race and this gave their message essential meaning.

Intellectuals and others concerned with race relations had to reckon increasingly with population factors. During the 1950's and 1960's the demographic scene reflected the broader fields of race relations in its volatility. By 1969 one quarter of the white and over half of the black people in the U.S. lived in cities. During the sixties 2.4 million blacks moved into and 2.1 million whites moved out of the urban centers. During the last three years of the decade the "black invasion" slowed down, but the rate of "white flight" tripled. This cityward migration of blacks tended to dramatize discriminatory practices based on race, particularly those in employment and housing.

Federal pressure to take corrective action for equal opportunities mounted steadily, and the Congress, under President Johnson's prodding, enacted two important statutes. The Voting Rights Act of 1965 suspended all literacy, knowledge, and character tests in states and counties where less than 50 percent of the voting-age population registered or voted in the November 1964 elections. In those areas where the process was slowed by local practice or ordinance, the Attorney General was empowered to authorize federal registrars to qualify voters. By December 1967, federal registrars in 58 southern counties had listed as eligible more than 158,000 voters, of whom about 5 percent were white. The number of Negroes registered by local officials in the South by the end of 1967 was well over 400,000. Every southern state had registered more than half of its black voting-age population; in Mississippi the pre-1965 registration of 6.7 percent had jumped to 59.8 percent by the close of 1967. Black registration still lagged behind that of whites, but the law was beginning to tell.

In the spring of 1968, Congress passed an open housing law which applied to nearly 80 percent of the nation's housing, and the U.S. Supreme Court followed in June with a sweeping decision, based on the Civil Rights Act of 1866, which prohibited racial discrimination in all sales and rentals of housing. The federal commitment was now clear, but the test of local implementation was still to come.

One device for making law meaningful has been the ballot box. In terms of elected officials alone, post-1965 Negro voters, with some white support, have been electing their own people to represent them. While the headlines told of the mayoralty victories of Carl Stokes in Cleveland and Richard Hatcher in Gary, of Charles Evers in Fayette, Mississippi, and of the bitterly close defeat of Councilman Thomas Bradley in Los Angeles in 1969, Negroes in state and local politics quietly ran for and won positions as city councilmembers, school board members, justices of the peace, and county supervisors. In Macon County, Alabama, Lucius D. Amerson was elected sheriff. In Grand Coteau, Louisiana, the voters elected a majority of three black councilmen who were faced with the gigantic problems of paving streets, installing sewers, modernizing the water system, and generally improving municipal services for all of the town's citizens. Black representation in the state legislatures and the Congress was upgraded with men and women who, like Georgia's Julian Bond and Brooklyn's Congresswoman Shirley Chisholm, were articulate, outspoken, and politically minded.

Black politicians, reflecting the sentiments of their constituents, were cool toward the nation's participation in the Vietnam war. In *Soul on Ice,* the fluent black nationalist Eldridge Cleaver observed that "the relationship between the genocide in Vietnam and the smiles of white men toward black Americans is a direct relationship. . . . The police do on the domestic level what the armed forces do on the international level: protect the way of life of those in power." Even blacks with more moderate views had difficulty understanding Vietnam. The nation seemed so quick to protect the rights of the South Vietnamese and so slow to do the same for black Americans at home.

As Vietnam added fuel to the fires of black aggressiveness, Stokely Carmichael contributed the strident slogan of "black power." Used first as a book title by Richard Wright in 1954, black power became a rallying cry for many blacks and an enigma for many whites. As a slogan, black power meant different things to different people. An Ohio welfare newsletter offered one homely definition: "A man who won't fight for his rights, don't have any." The black power cry called for unity to secure rights—particularly the right of decision wherever black people were affected—from the right to free choice of a President to that of the unhindered selection of a home. "Black power," asserted one advocate, "means everything for people who are black that white power means for people who are white."

Black power also stood, at first, for the exclusion of whites. "History has proven," wrote one black radical, "that there are almost no real white allies." Those whites who sought to work with blacks found themselves ostracized and then excluded from organizations like SNCC and CORE. But as the black nationalists became more revolutionary in outlook, the barriers of exclusion began to lower. The Black Panthers in 1969 appeared to change their stance and welcome white ideological brothers and sisters in search of a revolutionary method. "Black racism," said Panther chairman Bobby Seale, "is just as bad as white racism." This move back toward alliance across race lines could be either a bellwether for black radicals or just another instance of fracturing the nascent unity of the black power movement.

The growing cohesion among blacks gained strength from the pride in blackness, the rejection of white racism, the emphasis on black culture, and the striving for economic independence, all of which were symptomatic of the new "oneness." Yet the bitter division among the leadership told of wide cracks in the unifying effort. The split developed ostensibly over the technique of nonviolence, endorsed by men like Martin Luther King, Jr., Roy Wilkins, and Whitney Young, Jr., and rejected by Stokely Carmichael, Malcolm X, Eldridge Cleaver, H. Rap Brown, James Forman, and Nathan Hare. This issue obscured a bitter power struggle. Those who lined up for nonviolence generally had the ear of white politicians, foundations and other sources of funds, and large black and white followings. They were Negroes who had made it in the black and white worlds. Those who disparaged nonviolence were blocked from these channels and sought power by skillful exploitation of issues and by discrediting as Uncle Toms those who worked with the white establishment. On both sides, the leaders were able, magnetic, and intelligent, but the divisive character of their leadership hurt the drive for racial unity.

The brutal assassinations of Malcolm X and Martin Luther King removed the most respected men in each camp and set back the prospect for reconciliation. The outburst which followed King's murder loosed pent-up emotions which failed to sustain a significant thrust for unification or, at the least, mutual understanding. To some extent, these repercussions represented a generational split which further complicated efforts at unity.

Black youths who turned "Afro" in dress and manner, rejected the slow movement of integration, joined the Black Panthers, presented black demands to college and university authorities, and met in black nationalist conventions were a puzzle to their parents' generation, though probably a source of pride, too. The elders could appreciate the posture, even if they could not comprehend the content, of the young peoples' affirmations. "That *soul* you are always talking about didn't grow in a juke box," a middle-aged Negro admonished young black militants. "It was a long time a-growing and . . . that soul is warm and vibrant with humanity, with compassion, with love."

Soul was one of the credible distinctions which young militants emphasized. It was "more than a music style, a way of walking-that-walk or talking-that-talk." It was "an inner drive" which might manifest itself in walking or talking, but on a more profound level it "leads one knowingly in a more meaningful direction than synthetic capitalist Christian materialism. . . ."

Whether or not all blacks called it soul or defined it in that way, the black movement had an inner drive which was unique. Its immediate objective, in the words of a young actress, was "to view the world, blackly, . . . that is, purge yourself of all those years of white indoctrination and white ideology." This was the wellspring which produced movements for black theater and black art, black capitalism and black curriculum, black politics and a black nation-state.

Of all these activities, the black student movement probably received more publicity than any other, particularly during 1968 and 1969. The pivotal campus was that of San Francisco State College, where radical activity among black and white faculty members and students split the institution into warring camps and immobilized it.

The inspiration and the legacy of San Francisco State transcended race lines as campus disruptions took on a pattern, whether the issue was black demands, Vietnam, or student power. Administrators at Brandeis and the University of Michigan used a deft touch to turn black wrath into constructive programs. When Cornell administrators tried the same approach, black students occupied a building and marched out carrying guns. At Columbia, blacks and whites split early in the buildings-occupation phase of their operation, and the whites moved alone down the road toward total campus disruption. In such black institutions as Howard University, administrators faced angry radicals who were demanding that the institutions declare their independence of white control. The climax came in 1970 and 1971 at two disparate institutions, Jackson State College in Mississippi and the Attica Correctional Facility in New York, when controlling whites killed demanding blacks after frightening and fatiguing confrontations.

The explosion of the late 1960's and early 1970's over the issue of racial equality crossed economic, educational, and generational lines in the black community. It was fused by an intensification of race pride and resentment sharply etched by generations of black progress and white disdain. Centuries of second-class citizenship had eroded black trust in gradual methods and white promises. From this point of view, racism permeated white society and made it incapable of an integrated justice. Blacks argued that this racism must be eradicated, but until it was they would be the interpreters of things black. "It is stupid and unmanly," author Larry Neal stated, "to expect the 'other fellow' to tell our story." Indeed, it was time for their story to be told in their own words and in their own way. It was time for whites to listen—and to hear.

196

WITH ALL DELIBERATE SPEED

The United States Supreme Court rendered two separate Brown *v.* Board of Education *decisions, one in 1954 and the second in 1955. Both were written for a unanimous Court by the Chief Justice, Earl Warren. The first decided the principle that segregated schools were a denial of equal protection of the laws, guaranteed by the Fourteenth Amendment. The second, with the famous phrase "with all deliberate speed," laid down the bases for the transition to integrated education. As the first opinion states, these cases had a long history, including a reargument for clarification of the history of public education and the relevance of the Fourteenth Amendment to public education.*

These opinions actually cover several cases, coming from Kansas, South Carolina, Virginia, and Delaware, but they carry the name of the first case alphabetically by name. A separate case in the District of Columbia had a separate opinion since the District is governed by Congress. The Warren statements have been attacked as sociological rather than legal in basis. Whatever the merits of this argument, it is sufficient to point out that a great number of court decisions at various levels have a socio-legal nature, most noticeably in this instance the very case which this Court overturned, Plessy *v.* Ferguson.

The Court delayed an implementing decree in its first decision until it had further time to study the alternatives and the effect of its 1954 opinion. Its 1955 decision outlined the general steps required for implementation.

BROWN V. BOARD OF EDUCATION OF TOPEKA (KANSAS)

The plaintiffs contend that segregated public schools are not "equal" and cannot be made "equal," and that hence they are deprived of the equal protection of the laws. Because of the obvious importance of the question presented, the Court took jurisdiction. Argument was heard in the 1952 Term, and reargument was heard this Term on certain questions propounded by the Court.

Reargument was largely devoted to the circumstances surrounding the adoption of the Fourteenth Amendment in 1868. It covered exhaustively consideration of the Amendment in Congress, ratification by the states, then existing practices in racial segregation, and the views of proponents and opponents of the Amendment. This discussion and our own investigation convince us that, although these sources cast some light, it is not enough to resolve the problem with which we are faced. At best, they are inconclusive. The most avid proponents of the post-War Amendments undoubtedly intended them to remove all legal distinctions among "all persons born or naturalized in the United States." Their opponents, just as certainly, were antagonistic to both the letter and the spirit of the Amendments and wished them to have the most limited effect. What others in Congress and the state legislatures had in mind cannot be determined with any degree of certainty.

An additional reason for the inconclusive nature of the Amendment's history, with respect to segregated schools, is the status of public education at that time. In the South, the movement toward free common schools, supported by general taxation, had not yet taken hold. Education of white children was largely in the hands of private groups. Education of Negroes was almost nonexistent, and practically all of the race were illiterate. In fact, any education of Negroes was forbidden by law in some states. Today, in contrast, many Negroes have achieved outstanding success in the arts and sciences as well as in the business and professional world. It is true that public school education at the time of the Amendment had advanced further in the North, but the effect of the Amendment on Northern States was generally ignored in the congressional debates. Even in the North, the conditions of public education did not approximate those existing today. The curriculum was usually rudimentary; ungraded schools were common in rural areas; the school term was but three months a year in many states; and compulsory school attendance was virtually unknown. As a consequence, it is not surprising that there should be so little in the history of the Fourteenth Amendment relating to its intended effect on public education.

In the first cases in this Court construing the Fourteenth Amendment, decided shortly after its adoption, the Court interpreted it as proscribing all state-imposed discriminations against the Negro race. The doctrine of "separate but equal" did not make its appearance in this Court until 1896 in the case of *Plessy v. Ferguson* involving not education but transportation. American courts have since labored with the doctrine for over half a century. In this Court, there have been six cases involving the "separate but equal" doctrine in the field of public education. In more recent cases, all on the graduate school level, inequality was found in that specific benefits enjoyed by white students were denied to Negro students of the same educational qualifications. In none of these cases was it necessary to re-examine the doctrine to grant relief to the Negro plaintiff.

* * *

In approaching this problem, we cannot turn the clock back to 1868 when the Amendment was adopted, or even to 1896 when *Plessy v. Ferguson* was written. We must consider public education in the light of its full development and its present place in American life throughout the Nation. Only in this way can it be determined if segregation in public schools deprives these plaintiffs of the equal protection of the laws.

Today, education is perhaps the most important function of state and local governments. Compulsory school attendance laws and the great expenditures for education both demonstrate our recognition of the importance of education to our democratic society. It is required in the performance of our most basic public responsibilities, even service in the armed forces. It is the very foundation of good citizenship. Today it is a principal instrument in awakening the child to cultural values, in preparing him for later professional training, and in helping him to adjust normally to his environment. In these days, it is doubtful that any child may reasonably be expected to succeed in life if he is denied the opportunity of an education. Such an opportunity, where the state has undertaken to provide it, is a right which must be made available to all on equal terms.

We come then to the question presented: Does segregation of children in public schools solely on the basis of race, even though the physical facilities and other "tangible" factors may be equal, deprive the children of the minority group of equal educational opportunities? We believe that it does.

In *Sweatt v. Painter* in finding that a segregated law school for Negroes could not provide them equal educational opportunities, this Court relied in large part on "those qualities which are incapable of objective measurement but which make for greatness in a law school." In *McLaurin v. Oklahoma State Regents* the Court, in requiring that a Negro admitted to a white graduate school be treated like all other students, again resorted to intangible considerations: ". . . his ability to study, to engage in discussions and exchange views with other students, and, in general, to learn his profession." Such considerations apply with added force to children in grade and high schools. To separate them from others of similar age and qualifications solely because of their race generates a feeling of inferiority as to their status in the community that may affect their hearts and minds in a way unlikely ever to be undone. The effect of this separation on their educational opportunities was well stated by a finding in the Kansas case by a court which nevertheless felt compelled to rule against the Negro plaintiffs:

> "Segregation of white and colored children in public schools has a detrimental effect upon the colored children. The impact is greater when it has the sanction of the law; for the policy of separating the races is usually interpreted as denoting the inferiority of the negro group. A sense of inferiority affects the motivation of a child to learn. Segregation with the sanction of law, therefore, has a tendency to [retard] the educational and mental development of negro children and to deprive them of some of the benefits they would receive in a racial[ly] integrated school system."

What ever may have been the extent of psychological knowledge at the time of *Plessy v. Ferguson,* this finding is amply supported by modern authority. Any language in *Plessy v. Ferguson* contrary to this finding is rejected.

We conclude that in the field of public education the doctrine of "separate but equal" has no place. Separate educational facilities are inherently unequal. Therefore, we hold that the plaintiffs and others similarly situated for whom the actions have been brought are, by reason of the segregation complained of, deprived of the equal protection of the laws guaranteed by the Fourteenth Amendment.*

**Brown v. Board of Education of Topeka* [*Kansas*], 347 U.S., 483, 1954

197

A DEMAND FOR DYNAMIC LEADERSHIP

After the 1954 decision came anticlimax. The implementation of the decision was slow and progress toward equal rights seemed to move at a tortoise's pace. This analysis of the period, written in 1960, pulls no punches in its assessment. The swift acceleration of crises and their solutions after 1960 lend credence to this analysis while, at the same time, blunting some of its criticisms with the perspective of time. The NAACP has taken steps to revitalize its program; new leaders have been welcomed in the top hierarchy; and some student groups have measured their zeal with pragmatism. Nevertheless, this is an exciting document of its time.

Louis E. Lomax is a freelance magazine and television writer and author. His book, The Negro Revolt, *published several years after this article, includes portions of it.*

This new gospel of the American Negro is rooted in the theology of desegregation; its major prophets are Christ, Thoreau, Gandhi, and Martin Luther King. But its missionaries are several thousand Negro students who—like Paul, Silas, and Peter of the early Christian era—are braving incalculable dangers and employing new techniques to spread the faith. It is not an easy faith, for it names the conservative Negro leadership class as sinners along with the segregationists. Yet, this new gospel is being preached by clergymen and laymen alike wherever Negroes gather.

* * *

The demonstrators have shifted the desegregation battle from the courtroom to the market place, and have shifted the main issue to one of individual dignity, rather than civil rights. Not that civil rights are unimportant—but, as these students believe, once the dignity of the Negro individual is admitted, the debate over his right to vote, attend public schools, or hold a job for which he is qualified becomes academic.

* * *

This revolt, swelling under ground for the past two decades, means the end of the traditional Negro leadership class. Local organization leaders were caught flat-footed by the demonstrations; the parade had moved off without them. In a series of almost frantic moves this spring, they lunged to the front and shouted loud, but they were scarcely more than a cheering section—leaders no more. The students completed their bold maneuver by jabbing the leadership class in its most vulnerable spot: the Southern schoolteachers. Many of these, as the Norfolk *Journal and Guide* put it, "were ordered to stop the demonstrations or else!" Most Negro school administrators kept silent on the matter; a few of them, largely heads of private colleges, supported the students; while others—notably Dr. H. C. Trenholm of Alabama State College—were forced by white politicians to take action against the students. As a Negro reporter from New York, I talked with scores of Southern Negro leaders and they admitted without exception that the local leadership class was in dire difficulty.

National leadership organizations fared only slightly better. The NAACP rushed its national youth secretary, Herbert Wright, into the area to conduct "strategy and procedure" conferences for the students. Lester Granger, the executive director of the Urban League, issued a statement saying the demonstrations were "therapeutic for those engaged in them and a solemn warning to the nation at large" —this despite the fact that, in Mr. Granger's words, "the League does not function in the area of public demonstrations."

The NAACP does not always move with such swiftness when local groups, some of them laced with NAACP members, set off independent attacks on racial abuse. The Montgomery bus boycott is a classic case in point. But the impact of these new student demonstrations was such that the NAACP was forced to support the students or face a revolt by its Southern rank and file. This does not impeach the NAACP's motives for entering the demonstrations—its motives and work have the greatest merit—but it does illustrate the reversal of the power flow within the Negro community.

"The demonstrations are not something we planned," NAACP public-relations director Henry Moon told me. "The students moved on their own. We didn't know what was going on until it happened. However, it should be kept in mind that many of the students involved are NAACP people."

The NAACP's frank admission that it had no part in planning a demonstration against segregation that resulted in upwards of a thousand Negroes being jailed—coupled with its prompt defense of the demonstrators—marks the end of the great era of the Negro leadership class: a half-century of fiercely guarded glory, climaxed by the historic school desegregation decision of 1954, during which the NAACP by dint of sheer militancy, brains, and a strong moral cause became the undisputed commander-in-chief of the Negro's drive for equality. These demonstrations also ended a two-century-long *modus vivendi* based on the myth of the Negro leader.

* * *

There were three chief prerequisites for becoming a Negro leader: (1) approbation of the white community, (2) literacy (real or assumed), and (3) some influence over the Negro masses. Each community spawned an array of "professors," "doctors," (not medical men), "preachers," "bishops," "spokesmen" who sat down at the segregated arbitration table and conducted business in the name of the Negro masses.

These leaders received their credentials and power both from the white community and from the Negro masses, who stood humble before their white-appointed leaders. This status was heady stuff for the early twentieth-century Negro elite, many of whom could remember the snap of the master's whip, and they began to function as a social class. As a result, three generations of educated Negroes dreamed of an equal but separate America in which white power spoke only to black power and black power spoke only to God, if even to Him.

* * *

The decade of the 'fifties was an incredible era for the Negro leadership class, particularly for the NAACP. That the NAACP hung together at all is a monument to its vitality as well as to the effectiveness of its muffling curtain.

First off, by suing for school integration the NAACP immobilized the majority of the Negro leadership class. The entire structure of the Negro community was designed to function in a separate but equal America. Negro newspapers, in addition to being protest organs, were the social Bibles of Negro society. They had their "400" and a list of the year's best-dressed women. The Negro church was ofttimes more Negro than church. Negro businesses depended upon the concept of a Negro community for survival (as late as 1958 Negro businessmen in Detroit criticized the NAACP for holding its annual convention at a "white" downtown hotel, which meant that local Negro merchants failed to benefit from the gathering). The dilemma of the Negro teacher was even more agonizing. If Negroes really meant business about integration, then it was obvious that the Negro leadership class could remain leaders only by working to put themselves out of business.

* * *

Nevertheless, these were glamorous years for successful Negroes; almost all got the title of Negro leader. Their names and faces appeared on ads endorsing soap, cigarettes, whiskeys, and ladies' personal items. Adam Clayton Powell endured in Congress, always reminding his flock that, some ten years earlier, he was the first Negro to call the late Senator Theodore Bilbo, of Mississippi, a "cesspool"; Paul Robeson called a press conference and announced that Negroes would not fight with America against Russia; Jackie Robinson took a day off from the Brooklyn Dodgers to assure the House Un-American Activities Committee that Mr. Robeson was wrong. Indeed we would fight. Joe Louis, who had dispelled doubts during the dark days of Dunkirk by proclaiming, "America will win 'cause God is on our side," made an all-expense-paid visit to a Washington, D.C., courtroom and embraced the defendant, James Hoffa, in full view of the jury, peppered with Negroes. Father Divine announced that he brought about integration, and he had a white wife to prove it!

These incidents—some humorous, some tragic, but all of them significant—had a grave impact on the Negro leadership class; a less stout-hearted group would have exploded from so much internal combustion. But it was the tense drama of school integration that provided the bailing wire for a show of unity.

I was there and it was a moving and unforgettable experience to see Negro students at Clinton, Sturgis, Clay, and Little Rock dodge bricks as they raced to and from school under armed guard. It was a magnificent hour for these fortuitously elite youngsters, many of whom became international heroes. But few of us lost sight of the Negro masses in these cities. They were still called "Jim," "Mary," "Aunt Harriet," and "Uncle Job"; they had to buy clothes they were not allowed to try on; their homes were searched by police without warrants; their heads were bloodied, their jobs threatened if they dared protest. They darted in and out of drug and department stores where they dared not sit down. They were denied free access to the polls, and if they received a just day in court it was usually when all parties concerned were Negroes.

Despite the march of well-scrubbed, carefully selected Negro students into previously all-white schools, it was crystal clear that the fundamental question of the Negro's dignity as an individual had not been resolved. The glory was the NAACP's and nobody begrudged it. Yet, there was a widespread doubt that a nationally directed battle of attrition that took so long and cost so much to bring so little to so few would ever get to the heart of the issue.

* * *

The curtain had begun to lift; it had achieved a great good, for it had produced a facade of unity; yet it had cloaked some terrible wrongs, including the smothering of home-grown, local Negro leaders who, even then, sensed the restlessness of the masses. The Reverend Dr. Martin Luther King, Jr., was the lone successful exception, and even he came into international prominence mainly because the NAACP refused to help the Montgomery bus boycotters when they at first demanded something less than full integration.

* * *

Little Rock kept the NAACP in the foreground, while a near-fatal stiletto wound at the hands of a crazed Harlem woman—and internal difficulties with his own Montgomery Association—rendered Dr. King almost inactive for some eighteen months. But this year, Dr. King moved to Atlanta and began to give the lion's share of his time to the Southern Christian Leadership Council. Mr. Wilkins was on hand and the NAACP appeared as co-sponsor when the Council launched a South-wide voting drive on behalf of the Negro masses.

Congress was locked in a civil-rights debate that we all knew would culminate in some kind of legislation. Both Dr. King and Mr. Wilkins were on hand backstage as liberal congressmen planned their moves.

* * *

Negroes, particularly the youth, were restless; they were tired of compromises, piecemeal legislation, and token integration which, as Martin Luther King phrased it, "is a new form of discrimination covered up with certain niceties and complexities." A small but growing segment of the Negro population had joined a Muslim faith that preaches the superiority of the black man and the imminent destruction of the white man. Then there is the matter of Africa: hardly a week passes that that awakening giant's cries for "Free DOOM" don't ring out over the radio and television into the ears of American Negroes—ashamed, as they most certainly are, that they are still oppressed. The law, particularly in the South, was against them; but for the militant young people this was the time for all good Negroes to be in jail.

* * *

When I talked to the students and their mass supporters I heard them quote the *Wall Street Journal,* of all things, to show that they had hit the segregationists in the pocketbook. I also discovered that in March five Southern cities had already yielded to the demands of the demonstrators and were serving Negroes at lunch counters without incident. Eighteen other cities had interracial committees working to resolve the matter. In each case the students have made it plain that they will not accept segregation in any form.

But neither the students nor their real supporters dwelt unduly on such practical results. For them, individually and as a group, the victory came when they mustered the courage to look the segregationists in the face and say, "I'm no longer afraid!"

The genius of the demonstrations lies in their spirituality; in their ability to enlist every Negro, from the laborer to the leader, and inspire him to seek suffering as a badge of honor. By employing such valid symbols as singing, praying, reading Gandhi, quoting Thoreau, remembering Martin Luther King, preaching Christ, but most of all by suffering themselves—being hit by baseball bats, kicked, and sent to jail—the students set off an old-fashioned revival that has made integration an article of faith with the Negro masses who, like other masses, are apathetic toward voting and education.

Now the cook, the maid, the butler, and the chauffeur are on fire with the new faith. For the first time since slavery the South is facing a mass revolt against segregation. There is no total explanation for what has happened. All I know is that as I talked with the participants I realized that people were weary of the very fact of segregation. They were no longer content "to let the NAACP do it"; they wanted to get into the fight and they chose the market place, the great center of American egalitarianism, not because it had any

Joy and a sense of purpose are reflected in the faces and gestures of Martin Luther King and several youngsters at Marion, Alabama, in February 1965. The Civil Rights leader has just been released from jail at nearby Selma, where he was sparking voter registration drives.

overwhelming significance for them but because it was there—accessible and segregated. Tomorrow—and they all believe there will be a tomorrow—their target will be something else.

Few of the masses who have come to the support of these students realize that in attacking segregation under the banner of idealism they are fighting a battle they refused for five years to enter in the name of legalism. But there is a twinkle in the Southern Negro's eye. One gets the feeling that he is proud, now that he has come to full stature and has struck out with one blow against both segregation and the stifling control of Negro leaders.

In all truth, the Negro masses have never been flattered by the presence of these leaders, many of whom—justifiably or not—they suspected were Judas goats. The Negro masses will name leaders and will give them power and responsibility. But there will never again be another class of white-oriented leaders such as the one that has prevailed since 1900.*

198

EQUALITY NOW

The evidence of an insistent, no-holds-barred drive for civil rights by young people surrounded and permeated the equal rights movement, but what of the older, more circumspect leaders? Benjamin E. Mays, scholar and educator, has long been a respected name on both sides of the Mason-Dixon line. President of Morehouse College, a component of Atlanta University, Mays has been neither an extremist nor an "Uncle Tom." His thoughtful statement, placed in the perspective of autobiographical history, suggests the depth and the extent of the Negro revolution, as of 1960.

A PLEA FOR STRAIGHT TALK BETWEEN THE RACES

Many well-meaning intelligent people have argued since the May 17, 1954, decision of the United States Supreme Court outlawing segregation in public schools that communication between the races has broken down. They contend that, as a result, the racial situation in the South has grown worse. The plain truth is that, up to a few years ago, Negroes and white people in the South never had honest communication.

Honest communication is built on truth and integrity and upon respect of the one for the other. It is true that, for decades upon decades, Negroes and white people have talked to each other. But it was conversation between a "superior" and an "inferior," a "man" and a "boy," and conversation between "master" and "servant." In this relationship the truth could seldom, if ever, emerge.

For nearly a century the South made itself believe that Negroes and white people were really communicating. So convinced of this

*The Negro Revolt Against the Negro Leaders" by Louis Lomax from *Harper's Magazine*, June 1960. Copyright © 1960 by Louis Lomax. Reprinted by permission of Paul R. Reynolds, Inc., 599 Fifth Avenue, New York, N.Y. 10017.

were the white Southerners that they almost made the nation believe that they, and only they, knew the mind of the Southern Negro. They were sure that the Negro was satisfied with segregation and with his subordinate role in American life. If only the Communists, the Yankees, and the N.A.A.C.P. would leave the Negro alone, they said, he would live happily forever within the confines of legal segregation. All the Negro wanted was equality within the segregation pattern.

The fallacy in this argument lies in the fact that it was based on falsehood from the beginning. White people got their information from two main sources: one source was their cooks, maids, and chauffeurs. These servants wanted to hold their jobs, and so they told their white employers what they wanted to hear—the Negro is happy with segregation. Most of the white people of the South—and the North, too, for that matter—have never known the cultured and trained Negro. The white South's other source of information was equally deceptive. Many Negro leaders led white Southerners to believe that if the impossible doctrine of separate but equal could be attained—separate schools, but equal; separate jobs, but equal; separate hospitals and recreational facilities, but equal; separate transportation and separate eating establishments, but all equal—Negroes would be satisfied. Many of these Negro leaders courted the favor of the whites either because they were economically dependent upon them or feared that unfortunate economic and physical consequences would follow if they told white people the truth. If what is communicated is false, it can hardly be called communication.

Let me give one illustration. In 1942 a group of Southern Negro leaders met in Durham, North Carolina, to draw up a manifesto in which Southern Negroes would speak plainly to Southern whites, setting forth the aims and aspirations of the Negro people. It was a magnificent document except for one thing. We did not speak with complete candor. Considerable time was spent trying to decide whether we should say in that manifesto that we wanted to see legal segregation abolished in every area of American life. Those of us who wanted to speak with complete honesty on this point were overruled. Every Negro who met in Durham was opposed to legal segregation and wanted it abolished. But we didn't say it. Did we communicate the truth to the white South? Nevertheless, the manifesto was worth while, because out of this meeting came the Southern Regional Council, which in recent years has declared itself in favor of the abolition of a segregated society and is doing magnificient work in this time of crisis.

Negro members of the Commission on Interracial Cooperation, which was the forerunner of the Southern Regional Council, never did advocate the abolition of segregation. This is not to reflect discredit on the commission; it did a job that needed to be done, but honest communication hardly ever prevailed. I recall vividly a discussion held by Negro members of the Regional Council after one of their state meetings. They all admitted that they did not say what was in their hearts and minds. It was plainly acknowledged that if their true desires about the abolition of segregation had been expressed, the meeting would have been broken up and further meetings would have been impossible. The two races met and talked about what they thought was expedient. At that time, and up to about a decade ago, Negro-white relations were so sensitive that Negroes dared not challenge the institution of segregation. No Negro dared to advocate its abolition publicly. Negroes were hoping against hope that the "separate" would someday be made "equal."

* * *

We are now beginning to communicate without hypocrisy and without fear. The May 17, 1954, decision of the United States Supreme Court cleared the air for honesty between the races. The Negroes' contacts in wartime and through travel, and the uprising of suppressed peoples everywhere, have also helped to clear the air. Negroes do not wish to be branded as inferiors by being segregated, and they want to walk the earth as human beings with dignity. This idea was beautifully expressed by the Negro college students in Atlanta when they said, in "An Appeal for Human Rights": "We will use every legal and nonviolent means at our disposal to end segregation."

* * *

The demonstrations will continue, and the goals the students seek will be achieved. Their cause is just. Enlightened public opinion is sympathetic. Both political parties in their platforms approved the students' method of protest. The Negro students are determined to be free. Just before a thousand students of the six Atlanta Negro colleges marched through Atlanta to the Wheat Street Baptist Church, in defiance of state officials' threats and in celebration of the sixth anniversary of the Supreme Court decisions, they sang: "We will be free, We will be free, We will be free someday, Deep in our hearts, We will be free, We will be free someday." After they assembled in the Wheat Street Baptist Church, they sang: "That old Negro, He ain't what he used to be." For the first time since Emancipation, Negro youths are willing and proud to be arrested and serve time in jail for a cause they believe to be just.

Has communication broken down? The old hypocritical kind of communication between the races has broken down, and that is good. We can now build good human relations on truth, honesty, and sincerity.

Has progress in race relations been set back, as the conservatives claim? Not at all. I am convinced that as I travel throughout the South today I experience more friendly feeling toward me and receive more decent treatment than at any other time in my sixty years. I have never before felt so much like a free human being in the South as I do today.*

---

*Benjamin E. Mays, "A Plea for Straight Talk Between the Races," *The Atlantic Monthly*, December 1960, pp. 85–86. Copyright © 1960 by Benjamin E. Mays. Reprinted with permission of the author.

199

DISCRIMINATION IN THE 60'S

The Civil Rights Commission was established by law in 1957 and four years later submitted a massive report on its investigations of discrimination in voting, education, employment, housing, and police misconduct. This excerpt is the Commission's evaluation of President Eisenhower's Committee on Government Contracts, chaired by the Vice-President, Richard M. Nixon. Under President Kennedy, this committee was combined with another Eisenhower committee to form the Committee on Equal Employment Opportunity. The new committee was armed with authority to take direct action in cases which came to its attention, or which it uncovered, and to review compliance. In its first case in the spring of 1961, the new committee enunciated a "plan for progress" with a major aviation manufacturing company with a plant in Marietta, Ga., and this became the basis of future agreements with major government contractors.

Discrimination in Employment

When the President's Committee terminated activities, despite its many accomplishments, the goal of equal opportunity in employment by government contractors was far from attainment. This Commission's investigations in three cities—Atlanta, Baltimore, and Detroit—and a Commission hearing in Detroit revealed that in most industries studied, patterns of Negro employment by federal contractors conformed to local industrial employment patterns. In the automotive industry, for example, even though each of the three manufacturers contacted had adopted a companywide policy of nondiscrimination, employment patterns varied from city to city. In Detroit, Negroes constituted a substantial proportion—from 20 to 30 per cent—of the total work force. Although their representation in "nontraditional" jobs was slight, all companies employed them in all classifications other than management positions, and one company employed Negroes in administrative and management jobs as well. In Baltimore, each of the companies employed Negroes only in production work and not above the semiskilled level—as assemblers, repairmen, inspectors, and material handlers. In Atlanta, the two automobile assembly plants contracted employed no Negroes in assembly operations. Except for one driver of an inside power truck, all Negro employees observed were engaged in janitorial work—sweeping, mopping, or carrying away trash. Lack of qualified applicants cannot account for the absence of Negroes from automotive assembly jobs in Atlanta. Wage rates are relatively high for the locality and the jobs are in great demand. The work is at most semiskilled and educational requirements are extremely low (present employees averaging a third-grade education).

* * *

Although the federal nondiscrimination program may not have been effective in substantially increasing the over-all employment of Negroes, or the numbers employed above unskilled or semiskilled levels, the President's Committee did lay the groundwork for some advances. It established the machinery necessary for implementation of the nondiscrimination provision. It also publicized and, through education and persuasion, made some headway in selling the program to those responsible for its implementation. Through direct negotiation with government contractors, the Committee often brought about the opening of new job opportunities for Negroes, particularly in office and clerical, technical, and professional positions, and occasionally it opened new training opportunities as well. As a direct result of such negotiations, the automotive industry in Detroit first hired Negro office clerical employees about 3 years ago. Similarly, persuasion by Committee representatives resulted last year in the employment of Negroes for the first time by a large chemical company located in an all-white community near Detroit.

But such efforts were not always successful. The Committee lacked authority, it had only a vague charter, and its program was replete with weaknesses and loopholes. One of the most commonly voiced criticisms of the program concerned the inability of the applicant for employment to ascertain whether a company discriminating against him was a government contractor. The required notices "in conspicuous places" were not always helpful. Applicants often do not apply for employment at a plant, but go instead to a local public employment office, a recruitment source commonly used by government contractors. Such offices were often unable to determine which companies were current government contractors as no current and comprehensive list of such contractors was available. Thus employment offices could not effectively discharge their obligation "to cooperate with . . . appropriate agencies of the government in their efforts to secure compliance with nondiscrimination clauses in government contracts,"—though they might refer to the President's Committee any complaints they received of discrimination on the part of government contractors.

The complaint process suffered to some extent from a lack of uniform procedures among the contracting agencies in spite of the Committee's efforts at "standardization." More serious was the fact that by the time the complaint was settled, a job discriminatorily denied might well have ceased to exist. This was common in the construction industry. Perhaps this was inevitable since the Committee was concerned more with developing broad employment policies than with specific discriminatory acts, since it lacked enforcement powers, and since "negotiation, conciliation, and persuasion" are by their nature slow. Another difficulty was the division of authority between the contracting agencies and the Committee which occasionally led to buckpassing and to the shuttling back and forth of a case "for further action."

* * *

The Committee often attempted to foster minority group employment by urging the hiring of Negroes on a limited preferential basis, i.e., of giving preference to a Negro applicant where he and a white applicant were equally qualified. Although several contractors resisted this policy, others adopted it. Where the Committee was successful in securing Negro employment in nontraditional jobs such as clerical, technical, professional, and supervisory positions, it was generally only of a "token" nature. In the Lockheed plant in Marietta,

Ga., for example, two Negro secretaries were hired several years ago. One left shortly afterwards to take another position; the other was later laid off. When Commission representatives visited the plant in February 1961, there were no Negro clericals employed. (Often, however, the fact that Negro employment in nontraditional positions was of a token nature was due not so much to the company's reluctance to hire additional Negroes in these positions as to the lack of qualified Negro applicants.)

Aside from the infirmities of complaint and compliance procedures, the federal nondiscrimination program had several over-all weaknesses. First was the Committee's lack of authority to investigate complaints and to take—or even recommend—final action on them. The Committee nonetheless did make recommendations. Although the contracting agencies accepted those on the disposition of particular complaints, there were certain areas where cooperation was lacking. For instance, contracting agencies did not adopt the "firmer approach" recommended by Chairman Nixon with respect to disqualifying government contractors. Nor did the Committee receive full cooperation from other federal agencies. The Bureau of Employment Security, for example, refused to require state employment offices to notify the Committee of discriminatory job orders placed by government contractors. Here, as with the President's Committee on Government Employment Policy, stronger support from the White House was needed.

Further, the Committee was hampered by its lack of jurisdiction with respect to labor organizations. In the construction trades, for example, labor unions are the main—if not the sole—source of recruitment, and the unions, in effect, do the hiring. Accordingly, attempts to negotiate changes in employment practices or to force such changes by threat of legal action, with the contractors alone were generally ineffective. Building contractors sometimes preferred to lose the financial benefits of government contracts rather than alienate their source of labor by hiring nonunion employees or those not "cleared" by the unions. And few pressures could be brought on all-white labor organizations to persuade them to refer nonmembers. Where the bulk of commercial construction is unionized, even the threat of contract termination is a weak one, since most companies performing work under the contract would have to hire through the union. Often the pressure of public opinion was the only one available to the Committee, and this was rarely effective.

* * *

The Committee's most significant contribution may well have been its concentration, during the last few years of its existence, on the problems of motivation and training of minority group youth. In the surveys conducted by this Commission and by State Advisory Committees in several States as well as in the Committee's compliance surveys, one fact stands out: when new employment opportunities are opened to Negroes, there is often a dearth of qualified Negro applicants. Similarly, the Commission's survey of government contractors, conducted during the recent recession, found the contractors taking on employees only in hard-to-fill categories such as technical employees and engineers; even those companies which had adopted a policy of specifically recruiting Negro employees found it difficult to obtain qualified Negroes for these positions. A similar problem was encountered by companies seeking to hire Negro women in office clerical positions. Although one large automobile manufacturer in Detroit originally hired Negro women as office clericals about three years ago (though a program of affirmative recruitment) and expressed willingness to employ more, company representatives stated that there were few qualified Negro applicants for these jobs.

Part of the problem is sometimes an unwillingness on the part of Negroes to apply for jobs that have always been closed to them, coupled with lack of information as to jobs that have in fact been opened on a nondiscriminatory basis. Affirmative recruitment may be necessary during a transitional period to overcome past discriminatory employment practices. But even this initial recruitment may not be sufficient to counteract the feeling on the part of many Negroes that it is futile to apply for nontraditional jobs.

Another facet of the problem is the lack of adequately trained minority group members. Some Negro youth lack the motivation to continue their education and training. Others, particularly in the South, have limited their education to training in the social sciences (which, in the past, offered almost the only opportunities for Negro white collar employment). Where Southern Negro youth do attempt to acquire training in the natural and physical sciences, they find the opportunities for such training severely limited. Moreover, in the North as well as the South, training for Negroes under federally assisted vocational education programs is still geared almost exclusively to those jobs which have been traditionally open to them.*

200

PRESIDENTIAL COMMITMENT TO INTEGRATION

President Kennedy's message to Congress had as its primary purpose the exposition of a civil rights bill which he was going to support in Congress. But the message was more than a plea for a particular bill. It provided him with the opportunity to sum up for the nation the progress which his administration had made in the civil rights struggle and point out the various areas, some within and some without legislative prerogative, which still needed close attention.

With an ear to history, he chose a time close to the actual centennial of the final issuance of the Emancipation Proclamation and he used a tone which did no disservice to the party of Lincoln. Conscious of recent events at the University of Mississippi, he restated his position on desegregation in education and his obligation to uphold the law of the land.

No President before him had spoken with such complete commitment. His message left no room for doubt that the Executive branch was totally concerned with the right and duty of seeing that all citizens had equal opportunities under the

---

*Wallace Mendelson, *Discrimination, Based on the Report of the United States Commission on Civil Rights* (Prentice-Hall, Englewood Cliffs, N.J., 1962), 87-91. Copyright © 1962. Reprinted by permission of Prentice-Hall, Inc.

law. His continued reference to the abolition of segregation in various nooks and crannies in the Executive establishment itself carried Kennedy further in this direction than any of his predecessors and reinforced his stated commitment with evidence from areas directly under his jurisdiction.

President Kennedy's Message to Congress

February 28, 1963

* * *

The Negro baby born in America today—regardless of the section or state in which he is born—has about one half as much chance of completing high school as a white baby born in the same place on the same day—one third as much chance of completing college—one third as much chance of becoming a professional man—twice as much chance of becoming unemployed—about one seventh as much chance of earning ten thousand dollars per year—a life expectancy which is seven years less—and the prospects of earning only half as much.

No American who believes in the basic truth that "all men are created equal, that they are endowed by their Creator with certain unalienable Rights," can fully excuse, explain, or defend the picture these statistics portray. Race discrimination hampers our economic growth by preventing the maximum development and utilization of our manpower. It hampers our world leadership by contradicting at home the message we preach abroad. It mars the atmosphere of a united and classless society in which this Nation rose to greatness. It increases the costs of public welfare, crime, delinquency, and disorder. Above all, it is wrong.

Therefore, let it be clear, in our hearts and minds, that it is not merely because of the Cold War, and not merely because of the economic waste of discrimination, that we are committed to achieving true equality of opportunity. The basic reason is because it is right.

* * *

In the last two years, more progress has been made in securing the civil rights of all Americans than in any comparable period in our history. Progress has been made—through executive action, litigation, persuasion, and private initiative—in achieving and protecting equality of opportunity in education, voting, transportation, employment, housing, government, and the enjoyment of public accommodations.

But pride in our progress must not give way to relaxation of our effort. Nor does progress in the Executive Branch enable the Legislative Branch to escape its own obligations. On the contrary, it is in the light of this nation-wide progress, and in the belief that Congress will wish once again to meet its responsibilities in this matter, that I stress in the following agenda of existing and prospective action important legislative as well as administrative measures.

THE RIGHT TO VOTE

The right to vote in a free American election is the most powerful and precious right in the world—and it must not be denied on the grounds of race or color. It is a potent key to achieving other rights of citizenship. For American history—both recent and past—clearly reveals that the power of the ballot has enabled those who achieve it to win other achievements as well, to gain a full voice in the affairs of their state and nation, and to see their interests represented in the governmental bodies which affect their future. In a free society, those with the power to govern are necessarily responsive to those with the right to vote.

* * *

An indication of the magnitude of the over-all problem, as well as the need for speedy action, is a recent five-state survey disclosing over two hundred counties in which fewer than 15 per cent of the Negroes of voting age are registered to vote. This cannot continue. I am, therefore, recommending legislation to deal with this problem of judicial delay and administrative abuse in four ways:

First, to provide for interim relief while voting suits are proceeding through the courts in areas of demonstrated need, temporary federal voting referees should be appointed to determine the qualifications of applicants for registration and voting during the pendency of a lawsuit in any county in which fewer than 15 per cent of the eligible number of persons of any race claimed to be discriminated against are registered to vote.

* * *

Second, voting suits brought under the Federal Civil Rights statutes should be accorded expedited treatment in the federal courts, just as in many state courts election suits are given preference on the dockets on the sensible premise that, unless the right to vote can be exercised at a specific election, it is, to the extent of that election, lost forever.

An instructor with a drawing shows a new voter how to operate a voting machine. This "voting clinic" is one of a number set up in the South by the Christian Leadership Conference in Atlanta, Georgia.

Third, the law should specifically prohibit the application of different tests, standards, practices, or procedures for different applicants seeking to register and vote in federal election . . .

* * *

Fourth, completion of the sixth grade should, with respect to federal elections, constitute a presumption that the applicant is literate.

* * *

EDUCATION

Nearly nine years have elapsed since the Supreme Court ruled that state laws requiring or permitting segregated schools violate the Constitution. That decision represented both good law and good judgment—it was both legally and morally right. Since that time it has become increasingly clear that neither violence nor legalistic measures will be tolerated as a means of thwarting court-ordered desegregation, that closed schools are not an answer, and that responsible communities are able to handle the desegregation process in a calm and sensible manner.

* * *

The shameful violence which accompanied but did not prevent the end of segregation at the University of Mississippi was an exception. State-supported universities in Georgia and South Carolina met this test in recent years with calm and maturity, as did the state-supported universities of Virginia, North Carolina, Florida, Texas, Louisiana, Tennessee, Arkansas, and Kentucky in earlier years. In addition, progress toward the desegregation of education at all levels has made other notable and peaceful strides.

* * *

Despite these efforts, however, progress toward primary and secondary school desegregation has still been too slow, often painfully so.

* * *

I recommend, therefore, a program of federal technical and financial assistance to aid school districts in the process of desegregation in accordance with the Constitution.

* * *

EXTENSION AND EXPANSION OF THE COMMISSION ON CIVIL RIGHTS

The Commission on Civil Rights, established by the Civil Rights Act of 1957, has been in operation for more than five years and is scheduled to expire on November 30, 1963. During this time it has fulfilled its statutory mandate by investigating deprivations of the right to vote and denials of equal protection of the laws in education, employment, housing and administration of justice. The Commission's reports and recommendations have provided the basis for remedial action both by Congress and the Executive Branch.

* * *

I recommend, therefore, that the Congress authorize the Civil Rights Commission to serve as a national civil rights clearinghouse providing information, advice, and technical assistance to any requesting agency, private or public; that in order to fulfill these new responsibilities, the Commission be authorized to concentrate its activities upon those problems within the scope of its statute which most need attention; and that the life of the Commission be extended for a term of at least four more years.

EMPLOYMENT

* * *

The President's Committee on Equal Employment Opportunity, reconstituted by Executive Order in early 1961, has, under the leadership of the Vice-President, taken significant steps to eliminate racial discrimination by those who do business with the government. Hundreds of companies—covering seventeen million jobs—have agreed to stringent nondiscriminatory provisions now standard in all government contracts. One hundred four industrial concerns—including most of the Nation's major employers—have in addition signed agreements calling for an affirmative attack on discrimination in employment; and 117 labor unions, representing about 85 per cent of the membership of the AFL-CIO, have signed similar agreements with the Committee. Comprehensive compliance machinery has been instituted to enforce these agreements. The Committee has received over 1,300 complaints in two years—more than in the entire seven and a half years of the Committee's prior existence—and has achieved corrective action on 72 per cent of the cases handled—a heartening and unprecedented record. Significant results have been achieved in placing Negroes with contractors who previously employed whites only—and in the elevation of Negroes to a far higher proportion of professional, technical, and supervisory jobs. Let me repeat my assurances that these provisions in government contracts and the voluntary nondiscrimination agreements will be carefully monitored and strictly enforced.

* * *

PUBLIC ACCOMMODATIONS

No act is more contrary to the spirit of our democracy and Constitution—or more rightfully resented by a Negro citizen who seeks only equal treatment—than the barring of that citizen from restaurants, hotels, theaters, recreational areas and other public accommodations and facilities.

Wherever possible, this Administration has dealt sternly with such acts. In 1961, the Justice Department and the Interstate Commerce Commission successfully took action to bring an end to discrimination in rail and bus facilities. In 1962, the fifteen airports still maintaining segregated facilities were persuaded to change their practices, thirteen of them voluntarily and two others after the Department of Justice brought legal action. As a result of these steps, systematic segregation in interstate transportation has virtually ceased to exist. No doubt isolated instances of discrimination in transportation terminals, restaurants, rest-rooms, and other facilities will continue to crop up, but any discrimination will be dealt with promptly.

In addition, restaurants and public facilities in buildings leased by the federal government have been opened up to all federal employees in areas where previously they had been segregated. The General Services Administration no longer contracts for the lease of space in office buildings unless such facilities are available to all federal employees without regard to race. This move has taken place without fanfare and practically without incident; and full equality of facilities will continue to be made available to all federal employees in every state.

* * *

CONCLUSION

The various steps which have been undertaken or which are proposed in this Message do not constitute a final answer to the problems of race discrimination in this country. They do constitute a list of priorities—steps which can be taken by the Executive Branch and measures which can be enacted by the Eighty-eighth Congress. Other measures directed toward these same goals will be favorably commented on and supported, as they have been in the past—and they will be signed, if enacted, into law.

In addition, it is my hope that this Message will lend encouragement to those state and local governments—and to private organizations, corporations, and individuals—who share my concern over the gap between our precepts and our practices. This is an effort in which every individual who asks what he can do for his country should be able and willing to take part.

* * *

The program outlined in this Message should not provide the occasion for sectional bitterness. No state or section of this Nation can pretend a self-righteous role, for every area has its own civil rights problems.*

201

DR. KING IN DEFENSE OF HIS PRINCIPLES

The most dramatic action which Martin Luther King took in the name of the Southern Christian Leadership Conference was performed in the streets of Birmingham in the spring of 1963. Dismayed by the complete breakdown of negotiations between the races, the Reverend Fred Shuttlesworth invited King to Birmingham to assist in staging a gigantic demonstration. The strategy called for massive, nonviolent marches to flood the jails and place the city fathers in the untenable position of arresting large numbers of innocent people without facilities to house them.

Twice delayed by city elections which finally brought the more moderate of the two candidates, Albert Boutwell, into office, the campaign began just before Easter and was coupled with an economic boycott of the downtown area. At first the city police, directed by Eugene "Bull" Connor, the defeated candidate, were publicly nonviolent, but the cattle prods, water hoses, and polices dogs soon

*President John F. Kennedy's Message to Congress, Congressional Record 88th Congress, 1st Session, Feb. 28, 1963.

appeared. In accordance with plan, King demonstrated and was jailed. He used part of the time to reply to a public statement addressed to him and signed by eight clergymen. The letter was widely circulated as a stirring defense of King's methods and a skillful attack on the apathy of white Christian and Jewish churches.

The Birmingham conflict was resolved with the assistance of the United States Attorney-General's office and desegregation of lunch rooms, drinking fountains, and similar public places planned over a ninety-day period. The city's industrial community promised a non-discriminatory hiring policy and the channels to continue interracial discussions were established. The white extremists reacted with bombs to this agreement and the White House immediately sent in troops. The pact held and Birmingham was presented with and accepted the opportunity to create harmonious relationships between the two races on an equal basis.

LETTER FROM BIRMINGHAM JAIL

My Dear Fellow Clergymen:

* * *

I think I should indicate why I am here in Birmingham since you have been influenced by the view which argues against "outsiders coming in." I have the honor of serving as president of the Southern Christian Leadership Conference, an organization operating in every southern state, with headquarters in Atlanta, Georgia.

* * *

Several months ago the affiliate here in Birmingham asked us to be on call to engage in a non-violent direct-action program if such were deemed necessary. We readily consented, and when the hour came we lived up to our promise. So I, along with several members of my staff, am here because I was invited here. I am here because I have organizational ties here.

But more basically, I am in Birmingham because injustice is here. Just as the prophets of the eighth century B.C. left their villages and carried their "thus saith the Lord" far beyond the boundaries of their home towns, and just as the Apostle Paul left his village of Tarsus and carried the gospel of Jesus Christ to the far corners of the Greco-Roman world, so I am compelled to carry the gospel of freedom beyond my own home town. Like Paul, I must constantly respond to the Macedonian call for aid.

Moreover, I am cognizant of the interrelatedness of all communities and states. I cannot sit idly by in Atlanta and not be concerned about what happens in Birmingham. Injustice anywhere is a threat to justice everywhere. We are caught in an inescapable network of mutuality, tied in a single garment of destiny. Whatever affects one directly, affects all indirectly. Never again can we afford to live with the narrow, provincial "outside agitator" idea. Anyone who lives inside the United States can never be considered an outsider anywhere within its bounds.

You deplore the demonstrations taking place in Birmingham. But your statement, I am sorry to say, fails to express a similar concern for the conditions that brought about the demonstrations. I am sure that none of you would want to rest content with the superficial kind of social analysis that deals merely with effects and does not grapple with underlying causes. It is unfortunate that demonstrations are taking place in Birmingham, but it is even more unfortunate that the city's white power structure left the Negro community with no alternative.

* * *

We know through painful experience that freedom is never voluntarily given by the oppressor; it must be demanded by the oppressed. Frankly, I have yet to engage in a direct-action campaign that was "well timed" in the view of those who have not suffered unduly from the disease of segregation. For years now I have heard the word "wait!" It rings in the ear of every Negro with piercing familiarity. This "Wait" has almost always meant "Never." We must come to see, with one of our distinguished jurists, that "justice too long delayed is justice denied."

We have waited for more than 340 years for our constitutional and God-given rights. The nations of Asia and Africa are moving with jetlike speed toward gaining political independence, but we still creep at horse-and-buggy pace toward gaining a cup of coffee at a lunch counter. Perhaps it is easy for those who have never felt the stinging darts of segregation to say, "Wait." But when you have seen vicious mobs lynch your mothers and fathers at will and drown your sisters and brothers at whim; when you have seen hate-filled policemen curse, kick and even kill your black brothers and sisters; when you see the vast majority of your twenty million Negro brothers smothering in an airtight cage of poverty in the midst of an affluent society; when you suddenly find your tongue twisted and your speech stammering as you seek to explain to your six-year-old daughter why she can't go to the public amusement park that has just been advertised on television, and see tears welling up in her eyes when she is told that Funtown is closed to colored children, and see ominous clouds of inferiority beginning to distort her personality by developing an unconscious bitterness toward white people; when you have to concoct an answer for a five-year-old son who is asking: "Daddy, why do white people treat colored people so mean?"; when you take a cross-country drive and find it necessary to sleep night after night in the uncomfortable corners of your automobile because no motel will accept you; when you are humiliated day in and day out by nagging signs reading "white" and "colored"; when your first name becomes "boy" (however old you are) and your last name becomes "John," and your wife and mother are never given the respected title "Mrs."; when you are harried by day and haunted by night by the fact that you are a Negro, living constantly at tiptoe stance, never quite knowing what to expect next, and are plagued with inner fears and outer resentments; when you are forever fighting a degenerating sense of "nobodiness" —then you will understand why we find it difficult to wait. There comes a time when the cup of endurance runs over, and men are no longer willing to be plunged into the abyss of despair. I hope, sirs, you can understand our legitimate and unavoidable impatience.

You express a great deal of anxiety over our willingness to break laws. This is certainly a legitimate concern. Since we so diligently urge people to obey the Supreme Court's decision of 1954 outlawing segregation in public schools, at first glance it may seem rather paradoxical for us consciously to break laws. One may well ask: "How can you advocate breaking some laws and obeying others?" The answer lies in the fact that there are two types of laws; just and unjust. I would be the first to advocate obeying just laws. One has not only a legal but a moral responsibility to obey just laws. Conversely, one has a moral responsibility to disobey unjust laws. I would agree with St. Augustine that "an unjust law is no law at all."

Now, what is the difference between the two? How does one determine whether a law is just or unjust? A just law is a man-made code that squares with the moral law or the law of God. An unjust law is a code that is out of harmony with the moral law. To put it in the terms of St. Thomas Aquinas: An unjust law is a human law that is not rooted in eternal law and natural law. Any law that uplifts human personality is just. Any law that degrades human personality is unjust. All segregation statutes are unjust because segregation distorts the soul and damages the personality. It gives the segregator a false sense of superiority and the segregated a false sense of inferiority.

* * *

I must make two honest confessions to you, my Christian and Jewish brothers. First, I must confess that over the past few years I have been gravely disappointed with the white moderate. I have almost reached the regrettable conclusion that the Negro's great stumbling block in his stride toward freedom is not the White Citizen's Counciler or the Ku Klux Klanner, but the white moderate, who is more devoted to "order" than to justice; who prefers a negative peace which is the absence of tension to a positive peace which is the presence of justice; who constantly says: "I agree with you in the goal you seek, but I cannot agree with your methods of direct action"; who paternalistically believes he can set the timetable for another man's freedom; who lives by a mythical concept of time and who constantly advises the Negro to wait for a "more convenient season." Shallow understanding from people of good will is more frustrating than absolute misunderstanding from people of ill will. Lukewarm acceptance is much more bewildering than outright rejection.

* * *

You speak of our activity in Birmingham as extreme. At first I was rather disappointed that fellow clergymen would see my non-violent efforts as those of an extremist. I began thinking about the fact that I stand in the middle of two opposing forces in the Negro community. One is a force of complacency, made up in part of Negroes who, as a result of long years of oppression, are so drained of self-respect and a sense of "somebodiness" that they have adjusted to segregation; and in part of a few middle-class Negroes who, because of a degree of academic and economic security and because in some ways they profit by segregation, have become insensitive to the problems of the masses. The other force is one of bitterness

A tale of two cities: Birmingham, Alabama, September 11, 1963. Waving Confederate flags, students shout white supremacy slogans as they demonstrate near West End High School. Birmingham schools were beginning their second day of integrated classes.

and hatred, and it comes perilously close to advocating violence. It is expressed in the various black nationalist groups that are springing up across the nation, the largest and best-known being Elijah Muhammad's Muslim movement. Nourished by the Negro's frustration over the continued existence of racial discrimination, this movement is made up of people who have lost faith in America, who have absolutely repudiated Christianity, and who have concluded that the white man is an incorrigible "devil."

I have tried to stand between these two forces, saying that we need emulate neither the "do-nothingism" of the complacent nor the hatred and despair of the black nationalist. For there is the more excellent way of love and nonviolent protest. I am grateful to God that, through the influence of the Negro church, the way of nonviolence became an integral part of our struggle.

* * *

Let me take note of my other major disappointment. I have been so greatly disappointed with the white church and its leadership. Of course, there are some notable exceptions. I am not unmindful of the fact that each of you has taken some significant stands on this issue. I commend you, Reverend Stallings, for your Christian stand on this past Sunday, in welcoming Negroes to your worship service on a nonsegregated basis. I commend the Catholic leaders of this state for integrating Spring Hill College several years ago.

But despite these notable exceptions, I must honestly reiterate that I have been disappointed with the church. I do not say this as one of those negative critics who can always find something with the church. I say this as a minister of the gospel, who loves the

Atlanta, Georgia, September 6, 1966. Atlanta's mayor, Ivan Allen, surrounded by Negroes shouting "black power." Moments after this picture was taken the shouting stopped, and a rock and bottle-tossing riot broke out.

church; who was nurtured in its bosom; who has been sustained by its spiritual blessings and who will remain true to it as long as the cord of life shall lengthen.

* * *

Before closing I feel impelled to mention one other point in your statement that has troubled me profoundly. You warmly commended the Birmingham police force for keeping "order" and "preventing violence." I doubt that you would have so warmly commended the police force if you had seen its dogs sinking their teeth into unarmed, nonviolent Negroes. I doubt that you would so quickly commend the police if you were to observe their ugly and inhumane treatment of Negroes here in the city jail; if you were to watch them push and curse old Negro women and young Negro girls; if you were to see them slap and kick old Negro men and young boys; if you were to observe them, as they did on two occasions, refuse to give us food because we wanted to sing our grace together. I cannot join you in your praise of the Birmingham police department.

* * *

I wish you had commended the Negro sit-inners and demonstrators of Birmingham for their sublime courage, their willingness to suffer and their amazing discipline in the midst of great provocation. One day the South will recognize its real heroes. They will be the James Merediths, with the noble sense of purpose that enables them to face jeering and hostile mobs, and with the agonizing loneliness that characterizes the life of the pioneer. They will be old, oppressed, battered Negro women, symbolized in a seventy-two-year-old woman in Montgomery, Alabama, who rose with a sense of dignity and with her people decided not to ride segregated buses, and who responded with ungrammatical profundity to one who inquired about her weariness: "My feets is tired, but my soul is at rest." They will be the young high school and college students, the young ministers of the gospel and a host of their elders, courageously and nonviolently sitting in at lunch counters and willingly going to jail for conscience' sake. One day the South will know that when these disinherited children of God sat down at lunch counters, they were in reality standing up for what is best in the American dream and for the most sacred values in our Judaeo-Christian heritage, thereby bringing our nation back to those great wells of democracy which were dug deep by the founding fathers in their formulation of the Constitution and the Declaration of Independence.

* * *

Yours for the cause of Peace and Brotherhood,

Martin Luther King, Jr.*

202

AN INTERVIEW WITH A NEGRO INTELLECTUAL

Kenneth Clark, a professor of psychology at the City College of New York, sat down to talk with James Baldwin, an essayist, novelist, and dramatist, in front of the television cameras on May 24, 1963. They had both come from the now-famous meeting between Attorney-General Robert Kennedy and Negro intellectuals which ended in frustration on both sides, since the Negroes could not communicate their sense of urgency which had been heightened by the events in Birmingham, and the Attorney-General was unable to explain satisfactorily the political realities of the federal government's apparent inertia. Neither man had time to pull his thoughts together, to compose himself for a public appearance, and the result is an outpouring of raw thought and emotion, not always coherent but magnificently focused. In an appended note to the published version of this conversation, Clark identifies Baldwin as "a delicately tuned instrument of pure communication," using his skill and talents to revive the "conscience of America."

In an autobiographical note which prefaced his first book of essays, Notes of a Native Son, *Baldwin offers a simple and direct self-identification: "I want to be an honest man and a good writer."*

* * *

Clark: What school did you go to?

Baldwin: I went to P.S. 24 and I went to P.S. 139.

Clark: We are fellow alumni. I went to 139.

Baldwin: I didn't like a lot of my teachers, but I had a couple of teachers who were very nice to me; one was a Negro teacher. And I remember—you ask me these questions and I'm trying to answer you—I remember coming home from school, you can guess

*Abridgment of "Letter from Birmingham Jail" (April 16, 1963) in *Why We Can't Wait* by Martin Luther King, Jr. Copyright © 1963 by Martin Luther King, Jr. Reprinted by permission of Harper & Row, Publishers.

how young I must have been, and my mother asked me if my teacher was colored or white, and I said she was a little bit colored and a little bit white, but she was about your color. And as a matter of fact I was right. That's part of the dilemma of being an American Negro; that one is a little bit colored and a little bit white, and not only in physical terms but in the head and in the heart, and there are days—this is one of them—when you wonder what your role is in this country and what your future is in it; how precisely you are going to reconcile it to your situation here and how you are going to communicate to the vast heedless, unthinking, cruel white majority, that you are here. And to be here means that you can't be anywhere else. I could, my own person, leave this country and go to Africa, I could go to China, I could go to Russia, I could go to Cuba, but I'm an American and that is a *fact*.

* * *

Clark: Now I'd like to go back to the point that you made that the Harlem that you knew when you were growing up is not the Harlem now and see if we can relate this also even to the school.

Baldwin: Let's see. Let's see if we can. It was probably very important for me—I haven't thought of this for a long time—it was important at the point I was going to P.S. 24—the only Negro school principal as far as I know in the entire history of New York was the principal—a woman named Mrs. Ayer, and she liked me. And in a way I guess she proved to me that I didn't have to be entirely defined by my circumstances, because you know that every Negro child knows what his circumstances are though he can't articulate them, because he is born into a republic which assures him in as many ways as it knows how, and has got great force, that he has a certain place and he can never rise above it. And what has happened in Harlem since is that that generation has passed away.

Clark: Mrs. Ayer was a sort of a model in a sense.

Baldwin: She was a proof. She was a living proof that I was not necessarily what the country said I was.

Clark: Then it is significant, Jim, that we do not have a single Negro principal in the New York public school system today.

Baldwin: And it is *not* because "there ain't nobody around who can do it," you know. One's involved in a very curious and a very serious battle concerning which I think the time has come to be as explicit as one can possibly be. The great victims in this country of an institution called segregation (it is not a southern custom but has been for a hundred years a national way of life) the great victims are white people, the white man's children. Lorraine Hansberry said this afternoon—we were talking about the problem of being a Negro male in this society—Lorraine said she wasn't too concerned really about Negro manhood since they had managed to endure and to even transcend some fantastic things, but she was very worried about a civilization which could produce those five policemen standing on the Negro woman's neck in Birmingham or wherever it was, and I am too. I'm terrified at the moral apathy, the death of the heart, which is happening in my country. These people have deluded themselves for so long that they really don't think I'm human. I base this on their conduct, not on what they say, and this means that they have become in themselves moral monsters. It's a terrible indictment. I mean every word I say.

* * *

I think that one has got to find some way of putting the present administration of this country on the spot. One has got to force, somehow, from Washington, a moral commitment, not to the Negro people, but to the life of this country. It doesn't matter any longer—and I'm speaking for myself, Jimmy Baldwin, and I think I'm speaking for a great many other Negroes too—it doesn't matter any longer what you do to me; you can put me in jail, you can kill me. By the time I was seventeen, you'd done everything that you could do to me. The problem now is how are you going to save yourselves? It was a great shock to me—I want to say this on the air—the Attorney General did not know——

Clark: You mean the Attorney General of the United States?

Baldwin: Mister Robert Kennedy—didn't know that I would have trouble convincing my nephew to go to Cuba, for example, to liberate the Cubans in defense of a government which now says it is doing everything it can do, which cannot liberate me. Now, there are twenty million Negroes in this country, and you can't put them all in jail. I know how my nephew feels, I know how I feel, I know how the cats in the barbershop feel. A boy last week, he was sixteen, in San Francisco told me on television—thank God, we got him to talk, maybe somebody else ought to listen—he said, "I got no country. I got no flag." Now, he's only sixteen years old, and I couldn't say, "You do." I don't have any evidence to prove that he does. They were tearing down his house, because San Francisco is engaging, as most Northern cities now are engaged, in something called urban renewal, which means moving Negroes out; it means Negro removal, that is what it means. And the federal government is an accomplice to this fact. Now, we are talking about human beings; there's not such a thing as a monolithic wall or some abstraction called the Negro problem; these are Negro boys and girls, who at sixteen and seventeen don't believe the country means anything that it says and don't feel they have any place here on the basis of the performance of the entire country.

* * *

Clark: Could you react to the student non-violent movement which has made such an impact on America, which has affected both Negroes and whites and seems to have jolted them out of the lethargy of tokenism and moderation? How do you account for this, Jim?

Baldwin: Well, of course, one of the things I think that happened, Ken, really, is that in the first place, the Negro has never been as docile as white Americans wanted to believe. That was a myth. We were not singing and dancing down on the levee. We were trying to keep alive; we were trying to survive a very brutal system. The Negro has never been happy in "his" place. What those kids first of all proved—first of all they proved *that.* They come from a long line of fighters. And what they also prove—I want to get to your point, really—what they also prove is not that the Negro has changed, but that the country has arrived at a place where he can no longer contain the revolt. He can no longer, as he could do once—let's say I was a Negro college president, and I needed a new chemistry lab., so I was a Negro leader. I was a Negro leader because the white man said I was, and I came to get a new chemistry lab., "Please, suh," and the tacit price I paid for the chemistry lab. was controlled by the people I represented. And now I can't do that. When the boy said this afternoon—we were talking to a Negro student this afternoon who had been through it all, who's half dead and only about twenty-five. Jerome Smith. That's an awful lot to ask a person to bear. The country has sat back in admiration of all those kids for three or four or five years and has not lifted a finger to help them. Now, we all knew. I know you knew and I knew, too, that a moment was coming when we couldn't guarantee, that no one can guarantee, that he won't reach the breaking point. You can only survive so many beatings, so much humiliation, so much despair, so many broken promises, before something gives. Human beings are not by nature non-violent. Those children had to pay a terrible price in discipline, moral discipline, an interior effort of courage which the country cannot imagine, because it still thinks Gary Cooper, for example, was a man. I mean his image—I have nothing against him, you know, *him.*

Clark: You said something, that you cannot expect them to remain constantly non-violent.

Baldwin: No, you can't! You can't! And, furthermore, they were always, these students that we are talking about, a minority—the students we are talking about, not in Tallahassee. There were some students protesting, but there were many, many, many, many more students who had given up, who were desperate and whom Malcolm X can reach, for example, much more easily than I can.

Clark: What do you mean?

Baldwin: Well, Malcolm tells them—what Malcolm tells them, in effect, is that they should be proud of being black, and God knows that they should be. That is a very important thing to hear in a country which assures you that you should be ashamed of it. Of course, in order to do this, what he does is destroy a truth and invent a history. What he does is say, "You're better *because* you're black." Well, of course that isn't true. That's the trouble.

Clark: Do you think this is an appealing approach and that the Black Muslims in preaching black supremacy seek to exploit the frustration of the Negro?

Baldwin: I don't think, to put it as simply as I can, and without trying now to investigate whatever the motives of any given Muslim leader may be. It is the only movement in the country that you can call grass roots. I hate to say that, but it's true. Because it is the only—when Malcolm talks or the Muslim ministers talk, they articulate for all the Negro people who hear them, who listen to them. They articulate their suffering, the suffering which has been in this country so long denied. That's Malcolm's great authority over any of his audiences. He corroborates their reality; he tells them that they really exist.

Clark: Jim, do you think that this is a more effective appeal than the appeal of Martin Luther King?

* * *

Baldwin: Well, to leave Martin out of it for a moment. Martin's a very rare, a very great man. Martin's rare for two reasons: probably just because he *is;* and because he's a real Christian. He really believes in non-violence. He has arrived at something in himself which permits him—allows him to do it, and he still has great moral authority in the South. He has none whatever in the North. Poor Martin has gone through God knows what kind of hell to awaken the American conscience, but Martin has reached the end of his rope. There are some things Martin can't do; Martin's only one man. Martin can't solve the nation's central problem by himself. There are lots of people, lots of black people I mean, now, who "don't go to church no more" and don't listen to Martin, you know, and who anyway are themselves produced by a civilization which has always glorified violence unless the Negro has the gun so that Martin is undercut by the performance of the country. The country is only concerned about non-violence if it seems as if I'm going to get violent, because I worry about non-violence if it's some Alabama sheriff.

Clark: Jim, what do you see deep in the recesses of your own mind as the future of our nation, and I ask that question in that way because I think that the future of the Negro and the future of the nation are linked.

* * *

Baldwin: I'm both glad and sorry you asked me that question, but I'll do my best to answer it. I can't be a pessimist because I'm alive. To be a pessimist means that you have agreed that human life is an academic matter, so I'm forced to be an optimist; I'm forced to believe that we can survive whatever we must survive. But the future of the Negro in this country is precisely as bright or as dark as the future of the country. It is entirely up to the American people and our representatives, it is entirely up to the American people whether or not they are going to face and deal with and embrace the stranger whom they maligned so long. What white people have to do is try to find out in their own hearts why it was necessary to have a nigger in the first place. Because I'm not a nigger, I am a man, but if you think I'm a nigger, it means you need it. The question you got to ask yourself—the white population has got to ask itself, North and South, because it's one country and for a Negro there's no difference between the North and South; there's just a difference in the way they castrate you, but the fact of the castration is the American fact. If I'm not the nigger here and if you invented him—you, the white people, invented him, then you've got to find out why.*

---

*From "James Baldwin Talks with Kenneth B. Clark" from *The Negro Protest.* Copyright © 1963 by Kenneth B. Clark. Reprinted by permission of Beacon Press.

203

JOURNAL FROM A GEORGIA TOWN

These diary excerpts come from the pen of Dennis Roberts who, as a third year law student at the University of California at Berkeley, spent the summer of 1963 as law clerk for C. B. King, the Negro attorney in Albany who handled the bulk of the civil rights cases in Albany, Georgia.

GEORGIA JUSTICE

June 28: Today I saw Georgia justice in action. We were up at about seven a.m. We had all the witnesses to John Perdew's arrest meet at Shiloh Baptist Church to see if we could find anyone who could testify that he didn't throw a brick at a police car, as is charged. One of the kids gave me an announcement of a Klan meeting on July 6 in Albany; the Klan is quite active in this part of the State.

The trials started at nine a.m., presided over by Judge A. N. Durden of the Recorder's Court. The courtroom is upstairs in the city hall, above the jail and police station. It is an old room with uncomfortable wooden benches and ceiling fans, a far cry from the elegant Federal courtroom in Montgomery. One police officer sits tilted back in his chair by the door. The other policemen sit clustered around Chief Pritchett, across the room from the defense counsel table. With them sits a reporter for the *Albany Herald* and the city prosecutor.

I sat at counsel table with Attorney King, and before the first case was called, Rawls, solicitor for the city, demanded to know who "the white boy" sitting with King was. C. B. introduced me to the court as his law clerk, and the judge finally decided that I could stay. I think this was the only thing during the day that he decided in our favor.

The first case was *City of Albany v. Vera Giddens, Robert Cover, and Ralph Allen,* all SNCC workers. They were charged with distributing advertising matter. The city, as in every other case, offered very little testimony or proof. We showed that the publications were simply an announcement of a mass meeting to be held that night and a copy of *Student Voice,* a SNCC publication which the kids mimeograph every few days. Neither of these publications contained any advertising matter and they were clearly protected by the First Amendment. The Judge said $54 or fifteen days.

Next was *City v. Willie Ricks.* Ricks, a Negro field secretary with SNCC, was charged with disorderly conduct while attending a mass meeting held in one of the Negro housing projects. The judge said $200 and 60 days.

He was followed by *City v. Porter, et al,* which included Penny, Pete Titelman (both with SNCC), and five local Negroes, charged with disorderly conduct and failure to obey an officer. They testified that they were walking on a dirt path which serves as a sidewalk, two abreast, making no noise, on their way to a mass meeting and that Chief Pritchett came up and arrested them. He testified that they were sitting in the street blocking traffic. The testimony of five Negroes and two "outside agitators" didn't carry much weight against the testimony of the chief of police, so it was $193 or 30 days.

* * *

Every one of the defensive pleadings, which we spent all day and half the night working on, is summarily overruled. Attorney King hands it to the judge, who glances at it, lays it aside, and announces "overruled."

Every time the Chief testified, he just rambled on about the violence perpetrated by Negroes and the SNCC people, and Attorney King's objections only serve to fill the record.

The last case of the day was *City v. Mann, et al,* which was Wendy Mann, Cathy Cade, and Sue Wender, three white SNCC girls. They had been arrested on suspicion of vagrancy, held seventy-two hours, and then booked as vagrants. At the trial, we brought out for the record that they had advised the police they were employed by SNCC (at subsistence wages) and that they also had independent incomes or parental support; that the clothes they were wearing when arrested were brand new; and so on. The fathers of some of them were in court, including a very proper midwestern law professor. The judge delivered a speech about how they were obviously nice girls from fine upstanding homes and said that they should go back home and not be with these bad associates in Albany. Then he sentenced them to sixty days as vagrants, in the face of all the proof we had submitted.

* * *

The hardest concept to understand is that what is being demanded here in Albany, and elsewhere in the South, is simply the right to enjoy the most basic permissible constitutional conduct. It is as if the First Amendment didn't exist. Acts of brutality are common occurrences. Tuesday, King's parents had the window of their grocery store broken for the sixth time in two months. The police seem unable to find the guilty party. This goes on every day, every hour, on a hundred different levels. To be a Negro in the South is to be a snake in a swamp—invisible most of the time, but when seen, hated.

It is depressing for me to write this account. I guess I have been holding my feelings in me the whole time, and now each of these incidents fits together into a composite of inhumanity that is hard to face. I don't think I have ever felt so helpless in my life. Yet when people come into the office just to tell me they heard I came from California to help, when I feel this kind of warmth, when I see the integrity of a C. B. King or a Charles Sherrod, then it all seems right, and I couldn't want to be any place else.*

**The Progressive,* XXVIII (March 1964), 17–22. Reprinted by permission of *The Progressive.*

204

THE MARCH ON WASHINGTON

More than 200,000 people from all over the country jammed Washington, D.C., on August 28, 1963, to participate in the March on Washington. The March idea was more than twenty years old: back in 1941, A. Philip Randolph had used it to extract from President Roosevelt an executive order against discrimination in war industries. The idea came alive again in 1963, raised by Randolph and nursed by hundreds of local marches and demonstrations, by police dogs and water hoses in Southern cities, by frustrations growing out of a slow-moving Congress. As the idea gained acceptance, James Farmer of CORE took the initiative in organizing it, joined by King of the Southern Christian Leadership Conference, Wilkins of NAACP, Whitney Young of the National Urban League, and others. Churches of both races endorsed it, as did other nationwide organizations.

James Reston, an accomplished news analyst, was chief of the New York Times *Washington bureau. His balanced but probing story serves as a fitting introduction to the King speech which follows. The March was effective beyond the fondest hopes of the leaders and participants as the press generally commended the marchers for their conduct and their convictions. An elderly Memphis dressmaker who marched summed it all up: "Today is history."*

Washington, Aug. 28—Abraham Lincoln, who presided in his stone temple today above the children of the slaves he emancipated, may have used just the right words to sum up the general reaction to the Negro's massive march on Washington. "I think," he wrote to Gov. Andrew G. Curtin of Pennsylvania in 1861, "the necessity of being ready increases. Look to it." Washington may not have changed a vote today, but it is a little more conscious tonight of the necessity of being ready for freedom. It may not "look to it" at once, since it is looking to so many things, but, it will be a long time before it forgets the melodious and melancholy voice of the Rev. Dr. Martin Luther King Jr. crying out his dreams to the multitude.

It was Dr. King who, near the end of the day, touched the vast audience. Until then the pilgrimage was merely a great spectacle. Only those marchers from the embattled towns in the Old Confederacy had anything like the old crusading zeal. For many the day seemed an adventure, a long outing in the late summer sun—part liberation from home, part Sunday School picnic, part political convention, and part fish-fry.

But Dr. King brought them alive in the late afternoon with a peroration that was an anguished echo from all the old American reformers. Roger Williams calling for religious liberty, Sam Adams calling for political liberty, old man Thoreau denouncing coercion, William Lloyd Garrison demanding emancipation, and Eugene V. Debs crying for economic equality—Dr. King echoed them all.

"I have a dream," he cried again and again. And each time the dream was a promise out of our ancient articles of faith; phrases from the Constitution, lines from the great anthem of the nation, guarantees from the Bill of Rights, all ending with a vision that they might one day all come true.

Dr. King touched all the themes of the day, only better than anybody else. He was full of the symbolism of Lincoln and Gandhi, and the cadences of the Bible. He was both militant and sad, and he sent the crowd away feeling that the long journey had been worthwhile.

This demonstration impressed political Washington because it combined a number of things no politician can ignore. It had the force of numbers. It had the melodies of both the church and the theater. And it was able to invoke the principles of the founding fathers to rebuke the inequalities and hypocrisies of modern American life.

There was a paradox in the day's performance. The Negro leaders demanded equality "now," while insisting that this was only the "beginning" of the struggle. Yet it was clear that the "now," which appeared on almost every placard on Constitution Avenue, was merely an opening demand, while the exhortation to increase the struggle was what was really on the leaders' minds.

* * *

It is a question whether this rally raised too many hopes among the Negroes or inspired the Negroes here to work harder for equality

Below, at the climax of the March on Washington, tens of thousands gathered at the shrine of Abraham Lincoln.

when they got back home. Most observers here think the latter is true, even though all the talk of "Freedom NOW" and instant integration is bound to lead to some disappointment.

The meetings between the Negro leaders on the one hand and President Kennedy and the Congressional leaders on the other also went well and probably helped the Negro cause. The Negro leaders were careful not to seem to be putting improper pressure on Congress. They made no specific requests or threats, but they argued their case in small groups and kept the crowd off Capitol Hill.

Whether this will win any new votes for the civil rights and economic legislation will probably depend on the over-all effect of the day's events on the television audience.

* * *

Above all, they got over Lincoln's point that "the necessity of being ready increases." For they left no doubt that this was not the climax of their campaign for equality but merely the beginning, that they were going to stay in the streets until they could get equality in the schools, restaurants, houses and employment agencies of the nation, and that, as they demonstrated here today, they had found an effective way to demonstrate for changes in the laws without breaking the law themselves.*

DR. MARTIN LUTHER KING SPEAKS

Now is the time to make real the promises of democracy. Now is the time to rise from the dark and desolate valley of segregation to the sunlit path of racial justice. Now is the time to lift our nation from the quicksands of racial injustice to the solid rock of brotherhood. Now is the time to make justice a reality for all of God's children.

There will be neither rest nor tranquility in America until the Negro is granted his citizenship rights. The whirlwinds of revolt will continue to shake the foundations of our nation until the bright day of justice emerges.

And that is something that I must say to my people who stand on the threshold which leads to the palace of justice. In the process of gaining our rightful place we must not be guilty of wrongful deeds.

Again and again, we must rise to the majestic heights of meeting physical force with soul force. The marvelous new militancy which has engulfed the Negro community must not lead us to a distrust of all white people, for many of our white brothers as evidenced by their presence here today have come to realize that their destiny is tied up with our destiny.

There are those who are asking the devotees of civil rights, "When will you be satisfied?" We can never be satisfied as long as the Negro is the victim of the unspeakable horrors of police brutality. We can never be satisfied as long as our bodies, heavy with the fatigue of travel, cannot gain lodging in the motels of the highways and the hotels of the cities.

---

*James Reston, New York *Times,* August 29, 1963, 17. Copyright © 1963 by the New York Times Company. Reprinted by permission.

We can never be satisfied as long as our children are stripped of their selfhood and robbed of their dignity by signs saying "for whites only." We cannot be satisfied as long as the Negro in Mississippi cannot vote and the Negro in New York believes he has nothing for which to vote.

No, we are not satisfied and we will not be satisfied until justice rolls down like water and righteousness like a mighty stream.

Now, I am not unmindful that some of you have come here out of great trials and tribulations. Some of you have come fresh from narrow jail cells.

Continue to work with the faith that honor in suffering is redemptive. Go back to Mississippi, go back to Alabama, go back to South Carolina, go back to Georgia, go back to Louisiana, go back to the slums and ghettos of our Northern cities, knowing that somehow this situation can and will be changed. Let us not wallow in the valley of despair.

Now, I say to you today, my friends, so even though we face the difficulties of today and tomorrow, I still have a dream. It is a dream deeply rooted in the American dream. I have a dream that one day this nation will rise up and live out the true meaning of its creed: "We hold these truths to be self-evident, that all men are created equal."

I have a dream that one day on the red hills of Georgia the sons of former slaves and the sons of former slaveowners will be able to sit down together at the table of brotherhood.

I have a dream that one day even the state of Mississippi, a state sweltering with the people's injustice, sweltering with the heat of oppression, will be transformed into an oasis of freedom and justice.

I have a dream that my four little children will one day live in a nation where they will not be judged by the color of their skin, but by the content of their character.

This is our hope. This is the faith that I go back to the South with—with this faith we will be able to hew out of the mountain of despair a stone of hope.*

205

TRAGEDY AT JACKSON STATE

In May 1970 four students were killed at Kent State University in Ohio and two at Jackson State College in Mississippi. In each instance a long chain of events had created a potentially explosive situation, leading to a confrontation between the National Guardsmen and the local police on the one hand and the students on the other. While the underlying causes at both schools reflected the national mood, the events at Jackson State, a predominantly black institution, also involved deep-seated southern attitudes and behavior patterns. Three days before

*From "The March on Washington" in *I Have a Dream* by Martin Luther King, Jr. Copyright © 1963 by Martin Luther King, Jr. Originally appeared in *The New York Times* (August 29, 1963). Reprinted by permission of Joan Daves and The New York Times Company.

the Jackson State incident six black men had been fatally shot in the back by local police in Augusta, Georgia. The Jackson State tragedy is described and appraised in the following report by Ed Williams, a Mississippi journalist and free-lance writer.

JACKSON STATE

The deaths of two young black men at Jackson State College May 15, following other slayings at Kent State and in Augusta, Georgia, seem part of a national surge of violence which is taking the lives of America's disaffected, the antiwar students and the blacks. From a distance, at least, that pattern seems clear. But explanation totally in terms of malevolent forces and national moods is not sufficient.

In Jackson, as still throughout much of the South, old grievances, old wounds that are the heritage of a century must be taken into account in any evaluation of police and black student conflict. At Jackson State almost precisely three years earlier students had clashed with police in an incident that broke out when Jackson police came on campus in pursuit of a student who was alleged to have been speeding. Students at the time had seen the police intrusion as illustrative of the fact that the Jackson police did not respect the sovereignty of the campus security force. The violence of May 1970, however, was not traceable to one single event.

In the late night hours of Wednesday, May 13, 1970, young blacks, some of them probably Jackson State students and some street-corner toughs, began pelting cars on Lynch Street with rocks and bottles. Jackson police blocked access to a long segment of Lynch, a broad east-west thoroughfare in south Jackson which bisects the campus of Jackson State, a predominantly black (it has a smattering of whites) college of 4500 in a black business and residential area.

Around midnight, the situation worsened. State highway patrolman moved onto the campus. A bonfire burned on Lynch, and lawmen reported barrages of rocks and bottles. Officials later reported an abortive foray by blacks with the ROTC building as the apparent target. But the campus grew quiet in the early morning hours.

What started the trouble? Although the student government had organized a war protest a few days earlier, the disorder Wednesday night did not stem from a demonstration. It just erupted, without an immediate discernible cause. "It's a lot of things," said one student standing at a police roadblock. "The war, Cambodia, the draft, the governor, Mississippi. It's not just any one thing."

About 10:30 the next night, the rock and bottle throwing began anew. Police, aided by state highway patrolmen and National Guardsmen called to duty as a back-up force by Governor John Bell Williams, again blocked Lynch and other streets leading onto campus. Shortly before midnight, someone set fire to a dump truck parked for the night beside a sewage work site on Lynch. A city fire truck was summoned.

Jerry DeLaughter, Jackson correspondent for the Memphis, Tennessee, *Commercial-Appeal,* was at a roadblock one block north of Lynch when the fire truck pulled onto campus. DeLaughter said he saw a rapid series of flashes and heard reports which sounded like gunfire coming from the darkness nearby; but no one was hit, and apparently no gunshots—if they were gunshots—struck the fire truck.

Highway patrolmen and Jackson police also arrived on campus about midnight, traveling on Lynch. A contingent of about 75 highway patrolmen, armed and garbed in riot gear, moved from the burning truck east on Lynch to a spot near the front of Alexander Hall, a women's dormitory whose three wings form a trapezoid on the north side of the street, with Lynch as the long base.

A crowd of young blacks—students and nonstudents, men and women—had gathered in the inner yard of Alexander and near the entrance at the southwest end of the dormitory. Both men and women were inside. The patrolmen stopped, witnesses say, and faced Alexander.

Then without warning the scene exploded. Gunfire erupted, first in a sputter, then quickly in a deafening roar lasting a full 30 seconds. Students fled, stumbled and fell over one another, seeking cover.

Then the guns were silent.

Two blacks were found dead after the firing stopped: 21-year-old Phillip L. Gibbs, a JSC junior, married, father of an 11-month-old son; and 17-year-old James Earl Green, a local high school senior, whose sister said he had just received a tentative offer of a track scholarship to UCLA. Gibbs was found in the yard at Alexander, near the southwest entrance. Green was found across Lynch, near the cafeteria.

* * *

There is an almost irresistible tendency to look for parallels between Jackson State and Kent State. Here is my view:

The real similarities and differences between the two tragedies are best seen by comparing the symbolic roles of the antagonists on both campuses.

The highway patrol at Jackson State and the National Guard at Kent State were forces dispatched to establish order and protect property. Both were backed by, in a phrase favored by Governor Williams, "the majesty of the law." Students who did not cooperate with these forces, then, were lawbreakers in the eyes of the lawmen.

The highway patrol and the National Guard were representatives of white establishment America, thrown into an alien, hostile environment against an enemy hiding among a large mass of innocent bystanders. The role of the lawmen: to establish order. Their method: strike at the enemy. The result: the deaths of several bystanders, none of whom is accused of anything other than being present when the shooting started.

Because they did not retreat when confronted by duly constituted authorities, the students on both campuses got what they asked for, in the cold, quasi-legalistic view of many Americans.

Such a view ignores both law and humanity.

Few lawmen would suggest that the proper response to rocks

and bottles, even to an unseen sniper, is to fire point-blank into a mass of milling students. And if, in the final analysis, law allows such a response, humanity does not. If that is our best method of dealing with angry college students, law and justice have become hollow words, for a withering volley of gunfire does not distinguish between the guilty and the innocent. The men sworn to uphold the law, then, have become as lawless as the mob they see before them.

The confrontation at Jackson State is further complicated by the problem of race. Any confrontation between a white lawman and a black man in Mississippi is necessarily a racial confrontation. One hundred and fifty years of history, with its myths and horrors, make it so.

A deposition taken by the Lawyers Committee here contains an exchange between a lawyer and a highway patrolman about the use of the term "nigger." The lawyer asks if the patrolman considers it an offensive term, and the patrolman replies, "No, sir." The patrol has no policy about use of that term, the patrolman says, and he uses it several times during the taking of the deposition.

A black man who breaks a law, or is suspected of breaking a law, is more than merely a lawbreaker to many white Mississippi lawmen; he is a "nigger" lawbreaker, and that makes a difference.

In the eyes of white Mississippi, a black man who angrily throws a rock at a highway patrolman is more dangerous than a black service station attendant who kills a black tractor driver in a Saturday night brawl. That fact makes any confrontation between angry young blacks and white Mississippi lawmen a potential tragedy.

Possible solutions? Representative Robert Clark, the only black in the Mississippi legislature, suggested a third force; when blacks seem on the verge of violence, other blacks should step in. "We don't want any more armed white men on black campuses," said Clark. "They've proved they don't know what to do. We do."*

206

OUTBREAK AT ATTICA

Prison conditions leading to outbreaks of violence played their role in embittering race relations. Of these the worst by far was the uprising in September 1971 at the Attica Correctional Facility in upstate New York, during which the inmates called for an end to "brutal, dehumanized" conditions. At Attica, as elsewhere throughout the country, the problem of improving correctional policies in general was compounded by the racial divisions between the prisoners and the guards. At Attica most inmates were black and Puerto Rican (85 percent) whereas virtually all of the prison guards were white. An editorial in The Crisis *(October 1971), organ of the NAACP, reflected the prevailing sentiment among blacks.*

*From "Augusta, Georgia, and Jackson State University: Southern Episodes in a National Tragedy" by Ed Williams from *Southern Regional Council: Special Report*, pp. 45–48, 69–71. Reprinted by permission of the publishers, Southern Regional Council, Inc.

Inmates of the Attica Correctional Facility show their solidarity with their representatives in negotiation with Commissioner Oswald. The negotiations were only partially successful, and the uprising ended in tragedy.

THE ATTICA MASSACRE

The revolt of some 1200 prisoners at the Attica Correctional Facility in upstate New York last month and the harsh repression of that organized defiance of state authority at the cost of 43 lives was a monstrous tragedy compounded by an incredible conglomeration of error, misjudgment, racial hate, deceit, and contradictions. As the statement of the NAACP Board of Directors points out: "The blame for this massacre is shared by every one of the principals involved."

Because the prisoners were predominantly black and Puerto Rican and the guards, civilian employees, and law enforcement personnel white, the confrontation was significantly racial. One observer noted that the uprising was more of a race riot than a prison riot. Nevertheless, the prison rebels did include a white minority apparently without friction.

Basically the demands of the prisoners for reforms were reasonable and 28 of them were promptly granted by Correction Commissioner Russell G. Oswald. Whether the appearance on the scene of Governor Nelson A. Rockefeller could have achieved a satisfactory solution of the "nonnegotiable" demands for complete amnesty and the dismissal of the prison superintendent will now never be known. But it is abundantly clear that the Governor's adamant refusal to make a final attempt to arrive at a peaceable settlement was a ghastly blunder, costly in lives of prisoners and prison personnel and irreparably damaging to the Rockefeller image as a political liberal, a level-headed administrator, and a humanitarian champion of interracial justice. What also can be said is that the presence of the Governor could have bought postponement of the massive show of force at Attica, possibly saved some lives, and certainly helped preserve the Governor's reputation as a concerned public official.

The massacre of 33 prisoners and ten prison guards and civilian employees cannot be justified as the inevitable consequence of the intransigence of the prison insurgents. There has been no evidence that the prisoners offered resistance or were equipped to resist the armed assault upon cell block D, the citadel of defiance during their four-day rebellion. The early inflammatory report that the prisoners executed the hostages by slitting their throats was annihilated by the autopsy report of qualified physicians who found that all had died as a result of gunshot wounds. The Governor himself affirmed that the prisoners had no guns. The slain guards were the victims of the indiscriminate shooting of their would-be rescuers.

With black persons as principal targets, the result of the unleashing of armed law enforcement personnel was predictable—indiscriminate shooting. It happened in Orangeburg at South Carolina State College, 1968, and at Jackson State College in Mississippi, 1970. But the killings at the southern institutions were dwarfed by the massacre at Attica. In each instance, non-resisting persons were shot in the back, in flight, or lying down in surrender. The absence of resistance in the cell block was clear indication that the prisoners were ready to capitulate, that resort to firearms was unnecessary.

The prisoners all had criminal records and they talked tough. They could have carried out their threats to kill the white hostages. But they did not. In the end they turned out to be more restrained, less hate-filled, and more compassionate than the troops who slaughtered them. They were men, human beings, and insisted that they be so treated. They were, in a measure, the victims of their records and their rhetoric, as well as white racism. Their massacre cries aloud for immediate and sweeping reformation of the penal system throughout the country with emphasis on rehabilitation rather than on dehumanizing punishment, physical or psychic.*

**The Crisis,* October 1971, p. 241. Reprinted with permission of *The Crisis* Magazine, official publication of the NAACP.

CHAPTER THIRTEEN

Waves at Ebb Tide

Recent years have witnessed the formation of a substantial black middle class, but even for those blacks who have managed to escape poverty, the struggle is not yet over. Affluence brings its own problems, many of them internal, revolving around the questions, What does it mean to be a black person in America today? Can blacks retain their racial identity and still be assimilated into the larger American society? What unique contributions can they make to that society? How can middle-class blacks best help their brothers and sisters still trapped by poverty and discrimination? No consensus is likely to emerge in answer to these questions. Each individual must find his or her own answers.

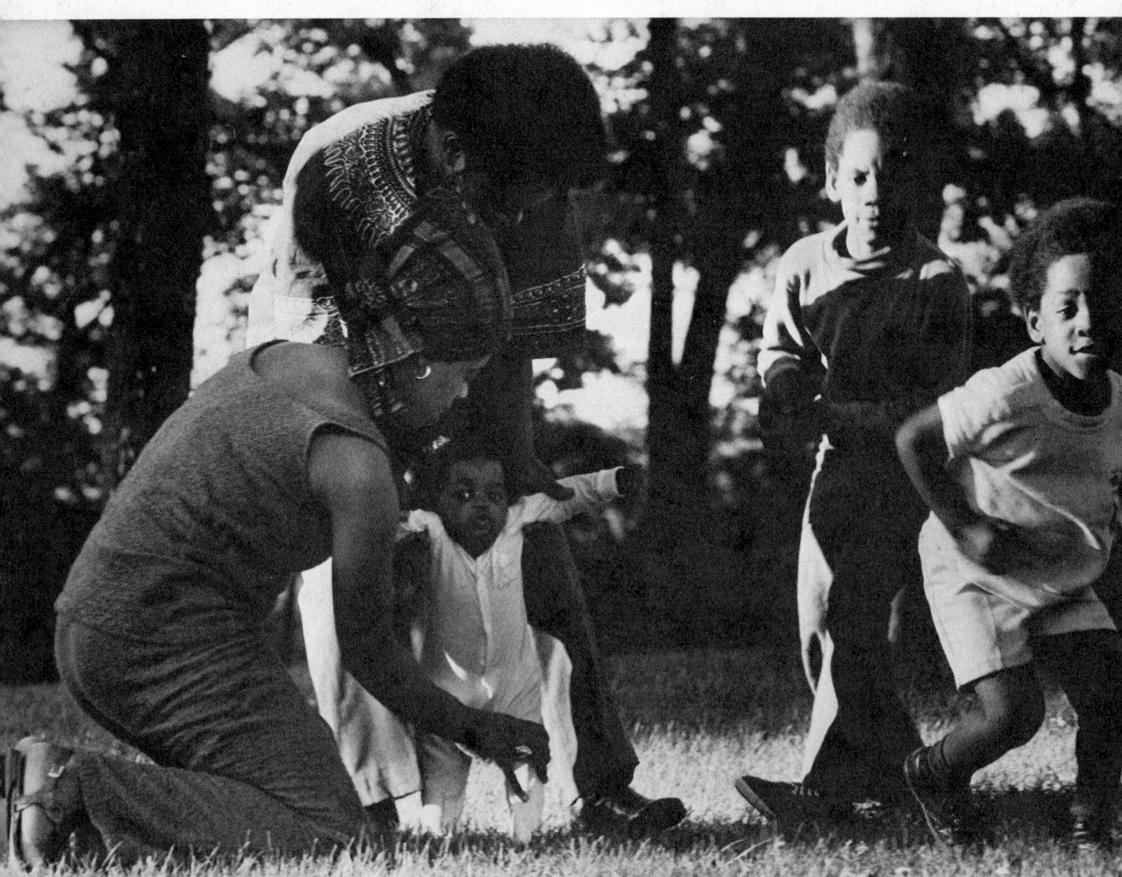

Waves at Ebb Tide

The first half of the 1970's was as defiant of pattern as any half-decade in our history. It was a period of extremes, from the bitter violence in cities and on campuses to the euphoria with which black Congressional leaders reacted to their first meeting with President Gerald Ford. It was a period, too, of progress and retrogression, to the extent that one can measure movement in the well-being of a minority. There was progress in the percentages of blacks voting, holding elective office, attending schools and colleges, and there was retrogression in economic areas like jobs, income, and housing. It was a period of cultural explosiveness, with black artists using an array of artistic artillery to express the oneness of their group, their hostility to oppression, and, at times, their optimism about the future.

It was the violence which first gripped a nation still bemused by Watts, Detroit, and similar riots in the previous decade. In the seventies the violence had an offbeat tempo—quick, concentrated, and apparently mindless. Prison outbreaks, a campus riot, and numberless police actions against the Black Panthers and local groups and individuals flashed in and out of public consciousness with numbing rapidity. Television viewers around the country watched northern white parents in Pontiac, Michigan, and Boston inveigh against busing to achieve integrated schools with the same passion exhibited by their southern counterparts a few years earlier.

Beneath the tragedy of racial violence in the early seventies lay a twin irony. Both the President, Richard M. Nixon, and his first Vice-President stood aggressively for the rigorous enforcement of law and order in the face of racial violence, yet both men were later forced to resign their offices because of their own illegal acts. On another level, racial violence accentuated a growing polarization between whites and blacks; masses of the former were convinced that blacks had initiated or deserved the violence imposed upon them, while masses of the latter were equally convinced that even the right to defend themselves was no longer protected. "I am more afraid of the police," a quiet, middle-aged, black grocer observed in 1971, "than I am of the Panthers." The repercussions of these ironic twists were as devastating a time bomb for American society as the racial violence which exposed them.

In 1972 the violence began to subside almost as quickly as it had arisen, leaving painful scars to cover still aching ills. As the nation became entwined in and entranced by the Watergate scandal, the voices of black aspirations and white resistance became nearly inaudible. Symbolically, the only black participant in the Watergate saga (members of the House Judiciary Committee excluded) was the security guard who had called the police to the Watergate building on the night of the break-in. Subsequently fired, he was unable to capitalize on his Watergate role or to locate steady work. But the lowered profile of racial hostility stemmed from more than a national preoccupation with White House immorality. Zealous police action against black militants and a fracturing of black leadership coupled with widespread emotional fatigue to bring about the relative quiet.

The lack of coordinated leadership was a significant liability for blacks in the 1970's. The Panthers fell to quarreling among themselves as early as 1971. Charles Evers, a nationally recognized political dynamo as mayor of Fayette, Mississippi, was indicted for alleged misappropriation of funds; Angela Davis, acquitted of complicity in a courtroom shoot-out, remained aloof; Roy Wilkins and Bayard Rustin discovered that their advanced age somewhat eroded their influence. Ralph D. Abernathy and Jesse Jackson were still struggling with regional images and the National Urban League's Vernon Jordan was preoccupied with his organization's mission. The Congressional Black Caucus was limited by its narrow political base and internal staffing problems. In the hyperbole of an octogenarian bookseller in Harlem in 1974, "We lack leaders who want to dig deep. . . . Now we have only would-be leaders: doctors who don't want any part of you unless you're sick, . . . lawyers who won't talk to you unless you're in jail, . . . preachers who won't give you the time of day unless they can sell Heaven to you."

Black political potential increased during the first half of the seventies without a comparable growth in black political power. The number of black Congressmen and Congresswomen almost doubled between 1969 and 1975; the number of state and locally elected officials jumped even more sharply in the same period. Large metropolitan areas like Los Angeles, Atlanta, and Detroit elected black mayors, as did smaller cities like Pritchard, Alabama; Raleigh, North Carolina; and Highland Park, Michigan. At the national level, however, the complaint of the Black Congressional Caucus to President Nixon in 1971 was still valid in the early months of President Ford's tenure: "The representatives of this administration by word and deed have at crucial points retreated from the national commitment to make Americans of all races and cultures equal in the eyes of their government."

A group of black college presidents had in 1970 expressed their disappointment with the Nixon administration, with a catalogue of failures which included the exclusion of blacks from domestic policy making, the absence of blacks from high levels in the Department of Justice, apathy on gun control, urban neglect, and inadequate protection of voting rights. Few of these issues were faced frontally by the White House, although an able black woman was appointed Deputy Solicitor General and more federal funds were released to black institutions of higher education.

Symptomatic of the President's posture was his 1971 pronouncement that executive action would be minimal in the enforcement of court decisions legitimizing busing to overcome dual school systems. This open invitation to opponents of busing to scuttle judicially mandated busing helped irritate the issue. The Supreme Court's 1974 decision in the Detroit case, invalidating a stiff but workable lower-court busing plan because it extended beyond the city limits, added to the confusion. Later that year a federal court in Boston approved a busing plan within the city and provoked busing opponents to active hostility and noncompliance.

White House inertia appeared to carry over to the Ford administration, although the presidential styles were different. After their initial positive reaction to President Ford's open manner and willingness to talk with them, black leaders found few changes to cheer about. The deepening recession and accelerating inflation, coupled with an absence of vigorous action by the President, reconfirmed this attitude, since blacks were far more vulnerable than whites to the early ravages of shortages, high prices, and industrial layoffs. The historic intransigence of labor unions to integration, symbolized at the highest level by the long-time AFL-CIO president, George Meany, persisted, so that even black union members complained about union-inspired job discrimination. The "Philadelphia Plan" to insure wider employment of minority workers on federally assisted construction projects slowly collapsed for lack of executive support after 1970. By 1975, without strong White House support for equal employment, without a solid base of union affiliation, or, as in the case of black members of the United Auto Workers, without seniority, black workers were among the first to feel the indignity and insecurity of unemployment.

The burden of discrimination and the challenge of separatism spurred the black community to continue organizing itself. Aware of the variety of voice and the complexity of class within their midst, black leaders like Roy Innis and Kenneth B. Clark scoffed at the idea of a single spokesperson for all blacks. "The time has passed," Clark asserted in 1969, "when self-appointed individual leaders . . . can speak for the masses of American Negroes." Instead leadership began to emerge, sporadically and responsively, as need dictated. The Reverend Jesse Jackson organized People United to Save Humanity (PUSH) in 1972, with a comprehensive program to upgrade the quality of life in black communities. Black ministers from the major black and white Protestant denominations came together in various organizations to find ways to combat white racism and revivify black leadership, while the National Office for Black Catholics monitored the same trends in its church. More radical black intellectuals devoted themselves to Pan-Africanism, a movement to unite the blacks of two continents into a vehicle of international strength. Black college students formed campus groups for study and action in defense of their rights and privileges. At local levels, civil rights groups and community organizations sprang up to assert and protect an enlarged role for black citizens.

One small but potentially strong leadership segment began to crystallize in the late sixties, only to feel the early pinch of recession in the mid-seventies. Blacks began moving into commercial activities, usually with a black clientele, and into industrial and scientific production, demonstrating management and technical skills which defied their detractors. The range of enterprises was as wide as the economy itself: from the production of metals, plastics, paper, and pharmaceuticals to employment and automobile agencies to financial institutions. By the end of 1974, minority businessmen and women were as a rule more affected by the economic downswing because their establishments were younger, less diversified, and without long-standing business, credit, and customer contacts, but few were ready to throw in the towel. Supporting them were the many black men and women who had entered industry and the professions and had moved up to influential positions in major financial, industrial, and communications corporations.

The most striking positive change in interracial tone took place in the South, sparked by a new burst of race pride which was expressed in both nonviolent and violent assertiveness. Southern industrial expansion and federal law exerted significant leverage, and some southern white leaders responded constructively to economic, political, and ideological influences. When Georgia's Governor Jimmy Carter declared in his 1971 inaugural address that "the time for racial discrimination is over," a black legislator remarked that this kind of white man's talk had heretofore taken place secretly and before an election, "not out in public after an election." A black union bricklayer quietly confirmed, "The peoples are not the same anymore. They won't listen to that old talk." Three years later, a white member of the Alabama Board of Education confided to Carl Rowan that "we're making progress, but God it seems slow."

Circumstantial evidence bore out both the change and its snail-like pace. Courtesies of address and the proprieties of customer attention became commonplace in most southern stores. "It's 'yes, sir' this and 'yes, sir' that nowadays," an elderly black resident of Perry, Georgia, observed. The metamorphosis went deeper than propriety and integrated public facilities. The media began to devote space and air time to black social and cultural events, recognizing their significance as news and as a distinctive pattern of American life. In cities, especially Atlanta, a new black upper class provided style and visibility in an urban setting.

Some called it a social revolution, but it did not sweep away all of the disabilities which gripped southern blacks. Urban slums in large and small cities continued to be home for too many black families. Police brutality or insensitivity remained a chronic complaint. Black income in the South still lagged behind that of whites by a significantly higher percentage than was true in other regions of the country. The job situation, while improved in some areas, was in others still precarious for blacks. Land ownership, which had seen a sixty-year decline among southern blacks, continued downward at such a pace that, beginning in southeastern South Carolina, efforts were organized to halt it. Social revolution or social reform, the pressing need for persistence was as apparent as its positive results by the mid-seventies, yet the enlarging economic crisis threatened to crush the poor, erode the stability of the prosperous, and rupture the rhythm of constructive change in the South.

The most telling turnaround of the late sixties and seventies was the artistic expression of black consciousness, spread wide and plumbed deep. "I want black children to have that black sense of self on which to build," Julius Lester told a white friend in 1970. This was the temper of black artists whose sudden access to channels of public communication led to an explosion of new books, plays, music, poetry, television, movies, dance, and other art forms.

That this occurred without substantive support from the white establishment made the flowering all the more dramatic. The talent for artistic creation had been in ferment in the black community for half a century or more, but in less than one decade black artists had overcome the resistance of major white organizations and gained access to the public.

It was the poets who established the new beachhead, men and women like Gwendolyn Brooks and Haki R. Madhubuti (Don L. Lee), Imamu Amiri Baraka (Leroi Jones) and Nikki Giovanni. They spoke in concrete black idiom as mystifying to most whites as it was comprehensible to most blacks. As Hoyt Fuller, the influential editor of *Black World,* observed, this poetry "grows directly out of the 'rap' tradition which black people have. It came about because of the need for communication." There followed in random sequence a breakthrough in the movies and television, beginning with detective films and serials, and reaching dramatic heights in *Sounder* and "The Autobiography of Miss Jane Pittman." Black actors and actresses were acknowledged for their talent, without the earlier restrictions of type casting. They had roles in sex films and Westerns, in social comedy and serious drama, blurring what had once been a clear distinction between black and other films. "Frankly," actor-athlete Fred Williamson commented, "the industry is so mixed up now, it isn't sure what's a black film and what isn't."

Black theater prospered, on its own terms on and off Broadway, using a range of dramatic vehicles from the traditional to the speculative. Black performers, often trained in urban community theaters, moved with greater freedom from black to integrated casts and back again. Even the most sacred of theatrical professions was breached; in 1971 five black women were professionally successful as directors. Black musicians and their black-created or oriented music were in great demand at concerts and in nightclubs, on television and radio. Black classical instrumentalists were less favored—less than 1 percent of the musicians in the fifty-four major symphony orchestras were black—and black conductors and soloists were still rare.

By 1975 the black communities in the United States had demonstrated two striking concepts which many whites were as yet slow to understand. The first was that a rich black way of life existed and thrived in this country, drawn from a wide variety of sources and experiences, and expressed in sometimes beautiful, sometimes brutal ways. This way of life touched every black person and was the basic context, the primary experience, out of which black people shaped their own lives, made their own judgments and decisions, and developed their own creativity.

The second concept which received a cool response in some quarters was that blacks have been and will continue to be a positive contributing force in American society, and that the black struggle for survival in this nation was a struggle for self-determining the dimensions and direction of that positive force. Having survived in this land for over three hundred years, black people remained cautious about the future. Their goal was still that of gaining the same control over their destiny that whites had over theirs.

To the extent that blacks as a group were more impoverished, less healthy, not so well employed or educated, less mobile, and more insecure than whites, this goal was far from realization. To the extent that blacks were now more politically active, more culturally explosive, more visible, more assertive, and more secure in their own black tradition, it was closer to realization.

Implosion in Washington

207

A SALUTE FROM AN HONORED GUEST: PRESIDENT JOHNSON

In a nationally televised address on March 31, 1968, President Johnson announced that he would not seek his party's nomination for reelection. As his term drew to a close, black groups formally voiced their affection and esteem. "In the field of civil rights, no man has done more," said Whitney M. Young, Jr., in referring to President Johnson at the annual Equal Opportunity Awards Dinner of the National Urban League held in New York on November 19, 1968. One month later, at the Sheraton-Carlton Hotel in Washington, a group of black presidential appointees would hold a reception for the retiring Chief Executive.

In introducing President Johnson at the Urban League Dinner, Whitney Young, Executive Director, announced that the League was establishing a $100,000 Lyndon Baines Johnson Scholarship at the University of Texas to aid black students pursuing careers in public affairs. President Johnson responded with a short speech, reminiscent and valedictory in tone, although ending with an eye to the future, as indicated by a favorite Winston Churchill story of his.

REMARKS IN NEW YORK CITY
AT THE ANNUAL EQUAL OPPORTUNITY AWARDS DINNER
OF THE NATIONAL URBAN LEAGUE, NOVEMBER 19, 1968

Mr. Linen, Mr. Young, directors and members of the National Urban League, ladies and gentlemen:

I wanted to come here tonight, not only to join you in paying tribute to an old friend and his fellow award winners, but to reaffirm my dedication to equal human rights in America.

A good many of you have sat by my side during the past five years and have tried to help me as I tried to keep America moving toward the only destiny that is worthy of her greatness—as a just and prosperous Nation, where opportunity is open to all.

I remember those hours—some bright with promise and some shadowed by tragedy. But all of them were filled with challenge to those of us who sought one America—one hopeful, free America, from which bigotry is banished and from which the races of man have learned tolerance and mutual respect.

There was the Civil Rights Act of 1964, and the struggle to write into law each American's right to a job, to equal treatment in public places, to justice in the expenditure of public funds. Many of you were there in that struggle.

Then there was Selma, and the Voting Rights Act of 1965 that grew out of it. Many of you joined me in saying that, despite the blind anger of some men and the apathy of other men, we shall overcome.

Then there were the riots of 1965, 1966, and 1967, when frustration turned into violence, and racists of both colors called for an Armageddon in which our dreams—as well as our cities—would go up in smoke. Many of you denounced that suicidal course, and called upon our great Nation to turn from self-destruction to self-renewal.

Then there was the Fair Housing Act of 1968 when at last we declared that Americans were not to be cordoned off against their will in racial ghettos.

Throughout this time, there were moments of grief, as when a great civil rights leader was shot down and his voice forever lost; moments of doubt, when it appeared that many of our people would respond to the racists and the demagogues who played upon their resentments and who played upon their fears; and moments of achievement and hope when great numbers of Negroes began voting all through the South, when black incomes began rising, when some of the highest offices in Government including the Supreme Court and the Cabinet were occupied for the first time by Negro Americans.

Many of you were there in the White House with me, at those moments. And many others of you were out in the cities—in the board rooms, in the personnel offices, at the editorial desks, in city halls, in the councils of labor—urging your fellow Americans to break down the bars that separate black Americans from a share in the common good.

Nothing that we have done in these years would have really been achieved without you.

Nothing that must be done in the years ahead can be achieved without you.

And if you are inclined—after these years of struggle and success in winning legal rights for all Americans—to rest for a while, consider where you are resting:

—with nonwhite incomes rising, but still only 60 percent of white incomes;

—with the number of nonwhite families earning $8000 a year almost doubling in the past five years, but with one family in three still living in poverty tonight;

—with unemployment among nonwhite married men less than half of what that unemployment was five years ago, but with one teenager in four looking tonight for work and being unable to find it;

—with the number of Negro professionals, white-collar workers, and craftsmen rising sharply, but with opportunities for millions still limited just to menial and custodial jobs;

—with mortality rates for Negro babies falling, but still it is three times those for white babies;

—with millions of Negro fathers better able to care for their families, but with one family in four headed by the mother—more than that in many ghetto areas.

So, it is true, we have come a long way. We have made a lot of verbal commitments. We have even changed a great many lives already for the better. But we are nowhere, nowhere in sight of where we must be before we can rest.

* * *

Back in the 1930's, we used to hear the opposition talk about "property rights" each time a proposal came up to establish a minimum wage, or to give labor the right to collective bargaining, or to try to control the spread of monopolies.

Well, I think some of us have sounded too cavalier in our response to that argument about property rights. For property rights are precious and they are necessary rights in our democratic society.

What we really objected to all along was that not enough people had property rights—because not enough people had property.

So what we have all been trying to do in these past two years is to increase the number of property holders and to increase the size of what they hold.

If we have planted one idea in the American consciousness I hope it is this: Every man, woman and child has at least one property right. It is the right to opportunity.

The task of government, business, and labor, of the news media, of the schools, and of the organizations like the Urban League, is to protect and to extend that right—to make it just as real for the child of Harlem as it is for the child of the most prosperous suburb.

When we break the barriers to his father's promotion, we do that.

When we put some living color into our TV ads, we do that. [*Laughter*]

When we expand our economy and when we resist those voices who call for a little more unemployment as medicine for inflation, we do that.

When we insist that the programs that we have begun be supplied with funds, and the rights that we have written together be enforced, then we do that.

I promise you one thing: For as long as I live, I shall remain joined with you in fighting for that right to opportunity.

* * *

I feel tonight like Winston Churchill is reputed to have felt one time when the little ladies of the Temperance Union came in, in the closing days of World War II, to complain to the Prime Minister about his drinking habits. The spokesman said: "Mr. Prime Minister, we are told that if all the brandy that you have drunk throughout this war were poured into this room it would come up to about here."

The Prime Minister looked at the floor, looked to the little lady's hand measuring about half the room, and then looked at the ceiling and said: "My dear little lady, so little have I done." Then he looked at the ceiling and said: "So much I have yet to do."

So as we look back over the five years that we have traveled this road and all that we have tried to do and those little things that we have done, we all, like Prime Minister Churchill, recognize that so little have we done, but so much we all have yet to do.*

208

A SUGGESTION FOR "BENIGN NEGLECT": DANIEL P. MOYNIHAN

Hailed as the liberal in the initial Nixon family of advisers, Daniel P. Moynihan, a former Harvard sociologist, played an enigmatic role in Washington until his appointment in 1972 as ambassador to India. Publicly Moynihan was loyal to the Nixon administration, as a presidential counselor must be. Privately the reports about his advice and his actions placed him at various points along the ideological spectrum, depending upon the issue and the reporter.

Moynihan's early advice to Richard Nixon relative to the President's developing relationship with the black community was leaked to the press and stirred up a storm of protest. The term "benign neglect" reflected the tone of the memorandum and critics were quick to underline an implicit Moynihan premise, that Nixon owed little to the black vote and had little chance of garnering it in 1972. The political overtones of this memorandum, couched as it was in the language of the social scientist, were particularly discouraging to black leaders since the administration began at a time of great and emotional expectations among black people, and especially among young black men and women.

As the new year begins, it occurs to me that you might find useful a general assessment of the position of Negroes at the end of the first year of your Administration, and of the decade in which their position has been the central domestic political issue.

In quantitative terms, which are reliable, the American Negro is making extraordinary progress. In political terms, somewhat less reliable, this would also appear to be true. In each case, however, there would seem to be countercurrents that pose a serious threat to the welfare of the blacks and the stability of the society, white and black.

1. Employment and Income

The nineteen-sixties saw the great breakthrough for blacks. A third (32 percent) of all families of Negro and other races earned $8000 or more in 1968 compared, in constant dollars, with 15 percent in 1960.

The South is still a problem. Slightly more than half (52 percent) of the Negro population lived in the South in 1969. There only 19 percent of families of Negro and other races earned over $8000.

Young Negro families are achieving income parity with young white families. Outside the South, young husband–wife Negro

---

Public Papers of the Presidents of the United States: Lyndon B. Johnson, 1968–1969, 2 vols. (Washington, D.C., 1970), II, 1140–1143.

families have 99 percent of the income of whites. For families headed by a male age 25 to 34, the proportion was 87 percent. Thus, it may be this ancient gap is finally closing.

Income reflects employment, and this changed dramatically in the nineteen-sixties. Blacks continued to have twice the unemployment rates of whites, but these were down for both groups. In 1969, the rate for married men of Negro and other races was only 2.5 percent. Teen-agers, on the other hand, continued their appalling rates: 24.4 percent in 1969.

Black occupations improved dramatically. The number of professional and technical employees doubled in the period of 1960–68. This was two and a half times the increase for whites. In 1969, Negro and other races provided 10 percent of the other-than-college teachers. This is roughly their proportion of the population (11 percent).

2. Education

In 1968, 19 percent of Negro children three and four years old were enrolled in school, compared to 15 percent of white children. Forty-five percent of Negroes 18 and 19 years old were in school, almost the equal of the white proportion of 51 percent. Negro college enrollment rose 85 percent between 1964 and 1968, by which time there were 434,000 Negro college students. (The total full-time university population of Great Britain is 200,000.)

Educational achievement should not be exaggerated. Only 16 percent of Negro high school seniors have verbal test scores at or above grade level. But blacks are staying in school.

3. Female-Headed Families

This problem does not get better, it gets worse. In 1969, the proportion of husband–wife families of Negro and other races declined once again, this time to 68.7 percent. The illegitimacy ratio rose again, this time to 29.4 percent of all live births. (The white ratio rose more sharply, but was still only 4.9 percent.)

Increasingly, the problem of Negro poverty is the problem of the female-headed family. In 1968, 56 percent of Negro families with income under $3000 were female-headed. In 1968, for the first time, the number of poor Negro children in female-headed families (2,241,000) was greater than the number in male-headed families (1,947,000).

4. Social Pathology

The incidence of antisocial behavior among young black males continues to be extraordinarily high. Apart from white racial attitudes, this is the biggest problem black Americans face, and in part it helps shape white racial attitudes. Black Americans injure one another. Because blacks live in de facto segregated neighborhoods and go to de facto segregated schools, the socially stable elements of the black population cannot escape the socially pathological ones. Routinely, their children get caught up in the antisocial patterns of the others.

* * *

5. Social Alienation

With no real evidence, I would nonetheless suggest that a great deal of the crime, the fire-setting, the rampant school violence, and other such phenomenon in the black community have become quasi-politicized. Hatred—revenge—against whites is now an acceptable excuse for doing what might have been done anyway. This is bad news for any society, especially when it takes forms which the Black Panthers seem to have adopted.

This social alienation among the black lower classes is matched, and probably enhanced, by a virulent form of anti-white feeling among portions of the large and prosperous black middle class. It would be difficult to overestimate the degree to which young, well-educated blacks detest white America.

6. The Nixon Administration

As you have candidly acknowledged, the relation of the Administration to the black population is a problem. I think it ought also to be acknowledged that we are a long way from solving it. During the past year, intense efforts have been made by the Administration to develop programs that will be of help to the blacks. I dare say, as much or more time and attention goes into this effort in this Administration than any in history. But little has come of it. There has been a great deal of political ineptness in some departments, and you have been the loser.

I don't know what you can do about this. Perhaps nothing. But I do have four suggestions.

First. Sometime early in the year, I would gather together the Administration officials who are most involved with these matters and talk out the subject a bit. There really is a need for a more coherent Administration approach to a number of issues. (Which I can list for you, if you like.)

Second. The time may have come when the issue of race could benefit from a period of "benign neglect." The subject has been too much talked about. The forum has been too much taken over [by] hysterics, paranoids, and boodlers on all sides. We may need a period in which Negro progress continues and racial rhetoric fades. The Administration can help bring this about by paying close attention to such progress—as we are doing—while seeking to avoid situations in which extremists of either race are given opportunities for martyrdom, heroics, histrionics, or whatever. Greater attention to Indians, Mexican-Americans, and Puerto Ricans would be useful. A tendency to ignore provocations from groups such as the Black Panthers might also be useful.

* * *

Third. We really ought to be getting on with research on crime. We just don't know enough. It is a year now since the Administration came to office committed to doing something about crime in the streets. But frankly, in that year I don't see that we have advanced either our understanding of the problem, or that of the public at large. (This of course may only reveal my ignorance of what is going on.)

At the risk of indiscretion, may I put it that lawyers are not professionally well-equipped to do much to prevent crime. Lawyers are not managers, and they are not researchers. The logistics, the ecology, the strategy and tactics of reducing the incidence of certain types of behavior in large urban populations simply are not things lawyers think about often.

We are never going to "learn" about crime in a laboratory sense. But we almost certainly could profit from limited, carefully done studies. I don't think these will be done unless you express a personal interest.

Fourth. There is a silent black majority as well as a white one. It is mostly working class, as against lower middle class. It is politically moderate (on issues other than racial equality) and shares most of the concerns of its white counterpart. This group has been generally ignored by the Government and the media. The more recognition we can give to it, the better off we shall all be. (I would take it, for example, that Ambassador [Jerome H.] Holland is a natural leader of this segment of the black community. There are others like him.)*

209

A GAME PLAN FOR BLACKS

During his campaign for the presidency in 1968, Richard M. Nixon repeatedly emphasized the necessity for black economic advancement, particularly black ownership of business. At a press conference held within a month after he had taken office, he was questioned as to whether "he and his administration had a serious problem of distrust among the blacks." The President replied that he hoped that "I can gain the respect and . . . eventually the friendship of black citizens and other Americans." Two years later the monthly Black Enterprise *assessed the Nixon administration's record in terms of one vital aspect of black life—business ownership and operation.*

THE GAME PLAN: A NEED FOR COMMITMENT

Not long ago, the Republican National Committee published a brochure entitled "Black Leadership in the Republican Administration" in which it proudly displayed the photographs of 150 blacks employed by the federal government. In visibility, they ranged from the well-known James Farmer, founder of the Congress of Racial Equality and then assistant secretary for administration of the Department of Health, Education, and Welfare, all the way to diligent but obscure career civil servants.

This group forms the core of Nixon's black leadership, or—as the President himself refers to his aides, as the Nixon team—then this group might be called Nixon's black team. Photographed together with the President, they projected an image of determination and harmony; and, indeed, the group could well be proud of its collective capability. Included in "black leadership" are two assistant secretaries of Housing and Urban Development, Samuel Jackson and Samuel Simmons; Assistant Secretary of Labor Arthur Fletcher, who is in charge of enforcing the "Philadelphia Plan"; Benjamin

*The New York Times, March 1, 1970, p. 69.

Holman, the director of the Community Relations Service; the chairman of the Equal Employment Opportunity Commission, William Brown 3d; as well as the three talented men pictured on the cover of this magazine—Robert Brown, a special assistant to the President, Abraham S. Venable, director of the Office of Minority Business Enterprise, and Arthur McZier, assistant administrator for minority enterprise in the Small Business Administration.

But despite the image of determination and harmony conveyed in the group picture—and with it the promise of tangible accomplishment—Nixon's black team seems to be far from winning any stunning victories for the cause of black economic development.

In fact, disenchantment rather than determination seems to be the order of the day. Farmer submitted his resignation last month and several others were reportedly ready to follow him, including Simmons, Venable, and even Brown.

The departure of even such top leaders alone will not mean, of course, the collapse of the black team. But in a very important way their leave-taking seems symptomatic of a distressing problem—the uncertainty of the cause they serve. Who is the President listening to, and precisely what are his intentions? What has been accomplished up to now? And, very important, who will carry out tomorrow's plan?

Does the Nixon Administration really have a plan to help black business?

That question, like larger aspects of Mr. Nixon's racial policies, continues to puzzle many in Washington and the nation as Republican control of the White House enters its third year. For whatever the concepts "black capitalism" and "minority enterprise" have produced in the way of accomplishments during the past 24 months, they clearly have also been the source of considerable conflict and confusion.

If one accepts the word of Commerce Secretary Maurice H. Stans, for example, they exemplify the Nixon cornucopia from which—as Mr. Stans explains in speech after speech—spews forth an ever-expanding array of help for minority firms that ranges from loans and guarantees to supply and service contracts.

But skeptics like the NAACP's Roy Wilkins and the chairman of Harlem's Freedom National Bank, Jackie Robinson, believe that if a Nixon cornucopia does exist, it has a hollow sound. The Nixon years, in their viewpoint, have brought little improvement in the chances of black businessmen and business aspirants who continue to struggle as before with Government paperwork and bureaucratic indifference in order to overcome their lack of capital and other handicaps.

For civil servants, a good number of them truly dedicated to the proposition that all men deserve a decent serving from the economic pie, the uncertain signals from the White House frequently have made its wishes difficult to comprehend. Too often, when Mr. Nixon could have easily cut through the uncertainty with an unmistakable commitment to adequate funding and staffing for policies forged by his subordinates, there has been total silence.

Perhaps the best way to clarify where Uncle Sam currently stands on the road to equal minority opportunity is to step back to the vantage point of January 1964. Uncle's big program for opening the door of business opportunity to blacks wasn't difficult to understand in those days—he simply didn't have one.

Among the first Government officials to recognize the injustice in this was Eugene P. Foley, then head of the Small Business Administration. Checking into Negro complaints that the agency had discriminated against black loan applicants since its creation a decade earlier, Mr. Foley learned that SBA could identify a grand total of 13 loans to Negro-owned companies during all that time. (Seven of these had been made in Philadelphia and six in Washington.)

A few other loans may have been overlooked because SBA records in those days carried no racial identification. But the conclusion was inescapable. Of several billion dollars that SBA had arranged in aid for small businesses, either in financing or in set-asides of Government contracts, a negligible fraction had gone to blacks.

Mr. Foley's response, the "6 X 6" program, was a rather startling innovation at the time. Experimentally in Philadelphia and later as a full-fledged SBA program extending to Harlem, Brooklyn, Washington, San Francisco, and Houston, it offered "disadvantaged" borrowers $6,000 for up to six years. By Mr. Foley's order, SBA did not require these clients to put up collateral or obtain a turndown by private banks, the practice with standard SBA loans.

During the year or so that the 6 X 6 program continued in force (it was to be followed by the Economic Opportunity Loan program, created by the basic antipoverty law of 1964 with a $15,000 ceiling) it generated 794 loans totaling $3.6 million. As for the black share, it amounted to slightly less than half the loans and the dollars—a contemptible trickle when measured against the comparative largesse of the cupboard today:

—Direct SBA and bank loans guaranteed by the agency currently are flowing to minority borrowers, most of them black, at the rate of $200 million a year.

—Procurement and service orders from Defense agencies, the General Services Administration, the Post Office, the Agriculture Department, and other arms of government are expected to exceed $55 million in the current fiscal year ending next June 30, nearly seven times the rate of only two years earlier.

—MESBICs, though still less numerous than predicted by Secretary Stans, continue to multiply. At the year-end, some 30 of the minority enterprise small business investment companies had been licensed by SBA and applications from another 15 or so were awaiting the agency's approval. The licensed companies represent $8 million in private capital plus an important pool of management assistance for blacks and other minority members. Together with the money that SBA offers MESBICs for relending to small minority firms, plus the loans that banks are willing to make the minority companies once MESBICs have backed them, the MESBIC program at its present intermediate level already promises $80 million to

$100 million in small firm financing.

—Management assistance for minority borrowers is improving. SBA has continued to strengthen staff procedures for helping blacks at its local offices. The Commerce Department's Office of Minority Business Enterprise (OMBE) recently announced funding for MEDIC Enterprises Inc. in Newark as its 18th affiliate. Professional staff members on the MEDIC payroll will identify business opportunities for minority members, help them develop a business plan, assist in getting financing, and follow up with management assistance once the client is set up in business.

—Private sector help, though crimped by the recession, shows measurable gains. One hundred and fourteen companies responding to a Commerce Department survey reported that as of June 30, 1970, 743 minority members were franchised to operate their retail outlets, an 83 percent rise from a year earlier.

Another survey of half the oil industry found that the companies queried had nearly 9300 minority-owned service stations, a 27 percent increase from June 1969.

Impressive as this catalogue appears, though, it's a lot less than what candidate Richard M. Nixon seemed to be promising blacks in the Bridges to Human Dignity speeches that he delivered over radio in April and May 1968. "In order to *have* human rights, people need property rights—and never has this been more true than in the case of the Negro today," he said on that occasion. "What do I mean by property? . . . essentially, the economic power that comes from ownership, and the security and independence that comes from economic power. . . ."

Addressing himself to the general need for ghetto renewal, Mr. Nixon went on to offer some intriguing specifics: "A New Enterprise program should be established to serve the Negro in the central city, helping black employees to become black employers." One feature of this program would be tax incentives for corporation executives to volunteer their time as business management teachers.

There might even be a "Domestic Development Bank roughly comparable in concept to the World Bank. This would make loans and guarantees for businesses that either are located in poverty areas or draw most of their employees from poverty areas, with preference given to those enterprises that are locally owned or that allow residents of the area to participate in ownership."

Then came the conventions and with them the commitment to Strom Thurmond and the Chicago riots; Republican nominee Nixon began to court the Silent Majority and nothing more was heard of ghetto renewal or New Enterprise.

Pierre Rinfret, the economist, and other liberals on the Nixon campaign staff nevertheless continued to believe that their candidate had something big in mind. Just three weeks before Election Day, *The Wall Street Journal* reported [its] expectation that tax incentives "totaling $2 billion to $3 billion a year" would be made available for urban needs, including black business development.

Yet, what really *was* in Mr. Nixon's mind?

"For all its eloquence," John M. Claughry, another adviser in the campaign, later was to write, "'Bridges' (the radio talks) left open almost as many questions as (they) answered. . . .

"What was not clear was whether 'black capitalism' (a term used only twice in the first speech, and not at all in the second) embraced consumer ownership—as in cooperative retail establishments. . . . Perhaps most crucially, it was not clear whether Nixon conceived of any kind of black ownership which extended broadly across the ghetto and to major profit-making industries, or whether he advocated merely the skimming off of the most talented ghetto dwellers to make them into 'Mom and Pop' store owners.

"Nixon's unwillingness to attempt any further refinement and exposition of the principles enunciated inspired widely varying interpretations of 'black capitalism.' Those who saw in it their own view of what should be done praised Nixon; those who saw in it some other view attacked him."

The tax incentive idea did get some consideration once the new administration took over in Washington, but for a variety of reasons never got past the thinking stage. Responsibility for the concept passed to Dr. Arthur Burns, a White House economic adviser and troubleshooter before Mr. Nixon appointed him chairman of the Federal Reserve Board. Dr. Burns soon found himself deep in weightier questions like the anti-inflation battle and tax reform, though, and couldn't give much attention to the incentive idea.

Other tax revenue increases that Nixon men were counting on to offset the income the Treasury would lose because of incentives never materialized. And there was also the steady opposition to tax concessions as "backdoor financing" expressed by Wilbur D. Mills, the Democratic chairman of the House Ways and Means Committee and a mighty force when it comes to writing tax law.

Administration sources insist the incentive approach still is alive as a possible way to encourage large corporations to deposit some of their cash in minority-owned banks; to establish minority procurement offices; and to loan their middle management executives to new minority firms for periods up to six months. Conceivably, the President may even recommend such steps in his State of the Union message this month. . . .

If the problems encountered in using tax incentives are understandable, though, it's not as easy to forgive the bureaucractic bog that Mr. Nixon has allowed to rise around the minority enterprise programs already in existence when he got to Washington. . . .*

---

*From "The Game Plan: A Need for Commitment," from *Black Enterprise,* January 1971, pp. 16–20. Reprinted by permission of *Black Enterprise.*

210

THE BUSING CONTROVERSY

The 1954 Brown *decision by the United States Supreme Court, which made desegregation the law of the land, was directed at those legally separate school systems in the South. Twenty years later 46 percent of the black children in the eleven states of the old Confederacy were attending predominantly white schools, but in the North and West, where segregation laws did not exist, only 28 percent of the black children sat in predominantly white schools.*

Behind these two statistics lay a persistent question: What is the most effective way to provide an educational experience of high quality to all students? The two most common responses have been either a continued emphasis on integrating all school systems or a massive dose of federal and state funds to upgrade school systems which prefer to remain separate. Beyond these two solutions were longer-range proposals dealing with teacher training, changes in school board and parent attitudes, curriculum revision, motivation research, and a host of others offered by private and government-sponsored panels of experts. But the pressure of lower court decisions narrowed the immediate choice to mixed or separate schools, first in the South, and later in the North and West, where segregated housing created segregated school districts.

In the late sixties and early seventies, some black leaders stood up for separatism with local control, but in too many instances the merits of this concept were lost in dispute—educational, financial, and political—among blacks, between blacks and whites, and among whites. On the other side were white and black leaders who pushed hard for integration by whatever means possible. By 1970 the chief means available to cities across the nation was cross-district busing, and this became the red flag to rally around or to attack.

President Nixon made it clear in 1972 that he was opposed to federally ordered busing and proposed, as an alternative, the expenditure of $2.5 billion to improve inner city schools. Proponents of an anti-busing constitutional amendment received his moral support but with a dash of cold water, since he told the nation in March 1972 that a constitutional amendment would take too long. After his reelection he fired the distinguished chairman of the Civil Rights Commission, Father Theodore M. Hesburgh, whose views on busing as an immediate step were uncompromising: "Unless black children are given a chance to get out of, and away from, these schools we now finally see are so bad, . . . then we have destroyed the last bridge out of the ghetto."

Some black leaders argued that the busing dispute obscured real issues like quality education and unequal educational opportunities, but the public seized upon it and made it a national controversy. The Detroit case focused on a plan which would mix children from the city and the suburbs by cross-district busing and the establishment of a metropolitan school system including the city and the suburbs. The U.S. Supreme Court, by a bare majority, decided against the plan.

BUSING: A FRAUDULENT ISSUE

There is a weirdly false and hollow note to the vast outcry against busing to achieve school integration—from President Nixon's ominous call for Congressional action to curb the Federal Courts to Governor Wallace's strident appeal to raw racism. For more than half a century busing of school children has been a commonplace adjunct to American educational facilities. Children have been bused to school for a wide variety of purposes, not the least of which has been to maintain a segregated educational system. Presently some 40 percent of all school children in the nation are bused to schools out of their neighborhoods. Of these, less than 3 percent are transported for the purpose of integration.

It is not busing of children that arouses hostility. Rather, it is transporting them from black to white areas or, particularly, from white to black neighborhoods. In other words, race is the sole issue. And no one who has not advocated abolition of all school busing or who has remained silent over the long years that Negro and Caucasian children have been bused long distances to maintain segregation can expect credibility when he avows that his present posture is not rooted in racism. There is no movement to halt busing of school children as such. No one raises a cry for the elimination of all busing. The clamor is for curbing busing for the constitutional purpose of desegregating schools.

Another aspect of the anti-busing alarum has been the spreading of a vicious half-truth, namely, that the integration forces believe black children cannot be educated without the presence of white children in the same classroom. In the broad sense of education for meeting and understanding the challenges and complexities of life in the United States of America during this last third of the twentieth century, the children of both races desperately need to know one another from an early age. For such preparation, the white child needs the presence of the black as much as the latter needs the former. Otherwise the nation faces the probability of disastrous racial polarization and large-scale conflict.

In the narrower, academic sense of education, the schools offering the best in modern training have long been, and remain, primarily the institutions provided for white children. These schools have the best facilities—libraries, laboratories, recreational space, buildings, and, often, teachers. If our black children are to have the best education they will have to attend schools where it is available, that is, schools attended by white children.

If they are to be able to compete with persons of other races in adulthood, they need to start in childhood. Such training is rarely, if ever, available in the ghetto. And, contrary to Mr. Nixon's roseate assurances, [it] cannot magically be made available within the next 12 or 36 months with the paltry expenditure of $2.5 billion nor with a more plausible $10 billion. Even were the President's proposal attainable, it would leave unmet the need of both black and white children for training for life as equals in a multiracial society.

The most tragic aspect of this whole phony issue is the bewilderment of that minority of black parents who have been misled into believing that integration is unimportant, undesirable, and demeaning. They are willing to sacrifice the future, the very survival, of their children in the suffocation of segregation. The race has too long been imprisoned behind the Jim Crow barriers. Now that these sinister bars are beginning to be levelled, thanks in large part to efforts of the NAACP, let no black person be beguiled into aiding those who would reinforce them and cripple another generation of our children.

Make no mistake. The issue is not busing. The issue is equal education.*

MILLIKEN V. BRADLEY

CHIEF JUSTICE BURGER'S MAJORITY DECISION

. . . Ever since *Brown v. Board of Education*, 347 U.S. 483 (1954), judicial consideration of school desegregation cases has begun with the standard that:

> "[I]n the field of public education the doctrine of 'separate but equal' has no place. Separate educational facilities are inherently unequal." 347 U.S., at 495.

This has been reaffirmed time and again as the meaning of the Constitution and the controlling rule of law.

The target of the *Brown* holding was clear and forthright: the elimination of state mandated or deliberately maintained dual school systems with certain schools for Negro pupils and others for White pupils.

* * *

Proceeding from these basic principles, we first note that in the District Court the complainants sought a remedy aimed at the *condition* alleged to offend the Constitution—the segregation within the Detroit City school district.

* * *

Viewing the record as a whole, it seems clear that the District Court and the Court of Appeals shifted the primary focus from a Detroit remedy to the metropolitan area only because of their conclusion that total desegregation of Detroit would not produce the racial balance which they perceived as desirable. Both courts proceeded on an assumption that the Detroit schools could not be truly desegregated—in their view of what constituted desegregation—unless the racial composition of the student body of each school substantially reflected the racial composition of the population of the metropolitan area as a whole. The metropolitan area was then defined as Detroit plus 53 of the outlying school districts.

* * *

The Michigan educational structure involved in this case, in common with most States, provides for a large measure of local control and a review of the scope and character of these local powers indicates the extent to which the inter-district remedy approved by the two courts could disrupt and alter the structure of public education in Michigan. The metropolitan remedy would require, in effect, consolidation of 54 independent school districts historically administered as separate units into a vast new super school district. . . . Entirely apart from the logistical and other serious problems attending large-scale transportation of students, the consoli-

---

**The Crisis*, June–July 1972, p. 185. Reprinted with permission of *The Crisis* Magazine, official publication of the NAACP.

dation would give rise to an array of other problems in financing and operating this new school system. Some of the more obvious questions would be: What would be the status and authority of the present popularly elected school boards? Would the children of Detroit be within the jurisdiction and operating control of a school board elected by the parents and residents of other districts? What board or boards would levy taxes for school operations in these 54 districts constituting the consolidated metropolitan area? What provisions could be made for assuring substantial equality in tax levies among the 54 districts, if this were deemed requisite? What provisions would be made for financing? Would the validity of long-term bonds be jeopardized unless approved by all of the component districts as well as the State? What body would determine that portion of the curricula now left to the discretion of local school boards? Who would establish attendance zones, purchase school equipment, locate and construct new schools, and indeed attend to all the myriad day-to-day decisions that are necessary to school operations affecting potentially more than three quarters of a million pupils? . . .

It may be suggested that all of these vital operational problems are yet to be resolved by the District Court, and that this is the purpose of the Court of Appeals' proposed remand. But it is obvious from the scope of the inter-district remedy itself that absent a complete restructuring of the laws of Michigan relating to school districts the District Court will become first, a *de facto* "legislative authority" to resolve these complex questions, and then the "school superintendent" for the entire area. This is a task which few, if any, judges are qualified to perform and one which would deprive the people of control of schools through their elected representatives.

* * *

The controlling principle consistently expounded in our holdings is that the scope of the remedy is determined by the nature and extent of the constitutional violation. . . . Before the boundaries of separate and autonomous school districts may be set aside by consolidating the separate units for remedial purposes or by imposing a cross-district remedy, it must first be shown that there has been a constitutional violation within one district that produces a significant segregative effect in another district. Specifically it must be shown that racially discriminatory acts of the state or local school districts, or of a single school district, have been a substantial cause of inter-district segregation. Thus an inter-district remedy might be in order where the racially discriminatory acts of one or more school districts caused racial segregation in an adjacent district, or where district lines have been deliberately drawn on the basis of race. In such circumstances an inter-district remedy would be appropriate to eliminate the inter-district segregation directly caused by the constitutional violation. Conversely, without an inter-district violation and inter-district effect, there is no constitutional wrong calling for an inter-district remedy.

The record before us, voluminous as it is, contains evidence of *de jure* segregated conditions only in the Detroit schools; indeed,

Under the gaze of police and newsmen, school buses bring young black students to predominantly white South Boston High School.

that was the theory on which the litigation was initially based and on which the District Court took evidence. . . . With no showing of significant violation by the 53 outlying school districts and no evidence of any inter-district violation or effect, the court went beyond the original theory of the case as framed by the pleadings and mandated a metropolitan area remedy. To approve the remedy ordered by the court would impose on the outlying districts, not shown to have committed any constitutional violation, a wholly impermissible remedy based on a standard not hinted at in *Brown I* and *II* or any holding of this Court.

* * *

We conclude that the relief ordered by the District Court and affirmed by the Court of Appeals was based upon an erroneous standard and was unsupported by record evidence that acts of the outlying districts affected the discrimination found to exist in the schools of Detroit. Accordingly, the judgment of the Court of Appeals is vacated and the case is remanded for further proceedings consistent with this opinion leading to prompt formulation of a decree directed to eliminating the segregation found to exist in Detroit city schools, a remedy which has been delayed since 1970.

Reversed and remanded.

JUSTICE MARSHALL'S DISSENT

. . . However imbedded old ways, however ingrained old prejudices, this Court has not been diverted from its appointed task of making "a living truth" of our constitutional ideal of equal justice under law. . . .

After 20 years of small, often difficult steps toward that great end, the Court today takes a giant step backwards. Notwithstanding a record showing widespread and pervasive racial segregation in the educational system provided by the State of Michigan for children in Detroit, this Court holds that the District Court was powerless to require the State to remedy its constitutional violation in any meaningful fashion. Ironically purporting to base its result on the principle that the scope of the remedy in a desegregation case should be determined by the nature and the extent of the constitutional violation, the Court's answer is to provide no remedy at all for the violation proved in this case, thereby guaranteeing that Negro children in Detroit will receive the same separate and inherently unequal education in the future as they have been unconstitutionally afforded in the past.

I cannot subscribe to this emasculation of our constitutional guarantee of equal protection of the laws and must respectfully dissent. Our precedents, in my view, firmly establish that where, as here, state-imposed segregation has been demonstrated, it becomes the duty of the State to eliminate root and branch all vestiges of racial discrimination and to achieve the greatest possible degree of actual desegregation. I agree with both the District Court and the Court of Appeals that, under the facts of this case, this duty cannot be fulfilled unless the State of Michigan involves outlying metropolitan area school districts in its desegregation remedy. Furthermore, I perceive no basis either in law or in the practicalities of the situation justifying the State's interposition of school district boundaries as absolute barriers to the implementation of an effective desegregation remedy. Under established and frequently used Michigan procedures, school district lines are both flexible and permeable for a wide variety of purposes, and there is no reason why they must now stand in the way of meaningful desegregation relief.

The rights at issue in this case are too fundamental to be abridged on grounds as superficial as those relied on by the majority today. We deal here with the right of all of our children, whatever their race, to an equal start in life and to an equal opportunity to reach their full potential as citizens. Those children who have been denied that right in the past deserve better than to see fences thrown up to deny them that right in the future. Our Nation, I fear, will be ill-served by the Court's refusal to remedy separate and unequal education, for unless our children begin to learn together, there is little hope that our people will ever learn to live together.

Desegregation is not and was never expected to be an easy task. Racial attitudes ingrained in our Nation's childhood and adolescence are not quickly thrown aside in its middle years. But just as the inconvenience of some cannot be allowed to stand in the way of the rights of others, so public opposition, no matter how strident, cannot be permitted to divert this Court from the enforcement of the constitutional principles at issue in this case. Today's holding, I fear, is more a reflection of a perceived public mood that we have gone far enough in enforcing the Constitution's guarantee of equal justice than it is the product of neutral principles of law. In the short run, it may seem to be the easier course to allow our great metropolitan areas to be divided up each into two cities—one white, the other black—but it is a course, I predict, our people will ultimately regret. I dissent.*

Explosion in Black Politics

211

A CALL TO ACTION

Since the Negro convention movement in the early decades of the nineteenth century, black men and women have assembled to develop strategies to strengthen their position in white America. Because their subordination to majority rule has been eased only gradually, the issues aired, the resolutions passed, and the tactics adopted have an almost eerie similarity to earlier conventions. Meeting for the first time in Gary, Indiana, in March 1972, the Black Political Convention resolved that "the American economic and political system ought to be given 'one more chance'" and set about to lay down the ground rules and construct a federation called the National Black Political Assembly "to develop mechanisms and strategies for the future economic and political empowerment of black people."

The assembly created a management structure with a representative 51-person steering committee known as the Black Political Council. The first officers included Congressman Charles Diggs of Michigan, Mayor Richard Hatcher of Gary, and, as secretary-general, Imamu Baraka of Newark. Faced with a continuing series of conflicts over methods, the assembly survived its birth pangs, although by 1974 it had still to make its mark. In March of that year, Little Rock was the site of its gathering and Central High School the scene of some of its meetings, sweet irony for a nation which had watched the bitter and bloody entrance of a handful of young blacks into that school not twenty years earlier.

The issues which immobilized the assembly transcended the usual struggles for power so familiar to activist organizations. The growing number of black elected officials created concern among assembly delegates that they would inundate the assembly in a politics-as-usual sea in which the white-led major political parties would still be dominant. The black politicians, on the other hand, feared the revolutionary posture of a Baraka and the latent activism of younger blacks would embarrass their more conservative constituencies. Few black elected officials attended the Little Rock meeting which devoted most of its time to workshops designed to show delegates how to organize at local levels. The theme of the assembly continued to be that which was so clearly articulated by Mayor Hatcher in his keynote address to the first assembly in his home city.

Richard Gordon Hatcher was the first black mayor of a major northern city, winning election in 1968. An attorney, he has been a strong voice for urban reform, not only because black people have become city dwellers, but because the health of the nation depends upon viable metropolitan areas. We need, he said in 1970, "the redevelopment of political structures which can take effective action." His 1972 speech elaborates on that theme.

---

*Milliken v. Bradley, 94 S. Ct. 3112 (1974).

Some of the white bourgeois news media have criticized us for welcoming all brothers and sisters. It is our convention. We shall determine who attends it. All black people are welcome. Thousands strong, we warmly embrace Angela Davis and Bobby Seale.

This convention can make history. Whether it does will depend on what we do here today. We must emerge from this convention with an independent national black political agenda, a dynamic program for black liberation that, in the process, will liberate all America from its current decadence.

Equally important, we must not leave this convention until we have built the mechanism to implement our program. Program must mesh with action. For this we must create a living organization.

And as we deliberate, as we plan, as we work—the banner waving over our heads must proclaim "unity." Without that unity, all is lost.

* * *

In 1969, black median income was *still* only 60 percent of white income, black unemployment was *still* twice that of white unemployment, and a black man with four years of high school *still* earned less money than a white man with an eighth-grade education.

In our infinite patience, we have tried year after year, election after election, to work with the two major political parties. We believed the pledges, believed the platforms, believed the promises, each time hoping they would not again be sold out . . . hoping . . . hoping . . . always hoping.

We are through believing. We are through hoping. We are through trusting in the two major white American political parties. Hereafter, we shall rely on the power of our own black unity.

We shall no longer bargain away our support for petty jobs or symbolic offices. If we are to support any political party, the price will now run high—very high.

First. We emphatically reject the role of adviser to the party's governing circles. Advisers are impotent. We are strong. Advisers do not vote on vital questions. We must have a vote in every decision which affects the party, black people and this country.

* * *

Second. Our sharing of power must take place on every political level, from precinct to ward, to county, to state, to Capitol Hill, to presidential cabinet.

Third. We are not concerned with minute tidbits of political power. We must be accorded the largest share of political power resulting from the following tests: our proportionate contribution to the party's vote, or the defeats that would occur were we to withhold that vote, or the importance of the black question on the American scene.

Whichever of these tests yields the greatest amount of political representation, that is what we must have.

Fourth. We shall name our own candidates for public office and our own party and governmental committee members. No political party to which we attach ourselves may any longer pick and choose the Toms and Sallys among us.

Fifth. The political party with which we identify ourselves must work from the bottom up, not the top down.

Before critical national decisions are made, they must be discussed in every nook and cranny of this country, from the tarpaper shacks in the Mississippi Delta to the pine hovels in the Appalachian Hills, from the rank and fetid basement apartments of 47th Street to the barrios of Spanish Harlem.

* * *

In considering when a political party may lay claim to our support and fidelity, we come now to the sixth and final point. It is by far the most crucial.

Who does the party represent? For whose benefit does it exist? What arouses its indignation? For whom does it have compassion? Who are its allies, and who its enemies? In short, *what does the political party stand for? What is its ideology?*

Preoccupation with power, while neglecting ideology, is the prelude to opportunism and betrayal.

This political convention will come to naught, it will be a disservice to the people, if the problems of power are permitted to overshadow the pressing issues of the day and our thoughtful solutions to them.

It is always a delicate balance we must maintain between the two—issues and program on one hand, power on the other. To neglect either is a disaster. And so let us consider issues and program.

We demand that any party which asks our support acknowledge the inhumanity every black man, woman, and child faces in a hundred different ways, each and every day of his existence, up and down the width and breadth of this vast country.

And we further demand that the party pledge, in bold script and deafening tones, the immediate liberation of black people from their long night of relentless indignities.

Poverty in the midst of opulence is madness. We demand employment, amply compensated, for every able man and woman, or else a governmental income which honorably sustains them.

Advanced education is not meant only for the children of the elite. We demand free college with adequate stipends for every student who will but make the grade.

We would not house animals where many wretched people dwell. We demand, for every family, a place to live which does not affront the eyes nor offend the nostrils.

No sin is greater than the early maiming of a child's intellect and spirit. We demand a healthy system of public education in which our children can grow and flower.

The state of medical care in the country is a national disgrace. We demand the finest medical and hospital care for every human being, and the absence of the ability to pay should not influence the quality of care.

We demand the eradication of heroin from the ghetto, now eating away the vitals of black youth. White society would never tolerate it in such epidemic proportions in suburbia.

* * *

Finally, we shall never forgive the massive support that a racist American government, and rapacious American corporations, have extended to the white barbarians who reign in the Union of South Africa, Angola, Rhodesia, and Mozambique. You may be sure that the 436 million dollars our government just gave Portugal, in violation of the United Nations' embargo, will be fully used against our brothers in the guerilla movement in Mozambique and Angola.

No self-respecting Afro-American can, without a sense of profound betrayal, offer one iota of further support to any political party which does not condemn American foreign policy with abhorrence, and pledge to end our savage repression of the struggling peoples in the Third World.

This convention signals the end of hip pocket politics. We ain't in nobody's hip pocket no more!

We are through with any political party, and many of us with any political system, which is not irrevocably committed to our first principles, pursued in tenacious action: The liberation of black people at home and the end of exploitation abroad.

We say to the two American political parties: This is their last clear chance; they have had too many already.

These are not idle threats. Only senile fools would think them so. The choice is theirs. To ignore our demands is to will the consequences. Those of us already disenchanted with the political system could conceivably turn to fearsome tactics, shattering the quiet routine of daily life. Those of us still committed to a political solution may then cross the Rubicon and form a third party political movement.

* * *

And when, if they leave us no choice—and if we form a third political movement, we shall take with us Chicanos, Puerto Ricans, Indians, Orientals, a wonderful kaleidoscope of colors.

And that is not all.

We shall also take with us the best of white America. We shall take with us many a white youth nauseated by the corrupt values rotting the innards of this society; many a white intellectual, revolted by the mendacity of the ruling ideology; many of the white poor, who have nothing to lose but the poverty which binds them; many a white ex-G.I., who dares to say "never again"; yes, and many of the white working class, too.

The sixties were an exciting decade, loaded with ferment, freedom rides, sit-ins, marches. It was all there—from the strains of "We Shall Overcome," sung warmly with arms linked—to the penetrating cries of black power, with fists raised. We buried some wonderful brothers and sisters who strode, like giants, across the decade, sweeping away injustice before them. And for each murdered martyr, a half-million black soldiers took his place. The '70's will be the decade of an independent black political thrust. Its destiny will depend upon us. . . .*

---

*From "Black Politics in the 70's" by Richard Gordon Hatcher from *The Black Scholar*, September 1972. Reprinted by permission of *The Black Scholar* and Richard Gordon Hatcher, Mayor, City of Gary, Indiana.

THE CONGRESSIONAL BLACK CAUCUS

Launched in 1969, the Congressional Black Caucus was designed to express the needs of black Americans in particular and the poor in general. Comprised of all the black members of the House of Representatives, all Democrats, and financed mainly by annual fund-raising dinners in Washington, the caucus introduces and supports legislation in a number of priority areas relating to the interests and well-being of its constituents. The official position on any matter is determined by a two-thirds vote, although such a vote is not binding on a member who dissents. In the following statements, both from the September 1973 issue of Focus, *Louis Stokes, who succeeded Charles C. Diggs as chairman of the caucus, and Augustus A. Adair, then its Executive Director, throw light upon the objectives and operations of the group.*

THE CAUCUS: PROGRESS THROUGH LEGISLATION

Louis Stokes

Many people have raised the questions: Why a separate caucus of black Congresspersons? Why is this necessary? What is the role of the Congressional Black Caucus? What are its primary objectives? And, since its organization in January 1969, what has the caucus done?

It is common knowledge that American politics began with coalitions based on common interests involving economic, social, religious, and ethnic groups. Today, on Capitol Hill, there are many caucuses, both formal and informal. Generally, these caucuses are based on partisan politics, political philosophy, geography, social issues, and special interests.

In this context, the Congressional Black Caucus is not a maverick organization. Instead, we are a coalition of Congresspersons deeply concerned about the issues, needs, and aspirations of minority Americans. We are, therefore, interested in developing, introducing, and passing progressive legislation which will meet the needs of millions of neglected citizens.

As Congresspersons, we realize that power politics is the name of the game. We have studied the rules. We comprehend the game and we are determined to have some meaningful input in the decisions of the legislative branch of the federal government. Furthermore, we have reached a point of political sophistication that provides us the knowledge and skill necessary not only to set our own agenda, but to determine our own frame of reference. In so doing, we move not against the current, but in fact with it, in seeking to make democracy what it ought to be for all Americans.

Initially, there were a number of misconceptions as to the role and responsibilities of the Congressional Black Caucus. Some felt that the caucus was trying to replace traditional civil rights groups. Still others felt that the caucus was trying to become the national forum or clearinghouse for a host of problems and issues confronting black Americans.

In fact, at first we were unclear about our proper role. Therefore, in the past year we have had to analyze what our resources are, what we should be doing, and how best to do it. And our conclusion is this: If we are to be effective, if we are going to make a meaningful contribution to minority citizens and this country, then it must be as legislators. This is the area in which we possess expertise—and it is within the halls of Congress that we must make this expertise felt.

This, essentially, is our mandate in the 93rd Congress, and to this end we have solicited and continue to seek financial resources for the maintenance of an excellent staff which provides us with the necessary professional services needed to accomplish these goals.

For over a year we have held hearings and conferences on subjects ranging from health to minority enterprise, from racism in the military to racism in the media. In the course of our investigations, we have assembled data which serve as the basis for a portion of our legislative program.

Thus far, the members of the Congressional Black Caucus have, as a body, sponsored or introduced bills in a number of areas which relate to the needs of our communities. Our legislative efforts had positive results in the recent attempt by Congress to rescue the Office of Economic Opportunity from presidential dismemberment, and to increase the minimum wage. We have united behind several pieces of anti-impoundment legislation, hoping to checkmate the administration's callous domestic policies. Our hearings on governmental lawlessness resulted in the Bureaucratic Accountability Act, a bill which would protect individuals' rights in their dealings with the federal government and strengthen the oversight powers of Congress. We have also joined together in support of a bill making Dr. Martin Luther King's birthday a national holiday.

Moreover, we have introduced legislation in every conceivable area. We are offering legislative alternatives to correct the problems of the elderly; improve and expand federally assisted child care centers; provide for direct election of the President; create a system of national health insurance; improve pension systems; grant equal representation to the residents of the District of Columbia; create jobs through public service employment; broaden the income tax base; require U.S. companies to abide by fair employment practices in South Africa; compensate innocent victims of violent crime; abolish the death penalty; improve the legal services program; and outlaw the unethical practice of psycho-surgery.

More importantly, the myriad bills that I mention here are only a fraction of our legislative efforts in this 93rd Congress.

As Congress moves to reassume its rightful place in our tripartite system of government, you can be assured that the Congressional Black Caucus will move progressively on several fronts. Where we can provide leadership for those colleagues who represent large minority constituencies, we shall. Where our causes can benefit by coalition politics, we shall coalesce. And whenever or wherever we can serve impoverished and minority citizens as legislators, unquestionably we shall.

Congressional Black Caucus members have pledged themselves to "developing, introducing, and passing progressive legislation designed to meet the needs of millions of neglected citizens." They felt that if they were to succeed in the effort to "promote the public welfare," as opposed to promoting the riches of the corporate elite, then it must be as legislators.

But this much-needed legislative undertaking requires that the four women and twelve men who comprise the Congressional Black Caucus not only be aware of the substantive objectives of proposed legislation, but also know the context of the bill. They have to know: (1) the sponsors; (2) the probable House and Senate supporters; (3) positions of major unions and industries; (4) the need for the legislation; (5) the administration's position; (6) the minority or opposing views; (7) the approximate cost if enacted; (8) the probable amendments or other floor strategies designed to kill, weaken, or enhance its passage; and scores of other variables.

The successful passage or prevention of passage of a substantive piece of legislation is a complicated and delicate process. A vital part of any rational strategy is a probing and informed source, succinctly analyzing the proposal and its probable impact.

The caucus staff felt that it could best aid the caucus members by providing them with weekly "legislative alerts" on key bills coming up for floor consideration. This, the staff felt, would provide the necessary uniformity in direction and information.

Each Thursday the staff meets informally to assess the probable activities of Congress for the coming week. A staffer obtains from the Whip's office the weekly calendar and other documents designed to inform Congress on probable weekly activity.

After a discussion of the legislative items, the staff decides which issues are of major import and who will analyze them. Within a given deadline, the written material is presented to the entire caucus staff. This is usually done to eliminate major flaws and to broaden the insight of the presentation.

Once the staff has read it and put it in final form, the alert is forwarded to each Congressional Black Caucus member. After this point, any number of things can happen. Usually key staff members from the caucus members' offices will call to discuss portions of the alert, looking forward to developing a floor strategy. Sometimes they wish to have a position distinguished or clarified. On still other occasions they may wish to know how many caucus members are supporting the position as written, or what members will offer amendments or make floor speeches.

At any rate, once an alert is issued there is invariably a great deal of discussion on the most effective strategy for the Congressional Black Caucus to take.

The alert is, essentially, an in-house document and as a rule is distributed only to offices of members of the Congressional Black Caucus.

No arbitrary guidelines are established to limit or increase the number of issues analyzed. Instead, the caucus staff, in its professional operation, decides the number of issues which will be reported. However, on occasion a caucus member will request legislative information or offer a suggestion of an important legislative item which deserves staff attention.

Among the main sources that the caucus staff utilizes are materials from the Congressional Research Service of the Library of Congress, committee and subcommittee reports, federal government documents, and information provided by various research groups. Although the alert is an independent staff product, caucus staffers make every effort to consult with caucus members (and their staffs) who have jurisdictional responsibilities to maximize the depth and assessment of the legislation. . . .*

213

GROWTH AT THE GRASSROOTS

In the fall of 1974, three black Chicago politicians announced that they would run in the 1975 Democratic primary as mayoral candidates. The announcements gave promise of future change in Chicago and underlined the importance of local black elected officials on the national scene. Black mayors and other officials in large and medium-sized cities had, by the end of 1974, become commonplace. As they looked beyond their local problems to the national arena, they came to rely on the National Black Caucus of Local Elected Officials (NBCLEO).

The NBCLEO objectives were restated late in 1974 by the vice-mayor of Richmond, Virginia, and NBCLEO chairman, Harry L. March, III. Writing to President Gerald Ford, March urged the President to "consciously raise serious domestic problems to the level of prominence formerly reserved for foreign policy." He also asked Ford to appoint black men and women to key positions. Early in 1975 William T. Coleman, Jr., became the first black Secretary of Transportation.

The significance of a national organization of local black officials had not been fully demonstrated during its infant years, but its potential for exercising political leverage grew, as suggested by the following article from Black Enterprise. *At the very least, as Mayor Richard Hatcher observed in the summer of 1974, it could help "reopen the closed channels of communication between American cities and American central government." Like its sister group, the Black Congressional Caucus, the NBCLEO reserved judgment on President Ford until his performance in appointments, funding, and overall recognition of black-related issues gave substance to his promises.*

THE "OTHER" BLACK CAUCUS

It was a sort of Golden Age of Black Mayors: Carl Stokes in Cleveland, 1967; Richard Hatcher in Gary, 1968; Charles Evers in Fayette, 1969; and Kenneth Gibson in Newark, 1970. With glamor they came, vanquishing racism, booting out corruption, saying profound, quotable things about relevant national issues. As a result, top urban management pros came to them with advice, foundation doors sprang open, local businessmen offered support, and

*Reprinted from "The Caucus: Progress Through Legislation," by Louis Stokes and Augustus A. Adair, in *Focus,* by permission of the Joint Center for Political Studies.

federal funding agency officials made themselves accessible. Problems weren't solved overnight, but foundations were laid.

At the same time, black people were also being elected to local office in dozens of other cities across the country. In small and medium-sized towns like Inkster, Michigan, and East Orange, New Jersey, they were becoming mayors, city councilmen, county commissioners. Elected without glamor, without national fanfare, and often without even knowing of each other's existence, they were in this Golden Age, but not of it.

Among them were few political pros; they were real estate dealers, insurance salesmen, workingmen. They lacked, for the most part, money, expertise, and most other resources necessary for dealing with the daily crises of urban administration. Adding to their woes, in some cases, was President Nixon's "new federalism," which decentralized government funding agencies and put purse strings in the hands of regional officials who seemed at times to have a knack for paralyzing proposals and requests with mounds of red tape.

As the number of black local elected officials grew to its present 880 (of a total of 1,860 blacks in elective office), those who attended the National League of Cities' annual congresses began meeting informally to talk over common problems. It was obvious to all that something needed to be done. It was important enough that they have a vehicle for communicating with each other, but even more important was the need for a unified black voice within the NLC. Each year at the Congress of Cities, representatives of the NLC's

Increasing numbers of blacks sought and won elective office in the 1970's. Here Virgil Calvert, mayoral candidate in East St. Louis, is surrounded by his supporters.

15,000 member cities participate in workshops, committee meetings, and floor sessions to hammer out a consensus on each of dozens of issues. This consensus becomes National Municipal Policy and the positions taken therein are lobbied for in Washington by the NLC staff. That lobby is generally conceded to be one of the strongest forces representing urban interests in Washington. With the nation's cities becoming blacker each year, the question of black interests in NLC policy statements was becoming increasingly vital.

At the NLC gathering in Atlanta in late 1970, the National Black Caucus of Local Elected Officials was formally organized. Mayor Robert Blackwell of Highland Park, Mich., a Detroit suburb of 35,000, was elected Chairman. Other officers and a 20-member steering committee were also selected. In a short statement of purpose, the new caucus recognized "the existence of problems peculiar to us with which we must deal within and without the National League of Cities and the United States Conference of Mayors," and voiced intention to "act and react in those situations where we believe our common interests so require."

Staff services for NBCLEO were arranged with the NLC and the Joint Center for Political Studies, a black-oriented research and information center in Washington which had been instrumental in helping caucus members organize. Clarence Townes, vice president of the Joint Center, believes that the caucus is potentially a "very powerful group" in the area of black/urban problems.

"The traditional method of government pacifying black folk is losing its effectiveness," Townes says. "As the number of black elected officials increases, government must respond to the needs of black folk through that leadership. The civil rights groups, which were the only representation black people had until recently, pressed government in some fairly nonspecific ways. What elected officials have the responsibility for doing is redirecting some of the flow of government services, 95 percent of which have been directed to white folks."

To that end, the caucus has already successfully moved to place blacks on all standing NLC committees, with special attention to the Community Development and Human Resources committees. Says Antonio Harrison, who serves as NBCLEO's staff liaison with NLC, "We want to infiltrate the whole structure of the League."

Though NBCLEO is so new that its "game plan" for strengthening black representation within NLC is rather indefinite, Harrison indicated that the general idea is to get caucus positions merged with those of the general body so as to avoid black-white floor fights. "I believe we can exert influence disproportionate to our numerical strength within the organization in much the same way as blacks influenced the Congress to pass strong civil rights measures in the sixties," he says. "We want to get our concerns filtered through the structure rather than play any mau-mau games."

Dr. Frank Reeves, executive director of the Joint Center, believes that NBCLEO's potential lies as much outside the NLC as in. "Almost more significant than getting positions on NLC committees is the fact of having a spokesman for the group," he says. "Previously, there has been no single voice for this category of black leaders. Hatcher, Stokes, and others spoke out on various issues, but they could not do it with the same weight as the official representatives of black elected officials."

* * *

Hopefully, NBCLEO's association with the Joint Center will help eliminate some of the problems peculiar to local black elected officials. Though many of the problems of cities like Highland Park, E. St. Louis, Compton, and others parallel those of every other urban area—crime, unemployment, education, health care, etc.—black elected officials frequently must overcome handicaps imposed as a result of their skin color before even starting to deal with them.

"White officials have the same basic problem, lack of adequate financial resources," points out Clarence Townes, "but often blacks, once elected, find they don't have those human resources that are so badly needed. Bankers and other people who would normally supply those resources are smiling at him, but he can't get any money—or advice."

Thus, NBCLEO finds itself in the rather unique position of having to run vigorously before it has begun to walk. Because those resources are often unavailable to officials of towns of 10,000 to 80,000—the constituencies of most black mayors are closer to the former figure and only about a half-dozen of them serve on a "full-time" basis—NBCLEO members hope that their organization, in conjunction with JCPS, will be able to establish national urban skills and information banks for minorities. Men like Mayor James Williams of E. St. Louis would have only to check with the centralized source to locate a top-flight urban planner or civil engineer who was available in another part of the country. Similarly, local officials who couldn't get local help would be able to find out immediately what agency or foundation had money available for a specific proposal. Direct economic benefits could also be realized by minority contractors who were notified by regional caucus members (who, in turn, had been notified by the central data bank) of contracts being let in other parts of the country on which they might bid.

* * *

Assessing NBCLEO's performance and possibilities is difficult at best. Because of the way in which the caucus functions within NLC, it is difficult for its leaders to point to specific items of NLC policy as results of NBCLEO action. It does seem safe to say, however, that until 1969 statements of NLC policy concerning minorities were limited to expressions of general agreement that nonwhites are indeed citizens of the United States, and, as such, entitled to all of the rights guaranteed by the Constitution and the Bill of Rights.

With the 1969 statement of National Municipal Policy there came a dramatic change, in some areas at least, from statements of passive agreement with Constitutional ideals to calls for specific affirmative action by government in behalf of the "disadvantaged and minorities." These included suggestions that funds and technical assistance be allocated "to encourage local entrepreneurship and indigenous industry in deprived areas" and that the Small Business

Administration be granted "increased authority and funds" and be required to "emphasize loans in areas which have substantial unemployment and loans or loan guarantees to 'high risk' ventures." NLC members also urged that legal assistance programs be allowed "to function in a commercial context and serve low-income area businesses much as larger law firms serve their business clients." Other suggestions were made for improvements in programs dealing with public assistance, health care, education, and unemployment. . . .*

Cycles and Circles:
The Economic Merry-Go-Round

214

BLUEPRINT FOR BLACK SELF-HELP

Of the newer black self-help organizations of the seventies, one of the most dynamic was Operation PUSH (People United to Save Humanity), an outgrowth of an earlier Chicago-based movement, Operation Breadbasket. The key figure in both organizations was Jesse L. Jackson, a close friend and associate of Martin Luther King, Jr., and like him a Baptist clergyman. Jackson had been with King only moments before the latter was fatally shot at a motel in Memphis, Tennessee, on April 4, 1968. Reminding one of a younger Frederick Douglass in appearance and platform eloquence, Jackson held that the church should address itself to social concerns, particularly to bread-and-butter issues.

Jackson made full use of picketing and boycotting to compel business firms to hire blacks, to market their products, and to use black-owned service companies. By shutting down construction projects, he forced unions and contractors to come to the negotiating table. His basic aim, he said, was to root out "America's internal disease." As one major step toward this end, he set forth his organization's proposals "to save the worker," his observations appearing in an article, "Completing the Agenda of Dr. King," in the July 1974 issue of Ebony.

COMPLETING THE AGENDA OF DR. KING

Six years ago, the nation and the world mourned the loss of Dr. Martin Luther King, Jr. Our state of grief was traumatic and real as we pondered the meaning of his assassination. We now understand that his murder was a pivotal act in a strategy designed to break up, dissolve, and scatter the coalition of progressive forces in our country that had won civil rights and abolished the racist insult of segregation.

Six years ago, the moral lights were snuffed out around us as

*From "The 'Other' Black Caucus," from *Black Enterprise,* January 1972, pp. 29–31, 33. Reprinted by permission of *Black Enterprise.*

demagogues and political assassins infused hopelessness and despair into the climate of a presidential election. When Dr. King was murdered in Memphis, we lost a great prophet who had done much to bring democracy within the reach of millions of blacks and other nonwhite and poor citizens. We lost a man who told the truth at a level where it shaped the nation's conscience and attitude and challenged the congenital deformity of racism in America. We also lost a great mobilizer—a force which coalesced divergent groups into a visible and viable movement for humanity. His tragic death by political assassination served to disintegrate and halt the movement he helped to initiate and build. Many who had followed him lost hope. They became bitter, despondent, and cynical. Often cloaked in blind rage, they dropped his agenda, his plan for progress and peace.

On April 4 of this year, in the city where the prophet died, our Operation PUSH satellite mobilized thousands of people in a great demonstration of hope and determination. We in PUSH are about the serious business of resurrecting the agenda for which Dr. King gave his life—to "Save the Worker." The threefold goal of our movement at this point in history is to secure the jobs of those already working (that has to be where we hold the line), to get the unemployed employed, and to get those working but not making a livable wage *organized.* That has to be the three-pronged thrust of our Civil Economics Movement.

Undergirding this basic economic thrust is the need to organize consumer power represented by the $51 billion per year in wages and salaries which the black community now earns. We must see that this money keeps circulating and gets institutionalized in the form of the growth of black-owned businesses and financial institutions. As workers and professionals, the black population is concentrated in the large urban centers of the country. In every one of these areas our community must raise the questions of how much taxes do we pay and in what banks are our taxes deposited? In many areas our children are the majority of those attending the public schools. How much of the insurance carried on our children by the various state and local school boards is with black-owned insurance companies? This combination of concerns, jobs, and the building up of institutions in our communities embraces the self-interest of the total community and is the basis for total community involvement.

* * *

We are aware that the "energy hoax" will eventually run its course—although we may be paying from 60¢ to 75¢ a gallon for gasoline by that time. But the basic economic rights outlined above must nevertheless be won. Whether the worker is an airline pilot or a skycap, whether a nurse or a longshoreman, that worker cannot pay bills and provide for a family and live in dignity when there are no jobs. Further, without the protection of legislation allowing for a moratorium on payment of major bills, and without extended unemployment compensation, millions of persons could lose their homes, could lose their on-the-job health insurance, and might even have to remove their children from schools. Their entire fundamental base for economic survival could be ripped off. Thus it is in pursuit of the goals of securing the jobs that black people already hold, of returning the unemployed to the labor force, and of organizing the unorganized workers that Operation PUSH has become so deeply involved. We have alerted the areas where there are satellites of PUSH—the various large industrial areas—and the work that we have initiated is taking place in many parts of the country. It is no longer confined to Chicago, nor is it confined to where I can physically go. People at the local levels have gotten the message! Ministers and local leaders of PUSH in a number of communities are visiting with workers in industrial plants as a regular style of organization—and that will bring good results. In this regard, I am especially encouraged by the number of young, able ministers who are coming forward to take up the mantle of leadership. They are carrying on, in a bold and dedicated way, the revolutionary democratic traditions of the Black Church. . . . A slow rebirth is also taking place among white ministerial leadership, some of which I met at Yale Divinity School during a recent lecture series. All these ministers, black and white, are in the vanguard of a new generation of ministers who, in the prophetic tradition, are committed to be watchmen on the wall in carrying the "good news to the captive."

Part of that "good news" is that Operation PUSH has not been, and cannot ever be, a one-issue organization. For whereas the energy situation affects us today, tomorrow will bring another situation with which black people will have to deal. Our current involvement in exposing the energy hoax will result, we hope, in stimulating public awareness that inflation and tax robbery and unemployment are *chronic* features of the U.S. economy. Our understanding of this is what determines our New Agenda.

Dr. King once made a profound assessment of the Civil Rights Era of our movement. He said: "The real significance of the civil rights struggle is the effects which it had on the psyche of the black man. We armed ourselves with the armor of dignity and respect; we straightened up our backs." There is a great lesson in that experience for organized labor today. Organized labor is challenged in this period of severe economic crisis to straighten up its back and regain the moral authority it once enjoyed when it, too, was a *movement* as well as an organization. We draw upon the spirit of struggle embodied in Dr. King's work when we declare that if we do not join forces to rebuild the human rights coalition, the American people will wallow in economic deprivation and moral and spiritual decay for generations to come.

* * *

The New Agenda of our movement is designed to give hope where there is now a sense of hopelessness and to mobilize into a mass movement those who are now immobilized by cynicism. The enlightened strategy of mass-movement-building requires that coalitions at the local community level be formed around issues, regardless of ethnicity: blacks in cooperation with Mexican Americans (Chicanos), Puerto Ricans, "American Indians," Asian Americans—

all the diverse segments of the population which also experienced much of the "benign neglect" that has been our experience, and who seek a constructive way out of the present crisis. In this regard we must give special recognition to the significance of women workers and the role they are playing today in clearing away the darkness and giving leadership to the struggle for regenerating America. This is particularly true of the recently organized Coalition of Labor Union Women which is destined to have a profoundly positive effect on organized labor in the struggle for a civilized society in our country.

The Watergate flood is surely destined to drown the wicked, but the righteous must organize an Ark. The multi-ethnic coalition we propose must mobilize around a New Agenda of economic rights. It cannot afford to allow itself to be led into the kind of trap that narrows our options down to choosing between a variety of Republican and Democratic Party presidential candidates—each of whom is trying to get George Wallace on his ticket. This kind of unprincipled compromise can only lead the nation into a kind of betrayal such as was seen in 1876 when the first Reconstruction was overthrown in the South. That betrayal at the presidential level carried America back into the dark ages of Ku Klux Klan terror and psychological depression.

We are moving toward 1976 with a clear vision and a sense of power. Our commitment to finish Dr. King's unfinished agenda is a commitment to guarantee a progressive and civilized future for ourselves and our children.*

215

FAIR HOUSING: A SLOW FRUIT

Racial exclusion and discrimination in housing continued to be a major economic problem to blacks in the seventies. In 1968 Congress established a ten-year program to achieve the goal it had first enunciated in the Housing Act of 1949: "a decent home and a suitable environment for every American family." In spite of explicit laws, backed by court decisions, the pattern of discriminatory housing had lost little of its sway by the mid-seventies. The problem of segregated housing was compounded by the reluctance of the Nixon administration to subsidize low-income developments or to grant housing allowances to low-income families.

Since its establishment by Congress as an independent agency in 1957, the United States Commission on Civil Rights has taken an interest in housing inequities. In February 1973 the commission issued a brochure, Understanding Fair Housing, *which pointed up some of the problems as well as some of the possibilities. The concluding section, "Prospects for the Future," is a combination balance sheet and call to action.*

PROSPECTS FOR THE FUTURE

One lesson learned from the civil rights experience in the 1960's

---

*"Completing the Agenda of Dr. King" by Reverend Jesse L. Jackson from *Ebony*, June 1974. Reprinted by permission of *Ebony* Magazine, copyright © 1974, by Johnson Publishing Company, Inc.

is there is no single path to resolving problems of racial injustice. The lesson was learned on a trial-and-error basis, as the Nation focused its attention piecemeal on civil rights issues—voting rights, jobs, public accommodations, and education—as though each provided the only solution. Housing came last.

Housing is one of the most complex and intractable areas in the civil rights field. A denial of the right to vote can be corrected instantly because thousands of disfranchised citizens can be registered to vote. While discrimination of the past is more difficult to overcome in employment and education, the Nation has achieved measurable results in these areas in a relatively short time.

In housing, the legacy of the past has a much stronger bearing on the present and future. Patterns of residence have developed over a period of decades in which government at all levels and private industry combined to establish a racially dual housing market—separate and unequal. The problem facing us now is not merely to end current discriminatory practices, but also to eliminate the effects of past discrimination and reverse the residential segregation that now exists. This is extraordinarily difficult and the answer does not lie in any single approach, whether it be adoption of a fair housing law or breaking down existing suburban barriers—racial and economic—to minority residence. Rather, it lies in an across-the-board effort in which all elements of the housing industry, public and private, become active participants.

Despite the complex and difficult problems that face us in reversing patterns of residential segregation, prospects for the future are not entirely gloomy. There is evidence of change in housing policy and practice—change that is still small and insubstantial, but which can provide the basis for the kind of large-scale effort necessary.

The Federal Government, which years ago was an active exponent of housing discrimination and residential segregation, now maintains strong laws and policies favoring equal housing opportunity. State and local governments have changed their official position. A few decades ago these governments were either indifferent to the problem of housing discrimination or were insistent upon residential segregation. Today 33 States, including the border and Southern States of Kentucky, Maryland, and Virginia, and literally thousands of municipalities, have fair housing laws. Likewise, the policies of the housing industry have changed. Trade associations of mortgage lenders and builders, which in earlier years took positions in support of racial discrimination, now pledge support of the principles of fair housing.

* * *

Nevertheless, a change in official policies, while a beginning, is not enough. The policies must be implemented if results are to be achieved. There are encouraging signs. In recent months HUD, which carries the major responsibility for enforcing the Federal Fair Housing Law, has issued a series of regulations in such areas as affirmative marketing requirements, site selection criteria, and fair housing advertising guidelines. These regulations are an effort to assure that HUD's programs of financial assistance advance the goals of fair housing. The General Services Administration, responsible for providing facilities for most Federal Agencies, has issued regulations concerning the selection of sites for Government installations to assure that lower-income and minority employees have access to housing. The Agencies that supervise mortgage lending institutions have started to accept their responsibilities under Title VIII by issuing regulations to assure that minority home buyers have equal access to mortgage credit.

At the State and local levels, there are small but encouraging signs of action to overcome obstacles to the exercise of free housing choice, particularly the suburban exclusion of lower-income minorities. Several States have passed laws aimed at overcoming the barrier of exclusionary zoning laws that keep out low- and moderate-income housing. Thus, Massachusetts has enacted an "Anti-Snob Zoning Law," which establishes a quota for low- and moderate-income housing for each town in the State. New York has established a State Urban Development Corporation with power to override local zoning laws and other exclusionary land use controls to provide low- and moderate-income housing. Furthermore, in some metropolitan areas, communities that previously viewed each other with hostility are cooperating to develop plans by which they will accept the responsibility for meeting a fair share of the lower-income housing needs of the entire area.

* * *

Private groups are increasingly active in the housing field. A few years ago, private activity was limited to the efforts of scattered fair housing councils and neighborhood stabilization organizations. Today the private fair housing movement has burgeoned, and the knowledge and the sophistication of those involved in the movement have expanded. These groups are engaged in monitoring the effect of Federal housing programs. They are pushing for innovative State and local legislation that will expand housing opportunities throughout the metropolitan areas. And they are urging basic changes in the operation of the private housing market.

None of these developments, singly or in combination, has yet had a significant impact in altering the patterns of segregated racial residence. They must be greatly strengthened if real change is to occur. Fair housing laws—Federal, State, and local—must be enforced much more vigorously than they are now. Federal housing programs must be designed more precisely to achieve equal housing opportunity goals. States and localities must recognize that metropolitan areas represent single social and economic units and take stringent measures to assure that housing is available to all. Private industry—builders, brokers, and lenders—must reevaluate their traditional practices so they can contribute to achieving the goals of fair housing, to which they now pay little more than lip service. The number of organizations and individuals working in the field of fair housing must expand and impress their convictions and strength upon public and private housing officials who may think that the fair housing movement is a passing fad.

In the last analysis, we must ask who benefits from fair housing? The obvious and immediate beneficiaries are, of course, minority group families, who, in an open housing market, gain the benefits of a free housing choice long denied them. But fair housing is of vital importance to us all. The dual housing market has bred a variety of ills from which our whole society is suffering: the physical decay and financial insolvency of our cities; the irrational proliferation of jurisdictions in metropolitan areas separated from each other by race and income; and the racial alienation and distrust that make us strangers to each other. This is the legacy that the present generation has inherited from the past. It is we who will determine which legacy we leave our children.*

216

LONG-RANGE OPTIMISM

In 1974 the U.S. Bureau of Census estimated that median black family income had fallen from 61 percent to 58 percent of median white family income between 1969 and 1973. In the same period, the bureau reported, earnings of black families had failed to keep up with price increases while white family earnings exceeded price levels by 6.1 percent.

While the slippage between black and white was obvious, these data masked a countermovement of black men and women into management and professional occupations, an accelerating trend since 1960. Between 1967 and 1972, the number of blacks in college doubled; between 1961 and 1971, the number of blacks earning over $10,000 a year more than doubled. Between 1960 and 1971, the number of black professionals and technicians increased by 128 percent while the number of black managers, officials, and proprietors almost doubled. In the words of a black official of a giant retail chain, "The placing of a black for show should be a thing of the past."

Paralleling the entrance of blacks into white-dominated corporate and professional structures, blacks increasingly established their own structures, generally at high risk. The suffocating blanket of inflation and economic stagnation that began in 1974 created enormous problems for these enterprises, which tended to concentrate in the retail trades. Their importance to the black community, however, transcended their immediate economic impact, since they stood as symbols of black economic achievement.

Andrew F. Brimmer, who wrote the article below, has been in the middle of national and black economic controversy for almost a decade. Appointed in 1966 to the prestigious Board of Governors of the Federal Reserve Bank, Brimmer spoke out forcefully and authoritatively on black economic matters until he resigned in 1974. He questioned whether black banks contributed significantly to the solutions of black economic problems, whether black industry could compete with the huge white corporate structure, whether minimum wage laws helped or hindered the employment of young unskilled workers. After resigning, Brimmer accepted a teaching position at Harvard as visiting professor of business administration and was elected the first black member of the Board of Directors of the DuPont Company.

---

*The United States Commission on Civil Rights, *Understanding Fair Housing* (Washington, D.C., U.S. Government Printing Office, 1973), pp. 17–18.

SHORT-RUN PROBLEMS WILL NOT HALT AN UPWARD TREND

The long-term prospects for black businesses appear promising, provided black entrepreneurs position themselves to take advantage of the opportunities unfolding before them. It is good to be able to say this, for the short-term prospects are not equally reassuring.

The current year will undoubtedly be a difficult one for black businessmen. Like their white counterparts, they will suffer from the combined effects of inflation and a sluggish economy, the latter the result partly of the energy crisis and partly of a slowdown already underway at the beginning of the year. As unemployment rises in the black community—at a faster pace, perhaps, than in the nation at large—black firms will be faced with a weak market for their products and services. As we shall see, however, even over the short run the outlook is not uniformly bleak.

Virtually every observer who has considered the matter agrees that 1974 will be a year of economic stagnation (perhaps even recession) and rapid inflation. Specific forecasts differ considerably both in their assumptions about economic policy and [in] their expectations for particular economic sectors. However, there appears to be broad agreement on a number of major points. For instance, even before the Arab oil boycott was imposed last November, economic activity in the United States was expected to slow down appreciably. The principal direct impact of the boycott, as was generally anticipated, has been on the automobile and travel industries. But the greatly increased prices of petroleum products have been felt throughout the economy and have given a sharp stimulus to the pace of inflation.

* * *

In retrospect, it is clear that the oil shortage had a severe impact on the economy last winter. Although the figures are subject to revision, it appears that the GNP declined by roughly 6 percent (at a seasonally adjusted annual rate) during the first quarter of 1974. For the second quarter, little or no expansion in real output is expected. However, economic activity should quicken in the second half of 1974. In fact, a number of economists expect real GNP to rise at an annual rate of about 4 percent in the final quarter. The pace of inflation is also expected to slow somewhat.

* * *

Given this unpromising outlook for the economy as a whole, the short-term economic prospects for blacks cannot be bright. In fact, it now appears that the black community once again will bear a disproportionate share of the burden of national economic adjustment, just as was the case during the 1970 recession.

In 1973, black workers improved their job situation noticeably, following several years of disappointing performance. The demand for labor remained strong throughout most of 1973. Despite the reduced growth of output after the first quarter, labor markets tightened as total employment expanded rapidly, and unemployment declined slightly. As a result, the black labor force increased rapidly and the labor force participation rate for blacks edged up, after remaining unchanged throughout 1972.

In 1973, jobs held by blacks climbed by 400,000 to a total of 9.3 million—an increase of 4.6 percent. In contrast, total employment rose by 3.7 percent. The expansion of factory employment, which is of crucial importance to black men, was especially noticeable. Unemployment among blacks declined slightly during 1973, after rising in the previous two years. For 1973 as a whole, the black unemployment rate averaged 8.9 percent—still more than twice the white rate of 4.3 percent. On the other hand, black workers raised their share of jobs in higher-skilled occupations and in high-wage industries. There was also some decline in their participation in low-wage sectors.

This improved job situation undoubtedly was paralleled by a significant rise in black income, though this cannot yet be documented, since Census Bureau figures on money income in 1973 will not be available until later this year. For 1972, the Bureau reported the total money income of blacks at $51.7 billion. This was 6.7 percent of the national total of $773 billion. Blacks, of course, constitute around 11.3 percent of the total population. If they had received the same fraction of total income, their cash receipts in 1972 would have amounted to $87.3 billion, or $35.6 billion more than they actually were. The explanation of this shortfall is widely known: The legacy of racial discrimination and deprivation has limited our ability to acquire marketable skills, while barring us from better-paying jobs.

In the absence of the official Census Bureau figures, one can estimate the racial distribution of total money income in 1973 from a comprehensive analysis of personal income figures published by the Commerce Department's Bureau of Economic Analysis and from Census Bureau data providing racial breakdowns. On this basis, I estimate that total money income for the nation as a whole was in the neighborhood of $870 billion last year. I also estimate that blacks received about $59 billion of this amount, or 6.8 percent of the total. This suggests that the total money income of blacks rose by about 15 percent in 1973, as against about 12.5 percent for the total population.

Blacks will not fare nearly as well during the current year. Slowdowns in production growth, combined with the adverse impact of the energy shortages, have resulted in layoffs in a number of industries and a rise in joblessness since last fall. In the first quarter of 1974, total employment growth slowed considerably, and the overall unemployment rate rose to an average of 5.2 percent (from 4.7 percent in the last quarter of 1973).

The number of jobless increased in most major labor force groups. Among black workers, the unemployment rate went up from an average of 8.6 percent in the final quarter of 1973 to 9.3 percent in the first three months of this year, while the jobless rate for whites rose from 4.2 to 4.7 percent. Most of the first quarter's increase in black unemployment occurred among men, while among white workers the two sexes were more nearly equally affected. If, as expected, the unemployment rate for the total labor force averages close to 6 percent for 1974 as a whole, then the rate for blacks may average close to 11 percent (maintaining the approximate 2:1 ratio of blacks to whites).

* * *

Since the progress of black businessmen is heavily dependent on the economic welfare of blacks generally, it appears that the current year will not be an especially good one for black enterprise. Nevertheless, black businessmen by no means should be excessively pessimistic about the short-term outlook. Thanks to their heavy concentration in retail trade and services, they can expect their total volume of sales to continue to grow—perhaps by as much as 8 percent.

Because of a lack of data, the recent experience of black firms cannot be assessed with precision. A careful consideration of a good deal of indirect evidence suggests, however, that black businesses made steady progress over the last few years.

The only comprehensive figures we have on black businesses were reported in the Census Bureau's "Survey of Minority Business Ownership" for 1969. In that year, blacks owned 163,000 firms, representing 1.4 percent of the national total of 12,021,000. These black firms had gross receipts of $4.474 billion, or 0.24 percent of the $1.89 trillion taken in by all U.S. businesses.

From published figures on business sales, trends in GNP, personal income, total consumer spending, and money income for both blacks and whites, one can make a rough estimate of the gross receipts of black businesses in 1973. In general, total business sales, GNP (in current dollars), and consumer expenditures all rose by 39 percent between 1969 and 1973. Total personal income rose by 38 percent. However, I estimate that total money income (as reported

The late sixties and early seventies saw more and more black men and women move into management and professional positions. Their importance to the black community is both economic and symbolic.

by the Census Bureau) rose by 44 percent and the money income of blacks rose 53 percent. Given the greatly increased efforts to stimulate business ownership among blacks since 1969, the number of black businesses has probably grown slightly faster than the number of businesses in the total economy. The increased emphasis on black identity should have led to increased patronage of black establishments by black consumers. Moreover, black firms have probably been able to cater somewhat more extensively to the market beyond the black community.

* * *

Looking beyond the short-term prospects for blacks in business and beyond the effects of the energy crisis, I would like to reiterate a few observations I have made previously about the long-term outlook. For some time, I have been troubled by the rather slow pace at which blacks are diversifying into new lines of business activity. I appreciate fully the reasons why black businessmen have historically concentrated mainly in retail trade and services. So long as racial segregation and discrimination restricted the access of blacks to housing and public accommodations, it was logical for black businessmen to concentrate on the limited demand for services that a predominantly low-income population was able to register in the market place. I also appreciate the extent to which traditional black businesses have been adversely affected by the abolition of legal restraints on access to public accommodations.

Such historical explanations, however, cannot alter the fact that black businessmen seem caught on a downhill course: While blacks are making some progress in expanding their modest share of the nation's business activity, the fields on which they are concentrating are contracting in comparison with the economy as a whole. During the seventies, the principal areas in which black-owned businesses are found—small-scale retail trade and personal services—will probably expand more slowly than will overall economic activity. Unless there is a major diversification of black-owned enterprises, blacks will end up with an even smaller share of the nation's business receipts in 1980 than they now get.

Moreover, a more diversified pattern of business activity alone will not be enough—it will have to be accompanied by a significant increase in the size and efficiency of black-owned firms. To achieve this latter goal will require much larger aggregations of equity capital than blacks have been able to mobilize to date. This, in turn, means that blacks will have to become more willing to adopt the corporation as a form of business organization and to rely far less on personal ownership. It also means that blacks must become increasingly willing to share in joint ventures with businessmen of other races and to tap the stream of risk capital flowing through the economy as a whole. Finally, blacks must be prepared to undertake, on a much more extensive scale, the hard task of acquiring the technical and managerial skills required to survive and prosper in the sophisticated business world unfolding before us.

In other words, if blacks want to have a truly meaningful role in the business world of the future, a new breed of entrepreneurs is needed. Blacks must be prepared to compete in a variety of new fields against a phalanx of nationwide corporations ever anxious to attract an increasing share of the rising income and expenditures of the black community. For black-owned firms, failure to diversify means stagnation and decline in the years ahead.*

Black Culture: Reaction and Resurgence

217

IF THEY TAKE YOU IN THE MORNING

Angela Davis was jailed in October 1970 as an accomplice in the murder of a San Rafael, California, judge by Jonathan Jackson on August 7, 1970. The shooting had taken place when Jackson attempted to free three convicts at gunpoint as they sat in the courtroom waiting to testify. Along with the judge, Jackson and two of the convicts were killed in the incident. Davis was charged with having knowingly supplied Jackson with the four guns he used in the abortive rescue attempt. Discharged four months earlier from her teaching position in philosophy at the University of California at Los Angeles because she was a Communist, Davis had been a friend of the slain Jonathan and of his better-known brother, George. The latter, author of the moving Soledad Brother: The Prison Letters of George Jackson, *would be shot to death a year later by San Quentin guards in an alleged jailbreak attempt.*

The imprisonment of Angela Davis made her a martyr to many, her thousands of sympathizers contending that she was being persecuted because of her race and her political opinions. Spearheaded by her fellow Communists, the cry "Free Angela" echoed around the world.

Holding that the seizure and jailing of Davis reflected a prevailing white American prejudice, James Baldwin, a best-selling black novelist and essayist, drafted an impassioned indictment of a society in which, as he saw it, blacks had long been systematically denigrated. Baldwin's searing phrases laid bare a mood which was deep-seated among black Americans and which would lose little of its force when Davis was subsequently found innocent by a trial jury.

DEAR SISTER . . .

One might have hoped that, by this hour, the very sight of chains on black flesh, or the very sight of chains, would be so intolerable a sight for the American people, and so unbearable a memory, that they would themselves spontaneously rise up and strike off the manacles. But no, they appear to glory in their chains; now, more than ever, they appear to measure their safety in chains and corpses. And so *Newsweek*, civilized defender of the indefensible, attempts to drown you in a sea of crocodile tears ("it remained to be seen what sort of personal liberation she had achieved") and puts you on its cover, chained.

* * *

I am something like 20 years older than you, of that generation, therefore, of which George Jackson ventures that "there are no

*From "Short-Run Problems Will Not Halt an Upward Trend" by Andrew F. Brimmer, from *Black Enterprise*, June 1974, pp. 27–30. Reprinted by permission of *Black Enterprise*.

healthy brothers—none at all." I am in no way equipped to dispute this speculation (not, anyway, without descending into what, at the moment, would be irrelevant subtleties), for I know too well what he means. My own state of health is certainly precarious enough. In considering you, and Huey, and George, and (especially) Jonathan Jackson, I began to apprehend what you may have had in mind when you spoke of the uses to which we could put the experience of the slave. What has happened, it seems to me, and putting it far too simply, is that a whole new generation of people have assessed and absorbed their history, and in that tremendous action have freed themselves of it and will never be victims again. This may seem an odd, indefensibly impertinent and insensitive thing to say to a sister in prison, battling for her life—for all our lives. Yet, I dare to say, for I think that you will perhaps not misunderstand me and I do not say it, after all, from the position of a spectator.

I am trying to suggest that you—for example—do not appear to be your father's daughter in the same way I am my father's son. At bottom, my father's expectations and mine were the same, the expectations of his generation and mine were the same, and neither the immense difference in our ages nor the move from the South to the North could alter these expectations or make our lives more viable. For, in fact, to use the brutal parlance of that hour, the interior language of that despair—he was just a nigger—a nigger laborer preacher, and so was I. I jumped the track but that's of no more importance here, in itself, than the fact that some poor Spaniards become rich bullfighters, or that some poor black boys become rich boxers, for example. That's rarely, if ever, afforded the people more than a great emotional catharsis, though I don't mean to be condescending about that either. But when Cassius Clay became Muhammad Ali and refused to put on that uniform (and sacrificed all that money) a very different impact was made on the people and a very different kind of instruction had begun.

The American triumph—in which the American tragedy has always been implicit—was to make black people despise themselves. When I was little, I despised myself. I did not know any better. And this meant—albeit unconsciously, or against my will, or in great pain—that I also despised my father. And my mother. And my brothers. And my sisters. Black people were killing each other every Saturday night out on Lenox Avenue, when I was growing up; and no one explained to them, or to me, that it was intended that they should; that they were penned where they were, like animals, in order that they should consider themselves no better than animals. Everything supported this sense of reality, nothing denied it; and so one was ready, when it came time to go to work, to be treated as a slave. So one was ready, when human terrors came, to bow before a white God and beg Jesus for salvation—this same white God who was unable to raise a finger to do so little as to help you pay your rent, unable to be awakened in time to help you save your child.

There is always, of course, more to any picture than can speedily be perceived and in all of this—groaning and moaning, watching, calculating, clowning, surviving and outwitting—some tremendous strength was nevertheless being forged, which is part of our legacy today. But that particular aspect of our journey now begins to be behind us. The secret is out; we are men!

But the blunt, open articulation of this secret has frightened the nation to death. I wish I could say "to life," but that is much to demand of a disparate collection of displaced people still cowering in their wagon trains and singing "Onward Christian Soldiers." The nation, if America is a nation, is not in the least prepared for this day. It is a day which the Americans never expected or desired to see, however piously they may declare their belief in "progress" and "democracy." These words, now, on American lips, have become a kind of universal obscenity; for this most unhappy people, strong believers in arithmetic, never expected to be confronted with the algebra of their history.

* * *

Or, to put it another way, as long as white Americans take refuge in their whiteness—for so long as they are unable to walk out of this most monstrous of traps—they will allow millions of people to be slaughtered in their name, and will be manipulated into and surrender themselves to what they will think of—and justify—as a racial war. They will never, so long as their whiteness puts so sinister a distance between themselves and their own experience and the experience of others, feel themselves sufficiently human, sufficiently worthwhile, to become responsible for themselves, their leaders, their country, their children, or their fate. They will perish (as we once put it in our black church) in their sins—that is, in their delusions. And this is happening, needless to say, already, all around us.

Only a handful of the millions of people in this vast place are aware that the fate intended for you, Sister Angela, and for George Jackson, and for the numberless prisoners in our concentration camps—for that is what they are—is a fate which is about to engulf them, too. White lives, for the forces which rule in this country, are no more sacred than black ones, as many and many a student is discovering, as the white American corpses in Vietnam prove. If the American people are unable to contend with their elected leaders for the redemption of their own honor and the lives of their own children, we, the blacks, the most rejected of the Western children, can expect very little help at their hands; which, after all, is nothing new. What the Americans do not realize is that a war between brothers, in the same cities, on the same soil, is not a racial war but a civil war. But the American delusion is not only that their brothers are all white but that the whites are all their brothers.

* * *

The enormous revolution in black consciousness which has occurred in your generation, my dear sister, means the beginning of the end of America. Some of us, white and black, know how great a price has already been paid to bring into existence a new people, an unprecedented nation. If we know, and do nothing, we are worse than the murderers hired in our name.

If we know, then we must fight for your life as though it were our own—which it is—and render impassable with our bodies the corridor to the gas chamber. For, if they take you in the morning, they will be coming for us that night.

Therefore peace.

Brother James*

218

MORE THAN A DEATH WISH

Huey P. Newton and Bobby Seale founded the Black Panther Party for Self-Defense in October 1966 at Oakland, California. The two collaborators wrote the initial platform and program and named Newton Minister of Defense. Reflecting the Marxist-Leninist orientation of the founders, the Black Panthers became a militant inner-city organization, attaining their peak importance in 1970, and in the process finding themselves a target for police harassment. Huey Newton was absent from party headquarters from 1968 to 1970, languishing in jail after being convicted for killing a policeman, a charge ultimately dismissed.

Whether in jail or out, Newton continued to read widely, impelled by a studious turn of mind. He was particularly stirred by the writings of Mao Tse-tung, Franz Fanon, Malcolm X, and W. E. B. DuBois. In January 1972 Newton announced that the Panthers were laying aside the "pick up the gun" approach, at least for the time being, in favor of community work and voter registration. Although the Panthers adopted a more concilatory stance, in line with the more pragmatic and immediate goals of inner-city betterment, this did not mean that they had become pacifists. Their long-range commitment to a no-holds-barred struggle against the ruling class was reaffirmed by Newton in his Revolutionary Suicide, *published in 1973. The following passage is taken from the opening chapter.*

REVOLUTIONARY SUICIDE: THE WAY OF LIBERATION

For twenty-two months in the California Men's Colony at San Luis Obispo, after my first trial for the death of Patrolman John Frey, I was almost continually in solitary confinement. There, in a four-by-six cell, except for books and papers relating to my case, I was allowed no reading material. Despite the rigid enforcement of this rule, inmates sometimes slipped magazines under my door when the guards were not looking. One that reached me was the May 1970 issue of *Ebony* magazine. It contained an article written by Lacy Banko summarizing the work of Dr. Herbert Hendin, who had done a comparative study on suicide among Black people in the major American cities. Dr. Hendin found that the suicide rate among Black men between the ages of nineteen and thirty-five had doubled in the past ten to fifteen years, surpassing the rate for whites in the same age range. The article had—and still has—a profound effect on me. I have thought long and hard about its implications.

The *Ebony* article brought to mind Durkheim's classic study

---

*From "Dear Sister . . ." by James Baldwin from *Manchester Guardian Weekly*, December 27, 1970, p. 31. Reprinted by permission of the author.

Suicide, a book I had read earlier while studying sociology at Oakland City College. To Durkheim all types of suicide are related to social conditions. He maintains that the primary cause of suicide is not individual temperament but forces in the social environment. In other words, suicide is caused primarily by external factors, not internal ones. As I thought about the conditions of Black people and about Dr. Hendin's study, I began to develop Durkheim's analysis and apply it to the Black experience in the United States. This eventually led to the concept of "revolutionary suicide."

To understand revolutionary suicide it is first necessary to have an idea of reactionary suicide, for the two are very different. Dr. Hendin was describing reactionary suicide: the reaction of a man who takes his own life in response to social conditions that overwhelm him and condemn him to helplessness. The young Black men in his study had been deprived of human dignity, crushed by oppressive forces, and denied their right to live as proud and free human beings.

A section in Dostoevsky's *Crime and Punishment* provides a good analogy. One of the characters, Marmeladov, a very poor man, argues that poverty is not a vice. In poverty, he says, a man can attain the innate nobility of soul that is not possible in beggary; for while society may drive the poor man out with a stick, the beggar will be swept out with a broom. Why? Because the beggar is totally demeaned, his dignity lost. Finally, bereft of self-respect, immobilized by fear and despair, he sinks into self-murder. This is reactionary suicide.

Connected to reactionary suicide, although even more painful and degrading, is a spiritual death that has been the experience of millions of Black people in the United States. This death is found everywhere today in the Black community. Its victims have ceased to fight the forms of oppression that drink their blood. The common attitude has long been: What's the use? If a man rises up against a power as great as the United States, he will not survive. Believing this, many Blacks have been driven to a death of the spirit rather than of the flesh, lapsing into lives of quiet desperation. Yet all the while, in the heart of every Black, there is the hope that life will somehow change in the future.

I do not think that life will change for the better without an assault on the Establishment,* which goes on exploiting the wretched of the earth. This belief lies at the heart of the concept of revolutionary suicide. Thus it is better to oppose the forces that would drive me to self-murder than to endure them. Although I risk the likelihood of death, there is at least the possibility, if not the probability, of changing intolerable conditions. This possibility is important, because much in human existence is based upon hope without any real understanding of the odds. Indeed, we are all—Black and white alike—ill in the same way, mortally ill. But before we die, how shall we live? I say with hope and dignity; and if pre-

---

*The power structure, based on the economic infrastructure, propped up and reinforced by the media and all the secondary educational and cultural institutions.

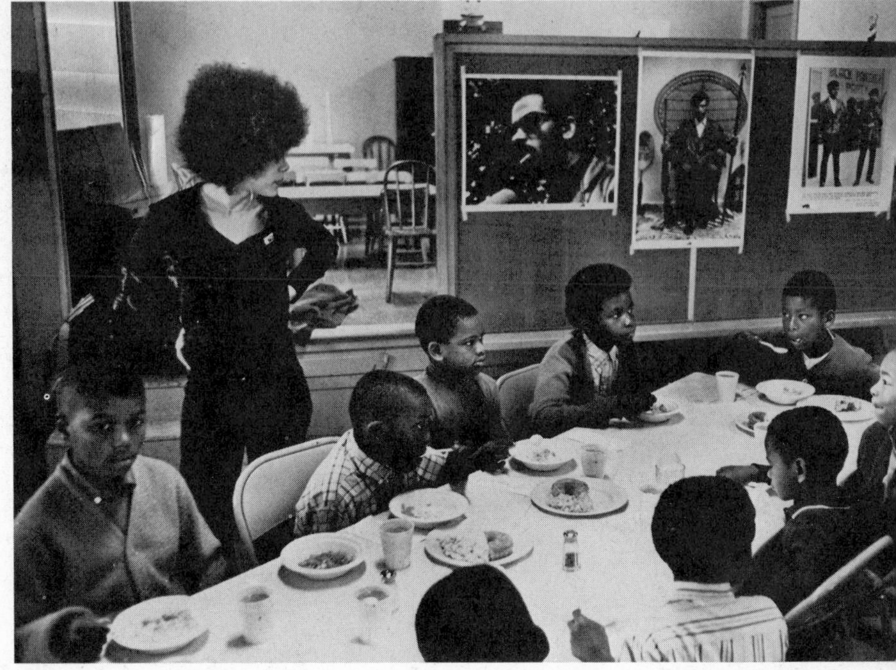

This Black Panther free breakfast program combines hot food for needy children with exposure to the history and philosophy of the Black Panther Party.

mature death is the result, that death has a meaning reactionary suicide can never have. It is the price of self-respect.

Revolutionary suicide does not mean that I and my comrades have a death wish; it means just the opposite. We have such a strong desire to live with hope and human dignity that existence without them is impossible. When reactionary forces crush us, we must move against these forces, even at the risk of death. We will have to be driven out with a stick.

Che Guevara said that to a reveolutionary death is the reality and victory the dream. Because the revolutionary lives so dangerously, his survival is a miracle. Bakunin, who spoke for the most militant wing of the First International, made a similar statement in his *Revolutionary Catechism*. To him, the first lesson a revolutionary must learn is that he is a doomed man. Unless he understands this, he does not grasp the essential meaning of his life.

When Fidel Castro and his small band were in Mexico preparing for the Cuban Revolution, many of the comrades had little understanding of Bakunin's rule. A few hours before they set sail, Fidel went from man to man asking who should be notified in case of death. Only then did the deadly seriousness of the revolution hit home. Their struggle was no longer romantic. The scene had been exciting and animated; but when the simple, overwhelming question of death arose, everyone fell silent.

Many so-called revolutionaries in this country, Black and white, are not prepared to accept this reality. The Black Panthers are not suicidal; neither do we romanticize the consequences of revolution in our lifetime. Other so-called revolutionaries cling to an illusion that they might have their revolution and die of old age. That cannot be.

I do not expect to live through our revolution, and most serious comrades probably share my realism. Therefore, the expression "revolution in our lifetime" means something different to me than it does to other people who use it. I think the revolution will grow in my lifetime, but I do not expect to enjoy its fruits. That would be a contradiction. The reality will be grimmer.

I have no doubt that the revolution will triumph. The people of the world will prevail, seize power, seize the means of production, wipe out racism, capitalism, reactionary intercommunalism—reactionary suicide. The people will win a new world. Yet when I think of individuals in the revolution, I cannot predict their survival. Revolutionaries must accept this fact, especially the Black revolutionaries in America, whose lives are in constant danger from the evils of a colonial society. Considering how we must live, it is not hard to accept the concept of revolutionary suicide. In this we are different from white radicals. They are not faced with genocide.

The greater, more immediate problem is the survival of the entire world. If the world does not change, all its people will be threatened by the greed, exploitation, and violence of the power structure in the American empire. The handwriting is on the wall. The United States is jeopardizing its own existence and the existence of all humanity. If Americans knew the disasters that lay ahead, they would transform this society tomorrow for their own preservation. The Black Panther Party is in the vanguard of the revolution that seeks to relieve this country of its crushing burden of guilt. We are determined to establish true equality and the means for creative work.

Some see our struggle as a symbol of the trend toward suicide among Blacks. Scholars and academics, in particular, have been quick to make this accusation. They fail to perceive differences. Jumping off a bridge is not the same as moving to wipe out the overwhelming force of an oppressive army. When scholars call our actions suicidal, they should be logically consistent and describe all historical revolutionary movements in the same way. Thus the American colonists, the French of the late eighteenth century, the Russians of 1917, the Jews of Warsaw, the Cubans, the NLF, the North Vietnamese—any people who struggle against a brutal and powerful force—are suicidal. Also, if the Black Panthers symbolize the suicidal trend among Blacks, then the whole Third World is suicidal, because the Third World fully intends to resist and overcome the ruling class of the United States. If scholars wish to carry their analysis further, they must come to terms with that four fifths of the world which is bent on wiping out the power of the empire. In those terms the Third World would be transformed from suicidal to homicidal, although homicide is the unlawful taking of life, and the Third World is involved only in defense. Is the coin then turned? Is the government of the United States suicidal? I think so.

With this redefinition, the term "revolutionary suicide" is not as simplistic as it might seem initially. In coining the phrase, I took two knowns and combined them to make an unknown, a neoteric phrase in which the word "revolutionary" transforms the word "suicide" into an idea that has different dimensions and meanings, applicable to a new and complex situation.

My prison experience is a good example of revolutionary suicide in action, for prison is a microcosm of the outside world. From the beginning of my sentence I defied the authorities by refusing to cooperate; as a result, I was confined to "lock-up," a solitary cell. As the months passed and I remained steadfast, they came to regard my behavior as suicidal. I was told that I would crack and break under the strain. I did not break, nor did I retreat from my position. I grew strong.

If I had submitted to their exploitation and done their will, it would have killed my spirit and condemned me to a living death. To cooperate in prison meant reactionary suicide to me. While solitary confinement can be physically and mentally destructive, my actions were taken with an understanding of the risk. I had to suffer through a certain situation; by doing so, my resistance told them that I rejected all they stood for. Even though my struggle might have harmed my health, even killed me, I looked upon it as a way of raising the consciousness of the other inmates, as a contribution to the ongoing revolution. Only resistance can destroy the pressures that cause reactionary suicide. . . .*

219

THE INTEGRITY OF THE BLACK INTELLECTUAL

It was probably no coincidence that Harold Cruse's provocative critique of his race's cultural posture was published just as the vitality and originality of black culture began to be recognized. Novelists like John Oliver Killens, Carlene Hatcher Polite, Earnest Gaines, and Gordon Parks treat race issues as universals, and the message is fresh. The same is true of playwrights, such as the four whose short plays became an evening of theater entitled "A Black Quartet": Ben Caldwell, Ronald Milner, Ed Bullins, and LeRoi Jones (Imamu Amiri Baraka.)

Actors and actresses, dancers, sculptors, painters, and, of course, critics, are contributing to this breakthrough; even Henry O. Tanner, whose work was done in the late nineteenth and early twentieth centuries, is being exhibited as "America's first major black painter." Cruse's examination is historical, polemical, and primarily centered on Harlem, but his criticism is penetrating. He believes that all efforts for political and economic self-sufficiency depend upon a cultural independence which is rooted in and supported by the community. He accuses black power advocates of being insufficiently prepared to exercise the authority they seek. The Negro's one great hope is the development of what he calls "a new synthesis and a social theory of action," drawing on the intellectual and cultural fruits of the black past. The future looks barren unless the black man begins "to know and understand his Afro-American history in the United States more profoundly."

---

*From *Revolutionary Suicide,* by Huey Newton, copyright © 1973 by Stronghold Consolidated Productions, Inc. Reprinted by permission of Harcourt Brace Jovanovich, Inc.

THE HARLEM BLACK ARTS THEATER—NEW DIALOGUE WITH THE LOST BLACK GENERATION

. . . As it turned out, it was in the new Harlem Black Arts Repertory Theater and School in May 1965, that I realized the full potential of the new young black generation. There, at a round-table discussion on Negro playwrights and the black theater, a young man, in his early twenties, discussed his views on the theater. He said, in effect, that *a black theater should be about black people, with black people, and only black people.* Immediately, there are startled objections to this radical idea, from both the panelists and the audience: "This is impossible, impractical, and anti-humanistic EXTREMISM!" . . . "Black people cannot close themselves off in a compartment separate from whites" . . . "Art is universal" . . . "Art is for everybody" . . . and so on. Then came the question: "*Suppose the Black Arts Theater wanted to put on a play with Negro and white characters?*" "You see," said the opponent with a smug smile, "you would have to eliminate such a play. You would limit the repertory of the Black Arts Theater. You would limit the range of your playwrights to writing only about black people." But the young man, the ranting extremist, said: "Oh no, it won't be that way—you dig? We have black actors who can play white roles—you dig? *They can be made up to play white people.*" In other words, this young man was intent on having a truly *black* theater, come what may. And the whole historical truth is, that this young man was absolutely right. Even I, who have been castigated and refuted for eighteen years by the theatrical integrationists for my views on the need for a purely ethnic Negro theater, could not have put the question so clearly. I would have made room for the mixed-cast play in a black theater repertory by having white people play white roles, whenever demanded. Beyond that, my own standards for a black theater would be one where Negroes themselves would finance the institution and man all the technical and administrative posts.

But Negro theatrical history has demonstrated time and time again the inexorability of the unique Negro-white aesthetic, that culturally false symbiosis that undermines and negates the black theater idea. First off, the Negro creative intellectual, as writer, artist, and critic has no cultural philosophy, no cultural methodology, no literary and cultural critique on himself, his people, or on America. Hence he cannot create, establish, and maintain a code of cultural ethics, an artistic standard, a critical yardstick, or any kind of cogent and meaningful critique on society that might enable him to fashion viable and lasting institutions in the cultural spheres that motivate progressive movements.

If any group of Negroes were to start a black theater in a black community without a well-thought-out rule of thumb on administration, Negro playwrights, white playwrights, Negro actors, white actors, Negro technicians, white technicians, Negro directors, white directors, Negro audience, white audience, Negro plays, mixed-cast plays, etc.—such a theater venture would soon collapse. Even if this theater group started with the hopes of becoming "for, or, about, and by" black people, *without a code*, it would soon be integrated out of existence. . . .

The Black Arts Repertory Theater and School was started by LeRoi Jones and others, and hence my reticence in this book in discussing much of Jones' work. Jones has come so far and so fast since 1961, and in the meantime been so contradictory, that it is difficult to place him. In 1961, after my own personal ideological tussle with the Jones-Shepp-Hicks contingent in Harlem, no one could have made me believe that in 1965 LeRoi Jones would start a Black Arts Repertory Theater and School in Harlem. But he did—in itself amazing, because Jones is not a ghetto product. Any of my personal early misgivings about Jones grew out of my critical responses to his different poses and postures. As it turns out these Jonesian posturings have not been all upstage antics, but rather the ambivalence of the supreme actor brazenly in search of just the right "role" that would best suit the purposes in life of the real man inside Jones. Nevertheless, it is my belief that his play, *The Slave*, stamps Jones as the most original dramatist Negroes have produced since Oliver Pitcher (who still remains unheard of by the general public). Nonetheless, the Black Arts Theater and School, after an auspicious beginning, lasted about seven months and collapsed. It had a very short, stormy, creative career that has left an indelible impression on the minds of both its supporters and detractors. The causes of this collapse deserve examination because they relate graphically to the general theme of this critique—the social role of the Negro creative intellectual. The Black Arts was not a failure in achievement, so much as a failure in its inability to deal with what had been achieved. With Jones, the radical, avant-garde, literary integrationist, turned nationalist, he did not go far enough in his understanding of nationalism. Moreover, he had too much to overcome—forty-five years of leadership mismanagement on this question. As a result, the Black Arts Theater began without the foundation of a tradition of cultural nationalism. Lacking this tradition, the role of the Negro creative intellectual as nationalist is not understood even by the nationalists themselves. . . .

LeRoi Jones, after establishing the Black Arts Theater, tried then to play the role of political spokesman on nationhood, in the absence of any official organization established to back up his political pronouncements about "destroying the system." Although again Jones was advised that these steps would have to be taken if the Black Arts was to be sustained, he failed to pay adequate attention. He made no attempt to link up a cultural institution with political and economic organization; without it, the Black Arts could not win the broader community support it needed to survive. Instead Jones attempted the triple-threat role of writer, cultural leader, and political spokesman, and consequently, all three roles were inadequately filled.

LeRoi Jones considered that to have established the Black Arts Theater was enough, but even so he did not pursue this cultural trend to its full potential. For example, his successful book, *Blues People*, suggested that much greater effort be mounted in the jazz field. Indeed, as jazz is his specialty, Jones' next step should have been to found a critical Negro jazz publication. Beyond that, Harlem could well use a jazz institute, a type of foundation that has never existed, to further the creative, economic, research, and educational interests of the jazz musician. The problem here is that, despite *Blues People*, the white jazz critics are still deciding the status and fortunes of Negro jazzmen. Cultural nationalism must be expressed by all possible organizational and educational means that might further and equalize the status of the Negro artist as creator, interpreter, or critic. Such an aim is certainly in consonance with the cultural development of the Negro community.

It is not the role of the Negro creative intellectual or writer to play the Big Leader Spokesman. His role as spokesman is to see what has to be done, point to it, and then explain why. He must be able to instruct others in what he cannot (or should not) do himself. Jones' failure to implement this kind of leadership in the Black Arts inevitably forced him into the position of being told by his "opposition" what to do—within the very institution he had founded. These oppositional elements in the Black Arts were dangerously irrational, misguided, negative, and disoriented. They represented the terrorist fringe of the nationalist wing—an alienated and psychotic separatism that has developed as a result of the long-standing cultural neglect and leadership default endemic to Harlem. This nihilistic fringe has its counterparts, no doubt, in all the great urban ghettoes, especially in the North. This trend is anti-middle class, anti-intellectual, anti-anything that resembles the establishment—from a college education to pressed-suit manners, whether Negro or white. Mainly it is anti-bourgeois—covering a rather broad spectrum of class "sins." This trend carries its separatism and black irrationality to such extremes that it bans Negro spokesmen from television, radio, and panel programs involving whites, among other things. In the absence of their own viable and positive program, the Afro-American nationalists will have severe difficulties with this trend. Unless many more representatives of the Negro middle classes and the intelligentsia become increasingly committed to basic political, economic, and cultural issues in the ghettoes, aggravated class conflict is in store for the Negro movement as a whole.

The experiences of LeRoi Jones in the Black Arts Theater reveal several hard truths about the nationalist wing. In dealing with Afro-American nationalist trends, Negro writers and other creative elements must maintain their own autonomy absolutely; they must not permit themselves to come under the domination of activists and politicians who do not favor cultural front activities. The political activists will attempt to either suppress or control the creative elements, and especially the writers. This is, of course, a problem of long standing for all radical or revolutionary movements, especially those of the Marxist Left. The Negro writer, who is nationalistically oriented, must, at all times, fight within movements to maintain his creative and critical independence within a reasonable context of the general aims of the movement. The American system, unlike the Soviet, Chinese, or African, has had its full flowering of the industrial revolution on the economic front; thus the Negro movement as a whole has no need for the politics of suppression and control of criticism and creativity. As a matter of fact, the precise cultural aim of the Negro movement *has* to be for the enhancement of criticism and creativity, not the other way around. . . .*

220

THE NEW RENAISSANCE

The Harlem Renaissance of the 1920's captured the attention of a limited audience—the black community, white intellectuals, and eventually historians. The New Renaissance of the 1970's attracted a national and international following. In part, this stemmed from technological changes in film making, television, audiotaping, photography, and transportation, all of which contributed to a greater and global exposure to the arts.

The impact of this new exposure to black artists has not been definitely measured, but black men and women in all fields of artistic endeavor have firmly established that they have something to say to the world and the talent with which to say it. In January 1975, for example, composer Carman Moore heard the premier performance of his "Gospel Fuse" by the San Francisco Symphony on a Wednesday night and came home on Thursday to hear the New York Philharmonic introduce his "Wild Fires and Field Songs."

The wider audience which saw and heard black artists and their works began to realize that, in addition to talent, the artists and their works often brought a new black dimension to the art form. It could appear in the character study in a novel or play, the color tone of a painting, or the beat of a poem or musical piece. Carman Moore was explicit in the piece performed by the San Francisco Symphony, an orchestra which had refused to continue employing a black timpanist. Moore said that he wrote "Gospel Fuse" for the conductor, Seiji Ozawa, not the orchestra, and revised it to include "a big timpani solo in the first few measures. I think that will get the message across out there."

The New Renaissance helped diffuse the racial tension which had gripped this nation for so long. The popular media capitalized on it, with commercial restraint, so that masses of viewers and readers became accustomed to the black dimension. In more rarified artistic and intellectual circles, the black men and women could compete on merit, with only whispers of incredulity from the dilettantes where once there had been shouts. The old spiritual which proclaimed a "new day a'comin'" had not yet been fulfilled, but, as the following articles by Warren Marr, II, and David Graham DuBois attest, in the arts it could be sung with greater assurance.

A SECOND RENAISSANCE?

Black culture has exploded! The productive amplitude of today's Negro in art, dance, literature, and music surpasses that of the celebrated Negro Renaissance of the Twenties, and the productivity seems only to have started. Producing in every art form, Negroes are now being recognized for their works not only by their own communities but by the population as a whole. Current productivity has been augmented by a rush of publishers, nearly all of

*Excerpted from "The Harlem Black Arts Theater—New Dialogue with the Lost Black Generation" in *The Crisis of the Negro Intellectual* by Harold Cruse. Reprinted by permission of William Morrow and Company, Inc. Copyright © 1967 by Harold Cruse.

whom are white, to reprint and reissue black literary works which in the past had been valued primarily by educated Negroes who took pride in their own racial culture. Heartening as all this may be, no God of Creativity yet has proclaimed the current era as the ultimate moment of black fulfillment. The obverse may be true—it may be only the beginning.

Energy for today's cultural explosion had accumulated for years. The late writer Langston Hughes and painters Aaron Douglas and Hale Woodruff, contributors to the Negro Renaissance, had been continuously prolific. So have painters such as Charles Alston, Ernest Crichlow, and Romare Bearden who came upon the scene a bit later. But now there was a vast new crop of competent artists led by the incomparable, world-renowned Jacob Lawrence, the first painter ever to win the coveted Spingarn Medal. Among sculptors, there was the late Augusta Savage and there is Selma Burke. The great Richmond Barthé left the United States, first for the island of Jamaica and then to Italy. While his name is not often heard here these days, persons who have seen Barthe in his Italian studios recently report that he is producing with a quality superseding that of his earlier work. Beginning to replace his name here were those of the Chicago-based sculptors Richard Hunt and John Rodin.

Similarly, in dance, literature, and music, new talent was developing across the nation, but comparatively few of the younger artists were getting significant recognition.

Then, in the autumn of 1967, came the massive retrospective art exhibit, "Evolution of the Afro-American Artist" at the College of the City of New York. Organized by Romare Bearden, by now a very successful painter, and Carroll Greene, who was just emerging to replace James Porter as the nation's leading contemporary authority on black art, the unprecedented assemblage of works by 53 black artists contained 150 paintings and sculptures dating from 1800 to 1950. It was reported as the first art survey of its kind, and the catalogue is still used as a prime source of information on Afro-American artists by major museums, galleries, and universities across the nation.

That exhibit hit New York like a bombshell. Enormous as the display area was, there was too little room to accommodate adequately the immense crowds (100,000 people) which flocked to see it. School teachers brought their children. Class after class, from all parts of the metropolitan area, and of every ethnic group, lined up in endless and noisy queues to await their turn to enter the Great Hall of the College of the City of New York. Sandwiched somewhere between were thousands of adults. Black art had arrived with a very loud bang.

* * *

From January 18 to April 6, 1969, the prestigious Metropolitan Museum presented an enormous spectacular called "Harlem On My Mind." It purported to exhibit "a 68-year history of the cultural capital of Black America." The exhibit missed and aroused the ire of many, both black and white. Its 225-page, $12.95, hardback catalogue was recalled. And the Harlem Cultural Council boycotted the exhibit because its consultative role had been abrogated. "Harlem On My Mind" fell flat on its face, but it helped accomplish one important thing—the determination of black folk to exhibit as they thought they should be exhibited. Who can say that the success of the Studio Museum of Harlem is not at least partially due to the Metropolitan's high-handed patronage?

In the winter of 1969, the Brooklyn Museum was smarter. It organized a major exhibit of African sculpture, using its best designers to create the displays. The result was spectacular—one of the most successful shows ever in its history. And black folk turned out in droves. Much of the success of that show was due to Mrs. Ruth Logan, a Negro public relations expert who knew how to reach the total black community.

In 1969, the NAACP, with the assistance of Carroll Greene in determining exhibitors, sponsored "Twelve Afro-American Artists" at the Nordness Galleries in New York, the first show of its type in a major New York gallery. Attention was brought to the works of Jack White, Charles McGee, Russ Thompson, Arthur Smith, Walter Williams, Arthur Coppedge, Alma W. Thomas, Norman Lewis, Felrath Hines, Carroll Sockwell, Noah Purifoy, and James Tanner. After the scheduled closing at Nordness, the works were kept together for showing at Gimbels New York and then were sent on national tour under the auspices of the Smithsonian Institution. Also *The Crisis*, in keeping with its 60-year tradition, featured paintings by some of these artists as cover illustrations.

Precedent was shattered in New York when a major exhibit of the works of Charles Alston was held at the Gallery of Modern Art (Huntington Hartford Museum) and again when the Museum of Modern Art built a major exhibit around the works of collagist Romare Bearden and sculptor Richard Hunt in 1971.

"Afro-American art has taken giant strides" between 1968 and 1970, said *The Art Gallery* in its second Afro-American issue of April, 1970. That magazine's editorial said further: "Several black artists who were virtually unknown in 1968 have emerged as major figures on the contemporary scene; black museums, galleries, and training and study programs have sprung up from coast to coast and border to border. More important, black youth has begun to awaken to the realization that the painting of pictures in a lonely loft can be as valid a source of community pride as the grabbing of rebounds before an audience of thousands; that personal identity and dignity are perhaps more readily achievable through the making of sculpture than in dubious battle in the prize ring."

In theatre, only a book-length treatment could list adequately the recent accomplishments. Charles Gordone's "No Place to Be Somebody" won the Pulitzer Prize in 1970. This was the first play by a Negro to receive such an award. And there are two other black Pulitzer Prize winners: Gwendolyn Brooks, poet laureate of the State of Illinois until she resigned in 1970 so that someone else could enjoy the status, and Moneta Sleet, ace photographer for *Ebony Magazine*.

James Earl Jones created an excitement in "The Great White

Hope" which not only kept that play a major production on Broadway but evoked similar box office attraction in the film version.

Broadway and Off-Broadway have seen numerous productions by and with black people. Ossie Davis, Douglas Turner Ward, and others have come to the fore as playwrights. And Pearl Bailey was the longest running of the ubiquitous Dollies in a superb all-black cast of *Hello, Dolly*.

The legendary Lafayette Theatre, where great stars like Ethel Waters and Abbey Mitchell once vied for attention, has reemerged at another location. Mel Gussow, in *The New York Times* of January 21, 1972, said:

> The New Lafayette Theater on Seventh Avenue at 137th Street is one of New York's most admirable cultural enterprises. It is a true community theater, in touch with its audience, and nurturing actors, playwrights, and technicians in surroundings that are flexible and stimulating to the imagination. The stage is surrounded by seats and bleachers, placed at angles and at various heights so that productions assume different shapes, depending on where you sit.
>
> One never knows what to expect when visiting the New Lafayette. It may be a new play by Ed Bullins (he and Robert Macbeth are the associate directors of the company), such as last season's memorable *The Fabulous Miss Marie,* which broke from its naturalistic frame to become both poetic and vaudevillian. Or it may be a ritualistic parable such as *The Psychic Pretenders,* a "pageant of the black passion in three motions," which played later.

Ossie Davis wrote the Broadway success *Purlie Victorious,* the later musical version of which was known simply as *Purlie.* Together with his talented wife, Ruby Dee, the versatile couple's performances range from movies made in Mexico to Shakespearean drama in Stratford, Connecticut.

Few movie actors ever become superstars but, since the production in 1965 of the low-budget *Lilies of the Field,* starring Sidney Poitier, who won an Oscar for his role, there can be no question but that this black man has become one of filmdom's biggest box office attractions. He had been nominated for an Oscar in 1958 for his role in *The Defiant Ones.* His more recent films include: *To Sir With Love, Guess Who's Coming to Dinner, Raisin in the Sun, In The Heat of the Night*, and *Mr. Tibbs.*

Other black movies have been produced in recent years, including *The Learning Tree, Cotton Comes to Harlem, Putney Swope, Shaft,* and *Georgia, Georgia.* Today's black films have a professionalism and quality that the sepia movies of past decades rarely, if ever, approached. And their attraction is so strong that many neighborhood movie houses in which seats usually go begging find long lines awaiting seats for current black shows.

* * *

Music seems always to have been an art form in which Negroes have participated to a great degree, but the United States has been so busy emulating and worshipping European musical forms that it has never quite recognized that the music of the Negro is this country's major contribution to world culture, nor that a major portion of our popular music stems from the black idiom.

Spirituals, jazz, gospel songs, and rock were born of the Negro. Spirituals are timeless. And the essence of jazz, whether it be gospel songs or rock, seems to be here to stay.

Few persons stop to realize that Dvorak's *New World Symphony* and much of George Gershwin's music are built around the black idiom. Few whites, such as Frankie Laine of an earlier year and Tom Jones of today, acknowledge that the style of performance which brought them success is a duplication of the traditional Negro style of song presentation. Few persons, white or black, comprehend that the elimination of the black influence and input would considerably minimize the quality and quantity of this nation's musical production.

As important as music is to black people, few Negroes from former eras managed to earn national reputations in what is regarded generally as serious music. Clarence Cameron White managed it with his violin and Hall Johnson achieved it with his choir. And of course there are the incomparable singers, Roland Hayes and Paul Robeson, Abbie Mitchell and Jules Bledsoe. Then came Marian Anderson, who was said to have had the greatest voice in a hundred years. But even these giants had to earn much of their reputations abroad before white America would accord them any real honor.

* * *

Here in this country, Miss Anderson's unique voice had passed its prime before her greatness was permitted, in 1955, to grace the Metropolitan Opera Company, the zenith for singers in America. Since then, the list of great Negro singers includes names such as Martina Arroyo, Grace Bumbry, Mattiwilda Dobbs, Leontyne Price, George Shirley, and Shirley Verrett.

This musical burst applies to singers only. Instrumentalists and conductors such as Everett Lee and Dean Dixon must still find their recognition in Europe. Most American symphonies say they have been unable to find qualified Negro instrumentalists. Consequently, symphonies remain lily-white. The two notable exceptions are Henry Lewis, who conducts the New Jersey Symphony Orchestra, and Andre Watts, a young concert pianist.

There are two significant national musical organizations—the National Association of Negro Musicians, which will hold its 53rd annual convention at the Commodore Hotel in New York in August, and the rather young Afro-American Opportunity Association, which is more aggressive than the older NANM in seeking rewarding exposure for black musicians.

* * *

The Renaissance was a first flowering of black culture. The inspiration deriving from that period nurtured today's prolific blossoming. This second unfolding which began in the Sixties, mammoth as it is, seems to be only a beginning.*

SOUNDER

Sounder comes out of Hollywood almost miraculously as a welcome alternative to the recent rush of black crime, violence, and

---

**The Crisis,* June–July 1972, pp. 198–203. Reprinted with permission of *The Crisis* Magazine, official publication of the NAACP.

loveless sex films. Its appearance should be applauded long and vociferously. All those responsible for this touching and honest film deserve our praise, particularly its screenwriter, Lonnie Elder.

Sounder, as Lonnie Elder has transformed the original book for the screen, is a gentle story about black survival in [the] racist U.S.A. during the Great Depression. In its quiet dignity and its pregnant and seething understatement, *Sounder* focuses on black people's love for one another, their courage against great odds, their determination to survive, their ability to withstand great pain and suffering, their rare and hardwon joys, and their faith in a better tomorrow.

Love, courage, determination, family loyalty, pain, suffering, joy, and faith are not the unique property of black people. They are basic human attributes and experiences. But racism in the U.S. is fed on the lie that black people are severely lacking in these attributes, these experiences. This nation's majority population is repeatedly led to believe that black people know little of the heights of spiritual love, of great courage in the face of adversity, of firm determination to attain, of the primacy of family loyalty. In the U.S., nonblacks are led to believe that our pain and suffering are borne lightly and that joy is derived from forever merrymaking in wasteful slovenness.

The *Cottons*, the *Shafts*, the *Melindas*, the *Superflys*, and the *Trouble Men* all perpetuate these lies. This is why they are pushed before the movie-going audience. And this is why they "succeed." Overlayed with a thick coating of carnal lust, violence, flashy clothes, expensive cars, and unbelievable exploits—not reserved for black films—the deeper message of these films is insidious: black people are somehow less than human, i.e., their love is purely animal; their courage is a simple animal reflex against the threat of physical harm; their determination is operative only for the achieving of transient and meaningless goals. Family life does not exist for black people according to these films. The life of the streets, night clubs, poolhalls, and sordid women is the source of our greatest joy. Our pain and suffering is a self-inflicted root.

The U.S. majority population believes these lies, particularly when used to explain the conditions of our very poor and our very disadvantaged. This is *Sounder's* greatest achievement. Its people are from among our most oppressed, doubly trapped in a land tenure as outdated and cruel as feudalism and judicial and social codes based on the evil of racism. *Sounder's* choice of people vividly points up this nation's two greatest contradictions: 20th-century industrial, technological, and scientific advances side by side with an 18th-century system of land ownership and cultivation, claimed by a democracy which embodies Hitlerite racism.

It matters not that some will argue *Sounder* is set in the 1930's. The continuing injustices of the antiquated land tenure system of our southland was guaranteed with the defeat of Populism in the 1890's. The continuing evils of racism were guaranteed with the defeat of Reconstruction in the preceding decade. For black people little has changed. Every black family in the U.S. knows the story of *Sounder*. For many it *is their* story. None of us is so far removed from our past as to have forgotten the Herculean efforts of our forefathers in keeping body and soul intact and raising children for something better than they had had. These efforts continue today for the majority of black Americans.

Some of our younger brothers and sisters erroneously maintain that *Sounder* is not relevant because it does not contain a call to revolution. *Sounder's* contribution rests on its undermining of the ideological bases upon which racism in the U.S.A. is built. It is not sufficient to assert our humanity among and between ourselves. The ideological foundations upon which claims of our inhumanity have been built and fed to the majority population must be destroyed. *Sounder* contributes to this effort magnificently.

Sounder speaks to the heroism of black survival, the heroism that is found in black people's ability to maintain dignity and ancestral humanity in the face of the odds that characterize racist/materialist America. It is from such heroic figures as depicted in *Sounder* that true revolutionaries are made.

Sounder's focus on the hardship and suffering, longings and hopes of a black family is so sharp, so crystal clear that a viewing of the film is painful for many of us. It is this pain that sends some of us out of the theater resentful. "Why expose our lives so that *all* can see," we protest. "Our pain, our suffering, the intensity of our rare moments of joy are ours alone. Those others can't understand."

Let them feel and know our pain and our suffering, our hopes and our longings. We must not let America do to us what it has done to the majority of people. Pain and suffering know no color line. Longing and hope lie deep and eternal in all humankind. If they have lost their faith, or if their faith seems to have been driven out of them, let us hold on to ours. Let us assert it. Perhaps by so doing we can rekindle theirs.*

---

*From a review of *Sounder* by David G. DuBois from *The Black Scholar*, January 1973, pp. 53–54. Reprinted by permission of *The Black Scholar*.

Suggestions for Further Reading

A. General Readings

Blaustein, Albert P., and Robert L. Zangrando. *Civil Rights and the American Negro: A Documentary History.* New York: Trident Press, 1968. Comprised of 98 documents (court decisions, statutes, manifestoes, executive orders, editorials, among others), this compilation traces the path of civil rights and liberties for black Americans. Its carefully selected contents include representations from blacks themselves, among them the celebrated antebellum school segregation case *Roberts* v. *Boston* and Martin Luther King's "Letter from a Birmingham Jail."

Foner, Philip S. *Organized Labor and the Black Worker, 1619–1973.* New York: Praeger Publishers, Inc., 1974. One of the major forces in the rise or fall of black workers has been their relationship to organized labor, a subject which badly needed the careful examination it receives from Foner. The wealth of illuminating detail and the subtlety of perception that mark this volume are to be expected from a productive scholar who is equally at home in labor history and black history.

Franklin, John Hope. *From Slavery to Freedom.* 4th ed. New York: Alfred A. Knopf, Inc., 1974. This is the best of the general histories portraying the role of the black American. Comprehensive and reliable, it is well organized and equally well written.

Hughes, Langston, Milton Meltzer, and C. Eric Lincoln. *A Pictorial History of Black Americans.* 4th ed. New York: Crown Publishers, Inc., 1974. A work that has sold more than a quarter of a million copies, this is a text-and-picture album. A flowing, smartly paced narrative adds to the effectiveness of the more than 1000 carefully selected illustrations.

McPherson, James M., Laurence B. Holland, James M. Banner, Nancy J. Weiss, and Michael D. Bell. *Blacks in America: Bibliographical Essays.* Garden City, N.Y.: Doubleday & Co., Inc., 1971. A highly useful combination bibliography and guide, this volume embraces black history and black cultural developments. Its arrangement, at once topical and chronological, is thoughtful; its grasp of the facts is sure; and its judgments are uniformly to be trusted.

Toppin, Edgar A. *A Biographical History of Blacks in America Since 1528.* New York: David McKay Co., Inc., 1971. Especially good as a reference, this is a two-pronged work. The first part is a readable and trustworthy account of the black past. A series of 145 sketches of black achievers, judiciously selected and clearly etched, follows.

B. The Early Period Through the Revolutionary War

Bedini, Silvio A. *Benjamin Banneker.* New York: Charles Scribner's Sons, 1972. Bedini's evaluation of Banneker as a mathematician and astronomer, based upon the Banneker writings he has unearthed, constitutes an important sidelight on the history of science in America. The author's overall assessment of Banneker as a symbol of the abilities of blacks is likewise soundly reasoned.

Davidson, Basil. *A History of West Africa to the Nineteenth Century.* Garden City, N.Y.: Anchor Books, 1966. The author surveys the ancestral homelands of the blacks who were brought to the New World. Dividing eight centuries into three periods, he touches upon not only political and military history, but also social organization, religion, and art. Included is a description of the slave trade with the Europeans and its effect on African life.

Herskovits, Melville J. *The Myth of the Negro Past.* New York: Harper & Row, Publishers, 1941. A classic study depicting the richness and complexity of the civilizations in the homelands of the blacks who were brought to the New World. That these transplanted Africans were "culturally naked" when they arrived on American shores is a myth, asserts anthropologist Herskovits.

Jordan, Winthrop D. *The White Man's Burden: Historical Origins of Racism in the United States.* New York: Oxford University Press, 1974. An abridgement of Jordan's highly acclaimed *White Over Black: American Attitudes Toward the Negro, 1550–1812* (1968), this work traces the origins and evolution of white-black relations during the colonial period and the formative years of the Republic. Drawing from many disciplines, the author reveals the pervasive anti-black sentiment in its many forms.

McManus, Edgar J. *Black Bondage in the North.* Syracuse, N.Y.: Syracuse University Press, 1973. Copiously documented, its style workmanlike and restrained, this is a detailed and rounded study of slavery in a region where it existed in its most complex forms in colonial America. Slavery died in the North during the Revolutionary War period but, as McManus points out, its legacy was long-lasting.

Quarles, Benjamin. *The Negro in the American Revolution.* Chapel Hill: The University of North Carolina Press, 1961. This work describes the varied roles of the blacks with both the Americans and the British, and it traces their lot as a result of the war and of their participation therein.

Wood, Peter H. *Black Majority: Negroes in Colonial South Carolina from 1670 Through the Stono Rebellion.* New York: Alfred A. Knopf, Inc., 1974. More numerous than the white population, the blacks in early South Carolina were significant contributors to the colony, their activities ranging broadly and in unexpected patterns. The author's revelations are supported by a scholarly outreach that is exceptional.

C. First Half of the Nineteenth Century

Aptheker, Herbert. *American Negro Slave Revolts.* New York: International Publishers Co., Inc., 1943. A path-breaking study of slave rebellions in the United States, this is a soundly documented work. It is to be noted, however, that the degree of overt militancy among slaves in the United States is still a matter of scholarly debate.

Berlin, Ira. *Slaves Without Masters: The Free Negro in the Antebellum South.* New York: Pantheon Books, Inc., 1974. Combining scholarship with a felicitous style, this comprehensive study goes beyond the things pre-Civil War southern free blacks had in common (chiefly the precarious nature of their liberties), unveiling the wide differences that existed among them. These differences notwithstanding, it was this group that would exercise the leadership roles among southern blacks during the Reconstruction period.

Fogel, Robert William, and Stanley L. Engerman. *Time on the Cross.* Vol. I, *The Economics of American Negro Slavery;* Vol. II, *Evidence and Methods, A Supplement.* Boston: Little, Brown and Co., 1974. Making use of quantitative methods, Fogel and Engerman challenge many of the traditional characterizations of the slave economy. Among other newer viewpoints, they hold that slave agriculture was more efficient than northern family farming, and that the day-to-day living conditions of the slaves compared favorably with those of free laborers.

Genovese, Eugene D. *Roll, Jordan, Roll: The World the Slaves Made.* New York: Pantheon Books, Inc., 1974. An analytical and interpretive survey of American slavery, with due attention to the behavior of the slaves themselves, this work is a landmark in the field. Wide ranging in its historical parallels and paradoxes, it is characterized by its breadth of learning. It is richly suggestive, the author not hesitating to advance a reasoned speculation of his own.

Litwack, Leon F. *North of Slavery: The Negro in the Free States, 1790–1860.* Chicago: The University of Chicago Press, 1961. This is a well balanced and thorough description of the lot of the Negro in the northern states during the antebellum period. These blacks were not bound to a master but, as Litwack makes clear, in their rights and opportunities they suffered badly in comparison with whites.

Osofsky, Gilbert, ed. *Puttin' on Ole Massa: The Slave Narratives of Henry Bibb, William Wells Brown, and Solomon Northup.* New York: Harper & Row, Publishers, 1969. Ranking high in readability and reliability, these autobiographies of Bibb, Brown, and Northup are fine examples of the slave as his own interpreter. Osofsky's revealing introduction is a thoughtful and persuasive essay on the significance of slave narratives.

D. Last Half of the Nineteenth Century

Cruden, Robert. *The Negro in Reconstruction.* Englewood Cliffs, N.J.: Prentice-Hall, Inc., 1969. Designed for "interested laymen and students," this is a clearly written work, broad but compact in its coverage. Familiar with the recent interpretations of this controversial period, Cruden describes the positive role of the blacks and the forces undermining their goal of equal status.

Durham, Philip, and Everett L. Jones. *The Negro Cowboys.* New York: Dodd, Mead & Co., 1965. In essence, this is the story of the blacks in the westward movement. Its fresh and somewhat unexpected information is heightened by its narrative style.

Harlan, Louis R. *Booker T. Washington: The Making of a Black Leader, 1856–1901.* New York: Oxford University Press, 1972. Booker T. Washington's path-breaking and many-faceted career was rooted in a variety of influences, including the kind of America in which he came to manhood. Harlan unravels these shaping forces in all their complexity in this sensitive portrait marked by exceptional scholarship, well-knit organization, and a flowing style.

Leckie, William H. *The Buffalo Soldiers, A Narrative of the Negro Cavalry in the West.* Norman, Okla.: The University of Oklahoma Press, 1967. This is a reliable study of the black recruits who formed the Ninth and Tenth Regiments during the quarter of a century after the Civil War, their primary scene of operations the southwestern plains. They discharged their assignments with efficiency despite working under disadvantages, many of which were rooted in race.

McPherson, James M. *The Negro's Civil War.* New York: Pantheon Books, Inc., 1969. Matching a wide breadth of topical coverage with an equally wide-ranging selection of documentary forms and types, this compilation of source materials describes the many roles of black men and women in the war that ended slavery.

Meier, August. *Negro Thought in America, 1880–1915; Racial Ideologies in the Age of Booker T. Washington.* Ann Arbor: The University of Michigan Press, 1963. Scholarly and authoritative, this is a carefully organized mine of information on black attitudes and behavior patterns at the turn of the century.

Sinkler, George. *The Racial Attitudes of American Presidents from Abraham Lincoln to Theodore Roosevelt.* Garden City, N.Y.: Doubleday & Co., Inc., 1971. Combining scholarship with a vivacity of style, this work is notable for its sensitive analysis of presidential ethnic politics as shaped by personal predilection, public opinion, and political expediency.

Washington, Booker T. *Up from Slavery.* 1901. A best-seller in America, and translated into more than a dozen foreign languages, this work tells the story of obstacles overcome. Here too the author sets forth his philosophy of race relations, basing his observations upon his personal experiences.

Woodward, C. Vann. *The Strange Career of Jim Crow.* 3rd ed. New York: Oxford University Press, 1974. This much-honored work described the origins, development, and numerous manifestations of the racial segregation of blacks. Woodward's contention that Jim Crow practices in the antebellum South were somewhat milder than those in the latter part of the nineteenth century aroused considerable critical reaction. Few, however, would question the book's contribution to the literature of race relations in America.

E. Twentieth-Century Focus

Aptheker, Herbert, ed. *The Autobiography of W. E. B. Du Bois.* New York: International Publishers Co., Inc., 1968. Written when Du Bois had passed his ninetieth birthday, this work discloses the full sweep of a many-sided and important career. Its reflections are informed by the insights of a mind that was vigorous to the last. The book contains 30 photographs and the editor has supplied a selective list of the Du Bois writings, plus a calendar of his public life.

Carmichael, Stokely, and Charles V. Hamilton. *Black Power: The Politics of Liberation in America.* New York: Random House, Inc., 1967. The black man's search for self-identity and self-determination are portrayed herein. The concept of black power is defined and defended.

Cleaver, Eldridge. *Soul on Ice.* New York: McGraw-Hill Book Co., 1968. This eloquent semi-autobiographical work of a former prison inmate and subsequent Black Panther spokesman appealed especially to the younger militants, employing their idioms of expression and articulating their aspirations.

Cronon, E. David. *Black Moses: The Story of Marcus Garvey and the Universal Negro Improvement Association.* Madison: The University of Wisconsin Press, 1955. A colorful, dramatic figure who caught the attention of the black masses with his advocacy of black pride and racial solidarity, combining them with a back-to-Africa theme, Garvey comes to life in this balanced biographical portrait.

Du Bois, W. E. B. *The Souls of Black Folk.* 1903. A moving group of interrelated essays on the past and present, offering a fresh insight into the beauty and frustrations of black life at the turn of the century, and a revealing portrait of Du Bois in his mid-thirties.

Lewis, David L. *King: A Critical Biography.* New York: Praeger Publishers, Inc., 1970. Measuring a person of King's proportions, a world figure in whom reflection and action were wed, is no easy task, but one which Lewis performs admirably. The result is a penetrating portrait, the product of a wealth of information, much of it fresh and revealing, filtered through a sensitive mind.

Locke, Alain, ed. *The New Negro.* New York: A. and C. Boni, 1925. Edited by a Rhodes scholar and professor of philosophy at Howard University, this treasury of essays, stories, and poems by contemporary blacks ushered in the so-called Harlem Renaissance. By example and exhortation this work called upon the "New Negro" to define and proclaim the role of blacks in American culture and letters.

Malcolm X, with Alex Haley. *The Autobiography of Malcolm X.* New York: Grove Press, Inc., 1965. The remarkable odyssey of Malcolm X from a life of crime to leadership in the black revolution, following his conversion to the Black Muslims, is traced. His insistence on proclaiming painful truths elicited a rising response from inner-city blacks.

Meier, August, and Elliott Rudwick. *CORE: A Study in the Civil Rights Movement, 1942–1968.* New York: Oxford University Press, 1973. This work describes the rise and decline of a major protest organization during a quarter of a century that witnessed many significant changes in American race relations. Sagacious and scholarly, its interpretations consistently revealing, this study illuminates the contemporary black thrust for equality.

Parris, Guichard, and Lester Brooks. *Blacks in the City: A History of the National Urban League.* Boston: Little, Brown and Co., 1971. The varied role of the Urban League in meeting the challenge of the unprecedented migration of blacks to the cities in the twentieth century, a movement having a profound effect upon the nation as well as upon the cities themselves, is examined in this objective study.

Spear, Allan H. *Black Chicago: The Making of a Negro Ghetto, 1890–1920.* Chicago: The University of Chicago Press, 1967. A careful analysis of the internal and external pressures on a black urban community, exploring structure and mobility in social and economic ferment.

Yette, Samuel F. *The Choice: The Issue of Black Survival in America.* New York: G. P. Putnam's Sons, 1971. A grim assessment of the odds against black Americans with a pessimistic prophecy as to their future.

Index